The Oxford Chinese Minidictionary

OXFORD
UNIVERSITY PRESS

OXFORD
UNIVERSITY PRESS

Great Clarendon Street, Oxford OX2 6DP

Oxford University Press is a department of the University of Oxford.
It furthers the University's objective of excellence in research, scholarship,
and education by publishing worldwide in

Oxford New York

Athens Auckland Bangkok Bogotá Buenos Aires Cape Town
Chennai Dar es Salaam Delhi Florence Hong Kong Istanbul Karachi
Kolkata Kuala Lumpur Madrid Melbourne Mexico City Mumbai Nairobi
Paris São Paulo Shanghai Singapore Taipei Tokyo Toronto Warsaw

with associated companies in Berlin Ibadan

Oxford is a registered trade mark of Oxford University Press
in the UK and in certain other countries

Published in the United States
by Oxford University Press Inc., New York

First published as the Oxford Starter Chinese Dictionary 2000
Published as the Oxford Chinese Minidictionary 2001

British Library Cataloguing in Publication Data

Data available

Library of Congress Cataloging in Publication Data

Data available

ISBN 0-19-860364-9

10 9 8 7 6 5 4 3 2

Typeset by Graphicraft Limited
Printed in Great Britain by
Charles Letts (Scotland) Ltd.

Contents

Proprietary terms

This dictionary includes some words which are, or are asserted to be, proprietary names or trade marks. Their inclusion does not imply that they have acquired for legal purposes a non-proprietary or general significance, nor is any other judgement implied concerning their legal status. In cases where the editor has some evidence that a word is used as a proprietary name or trade mark, this is indicated by the symbol ®, but no judgement concerning the legal status of such words is made or implied thereby.

Introduction

The *Oxford Chinese Minidictionary* represents a major departure from traditional bilingual dictionaries on several fronts. It approaches the specific needs of the English-speaking learner of Chinese from a very different angle.

It looks different

The dictionary page is refreshingly uncluttered, with streamlined typeface and symbols providing a consistent structure for the information both in English and Chinese. Subdivisions of text are clearly indicated using Arabic numerals. Points of basic grammar are reinforced using the ! signs, and informal or colloquial usage is marked ✶ for Chinese.

It provides essential information in a new way

Every effort has been made to approach the foreign language from the point of view of the beginner who may be unfamiliar with the conventions of the more traditional bilingual dictionary.

Parts of speech and grammatical terms are all given in abbreviated form with a glossary providing explanations and examples of different parts of speech in use. More complex grammatical issues are dealt with in short notes at appropriate points in the text. All Chinese headwords and examples are presented in both *pinyin* (the Chinese phonetic system) and Chinese characters to make the dictionary more user-friendly for beginners. Only simplified characters are used.

The language used in examples and in sense
indicators (or signposts to the correct translation) is
carefully screened and reflects current English and
Chinese as it is based on up-to-date corpus
information.

Both varieties of English — British and American
— are covered and clearly labelled on the English-
Chinese side, while users on both sides of the
Atlantic will recognize the appropriate English-
language equivalent for items in the Chinese-
English part of the dictionary.

The two sides of the dictionary have distinct functions

Each side of the dictionary is shaped by its specific
function. The Chinese-English side is designed to
capitalize on what English speakers know about
their language, hence the more streamlined
presentation of English-language information. The
Oxford Chinese Minidictionary provides generous
coverage of those aspects of Chinese which are less
easy to decode for English speakers.

The English-Chinese side is longer, providing the
user of the foreign language with maximum
guidance in the form of detailed coverage of
essential grammar, clear signposts to the correct
translation for a particular context, and lots of
examples.

The *Oxford Chinese Minidictionary* is unique as an
accessible and user-friendly introduction to the
Chinese language.

How to use the dictionary

The English into Chinese side

The English into Chinese side of the dictionary attempts to give full guidance on how to write and speak correctly in Chinese. Plenty of examples are given to demonstrate not only the translation of words into Chinese but also hints about their usage in Chinese sentences. You will find additional information on grammatical points, such as the use of words in certain contexts, in the grammatical notes that occur within the entries on certain words. These notes are designed to help you produce correct Chinese in areas where mistakes are frequently made. Information about alternative pronunciations is also given in these notes.

If you are unable to translate an English word into Chinese because you cannot find it in the wordlist, try to use another word with the same or a similar sense, or choose another form of wording which will enable you to find what you're looking for. For instance, if you want to translate the adjective *complex* but cannot find it in the dictionary, you could try *complicated* as an alternative, which gives *fùzá* 复杂 as the Chinese equivalent.

The Chinese into English side

The Chinese into English side of the dictionary is organized alphabetically by *pinyin* spelling. If you already know the *pinyin* romanization for a word, you can go straight to the Chinese-English side and look it up alphabetically. Words that have the same *pinyin* spelling but different tones are arranged according to tone, with the first tone first, followed by the second, third, fourth, and neutral tones. (See the section on **Tones in Mandarin Chinese** for information on tones.) Thus *fán* will come before *fǎn*, and *bǎ* will come before *bà*. Words beginning with the same character are grouped together to give a sense of the semantic range of that character. Words that begin with different characters having the same romanization and tone are arranged according to the number of strokes in the character, with the smaller number first. Thus *jiān* 尖 comes before *jiān* 肩 because the former has six strokes and the latter eight strokes. If words or compounds begin with the same character, romanization, and tone, they are arranged alphabetically according to the first letter of the second syllable or word in *pinyin*. For example, *miànqián* comes before *miàntiáor*.

In the cases of *yi* 一 (one) and *bu* 不 (not), where the tone of the character changes depending on the character that follows it (see the subsection on **Tone Changes** in the section on **Tones in Mandarin Chinese**), all words and compounds beginning with the character in question are listed together, regardless of tone, and are arranged alphabetically by the *pinyin* romanization of the second character in the word or compound. For instance, *bùguǎn* 不管 is listed before *búyào* 不要 because g comes before y in the alphabet, even though *bu* in the first has a fourth tone and *bu* in the second has a second tone.

If you have only the Chinese character but do not know how it is pronounced, or spelled in *pinyin*, you can use the **Radical Index** and the **Character Index** in the **Index** section to find the pronunciation.

How to use the Index

The **Index** is divided into the **Radical Index** and
the **Character Index**. The **Character Index** lists
every character that is either a headword or the first
character of a headword in the dictionary. It lists
them by radical and provides their *pinyin*
romanization, which is the key to finding them in
the Chinese-English side.

To find a character in the **Character Index**, you
need first to identify the radical under which the
character is categorized. The **Radical Index**
provides a list of radicals and their numbers in
order of their appearance in the **Character Index**.
These radicals are listed according to the number of
strokes used to write them, with the smallest
number of strokes coming first. When you have
identified the most likely radical of a character,
note its radical number in the **Radical Index**, and
use this number to find the radical in the
Character Index. Because it is sometimes difficult
to figure out which radical is used to categorize any
given character, the **Character Index** lists some
characters under more than one radical for your
convenience. For example, the character 胃 is listed
both under the 田 radical and the 月 radical in the
Character Index.

The **Character Index** lists each radical by
number, followed by all the characters categorized
under that radical. The characters under each
radical are listed according to the number of
strokes beyond those needed to write the radical
portion of the character. For instance, supposing
you are looking for the character 树 in the **Index**.
You guess that it is probably listed under the radical
(木), which is often called the *tree radical*. This

radical is Number 81 in the **Radical Index**. To find
the pronunciation of 树, first find where radical 81
is in the **Character Index**. You will see all the
characters having this radical listed below it. The
tree radical has four strokes. Now count the number
of strokes that remain after you have written those
four strokes. The answer is five. If you look down
the list of characters to the subsection entitled "Five
Strokes", you will see that the character 树 is listed
within that group. The listing tells you that the
character is pronounced *shù*; now you can look up
shù in the Chinese-English side.

By following this procedure, you should be able
to find any character you are looking for, providing
that it is in the dictionary as a headword or the first
character of a headword. If you have trouble finding
a character in the **Character Index**, first check
above or below in the list under that radical, in case
your stroke count was incorrect. It is best to write
the character down as you count, being sure to
write it using the proper strokes and stroke order.
If you still cannot find it, the character is probably
listed under a different radical, and you will need to
start again from the beginning of the process
described above, looking under a different radical.
Beginners sometimes find this process frustrating,
but if you keep trying, it will become easier.

Each Chinese character corresponds to a syllable
in *pinyin*, but a Chinese word can consist of more
than one character. There is no obvious way to
distinguish word boundaries in a written text
unless one knows what the characters and words
mean. Because only headwords and first characters
of headwords are indexed in this dictionary, the
absence of a character from the **Index** does not

mean that it is not in the dictionary. It could be the
second or third character in a word or expression,
whose first character is in the **Character Index**. If
the character you are looking for happens to be
such a second, third, or fourth character, you may
not find it in the **Index**. In that case you must look
back at your text to see if it might be the latter part
of a word beginning with a different character. For
instance, if you find the character *bì* 壁 in your text,
and try to look it up in the dictionary, you will not
find it in the **Index** or under *bì* in the Chinese into
English side. However, after looking again at your
text you may find that it occurs after the character
gé 隔, as the second character of the word *gébì* 隔壁
(= next door). You can then try looking up *gébì* 隔壁
under *g* in the dictionary. Sometimes the
Character Index gives you more than one
pronunciation. It is best to check all the different
pronunciations until you learn which one is used
for the meaning of the character you are looking
for.

Tones in Mandarin Chinese

Chinese is a tonal language. In Mandarin Chinese, there are four tones, indicated respectively by the tone marks ‾, ⁄, ∨ and ⟍.

Tone	Tone mark	Description	Example
First tone	‾	high, level pitch	tī 踢 = kick
Second tone	⁄	starting high and rising	tí 提 = lift
Third tone	∨	falling first, then rising	tǐ 体 = body
Fourth tone	⟍	starting high and falling	tì 替 = replace

As can be seen from the fourth column above, the tone is marked above the vowel in the romanized syllable. It is marked only in the *pinyin* romanization, not in the characters. Some words have unstressed syllables. These are toneless, and are not given tone marks. For example, in *wǒmen* 我们(= we, us), the syllable *men* is toneless and therefore has no tone mark on it. This type of syllable is often called a neutral tone syllable.

Tone Changes

Sometimes the tone of a syllable or a word changes according to the tone of the syllable that follows it.

1. The negative adverb *bù* 不 (=not)

Normally, the negative adverb *bù* 不 is pronounced in the fourth tone:

wǒ **bù** tīng yīnyuè 我不听音乐
= *I don't listen to music*
wǒ **bù** xué Zhōngwén 我不学中文
= *I don't study Chinese*
wǒ **bù** mǎi Zhōngwén shū 我不买中文书
= *I don't buy Chinese books*

However, when it is followed by a fourth-tone syllable, its tone changes to the second tone.

wǒ **bú** shì Zhōngguórén 我不是中国人
= *I'm not Chinese*

2. The numeral *yī* — (=one)

When read in isolation, in counting, or in reading numbers, the numeral *yī* — is pronounced in the first tone.

yī, èr, sān, sì ... 一, 二, 三, 四 ... = *1, 2, 3, 4 ...*
yījiǔjiǔbā 一九九八 = *1998*

However, when the numeral *yī* — precedes a first-, second-, or third-tone syllable, its tone changes to the fourth tone.

yìzhāng zhǐ 一张纸 = *a piece of paper*
yìpán cídài 一盘磁带 = *a tape*
yìběn shū 一本书 = *a book*

When it is followed by a fourth-tone syllable, its tone changes to the second tone.

yíliàng qìchē 一辆汽车 = *a car*

3. A third-tone syllable preceding another third-tone syllable

When a third-tone syllable precedes another third tone, it is pronounced in the second tone even though the tone mark remains the same.

wǔběn shū 五本书 = *five books*
nǐ hǎo! 你好 = *hello!*
hǎohǎo xuéxí 好好学习 = *study well*

The structure of Chinese-English entries

headword · · · **bǎohù** 保护 **1** *vb* protect, safeguard · · · translations

numbers indicating grammatical categories · · · **2** *n* protection

Chinese characters
pinyin

part of speech

běibiān 北边 *n* the North, the north side, on the north **!** *This term can also be used to refer either to the northern border or what is north of the border;*

explanatory note

example of its use · · · Měiguó de běibiān shì Jiānádà 美国 的北边是加拿大 north of the United States of America is Canada

cross-reference to headword · · · **shàngmian** 上面 ▶ **shàngbian** 上边

optional use

Shèngdàn(jié) 圣诞 (节) *n* Christmas (Day)

yánjiū 研究 **1** *vb* study, do research; *(for problems, suggestions, applications)* consider, discuss **2** *n* research, study; **yánjiūhuì** 研究会 research association; **yánjiūshēng** 研究生 research student, postgraduate student; **yánjiūsuǒ** 研究所 research institute

compounds presented at end of entry

indicator which spells out the sense of the headword · · · **yuán** 员 *n* (of a profession, party, or other organisation) member, personnel, staff; [dǎng | hǎi | chúshī | shòuhuò] yuán [党 | 海 | 炊事 | 售货] 员 [party member | sailor | cook | shop assistant]

example indicating generative structure

page number cross-reference to a usage section

zhāng 张 *mw* ▶ **213** (for flat things such as paper, paintings, tables, etc.)

The structure of
English-Chinese entries

pinyin · Chinese character · translations · symbol drawing attention to register

headword · separate senses of the headword

cool *adj* (*fresh, not hot*) liáng 凉, liángkuai 凉快; a cool drink yíge lěngyǐn 一个冷饮; it's much cooler today jīntiān liángkuai duō le 今天凉快多了; (*calm*) lěngjìng 冷静; (*fashionable*) kù 酷▪:

numbers indicating grammatical categories · numeral plus measure word

dance 1 *vb* tiàowǔ 跳舞 **2** *n* a dance yíge wǔdǎo 一个舞蹈

indicators which spell out the different senses of the headword

director *n* (*of a film or play*) dǎoyǎn 导演; a director yíge dǎoyǎn 一个导演; a director (*of a research institute or department*) yíge suǒzhǎng 一个所长, yíge zhǔrèn 一个主任; (*of a factory*) yíge chǎngzhǎng 一个厂长; (*of a company*) yíge zǒngcái 一个总裁

part of speech made clear · indicator of optional use

except *prep* chúle...(yǐwài)...dōu 除了...(以外)...都

separate entries for compounds

fireman *n* a fireman yíge xiāofáng duìyuán 一个消防队员

fire station *n* a fire station yíge xiāofángzhàn 一个消防站

phrasal verbs

kick *vb* tī 踢; to kick someone tī mǒurén 踢某人; he didn't kick the ball tā méi tī qiú 他没踢球; **kick off** (*in a football match*) kāiqiú 开球; **kick out** to kick someone out bǎ mǒurén gǎnchūqu 把某人赶出去

example indicating generative structure

plenty *pron* to have plenty of [time | money | friends...] yǒu hěn duō [shíjiān | qián | péngyou] 有很多 [时间 | 钱 | 朋友]

information on correct grammatical usage

population *n* rénkǒu 人口! Note that rénkǒu 人口 is uncountable and does not have a measure word; a population of one million yìbǎiwàn rénkǒu 一百万人口

Glossary of grammatical terms

This section explains the basic terms that are used in this dictionary to help you to find the information that you need.

Adjective An adjective is used to add extra information to a noun — *an **experienced** worker, a **beautiful** girl, a **black** cat*. In Chinese: *yíge **yǒu jīngyàn de** gōngrén* 一个有经验的工人, *yíge **piàoliang de** gūniang* 一个漂亮的姑娘, *yìzhī **hēi** māo* 一只黑猫. As can be seen in the examples above, the Chinese adjective is often followed by *de* 的 when used to modify a noun. In some Chinese grammar books, some Chinese adjectives are called stative verbs, because the adjective indicates the state of the subject, and the Chinese equivalent of the verb *be* is not used.

> *he **is** tired* = tā__lèi le 他__累了
> *these students **are** very **intelligent*** = zhèxiē xuésheng __ hěn cōngming 这些学生__很聪明

Adverb An adverb is used to add extra information to a verb, an adjective, or another adverb — *to walk **slowly**, **extremely** satisfied, **quite** frequently*. In Chinese: ***hěn mànde** zǒu* 很慢地走, ***fēicháng** mǎnyì* 非常满意, ***xiāngdāng** pínfán* 相当频繁. When used to modify a verb, the Chinese adverb is often followed by *de* 地.

Auxiliary verb An auxiliary verb is a verb, such as *be, do, have*, which is used to form a particular tense or grammatical function of another verb, or to form an interrogative, negative, or imperative sentence. Here are some English examples: *it **is***

raining; **did** *you see him?*; *she **didn't** come*; *he **has** left*; ***don't** go!*.

Comparative The comparative, as its name indicates, is the form of the adjective or adverb which enables us to compare two or more nouns or pronouns. In English, this is usually done by putting *more*, *less*, or *as* before the appropriate adjective or adverb, or by changing the base form to the comparative form ending in -*er*. Chinese adjectives and adverbs do not have comparative forms. The comparison is usually indicated by *bǐ* 比, the Chinese equivalent of *than*, as can be seen in the following examples:

*my mother is **more** patient (**than** my father)* = wǒ māma (**bǐ** wǒ bàba) nàixīn 我妈妈 (比我爸爸) 耐心
*he has **less** money (**than** I have)* = tāde qián (**bǐ** wǒde) shǎo 他的钱 (比我的) 少
*Tom is taller (**than** his father)* = Tāngmǔ (**bǐ** tā bàba) gāo 汤姆 (比他爸爸) 高
*he walked **more** slowly (**than** my mother)* = tā (**bǐ** wǒ māma) zǒu de màn 他 (比我妈妈) 走得慢
*he is **as** tired **as** I am* = tā **hé** wǒ **yíyàng** lèi 他和我一样累

Note that when the comparison is implied, that is, when *bǐ* 比 (= *than*) is not used, the Chinese adjective has a sense of comparison by itself, as in the example below.

A: *Of you two, who is **older**?* = nǐmen liǎ rén shéi **dà**? 你们两人谁大?
B: *I'm **older*** = wǒ **dà** 我大
C: *Yes. I'm **younger*** = duì, wǒ **xiǎo** 对, 我小

If the sentence describes the state or condition of the subject, and no comparison is implied, it is

necessary to add the adverb **hěn** 很 (= *very*) before
the adjective, as in the example below. Otherwise,
the sentence has a sense of comparison.

she is tall = tā **hěn** gāo 她很高

Conditional A conditional sentence is one in
which the statement contained in the main clause
can only be fulfilled if the condition stated in the
subordinate clause is also fulfilled. This condition is
usually introduced by *if* in English and *rúguǒ* 如果
in Chinese.

If it is fine tomorrow, we'll go to the seaside = rúguǒ
míngtiān tiānqì hǎo, wǒmen jiù qù hǎibiān 如果明天
天气好，我们就去海边
I would go travelling if I had lots of money = rúguǒ
wǒ yǒu hěn duō qián, wǒ jiù qù lǚxíng 如果我有很
多钱，我就去旅行

Conjunction A conjunction can be either (i) a
word like *and* or *but* which is used to join words or
simple sentences together, or (ii) a word like *when*,
although, *if*, *where*, which is used to form a complex
sentence. Note that *and* is not translated into
Chinese when it joins two simple sentences or two
verbal phrases. See the following examples:

(i) *Britain and China* = Yīngguó **hé** Zhōngguó 英国
和中国
he is tired but happy = tā hěn lèi **dànshì** hěn
gāoxìng 他很累但是很高兴
I went to Beijing and she went to Shanghai = wǒ
qùle Běijīng, ___ tā qùle Shànghǎi 我去了北京，
___她去了上海
she went to the shop and bought some apples
= tā qù shāngdiàn ___ mǎile yìxiē píngguǒ 她去
商店___买了一些苹果

(ii) *he has agreed to help me **even though** he is busy* = suīrán tā hěn máng, dàn tā tóngyì bāngzhù wǒ 虽然他很忙, 但他同意帮助我
***when** I was about to go out, the telephone rang* = wǒ zhèngyào chūqù de shíhou, diànhuà líng xiǎng le 我正要出去的时候, 电话铃响了

Determiner A determiner is used before a noun in order to identify more precisely what is being referred to. Here are some examples:

the book = zhèběn shū 这本书
my book = wǒde shū 我的书
that book = nàběn shū 那本书
these books = zhèxiē shū 这些书
some books = yìxiē shū 一些书

Note that the English determiner *a* is usually translated into Chinese as a numeral plus an appropriate nominal measure word:

a book = yìběn shū 一本书

Exclamation An exclamation is a word or phrase conveying a reaction such as surprise, shock, disapproval, indignation, amusement, etc. In both English and Chinese, it is usually followed by an exclamation mark.

Excellent! = Hǎo jí le! 好极了!
What nice weather! = Duōme hǎo de tiānqì a! 多么好的天气啊!

Imperative An imperative sentence is used to indicate an order, command, prohibition, suggestion, etc.

come here quickly = kuài lái 快来
don't go out = bié chūqu 别出去
let's go = zánmen zǒu ba 咱们走吧

Infinitive The infinitive is a form of the verb which has no indication of person or tense. In English, it is often preceded by *to*, as in *to walk*, *to run*, *to read*, *to receive*. In Chinese, there is no word like *to* or any change of form to indicate the infinitive.

Measure word ▶ Nominal measure word, Verbal measure word

Nominal measure word In Chinese, a numeral cannot quantify a noun by itself. It has to be accompanied by the measure word that is appropriate for the noun that is being used. Each noun has a specific measure word or set of measure words that can be used with it. There is often a link between the measure word and the shape of the object. In expressions of quantification, the numeral comes first, followed by the measure word and the noun. When the determiner *this* or *that* is used, an appropriate measure word is also required. As can be seen in the examples below, we have put the numeral/determiner and the measure word together as one word in *pinyin* to correspond to the numeral or the determiner in English. Note that some nominal measure words can also be used as verbal measure words. (For a list of common nominal measure words and examples of their use, see the section on **Measure Words** on page 213)

a computer = yìtái jìsuànjī 一台计算机
four dictionaries = sìběn cídiǎn 四本词典
this student = zhège xuésheng 这个学生
that river = nàtiáo hé 那条河

Noun A noun is used to identify a person, an animal, an object, an idea, or an emotion. It can also be the name of an individual, a company, or an institution.

> *student* = xuésheng 学生
> *dog* = gǒu 狗
> *table* = zhuōzi 桌子
> *plan* = jìhuà 计划
> *happiness* = xìngfú 幸福
> *Peter* = Bǐdé 彼得
> *America* = Měiguó 美国

Number A number, as a part of speech, refers to numerical figures, such as *five*, *twenty*, *thousand*, etc., or words indicating quantity. As a grammatical concept, it refers to the state of being either singular or plural. Nouns in English usually change to their plural forms by adding -s to the end: *a table*, *two tables*. Chinese nouns usually do not change to form singular and plural.

> *a table* = yìzhāng zhuōzi 一张桌子
> *two tables* = liǎngzhāng zhuōzi 两张桌子

Occasionally, *-men* -们 can be attached to the end of a noun to mark the plural form, but it is optional and applies only to nouns referring to animate entities:

> *students* = xuésheng(**men**) 学生(们)
> *workers* = gōngrén(**men**) 工人(们)

Object The object of a sentence is the word or group of words which is immediately affected by the action indicated by the verb. In the following English sentence, the word *child* is the subject, *broke* is the verb and *a cup* is the object. Similarly, in the Chinese translation, *zhège háizi* 这个孩子 is the subject, *dǎpòle* 打破了 is the verb and *yíge chábēi* 一个茶杯 is the object.

the child broke a cup = zhège háizi dǎpòle yíge chábēi 这个孩子打破了一个茶杯

There may be two kinds of object in a sentence, a direct object and an indirect object. In the example above, *a cup* and *yíge chábēi* 一个茶杯 are strictly direct objects. However, in the following English sentence, *he* is the subject, *gave* is the verb, *the child* is the indirect object and *a cup* is the direct object. Similarly, in the Chinese translation, *tā* 他 is the subject, *gěile* 给了 is the verb, *zhège háizi* 这个孩子 is the indirect object and *yíge chábēi* 一个茶杯 is the direct object. In general terms, the indirect object indicates the person or thing which 'benefits' from the action of the verb upon the direct object.

he gave the child a cup = tā gěile zhège háizi yíge chábēi 他给了这个孩子一个茶杯

Phrasal verb A phrasal verb is a verb combined with a preposition or an adverb and having a particular meaning. For example, *to run away*, meaning to flee, and *to see to something*, meaning to ensure that something is done, are phrasal verbs. If you look up *to run away* for example, you will see that the phrasal verbs beginning with the word *run* are listed after all the other meanings of the word *run*, in alphabetical order of the following adverb or preposition.

Pinyin Designed in the People's Republic of China during the mid-1950s, *pinyin* is a phonetic system of the Chinese language. It adopts the roman alphabet to represent phonemic sounds in Mandarin Chinese. In this dictionary, all Chinese headwords, translations, and examples are given first in *pinyin* and then in Chinese characters.

Preposition A preposition is a word, such as *under, beside, across, in,* which is usually followed by a noun in English. In Chinese, the preposition often consists of two parts, such as *zài ... xiàmian* 在 ...下面 (= *under*), and the noun is placed between them, as in the examples below.

> *under the table* = **zài** zhuōzi **xiàmian** 在 桌子下面
> *beside the road* = **zài** lù **pángbiān** 在路旁边
> *in the garden* = **zài** huāyuán **lǐ** 在花园里

Most preposition + noun groups indicate movement

> *he ran **towards the house*** = tā **cháo** nàzuò fángzi pǎoqù 他朝那座房子跑去

position

> *your books are **on the table*** = nǐde shū **zài zhuōzi shang** 你的书在桌子上

or time

> *I'll be there **at 4 o'clock*** = wǒ **sì diǎnzhōng** huì dào nàr 我四点钟会到那儿

Pronoun A pronoun is used instead of a noun in order to avoid repeating it unnecessarily. There are the personal pronouns *I, you, he, she, it, we, you* (plural), *they*; the possessive pronouns *mine, yours, his, hers, its, ours, yours* (plural), *theirs*; the interrogative pronouns used in questions *who, which, what*; the demonstrative pronouns *this, that, these, those*; the relative pronouns used in relative clauses *who, which, whose*; and the reflexive pronouns *myself, yourself, himself, herself, itself, ourselves, yourselves, themselves*. To find the Chinese equivalents of these pronouns, please look them up in the English-Chinese side of the dictionary.

Reflexive pronoun ▶ Pronoun

Relative pronoun ▶ Pronoun

Subject The subject of a sentence is often the word or group of words which performs the action indicated by the verb. In the sentence *John laughed*, *John* is the subject of the verb *laughed*. Of course, the verb doesn't necessarily express an action as such. For example, in the sentence *John is tall*, *John* is the subject of the verb *is*. In the Chinese sentence *Yuēhàn xiào le* 约翰 笑了, *Yuēhàn* 约翰 is similarly the subject of the verb *xiào le* 笑了, and in the sentence *Yuēhàn hěn gāo* 约翰 很高, *Yuēhàn* 约翰 is the subject of *hěn gāo* 很高.

Superlative The superlative is the form of the adjective or adverb which is used to express the highest or lowest degree. In English, the adjective or adverb is usually preceded by *most* or *least*. Some adjectives and adverbs (usually of one syllable) have their own form: *best, worst, biggest, smallest, fastest, slowest*, etc. In Chinese, the superlative is formed by putting *zuì* 最 before the adjective or adverb.

> *most important* = **zuì** zhòngyào 最重要
> *least important* = **zuì bú** zhòngyào 最不重要
> *most carefully* = **zuì** zǐxì 最仔细
> *least carefully* = **zuì bù** zǐxì 最不仔细
> *smallest* = **zuì** xiǎo 最小

Tense The tense of a verb expresses whether the action takes place in the past, present, or future. Unlike English verbs, Chinese verbs do not have any particular form to express tense; the time of the action is usually indicated by the adverb or in the context.

Present tense

he is telephoning his friends = tā zài gěi tāde péngyou dǎ diànhuà 他在给他的朋友打电话

Past tense

I didn't go = wǒ méi qù 我没去

Future tense

they will come tomorrow = tāmen míngtiān lái 他们明天来

Tone Please see the section on **Tones in Mandarin Chinese** on page xiii.

Verb The verb propels the sentence along, telling us what is happening. Note these examples:

Paul bought a new car = Bǎoluó mǎile yíliàng xīn chē 保罗买了一辆新车
The flood caused a lot of damage = shuǐzāi zàochéngle hěn dàde sǔnhài 水灾造成了很大的损害

Sometimes, of course, the verb doesn't describe an action, but rather a state of affairs:

He has a problem = tā yǒu yígè wèntí 他有一个问题
The damage appears quite serious = sǔnhài kànlái xiāngdāng yánzhòng 损害看来相当严重
I am ill = wǒ bìng le 我病了

Note that the verb *am* in the sentence *I am ill* is not translated into Chinese. See the entry on **Adjective** in the glossary above.

Verbal measure word Verbal measure words are generally used to indicate the number of times an action or state occurs. As in the case of nominal measure words, the numeral and verbal measure word are spelled together as one *pinyin* word in this dictionary. The numeral + measure word unit is preceded by the verb and is usually followed by the object, if there is one (i.e. if the verb is transitive). For a list of common verbal measure words and examples of their use, see the section on **Measure words** on page 213.

> *I've been to Hong Kong twice* = wǒ qùguo liǎng**cì** Xiānggǎng 我去过两次香港
> *he nodded his head several times* = tā diǎnle jǐ**xià** tóu 他点了几下头

Index

1. Radical Index

2. Character Index

橡 xiàng
橘 jú

---

(82)
犬

状 zhuàng
哭 kū
臭 chòu
献 xiàn

---

(83)
歹

列 liè
死 sǐ
残 cán

---

(84)
车

车 chē
军 jūn
转 zhuǎn;
     zhuǎn
轮 lún
软 ruǎn
轻 qīng
较 jiào
辅 fǔ
辆 liàng
输 shū

---

(85)
戈

划 huá
成 chéng
戏 xì
我 wǒ
或 huò
战 zhàn
裁 zāi
裁 cái
戴 dài

---

(86)
比

比 bǐ
毕 bì

---

(87)
瓦

瓶 píng

---

(88)
止

止 zhǐ
正 zhēng;
     zhèng

此 cǐ
步 bù
武 wǔ
肯 kěn
歪 wāi

---

(89)
支

敲 qiāo

---

(90)
日

日 rì

**One to five
strokes**

旧 jiù
早 zǎo
时 shí
明 míng
昏 hūn
春 chūn
是 shì
显 xiǎn
星 xīng
昨 zuó

**Six or more
strokes**

晒 shài
晓 xiǎo

翅	chì
翻	fān

譬	pì

短	duǎn
登	dēng

(151)
艮 (阝)

良	liáng
艰	jiān
即	jí
既	jì

(155)
麦

麦	mài

(159)
酉

酒	jiǔ
配	pèi
酱	jiàng
酸	suān
醉	zuì
醋	cù
醒	xǐng

(152)
糸

系	xì
紧	jǐn
累	lèi
紫	zǐ
繁	fán

(156)
走

走	zǒu
赶	gǎn
起	qǐ
越	yuè
趁	chèn
趋	qū
超	chāo
趣	qù
趟	tàng

(160)
辰

唇	chún

(153)
辛

辛	xīn
辞	cí
辣	là

(157)
赤

赤	chì

(161)
豕

家	jiā
象	xiàng

(154)
言

警	jǐng

(158)
豆

豆	dòu

(162)
卤

卤	lǔ

Abbreviations

adjective	adj
adjectival noun	adj n
adverb	adv
auxiliary verb	aux vb
conjunction	conj
determiner	det
measure word	mw
nominal measure word	nmw
verbal measure word	vmw
noun	n
number	num
preposition	prep
pronoun	pron
reflexive pronoun	ref pron
relative pronoun	rel pron
verb	vb
prefix	prf
exclamation	exc
particle	pt
suffix	suf

ā 阿 *prf* (*informal name prefix especially in Yangtze delta region*) **ā Q** 阿 Q Ah Q

Ālābó 阿拉伯 *n* Arabia

āyí 阿姨 *n* (*child's word for a woman of his or her mother's generation*) auntie; (*child's word for a child-minder*) nanny, baby-sitter

ā 啊 **1** *exc* (*to express surprise*) Oh! Ah!; **ā, nǐ lái le!** 啊，你来了! Ah, here you are! **2** *pt* (*placed at the end of a sentence to express admiration, warning, or request*) **duō hǎo de tiānr ā!** 多好的天儿啊! what a beautiful day!; **bié chídào a!** 别迟到啊! don't be late!; **nǐ kuài lái a!** 你快来啊! come here quickly!

āi 哎 *exc* (*to express surprise or discontent*) **āi, nǐ bǎ qián fàng zài nǎli le?** 哎，你把钱放在哪里了? but where did you put the money?

āiyā 哎呀 *exc* (*expressing surprise*) My goodness!; **āiyā, wǒde qiánbāo diū le!** 哎呀，我的钱包丢了! Oh dear, I've lost my wallet!

āi 挨 *vb* ▶ *See also* **ái** 挨. (*get close to, be next to or near to*) **tā jiā āizhe xuéxiào** 他家挨着学校 his house is next to the school; (*in sequence, by turns*) **shénme shíhòu néng āidào wǒ?** 什么时候能挨到我? when can it be my turn?

ái 挨 *vb* ▶ *See also* **āi** 挨. suffer, endure; **ái dòng** 挨冻 suffer from the freezing cold; **ái mà** 挨骂 get a scolding; **ái dǎ** 挨打 get a beating, come under attack

ái 癌 *n* cancer; **áizhèng** 癌症 cancer

ǎi 矮 *adj* (*in stature*) short; (*of inanimate objects*) low

ài 爱 *vb* (*if the object is a person*) love, be fond of; **wǒ ài nǐ** 我爱你 I love you; (*if the object is an activity*) like, love; **wǒ ài tīng nàge gùshi** 我爱听那个故事 I like to hear that story

àihào 爱好 1 vb be keen on; **àihào dǎ wǎngqiú** 爱好打网球 be keen on tennis 2 n hobby; **qí mǎ shì tāde àihào** 骑马是她的爱好 horse-riding is her hobby **!** Note that **hào** 好 in this essentially verbal usage is fourth tone.

àihù 爱护 vb cherish, treasure, protect; **àihù zìjǐ de shēntǐ** 爱护自己的身体 take good care of one's own health

àiqíng 爱情 n (between lovers) love, affection

àiren 爱人 n husband or wife, lover, spouse; **wǒde àiren shì lǎoshī** 我的爱人是老师 my wife/husband is a teacher

àixí 爱惜 vb cherish, treasure, use sparingly

ān 安 1 adj peaceful, secure, content; **xīnlǐ bù ān** 心里不安 feel worried 2 vb install; settle down; **ān jiā** 安家 settle a family down in a place

āndìng 安定 1 vb (for a family, system, etc.) settle down in peace; **xíngshì yǐjīng āndìngxiàlai le** 形势已经安定下来了 the situation has calmed down; stabilize 2 adj settled, stable, secure; **yíge āndìng de shèhuì huánjìng** 一个安定的社会环境 a stable social environment

ānjìng 安静 adj peaceful, quiet; **qǐng ānjìng!** 请安静! please be quiet!

ānpái 安排 1 vb arrange, plan, fix up; **ānpái shísù** 安排食宿 arrange room and board 2 n arrangements

ānquán 安全 1 adj safe, secure; **zhèlǐ bù ānquán** 这里不安全 this place is not safe; **ānquándài** 安全带 safety belt 2 n safety, security; **bǎohù tāmende ānquán** 保护他们的安全 preserve their safety

ānwèi 安慰 1 vb comfort, console 2 n comfort, reassurance

ānxīn 安心 vb feel at ease, be relieved; **shǐ tā ānxīn** 使她安心 make her feel at ease

ānzhuāng 安装 vb install; **ānzhuāng jìsuànjī** 安装计算机 have a computer installed

àn 按 1 prep according to, by; **qǐng nǐ àn wǒ shuō de zuò** 请你按我说的做 please do it the way I told you; **àn yuè suàn** 按月算 calculate by the month 2 vb press, push down; **ànxià**

diànniǔ 按下电钮 press down the button; restrain, control; tā àn bú zhù zìjǐ de fènnù 他按不住自己的愤怒 he cannot restrain his anger

ànshí 按时 *adv* on time, on schedule; huǒchē huì ànshí dào ma? 火车会按时到吗? will the train arrive on time?

ànzhào 按照 *prep* according to, based on; ànzhào tāmende àihào, wǒ gěi tāmen měige rén mǎile yíjiàn lǐwù 按照他们的爱好, 我给他们每个人买了一件礼物 I bought each of them a present according to their hobbies

àn 岸 *n* bank, shore, coast; [hǎi | hú | hé] àn [海|湖|河]岸 [seashore | lake shore | river bank]; shàng àn 上岸 go ashore

àn 暗 *adj* dark, dim, dull; nàjiān wūzi hěn àn 那间屋子很暗 that room is very dark; hidden, secret; wǒmen zài àn chù guānchá dírén de xíngdòng 我们在暗处观察敌人的行动 we were observing the enemy's actions from a hidden position

āngzāng 肮脏 *adj* dirty, filthy

Àolínpǐkè Yùndònghuì 奥林匹克运动会 *n* the Olympic Games

Àodàlìyà 澳大利亚 *n* Australia

àohuǐ 懊悔 *adj* regret, feel remorse, repent

àonǎo 懊恼 *adj* annoyed, upset, vexed

àomàn 傲慢 *vb* arrogant, haughty

Bb

bā 八 *num* eight

bāyuè 八月 *n* August

bá 拔 *vb* pull, pull out, uproot; bá yá 拔牙 extract a tooth or have a tooth extracted; (for people of talent) choose, select; xuǎnbá 选拔 select from a number of candidates; capture, seize

bǎ 把 **1** mw ▶213 *(for objects with a handle or with something a person can hold)*; *(for things that can be grouped in bunches or bundles)* bunch, bundle; handful **2** prep *1 As a preposition, bǎ* 把 *acts as a structural device that brings the object from the post-verbal position to the pre-verbal position. The object of the preposition* bǎ *is also the object of the verb*; wǒ xiǎng bǎ tā mài le 我想把它卖了 I want to sell it; háizimen bǎ táng dōu chīwán le 孩子们把糖都吃完了 the children ate all the sweets; xiān bǎ liànxí zuòwán 先把练习作完 finish the exercises first; tā bǎ wǒ qìhuài le 他把我气坏了 he made me very angry; bǎ quán jiā jiàoqǐlai 把全家叫起来 awaken the whole family

bàba 爸爸 *n* father, dad, papa

ba 吧 *pt (used to make a mild imperative sentence)* zánmen zǒu ba 咱们走吧 let's go; gěi wǒ shū ba 给我书吧 give me the book; gěi nǐ ba 给你吧 here, you take it; chī bǐnggān ba? 吃饼干吧? how about having a biscuit?; bié gàosu tā ba 别告诉他吧 better not tell him; *(used to imply agreement)* jiù zhèyàng ba 就这样吧 OK, let's leave it like that; *(used to imply a degree of certainty)* tā jīntiān lái ba? 他今天来吧? he is coming today, isn't he?; *(to express unwillingness, reluctance, or hesitation)* nǐ quèshí xiǎng mǎi, nà nǐ jiù qù mǎi ba 你确实想买，那你就去买吧 if you really want to buy it, go and buy it then

bái 白 **1** *adj* white; pure, plain, blank; báifàn 白饭 plain rice; kòngbái 空白 blank; báihuà 白话 vernacular Chinese, modern Chinese **2** *adv* in vain, to no effect; bái pǎo yītàng 白跑一趟 make a trip for nothing; bái fèi jìn 白费劲 waste one's effort; free of charge; bái sòng 白送 give as a gift; qīngbái 清白 clean, pure

báicài 白菜 *n* Chinese cabbage

báitiān 白天 *n* daytime, day

bǎi 百 *num* hundred, unit of a hundred

bǎi 摆 *vb* put, place, arrange; sway, wave; xiàng mǒurén bǎi shǒu 向某人摆手 wave one's hand at someone

bài 败 *vb* be defeated in a battle or contest; **tāmen bài de hěn cǎn** 他们败得很惨 they suffered a heavy defeat; (*of an enemy or opponent*) defeat; **dǎbài** 打败 defeat; spoil, ruin; **bàihuài míngyù** 败坏名誉 to spoil one's reputation; wither

bān 班 **1** *n* class; **èrniánjí yǒu sānge bān** 二年级有三个班 there are three classes in second grade; shift, duty; **shàng bān** 上班 go to work; [**zǎo** | **zhōng** | **yè**] **bān** [早 | 中 | 夜] 班 [morning | afternoon | night] shift; squad **2** *mw* ▶ **213** (*for scheduled services of public transportation*)

bānzhǎng 班长 *n* head of a class, squad, or team

bān 搬 *vb* take away, move, remove; move house; **tā bānzǒu le** 他搬走了 he moved away

bǎn 板 *n* board, plank, plate

bàn 办 *vb* handle, manage, attend to; **méiyǒu qián, zěnme bàn?** 没有钱, 怎么办? what will we do if we have no money?; **zhèjiàn shì tā bàn bù wán** 这件事他办不完 he can't finish this; set up, run; **bàn xuéxiào** 办学校 run a school; **bàn gōngsī** 办公司 set up a company; hold, have; **bàn yícì zuòwén bǐsài** 办一次作文比赛 hold a writing competition; **bàn zhǎnlǎnhuì** 办展览会 hold an exhibition

bànfǎ 办法 *n* way, method, way to handle a problem

bàngōng 办公 *vb* handle official business

bàngōngshì 办公室 *n* office

bànshì 办事 *vb* handle affairs, handle a matter, work

bàn 半 *adj* half; **bànge píngguǒ** 半个苹果 half an apple; **yígebàn yuè** 一个半月 one and a half months; partly, about half; **tā chīle yíbàn jiù zǒu le** 他吃了一半就走了 he ate about half his meal and then left

bàndǎotǐ 半导体 *n* semi-conductor, transistor

bàntiān 半天 *n* half a day; for a long time, quite a while; **tā yǐjīng shuōle bàntiān le** 他已经说了半天了 he has already been talking for a long time

bànyè 半夜 *n* midnight, in the middle of the night; half a night; **qián bànyè** 前半夜 first half of the night; **hòu bànyè** 后半夜 second half of the night

bāng 帮 vb help, assist; **wǒ kěyǐ bāng nǐ** 我可以帮你 I can help you

bāngmáng 帮忙, **bāng...máng** 帮...忙 vb help, lend a hand, do a favour; **tā bú yuànyì bāngmáng** 他不愿意帮忙 he is not willing to help; **tā xǐhuān bāng biérén de máng** 她喜欢帮别人的忙 she likes to help other people

bāngzhù 帮助 vb help, assist; **wǒ yuànyì bāngzhù nǐ** 我愿意帮助你 I am willing to help you

bǎngyàng 榜样 n good example, model; **wèi dàjiā zuòchū yíge bǎngyàng** 为大家作出一个榜样 set an example for everyone

bàngwǎn 傍晚 n at dusk, toward evening or nightfall

bāo 包 1 n parcel, package, bundle; bag 2 mw ▶213 package, packet, bundle 3 vb wrap with paper, cloth, or some other material; **bǎ dōngxi bāoqǐlai** 把东西包起来 wrap things up; **bāo jiǎozi** 包饺子 make jiǎozi (Chinese dumplings); assure, guarantee; **bāo nǐ gāoxìng** 包你高兴 You'll be happy, I assure you; hire, charter; **bāo yíliàng chūzūchē** 包一辆出租车 hire a taxi; **bāojī** 包机 a chartered plane

bāokuò 包括 vb include, consist of, comprise

bāozi 包子 n steamed stuffed bun

báo 薄 adj thin, slight, insubstantial; (how a person is treated) coldly, shabbily; **dài tā bù báo** 待他不薄 treat him generously

bǎo 饱 adj (to describe a person after eating) full, replete; **wǒ chībǎo le** 我吃饱了 I have eaten my fill; (to describe a thing) full, plump

bǎoguì 宝贵 adj valuable, precious

bǎo 保 vb protect, defend, safeguard; keep, maintain, preserve; **bǎo xiān** 保鲜 keep something fresh; guarantee, ensure; **bǎo zhì bǎo liàng** 保质保量 ensure both quality and quantity

bǎochí 保持 vb keep, maintain; **bǎochí ānjìng** 保持安静 keep quiet

bǎocún 保存 vb preserve, conserve, keep; **bǎocún de hěn wánzhěng** 保存得很完整 be well preserved, be intact

bǎohù 保护 1 *vb* protect, safeguard 2 *n* protection

bǎohùrén 保护人 *n* guardian

bǎoliú 保留 *vb* retain, keep; réngjiù bǎoliú yǐqián de tàidu 仍旧保留以前的态度 still retain one's former attitude; hold or keep back, reserve; bǎoliú (...de) quánlì 保留 (...的) 权利 reserve the right (to...)

bǎoshǒu 保守 *adj* conservative

bǎowèi 保卫 *vb* defend, protect, safeguard

bǎoxiǎn 保险 *n* insurance

bǎozhèng 保证 1 *vb* pledge, guarantee, assure; bǎozhèng fù kuǎn 保证付款 pledge or guarantee to pay 2 *n* guarantee

bào 抱 *vb* embrace, enfold, carry in the arms; (when referring to a child) adopt; cherish, harbour; tā duì zhèjiàn shì bào hěn dà de xīwàng 他对这件事抱很大的希望 he has a lot of hope for that matter

bàoqiàn 抱歉 1 *adj* sorry; hěn bàoqiàn 很抱歉 I'm sorry 2 *vb* apologize

bào 报 *n* newspaper; [rì | wǎn | zǎo] bào [日 | 晚 | 早] 报 [daily | evening | morning] paper; periodical, journal; yuèbào 月报 monthly journal; zhōubào 周报 weekly; bulletin, report; jǐngbào 警报 alarm, warning; xǐbào 喜报 good news

bàochóu 报仇 *n* revenge

bàodào 报到 *vb* report for work, check in, register

bàodào, bàodǎo 报道, 报导 1 *vb* report or cover the news 2 *n* news reporting, story; guānyú dìzhèn de bàodào 关于地震的报道 reports about the earthquake

bàogào 报告 1 *vb* report, make known; yīnggāi xiàng jīnglǐ bàogào 应该向经理报告 should report it to the manager 2 *n* report, speech, lecture; zuò bàogào 做报告 make a speech

bàomíng 报名 *vb* register, sign up

bàozhǐ 报纸 *n* newspaper, newsprint

bēi 杯 n cup, glass, tumbler; **yìbēi chá** 一杯茶 a cup of tea;
(as a prize) cup, trophy; **Shìjiè Bēi** 世界杯 the World Cup

bēizi 杯子 n cup, glass, mug

bēi 背 vb carry on one's back; bear, shoulder; **tā bēizhe
chénzhòng de jīngshén fùdān** 他背着沉重的精神负担
he has a heavy load on his mind

bēitòng 悲痛 adj grieved, feeling melancholy

bēi 碑 n large stone tablet or stele used for commemorative
purposes; **jìniàn bēi** 纪念碑 commemorative monument; **mùbēi**
墓碑 tombstone

běi 北 n north; **Huáběi** 华北 North China; **Běijí** 北极 North
Pole

běibiān 北边 n the North, the north side, on the north ! This
term can also be used to refer either to the northern border or
what is north of the border; **Měiguó de běibiān shì Jiānádà**
美国的北边是加拿大 north of the United States of America is
Canada

běibù 北部 n north, northern section or part; **Sūgélán zài
Yīngguó de běibù** 苏格兰在英国的北部 Scotland is in the
north of Britain

běifāng 北方 n the north; the northern part of China, the area
north of the Yangtze River

Běijīng 北京 n Beijing, the capital of China; **Běijīng kǎoyā**
北京烤鸭 Peking duck

bèi 背 n the back of the body, the back of an object; **zài mǎ bèi
shàng** 在马背上 on the back of the horse

bèihòu 背后 n behind, at the back, to the rear; **tā duǒ zài
mǔqīn bèihòu** 他躲在母亲背后 he hid behind his mother;
behind someone's back; **tā cháng zài rénjiā de bèihòu luàn shuō**
她常在人家的背后乱说 she often gossips behind people's
backs

bèimiàn 背面 n reverse side; **xiàngpiàn de bèimiàn** 相片的
背面 the back of the photograph

bèi 倍 *n* times, -fold; **shíbèi** 十倍 ten times; X **bǐ** Y **zhòng shíjǐbèi** X 比 Y 重十几倍 X is more than ten times heavier than Y

bèi 被 *prep* by! *The preposition* 被 *is used in a passive sentence and usually marks the agent in a passive construction*; **wǒ de háizi bèi tā dǎ le** 我的孩子被他打了 my child was hit by him; **tā zuìjìn bèi cítuì le** 他最近被辞退了 he was recently discharged from his job

bèizi 被子 *n* quilt, duvet

běn 本 **1** *n* edition of a book; **Yīngwén běn** 英文本 English edition **2** *mw* ▶ **213** (for things that are bound, such as books, magazines, etc.) **3** *adj* one's own, oneself, personally; **wǒ běnrén bù zhīdào** 我本身不知道 I personally don't know; **tā běnrén méiyǒu qù** 他本人没有去 he didn't go himself; this, current, present; **běn xiào** 本校 our school; **běn nián** 本年 this year; *(when referring to a place)* native; **běndì rén** 本地人 a native of this place **4** *adv* originally; **wǒ běn xiǎng qù, kěshì hòulái méi qù** 我本想去, 可是后来没去 originally I wanted to go, but in the end I didn't go

běnlái 本来 **1** *adv* originally, at first; **wǒ běnlái xiǎng zài cānguǎn chīfàn, kěshì tài wǎn le** 我本来想在餐馆吃饭, 可是太晚了 I originally wanted to eat at a restaurant, but it was too late **2** *adj* original; **wǒ běnlái de xiǎngfǎ** 我本来的想法 my original idea

běnlǐng 本领 *n* skill, ability, capability

běnshì 本事 *n* ability

běnzhì 本质 *n* essence, true nature

běnzi 本子 *n* notebook, exercise book

bèn 笨 *adj* (of a person's mental ability) slow, stupid, dull; (of a person's movements) clumsy, awkward; **tiàowǔ wǒ xué bú huì; wǒ tài bèn!** 跳舞我学不会; 我太笨! I can't learn how to dance; I'm too clumsy!

bī 逼 *vb* force, compel, press; press for extort; **bī gòng** 逼供 extort a confession; **bīsǐ** 逼死 hound to death; **bī zū** 逼租 press for payment of rent; press on towards, press up to, close in on; **bījìn** 逼近 draw close to, press hard upon (as an army to a city)

bízi 鼻子 *n* nose

bǐ 比 **1** *prep* compared with, than; **tā bǐ wǒ gāo** 他比我高 he is taller than I am; **nǐ fùqīn bǐ nǐ mǔqīn dà jǐ suì?** 你父亲比你母亲大几岁? how many years older than your mother is your father?; (*comparison over time*) **tā yìtiān bǐ yìtiān jiēshi** 他一天比一天结实 he gets stronger every day; (*indicating a score of a match or game*) **wǔ bǐ sān** 五比三 five to three **2** *vb* compare, emulate; **bǎ hóng de gēn lán de bǐyibǐ** 把红的跟蓝的比一比 make a comparison between the red one and the blue one **3** **bǐfāng (shuō)** 比方(说) for example, such as **4** **bǐrú (shuō)** 比如(说) for example, such as

bǐjiào 比较 **1** *adv* quite, relatively, rather; **wǒ bǐjiào xǐhuān dú shū** 我比较喜欢读书 I rather enjoy reading **2** *vb* compare, contrast; **bǐjiào liǎngjiàn yīfu de zhìliàng** 比较两件衣服的质量 compare the qualities of the two items of clothing

bǐlì 比例 *n* ratio, proportion; **nán-nǚ xìngbié bǐlì** 男女性别比例 the ratio of males to females

bǐsài 比赛 **1** *vb* compete; **gēn Yīnggélán duì bǐsài** 跟英格兰队比赛 have a match against the English team **2** *n* match, competition

bǐ 笔 **1** *n* pen, brush; stroke, touch of the brush; **zhège zì de bǐhuà** 这个字的笔划 the strokes that make up this Chinese character; **zhège zì de dìyībǐ** 这个字的第一笔 the first stroke of the character **2** *mw* ▶ **213** (*for sums of money*); (*for deals in business or trade*)

bǐjì 笔记 *n* notes; **bǐjìběn** 笔记本 notebook

bìrán 必然 *adj* inevitable, certain; **yíge bìrán de guīlǜ** 一个必然的规律 an inexorable law

bìxū 必须 *vb* must, have to; **nǐ bìxū lái** 你必须来 you must come

bìyào 必要 *adj* necessary

bìyè 毕业 *vb* graduate, finish school

bì 闭 *vb* shut, close; **bìshàng yǎnjīng** 闭上眼睛 close one's eyes; **bì zuǐ!** 闭嘴! hold your tongue!, shut up!

bì *vb* avoid, stay away from, hide; **bì fēng yǔ** 避风雨 get out of the wind and rain; **bìnàn** 避难 run away from trouble, escape calamity, seek asylum; prevent, keep away, repel; **bìyùn** 避孕 contraception

bìmiǎn 避免 *vb* avoid, refrain from, avert

biān 边 *n* side; [nǎ | zhè | běi | shàng | xià] **biān** [那 | 这 | 北 | 上 | 下] 边 [over there | over here | the north | above | below]; frontier, border; **biānjiāng** 边疆 border; **biānjiè** 边界 border; limit, edge; **shùlín biān** 树林边 the edge of a forest; close by; **zhàn zài chuāng biān** 站在窗边 stand by the window

biān...biān... 边...边... *conj* ! Biān 边 is used before two different verbs to indicate simultaneous actions. It is sometimes expressed as yìbiān...yìbiān... 一边...一边...; (yì) biān chī (yì) biān tán (一)边吃(一)边谈 eat and talk at the same time; **yìbiān tīng yīnyuè yìbiān kàn shū** 一边听音乐一边看书 read while listening to music

biān 编 *vb* edit, arrange in order, compile; **biān cídiǎn** 编词典 edit or compile a dictionary; weave, plait

biǎn 扁 *adj* flat; **lúntāi biǎn le** 轮胎扁了 the tyre has become flat

biàn 变 *vb* change, become different; **xiànzài Zhōngguó biàn le** 现在中国变了 China has changed now; transform, change, turn; **biàn huàishì wéi hǎoshì** 变坏事为好事 turn a bad thing into a good thing

biànchéng 变成 *vb* change into; **bǎ hēi zì biànchéng hóng zì** 把黑字变成红字 turn the black characters into red ones

biànhuà 变化 **1** *vb* change, vary **2** *n* change

biàn 便 ▶ See also **pián** 便. **1** *adv* then; **tiān yí liàng tā biàn shàngbān qù le** 天一亮她便上班去了 she left for work as soon as it was light **2** *adj* convenient; **biànlì** 便利 convenient

biàntiáo 便条 *n* an informal note

biàn 遍 **1** *mw* ▶213 (to indicate the number of times an action or state occurs) time ! Note that biàn 遍 is different from cì 次 in that it emphasizes the whole process from the beginning to

the end. **2** *adv* everywhere, all over; **yóu biàn quán shìjiè** 游遍
全世界 travel all over the world

biǎodiǎn 标点 *n* punctuation; **biāodiǎn fúhào** 标点符号
punctuation mark

biāozhǔn 标准 **1** *n* standard; **biāozhǔnhuà** 标准化
standardization **2** *adj* standard; **nǐde Zhōngguó huà hěn
biāozhǔn** 你的中国话很标准 your Chinese is very good

biǎo 表 *n* table, form, list; **shíjiānbiǎo** 时间表 timetable,
schedule; **shēnqǐngbiǎo** 申请表 application form; meter, gauge;
watch; **shǒubiǎo** 手表 wrist watch; the relationship between
children with two common grandparents but without sharing
the same paternal grandfather; **biǎogē** 表哥 elder male cousin;
biǎodì 表弟 younger male cousin; **biǎojiě** 表姐 elder female
cousin; **biǎomèi** 表妹 younger female cousin

biǎodá 表达 *vb* (thoughts and feelings, ideas) express

biǎomiàn 表面 *n* surface, face, outside appearance

biǎomíng 表明 *vb* make known, make clear, state clearly

biǎoshì 表示 **1** *vb* show, express, indicate **2** *n* gesture,
manifestation

biǎoxiàn 表现 **1** *vb* show, display, manifest; show off;
tā xǐhuān biǎoxiàn zìjǐ 他喜欢表现自己 he likes to show off;
behave **2** *n* expression, manifestation; behaviour

biǎoyǎn 表演 **1** *vb* perform, act, play **2** *n* performance

biǎoyáng 表扬 *vb* praise

bié 别 **1** *adv* (*negative imperative*) not; **bié** [**qù** | **zǒu** | **chī**] 别
[去 | 走 | 吃] don't [go | leave | eat]; **wǒ ràng tā bié lái** 我让他别来
I told him not to come **2** *adj* other, another; **bié chù** 别处
elsewhere, another place; **nǐ hái yào bié de (dōngxi) ma?** 你还
要别的 (东西) 吗? do you want anything else?

biéren 别人 *n* others, other people; **biéren dōu shuō yǒu yìsi**
别人都说有意思 other people all say it's interesting

bīnguǎn 宾馆 *n* hotel, guesthouse

bīng 冰 *n* ice

bīngqiú 冰球 *n* ice hockey

bīng 兵 *n* soldier, troops

bǐnggān 饼干 *n* biscuit, cracker, cookie

bìng 并 **1** *adv* (*used before a negative for emphasis*) actually, in reality, in fact; **tā bìng méi qù** 他并没去 he actually didn't go **2** *conj* and, also

bìngqiě 并且 *conj* and ! Often used in a pattern with búdàn 不但 to mean not only...but also....; **tā yǒu bìng cōngmíng bìngqiě hěn hǎokàn** 他不但很聪明并且很好看 he is not only intelligent but also very handsome; moreover, besides

bìng 病 **1** *vb* be ill, become ill; **tā bìng le** 他病了 he is ill **2** *n* disease, ailment; **tā yǒu bìng** 他有病 he has an illness; **tā shēng bìng le** 他生病了 he has become ill; **kàn bìng** 看病 examine someone who is ill, be examined by a doctor, see a doctor

bìngfáng 病房 *n* hospital ward, hospital room

bìngjūn 病菌 *n* bacteria, germs

bìngrén 病人 *n* ill person, patient

bōli 玻璃 *n* glass; **bōli bēi** 玻璃杯 a glass

bófù 伯父, **bóbo** 伯伯 *n* father's elder brother, uncle

bómǔ 伯母 *n* aunt, wife of father's elder brother

bózi 脖子 *n* neck

bǔ 补 *vb* mend, patch, repair; fill, supply, make up for; **bǔ kòngquē** 补空缺 fill a vacancy; nourish; **bǔ shēntǐ** 补身体 build up health; **bǔ xuě** 补血 enrich the blood

bǔchōng 补充 **1** *vb* replenish, supplement **2** *adj* supplementary; **bǔchōng cáiliào** 补充材料 supplementary materials

bǔkè 补课 *vb* make up for a missed lesson; **gěi xuésheng bǔkè** 给学生补课 give tutorials to students who have missed classes

bǔxí 补习 *vb* take lessons after school or work, have remedial lessons; **bǔxíbān** 补习班 special class for supplementary learning

bǔ 捕 *vb* catch, seize, arrest

bú 不, **bù** 不! As is true of **yī** 一, the tone on bu 不 changes depending on the tone of the word that follows it. It is pronounced **bù** before words in first, second, and third tone, but **bú** before the fourth tone. Because the tone changes for bu 不 do not indicate any difference in meaning, but only of pronunciation, combinations beginning with bu 不 are listed in alphabetical order below, regardless of tone; *adv* (used to form a negative) no, not; **wǒ bù kěn qù** 我不肯去 I'm not willing to go; (used to indicate negative potentiality) **tā bā diǎn yǐqián zuò bù wán zuòyè** 他八点以前做不完作业 he won't be able to finish his homework by 8 o'clock

búbì 不必 *vb* need not, be unnecessary; **wǒmen jīntiān búbì shàngkè** 我们今天不必上课 we don't have to attend class today

búcuò 不错 *adj* correct, right; **nǐde jìsuàn yìdiǎnr dōu búcuò** 你的计算一点儿都不错 your calculations were completely correct; (to indicate that what has been said is right) **búcuò, tā míngtiān yào lái** 不错, 他明天要来 yes, he will come tomorrow; (colloquial) not bad, pretty good; **tāde zuòwén búcuò** 他的作文不错 his essay was pretty good

búdà 不大 *adv* not very, not too; **jiàqián búdà piányi** 价钱不大便宜 the prices are not very cheap; not often; **tā wǎnshang búdà niànshū** 他晚上不大念书 he doesn't study in the evening very often

búdàn 不但 *conj* ! Usually used in a sentence pattern with **érqiě** 而且 or **bìngqiě** 并且 in the form búdàn... érqiě/bìngqiě 不但... 而且/并且... to mean not only...but also.... not only; **tā búdàn yǎnjīng bù hǎo, érqiě jìxìng yě bù kěkào** 他不但眼睛不好, 而且记性也不可靠 not only is his eyesight bad but his memory is also unreliable

bùdébù 不得不 *vb* have no choice or option but to, cannot but, have to; **tā bùdébú qù** 他不得不去 he has to go

bùdéliǎo 不得了 **1** *adj* extremely serious, important, extreme; **zhè bú shì shénme bùdéliǎo de wèntí** 这不是什么

不得了的问题 this is not such a desperate matter **2** *adv* (used after de 得 as a complement) extremely, exceedingly; **tā gāoxìng dé bùdéliǎo** 她高兴得不得了 she is overjoyed

búduàn 不断 *adv* unceasingly, continuously, in an uninterrupted fashion; **búduàn de késou** 不断地咳嗽 cough continuously

bù gǎn dāng 不敢当！ *This is a polite expression in reply to a compliment;* thank you! you're flattering me! I don't deserve it

bùguǎn 不管 *conj* no matter what or how; **bùguǎn dào shénme dìfang qù dōu xíng** 不管到什么地方去都行 it doesn't matter where we go, it will be fine with me

búguò 不过 **1** *conj* but, however; **dàxiǎo kěyǐ, búguò yánsè bù xíng** 大小可以，不过颜色不行 the size is fine, but the colour won't do **2** *adv* only, merely; **tā búguò shì ge háizi** 他不过是个孩子 he's only a child **3** *superlative emphatic* **zài** [**hǎo** | **jiǎndān** | **xìngyùn**] **búguò le** 再[好 | 简单 | 幸运]不过了 couldn't be [better | simpler | luckier]

bù hǎoyìsi 不好意思 *adj* feel embarrassed, be ill at ease, find embarrassing

bùjǐn 不仅 not only; **zhè bùjǐn shì tāzìjǐ de kànfǎ** 这不仅是他自己的看法 this is not only his personal view; **bùjǐn rúcǐ** 不仅如此 not only that, moreover

bùjiǔ 不久 *adv* soon, before long; **nǐmen bùjiǔ jiù yào bìyè le** 你们不久就要毕业了 soon you will graduate; not long after, soon after; **xiàle kè bùjiǔ jiù kāishǐ xiàyǔ le** 下了课不久就开始下雨了 not long after class ended it began to rain

búlùn 不论 *conj* no matter what, it doesn't matter; **búlùn nǐ zuò shénme shì, dōu yào zuò hǎo** 不论你做什么事，都要做好 it doesn't matter what you do, you must do it well

bùpíng 不平 *adj* indignant, resentful; unjust

bùrán 不然 *conj* or else, otherwise, if not; **nǐ děi fùxí shēngcí, bùrán huì dōu wàng le** 你得复习生词，不然会都忘了 you must revise the new words or else you'll forget them all

bùrú 不如 *vb (before a noun)* not as...as, not measure up to, compare unfavourably with; **wǒ Hànyǔ shuō de bùrú tā liúlì** 我汉语说得不如她流利 my spoken Chinese is not as fluent as hers; *(before a clause)* had better; **nǐ bùrú jīntiān niànshū** 你不如今天念书 you had better study today

bùshǎo 不少 *adj* quite a bit, quite a few; **bùshǎo qián** 不少钱 quite a large amount of money

bùtóng 不同 *adj* different, distinct

bùxíng 不行 *vb* it's out of the question, it's not allowed; be no good, won't work

bùxìng 不幸 **1** *adj* unfortunate, unlucky, sad **2** *n* misfortune

bù xǔ 不许 *vb* not allow; **wǒde mǔqīn bù xǔ wǒ chū mén** 我的母亲不许我出门 my mother doesn't allow me to leave the house; must not, be forbidden; **nǐ bù xǔ chōu yān** 你不许抽烟 you mustn't smoke

bú yào 不要 *vb* don't; **bú yào nàyàng wúlǐ** 不要那样无礼 don't be so rude

bú yàojǐn 不要紧 **1** *adj* not important; not serious; **wǒde shāng bú yàojǐn** 我的伤不要紧 my injury is not serious **2 búyàojǐn** 不要紧 it doesn't matter

bùyídìng 不一定 *adv* not necessarily; **wǒ bùyídìng néng qù** 我不一定能去 I won't necessarily be able to go

bú yòng 不用 *vb* need not; **bú yòng jǐnzhāng** 不用紧张 you needn't be nervous

bù 布 *n* cloth, cotton cloth

bùzhì 布置 *vb* fix up, arrange, decorate; **bùzhì bàngōngshì** 布置办公室 decorate the office; assign, arrange; **bùzhì zuòyè** 布置作业 assign homework

bù 步 *n* step, pace; stage, step, procedure; condition, situation, state; **nǐ zěnme luòdào zhè yí bù** 你怎么落到这一步 how could you get yourself into such a situation?

bù 部 **1** *n* part, area, section; **xī bù** 西部 the western part; unit, ministry, department; **wàijiāo bù** 外交部 Ministry of Foreign

Affairs; **biānjí bù** 编辑部 editorial board or office **2** *mw* ▶ **213** *(for novels, films, etc.)*

bùduì 部队 *n* army; troops, unit in a military force

bùfen 部分 *n* part, section, portion; **dìyī bùfen** 第一部分 Part One

bùmén 部门 *n* department or branch in a government, company, etc.

bùzhǎng 部长 *n* minister, head of a department; **wàijiāo bù bùzhǎng** 外交部长 Minister of Foreign Affairs

Cc

cā 擦 *vb* wipe, clean; (spread on) **zài liǎn shang cā yóu** 在脸上擦油 put cream on one's face

cāi 猜 *vb* guess, conjecture, speculate

cāixiǎng 猜想 *vb* suppose, guess, suspect

cái 才 **1** *n* ability, talent, gift **2** *adv* just; **diànyǐng cái kāishǐ** 电影才开始 the film has just started; so late; **nǐ zěnme cái lái** 你怎么才来 why are you so late?; only; **tā cái shísān suì** 他才十三岁 he is only 13 years old; then and only then; **wǒmen děi děng tā huílai yǐhòu, cái néng zǒu** 我们得等他回来以后，才能走 we have to wait until he comes back; then we can go

cáinéng 才能 *n* ability, talent

cáizǐ 才子 *n* talented scholar

cáiliào 材料 *n* material, data

cáichǎn 财产 *n* property

cáifù 财富 *n* wealth

cáizhèng 财政 *n* finance

cáifeng 裁缝 *n* tailor, dressmaker

cáipàn 裁判 *n* referee, umpire, judge

cǎi 采 *vb* pick, gather

cǎifǎng 采访 *vb (by a news reporter)* gather material, cover news, interview

cǎigòu 采购 *vb* purchase, buy

cǎiqǔ 采取 *vb* adopt, take; **cǎiqǔ jǐnjí cuòshī** 采取紧急措施 take emergency steps

cǎiyòng 采用 *vb* adopt for use, use; **cǎiyòng xīn jìshù** 采用新技术 adopt new techniques

cǎisè 彩色 *n* colour, multicolour; **cǎisè diànshì** 彩色电视 colour television

cǎi 踩 *vb* step on

cài 菜 *n* vegetable; *(food in general)* food; **mǎi cài** 买菜 shop for food; dish, course

càidān 菜单 *n* menu

cānguān 参观 *vb* visit, look around

cānjiā 参加 *vb* join, take part in; attend; **cānjiā huìyì** 参加会议 attend meetings

cānkǎo 参考 **1** *vb* consult, refer to **2** *n* **cānkǎo shū** 参考书 reference book

cānmóu 参谋 **1** *n* adviser, staff officer; **cānmóu zhǎng** 参谋长 chief of staff **2** *vb* give advice

cān 餐 *n* food, meal; [Xī | Zhōng | wǔ | yě] **cān** [西 | 中 | 午 | 野] 餐 [Western food | Chinese food | lunch | picnic]

cānchē 餐车 *n* dining car, restaurant car

cāntīng 餐厅 *n* dining room, dining hall

cánfèi 残废 *adj* disabled, physically handicapped

cánkù 残酷 *adj* cruel, ruthless, brutal

cánkuì 惭愧 *adj* feel ashamed

cǎn 惨 *adj* miserable, pitiful, tragic

cànlàn 灿烂 *adj* magnificent, splendid, bright

cāngkù 仓库 *n* warehouse, storehouse

cāngbái 苍白 *adj* pale

cāngying 苍蝇 *n* fly

cāng 舱 *n* cabin; **kècāng** 客舱 passenger cabin; **huòcāng** 货舱 a (ship's) hold

cáng 藏 *vb* hide, store, put by

cāochǎng 操场 *n* playground, sports ground, drill ground

cǎo 草 *n* grass, straw

cǎodì 草地 *n* grassland, meadow, lawn

cǎoyuán 草原 *n* steppe, grasslands, prairie

cè 册 *mw* ▶ 213 (for books or volumes of books) volume, book; (for copies of books) copy

cèsuǒ 厕所 *n* lavatory, toilet, loo

cèyàn 测验 **1** *vb* test **2** *n* test

cèlüè 策略 *n* tactics, strategy

céng 层 **1** *mw* ▶ 213 storey, floor; (for a layer, coat, sheet) **2** *n* floor; **wǒde fángjiān zài sāncéng** 我的房间在三层 my room is on the third floor ! Note that Chinese is similar to US usage where the 1st floor is the ground floor, whereas in British English the storey above the ground floor is called the 1st floor.

céng 曾 *adv* once, formerly, sometime ago; **tā céng zuòguo zhèzhǒng gōngzuò** 他曾做过这种工作 he did this kind of work once before

céngjīng 曾经 *adv* once, formerly; **tāmen céngjīng shì hǎo péngyou** 他们曾经是好朋友 they were once good friends

chāzi 叉子 *n* fork

chā 插 *vb* stick in, insert; interpolate; insert; **tā bànjù huà yě chā bú jìnqu** 他半句话也插不进去 he couldn't get a word in edgeways

chá 茶 *n* tea

chábēi 茶杯 *n* teacup

chádiǎn 茶点 *n* tea and snacks, tea and biscuits

cháguǎn 茶馆 *n* teahouse

cháhú 茶壶 *n* teapot

cháyè 茶叶 *n* tea leaves

chá 查 *vb* check, examine, inspect; look into, investigate, find out; look up, consult; **chá zìdiǎn** 查字典 consult a dictionary

chà 差 **1** *vb* differ from, fall short of; **chà de yuǎn** 差得远 differ substantially **2** *adj* wanting, short of; **hái chà liǎng kuài qián** 还差两块钱 still two yuan short; **chà wǔ fēn qī diǎn** 差五分七点 five minutes to seven

chàbuduō 差不多 *adj* almost, nearly; **tā líkāi chàbuduō liǎng nián le** 他离开差不多两年了 he's been gone nearly two years now; about the same, similar

chàdiǎnr 差点儿 *adv* almost, nearly, on the verge of; **tā chàdiǎnr shībài** 她差点儿失败 she very nearly failed

chāi 拆 *vb* take apart, tear open; pull down, demolish; unravel; **bǎ yíjiàn jiù máoyī chāi le** 把一件旧毛衣拆了 unravel an old jumper

chǎnliàng 产量 *n* output, yield

chǎnpǐn 产品 *n* product, produce

chǎnshēng 产生 *vb* produce, engender, bring about; emerge, come into being

cháng 长 *adj* long

Chángchéng 长城 *n* the Great Wall

chángchù 长处 *n* good qualities, strong points

chángdù 长度 *n* length

Chángjiāng 长江 *n* Yangtze River, Yangtse River

chángjiǔ 长久 *adj* long-lasting, long-term

chángqī 长期 *n* a long period of time, long-term

chángtú 长途 *n* long-distance; **chángtú diànhuà** 长途电话 long-distance telephone call

cháng 尝 *vb* taste, try the flavour of

cháng 常, **chángcháng** 常常 *adv* frequently, often

chǎng 场 **1** *mw* ▶ **213** (*for the whole process of being ill*); (*for a natural disturbance, war, disaster, etc.*); (*for a show, performance, game, or debate*); (*to indicate the occasion on which a state or an action occurs*) **2** *n* site, spot, place where people gather; (*for ballgames*) court, field, ground; [lánqiú | páiqiú | zúqiú | wǎngqiú] **chǎng** [篮球 | 排球 | 足球 | 网球] 场 [basketball court | volleyball court | football field | tennis court]; stage; **dēng chǎng** 登场 come on stage

chàng 唱 *vb* sing

chànggē 唱歌 *vb* sing songs

chāo 抄 *vb* copy, transcribe; plagiarize

chāoxiě 抄写 *vb* make a clear copy

chāo 超 *vb* exceed, surpass, overtake

chāoguò 超过 *vb* outstrip, surpass, exceed

chāojí shìchǎng 超级市场 *n* supermarket

cháo 朝 **1** *prep* facing, towards; **cháo Lúndūn kāi** 朝伦敦开 drive towards London **2** *vb* face, towards; **zhè fángzi cháo nán** 这房子朝南 this house faces south **3** *n* dynasty or period; **Hàn cháo** 汉朝 the Han Dynasty

Cháoxiān 朝鲜 *n* North Korea

cháo 巢 *n* nest

chǎo 吵 **1** *vb* quarrel, wrangle, squabble; **wèi yìxiē xiǎoshì chǎojià** 为一些小事吵架 bicker over small matters **2** *adj* noisy

chǎojià 吵架 *vb* quarrel, have an argument

chǎonào 吵闹 *vb* make a fuss, make trouble

chǎozuǐ 吵嘴 *vb* quarrel, bicker

chǎo 炒 *vb* stir-fry

chē 车 *n* vehicle, car, bus

chēdài 车带 *n* tyre on a car or bicycle

chējiān 车间 *n* workshop

chēpiào 车票 *n* bus ticket, train ticket

chēzhàn 车站 *n* station, stop

chèdǐ 彻底 *adj* thorough

chén 沉 **1** *vb* sink, sink down, lower **2** *adj* shuì de hěn chén 睡得很沉 sleep soundly, sleep deeply; heavy

chénmò 沉默 *adj* reticent, uncommunicative; silent

chénzhòng 沉重 *adj* heavy

chénliè 陈列 *vb* display, exhibit

chènshān 衬衫 *n* shirt

chènyī 衬衣 *n* underclothes, shirt

chèn 趁 *vb* take advantage of, avail oneself of; **chèn zhège jīhuì xiūxi yíxià** 趁这个机会休息一下 take this opportunity to have a rest

chēng 称 *vb* name, call; **wǒmen dōu chēng tā shūshu** 我们都称他叔叔 we all call him Uncle; weigh; state, say

chēngzàn 称赞 *vb* praise, acclaim, commend

chéng 成 *vb* become, change to, develop into; **tā chéngle yíge dàifu** 他成了一个大夫 he became a doctor; accomplish, succeed; **zhèbǐ jiāoyì méi chéng** 这笔交易没成 the deal did not succeed

chéngfèn 成分(成份) *n* composition, component part, ingredient; one's class status or family background

chénggōng 成功 **1** *vb* succeed **2** *n* success

chéngguǒ 成果 *n* accomplishment, achievement

chéngjī 成绩 *n* achievement, success

chéngjiā 成家 *vb* (referring to a man) get married

chéngjiù 成就 *n* achievement, accomplishment, attainment

chénglì 成立 *vb* set up, found, establish

chéngnián 成年 *vb* grow up, come of age

chéngrén 成人 *n* adult

chéngshú 成熟 **1** *vb* ripen, mature **2** *adj* ripe, mature

chéngwéi 成为 *vb* become, change to, develop into

chéngzhǎng 成长 *vb* grow up

chéngkěn 诚恳 *adj* sincere

chéngshí 诚实 *adj* honest

chéng 城 *n* city, town; city wall, wall

chéngshì 城市 *n* town, city

chéngzhèn 城镇 *n* cities and towns, town

chéngrèn 承认 *vb* admit, acknowledge, recognize; give diplomatic recognition to, recognize

chéngshòu 承受 *vb* bear, endure

chéng 乘 *vb* ride; **chéng** [huǒchē | fēijī | gōnggòng qìchē] **lǚxíng** 乘[火车/飞机/公共汽车]旅行 travel by [train | plane | bus]; take advantage of; (*in mathematical operations*) multiply; **wǔ chéng sān děngyú shíwǔ** 五乘三等于十五 five times three equals fifteen

chéngwùyuán 乘务员 *n* train attendant, conductor, ticket collector

chéngdù 程度 *n* level, degree, extent

chī 吃 *vb* eat

chīcù 吃醋 *adj* be jealous

chījīng 吃惊 *vb* be startled, be shocked, be amazed; **dà chī yì jīng** 大吃一惊 be greatly surprised

chídào 迟到 *vb* be late

chǐ 尺 *n* (*unit of length, 1/3 metre*) chi

chǐzi 尺子 *n* (*to measure length*) ruler

chǐcùn 尺寸 *n* size, measurement, dimension

chìdào 赤道 *n* equator

chìbǎng 翅膀 *n* wing

chōngfèn 充分 *adj* full, ample, abundant

chōngmǎn 充满 *vb* be full of, be brimming with

chōngzú 充足 *adj* adequate, ample, abundant

chōng 冲 *vb* pour boiling water on; **chōng chá** 冲茶 make tea; rinse, flush, wash away; **chōng cèsuǒ** 冲厕所 flush the toilet; charge, rush, dash; **chōng jìn fángzi** 冲进房子 rush into the house; (*for film*) develop; **chōng jiāojuǎn** 冲胶卷 develop a roll of film

chōngtū 冲突 *n* conflict, clash

chóngzi 虫子 *n* insect, worm

chóng 重 *vb* ▶ See also **zhòng** 重. over again; **chóng fǎng Yīngguó** 重访英国 revisit the U.K.

chóngdié 重叠 *vb* overlap, pile on top of one another

chóngfù 重复 *vb* repeat, duplicate

chóngxīn 重新 *adv* again, anew, afresh

chónggāo 崇高 *adj* lofty, high

chǒng'ài 宠爱 *vb* dote on, make a pet of someone

chōu 抽 *vb* take out (*from in between*); **cóng shūjià shang chōuchū yìběn shū** 从书架上抽出一本书 take a book from the shelf; (*cigarette, pipe*) smoke; (*water*) draw; **chōu shuǐ** 抽水 draw water (*from a well, etc.*); lash, whip, thrash

chōuxiàng 抽象 *adj* abstract

chōuyān 抽烟 *vb* smoke (a cigarette or a pipe)

chóu 愁 *vb* worry, be anxious; **bié chóu** 别愁 don't worry

chǒu 丑 *adj* ugly, disgraceful

chòu 臭 *adj* smelly, stinking, foul; **chòu jīdàn** 臭鸡蛋 rotten egg; **chòu dòufu** 臭豆腐 fermented beancurd

chū 出 *vb* go or come out; issue, put forth; produce, turn out, publish; **chū xīn shū** 出新书 publish new books; arise, happen, occur; **chū shìgù** 出事故 there was an accident; exceed, go beyond; **bù chū sān nián** 不出三年 within three years; vent; **chū qì** 出气 vent one's spleen, express one's anger

chūbǎn 出版 *vb* publish

chūbǎnshè 出版社 *n* publishing company, publishing house

chūfā 出发 *vb* set out, start off; start, proceed

chūfādiǎn 出发点 *n* starting point, point of departure

chūguó 出国 *vb* go abroad, leave the country

chūkǒu 出口 **1** *vb* export **2** *n* export; exit

chūlai 出来 *vb* come out; (*after a verb to indicate movement in an outward direction or a completed action*) **bǎ qián náchūlai** 把钱拿出来 take out the money; **xiàngpiàn xǐchūlai le** 相片洗出来了 the photographs have been developed; **tā xiǎngchūlaile yíge hǎo bànfǎ** 他想出来了一个好办法 he thought of a good solution

chūlù 出路 *n* a way out, a solution to a problem

chūmíng 出名 *adj* famous, well-known

chūqu 出去 *vb* go out, get out; (*after a verb to indicate movement in an outward direction*) **cóng wūlǐ pǎochūqu** 从屋里 跑出去 run out from the room

chūsè 出色 *adj* excellent, outstanding, remarkable

chūshēng 出生 *vb* be born

chūxí 出席 *vb* (*when speaking of a meeting, banquet, etc.*) attend, be present

chūxiàn 出现 *vb* appear, emerge, come to light

chūyuàn 出院 *vb* leave hospital, be discharged from hospital after recovery

chūzū qìchē 出租汽车 *n* taxi

chū 初 1 *adj* early; chū [dōng | chūn | xià | qiū] 初 [冬 | 春 | 夏 | 秋] early [winter | spring | summer | autumn]; elementary, rudimentary; **chūzhōng** 初中 *(abbreviation of* chūjí zhōngxué 初级中学*)* junior middle school, junior high school; *(used to enumerate days of the lunar month up to ten)* chū [yī | èr | sān | sì...] 初 [一 | 二 | 三 | 四...] the [first | second | third | fourth...] day of a lunar month 2 *n* beginning; [zhège yuè | míngnián | shàngge shìjì] chū [这个月 | 明年 | 上个世纪] 初 the beginning of [this month | next year | the last century]

chūbù 初步 *adj* initial, preliminary, tentative

chūjí 初级 *adj* elementary, primary

chú 除 *vb* get rid of, do away with, remove; **chúdiào** [huài xíguàn | jiù sīxiǎng] 除掉 [坏习惯 | 旧思想] get rid of [bad habits | old ways of thinking]; divide; **sān chú liù dé èr** 三除六得二 six divided by three equals two

chúfēi 除非 *conj* ! *When* chúfēi 除非 *is used, it is often necessary to use* fǒuzé 否则 *or* bùrán 不然 *at the beginning of the main clause to indicate the necessary consequence of the clause introduced by* chúfēi 除非; only if, unless; **chúfēi tiānqì bù hǎo, fǒuzé wǒmen míngtiān qù hǎibiān wánr** 除非天气不好，否则我们明天去海边玩儿 we'll go to the seashore tomorrow unless the weather isn't good

chúle ... (yǐwài) 除了...(以外) *prep* ! *Note that the use of* yǐwài 以外 *is optional; (used with* dōu 都 *or* yě 也*)* except; **chúle tā (yǐwài), biéren dōu bú huì chàng zhèshǒu gē** 除了她 (以外)，别人都不会唱这首歌 no one can sing this song except her; *(used with* hái 还*)* apart from, besides, in addition to...; **tā chúle kànshū yǐwài, hái xiězuò** 她除了看书以外，还写作 in addition to reading she also does some writing

chúfáng 厨房 *n* kitchen

chǔ 处 *vb* deal with, handle; **chǔ shì** 处事 handle affairs, manage matters; be in a certain position *(literal or figurative)*; **chǔyú** 处于 *(literal or figurative)* to be located in a place or position; **tā chǔyú bú lì dìwèi** 他处于不利地位 he is in a disadvantageous position

chǔfèn 处分 **1** n disciplinary action, punishment **2** vb take disciplinary action against, punish

chǔlǐ 处理 **1** vb handle, deal with, dispose of; **chǔlǐ jiāwù** 处理家务 do household chores; **chǔlǐ jiàgé** 处理价格 reduced price, bargain price; **chǔlǐpǐn** 处理品 goods sold at reduced or sale prices **2** n handling, treatment, disposal

chù 处 n place; **tíngchēchù** 停车处 car park, parking lot; point, feature; **gòngtóng zhī chù** 共同之处 common feature; department, office; **mìshūchù** 秘书处 secretariat

chuān 穿 vb wear, put on, be dressed in; pierce through, penetrate; **chuāntòu** 穿透 penetrate; pass through, cross; **chuānguò mǎlù** 穿过马路 cross the road; **chuānshang** 穿上 put on; **chuānshang nǐde dàyī** 穿上你的大衣 put on your coat

chuán 传 vb pass, pass on; (for news, rumours, etc.) spread, transmit; hand down; (for heat, electricity, etc.) transmit, conduct

chuánbō 传播 vb propagate, disseminate, spread

chuánrǎn 传染 vb infect, catch; **chuánrǎngěile tā** 我把感冒传染给了他 he caught my cold

chuánshuō 传说 n rumour, legend

chuántǒng 传统 n tradition, conventions

chuánzhēn 传真 n facsimile, fax

chuán 船 n boat, ship

chuāng(hu) 窗(户) n window

chuáng 床 **1** n bed; **shàng chuáng shuìjiào** 上床睡觉 go to bed, get into bed **2** mw ▶ **213** (for quilt, blanket, sheet)

chuángdān 床单 n (bed) sheet

chuǎng 闯 vb rush, force one's way in or out

chuàng 创 vb initiate, achieve for the first time, innovate; **chuàng jìlù** 创记录 set a record

chuàngzào 创造 **1** vb create, produce, bring about **2** n creation

chuàngzuò 创作 **1** vb (works of art or literature) create, write, produce **2** n literary or artistic creation

chuī 吹 vb blow, exhale; **chuī yìkǒu qì** 吹一口气 blow out a puff of air; (wind instruments) play; **chuī dízi** 吹笛子 play the flute; (colloquial) brag, boast; (colloquial, referring to a relationship) break off, break up, fall through; **tāmen liǎ chuī le** 他们俩吹了 they have broken up; **chuīmiè** 吹灭 blow out; **bǎ làzhú chuīmiè** 把蜡烛吹灭 blow out the candle

chuīniú 吹牛 vb brag, boast

chuīxū 吹嘘 vb brag, boast

chūn 春 n (the season) spring; **chūnjì** 春季 spring season

Chūnjié 春节 n Spring Festival, the Chinese New Year

chūntiān 春天 n spring, springtime

chúncuì 纯粹 adj pure, simple

chún 唇 n lip

cí 词 n word, term; speech, statement; **kāimùcí** 开幕词 opening speech

cídiǎn 词典 n dictionary, lexicon

cíhuì 词汇 n vocabulary

cízhí 辞职 vb leave or quit a job, resign

cídài 磁带 n (magnetic) tape

cǐ 此 det this; **cǐ** [chù | rén] 此 [处 | 人] this [place | person]

cǐwài 此外 adv besides, moreover, in addition

cì 次 mw ▶ 213 (for events such as examinations, accidents, experiments, etc.); (to indicate the number of times an action or state occurs) time

cì 刺 **1** vb prick, stab; irritate, criticize **2** n thorn

cìshā 刺杀 vb assassinate

cōngmáng 匆忙 adv hurriedly, hastily

cōngmíng 聪明 adj intelligent, bright, clever

cóng 从 *prep* (used to indicate the starting point) from; **cóng Běijīng chūfā** 从北京出发 start off from Beijing; **cóng lǐlùnshàng jiǎng** 从理论上讲 theoretically speaking

cóng bù/méi 从不/没 *adv* never; **wǒ cóng bù hē jiǔ** 我从不喝酒 I never drink wine; **wǒ cóng méi qùguo Yìdàlì** 我从没去过意大利 I've never been to Italy

cóngcǐ 从此 *adv* from now on, henceforth

cóng...dào... 从...到... *prep* from...to...; **cóng zǎoshàng jiǔ diǎn dào wǎnshàng bā diǎn** 从早上九点到晚上八点 from 9:00 am to 8:00 pm

cóng'ér 从而 *conj* thus, and then, and then proceed to

cónglái 从来 *adv* always, all along ! Note that cónglái 从来 *normally precedes the negative word* bù 不 *or* méi 没; **wǒ cónglái méi jiànguo tā** 我从来没见过他 I have never seen him before; **tā cónglái bù hē jiǔ** 他从来不喝酒 he never drinks wine

cóng...qǐ 从...起 *prep* from...on, from...forward; **cóng xiànzài qǐ...** 从现在起... from now on...

cóngqián 从前 *adv* before, in the past, formerly

cóngshì 从事 *vb* go in for, be engaged in

còuqiǎo 凑巧 *adv* luckily, by coincidence

còuhe 凑合 *vb* gather together, get together; **tāmen měige zhōumò dōu còuhe zài yìqǐ hē chá liáotiān** 他们每个周末都凑合在一起喝茶聊天 every weekend they get together for tea and have a chat; make do; **tā yìzhí zài còuhezhe yòng nàtái jiù jisuànjī** 他一直在凑合着用那台旧计算机 he has been making do with that old computer all along; do in a pinch, be OK, be not too bad; 'nàbù Měiguó diànyǐng zěnmeyàng?'—'hái còuhe' '那部美国电影怎么样?'—'还凑合' 'how was that American film?'—'it wasn't too bad'

cū 粗 *adj* thick; careless, negligent

cūxīn 粗心 *adj* careless, thoughtless

cùjìn 促进 *vb* promote, advance, accelerate

cù 醋 *n* vinegar; (*in love affairs*) jealousy

cuī 催 *vb* hurry, urge, speed up

cūn 村 *n* village

cūnzhuāng 村庄 *n* village

cūnzi 村子 *n* village

cún 存 *vb* store, keep, preserve; place something for safe keeping, deposit; **bǎ qián cún zài yínháng lǐ** 把钱存在银行里 save money in a bank; exist, live, survive

cúnfàng 存放 *vb* leave in someone's care

cúnkuǎn 存款 *n* deposit account, bank savings

cúnzài 存在 *vb* exist

cùn 寸 *n* (*a unit of length, 1/30 metre*) *cun*

cuòshī 措施 *n* measure, step, suitable action

cuò 错 **1** *adj* wrong, mistaken, erroneous; **cuò zì** 错字 wrong Chinese character **2** *n* mistake, error, fault; **zhè búshì nǐde cuò** 这不是你的错 it's not your fault **3** *adv* by mistake, in the wrong way; **zuòcuò le** 做错了 made a mistake; **zuòcuòle chē** 坐错了车 took the wrong bus

cuòguò 错过 *vb* miss, let slip; **bié cuòguò zhège hǎo jīhuì** 别错过这个好机会 don't miss this good opportunity

cuòwù 错误 *n* mistake, error

Dd

dā 搭 *vb* put up, put together, construct; **dā yíge xiǎo péng** 搭一个小棚 put up a shed/arbour; join up with, establish contact; **dā huǒ** 搭伙 join a group; **dāshang guānxi** 搭上关系 establish contact; (*a ship, train, plane, etc.*) go by, go aboard; **dā** [chuán | huǒchē | chē] 搭 [船 | 火车 | 车] go by [ship | train | car]

dāyìng 答应 *vb* respond, reply; **méi rén dāyìng** 没人答应 no one answered; agree, promise; **tā dāyìng qù** 他答应去 he agreed to go

dádào 达到 *vb* attain, reach; **dádào mùdì** 达到目的 attain a goal

dá 答 *vb* answer, reciprocate

dá'àn 答案 *n* answer, solution

dáfù 答复 *vb* (in a formal way) reply, answer

dájuàn 答卷 *n* answer booklet, answer sheet

dǎ 打 *vb* hit, strike, beat; **dǎ rén** 打人 hit a person; fight, make (war); (when talking about an object) break, smash, destroy; **dǎpò jìngzi** 打破镜子 break a mirror; (when talking about prejudice, tradition, record, relationship, etc.) **dǎpò** [piānjiàn | jiù chuántǒng | jìlù] 打破 [偏见 | 旧传统 | 纪录] [dispel a prejudice | break an old tradition | break a record]; (for games played with the hands, some musical instruments) play; **dǎ qiú** 打球 play a (ball) game; **dǎ tàijíquán** 打太极拳 practice taiji boxing; **dǎ pái** 打牌 play cards; **dǎ gǔ** 打鼓 play a drum/drums; type on a typewriter, use a keyboard on a computer; **dǎzì** 打字 type, typing; send, dispatch; **dǎ** [diànbào | diànhuà] 打 [电报 | 电话] [send a telegram | make a phone call]; (other uses) **dǎ chái** 打柴 gather firewood; **dǎ gōng** 打工 do odd jobs; **dǎ liè** 打猎 go hunting; **dǎ máoyī** 打毛衣 knit a sweater; **dǎ qì** 打气 (for tyres) inflate with air; (for people) encourage, boost morale; **dǎ qiāng** 打枪 fire a gun; **dǎ shuǐ** 打水 fetch water; **dǎ yóu** 打油 buy oil; **dǎ yú** 打渔 catch fish

dǎbài 打败 *vb* defeat

dǎbàn 打扮 *vb* dress up, deck out, make up

dǎdǎo 打倒 *vb* down with..., overthrow

dǎjī 打击 *vb* attack, hit, strike

dǎjià 打架 *vb* fight, come to blows

dǎkāi 打开 *vb* open (something)

dǎ pēntì 打喷嚏 *vb* sneeze

dǎrǎo 打扰 *vb* bother, disturb, trouble

dǎsǎo 打扫 *vb* (when referring to housework) clean, sweep

dǎsuàn 打算 **1** *vb* intend to, plan to **2** *n* intention, plan

dǎtīng 打听 *vb* ask about, inquire about

dǎzhàng 打仗 *vb* fight, make war

dǎ zhāohu 打招呼 *vb* greet politely, make a sign of greeting politely

dǎzhēn 打针 *vb* inject, give or have an injection

dǎzì 打字 *vb* type, word-process, key in

dǎzìjī 打字机 *n* typewriter

dà 大 **1** *adj* big, large, major; heavy, strong; **fēng hěn dà** 风很大 the wind is strong; (when referring to sound) loud; (when referring to age) old, elder; **háizi duō dà le?** 孩子多大了? how old is the child?; **dà jiě** 大姐 elder sister **2** *adv* (to a great extent, to an extreme) **dà nào** 大闹 create a major disturbance; (after a negative) not very, not often; **bú dà hǎo** 不大好 not very good; **bú dà huì** 不大会 cannot (do something) very well

dàdǎn 大胆 *adj* bold, daring, audacious

dàduōshù 大多数 *n* the great majority

dàgài 大概 **1** *adj* general, approximate; **yíge dàgài de yìnxiàng** 一个大概的印象 a general impression **2** *adv* probably

dàhuì 大会 *n* large meeting, plenary session

dàhuǒr 大伙儿 *pron* we all, you all, everyone; **zhè shì wǒmen dàhuǒr de yìjiàn** 这是我们大伙儿的意见 this is the view that we all take

dàjiā 大家 *pron* (often used with **dōu** 都 when it's the subject of a sentence) everybody, everyone; **dàjiā dōu xǐhuān tā** 大家都喜欢他 everyone likes him

dàjiē 大街 *n* main road, boulevard, avenue

dàliàng 大量 **1** *adj* large amount of, a great quantity of; **dàliàng de liángshi** 大量的粮食 a large quantity of food **2** *adv* in large numbers, by a great quantity; **dàliàng xuějiǎn jīngfèi** 大量消减经费 reduce expenses by a large amount

dàlù 大陆 *n* mainland, continent

dàmǐ 大米 *n* uncooked white rice

dàpī 大批 *adj* large quantity/number of; **yí dàpī xuésheng** 一大批学生 a large group of students

dàren 大人 *n* adult, grown-up

dàshēng 大声 *adv* loudly; **dàshēng jiào** 大声叫 call out in a loud voice

dàshǐ 大使 *n* ambassador

dàshǐguǎn 大使馆 *n* embassy

dàtǐshàng 大体上 *adv* for the most part, generally, more or less

dàxiǎo 大小 *n* size

dàxíng 大型 *adj* large-scaled, large-sized, large; **dàxíng fādòngjī** 大型发动机 large-sized motor

dàxué 大学 *n* university, college; **shàng dàxué** 上大学 attend university

dàyī 大衣 *n* coat, overcoat

dàyuē 大约 *adv* approximately, about; **dàyuē yào yíge xiǎoshí** 大约要一个小时 it will take about one hour

dāi 呆 **1** *adj* slow-witted, dull; (*with fear or amazement*) blank, wooden; **tā zhàn zài nàr fā dāi** 他站在那儿发呆 he stood there staring blankly **2** *vb* stay; **dāi zài jiālǐ** 呆在家里 stay at home

dāi 待 *vb* ▸ See also **dài** 待. stay

dàifu 大夫 *n* doctor, physician

dài 代 **1** *n* historical period; **Táng dài** 唐代 the Tang Dynasty; generation; **xīn yídài** 新一代 a new generation **2** *vb* on behalf of; **qǐng dài wǒ wènhòu tā** 请代我问候他 please give him my greetings; acting; **dài zǒnglǐ** 代总理 acting premier

dàibiǎo 代表 **1** *n* representative **2** *vb* represent

dàijià 代价 *n* cost, price to pay for

dàitǐ 代替 *vb* stand in place of, substitute

dài 带 **1** *n* belt, ribbon; tyre; region, area; **zài Huánghé yídài** 在黄河一带 in the region of the Yellow River **2** *vb* take, bring along, bring; **kěyǐ dài háizi qù ma?** 可以带孩子去吗? can we take children with us?; have with, attached, included; **yíkuài dài rìlì de shǒubiǎo** 一块带日历的手表 a date watch, a calendar watch; (*when talking about children*) look after, bring up; **tāde zǔmǔ bǎ tā dài dà** 他的祖母把他带大 his grandmother raised him

dài 待 *vb* ▶ *See also* **dāi** 待. treat, deal with; wait for, await; **dài dào míngtiān** 待到明天 wait until tomorrow

dài 袋 *n* bag, sack; **yídài tǔdòu** 一袋土豆 a sack of potatoes

dài 戴 *vb* (*on the head, neck, or wrist*) put on, wear

dānrèn 担任 *vb* assume the responsibility for, hold the position of

dānxīn 担心 *vb* worry about, be concerned that

dān 单 **1** *adj* single, of one unit, simple; **dānrén chuáng** 单人床 single bed; (*referring to numbers*) odd; **dān shù** 单数 odd number **2** *adv* singly, separately; **bǎ zhèběn shū dān fàng** 把这本书单放 keep this book in a separate place **3** *n* (*for a bed*) sheet; bill, list; **dānzi** 单子 list

dāncí 单词 *n* (*as a linguistic unit*) word

dāndiào 单调 *adj* monotonous, dull, drab

dāndú 单独 *adj* alone

dānwèi 单位 *n* unit of measurement; organizational unit; **gōngzuò dānwèi** 工作单位 work unit

dǎnliàng 胆量 *n* courage

dàn 但 *conj* ▶ *See also* **búdàn** 不但. but, yet, nevertheless

dànshì 但是 *conj* but, however, yet

dànyuàn 但愿 *vb* I wish, if only

dànzi 担子 *n* load, burden, task

dànshēng 诞生 *vb* be born, emerge, come into being

dàn 淡 *adj* lacking salt; **tā zuò de cài tài dàn** 他做的菜太淡 the dishes he cooks are not salty enough; **dàn shuǐ hú** 淡水湖 freshwater lake; tasteless, insipid, weak; **zhèbēi chá tài dàn** 这杯 茶太淡 this cup of tea is too weak; (*in colour*) light; **dàn lǜ** 淡绿 pale green, light green; slack, poor; **dànjì** 淡季 low season, slack season

dàn 蛋 *n* egg; **dànbái** 蛋白 egg white, protein; **dànhuáng** 蛋黄 egg yolk

dàngāo 蛋糕 *n* cake

dāng 当 ▶ See also **dàng** 当. **1** *vb* act in the role of, undertake/occupy the position of; **dāng lǎoshī** 当老师 be a teacher, work as a teacher **2** *prep* (*when referring to a certain time or place*) when, at, whilst; **dāng...de shíhòu** 当...的时候 when..., at the time...; **dāng wǒ dào de shíhòu, tā yǐjīng zǒu le** 当我到的时候, 他已经走了 when I arrived, he had already left

dāngchǎng 当场 *adv* on the spot, there and then, red-handed

dāngdài 当代 *n* contemporary, the present age

dāngdì 当地 *adj* local; **dāngdì shíjiān** 当地时间 local time

dāngjīn 当今 *adv* now, at present, nowadays

dāngnián 当年 *adv* ▶ See also **dàngnián** 当年. in those years

dāngqián 当前 **1** *adj* present, current **2** *adv* at present

dāngrán 当然 *adv* of course, naturally

dāngshí 当时 *adv* at that time

dāngxīn 当心 *vb* be careful, look out

dǎng 挡 *vb* stand in the way of, bar, block; **dǎngzhù dàolù** 挡住 道路 bar the way

dǎng 党 *n* political party

dǎngyuán 党员 *n* party member

dàng 当 *vb* ▶ See also **dāng** 当. treat as, regard as; equal to; think that, take it to be that

dàngnián 当年 *adv* ▶ *See also* **dāngnián** 当年. in the same year, that very year

dàngzuò 当做 *vb* consider as, take as

dāo 刀 *n* knife, sword, razor

dāozi 刀子 *n* knife, penknife

dǎo 岛 *n* island

dǎo 倒 *vb* ▶ *See also* **dào** 倒. fall, fall down; tā dǎo zài dì shang le 他倒在地上了 he fell down to the ground; collapse, be overthrown, close down; go bankrupt; change, exchange; **dǎo chē** 倒车 change a train/bus

dǎobì 倒闭 *vb* close down, go bankrupt

dǎoméi 倒霉 *adj* unlucky, have bad luck

dào 到 **1** *vb* arrive, reach; go to ! *Often used with* qù 去 *or* lái 来 *in the pattern* dào...qù 去 *or* dào...lái 来: dào Lúndūn qù 到伦敦去 go to London; dào Běijīng lái 到北京来 come to Beijing **2** *vb* (*used after other verbs to indicate successful attainment*) [mǎi | zhǎo | bàn] 到 [买 | 找 | 办] 到 manage to [buy | find | accomplish] something; (*used with the negative* bù 不 *to indicate impossible attainment*) [kàn | tīng | zuò] bú dào [看 | 听 | 做] 不到 be unable to [see | hear | do] something; (*used with the negative* méi 没 *to indicate unsuccessful attainment*) tā méi mǎidào 他没买到 he was unable to buy it **3** *prep* until, to, towards; yì tiān dào wǎn 一天到晚 from morning to night; huì yìzhí kāi dào bā diǎnzhōng 会一直开到八点钟 the meeting lasted until 8 o'clock

dàochù 到处 *adv* in all places, everywhere

dàodá 到达 *vb* arrive, reach

dàodǐ 到底 *adv* after all, really; in the end, at last, finally; to the end, to the finish

dào 倒 ▶ *See also* **dǎo** 倒. **1** *vb* pour, pour out, dump; reverse, go backwards; **dào chē** 倒车 reverse the car **2** *adv* back, in the opposite direction; upside down; guàdào le 挂倒了 hang upside down; (*for emphasis*) indeed, after all, on the contrary; **dào shì** 倒是 (*used in a question to find out the fact of a matter*) (really)...or not?; **nǐ dào shì qù bú qù?** 你倒是去不去? are you really going or not?

dào 道 1 *n* road, way, path; way, method 2 *adj* Taoist, Daoist 3 *vb* speak, say, or tell 4 *mw* ▶ **213** (for orders issued by an authority, questions on an examination); (for things in the shape of a line); (for courses in a meal)

dàodé 道德 *n* morality, ethical code, ethics

Dàojiào 道教 *n* Taoism, Daoism

dàolǐ 道理 *n* teaching, doctrine, principle; reason, sense; **yǒu dàolǐ** 有道理 make sense, be reasonable

dàolù 道路 *n* way, road, course

dàoqiàn 道歉 *vb* apologize

de 的 *pt* ! The particle de 的 is often used to transform a word, phrase, or clause to modify a noun or noun phrase. It can also be used to transform an adjective into a noun or a verb phrase into a noun phrase; of; **xuéxiào de guīdìng** 学校的规定 the rules of the school; (to indicate possession) **wǒ māma de shū** 我妈妈的书 my mother's book; (after an adjective to modify a noun) **měilì de gūniang** 美丽的姑娘 a beautiful girl; (after a clause to make it modify a noun) **tā mǎi de shū** 他买的书 the books he bought; (after an adjective to transform it into a noun) **hóng de shì wǒde** 红的是我的 the red one is mine; (after a verb phrase to transform it into a noun phrase) **tā shuō de bù hǎotīng** 他说的不好听 what he said was not pleasant; (in the **shì...de** 是... construction for emphasis) **wǒ shì zuótiān dào de** 我是昨天到的 I arrived yesterday

de 得 *pt* (used between two verbs to indicate possibility) ! Note that the first verb indicates the action, while the second indicates a possible result or attainment; **bān de dòng** 搬得动 be able to move it; **zuò de dào** 做得到 be able to do it ! In expressions like these, the possibility is negated by the use of bu 不 in place of de 得, thus the expressions **bān bú dòng** 搬不动, **zuò bú dào** 做不到 mean be unable to move and be unable to do; (used between a verb and an adjective or a clause to indicate degree or extent) **pǎo de kuài** 跑得快 run fast; **bìng de hěn lìhai** 病得

很厉害 be very ill; **lèi de tóu tòng** 累得头痛 be tired to the point of having a headache; *(used in a negative form to advise someone strongly against doing something)* [**shuō** | **gàn** | **chī**] **bù dé** [说 | 干 | 吃] 不得 mustn't/can't [*say* | *do* | *eat*] (something)

dé 得 *vb* get, have, obtain; *(when used with bu 不)* **bù dé** 不得 disallow, prohibit

dédào 得到 *vb* obtain, receive, gain

dézuì 得罪 *vb* offend

de 地 *pt* ▶ *See also* **dì** 地. *(used after an adjective to form an adverb, equivalent to -ly in English)* **cōngmáng de jìnlai** 匆忙地进来 rush in hurriedly

Déguó 德国 *n* Germany

Déwén 德文 *n* German language (usually written)

Déyǔ 德语 *n* German language (usually spoken)

děi 得 *vb* have to, must; **xuésheng děi niànshū** 学生得念书 students have to study; require; **mǎi zhèběn shū děi duōshǎo qián?** 买这本书得多少钱? how much money will I need to buy this book?

dēng 灯 *n* lamp, light; **diǎn dēng** 点灯 light a lamp

dēng 登 *vb (for a bus, train, or other vehicle)* mount, ascend, board; land, alight; **dēng lù** 登陆 land on shore, disembark; publish, print; **dēng bào** 登报 print in a newspaper

dēngjì 登记 *vb* register

děng 等 **1** *vb* wait, await **2** *n* grade, class **3** *pron (used at the end of an enumeration)* etc., and so on; **děngděng** 等等 and so on, etc.; **děngdeng** 等等 wait a moment

děngdài 等待 *vb* wait, wait for

děnghòu 等侯 *vb* wait, wait for

děngyú 等于 *vb* be equal to, be equivalent to; be the same as, amount to, be tantamount to

dèng(zi) 凳(子) *n* stool, bench

dī 低 **1** *adj* low **2** *vb* lower; **dī tóu** 低头 bow one's head

dī 滴 *mw* ▶**213** drop

díquè 的确 *adv* indeed, really

dírén 敌人 *n* enemy

dǐxia 底下 *prep* under, below, beneath; **zhuōzi dǐxia** 桌子底下 under the table

dì 地 *n* ▶ *See also* **de** 地. the ground, floor; earth, soil; place, location

dìbù 地步 *n* situation, condition; extent, point

dìdài 地带 *n* area, region

dìdiǎn 地点 *n* place, location

dìfang 地方 *n* place

dìfāng 地方 *adj* local

dìlǐ 地理 *n* geography

dìmiàn 地面 *n* ground, the earth's surface

dìqiú 地球 *n* the earth, the globe

dìqū 地区 *n* district, area

dìtiě 地铁 *n* underground, subway, tube

dìtú 地图 *n* map

dìwèi 地位 *n* status, social position

dìxià 地下 *n* underground

dìxiàshì 地下室 *n* basement, cellar

dìzhèn 地震 *n* earthquake

dìzhǐ 地址 *n* address

dìzhǔ 地主 *n* landlord

dìdi 弟弟 *n* younger brother

dì 递 *vb* hand over, pass

dì 第 *pt* (used to indicate ordinal numbers) **dìyī cì** 第一次 first time; **dìyī míng** 第一名 number one, champion, winner; **dì'èr tiān** 第二天 the next day; **dìjǐ kè?** 第几课? which lesson?

diāndǎo 颠倒 **1** vb reverse, invert, turn upside down **2** adj muddled, confused, upside down

diǎn 点 **1** n dot, drop, speck; (in decimals) point; sān diǎn liù 三点六 three point six; (used in time expressions, referring to hours on the clock) o'clock; sān diǎn zhōng 三点钟 3 o'clock; (when talking about abstract ideas) point; xiàmian liǎng diǎn 下面两点 the following two points, the two points below **2** mw ▶ 213 (for suggestions, requirements, ideas, opinions) **3** vb touch slightly; mark, punctuate; tick off on a list, check; choose; diǎn cài 点菜 select dishes from a menu; (as fire or flame) light; diǎn dēng 点灯 light a lamp **4** adv a little, slightly; [hǎo | dà | xiǎo] diǎnr [好 | 大 | 小] 点儿 a little [better | bigger | smaller]

diǎn míng 点名 vb take a roll call, check names on a list, mention by name

diǎn tóu 点头 vb nod the head

diǎnxin 点心 n light refreshments, pastry, snacks

diàn 电 **1** n electricity **2** adj electric

diànbào 电报 n telegram, cable

diànbīngxiāng 电冰箱 n refrigerator, fridge

diànchē 电车 n trolley, street car, tram

diàndēng 电灯 n electric light

diànfēngshàn 电风扇, **diànshàn** 电扇 n electric fan

diànhuà 电话 n telephone

diànnǎo 电脑 n computer

diànshì 电视 n television, TV

diànshìtái 电视台 n television station

diàntái 电台 n radio station

diàntī 电梯 n lift, elevator, escalator

diànyǐng 电影 n film, movie

diànyǐngyuàn 电影院 n cinema, movie theatre

diànzǐ 电子 **1** n electron **2** adj electronic

diàn 店 *n* store, shop; inn, hotel

diào 吊 *vb* pull up by a rope, hang, suspend

diào 钓 *vb* fish, angle; **diào yú** 钓鱼 to fish

diào 调 ▶ *See also* **tiáo** 调. **1** *n* melody, tune **2** *vb* (*when talking about troops or personnel*) transfer, move, send; change direction, turn, exchange

diàochá 调查 **1** *vb* investigate **2** *n* investigation

diào 掉 *vb* fall down, drop, come off; (*used after such verbs as* **shī** 失, **qù** 去, **mài** 卖, **táo** 逃, **wàng** 忘, **miè** 灭, **rēng** 扔, *and* **cā** 擦 *to indicate loss, end of supply*) **shīdiào** 失掉 lose; **qùdiào** 去掉 get rid of; **màidiào** 卖掉 sell off, sell out; lose, be missing; turn, turn round; **diàoguò tóu lai** 掉过头来 turn the head round; change, exchange; **diàohuàn** 掉换 exchange

diē 跌 *vb* fall down; (*of prices*) fall

dǐng 顶 **1** *n* top, summit **2** *adj* topmost, extreme; **dǐng tóu** 顶头 furthest end, top **3** *adv* very, extremely, most; **dǐng hǎo** 顶好 the best, the greatest **4** *vb* carry on the head; push the head against; go against **5** *mw* ▶ 213 (*for hats, caps, or things with a top*)

dìng 定 **1** *adv* definitely, certainly **2** *adj* stable, calm **3** *vb* decide, fix, settle

dìng qī 定期 **1** *vb* set a date **2** *adv* regularly

dìng 订 *vb* make an agreement, cement a relationship; **dìnghūn** 订婚 become engaged; **dìng hétong** 订合同 make a contract; subscribe to, order, book; **dìng zázhì** 订杂志 order a magazine; **dìng fángjiān** 订房间 book a room

diū 丢 *vb* lose; **tā diūle yíjiàn dōngxi** 他丢了一件东西 he lost something; throw, cast, toss; put or lay aside

dōng 东 *n* east; **dōng** [**biān** | **bù** | **fāng** | **miàn**] 东 [边 | 部 | 方 | 面] eastern [side | part | direction | side]

dōngběi 东北 *n* northeast, Manchuria, the three provinces of Heilongjiang, Jilin, and Liaoning

dōngfāng 东方 *n* east; the Orient

dōngnán 东南 *n* southeast

dōngxi 东西 *n* thing, things; **mǎi dōngxi** 买东西 go shopping, buy things

dōng 冬 *n* winter; **dōngtiān** 冬天 winter

dǒng 懂 *vb* understand

dǒngdé 懂得 *vb* understand, know

dǒngháng 懂行 *vb* know a business, be experienced in a profession

dǒngshì 懂事 *adj* sensible, wise

dòng 动 *vb* move; start action; stir, arouse; use

dòngjìng 动静 *n* stirring noises, sound of people speaking or moving about; movement, activity

dònglì 动力 *n* power; driving force, motive, impetus

dòngrén 动人 *adj* moving, touching

dòngshēn 动身 *vb* embark on a journey, set off

dòngshǒu 动手 *vb* start, make a move to; raise a hand to fight or hit; touch; **qǐng wù dòngshǒu！** 请勿动手! please don't touch!

dòngwù 动物 *n* animal

dòngwùyuán 动物园 *n* zoo

dòngyuán 动员 *vb* mobilize

dòngzuò 动作 *n* action, movement

dòng 冻 *vb* freeze; **dòngsǐ** 冻死 freeze to death

dòng 洞 *n* hole, cave

dòng 栋 *mw* ▶ 213 (for buildings)

dōu 都 ! Can also be pronounced dū 都 *with a different meaning; adv* all, both; **tāmen dōu hěn hǎo** 他们都很好 they are all well; **dōu shì wèile zhuàn qián** 都是为了赚钱 it's all to make money; (*when used with a negative*) ! *Note that* bù 不 *before* dōu 都 *means* not all do *or* some don't; *while* dōu 都 *before* bù 不 *means* none do; **tāmen dōu bú huì chànggē** 他们

都不会唱歌 none of them can sing well; **tāmen bù dōu huì chànggē** 他们不都会唱歌 they can't all sing well; (*when used with the interrogative* **shénme** 什么 *what*) everything; **nǐ shénme dōu huì** 你什么都会 you can do everything; (*when used with the interrogative* **shénme** 什么 *and a negative*) nothing, not anything; **tā shénme dōu méi zuò** 他什么都没做 he hasn't done anything; (*when used with the interrogative* **shéi** 谁 *who*) everyone; **shéi dōu zhīdào** 谁都知道 everyone knows; (*when used with the interrogative* **shéi** 谁 *and a negative*) no one; **shéi dōu bù chuān zhèzhǒng yīfu** 谁都不穿这种衣服 no one wears clothing like this; (*in the pattern* **lián...dōu...** 连... 都...) even ! Note that in practice when the first element of this pattern is omitted, the word **dōu** 都 alone retains the sense of the pattern and means even; **lián zhège wèntí tā dōu bù dǒng** 连这个问题他都不懂 he can't even understand this kind of question; **tā yīfu dōu méi xǐ** 他衣服都没洗 he didn't even wash his clothes; already

dòuzhēng 斗争 1 *vb* struggle, fight, strive 2 *n* struggle, combat

dòufu 豆腐 *n* beancurd, tofu

dòu 逗 1 *vb* tease 2 *adj* funny

dòuliú 逗留 *vb* stay (for a short time), stop over

dúlì 独立 1 *vb* be independent, become independent: **zhège guójiā dúlì le** 这个国家独立了 this country became independent 2 *n* independence 3 *adj* independent; **nàge háizi hěn dúlì** 那个孩子很独立 that child is very independent

dúshēn 独身 *adj* single, unmarried

dúshēngnǚ 独生女 *n* only daughter

dúshēngzǐ 独生子 *n* only son

dúzì 独自 *adj* alone, by oneself

dú 读 *vb* read; read aloud; study (at school, college, or university): **dú dàxué** 读大学 study at university

dúshū 读书 *vb* study, read books; attend school

dúzhě 读者 *n* reader

dǔ 堵 **1** vb obstruct, block up **2** mw ▶ **213** (for walls)

dùzi 肚子 n stomach, belly

dù 度 **1** n (unit or measurement for angles, temperature, etc.) degree; **língxià sān (shèshì)dù** 零下三 (摄氏)度 3 degrees below zero centigrade; **sānshíèr huáshìdù** 三十二华氏度 32 degrees Fahrenheit; occasion, time **2** vb spend, pass

dù(guò) 度(过) vb spend, pass

dù 渡 vb (when talking about a body of water) cross over; **dù** (**hé** | **Chángjiāng** | **hǎi**) 渡 (河 | 长江 | 海) cross (a river | the Yangtze River | an ocean); (a difficulty, or a period of time) go through; **dùguò kùnnan shíqī** 渡过困难时期 go through a difficult time

duān 端 **1** n (of a long, narrow object) end, end point **2** vb hold something level with the hand(s)

Duānwǔjié 端午节 n Dragon Boat Festival **!** It falls on the fifth day of the fifth month of the lunar calendar.

duǎn 短 **1** adj (in length) short **2** n weak point, fault

duǎnchù 短处 n shortcoming

duǎnqī 短期 n short-term

duàn 段 mw ▶ **213** (for lengths of road, cable, etc.) section, segment; (for periods of time) period, length; (for units of writing, articles, speeches, etc.) piece, passage, paragraph

duàn 断 vb break, cut off

duàndìng 断定 vb conclude, decide, judge

duànduàn xùxù 断断续续 adv intermittently, on-and-off

duànliàn 锻炼 vb do physical training, take exercise, improve one's physical fitness

duī 堆 **1** vb heap up, pile up **2** n pile, stack, heap; **yìduī dōngxi** 一堆东西 a pile of things

duì 队 n team, group; a queue/line of people

duìwu 队伍 n troops, ranks

duìyuán 队员 n member of a team

duìzhǎng 队长 *n* captain of a team, team leader

duì 对 **1** *adj* correct, accurate, right **2** *prep* (*introducing a target, aim*) to, towards, with; **duì wǒ shēngqì** 对我生气 angry with me; regarding, about, on; **duì zhèjiàn shì de kànfǎ** 对这件事的看法 views on this matter; (*in sports*) against; **Sūgélán duì Yīnggélán** 苏格兰对英格兰 Scotland vs. England **3** *vb* treat, deal with; face; **chuānghu duìzhe huāyuán** 窗户对着花园 the window faces the garden **4** *mw* ▶ 213 pair, couple; **duì wǒ lái shuō** 对我来说 in my view, as far as I'm concerned

duìbǐ 对比 **1** *vb* contrast, compare **2** *n* comparison, contrast; ratio, correlation

duìbuqǐ 对不起 *vb* let someone down, act unworthily toward; **nǐ yǒu shénme duìbuqǐ tā de shì ma?** 你有什么对不起他的事吗? did you let him down in some way?; sorry, I'm sorry, excuse me

duìdài 对待 *vb* treat, handle, deal with

duìfāng 对方 *n* (*in negotiations, games, competitions*) the other party, opposite side

duìfu 对付 *vb* deal with, cope with; serve for the time being, make do

duìhuà 对话 *n* dialogue

duìmiàn 对面 *prep* opposite

duìxiàng 对象 *n* goal, objective; boyfriend, girlfriend, partner

duìyú 对于 *prep* with regard to

dūn 吨 *n* (*a unit of weight*) ton

dūn 蹲 *vb* squat

dùn 顿 *mw* ▶ 213 (*for meals*); (*for actions that take place in single sessions*)

duō 多 **1** *adj* many, much, more; more than; **wǔshí duō yuán** 五十多元 over fifty yuan (*between fifty and sixty*) extra, additional; **duōle sān yīngbàng** 多了三英镑 three pounds extra **2** *adv* (*to indicate degree or extent in comparison*) much, a great deal; **jīntiān tiānqì hǎo duō le** 今天天气好多了 the weather is a lot better today; (*in questions asking for a number, degree, age, etc.*) **duō dà** [niánlíng | suìshù] 多大 [年龄 | 岁数] how old?; **duō dà de** [fángjiān | xié]? 多大的 [房间 | 鞋]? [how big a room? | what size shoes?]; (*in comparisons, after a verb, expressing a large extent*) much, a lot; [hǎo | nán | kěxiào] **de duō** [好 | 难 | 可笑] 得多 much [better | harder | funnier]

duō(me) 多(么) *adv* (*to exclaim about the high degree to which an action is done*) such...! what a...!; **nǐ fùmǔ duō(me) ài nǐ a!** 你父母多(么)爱你啊! your parents love you so much!; (*to exclaim or ask about the extent of a quality*) **duō(me) kě'ài de háizi!** 多(么)可爱的孩子! what a lovable child!

duōshǎo 多少 *det* (*as an interrogative*) how many? how much?; **duōshǎo** [rén | tiān | běn shū | gōnglǐ] 多少 [人 | 天 | 本书 | 公里] how many [people | days | books | kilometres]; (*to indicate an uncertain amount*) how many, how much; **wǒ bù xiǎng zhīdào tā yǒu duōshǎo qián** 我不想知道他有多少钱 I don't want to know how much money he has

duōshù 多数 *n* majority, most

duōyú 多余 *adj* extra, excess, surplus

duó 夺 *vb* rob, snatch, seize by force; strive for, win

duóqǔ 夺取 *vb* seize by force

duǒ 朵 *mw* ▶ **213** (for flowers, clouds)

duǒ 躲 *vb* hide oneself away from, avoid, dodge

Ee

Éguó 俄国 *n* Russia

Éwén 俄文 *n* Russian language (usually written)

Éyǔ 俄语 *n* Russian language (usually spoken)

é 鹅 *n* goose

è 饿 **1** *adj* hungry; **wǒ è le** 我饿了 I'm hungry **2** *vb* starve; **èsǐ** 饿死 starve to death

értóng 儿童 *n* children

érzi 儿子 *n* son

ér 而 *conj* (connecting two adjectives, two verbs, etc.) and; **cōngming ér yǒnggǎn** 聪明而勇敢 intelligent and brave; (connecting an affirmative clause with a negative clause) but, yet, while; **tā zhǐ xiǎng zìjǐ, ér bù xiǎng biéren** 他只想自己, 而不想别人 he thinks only of himself and not of others; (connecting an adverb of manner with a verb) **qiāoqiāo ér qù** 悄悄而去 depart quietly; (connecting the cause of an action with the action itself) because of, on the grounds of; **tā yīnwèi gōngzuò ér fàngqì xiū jià** 他因为工作而放弃休假 he gave up his holidays because of his work; **bú shì...ér shì...** 不是...而是... not...but...; **wǒ bú shì Měiguórén ér shì Jiānádàrén** 我不是美国人而是加拿大人 I am not an American but a Canadian

érqiě 而且 *conj* and also, moreover, in addition; **búdàn...érqiě...** 不但... 而且... not only...but also...; **tā búdàn lèi érqiě bù shūfu** 他不但累而且不舒服 he's not only tired but also unwell

ěrduo 耳朵 *n* ear

èr 二 *num* two **!** Note that when used with a measure word, **èr** 二 usually changes to **liǎng** 两; ▶ See also **liǎng** 两.

èryuè 二月 *n* February

Ff

fā 发 *vb* ▶ See also **fà** 发. send out, issue; **fā hěn duō xìn** 发很多信 send out a lot of letters; start, grow, develop; **fā yá** 发芽 put out shoots; get into a state, become; **fā** [jí | nù | hóng] 发 [急 | 怒 | 红] [become agitated | get angry | turn red]; break out in, have a sensation of; **fā** [má | yǎng] 发 [麻 | 痒] get [pins and needles | itchy]

fābiǎo 发表 *vb* publish, issue; express, state

fācái 发财 *vb* get rich, make lots of money

fāchū 发出 *vb* send out, issue; fāchū tōngzhī 发出通知 send out notification; give off, give out, give rise to; fāchū guāngliàng 发出光亮 emit light

fādá 发达 *adj* prosperous, flourishing, developed

fādòng 发动 *vb* launch, start; mobilize

fādòngjī 发动机 *n* engine, motor

fādǒu 发抖 *vb* shiver, tremble

fāhuī 发挥 *vb* give play to, bring into play, give free rein to; fāhuī tāde cáinéng 发挥他的才能 give full play to his talents; (when talking about an idea, a theme, etc.) develop, expand on, elaborate; bǎ zhège tímù zài fāhuī yíxià 把这个题目再发挥一下 develop this topic further

fā huǒ 发火 *vb* catch fire; become angry, lose one's temper

fāmíng 发明 **1** *vb* invent **2** *n* invention

fāshāo 发烧 *vb* have or run a fever, have a high temperature

fāshēng 发生 *vb* occur, happen, take place

fāxiàn 发现 **1** *vb* discover, find **2** *n* discovery

fāyán 发言 *vb* speak, make a speech/statement

fāyáng 发扬 *vb* develop, expand, carry on

fāyīn 发音 **1** *vb* pronounce **2** *n* pronunciation

fāzhǎn 发展 **1** *vb* develop, expand **2** *n* development

fá 罚 *vb* punish, penalize

fákuǎn 罚款 *vb* fine, make someone pay a penalty

fǎ 法 *n* law, method

Fǎguó 法国 *n* France; Fǎguórén 法国人 French people, Frenchman, Frenchwoman

fǎlǜ 法律 *n* law

fǎtíng 法庭 *n* court of law

Fǎwén 法文 *n* French language (usually written)

Fǎyǔ 法语 *n* French language (usually spoken)

fǎyuàn 法院 *n* court of law

fǎzi 法子 *n* way, method

fà 发 *n* ▶ See also **fā** 发. hair

fānqié 番茄 *n* tomato

fān 翻 *vb* (when talking about sheets, pages in a book) flip, thumb through; turn, turn over; translate; cross, get over; **fānguò nàzuò shān** 翻过那座山 cross that mountain; rummage, search; **tā zài fān wǒde shūbāo** 他在翻我的书包 he is searching my book bag; multiply; **fān yīfān** 翻一番 double, increase two-fold

fānyì 翻译 **1** *vb* translate, interpret **2** *n* translator, interpreter; translation

fán (shì) 凡 (是) *adv* every, all ! *The term* **fán shì** 凡是 *is used at the beginning of a sentence and followed by a noun or noun-clause to mean* whatever *or* whoever. *The subject of the sentence, thus defined, is usually followed by* **dōu** 都; **fán (shì) tā mǎi de dōu hěn piàoliang** 凡 (是) 她买的都很漂亮 everything she buys is attractive

fán 烦 **1** *adj* irritated, annoyed, vexed; tired of **2** *vb* trouble, bother

fánnǎo 烦恼 *adj* worried, vexed

fánróng 繁荣 **1** *adj* prosperous **2** *vb* make prosperous **3** *n* prosperity

fǎndòng 反动 *adj* reactionary

fǎnduì 反对 *vb* oppose, object, combat

fǎnfù 反复 *adv* again and again, over and over

fǎnkàng 反抗 *vb* resist, oppose, react against

fǎnmiàn 反面 *n* reverse side, wrong side; negative side, opposite side

fǎnyìng 反映 1 *vb* reflect, mirror; report, make known, express; **xiàng lǐngdǎo fǎnyìng** 向领导反映 make something known to one's superiors 2 *n* reflection

fǎnyìng 反应 1 *vb* react 2 *n* reaction

fǎnzhèng 反正 *adv* in any case, anyway

fǎnhuí 返回 *vb* return, go back

fàn 犯 *vb* (*when talking about the law, rules*) offend, violate; (*when talking about a mistake, a crime, etc.*) commit; **fàn cuòwu** 犯错误 make a mistake; (*when talking about an old illness*) have another attack of

fàn 饭 *n* cooked rice, food, a meal

fàndiàn 饭店 *n* hotel, restaurant

fànguǎn 饭馆 *n* restaurant

fàntīng 饭厅 *n* dining hall, dining room

fànwéi 范围 *n* scope, sphere, jurisdiction

fāng 方 1 *n* direction; [dōng | nán | xī | běi] fāng [东 | 南 | 西 | 北] 方 the [east | south | west | north]; side, party; **dān fāng** 单方 one side, unilateral 2 *adj* square; **fāngkuàizì** 方块字 Chinese characters

fāng'àn 方案 *n* plan, scheme

fāngbiàn 方便 1 *adj* convenient 2 *vb* to go to the lavatory

fāngfǎ 方法 *n* way, method

fāngmiàn 方面 *n* aspect, respect, side; **yì fāngmiàn...yì fāngmiàn...** 一方面… 一方面… on the one hand...on the other hand...

fāngshì 方式 *n* method, style, formula

fāngxiàng 方向 *n* direction

fāngyán 方言 *n* dialect

fāngzhēn 方针 *n* policy, guiding principle

fáng 防 *vb* prevent, guard against, defend against

fángzhǐ 防止 *vb* prevent

fángdōng 房东 n landlord

fángjiān 房间 n room

fángzi 房子 n house, building, room

fángzū 房租 n rent

fǎngwèn 访问 1 vb visit, call on 2 n visit

fǎngfú 仿佛 1 vb seem as if 2 adv apparently, seemingly

fǎngzhī 纺织 n spinning; weaving textiles

fàng 放 vb put down, place; let go, release (physically); **bié fàng tā** 别放他 don't release him; (emotionally or psychologically) **fàng shēng dà kū** 放声大哭 burst into tears; (when talking about something that explodes or fires) let off, fire, shoot; **fàng [pào | qiāng | yānhuǒ]** 放 [炮 | 枪 | 烟火] (fire a cannon | shoot a gun | let off fireworks) tend, herd; **fàng [niú | yáng]** 放 [牛 | 羊] pasture [cows | sheep]; readjust slightly; **dǎnzi fàng dà diǎnr** 胆子放大点儿 be a bit braver; (film, recording, etc.) show, play

fàngdà 放大 vb enlarge, magnify

fàngjià 放假 vb go on holiday/vacation, have a day off

fàngqì 放弃 vb give up, abandon, forego

fàngsōng 放松 vb relax, loosen

fàngxué 放学 vb let out of school, classes are over

fàngxīn 放心 vb feel relieved, set one's mind at rest, be at ease; **fàngxīn bú xià** 放心不下 can't relax, feel anxious

fēi 飞 vb fly

fēijī 飞机 n aircraft, aeroplane, airplane

fēixíng 飞行 n flight, flying

fēi...bù kě 非... 不可 vb (emphatic) must, have to; **fēi qù bù kě** 非去不可 must, will inevitably, will be bound to; **tā fēi chídào bù kě** 他非迟到不可 he will definitely be late; insist on

fēicháng 非常 adv very, extremely, unusually

Fēizhōu 非洲 n Africa

féi 肥 *adj* fat; (*when talking about clothes*) loose, large; (*of soil*) fertile, rich

féizào 肥皂 *n* soap

fèi 废 *adj* useless, waste, discarded

fèi 肺 *n* lungs

fèi 费 **1** *vb* expend, consume, waste; **fèi shíjiān** 费时间 be time-consuming, take a long time **2** *n* fee, fees

fèiyòng 费用 *n* expense, expenses, cost

fēn 分 **1** *vb* separate, divide; distinguish; **bù fēn hǎo huài** 不分好坏 not to distinguish the good from the bad; divide, share, receive a share of; **fēndào yìfēn jiǎngjīn** 分到一份奖金 get a share of the prize money; distribute; **bǎ zhèxiē dōngxi fēn gěi biérén** 把这些东西分给别人 distribute these things to others **2** *adj* (*describing an organization*) branch, sub-; **fēn gōngsī** 分公司 a branch company **3** *n* (*of a dollar*) cent; (*of Chinese currency, RMB*) fen; (*of an hour*) minute; (*to represent a point or mark*) point, mark; **dé qī fēn** 得七分 get seven points; **...fēn zhī... ...**分之... (*to represent a fraction or parts of the whole*) **sān fēn zhī èr** 三分之二 two thirds

fēnbié 分别 **1** *vb* part, leave each other, say good-bye to each other; separate, distinguish, differentiate **2** *adv* differently; separately, respectively

fēnkāi 分开 *vb* separate, part

fēnpèi 分配 *vb* assign, distribute

fēnshǒu 分手 *vb* part company, separate, say good-bye

fēnshù 分数 *n* mark, grade

fēnxī 分析 **1** *vb* analyze **2** *n* analysis

fēnfù 吩咐 *vb* tell, order, instruct

fēnfēn 纷纷 *adv* in quick succession, one right after another; in profusion and confusion

fénmù 坟墓 *n* grave, tomb

fěnbǐ 粉笔 *n* chalk

fěnhóng 粉红 n pink

fèn 份 mw ▶ 213 portion, share; (for copies of newspapers, magazines, or manuscripts)

fèndòu 奋斗 vb struggle/strive toward a goal

fènnù 愤怒 1 adj angry 2 n anger, indignation

fēngfù 丰富 1 adj plentiful, abundant 2 vb enrich

fēngshōu 丰收 n good harvest, bumper harvest

fēng 风 n wind, breeze, storm; custom, practice, habit

fēnggé 风格 n style

fēngjǐng 风景 n scenery, landscape, view

fēnglì 风力 n wind power, force of the wind

fēngshuǐ 风水 n geomancy

fēngsú 风俗 n social customs

fēng 封 1 mw ▶ 213 (for letters, telegrams) 2 vb seal, close

fēngjiàn 封建 adj feudal

fēng 疯 adj mentally unbalanced, mad, crazy

fēng 蜂 n bee, wasp

fēngmì 蜂蜜 n honey

féng 逢 vb meet, come upon, chance upon; **féng nián guò jié** 逢年过节 on New Year's Day or other festivals

fěngcì 讽刺 vb satirize

Fójiào 佛教 n Buddhism

fǒurèn 否认 vb deny

fǒudìng 否定 vb deny, negate, decide in the negative

fǒuzé 否则 conj if not or else, otherwise

fūfù 夫妇 n husband and wife, Mr. and Mrs.

fūqī 夫妻 n husband and wife

fūren 夫人 n Mrs., Madam, wife; **Zhōu Fūren** 周夫人 Mrs. Zhou

fú 扶 *vb* support with the hand; **fúzhe lǎorén zhànqǐlai** 扶着老人站起来 help the elderly person stand up; place one's hands on somebody/something for support; **tā fúzhe qiáng zǒu** 她扶着墙走 she walked along holding the wall for support

fúcóng 服从 *vb* obey, be subordinate to

fúwù 服务 **1** *vb* serve, provide service to **2** *n* service

fúwùyuán 服务员 *n* attendant, steward, waiter

fúzhuāng 服装 *n* costume, outfit, uniform

fú 浮 float, drift

fúhé 符合 *vb* conform to, fit, coincide; **fúhé tāde àihào** 符合他的爱好 suit his hobby

fú 幅 *mw* ▶ **213** (*for paintings, works of calligraphy*)

fǔdǎo 辅导 *vb* advise/coach in studies, give tutorials to

fú 福 *n* good fortune, blessing, happiness

fǔbài 腐败 *adj* rotten, decayed, corrupt

fùmǔ 父母 *n* parents

fùqin 父亲 *n* father

fù 付 *vb* pay; **fù** [**fángzū** | **shuì** | **lìxí**] 付 [房租 | 税 | 利息] pay [the rent | taxes | interest]

fùnǚ 妇女 *n* woman

fùdān 负担 **1** *n* burden, load **2** *vb* bear (a burden), shoulder (a burden)

fùzé 负责 **1** *vb* be responsible for, be in charge of **2** *adj* responsible; conscientious; **tā duì gōngzuò bú tài fùzé** 他对工作不太负责 he is not very conscientious in his work

fùjìn 附近 **1** *adj* nearby, close **2** *adv* closely, nearby, in the vicinity of

fù 服 *mw* ▶ **213** (*for doses of Chinese medicine*)

fùyìn 复印 *vb* photocopy, duplicate

fùxí 复习 *vb* review, revise

fùzá 复杂 *adj* complicated, complex

fù 副 **1** *mw* ▸ **213** (for things that come in pairs or sets) set, pair; (for facial expressions) **2** *adj* deputy, assistant, vice-; **fù xiàozhǎng** 副校长 vice-principal; subsidiary, secondary; **fù zuòyòng** 副作用 side-effect

fù 富 *adj* wealthy, rich

....

Gg

gāi 该 **1** *vb* should, ought to; **wǒ gāi zǒu le** 我该走了 I must leave now, I have to go; be one's turn to do something; **gāi wǒ le** 该我了 it's my turn **2** *det* this, that, the above-mentioned; **gāi xuéxiào** 该学校 that school

gǎi 改 *vb* change, transform; alter, correct; **gǎi zuòyè** 改作业 correct students' homework

gǎibiàn 改变 **1** *vb* change, alter, transform **2** *n* change

gǎigé 改革 **1** *vb* reform **2** *n* reform

gǎijìn 改进 **1** *vb* improve, make better **2** *n* improvement

gǎiliáng 改良 *vb* change for the better, improve, reform

gǎishàn 改善 **1** *vb* improve, better **2** *n* improvement

gǎizào 改造 **1** *vb* transform, reform, remould **2** *n* transformation, reform

gǎizhèng 改正 *vb* correct, amend, put right

gài 盖 *vb* build, construct; cover; apply, affix with; **gài zhāng** 盖章 apply a chop/seal

gàizi 盖子 *n* cover, lid

gàikuò 概括 **1** *vb* summarise, generalise **2** *n* summary

gàiniàn 概念 *n* concept, notion, idea

gān 干 *adj* ▶ See also **gàn**. dry; (taken into nominal kinship)
gān érzi 干儿子 nominally adopted son

gānbēi 干杯 *vb* (when drinking a toast) "Bottoms up!"

gāncuì 干脆 1 *adj* straightforward, frank, clear-cut 2 *adv* simply, just

gānjìng 干净 *adj* clean

gānshè 干涉 1 *vb* interfere with 2 *n* interference

gānzào 干燥 *adj* dry, arid

gān 杆 *n* pole, post, stake

gān 肝 *n* liver

gǎn 赶 *vb* (an animal, an enemy) drive, drive away; **bǎ tā gǎnzǒu** 把他赶走 chase him away; catch up; hurry, rush; **gǎn huí jiā** 赶回家 hurry home; catch; **gǎn chē** 赶车 catch the bus

gǎnjǐn 赶紧 *adv* speedily, at once, hurriedly

gǎnkuài 赶快 *adv* in a hurry, hurriedly, at once

gǎnshàng 赶上 *vb* catch up with

gǎn 敢 1 *vb* dare, venture, be certain 2 *adj* bold, daring

gǎndào 感到 *vb* feel, sense

gǎndòng 感动 1 *vb* (referring to the emotions) move, be moved, touch 2 *adj* moving, touching

Gǎn'ēnjié 感恩节 *n* Thanksgiving, Thanksgiving Day

gǎnjī 感激 *vb* feel grateful, be thankful

gǎnjué 感觉 1 *vb* sense, feel, perceive 2 *n* perception, feeling

gǎnmào 感冒 1 *vb* catch cold, have a cold 2 *n* cold, flu

gǎnqíng 感情 *n* feelings, emotions, sentiments; affection

gǎnxiǎng 感想 *n* impressions, feelings

gǎnxiè 感谢 1 *n* thanks, gratitude 2 *vb* thank, be grateful

gǎn xìngqù 感兴趣 *vb* be interested in ! The preposition **duì** 对 *is used to introduce the object of interest expressed by* in *in English, and the prepositional phrase comes before the verb;*

wǒ duì yǔyán gǎn xìngqù 我对语言感兴趣 I am interested in languages

gàn 干 vb ▶ See also **gān**. do, work; nǐ xiǎng gàn shénme? 你想干什么? what do you want to do?; **gànmá?** 干吗? why? why on earth?; nǐ gànmá mǎi zhèběn shū? 你干吗买这本书? why on earth did you buy this book?; nǐ gànmá? 你干吗? what are you doing?

gànbù 干部 n cadre, government official

gàn huó(r) 干活(儿) vb work, work on a job, do some work

gāng 刚 adv (referring to something that is happening or about to happen) just this minute, just now, just about to; tā gāng yào zǒu 他刚要走 he is just about to leave; (referring to something that has just happened) only a short time ago, just; tā gāng zǒu 他刚走 he has just left; (when talking about suitability) exactly; zhèshuāng xié gāng hǎo 这双鞋刚好 this pair of shoes fits perfectly; (when talking about quantity) just, no more than; gāng shíbā suì 刚十八岁 just eighteen years old

gāngcái 刚才 adv just now, just a few minutes ago

gānggāng 刚刚 adv just now, just a few minutes ago; just, only, exactly

gāng 钢 n steel

gāngbǐ 钢笔 n fountain pen

gāngqín 钢琴 n piano

gǎng 港 n port, harbour

gǎngkǒu 港口 n port, harbour

gāo 高 1 adj tall, high; advanced, superior; gāojí 高级 high level 2 adv in a high/loud voice, loudly; gāo hǎn 高喊 shout at the top of one's voice

gāodà 高大 adj tall and big

gāoděng 高等 adj high level, advanced; gāoděng jiàoyù 高等教育 higher education

gāodù 高度 1 n altitude, height 2 adv highly, to a high degree

gāosù gōnglù 高速公路 *n* motorway

gāoxìng 高兴 *adj* happy, pleased, in high spirits

gāoyuán 高原 *n* plateau, highland

gāozhōng 高中 *n* (abbreviation of **gāojí zhōngxué** 高级中学)
senior middle school, senior high school

gǎo 搞 *vb* (work, a task, etc.) do, work; **gǎo gōngzuò** 搞工作
do work; set up, establish, arrange; be involved in

gào 告 *vb* tell, inform, notify; accuse, sue; **gào mǒurén** 告某人
sue someone

gàobié 告别 *vb* take leave of, say good-bye to

gàojiè 告诫 *vb* warn, admonish

gàosu 告诉 *vb* tell, inform, let know

gēge 哥哥 *n* elder brother

gēbo 胳膊 *n* arm

gē 搁 *vb* place, put down; **gēxia** 搁下 put down; put aside, put
to one side, shelve; **gē zài yìbiān** 搁在一边 put aside

gē 割 *vb* cut, cut down, lop off

gē 歌 *n* song

gējù 歌剧 *n* opera

gēqǔ 歌曲 *n* song

gémìng 革命 **1** *vb* revolt, carry out a revolution **2** *n*
revolution

géwài 格外 *adv* especially, all the more

gé 隔 **1** *vb* divide, separate, partition; be separated by **2** *adv*
(when talking about an interval of time) later, afterwards, every
other; **gé yìtiān zài lái** 隔一天再来 come back a day later; **gé
yìtiān dǎ yícì diànhuà** 隔一天打一次电话 phone every other
day; (when talking about a physical distance) apart, at a distance
of; **gé yìtiáo mǎlù** 隔一条马路 one street apart; **géchéng...**
隔成... separate into, partition into; **bǎ yīge wūzi géchéng
liǎngjiān** 把一个屋子隔成两间 partition one room into two

gébì 隔壁 *n* next door

gè 个 *mw* ▶213！ *This is the most common measure word. It can take the place of many nominal measure words, and is handy to use if one does not know the measure word that is specific to a particular noun. It usually has a neutral tone, but has a fourth tone when stressed.*

gèbié 个别 *adj* several; very few, rare

gèrén 个人 **1** *n* oneself, one's own; zhè shì wǒ gèrén de yìjiàn 这是我个人的意见 this is my personal view; (*as an abstract concept*) the individual **2** *adj* individual, private; gèrén zhǔyì 个人主义 individualism

gètǐ 个体 *adj* individual, self, private

gèzi 个子 *n* height, stature, build

gè 各 *det* each, every; gè chù 各处 every place, everywhere

gèzhǒng 各种 *pron* every kind, all kinds; gèzhǒng bù tóng... 各种不同... all kinds of..., different kinds of...; gèzhǒng bù tóng de shuǐguǒ 各种不同的水果 all kinds of fruit

gèzì 各自 *det* each, respective

gěi 给！ *Can also be pronounced* jǐ *with a different meaning.* **1** *vb* give; tā gěi wǒ yìběn shū 他给我一本书 he gave me a book; (*used with* jiào 叫, *ràng* 让, *or* bǎ 把 *before the main verb for emphasis*) tāmen bǎ tā dǎ le 他们把他打了 they gave him a beating **2** *prep* (*when handing over or transferring something to someone*) to, with, for; [jiāo | sòng | jièshao] gěi tā [交 | 送 | 介绍] 给他 [hand over | give | introduce] to him; (*when doing something for someone*) for, on behalf of, for the benefit of; gěi tā [zuòfàn | mǎi shū | shōushi wūzi] 给他 [做饭 | 买书 | 收拾屋子] [cook | buy books | clean his room] for him; (*when introducing the recipient of an action, often translated as let, allow*) gěi wǒ kànkan 给我看看 let me have a look; wǒ gěi nǐ kàn yíjiàn dōngxi 我给你看一件东西 let me show you something; (*indicating the passive voice*) by; wǒde shū gěi xiǎotōu tóuzǒu le 我的书给小偷偷走了 my book was stolen by me; **gěi...kàn** 给...看 show (to someone) qǐng nǐ bǎ nàshuāng xié gěi wǒ kànkan 请你把那双鞋给我看看 please show me that pair of shoes

gēn 根 **1** *mw* **▶ 213** *(for long, thin objects)* **2** *n (of a plant or tree)* root; *(of a structure)* foot, base, basis; cause, origin, source

gēnběn 根本 **1** *n* root, foundation, base **2** *adj* basic, fundamental, essential **3** *adv* radically, thoroughly; **tā méiyǒu gēnběn gǎibiàn tāde tàidù** 他没有根本改变他的态度 his attitude hasn't radically changed; *(in the negative)* at all, simply; **wǒ gēnběn bù zhīdào** 我根本不知道 I have no idea

gēnjù 根据 **1** *prep* on the basis of, according to, in the light of; **gēnjù tā shuō de huà...** 根据他说的话... according to what he said... **2** *n* basis, grounds; **nǐ yǒu shénme gēnjù shuō zhèzhǒng huà?** 你有什么根据说这种话? on what basis do you say this? **3** *vb* base on

gēn 跟 **1** *prep* together with, with; **wǒ gēn nǐ yìqǐ qù** 我跟你一起去 I'll go with you; to, towards; **gēn tā shuōhuà** 跟她说话 speak to her; *(with certain verbs)* from; **gēn tā jiè shū** 跟他借书 borrow books from him; **gēn tā xué Zhōngwén** 跟他学中文 I am learning Chinese from him **2** *conj (when connecting two nouns or noun phrases)* and, with; **wǒ gēn tā shì tóngshì** 我跟他是同事 he and I are colleagues **3** *vb* follow, accompany; **qǐng gēnzhe wǒ shuō** 请跟着我说 please say after me

gēnqián 跟前 *n* in front of, near

gēngdì 耕地 **1** *vb* plough, till **2** *n* cultivated land, arable land

gèng 更 *adv* still more, even more; **gèng [hǎo | dà | yǒuqù]** 更 [好 | 大 | 有趣] even [better | bigger | more interesting]

gèngjiā 更加 *adv* still more, even more; **gèngjiā kěpà** 更加可怕 even more frightening

gōngchǎng 工厂 *n* factory, plant

gōngchéng 工程 *n (as a field of study or work)* engineering; project, engineering project, construction work; **gōngchéngshī** 工程师 engineer

gōngfu 工夫 *n* free time, leisure time; **wǒ méi yǒu gōngfu** 我没有工夫 I don't have time; work, effort; **huāle hěn dà de gōngfu** 花了很大的工夫 put in a lot of effort; ability, skill

gōnghuì 工会 *n* labour union, trade union

gōngjù 工具 *n* tool, instrument

gōngrén 工人 *n* worker, workman

gōngyè 工业 **1** *n* industry **2** *adj* industrial; **gōngyèhuà** 工业化 industrialization

gōngyìpǐn 工艺品 *n* handicraft item

gōngzī 工资 *n* wages, salary

gōngzuò 工作 **1** *vb* work **2** *n* work, job, employment

gōngān 公安 *n* public security; **gōngānjú** 公安局 public security bureau

gōngbù 公布 *vb* make public, announce

gōngfèi 公费 *adj* at public/state expense, publicly funded; **gōngfèi lǚxíng** 公费旅行 travel at state expense

gōngchǐ 公尺 *n* metre

gōngfēn 公分 *n* centimetre

gōnggòng 公共 *adj* public, common, communal

gōnggòng qìchē 公共汽车 *n* bus; **gōnggòng qìchē zhàn** 公共汽车站 bus stop

gōngjīn 公斤 *n* kilogram

gōngkāi 公开 **1** *adj* open, public, open to the public **2** *vb* make public

gōnglǐ 公里 *n* kilometre

gōnglù 公路 *n* highway

gōngmín 公民 *n* citizen

gōngpíng 公平 *adj* fair, just, reasonable

gōngshè 公社 *n* commune

gōngsī 公司 *n* corporation, company, firm

gōngyòng 公用 *adj* public; **gōngyòng diànhuà** 公用电话 public telephone

gōngyuán 公园 *n* park

gōngyuán 公元 *n* A.D., the Christian era; or C.E., the Common Era; **gōngyuánqián** 公元前 B.C., before Christ, or B.C.E., Before Common Era

gōngfu 功夫 *n* martial arts, kung-fu, skill

gōngkè 功课 *n* schoolwork, homework, assignment

gōngláo 功劳 *n* contribution, credit, service

gōngjī 攻击 *vb* attack, assault

gōng 供 *vb* supply, provide, support; **gōng de qǐ** 供得起 be able to support financially

gōngjǐ 供给 *vb* supply, provide, furnish; **tā mǔqīn gōngjǐ tā dúshū** 他母亲供给他读书 his mother supports his studies

gōngyìng 供应 *vb* supply

gǒnggù 巩固 **1** *adj* (of a foundation, organization, ambition) strong, firm, solid **2** *vb* consolidate, strengthen

gòng 共 *adv* together; **gòngshì** 共事 work together; in all, altogether; **zhège bān gòng yǒu èrshímíng xuéshēng** 这个班共有二十名学生 in all there are twenty students in this class

Gòngchǎndǎng 共产党 *n* the Communist Party

gòngchǎn zhǔyì 共产主义 *n* communism

gònghéguó 共和国 *n* republic

gòngtóng 共同 **1** *adj* common **2** *adv* together, jointly

gòngxiàn 贡献 **1** *vb* contribute, dedicate, devote **2** *n* contribution

gǒu 狗 *n* dog

gòuchéng 构成 *vb* constitute, make up

gòuzào 构造 *n* construction, structure

gòu 够 **1** *adj* enough, sufficient, adequate **2** *adv* rather, quite; **gòu lèi** 够累 rather tired **3** *vb* (when referring to a certain standard, etc.) attain, reach, be up to; **tā** [gòu dé shàng | gòu bù shàng] **hǎo xuéshēng** 他 [够得上 | 够不上] 好学生 he [is | is not] good enough to be a good student

gūlì 孤立 *adj* isolated

gūjì 估计 **1** *vb* estimate, appraise, reckon **2** *n* estimate, appraisal

gūniang 姑娘 *n* girl, young girl

gūgu 姑姑 *n* aunt, father's sister

gútou 骨头 *n* bone; **gútou jiàzi** 骨头架子 skeleton

gǔ 古 *adj* ancient, old, old-fashioned

gǔwén 古文 *n* ancient Chinese, classical Chinese

gǔdài 古代 *n* ancient times, antiquity

gǔdiǎn 古典 *adj* classical

gǔjì 古迹 *n* historic site, place of historic interest

gǔlǎo 古老 *adj* ancient, age-old

gǔ 鼓 *n* drum

gǔchuī 鼓吹 **1** *vb* advocate **2** *n* advocacy

gǔdòng 鼓动 *vb* incite, instigate, agitate

gǔlì 鼓励 **1** *vb* encourage, urge **2** *n* encouragement

gǔwǔ 鼓舞 **1** *vb* encourage, inspire, hearten **2** *n* inspiration, encouragement

gǔzhǎng 鼓掌 **1** *vb* applaud, clap one's hands **2** *n* applause

gùshi 故事 *n* story, tale

gùxiāng 故乡 *n* home town, native place

gùyì 故意 *adv* intentionally, deliberately, purposely

gù 顾 *vb* turn round to look at; take care of, look after, manage; pay attention to, attend to, take into consideration

gùkè 顾客 *n* customer, client

guā 瓜 *n* melon, gourd

guā 刮 *vb* scrape; **guā húzi** 刮胡子 shave; (*as the wind*) blow

guà 挂 *vb* (*when speaking of a painting, poster, etc.*) hang up, suspend; **qiáng shang guàzhe yìzhāng huà** 墙上挂着一张画

a picture is hanging on the wall; ring, phone, call; **gěi mǒurén guà diànhuà** 给某人挂电话 phone someone; be concerned about; **guà zài xīn shang** 挂在心上 keep in mind; register; hang up a receiver; **guàshang** 挂上 (when speaking of a telephone) hang up

guàhào 挂号 **1** vb (at a hospital, at a doctor's office, etc.) register, take a number **2** adj registered; **guàhàoxìn** 挂号信 registered letter

guǎi 拐 vb (when speaking of walking, riding, cycling, driving, etc.) turn; **wàng zuǒ guǎi** 往左拐 turn to the left; limp

guài 怪 **1** adj strange, odd, peculiar **2** vb blame

guàibude 怪不得 conj no wonder, so that's why

guān 关 vb close, shut, lock; turn off, shut off; (as a business, school or factory) close down; concern, involve; **zhè bù guān nǐde shì** 这不关你的事 it's none of your business, this doesn't concern you; **guāndiào** 关掉 close, shut, turn off; **guānshang** 关上 close, turn off; **bǎ mén guānshang** 把门关上 close the door

guānjiàn 关键 n (when talking about issues, problems, matters) key, crux

guānhuái 关怀 vb show loving care for, show solicitude to

guānmén 关门 vb close a door; (when speaking of a shop, store, or business) close, shut

guānxi 关系 **1** n relationship, connection, tie; bearing, relevance, consequence; **méi(yǒu) guānxi** 没(有)关系 it doesn't matter, don't worry, never mind; (explaining a cause or reason) **yóuyú shēntǐ de guānxi, tā jīntiān méiyǒu lái** 由于身体的关系, 他今天没有来 because of his health, he didn't come today **2** vb concern, affect, involve; **zhè guānxidào rénmín de shēnghuó** 这关系到人民的生活 this concerns the life of the people

guānxīn 关心 **1** vb concern oneself with, pay great attention to **2** n concern, care

guānyú 关于 *prep* about, concerning, with respect to; **guānyú jīngjì de wèntí** 关于经济的问题 the economic problem

guānzhào 关照 *vb* look after, keep an eye on

guānchá 观察 **1** *vb* observe, examine **2** *n* observation

guāndiǎn 观点 *n* point of view, standpoint, viewpoint

guānkàn 观看 *vb* watch, view

guānniàn 观念 *n* concept

guānzhòng 观众 *n* audience, spectator, viewer

guān 官 *n* government official, officer; government

guǎn 管 **1** *vb* run, manage, be in charge of; **zhèjiàn shì shéi lái guǎn?** 这件事谁来管? who will take care of this matter?; mind, attend to, bother about; **bié guǎn wǒ** 别管我 don't concern yourself about me **2** *n* pipe, tube

guǎnlǐ 管理 **1** *vb* manage, run **2** *n* management

guǎnzi 管子 *n* tube, pipe

guànjūn 冠军 *n* champion

guànchè 贯彻 *vb* implement thoroughly, carry out, put into effect

guàntou 罐头 *n* tin, can

guāng 光 **1** *n* light, ray; brightness, shine, lustre; glory, honour **2** *adj* smooth, shiny; bare, naked; **guāngzhe tóu** 光着头 be bareheaded; used up; **shuǐguǒ màiguāng le** 水果卖光了 the fruit is completely sold out **3** *adv* solely, merely, alone; **guāng shuō bù néng jiějué wèntí** 光说不能解决问题 we cannot solve the problem solely by talking

guānghuī 光辉 **1** *n* splendour, brilliance, glory **2** *adj* splendid, brilliant, glorious

guāngmíng 光明 **1** *adj* bright, promising; open, above-board **2** *n* light

guāngróng 光荣 **1** *adj* glorious, honourable **2** *n* glory, honour, credit

guāngxiàn 光线 *n* light, ray

guǎngbō 广播 **1** *vb* (*on radio or television*) broadcast **2** *n* broadcast; **guǎngbō diàntái** 广播电台 broadcasting station; **guǎngbōyuán** 广播员 announcer, broadcaster

guǎngchǎng 广场 *n* public square

guǎngdà 广大 *adj* vast, broad, extensive; numerous

guǎngfàn 广泛 *adj* wide-ranging, widespread, extensive

guǎnggào 广告 *n* advertisement; **guǎnggào pái** 广告牌 hoarding

guǎngkuò 广阔 *adj* vast, wide, broad

guàng 逛 *vb* stroll, roam; **guàng shāngdiàn** 逛商店 go window shopping

guī 归 *vb* go back to, return, give back to; turn over to..., be for...to handle, be up to...; **zhèjiàn shì guī tā chǔlǐ** 这件事归他处理 this matter is for him to handle

guīdìng 规定 **1** *vb* regulate, prescribe, stipulate **2** *n* rule, regulation

guīlǜ 规律 *n* law (of nature), regular pattern

guīmó 规模 *n* scale, scope, magnitude; **dà guīmó** 大规模 large-scale

guīzé 规则 *n* rule, regulation

guǐ 鬼 *n* devil, ghost; (*suffix used in some terms of criticism or abuse*) (**lǎn** | **jiǔ**] **jiǔ** 懒 | 酒] 鬼 [lazy bones | drunkard]

guì 贵 *adj* expensive, costly; precious, valuable; noble, honoured; **guì bīn** 贵宾 honoured guest; (*polite word*) your; **nín guìxìng?** 您贵姓? your surname please?

guì 跪 *vb* kneel

gǔn 滚 *vb* (*for round things*) roll; (*abusive command*) **gǔnchūqù!** 滚出去! get out of here! shove off!; **gǔnkāi!** 滚开! shove off! scram!

gùnzi 棍子 *n* rod, stick

guō 锅 n pot, pan, cooker

guó 国 n country, nation, state

guófáng 国防 n national defence

guójí 国籍 n nationality

guójì 国际 adj international

guójiā 国家 n country, nation, state

guómín 国民 adj national; **Guómíndǎng** 国民党 Nationalist Party, Kuomintang (KMT)

guóqí 国旗 n national flag

guóqìng 国庆 n National Day; **Guóqìng Jié** 国庆节 National Day

guówáng 国王 n king

guóyíng 国营 adj state-operated, state-run

guóyǔ 国语 n (used primarily in Taiwan) Mandarin Chinese

guǒrán 果然 adv indeed, sure enough, as expected

guò 过 **1** vb cross, pass, pass over; **guò** [jiē | hé | qiáo] 过 [街 | 河 | 桥] cross a [street | river | bridge]; (a series of things, a process) go through; (when talking about time, a holiday, a special day, etc.) spend, celebrate; **guò rìzi** 过日子 spend one's days; **guò shēngri** 过生日 celebrate one's birthday; exceed, go beyond; (used after a verb to indicate a result) past, through, over; [tiào | fēi | zǒu] **guò** [跳 | 飞 | 走] 过 [jump over | fly over | walk past]; (used after a verb to indicate completion of an action) finished, over; **chīguò fàn yǐhòu** 吃过饭以后 after eating; (used after de 得 to indicate potentiality) be better than, surpass, get the better of; [shuō | pǎo | dǎ] **de guò** [说 | 跑 | 打] 得过 out [argue | run | fight] **2** adv exceedingly, excessively, too; **guò** [dà | duō | gāo] 过 [大 | 多 | 高] exceedingly [big | many | tall]; over, around, over to the other side **3** prep after, over; **guò yīhuǐr zài lái** 过一会儿再来 come back in a little while

guo 过 pt (after a verb to indicate or emphasize past experience) have (ever), have (never); **nǐ qùguo Zhōngguó ma?** 你去过中国吗? have you ever been to China? ❗ To express this *idea in the negative,* **méi (yǒu)** 没 (有), *rather than* **bù** 不, *is used before the main verb;* **tā méi shàngguo xué** 他没上过学 he has never attended school

guòchéng 过程 *n* process, course

guòfèn 过分 *adj* excessive

guòlái 过来 *vb* come over, come here; **qǐng nǐ guòlái ba** 请你过来吧 please come over here; *(after a verb to indicate a direction towards the speaker)* **bǎ shū náguòlái** 把书拿过来 bring the book over (to me); *(after a verb to indicate returning to a normal state)* **xǐngguòlái** 醒过来 wake up, regain consciousness

guò nián 过年 *vb* celebrate the New Year, spend the New Year

guòqù 过去 **1** *n* the past **2** *adj* former, previous

guòqu 过去 *vb* go through, get through; **qǐng ràng wǒ guòqu** 请让我过去 please let me get through; *(after a verb to indicate a direction away from the speaker)* **zǒuguòqu** 走过去 walk over (there); *(after a verb to indicate changing from a normal state)* **tā hūnguòqu le** 他昏过去了 he's lost his consciousness; *(after a verb to indicate success or attainment)* **tā hùnguòqu le** 他混过去了 he got through by cheating

Hh

hāhā 哈哈 *exc (to express laughter)* ha ha!; *(to express satisfaction)* Aha!

hái 还 *adv* ▶ *See also* **huán** 还. still, yet; *(when making comparisons)* even more, still more; **tā bǐ wǒ hái gāo** 他比我还高 he is even taller than I am; also, too, in addition; rather, fairly; *(for emphasis)* **zhè hái bù róngyì!** 这还不容易! this couldn't be easier!, this is very easy!; *(indicating something unexpected)* **wǒ hái zhēn wàngle tāde míngzi** 我还真忘了他的名字 I really have forgotten his name; **hái...ne** 还... 呢 still, yet; (*continuing, in suspense*) **wǒ hái méiyǒu chī fàn ne** 我还没有吃饭呢 I still haven't eaten

háishì 还是 **1** *adv* still, all the same, nevertheless; ought to, had better; **nǐ háishì bú qù ba** 你还是不去吧 you'd better not go **2** *conj* or

háizi 孩子 *n* child, children, son or daughter

hǎi 海 *n* sea, ocean

hǎi'àn 海岸 *n* coast, seashore

hǎibiān 海边 *n* seashore, beach

hǎiguān 海关 *n* customs house, customs

hǎijūn 海军 *n* navy

hǎiwài 海外 *adv* overseas, abroad

hǎixiá 海峡 *n* strait

hǎiyáng 海洋 *n* seas and oceans, ocean

hài 害 **1** *n* evil, harm, calamity; disadvantage, damage, injury **2** *vb* harm, impair, cause trouble to; kill, murder; suffer from (an illness or disease), become ill; **hài bìng** 害病 become ill

hàichu 害处 *n* harm

hàipà 害怕 *vb* fear, be afraid

hán 含 *vb* hold in the mouth; contain

hánjià 寒假 *n* winter holiday, winter vacation

hánlěng 寒冷 *adj* bitterly cold

Hánguó 韩国 *n* South Korea

hǎn 喊 *vb* shout, call, yell

Hànyǔ 汉语 *n* Chinese language

Hànzì 汉字 *n* Chinese characters

Hànzú 汉族 *n* Han nationality

hàn 汗 *n* sweat, perspiration; **chū hàn** 出汗 sweat, perspire

háng 行 ▸ *See also* **xíng** 行. **1** *n* line, row; trade, profession, line of business; **nǐ xǐhuan zhè yì háng ma?** 你喜欢这一行吗? do you like this profession? **2** *mw* ▸ **213** *(for things that form a line)*

hángkōng 航空 *n* aviation, aeronautics; **hángkōngxìn** 航空信 airmail letter

háobù 毫不 *adv* not in the least, not at all, not the slightest

háowú 毫无 *adv* without the slightest

hǎo 好 ▸ *See also* **hào** 好. **1** *adj* good, fine, alright; in good health, well; *(in comparisons)* better **2** *adv* well; easy to; **kuàizi hǎo yòng** 筷子好用 chopsticks are easy to use; good to (taste, smell, etc.); **hǎo** [**chī** | **hē**] 好 [吃 | 喝] good [to eat | to drink]; *(emphatic)* how...! so...! very...!; **hǎo lěng de tiānqì!** 好冷的天气! how cold the weather is!; *(when used after a verb to indicate completion)* done, finished, ready; **wǒ zuòhǎo le** 我做好了 I have finished doing it **3** *conj* so as to, so that; **jīntiān xiàwǔ wǒ yào bǎ zuòyè zuòwán, wǎnshàng hǎo qù kàn diànyǐng** 今天我要把作业做完, 晚上好去看电影 this afternoon I want to finish all my homework so that I can go to the cinema this evening

hǎochī 好吃 *adj* good to eat, tasty, delicious

hǎochu 好处 *n* good point, benefit, advantage; profit, gain

hǎohāor (de) 好好儿(地) *adv* properly, carefully, thoroughly; **nǐmen yào hǎohāor de yánjiū yíxià** 你们要好好儿地研究一下 you should research this thoroughly

hǎo jiǔ 好久 *adv* for a long time, a long time since; **hǎo jiǔ bú jiàn** 好久不见 haven't seen you for a long time, 'long time no see'

hǎokàn 好看 *adj* good-looking, nice-looking, attractive; *(as a book, movie, etc.)* interesting

hǎotīng 好听 *adj* pleasing to the ear, pleasant to listen to

hǎo róngyì 好容易, **hǎo bu róngyì** 好不容易 *adv* with difficulty, with great effort

hǎowánr 好玩儿 *adj* interesting, amusing, fun

hǎoxiàng 好象 *vb* seem as if, seem as though, be like

hǎoxiē 好些 *adj* quite a few, a good many of, a great deal of

hào 号 *n* mark, sign, signal; (*of size, house, room, telephone*) number; date, day; jīntiān shísān hào 今天十三号 today is the 13th; horn, bugle call

hàomǎ 号码 *n* number

hàozhào 号召 **1** *vb* call, appeal to, attract **2** *n* call, appeal

hào 好 *vb* ▶ See also **hǎo** 好. like, love, be fond of; hào xué 好学 like studying, be eager to learn; be apt to, be liable to, have a tendency to; hào shēngqì 好生气 apt to lose one's temper

hē 喝 *vb* drink; drink liquor, drink an alcoholic beverage; hēzuì 喝醉 get drunk

hé 合 **1** *vb* come together, join, combine; (*as eyes, etc.*) close, shut; bǎ yǎnjing héqilai 把眼睛合起来 close your eyes; agree, suit, accord with; be equal to, add up to, be equivalent to; yì yīngbàng hé shísān kuài Rénmínbì 一英镑合十三块人民币 one pound sterling is equal to thirteen *yuan* in Renminbi **2** *adj* suitable **3** *adv* jointly, together with others; hé bàn 合办 run jointly

héfǎ 合法 *adj* legal

hésuàn 合算 *adj* worthwhile

hélǐ 合理 *adj* reasonable, rational

héshì 合适 *adj* suitable, fitting, appropriate

hétong 合同 *n* contract, agreement

hézuò 合作 **1** *vb* co-operate, collaborate, work together **2** *n* co-operation, collaboration

hé 和 **1** *conj* (*connects parallel expressions*) and, together with **2** *prep* with; wǒ hé nǐ yíkuàir qù 我和你一块儿去 I'll go with you; (*denoting relations, etc.*) tā hé wǒ yíyàng gāo 他和我一样高 he is as tall as I am

hépíng 和平 *n* peace

héqì 和气 *adj* polite, kind, gentle

hé 河 *n* river

hébì 何必 *adv* what need...?, why bother...?, there is no need to...

hékuàng 何况 *conj* let alone, not to speak of; **zhège wèntí lián lǎoshī dōu bù dǒng, hékuàng wǒmen xuéshēng ne** 这个问题连老师都不懂，何况我们学生呢 even the teacher cannot understand this problem, let alone we students

hé 盒 *n* box, case; **yìhé cháyè** 一盒茶叶 a box of tea

hézi 盒子 *n* box, case

hēi 黑 *adj* black; **hēisè** 黑色 black in colour; (*when talking about weather*) dark; **tiān hēi le** 天黑了 it's getting dark

hēi'àn 黑暗 **1** *adj* black, dark; **hēi'àn de yímiàn** 黑暗的一面 the dark side **2** *n* darkness

hēibǎn 黑板 *n* chalk board, blackboard

hēi 嘿 *exc* hey!

hénjì 痕迹 *n* trace, track, mark

hěn 很 *adv* very, quite, very much

hèn 恨 **1** *vb* hate **2** *n* hate, hatred, regret

héng 横 *adj* horizontal, across, sideways

hóng 红 *adj* red

hóng chá 红茶 *n* black tea

hónglǜdēng 红绿灯 *n* traffic lights

hóngqí 红旗 *n* red flag/banner

hóngshuǐ 洪水 *n* flood

hóuzi 猴子 *n* monkey

hòu 后 **1** *adv* later **2** *adj* rear, back, the latter **3** *prep* after, behind; **wǔfàn hòu** 午饭后 after lunch **4** *conj* after

hòubian 后边 *n* back, rear

hòudài 后代 *n* descendant, later generations

hòuguǒ 后果 *n* result, consequence

hòuhuǐ 后悔 *vb* regret, feel regretful

hòulái 后来 *adv* later on, afterwards

hòumén 后门 *n* back door (literally and figuratively)

hòumian 后面, **hòutou** 后头 *adv* at the back, in the rear, behind; later

hòunián 后年 *n* the year after next, two years from now

hòutiān 后天 *n* the day after tomorrow

hòu 厚 *adj* thick; deep, profound; large, substantial, generous

hū 呼 *vb* call, call out, shout; exhale, breathe out

hūxī 呼吸 **1** *vb* breathe **2** *n* breath, breathing, respiration

hūrán 忽然 *adv* suddenly, all of a sudden

hūshì 忽视 *vb* ignore, overlook

húluàn 胡乱 *adv* blindly, confusedly, recklessly

húshuō 胡说 **1** *vb* talk nonsense **2** *n* nonsense; **húshuō bādào** 胡说八道 total nonsense, utter rubbish

hútòng 胡同 *n* lane, alley

húzi 胡子 *n* beard, moustache

hú 壶 *n* kettle, pot; **yìhú kāfēi** 一壶咖啡 a pot of coffee

hú 湖 *n* lake

hútu 糊涂, **húlihútu** 糊里糊涂 *adj* confused, muddle-headed

hù 户 **1** *n* door **2** *mw* ▶ 213 (for households)

hùxiāng 互相 *adv* mutual, mutually

hùshi 护士 *n* (medical) nurse

hùzhào 护照 *n* passport

huā 花 **1** *n* flower, blossom, bloom **2** *adj* multicoloured, variegated **3** *vb* (of money, time, etc.) spend, expend; **huā** [qián | shíjiān] 花 [钱 | 时间] [spend money | take time, be time-consuming]

huāfèi 花费 *n* expenditure, expenses

huāyuán 花园 *n* flower garden, garden

huáqiáo 华侨 *n* overseas Chinese

huárén 华人 *n* Chinese person with a non-Chinese nationality

huá 划 *vb* ▶ See also **huà** 划. (*a boat, etc.*) paddle, row; make a scratch/cut, be scratched/cut

huá 滑 *adj* slippery, slick, smooth; cunning, crafty

huábīng 滑冰 *vb* skate, ice skate

huáxuě 滑雪 *vb* ski

huà 化 *vb* transform, change, turn into; melt, dissolve; (*after an adjective or noun to form a verb*) -ise or -ize; **xiàndàihuà** 现代化 modernization

huàxué 化学 *n* chemistry; **huàxué chéngfèn** 化学成分 chemical composition; **huàxué fǎnyìng** 化学反应 chemical reaction

huà 划 ▶ See also **huá** 划. **1** *vb* (*a boundary between regions, classes, etc.*) delineate, draw (a line); appropriate, assign, transfer **2** *n* (*when speaking of a Chinese character*) stroke

huà 画 *vb* paint, draw; **huà huàr** 画画儿 draw/paint a picture

huà(r) 画（儿） *n* drawing, painting, picture

huàbào 画报 *n* pictorial, illustrated magazine/newspaper

huà 话 *n* speech, language, words

huàjù 话剧 *n* play, modern drama

huái 怀 **1** *n* arms, heart, bosom **2** *vb* cherish, harbour (feelings)

huáiniàn 怀念 *vb* miss, cherish the memory of, think of

huáiyí 怀疑 *vb* doubt, suspect

huáiyùn 怀孕 *vb* be pregnant, get pregnant

huài 坏 **1** *adj* bad; broken, ruined; (*as food or other perishables*) spoiled **2** *vb* go bad, become spoiled, get out of order; **mǐfàn huài le** 米饭坏了 the rice has gone bad **3** *adv* (*when used after an* *adjective, showing an extreme extent* [lèi | kě | qì] **huài le** [累 | 渴 | 气] 坏了 terribly [tired | thirsty | angry]

huàichu 坏处 *n* harm, fault, disadvantage

huānlè 欢乐 *adj* happy, merry

huānsòng 欢送 *vb* send off; **huānsònghuì** 欢送会 farewell party, send-off

huānxǐ 欢喜 **1** *adj* happy, delighted **2** *vb* like, be fond of, delight in

huānyíng 欢迎 *vb* welcome, greet

huán 还 ▶ *See also* **hái** 还. go/come back, return, repay; **qǐng nǐ bǎ qián huán gěi tā** 请你把钱还给他 please return the money to him

huán 环 *n* ring, hoop, link

huánjìng 环境 *n* environment, surroundings, circumstances

huǎnmàn 缓慢 *adj* slow, sluggish

huànxiǎng 幻想 *n* fantasy, illusion

huànxǐng 唤醒 *vb* awaken (someone), wake (someone) up

huànqǐ 唤起 *vb* call, arouse

huàn 换 *vb* exchange, trade; **huàn yíjù huà shuō** 换一句话说 to put it another way, in other words

huàn 患 *vb* (*when talking about an illness, etc.*) contract, suffer from

huāng 荒 *adj* waste; barren, deserted, uncultivated

huāng(zhāng) 慌(张) *adj* flurried, flustered, confused

huángdì 皇帝 *n* emperor

huáng 黄 *adj* yellow

huángguā 黄瓜 *n* cucumber

Huánghé 黄河 *n* Yellow River

huánghūn 黄昏 *n* dusk

huángyóu 黄油 *n* butter

huǎng(huà) 谎(话) *n* lie, falsehood; **shuō huǎng** 说谎 tell a lie

huī 灰 **1** *adj* grey **2** *n* ash, dust

huīchén 灰尘 *n* dust, dirt

huī 挥 *vb* wield, wave

huīfù 恢复 **1** *vb* recover, restore, re-establish **2** *n* recovery, restoration

huí 回 **1** *vb* return, go back; answer, reply, reciprocate; turn round **2** *mw* ▶ **213** (for times, occurrences)

huídá 回答 **1** *vb* answer, reply **2** *n* answer, response

Huíjiào 回教 *n* Islam

huílai 回来 *vb* come back, return; (when used after a verb to indicate action coming back toward the speaker) **bǎ yàoshi jiāohuílai** 把钥匙交回来 hand back the key

huíqu 回去 *vb* go back, return; (when used after a verb to indicate action going back to the place of origin) **bǎ shū huánhuíqu** 把书还回去 return the book

huítóu 回头 **1** *vb* turn the head round; repent, change one's ways **2** *adv* later; **wǒ huítóu qù kàn tā** 我回头去看她 I'll go and see her later

huíxiǎng 回想 *vb* think back, recollect, recall

huíxìn 回信 **1** *vb* reply to a letter, write in reply **2** *n* letter of reply

huíyì 回忆 **1** *vb* recall, recollect **2** *n* reminiscence, recollection

huǐ 毁 *vb* destroy, ruin

huì 汇 **1** *vb* remit; converge, gather together; collect **2** *n* compilation, collection

huì 会 **!** Can also be pronounced **kuài** 会 with a different meaning. **1** *vb* know how to, be able to, can; **huì yòng jìsuànjī** 会用计算机 be able to use a computer, know how to use a computer; be likely to, be going to, be sure to; **huì bú huì xià yǔ?**

会不会下雨？ is it going to rain?; be accomplished in, be skilful in, be good at; tā huì hěn duō zhǒng wàiyǔ 他会很多种外语 he can speak many foreign languages; *(when used after a verb to indicate accomplishment)* acquire, master, command; tā xuéhuìle zhège jìshù 他学会了这个技术 he has mastered the technique; *(to express future tense)* will, shall; kǒngpà nǐ huì tài lèi le 恐怕你会太累了 I'm afraid you'll be too tired; get together, meet, assemble **2** *n* meeting, conference, party; association, society, union

huìchǎng 会场 *n* meeting place, conference centre, assembly hall

huìhuà 会话 **1** *vb* to engage in a conversation/dialogue **2** *n* conversation, dialogue

huìjiàn 会见 **1** *vb* meet with **2** *n* a meeting

huìkè 会客 *vb* receive a visitor/guest; huìkè shíjiān 会客时间 visiting hours; huìkèshì 会客室 reception room

huìtán 会谈 **1** *vb* hold negotiations, talk, discuss **2** *n* negotiation, discussion, talk

huìyì 会议 *n* meeting, conference

húnshēn 浑身 *adv* from head to toe, the whole body

hūnmí 昏迷 **1** *vb* faint, lose consciousness, be in a coma **2** *n* coma

hūnlǐ 婚礼 *n* wedding ceremony, wedding

hūnyīn 婚姻 *n* marriage

hùn 混 *vb* confuse, mix up; pass for, pass off as; tā hùnjìnle huìchǎng 他混进了会场 he conned his way into the conference hall; live aimlessly, muddle along, drift along; tā zài Xiānggǎng hùnle yì nián 他在香港混了一年 he idled away a year in Hong Kong; get along with; wǒ gēn tā hùn de búcuò 我跟他混得不错 I get along with him rather well

hùnluàn 混乱 *n* chaos, disorder, confusion

huó 活 **1** *vb* live, be alive **2** *adj* alive, lively

huór 活儿 *n* work; **gàn huór** 干活儿 to work; product

huódòng 活动 **1** *n* activity, event **2** *vb* move about, get exercise **3** *adj* loose, movable, mobile

huópo 活泼 *adj* lively, vivid

huóyuè 活跃 **1** *vb* invigorate, animate **2** *adj* lively, active, dynamic

huǒ 火 *n* fire; anger, temper; firepower, firearms, ammunition

huǒchái 火柴 *n* match

huǒchē 火车 *n* train; **huǒchēzhàn** 火车站 railway station

huǒjī 火鸡 *n* turkey

huǒjiàn 火箭 *n* rocket

huǒyào 火药 *n* gunpowder

huǒ 伙 *mw* ▶ **213** ! *This measure word usually has a negative connotation; (for groups or bands of people)*

huǒbàn 伙伴 *n* partner, companion

huǒshí 伙食 *n* meals, food, board

huò(zhě) 或 (者) **1** *conj* or, either...or...; **huòzhě zuò huǒchē qù, huòzhě zuò qìchē qù, dōu kěyǐ** 或者坐火车去，或者坐汽车去，都可以 we can go either by train or by car **2** *adv* maybe, perhaps, probably

huò 货 *n* goods, products, commodities

huòbì 货币 *n* money, currency

huòwù 货物 *n* goods, products, merchandise

huò(dé) 获 (得) *vb* obtain, acquire, gain; win, achieve; reap, harvest

huò 祸 *n* misfortune, disaster

Jj

jīhū 几乎 *adv* almost, nearly

jīchǎng 机场 *n* airport

jīchuáng 机床 *n* machine tool

jīguān 机关 *n* organization, agency

jīhuì 机会 *n* opportunity

jīqì 机器 *n* machine; **jīqì rén** 机器人 robot

jīxiè 机械 **1** *n* machinery, mechanism, engine **2** *adj* mechanical

jī 鸡 *n* chicken

jīdàn 鸡蛋 *n* (of a chicken) egg **!** Note that in Chinese the kind of egg has to be specified; **jīdàn** 鸡蛋 is not used for the egg of any animal other than a chicken.

jījí 积极 *adj* positive, affirmative, optimistic; active, energetic, vigorous

jījíxìng 积极性 *n* positive attitude, zeal, enthusiasm

jīlěi 积累 *vb* accumulate, build up

jīběn 基本 *adj* basic, fundamental, essential

jīchǔ 基础 **1** *n* foundation, basis **2** *adj* basic, elementary

jīdòng 激动 *adj* moving, exciting; excited, moved

jīliè 激烈 *adj* heated, intense, sharp

jí 及 *conj* (used between nouns or noun phrases; the noun after jí 及 is often less important than the one before it) and, and including

jígé 及格 *vb* (when speaking of a test or examination) pass, reach an acceptable standard

jíshí 及时 *adj* **1** *adj* timely **2** *adv* on time; right away, promptly, without delay

jí 级 *n* grade, rank, quality; (*in school*) year, class, grade

jí 极 *adv* extremely, exceedingly, to the highest degree; **...jí le ...** 极了 (*follows an adjective when indicating an extreme degree*) extremely; **hǎochī jí le** 好吃极了 extremely delicious

jíqí 极其 *adv* extremely, exceptionally

jí 即 *vb* (*equivalent to jiùshì* 就是) be, be exactly, be none other than; that is, i.e.

jíjiāng 即将 *adv* will, going to, about to

jíshǐ 即使, **jíbiàn** 即便 *conj* even if, even though, even

jí 急 *adj* anxious, worried, uneasy; in a hurry; angry, annoyed, impatient; (*as a wind, a storm, or water in a river*) violent, strong, fast; urgent, pressing

jímáng 急忙 *adv* in a hurry, hurriedly, hastily

jí 集 **1** *vb* collect, gather, assemble **2** *n* collection, anthology; volume, part; market, fair; **gǎn jí** 赶集 go to market

jíhé 集合 *vb* gather together

jítǐ 集体 **1** *n* collective **2** *adj* collective

jízhōng 集中 **1** *vb* concentrate, amass, put together; centralize **2** *adj* concentrated, centralized

jǐ 几 *det* (*when unstressed*) a few, several **!** *Note that when used with numerals, the meaning of jǐ 几 changes depending on whether it comes before or after the numeral. The phrase jǐ shí bù 几十步 means several tens of steps, i.e., 20, 30, 40, etc. (sometimes translated as dozens or scores, while the phrase shíjǐ bù 十几步 means more than 10 steps, that is, over 10 but under 20; (when stressed) how many?; xiànzài jǐ diǎn le? 现在几点了? what time is it now?*

jǐ 己 *n* oneself, one's own

jǐ 挤 **1** *vb* crowd, press, squeeze; push, jostle; (*by squeezing an animal's udder*) milk **2** *adj* crowded

jìhuà 计划 **1** *n* plan, project **2** *vb* plan, arrange, map out; **jìhuà shēngyù** 计划生育 family planning, birth control

jìsuàn 计算 **1** *vb* compute, calculate **2** *n* calculation

jìsuànjī 计算机 *n* computer

jì 记 *vb* remember, keep in mind; record, note, jot down

jìde 记得 *vb* remember

jìlù 记录 **1** *vb* record, take notes, keep minutes **2** *n* (*of meetings, etc.*) minutes, notes, record; (*in athletics, etc.*) record

jìyì 记忆 **1** *vb* remember, recall **2** *n* memory, memories

jìzhě 记者 *n* reporter, journalist

jìzhu 记住 *vb* remember, keep in mind, learn by heart

jìlù 纪律 *n* discipline

jìniàn 纪念 **1** *vb* commemorate, observe **2** *n* souvenir, memento, keepsake; **yíge jìniànpǐn** 一个纪念品 a souvenir; commemoration, memorial, anniversary

jìshù 技术 *n* technique, skill

jìshùyuán 技术员 *n* technician

jì(jié) 季(节) *n* season

jì 既 *conj* since, now that; **jì...yě/yòu...** 既...也/又... both...and..., as well as; **zhège rén jì nǔlì, yòu cōngming** 这个人既努力又聪明 this person is both hardworking and intelligent

jìrán 既然 *conj* since, now that, as

jìxù 继续 *vb* continue, carry on

jì 寄 *vb* send, post, mail

jiā 加 *vb* (*as a mathematical function*) add, plus; increase, raise

jiāgōng 加工 *vb* (*of raw materials*) process into a finished product

Jiānádà 加拿大 *n* Canada

jiāqiáng 加强 *vb* strengthen, reinforce

jiāyǐ 加以 **1** vb add more, apply additionally **2** conj in addition, moreover

jiā 夹 **1** vb pinch, squeeze, compress; (with chopsticks, pincers, etc.) pick up, hold; place between, insert between; mix, mingle **2** n tweezers, pincers, pliers; fastener; clip; folder

jiā 家 **1** n home, family, household; (when it follows a subject or field) a specialist, a professional; **kēxuéjiā** 科学家 scientist; school of thought **2** mw ▶ 213 (for families, enterprises, restaurants, hotels, etc.)

jiājù 家具 n furniture

jiātíng 家庭 n family, home

jiāxiāng 家乡 n home town, native place

jiǎ 假 adj ▶ See also **jià** 假. false, artificial, fake

jiàgé 价格 n price, charge

jiàqian 价钱 n price, charge

jiàzhí 价值 n value, worth, cost

jià 架 **1** mw ▶ 213 (for aeroplanes, pianos, cameras, etc.) **2** n stand, rack, shelf; structure, scaffold **3** vb: erect, put up; support, help

jià 假 n ▶ See also **jiǎ** 假. holiday, vacation, leave of absence

jiàtiáo 假条 n leave permit, permit to take leave, doctor's certificate; application for leave

jiān 尖 **1** adj sharp, pointed; sharp in sound, shrill; (of the senses) keen, acute; [ěrduo | bízi] **jiān** [耳朵 | 鼻子] 尖 have an acute sense of [hearing | smell] **2** n sharp tip/point, hook

jiānruì 尖锐 adj (of objects) sharp, pointed; (of perception, analysis, thought, etc.) penetrating, incisive, sharp; (of sound) shrill, piercing; (of activity, struggle, opposition) intense, acute

jiānchí 坚持 **1** vb hold firmly to, persist in, insist **2** adj persistent, insistent

jiāndìng 坚定 adj firm, resolute, determined

jiānjué 坚决 **1** *adj* resolute, decided, determined **2** *adv* decidedly, determinedly

jiānqiáng 坚强 *adj* strong, solid

jiān 间 **1** *mw* ▶ **213** (for rooms) **2** *n* room **3** *prep* between, amongst

jiān 肩 *n* shoulder

jiānjù 艰巨 *adj* extremely difficult

jiānkǔ 艰苦 **1** *adj* hard, difficult, tough **2** *n* hardship, difficulty

jiǎnchá 检查 **1** *vb* inspect, examine **2** *n* inspection, examination

jiǎndān 简单 *adj* simple, easy, uncomplicated

jiǎn 拣 *vb* choose, pick out, select

jiǎn 捡 *vb* pick up, gather

jiǎn 剪 *vb* (with scissors) cut, clip, cut off

jiǎn 减 *vb* subtract, minus, take away; decrease, reduce, cut

jiǎnqīng 减轻 *vb* lighten, reduce, mitigate

jiǎnshǎo 减少 *vb* diminish, reduce, decrease

jiàn 见 *vb* see, catch sight of; meet; call on, visit, have an interview with; appear, manifest, be evident; (used as a suffix to certain verbs to indicate successful perception by the senses) [kàn | tīng | wén] 见 [see | hear | smell]

jiànmiàn 见面 *vb* meet (face to face)

jiàn 件 *mw* ▶ **213** (for luggage, clothes, furniture, matters, etc.)

jiàn 建 *vb* build, construct; establish, found, create

jiànlì 建立 **1** *vb* establish, set up, create **2** *n* establishment

jiànshè 建设 **1** *vb* build up, construct **2** *n* construction

jiànyì 建议 **1** *vb* suggest, recommend, give advice **2** *n* suggestion, recommendation, proposal

jiànzhù 建筑 **1** *n* building, structure; architecture **2** *vb* build, construct

jiànkāng 健康 **1** *adj* healthy, vigorous, robust **2** *n* health

jiànjiàn 渐渐 *adv* gradually, step by step

jiàn 箭 *n* arrow

jiāng 江 *n* river; the Changjiang (Yangtze) River; **Jiāng nán** 江南 south of the Yangtze River

jiāng 将 **1** *adv* about to, going to; **jiāng kāishǐ** 将开始 about to begin; *(when indicating future tense)* will, shall, be going to **2** *prep (used to introduce a verbal phrase by placing the object before the verb; functions like bǎ 把)* **jiāng tāde xíngli ná huí jiā** 将他的行李拿回家 take his luggage back home

jiānglái 将来 **1** *n* future **2** *adv* in the future

jiāngyào 将要 *vb* will, be going to, be about to; **jiāngyào shàngkè de shíhou...** 将要上课的时候... when the lesson is about to start...

jiǎng 讲 *vb* say, tell, remark; talk, discuss, negotiate; explain, interpret; pay attention to, be particular about

jiǎnghuà 讲话 *vb* talk, speak, converse

jiǎngzuò 讲座 *n* lecture

jiǎng 奖 **1** *n* prize, award **2** *vb* praise, commend, reward

jiǎngxuéjīn 奖学金 *n* scholarship

jiàng 降 *vb* descend, fall, drop; lower, reduce, cut down

jiàngdī 降低 *vb* lower, drop, reduce

jiàngluò 降落 *vb (when talking about an aeroplane)* descend, land

jiàngyóu 酱油 *n* soy sauce, soya sauce

jiāo 交 *vb* hand in, hand over, give up; meet, join, come into contact with; befriend, associate with; **jiāo péngyou** 交朋友 make friends

jiāohuàn 交换 **1** *vb* exchange, swap, interchange **2** *n* exchange, interchange, swap

jiāojì 交际 **1** n social interaction, communication **2** vb be socially active, interact with people

jiāoliú 交流 **1** vb exchange, interchange **2** n exchange, interchange

jiāotán 交谈 vb converse, have a chat

jiāotōng 交通 n communications, transportation; traffic

jiāoqū 郊区 n suburban district, suburbs

jiāo'ào 骄傲 **1** adj proud, arrogant, haughty; wǒ wèi nǐ jiāo'ào 我为你骄傲 I'm proud of you **2** n pride, conceit

jiāo 教 ! Can also be pronounced jiào with a different meaning; vb teach, train, instruct; jiāoshū 教书 teach

jiǎo 角 n (a unit of Chinese money); yì jiǎo qián 一角钱 ten fen, 1/10 of a yuan; corner; (in geometry) angle; (of an animal) horn, antler

jiǎozi 饺子 n boiled dumpling filled with meat and vegetable

jiǎo 脚 n (part of the body) foot; (of an object, mountain, structure, etc.) base, foot, leg

jiào 叫 **1** vb call out, cry out, shout; (as a taxi) summon, order, hire; name, call, address as; tā jiào wǒ lǎoshī 他叫我老师 he calls me 'Teacher'; be named, be called; tā jiào shénme míngzi? 她叫什么名字? what is her name?; tell, order; let, allow, permit; tā bú jiào wǒ kàn tāde shū 她不叫我看她的书 she won't let me read her book **2** n (of a bird or animal) call, cry; [gǒu | niǎo] jiào [狗 | 鸟] [dog's bark | bird's call] **3** prep (when used to introduce the agent in a passive construction) by; tā jiào lǎoshī pīpíngle yídùn 他叫老师批评了一顿 he was given a reprimand by the teacher

jiàozuò 叫做, **jiàozuò** 叫作 vb (when giving the name or term for something) be called, be known as; zhè jiàozuò làngfèi 这叫做浪费 this is called being wasteful

jiàocái 教材 n (textbooks, etc.) teaching materials

jiàoliàn 教练 n (in sports, etc.) coach, instructor

jiàoshī 教师 n teacher

jiàoshì 教室 *n* classroom

jiàoshòu 教授 *n* professor

jiàoxué 教学 **1** *vb* teach **2** *n* teaching

jiàoxùn 教训 **1** *vb* teach (someone a lesson), lecture (someone for wrongdoing); reproach, reprimand, chide **2** *n* lesson, teaching, moral; **cóng shìgù zhōng xīqǔ jiàoxùn** 从事故中吸取教训 learn a lesson from the accident

jiàoyù 教育 **1** *vb* teach, educate, inculcate **2** *n* education

jiàoyuán 教员 *n* teacher, instructor

jiào 较 **1** *vb* compare **2** *adv* comparatively, relatively **3** *prep* compared with, than

jiēduàn 阶段 *n* (of development) stage, phase

jiējí 阶级 *n* (social) class

jiēshi 结实 *adj* (when talking about objects) strong, durable, solid; (of people) sturdy, tough, strong

jiē 接 *vb* (when referring to guests or visitors) meet, receive, welcome, pick up; (when speaking of a letter, a ball, etc.) receive, take hold of, catch; (for the telephone, etc.) answer, accept, take over; connect, join, unite

jiēchù 接触 **1** *vb* touch, come into contact with, meet up with **2** *n* contact

jiēdài 接待 **1** *vb* (when referring to guests or visitors) receive, host, admit **2** *n* reception

jiēdào 接到 *vb* receive

jiējiàn 接见 *vb* (when referring to guests or visitors) receive, meet

jiējìn 接近 **1** *vb* approximate, come close to, approach **2** *adj* close to, near to, on intimate terms with

jiēshòu 接受 *vb* receive, take, accept

jiēzhe 接着 **1** *vb* follow, carry on, catch **2** *adv* right afterwards, following

jiē 街 *n* road, street, thoroughfare; downtown, shopping district

jiēdào 街道 *n* road, street

jié 节 **1** *n* (of an object) segment, section, division; sequence of events, proceedings, programme; festival, holiday **2** *vb* save, economize **3** *mw* ▶ 213 (for sections of things) section, length, segment; (for torch batteries, railway carriages, class periods at school)

jiémù 节目 *n* (of a performance, or on radio or TV) programme, item on a programme

jiérì 节日 *n* festival day, holiday

jiéshěng 节省 **1** *vb* save, economize **2** *adj* economical, thrifty, frugal

jiéyuē 节约 **1** *vb* economize, save **2** *n* austerity

jiégòu 结构 *n* structure, construction, composition

jiéguǒ 结果 **1** *n* result, outcome **2** *adv* consequently, finally, as a result

jiéhé 结合 **1** *vb* join together, unite, marry; combine, integrate **2** *n* unity, combination

jiéhūn 结婚 **1** *vb* marry, get married **2** *n* marriage

jiélùn 结论 *n* (of an argument or statement) conclusion; (of a law case) conclusion, verdict

jiéshù 结束 *vb* finish, conclude, wind up

jiějie 姐姐 *n* elder sister

jiěmèi 姐妹 *n* sisters

jiě 解 *vb* loosen, untie, unfasten; free, relieve, put an end to; dispel, dissolve, be dissolved; understand, comprehend, realize; solve, explain, interpret

jiědá 解答 *vb* answer, explain, solve

jiěfàng 解放 **1** *vb* liberate, set free, emancipate **2** *n* liberation, emancipation

jiějué 解决 *vb* settle, solve, resolve; dispose of, finish off; **tā bǎ nàxiē shèng fàn quán jiějué le** 他把那些剩饭全解决了 he finished off the food that was left over

jiěshì 解释 **1** *vb* explain, clarify, interpret **2** *n* explanation, interpretation

jièshào 介绍 *vb* introduce, present, recommend; **wǒ gěi nǐ jièshào jièshào** 我给你介绍介绍 let me introduce you

jiè 届 *mw* ▶213 (for regular sessions, conferences, sports tournaments, terms of office, etc.); (for students graduating in the same year) year, class, grade

jiè 界 *n* boundary; world, circle; [zìrán | xuéshù | shāngyè] jiè [自然 | 学术 | 商业] 界 [natural world | academic circles | business circles]

jiè 借 *vb* borrow; **gēn tā jiè qián** 跟他借钱 borrow money from him; lend; **wǒ bǎ wǒde cídiǎn jiè gěi tā** 我把我的词典借给他 I lent my dictionary to him; use, make use of, take advantage of

jīn 斤 *n* (a unit in the Chinese weight system) 1/2 kilogram

jīnnián 今年 *n* this year, the current year

jīnhòu 今后 *adv* from now on, in the future, hereafter

jīntiān 今天 *n* today; nowadays, the present

jīn 金 **1** *n* gold **2** *adj* golden

jīnshǔ 金属 *n* metal, metal product

jǐn(jǐn) 仅(仅) *adv* only, merely, just; barely, scarcely

jìn 尽 *adv* ▶ See also **jǐn** 尽. to the greatest extent, to the utmost, furthest; **jìn** [zǎo | dōngbian | shàngmian] 尽 [早 | 东边 | 上面] [as soon as possible | the easternmost | the highest]

jǐnguǎn 尽管 **1** *adv* freely, with no hesitation, without restriction **2** *conj* in spite of, even though, even if; **jǐnguǎn...dōu/yě/hái...** 尽管...都 / 也 / 还... although...still, in spite of...still; **jǐnguǎn tā shēntǐ bù hǎo, kě hái jìxù gōngzuò** 尽管她身体不好，可还继续工作 in spite of her ill health, she still continues to work

jìnliàng 尽量, **jǐnliàng** 尽量 *adv* to the fullest extent, as much as possible, to one's utmost

jǐn 紧 1 *adj* tight, taut, tense; urgent, important, pressing; near, close 2 *adv* tightly, closely

jǐnjí 紧急 *adj* urgent, pressing, critical

jǐnzhāng 紧张 *adj* (*of a person*) tense, nervous, intense; (*of a situation or supply*) critical, tight, short

jìn 进 *vb* enter, go into, come into; advance, move forward, go ahead; (*used after a verb to indicate inward direction*) into, in; zǒujìn shāngdiàn 走进商店 walk into the store

jìnbù 进步 1 *n* progress, advancement, improvement 2 *vb* advance, make progress, improve 3 *adj* progressive

jìngōng 进攻 1 *vb* attack, assault 2 *n* assault, offensive, attack

jìnhuà 进化 *vb* evolve, develop

jìnkǒu 进口 1 *vb* (*as goods, products, etc.*) import 2 *n* import

jìnlai 进来 *vb* (*when indicating a movement toward the speaker*) enter, come in; zǒujìnlai 走进来 walk in

jìnqu 进去 *vb* (*when indicating a movement away from the speaker*) enter, go in; zǒujìnqu 走进去 walk in

jìnrù 进入 *vb* enter, go into, penetrate; be admitted to

jìnxíng 进行 *vb* proceed, go ahead, carry on; undertake, engage in

jìnxiū 进修 1 *vb* receive further training, pursue further studies 2 *n* further training

jìnyíbù 进一步 1 *vb* go a step further 2 *adv* further 3 *adj* better

jìn 近 *adj* (*in place or time*) near, nearby, close; intimate, closely related

jìnlái 近来 *adv* recently, of late, lately

jìn 尽 ▶ See also **jǐn** 尽. 1 *vb* exhaust, use up, come to an end; do one's utmost, try one's best, live up to 2 *adv* exhaustively, exclusively, to the highest degree

jìn 劲 *n* (*physical*) strength, energy, force; (*mental or spiritual*) vigour, drive, spirit; air, manner, expression; **kàn tā nà jǐnzhāng jìnr** 看他那紧张劲儿 notice how nervous he is; interest, relish, gusto; **xué shùxué zhēn méi jìnr** 学数学真没劲儿 I don't have any interest in studying mathematics

jìnzhǐ 禁止 *vb* forbid, prohibit, ban

jīngjù 京剧, **jīngxì** 京戏 *n* Peking opera

jīng 经 *vb* (*when talking about a place or an experience*) go through, pass through, via; manage, deal in; stand, endure; **tā jīng bù qǐ zhèzhǒng dǎjī** 她经不起这种打击 she can't stand this kind of blow

jīngcháng 经常 *adv* frequently, often, regularly

jīngguò 经过 **1** *vb* (*when talking about a place or experience*) pass by, pass through, go through **2** *prep* as a result of, after, through; by means of **3** *n* process, course

jīngjì 经济 *n* economy, economics; financial condition, income

jīnglǐ 经理 *n* manager, director

jīnglì 经历 **1** *vb* experience, undergo **2** *n* experience, past career

jīngyàn 经验 *n* experience

jīngqí 惊奇 *adj* surprised, amazed

jīngrén 惊人 *adj* astonishing, amazing, alarming

jīngyà 惊讶 *adj* surprised, amazed, astonished

jīngcǎi 精彩 *adj* brilliant, splendid, wonderful

jīnglì 精力 *n* energy, vitality, vigour

jīngshén 精神 **1** *n* mind, consciousness; gist, essence, spirit **2** *adj* spiritual, mental

jīngshen 精神 **1** *n* vigour, vitality, drive **2** *adj* vigorous, lively, spirited

jǐng 井 *n* well

jǐngsè 景色 *n* scenery, landscape, scene

jīngchá 警察 n police, police officer, policeman

jǐnggào 警告 vb warn, caution, admonish

jìngsài 竞赛 **1** vb compete, race **2** n competition, race, contest

jìngzhēng 竞争 **1** vb compete **2** n competition

jìng'ài 敬爱 adj respectful, honourable, esteemed

jìnglǐ 敬礼 vb salute, give a salute; give a greeting; (when closing a letter respectfully) **cǐ zhì jìnglǐ** 此致敬礼 with best wishes

jìng 静 adj quiet, peaceful, still

jìngzi 镜子 n mirror; **zhào jìngzi** 照镜子 look at one's reflection in the mirror; lens, glass, spectacles; **fàngdà jìng** 放大镜 magnifying glass, magnifier

jiūzhèng 纠正 **1** vb correct (a mistake), put right **2** n correction

jiūjìng 究竟 adv after all, in the end; actually, exactly

jiǔ 九 num nine

jiǔyuè 九月 n September

jiǔ 久 adv for a long time, long since

jiǔ 酒 n wine, liquor, alcoholic drink

jiù 旧 adj old, used; former, past; old-fashioned, outdated

jiù 救 vb save, rescue, help

jiù 就 **1** adv soon, immediately, right away; (sooner or earlier than expected) already, as early as, as soon as; **tā zuótiān jiù lái le** 他昨天就来了 he arrived yesterday; as soon as, right after; **tā chīle fàn jiù zǒu le** 他吃了饭就走了 he left as soon as he had eaten; only, just, alone; precisely **2** conj (when used in a complex sentence with the second clause introduced by **yě** 也) even if, even though; **nǐ jiù bù qǐng wǒ, wǒ yě huì lái** 你就不请我，我也会来 even if you don't invite me, I'll still come; (when introducing a subsequent action) then; **zhǐyào nǐ yuànyì, wǒ jiù gēn nǐ yìqǐ qù** 只要你愿意，我就跟你一起去 I'll go with you if you wish; (when used between two identical words or phrases to indicate that one is making a concession) what's done is done, nothing can be done about it; **tā bù lái jiù bù lái ba, fǎnzhèng wǒmen bù néng qiángpò tā lái** 他不来就不来吧，反正我们不能强迫他来 if he doesn't come, he doesn't come; anyway, we cannot force him to come; (when used with **běnlái** 本来, to mean all along, from the start) **tā běnlái jiù bù xiǎng xué Déyǔ** 他本来就不想学德语 he never wanted to study German **3** prep according to, with regard to

jiùshì 就是 **1** adv precisely; (used with **le** 了 at the end of a sentence to indicate an affirmative and positive sense) just; **bié dānxīn nǐde gōngzuò, huí jiā hǎohǎo xiūxi jiùshì le** 别担心你的工作，回家好好休息就是了 don't worry about your work, just go home and get a good rest **2** conj (when used in the sense of either...or...) or; **búshì...jiùshì...** 不是...就是... either...or...; **tā búshì zài túshūguǎn jiùshì zài shítáng** 他不是在图书馆就是在食堂 he is either in the library or in the dining hall; even if, even; **jiùshì...yě** 就是...也 even..., even if....; **jiùshì tā qù, wǒ yě bú qù** 就是他去，我也不去 I won't go even if he goes

jiùjiu 舅舅 n mother's brother, uncle

jūzhù 居住 vb live, reside, dwell

júzhǎng 局长 n (of an office, bureau, department, etc.) head, director, chairperson

júzi 橘子 n orange, tangerine; **júzi shuǐ/zhī** 橘子水/汁 orange juice

jǔ 举 vb raise, lift, hold up; (an example, etc.) cite; enumerate; **jǔ yíge lìzi** 举一个例子 cite as an example

jǔbàn 举办 vb (when talking about an exhibition, competition, etc) hold, run

jǔxíng 举行 vb (when talking about a meeting, ceremony, discussion, etc) hold, conduct

jù 句 **1** n sentence, line of verse **2** mw ▶ 213 (for lines, sentences, units of speech, poetry, etc.)

jùzi 句子 n (when talking about language) sentence

jùdà 巨大 adj great, enormous, huge

jùjué 拒绝 1 vb refuse, reject, turn down 2 n refusal

jùbèi 具备 vb (when speaking of necessary conditions, qualifications, or requirements) have, possess

jùtǐ 具体 adj concrete, specific, particular

jùyǒu 具有 vb have, possess, be equipped with

jùlèbù 俱乐部 n club

jù 剧 n drama, play, opera

jùchǎng 剧场 n theatre

jù 据 1 vb occupy, seize 2 prep according to; **jùshuō** 据说 it is said, they say, I hear

jùlí 距离 1 n distance, gap, separation 2 prep apart/away from, at a distance from; **wǒ jiā jùlí Běijīng sānshí gōnglǐ** 我家距离北京三公里 my house is thirty kilometres from Beijing

juǎn 卷 1 vb roll up; **juǎnqǐlai** 卷起来 roll up; sweep off, carry along 2 n roll, scroll

jué 决 adv (used before a negative word) definitely, certainly; **wǒ jué bù tóngyì** 我决不同意 under no circumstances will I agree

juédìng 决定 1 vb decide, make up one's mind 2 n decision, resolution

juéxīn 决心 1 n determination, resolution, decision 2 vb determine, be determined

juéde 觉得 vb feel, think

juéwù 觉悟 1 vb become aware of, become awakened, realize 2 n consciousness, awareness, understanding

juéduì 绝对 1 adj absolute 2 adv absolutely, definitely

jūn 军 n (an armed force as a whole) the army, the military

jūnduì 军队 n army, armed force

jūnshì 军事 1 n military affairs, military matters 2 adj military

Kk

kāfēi 咖啡 *n* coffee; **kāfēi guǎn** 咖啡馆 café

kǎchē 卡车 *n* lorry, truck

kāi 开 *vb* open; *(a vehicle or engine)* operate, start, run; **kāi chē** 开车 drive a car; *(a business, shop, store)* open, be in business; *(a business, shop, store, factory)* set up, establish, run; *(as a ship, vehicle, or troops on a journey or expedition)* set off, start away; *(land, waterway, etc.)* open up, develop, reclaim; *(flowers, trees, etc.)* blossom, bloom; *(a switch, engine, heat)* turn on; *(as a restriction, ban, etc.)* remove, lift, allow; *(meeting, exhibition, performance, school, class)* hold, begin, start; *(setting out in detail)* write, list, itemize; **kāi yàofāng** 开药方 write a prescription; *(for water)* boil; **shuǐ kāi le** 水开了 the water is boiling; *(after a verb to indicate outward movement, getting out of the way, etc.)* away, off, out; [chuánkāi | zǒukāi | duǒkāi] [传开 | 走开 | 躲开] [spread around | get out of the way | step aside]

kāifàng 开放 **1** *vb* open to the public, allow public use; be open; **duì wài kāifàng** 对外开放 be open to the outside **2** *adj* liberal, open

kāihuì 开会 *vb* hold a meeting

kāiguān 开关 *n* switch

kāikè 开课 *vb (an academic course or class)* give a course, teach; *(referring to a school or university term)* begin, start

kāimíng 开明 *adj* liberal, enlightened, progressive

kāimù 开幕 *vb* raise the curtain, begin the show; open, inaugurate

kāipì 开辟 *n (a country, route, road, source of revenue, etc.)* open up, develop, utilize

kāishǐ 开始 **1** *vb* begin, start, commence **2** *n* beginning, start, outset

kāitóu 开头 n beginning, opening

kāi wánxiào 开玩笑 vb make fun of, crack a joke; gēn tā kāi wánxiào 跟他开玩笑 make fun of him

kāixīn 开心 vb feel happy

kāixué 开学 vb open/begin/start school

kāiyǎn 开演 vb begin/start a performance, raise the curtain

kāizhǎn 开展 vb develop, carry out, launch

kān 看 vb ▶ See also **kàn** 看. look after, take care of; kān háizi 看孩子 look after a child

kǎn 砍 vb chop, cut, cut down

kàn 看 vb ▶ See also **kān** 看. look, look at, watch; (silently) read; think, consider, regard as; wǒ kàn tā tài shòu le 我看她太瘦了 I think she's too thin; visit, call on; (in changeable circumstances) depend on; yào kàn tā máng bù máng 要看他忙不忙 that depends on whether he's busy or not; (after a verb, especially when used in reduplicated form) just...and see, try...and see; shìshi kàn 试试看 try and see (how it is, etc.); wènwèn kàn 问问看 ask and see (what the person says, etc.)

kànbìng 看病 vb (when talking about a patient seeing a doctor) see the doctor, have an examination; (when talking about a doctor seeing a patient) see, examine, treat

kànbuqǐ 看不起 vb look down on, scorn, despise; tā kànbuqǐ wǒ 他看不起我 he looks down on me

kànchéng 看成 vb treat as, regard as, consider as

kàndài 看待 vb regard, treat

kàndào 看到 vb catch sight of, see, notice

kànfǎ 看法 n viewpoint, view, way of thinking

kànjiàn 看见 vb (implying perception as well as looking) see; wǒ zuìjìn méi kànjiàn tā 我最近没看见他 I haven't seen him recently ! When used to negate the verb, bù 不 comes between the two syllables of this word; wǒ kàn bú jiàn nǐ 我看不见你 I can't see you; (when used in the negative, taking on a passive *sense*) (dis)appear, become (in)visible; **húrán tā kàn bú jiàn le** 忽然他看不见了 he suddenly disappeared

kàn(qǐ)lai 看 (起)来, **kàn yàngzi** 看样子 *vb* it looks as if, it seems that, it appears that; [**kànlai** | **kàn yàngzi**] **yào xiàyǔ** [看来 | 看样子] 要下雨 it looks like rain

kāngkǎi 慷慨 *adj* generous, vehement

káng 扛 *vb* carry on the shoulder/shoulders

kàngyì 抗议 1 *vb* protest 2 *n* protest

kǎo 考 *vb* examine, give/take an examination/test; investigate; **kǎoshang** 考上 *(to attain entry to a school or university)* to pass entrance exams; **kǎoshang dàxué** 考上大学 pass the entrance examination to enter university

kǎolǜ 考虑 *vb* consider, weigh, think over

kǎoshì 考试 1 *vb* take/give an examination 2 *n* examination, test

kǎoyàn 考验 *n* test, trial

kǎo 烤 *vb* roast, bake; **kǎohuǒ** 烤火 warm oneself next to a fire

kào 靠 1 *vb* lean on, lean against; depend upon, rely on; *(a person or a livelihood for a living)* depend on; **tā kào mài jìsuànjī shēnghuó** 他靠卖计算机生活 he relies on selling computers for a living; approach, get near to 2 *prep* near, towards, along; **kào běibù yǒu hěnduō shān** 靠北部有很多山 there are many mountains towards the north

kē 科 1 *n* area/branch of study; **wénkē** 文科 the humanities; **lǐkē** 理科 the sciences; administrative unit, section, department

kējì 科技 *n (abbreviation of* **kēxué jìshù** 科学技术*)* science and technology

kēxué 科学 *n* science

kēxuéjiā 科学家 *n* scientist

kēxuéyuàn 科学院 *n* academy of sciences

kēyán 科研 *n (abbreviation of* **kēxué yánjiū** 科学研究*)* scientific research

kēzhǎng 科长 n section chief

kē 棵 mw ▶213 (for trees, plants)

kē 颗 mw ▶213 (for small, round things such as pearls, teeth, and hearts; also for things that appear small such as stars, satellites and planets); (for bullets, bombs, etc.)

késou 咳嗽 vb cough

kě 可 1 vb may, can, be permitted; approve 2 adv (for emphasis) indeed, certainly, surely; **kě bié wàng le** 可别忘了 mind you, don't forget it 3 conj but, yet, however

kě'ài 可爱 adj lovely, beloved; lovable, cute

kěkào 可靠 adj reliable, trustworthy, dependable

kělián 可怜 1 adj meagre, inadequate, pitiable; poor, helpless, pitiful 2 vb have pity on, feel sorry for, be merciful to; **wǒ hěn kělián tā** 我很可怜他 I feel very sorry for him

kěnéng 可能 1 adj possible, probable; **zhè shì kěnéng de** 这是可能的 this is possible 2 vb may, might; **tā kěnéng yào qù** 他可能要去 he may want to go 3 n possibility; **méiyǒu kěnéng** 没有可能 there is no possibility

kěnéngxìng 可能性 n possibility

kěpà 可怕 adj frightful, terrible, dreadful

kěshì 可是 conj but, yet, however

kěxī 可惜 n pity; **shízài tài kěxī le** 实在太可惜了 it's really such a shame

kěxiào 可笑 adj laughable, funny

kěyǐ 可以 1 vb may, can, may be permitted to; **nǐ yě kěyǐ cānjiā** 你也可以参加 you too can take part in it 2 adj fine, OK, not bad; **wǒmen de shēnghuó hái kěyǐ** 我们的生活还可以 our life is pretty good

kě 渴 adj thirsty

kè 克 n (unit of weight) gram

kèfú 克服 vb (as a difficulty, hardship, inconvenience) overcome, surmount, conquer

kè 刻 **1** *n* quarter of an hour **2** *vb* carve, engrave, inscribe

kèkǔ 刻苦 *adj* hard-working, willing to endure hardships; frugal, austere

kèguān 客观 *adj* objective

kèqi 客气 *adj* polite, courteous, standing on ceremony; unassuming, modest, humble

kèren 客人 *n* guest, visitor

kètīng 客厅 *n* living room

kè 课 *n* (*in school or university*) class; [shàng | xià] kè [上 | 下] 课 [start | finish] class; course, subject; lesson; Dìyī kè 第一课 Lesson One

kèběn 课本 *n* textbook

kèchéng 课程 *n* course of study, curriculum; **kèchéng biǎo** 课程表 school time-table, lecture list

kètáng 课堂 *n* classroom

kètí 课题 *n* question for study, research project

kèwén 课文 *n* (*of a lesson or in a book*) text

kěn 肯 *vb* be willing to, consent to

kěndìng 肯定 **1** *vb* affirm, confirm **2** *adj* affirmative, positive, certain

kōng 空 **1** *adj* empty, vacant **2** *adv* in vain **3** *n* air, sky, space

kōngjiān 空间 *n* empty space; (*beyond the earth's orbit*) space

kōngjūn 空军 *n* airforce

kōngtiáo 空调 *n* (*abbreviation of* kōngqì tiáojié qì 空气调节器) air conditioner

kōngqì 空气 *n* air, atmosphere; (*in a figurative sense: social, political, aesthetic, etc.*) atmosphere; jīntiān xuéxiào de kōngqì hěn jǐnzhāng 今天学校的空气很紧张 there is a tense atmosphere at school today

kōngqián 空前 **1** *adj* unprecedented **2** *adv* in an unprecedented fashion

kōngzhōng 空中 *n* in the sky, in the air; **kōngzhōng xiǎojiě** 空中小姐 air hostess

kǒng 孔 1 *n* opening, hole, empty space 2 *adj* Confucian

Kǒngzǐ 孔子 *n* Confucius

kǒngpà 恐怕 1 *adv* probably, perhaps 2 *vb* be afraid that, think that; **kǒngpà tā bù lái le** 恐怕他不来了 I'm afraid he's not coming

kòngr 空儿 *n* empty space, vacant space; leisure, spare time; **wǒ méiyǒu kòngr** 我没有空儿 I don't have time

kòngzhì 控制 1 *vb* control, dominate 2 *n* control, hold

kǒu 口 1 *n* mouth; (*of a river, building, etc.*) opening, entrance; cut, wound, tear 2 *mw* ▶ **213** (for the number of people in a family or village); (for spoken languages, used with the verb "speak" and with the number one, yì 一)

kǒudài 口袋 *n* pocket, bag, sack

kǒuhào 口号 *n* slogan

kǒuqì 口气 *n* tone, note, implication

kǒutóu 口头 *adj* oral

kǒuyīn 口音 *n* accent

kǒuyǔ 口语 *n* spoken language

kòu 扣 1 *vb* button, fasten; deduct, reduce; (for a criminal) detain, arrest 2 *n* button; **kòuzi** 扣子 button; **kòushang** 扣上 button up

kū 哭 *vb* cry, weep

kǔ 苦 1 *adj* (in taste) bitter; (in life) bitter, difficult, painful 2 *adv* painstakingly, earnestly, at one's utmost 3 *n* hardship, suffering, misery 4 *vb* cause (someone) suffering

kǔnán 苦难 *n* hardship, misery, suffering

kùzi 裤子 *n* trousers

kuājiǎng 夸奖 *vb* praise, commend

kuāzhāng 夸张 *vb* exaggerate, overstate

kuǎ 垮 *vb* collapse, fall

kuà 跨 *vb* step astride, step across, take a step; (*when talking about a horse or other animal for riding*) mount; transcend, go beyond, go over; **kuà dìqū** 跨地区 transregional

kuài 块 **1** *n* piece, lump, cube; **bīng kuài** 冰块 ice cubes; (*units of money*) dollar, yuan; **liùbái kuài qián** 六百块钱 six hundred yuan **2** *mw* ▶ 213 (*for things that come in chunks or solid pieces*) (*for things that are shaped like sheets*); (*for slices, sections, divisions, etc.*)

kuài 快 **1** *adj* fast, quick; (*of a knife*) keen, sharp; **zhèbǎ jiǎnzi hěn kuài** 这把剪子很快 this pair of scissors is very sharp; (*when used with a negative*) pleased, happy, joyful; **xīn zhōng bú kuài** 心中不快 heavy-hearted **2** *adv* almost, soon, about to; **tā kuài yào bìyè le** 她快要毕业了 she will graduate soon; quickly; **kuài huílai** 快回来 come back quickly **3** *vb* hurry; **kuài diǎnr!** 快点儿! hurry up! quickly!

kuàihuo 快活 *adj* happy, cheerful

kuàilè 快乐 **1** *adj* happy, joyful **2** *n* happiness, joy

kuàizi 筷子 *n* chopsticks

kuān 宽 *adj* wide, broad; generous, broad-minded, liberal

kuǎn 款 *n* fund, funds, money

kuáng 狂 *adj* mad, deranged, crazy

kuàngqiě 况且 *adv* moreover, besides

kuàng 矿 *n* ore/mineral deposit; mine, excavation

kǔn 捆 **1** *vb* tie into a bundle, bind up, tie up; **kǔnqǐlai** 捆起来 tie up **2** *n* bundle

kùn 困 **1** *adj* sleepy; in difficulty, stranded, hard-pressed **2** *vb* surround

kùnnan 困难 **1** *n* difficulty, quandary, hardship **2** *adj* difficult, hard to cope with

kuòdà 扩大 **1** *vb* enlarge, expand, spread out **2** *n* expansion

LI

lā 拉 *vb* pull, drag; haul, transport by vehicle; (*certain musical instruments*) play; **lā** [**xiǎotíqín** | **shǒufēngqín**] 拉 [小提琴 | 手风琴] play the [violin | accordion]; extend, extenuate, draw out; implicate, drag in; **lā guānxi** 拉关系 use one's influence/connections; **lā dùzi** 拉肚子 have diarrhoea; **lākāi** 拉开 pull open; space out, widen; **lāshang** 拉上 (*curtains, etc.*) draw, close

lājī 垃圾 *n* rubbish, garbage, trash

la 啦 *pt (a fusion of* le 了 *and a* 啊, *which incorporates the function of* le 了 *while denoting exclamation or interrogation*) **tā yǐjīng dāying la!** 他已经答应啦! he has already agreed!

lǎbā 喇叭 *n* horn or other brass wind instrument; loudspeaker

là 辣 *adj* hot, spicy, peppery

làjiāo 辣椒 *n* hot pepper, chili pepper

làzhú 蜡烛 *n* candle

lái 来 **1** *vb* come, arrive; do; **ràng wǒ lái** 让我来 let me do it; bring; **zài lái yìwǎn fàn** 再来一碗饭 bring another bowl of rice; (*when following a verb to indicate direction of action*) **qǐng nǐ guòlái** 请你过来 please come over here; (*when following* dé 得 *or* bù 不 *to indicate possibility*) **chī** [**de** | **bù**] **lái** 吃 [得 | 不] 来 [it is | it is not] to (someone's) taste ! *The word* lái 来 *regularly follows certain verbs as a complement, such as* qǐ 起 *in* qǐlái 起来, chū 出 *in* chūlái 出来, guò 过 *in* guòlái 过来, *and so forth. For these expressions, see the verbs that precede* lái 来. *In other instances it follows a verb as a directional complement, as in* shànglai 上来 come up, *and* xiàlai 下来 come down. **2** *prep* (*with time expressions*) since, for, during; **sān nián (yǐ)lái** 三年 (以)来 during the past three years **3** *adv* (*following a numeral that acts as an adjective*) about, approximately, over; **shí lái ge** 十来个 over ten; (*when preceding the main verb, to indicate purpose*) to, in order to

láibují 来不及 *vb* be unable to do in time, lack sufficient time for

láidejí 来得及 *vb* be able to do in time, have enough time for

láihuí 来回 **1** *adv* back and forth, to and fro **2** *n* return journey, round trip

láiwǎng 来往 **1** *vb* come and go **2** *n* contacts, dealings

láixìn 来信 *n* your letter, a letter from...

lái zì 来自 *vb* come from, originate from

lán 拦 *vb* hinder, obstruct, block

lán 蓝 *adj* blue

lánqiú 篮球 *n* basketball

lǎn 懒 *adj* lazy, idle, indolent; sluggish, drowsy

làn 烂 *adj* (*of fruit, a wound, etc.*) rotten, over-ripe, festering; (*of clothes, cloth*) ragged, worn-out; (*of meat, stew, etc.*) well-done, thoroughly cooked

láng 狼 *n* wolf

lǎngdú 朗读 *vb* read aloud

làng 浪 *n* wave

làngfèi 浪费 **1** *vb* waste, squander **2** *adj* extravagant, wasteful **3** *n* extravagance, waste

làngmàn 浪漫 *adj* romantic

lāo 捞 *vb* trawl, dredge, drag for (fish, etc.)

láodòng 劳动 *vb* work, labour, toil

láojià 劳驾 *vb* (*polite expression*) excuse me...? may I trouble you...? would you mind...?

lǎo 老 **1** *adj* old, elderly, aged; long-term, of long standing; **lǎo péngyou** 老朋友 an old friend; old-fashioned, outdated; (*of meat*) tough; (*of vegetation*) overgrown; (*prefix before ordinal numbers to differentiate between children of a family*) **lǎo** [dà | èr...] 老 [大 | 二..] [eldest | second eldest...]; (*courteous or affectionate prefix to a name, title, or relationship*) **lǎo** [Zhāng | xiānsheng | dàgē]

老 [张 | 先生 | 大哥] [my pal Zhang | Sir | dear elder brother] **2** *adv* always, ever, keep on; **tā lǎo zhème shuō** 他老这么说 he always says this; **lǎoshì** 老是 always, ever, keep on; (*with a negative*) hardly ever, rarely, seldom; **tā lǎoshì bú niànshū** 他老是不念书 he hardly ever studies

lǎobǎixìng 老百姓 *n* common people, ordinary people

lǎobǎn 老板 *n* boss, employer, shopkeeper

lǎodàmā 老大妈, **dàmā** 大妈 *n* (*respectful address for an older woman*) Madam, granny, aunty

lǎodàniáng 老大娘 *n* (*respectful address for an older woman*) Madam, granny, aunty

lǎodàye 老大爷, **dàye** 大爷 *n* (*respectful address for an older man*) Sir, grandpa

lǎohǔ 老虎 *n* tiger

lǎojiā 老家 *n* hometown, old home

lǎoshī 老师 *n* teacher

lǎoshi 老实 **1** *adj* honest, frank, trustworthy; well-behaved; simple-minded, naive **2** *adv* honestly, truthfully

lǎoshǔ 老鼠 *n* mouse, rat

lǎotàitai 老太太 *n* (*term of respect for an elderly woman*) Madam, old lady

lǎotóur 老头儿 *n* (*rude word for an old man*) old man

lè 乐 ! *Can also be pronounced* yuè *with a different meaning*; *adj* happy, joyful

lèguān 乐观 **1** *adj* optimistic, positive **2** *n* optimism

lèqù 乐趣 *n* pleasure, joy

le 了 *pt* ▶ *See also* liǎo 了. (*indicating a past event*) **tā shàngge xīngqī qù le** 他上个星期去了 he went last week; (*indicating a completed action*) **tā zǒu le** 他走了 he has gone; (*indicating a change of situation or state*) **tā bìng le** 他病了 he's been taken ill; '**huǒchē láile méiyǒu?**'—'**méi lái**' '火车来了没有?'—'没来' 'has the train come?'—'no, it hasn't' ! *Note that* le 了 *is usually* *negated with méi* 没, *rather than with* bù 不; (*used with* bù 不 *to mean* no longer, not any more) **wǒ bù xiě le** 我不写了 I'm not writing (it) any more; (*used with* búyào 不要 *or* bié 别 *to stop someone from doing something*) **búyào jiǎng le** 不要讲了 stop talking about it, don't talk about it any more

léi 雷 *n* thunder; **léiyǔ** 雷雨 thunderstorm

lèi 泪 *n* tear, tears, teardrop

lèi 类 **1** *n* category, sort, type **2** *mw* ▶ **213** kind of, sort of

lèisì 类似 **1** *vb* resemble, be similar to, be like **2** *adj* similar, like

lèi 累 *adj* tired, fatigued, weary

lěng 冷 *adj* cold

lěngjìng 冷静 *adj* calm, sober, clear-headed

lěngyǐn 冷饮 *n* cold drink

límǐ 厘米 *n* centimetre

lí 离 **1** *vb* leave, part, separate from **2** *prep* from, off, away from; **xuéxiào lí zhèr sān yīnglǐ lù** 学校离这儿三英里路 the school is three miles from here

líhūn 离婚 *vb* divorce, be divorced

líkāi 离开 *vb* depart, leave, separate

lí 梨 *n* pear

lǐ 礼 *n* ceremony, ritual; propriety, courtesy, manners; gift, present

lǐbài 礼拜 *n* week; (*used for the days of the week*) **lǐbài** [yī | èr | sān…] 礼拜 [一 | 二 | 三…] [Monday | Tuesday | Wednesday…]

lǐbàitiān 礼拜天, **lǐbàirì** 礼拜日 *n* Sunday

lǐmào 礼貌 **1** *n* courtesy, politeness, manners **2** *adj* polite, courteous

lǐtáng 礼堂 *n* assembly hall, auditorium

lǐwù 礼物 *n* present, gift

lǐ 里 **1** *n* (unit of length, 1/2 kilometre) Chinese mile, lǐ **2** *prep* in, inside, among; **wū lǐ** 屋里 in the room

lǐbian 里边, **lǐmiàn** 里面 **1** *prep* inside, in, within; **wūzi lǐbian yǒu sānge rén** 屋子里边有三个人 there are three people in the room **2** *n* inside, within; **tā zài lǐbian** 他在里边 he is inside

lǐtou 里头 (*informal, colloquial*) ▶ **lǐbian** 里边

lǐfà 理发 *vb* have a haircut, have one's hair cut/styled

lǐjiě 理解 **1** *vb* understand, comprehend **2** *n* understanding, comprehension

lǐkē 理科 *n* (*a branch of learning*) science, natural sciences

lǐlùn 理论 *n* theory, theoretical idea

lǐxiǎng 理想 *n* ideal, dream

lǐyóu 理由 *n* reason, argument

lìshǐ 历史 *n* history, record of the past

lì 力 *n* strength, power, force

lìliang 力量 *n* strength, force, power

lìqi 力气 *n* physical strength, effort, energy

lì 立 *vb* stand; establish, set up, erect

lìchǎng 立场 *n* standpoint, position, point of view

lìfāng 立方 *n* cube; cubic metre; **sān lìfāng shāzi** 三立方沙子 three cubic metres of sand

lìjí 立即 *adv* immediately, right away

lìkè 立刻 *adv* immediately, right away

lìhai 利害, 厉害 *adj* (*when talking about the weather, etc.*) severe, extreme; **zhèr de tiānqì rè de lìhai** 这儿的天气热得利害 the weather here is extremely hot; (*as a teacher or disciplinarian*) formidable, strict

lìxī 利息 *n* (*when talking about finance*) interest

lìyì 利益 *n* interest, benefit

lìyòng 利用 *vb* utilize, make use of, take advantage of

lì 例 *n* example, case, instance; **lìrú** 例如 for example, for instance, such as

lìwài 例外 *n* exception

lìzi 例子 *n* example, instance

lì 粒 *mw* ▶ **213** (for small, round things, such as peas, peanuts, bullets, or grains)

liǎ 俩 *num* (colloquial) two; some, several

lián 连 **1** *vb* connect, link, join **2** *adv* in succession, one after the other; even, including; **lián...dōu/yě...** 连...都/也... even...; **lián tā dōu bù zhīdào** 连他都不知道 even he doesn't know

liánjiē 连接 *vb* join, link

liánmáng 连忙 *adv* promptly, at once

liánxù 连续 *adv* continuously, successively, one after the other; **liánxùjù** 连续剧 (on TV or radio) a serial, a series

liánhé 联合 *vb* unite, join together, ally

Liánhéguó 联合国 *n* the United Nations

liánhuān 联欢 **1** *vb* have a get-together/party **2** *n* social get-together

liánxì 联系 **1** *vb* connect, make connections with, link **2** *n* connection, link

liǎn 脸 *n* face; self-respect, honour; **diū liǎn** 丢脸 lose face

liàn 练 *vb* train, practise, drill

liànxí 练习 **1** *vb* practise, exercise **2** *n* practise, drill; **liànxíbù/běn** 练习簿/本 exercise book

liàn'ài 恋爱 *n* love, love affair

liánghǎo 良好 *adj* good, well

liáng 凉 ▶ See also **liàng**. **1** *adj* cool, cold; discouraged, disappointed **2** *n* cold, flu; **zháo liáng** 着凉 catch cold

liángkuai 凉快 *adj* cool, pleasantly cool

liáng 量 *vb* ▶ *See also* **liàng** 量. *(for length, weight, distance, etc.)* measure

liángshi 粮食 *n* food, provisions, grain

liǎng 两 **1** *num* ! *Note that* liǎng 两 *is like* èr 二 *but tends to be used in combination with measure words and nouns to specify two of something;* two; **liǎngzhāng zhǐ** 两张纸 two sheets of paper **2** *det* ! *Note that* liǎng 两 *in this sense is usually unstressed;* a few, some, a couple of; **shuō liǎng jù** 说两句 speak a few words **3** *pron* both **4** *n* *(traditional unit of weight equivalent to 1.33 English ounces or 0.05 kilo)*; **yì liǎng jiǔ** 一两酒 an ounce of liquor

liàng 亮 **1** *adj* bright, light, shiny **2** *vb* get light, be light, be switched on

liàng 凉 *vb* ▶ *See also* **liáng** 凉. cool, allow to cool

liàng 晾 *vb* dry in the air/sun

liàng 辆 *mw* ▶ **213** *(for vehicles)*.

liàng 量 *n* ▶ *See also* **liáng** 量. amount, quantity, capacity

liáo 聊 *vb* chat idly; **wǒ xiǎng gēn nǐ liáoliáo** 我想跟你聊聊 I'd like to have a chat with you

liáotiānr 聊天儿 *vb* chat to pass the time of day

liǎo 了 *vb* ▶ *See also* **le** 了. ! *Can also be pronounced* liào *with a different meaning;* finish, end; **wǒ shénme shíhou néng liǎole zhèjiàn shì?** 我什么时候能了了这件事? when will I be able to finish this task?; *(after* dé 得 *or* bù 不 *to indicate the possibility or impossibility of accomplishing or finishing something)*; **zhège bēibāo zhuāng [de | bu] liǎo zhèxiē dōngxi** 这个背包装[得 | 不] 了这些东西 this backpack [can | cannot] hold these things

liǎobuqǐ 了不起 *adj* extraordinary, astounding, amazing

liǎojiě 了解 **1** *vb* understand, comprehend, know; find out, inquire; **liǎojiě yíxià zhèr de shēnghuó** 了解一下这儿的生活 find out about the life here **2** *n* understanding, knowledge

liè 列 **1** vb list, arrange in order, enumerate **2** mw ▶**213** (for trains)

lièchē 列车 n train; **lièchēyuán** 列车员 train attendant

línjū 邻居 n neighbour

lín 临 **1** vb face, overlook; (when talking about problems, decisions) face, confront **2** adv on the point of, upon coming to...; **lín zǒu** 临走 about to depart

línshí 临时 **1** adj temporary, provisional, last-minute **2** adv at the time, at the last moment, when the time comes; **tā línshí juédìng bú qù Běijīng le** 他临时决定不去北京了 he made a last-minute decision not to go to Beijing

línyù 淋浴 n shower

línghún 灵魂 n spirit, soul, mind

línghuó 灵活 adj (referring to mental capacities, etc.) quick-witted, resourceful, agile; (when describing actions, movements, etc.) nimble, quick; (when talking about the quality of material objects) flexible, elastic

líng 铃 n bell, small bell

líng 零 num zero, nought

língqián 零钱 n small change, pocket money

líng 龄 n age, years; length of time, duration

lǐng 领 **1** vb lead, command, usher; (as a prize, award, pension, etc.) receive, draw, get **2** n neck, collar

lǐngdǎo 领导 **1** vb lead, be a leader **2** n leadership, guidance

lǐngdài 领带 n tie, necktie

lǐnghuì 领会 vb understand, comprehend

lǐngtǔ 领土 n territory

lǐngxiù 领袖 n leader, chief

lìng 另 **1** adj another, other; **lìng yì fāngmiàn...** 另一方面... another aspect..., on the other hand... **2** adv separately, another; **lìng zhǎo yígè fāngfǎ** 另找一个方法 look for another method

lìngwài 另外 **1** *adj* separate, other, another; **lìngwài yíge rén** 另外一个人 another person **2** *adv* separately, besides, in addition; **lìngwài xiě yíge jùzi** 另外写一个句子 write another sentence

liú 留 *vb* keep, preserve, save; stay, remain, linger; allow to stay, ask to stay, detain; **wǒ xiǎng liú nǐ zài wǒ jiā jǐ tiān** 我想留你在我家住几天 I would like you to stay at my house for a few days; leave, leave behind; **bǎ shūbāo liú zài jiā lǐ** 把书包留在家里 leave the satchel at home

liúniàn 留念 **1** *vb* accept/keep as a souvenir **2** *n* souvenir, keepsake

liúxué 留学 *vb* study abroad; **liúxuéshēng** 留学生 student studying abroad

liú 流 **1** *vb* flow **2** *n* flow, stream, current; [hé | diàn | qì] liú [河 | 电 | 气] 流 [river | electric current | air current]; class, grade

liúchuán 流传 *vb* spread, circulate, pass down

liúlì 流利 *adj* fluent, smooth

liúmáng 流氓 *n* hooligan, gangster, rogue

liúxíng 流行 *adj* popular, fashionable, prevalent

liù 六 *num* six

liùyuè 六月 *n* June

lóng 龙 *n* dragon

lóng 聋 *adj* deaf, hearing impaired

lóu 楼 *n* (of more than one story) building, tower; storey, floor; **yì lóu** 一楼 ground floor (British English), first floor (US English) **lóushàng** 楼上 upstairs; **lóuxià** 楼下 downstairs

lóutī 楼梯 *n* stairs, stairway

lòu 漏 *vb* leak, flow/drip out; disclose, divulge; leave out, omit, be missing

lòu 露 ▸ **lù** 露

lǔyā 卤鸭 *n* pot-stewed duck

lùdì 陆地 *n* dry land, land

lùxù 陆续 *adv* in succession, one after another

lù 录 *vb* (on tape) record, copy

lùxiàng 录像 **1** *vb* make a video recording, record on videotape **2** *n* video recording; **lùxiàngdài** 录像带 video tape; **lùxiàngjī** 录像机 video cassette recorder, VCR

lùyīn 录音 **1** *vb* make a sound recording, tape-record, tape **2** *n* sound recording, audio-tape; **lùyīndài** 录音带 magnetic tape, tape; **lùyīnjī** 录音机 tape recorder

lù 鹿 *n* deer

lù 路 *n* road, path, route; journey; distance; way, means; (*referring to the number of a bus route, etc.*) route; **yāo líng sì lù (qìchē)** 104路 (汽车) No. 104 (bus)

lùguò 路过 *vb* pass by/through (a place)

lùkǒu 路口 *n* crossing, intersection

lùshang 路上 *adv* on the way, on the road

lùxiàn 路线 *n* route, line, approach

lù 露 *vb* show, reveal, betray

lùtiān 露天 *n* in the open air, open-air, outdoors

lǚguǎn 旅馆 *n* hotel

lǚkè 旅客 *n* traveller, passenger, hotel guest

lǚtú 旅途 *n* journey, trip, route

lǚxíng 旅行 *vb* travel, journey, trip; **lǚxíngshè** 旅行社 travel service, travel agency

lǚyóu 旅游 *vb* tour, travel

lùshī 律师 *n* solicitor, barrister, lawyer

lǜ 绿 *adj* green

luàn 乱 **1** *adj* in a mess, in confusion, in turmoil **2** *adv* in a disorderly manner, recklessly

luànqībāzāo 乱七八糟 *adj* in a mess, in a muddle, in confusion

lüè 略 1 *vb* omit, leave out 2 *adv* slightly, a little, briefly

lúnchuán 轮船 *n* steamer, steamship, steamboat

lùnwén 论文 *n* thesis, dissertation, treatise

Lúndūn 伦敦 *n* London

luóbo 萝卜 *n* turnip, radish

luò 落 *vb* fall, drop, come down; lower; **bǎ liánzi luòxiàlai** 把帘子落下来 lower the blinds; (*referring to the sun or moon*) set, go down; **tàiyáng luò shān le** 太阳落山了 the sun has set; lag behind, fall behind, decline; leave behind, result in

luòhòu 落后 1 *adj* backward, behind the times 2 *vb* fall behind, be backward

Mm

mā 妈 *n* mother; **māma** 妈妈 mother, mum

máfan 麻烦 1 *vb* trouble, bother; **máfan nǐ le** 麻烦你了 sorry to have troubled you 2 *adj* troublesome, bothersome, annoying 3 *n* trouble, bother

mǎ 马 *n* horse

mǎhu 马虎 *adj* careless, casual, in a sloppy manner

mǎkè 马克 *n* (*unit of German currency*) mark

mǎlù 马路 *n* street, avenue

mǎmǎhūhū 马马虎虎 *adj* so-so; careless, casual

mǎshàng 马上 *adv* immediately, at once; **wǒ mǎshàng jiù lái** 我马上就来 I'll be right there

mǎtou 码头 *n* dock, pier, wharf

mà 骂 *vb* curse, swear, scold

ma 吗 *pt* (*used to turn a declarative sentence into a question*) **shì nǐ ma?** 是你吗? is it you?

ma 嘛 *pt* (used to show that something is obvious) zhè shì wǒde ma! 这是我的嘛! obviously this is mine!; (used to mark a pause) zhège wèntí ma, wǒ lái jiějué 这个问题嘛，我来解决 as for this question, let me solve it

mái 埋 *vb* bury, hide in the ground

mǎi 买 *vb* buy, purchase; mǎi dōngxi 买东西 go shopping, buy things **!** Note that in expressions denoting buying something for someone, the English word for is rendered as gěi 给; nǐ gěi tā mǎi shū ma? 你给她买书吗? do you buy books for her?; mǎi de qǐ 买得起 able to afford

mǎimai 买卖 *n* business, trade; zuò mǎimai 做买卖 do business, engage in a trade

mài 迈 *vb* take a step, stride; màiguò 迈过 step over

mài(zi) 麦(子) *n* wheat

mài 卖 *vb* sell, sell for; nàtái diànshìjī mài duōshǎo qián? 那台电视机卖多少钱? how much is the TV selling for?; mài gěi... 卖给... sell to; nǐ bǎ jìsuànjī mài gěi shéi? 你把计算机卖给谁? to whom are you selling the computer?; **mài** [de | bù] **chū(qu)** 卖 [得 | 不] 出 (去) [able to | unable to] sell (well)

mántou 馒头 *n* steamed bun, steamed bread

mǎn 满 **1** *adj* full, filled; whole, entire; mǎn tiān xīngxing 满天星星 the sky is filled with stars; satisfied, content, satisfactory **2** *adv* quite, rather; mǎn shūfu 满舒服 quite comfortable **3** *vb* reach, reach the limit of; tā hái bù mǎn shíbā suì 他还不满十八岁 he still hasn't reached the age of 18

mǎnyì 满意 **1** *adj* satisfied, pleased **2** *vb* be pleased, be satisfied

mǎnzú 满足 **1** *vb* be content, be satisfied; fulfill, satisfy, meet **2** *adj* satisfied, content

màn 慢 **1** *adj* slow **2** *adv* slowly

máng 忙 *adj* busy, occupied, bustling; nǐ máng shénme? 你忙什么? what are you so busy doing? what are you doing?; diànhuà xiànlù hěn máng 电话线路很忙 the telephone lines are busy; **mángbúguòlái** 忙不过来 (*referring to too much work*) unable to manage; **mángzhe...** 忙着... be busy doing...; **mángzhe xiě zuòwén** 忙着写作文 busy writing an essay

māo 猫 *n* cat; **xiǎomāo** 小猫 kitten

máo 毛 *n* (*a unit of Chinese money*) ten fen, 1/10 of a yuan; **wǔ máo qián** 五毛钱 five mao; hair on the body, fur; feather, down; wool

máobǐ 毛笔 *n* writing brush

máobìng 毛病 *n* trouble, defect; **zhèliàng qìchē chángcháng chū máobìng** 这辆汽车常常出毛病 this car often breaks down; illness; fault, shortcoming, bad habit

máojīn 毛巾 *n* towel

máoyī 毛衣 *n* jumper, sweater

máodùn 矛盾 **1** *n* contradiction, inconsistency **2** *adj* contradictory, inconsistent

mào 冒 *vb* risk, brave, take risks; **mào** [xuě | yǔ | sǐ] 冒 [雪 | 雨 | 死] [brave the rain | brave the snow | risk death]; falsify, feign; **mào** [míng | pái] 冒 [名 | 牌] falsify [a name | a brand]; emit, give off, spew forth; **mào** [qì | yān | hàn] 冒 [气 | 烟 | 汗] [be steaming | emit smoke | sweat]

màoyì 贸易 *n* trade, commerce, economic exchange

màozi 帽子 *n* hat, cap

mào 貌 *n* appearance, looks

méi 没 **1** *adv* (*when negating a completed action, an ongoing action, or a past experience*) not; **wǒ méi qù** 我没去 I didn't go; **tā méi zài kàn diànshì** 他没在看电视 he was not watching TV; **wǒ méi qùguo Běijīng** 我没去过北京 I have never been to Beijing **2** *vb* (*short for* **méi yǒu** 没有) not have, there is not; **méicuò** 没错 it's right, you're right; **méi fǎzi** 没法子 no way, it can't be helped; **méi guānxi** 没关系 it doesn't matter, it's alright, don't worry; **méi shénme** 没什么 it's nothing, it doesn't matter, never mind; **méishìr** 没事儿 it's alright, it's not important, it doesn't matter; be free, have nothing pressing to do; **wǒ méi shì, kěyǐ bāng nǐ** 我没事, 可以帮你 I'm free;

I can help you; **méixiǎngdào...** 没想到... unexpectedly, I never imagined..., I was surprised that...; **méi yìsi** 没意思 dull, uninteresting, boring; **méi yòng** 没用 useless, of no use; **méi (yǒu) le** 没 (有) 了 be gone, be used up, have disappeared

méiyǒu 没有 adv (when negating a completed action) haven't, hasn't, didn't; **tā hái méiyǒu shuìzháo** 他还没有睡着 he hasn't fallen asleep yet; (when negating a past experience) haven't...before, hasn't...before, hasn't...ever...; **nǐ méiyǒu jiànguo tā** 你没有见过他 you haven't met him before; less than; **qián méiyǒu sāntiān jiù huāwán le** 钱没有三天就花完了 the money was spent in less than three days; **méiyǒu...yǐqián** 没有... 以前; **tā méiyǒu jiéhūn yǐqián hěn jìmò** 他没有结婚以前很寂寞 he was very lonely before he got married

méi 煤 n coal

méiqì 煤气 n gas, coal gas

měi 每 det every, each; **měi cì** 每次 every time; **měi...dōu...** 每...都...; **měi yíge háizi dōu xǐhuan chī táng** 每一个孩子都喜欢吃糖 every child likes to eat sweets

měi 美 1 adj pretty, beautiful; high-quality, good, happy 2 n beauty, perfection; (short for Měiguó 美国) America; [Běi | Nán] Měizhōu [北 | 南] 美洲 [North | South] America

Měiguó 美国 n the United States of America, USA; **Měiguórén** 美国人 an American, a person from the USA

měihǎo 美好 adj good, desirable, bright

měilì 美丽 adj beautiful

měishù 美术 n art, fine arts

měishùguǎn 美术馆 n art gallery

měiyuán 美元, **měijīn** 美金 n American dollar

mèimei 妹妹 n younger sister

mēn 闷 ▶ See also **mèn** 闷. adj stuffy, close

mén 门 1 n door, gate, entrance; family, house 2 mw ▶213 (for academic courses, subjects or disciplines)

ménkǒu 门口 n doorway, gateway, entrance

mèn 闷 adj ▸ See also **mēn** 闷. bored, depressed

men 们 pt (used to make plural forms of personal pronouns or nouns referring to animate entities) [wǒmen | nǐmen | tāmen | 我们 | 你们 | 他们] [we | you | they]; [xuéshengmen | háizimen | péngyoumen] [学生们 | 孩子们 | 朋友们] [students | children | friends]

mèng 梦 n dream: zuò mèng 做梦 have a dream

mí 迷 1 vb be confused, be lost; be fascinated by 2 n fan, enthusiast; wǎngqiú mí 网球迷 tennis fan

míxìn 迷信 n superstition

míyǔ 谜语 n riddle, conundrum

mǐ 米 n husked rice, uncooked rice, grain; metre

mǐfàn 米饭 n cooked rice

mìmì 秘密 1 n secret 2 adj secret, confidential 3 adv secretly

mìshū 秘书 n secretary, clerk

mì 密 1 adj dense, thick, close; intimate, close, secret 2 adv secretly, intimately

mìqiè 密切 1 adj (of relationships) close, intimate 2 adv carefully, closely, attentively

mì 蜜 n honey

mìfēng 蜜蜂 n bee, honeybee

miánhuā 棉花 n cotton

miányī 棉衣 n cotton-padded jacket or other items of clothing

miǎnbùliǎo 免不了 adj unavoidable

miǎndé 免得 conj so that...not..., so as not to, so as to avoid; miǎndé shēngbìng 免得生病 so as to avoid getting sick

miǎnqiǎng 勉强 1 adv reluctantly, grudgingly; tā miǎnqiǎng dāyingle wǒ 他勉强答应了我 he promised me reluctantly; barely enough, narrowly; tā miǎnqiǎng tōngguòle kǎoshì 他勉

强通过了考试 he narrowly passed the examination **2** *adj* inadequate, unconvincing, far-fetched; **tāde jiěshì hěn miǎnqiǎng** 他的解释很勉强 his explanation is quite unconvincing **3** *vb* force (someone to do something); **bié miǎnqiǎng tā** 别勉强她 don't force her; do with difficulty, manage with a great effort; **bìngrén miǎnqiǎng chīle diǎnr fàn** 病人勉强吃了点儿饭 the patient has managed to eat some food

miàn 面 **1** *n* face; surface, top side, outside; side, dimension, aspect; wheat flour, flour, powder **2** *vb* face **3** *adv* personally, directly **4** *mw* ▶ **213** *(for flat, smooth objects, such as mirrors, flags, etc.)*

miànbāo 面包 *n* bread

miànduì 面对 *vb* face, confront

miànfěn 面粉 *n* flour, wheat flour

miànjī 面积 *n* area, surface area

miànmào 面貌 *n* *(of people)* facial features, looks, appearance; *(of things)* appearance, look

miànqián 面前 *adv* in front of (someone), to one's face; **bié zài lǎoshī miànqián shuō zhèzhǒng huà** 别在老师面前说这种话 don't say such things in front of the teacher

miàntiáor 面条儿 *n* noodles

miáoshù 描述 *vb* describe

miáoxiě 描写 *vb* describe, depict, delineate

miǎo 秒 *n* second, 1/60 of a minute; **yì miǎozhōng** 一秒钟 one second

miào 妙 *adj* miraculous, wonderful, excellent; ingenious, clever, skilled

miào 庙 *n* temple

miè 灭 *vb* *(as a light, fire, etc.)* extinguish, put out, go out; *(by killing)* exterminate, obliterate, wipe out

míngē 民歌 *n* folk song

mínjiān 民间 *adj* of the common people, popular, folk

mínzhǔ 民主 **1** *n* democracy **2** *adj* democratic

mínzú 民族 *n* race, tribe, nation; **shǎoshù mínzú** 少数民族 minority nationality, ethnic group

míng 名 **1** *n* name; fame, reputation; pretext, surface meaning; **yǐ...wéi míng** 以...为名 in the name of..., under the pretext of... **2** *adj* famous, well-known **3** *mw* ▶ **213** (for persons with professional or prominent social identities)

míngshèng 名胜 *n* famous site, place of interest, scenic spot

míngzi 名字 *n* name, given name, first name

míngbai 明白 **1** *adj* clear, obvious, plain; frank, explicit, unequivocal; sensible, reasonable **2** *vb* understand, realize, know

míngliàng 明亮 *adj* bright, well-lit, shining; (of understanding) clear

míngnián 明年 *n* next year

míngquè 明确 **1** *adj* clear, definite **2** *vb* clarify, specify

míngtiān 明天 *n* tomorrow

míngxiǎn 明显 *adj* obvious, clear, evident

míngxīng 明星 *n* famous person, star

mìng 命 *n* life; lot, fate, destiny; order, command

mìnglìng 命令 **1** *n* command, order **2** *vb* command, order

mìngyùn 命运 *n* destiny, fate

mō 摸 *vb* touch gently, feel, stroke; grope for, feel for; search for, try to find out, figure out

mófàn 模范 *n* ! *The word mó is sometimes pronounced mú with a different meaning*; model, fine example

mófǎng 模仿 **1** *vb* copy, imitate, model after **2** *n* copy, imitation, model

móxíng 模型 *n* model, pattern

mótuōchē 摩托车 *n* motorbike, motorcycle, motor bicycle

mó 磨 *vb* rub, wear down, wear away; sharpen, polish, grind; **mó dāo** 磨刀 sharpen a knife; waste time, while away time; **mó shíjiān** 磨时间 kill time; torment, bother, put through the grind

mǒ 抹 *vb* apply, smear, put on; wipe, erase

mòshēng 陌生 *adj* strange, unfamiliar; **mòshēng rén** 陌生人 stranger

mò 墨 **1** *n* ink, ink stick **2** *adj* black, dark

mòshuǐ 墨水 *n* ink

mǒu 某 *det* certain, some; **mǒurén** 某人 a certain person, someone; **mǒumǒu...** 某某... such-and-such..., so-and-so

múyàng 模样 *n*！*The word mú is sometimes pronounced mó with a different meaning:* appearance, shape, look

mǔ 母 **1** *n* mother; aunt, elder female relative; [zǔmǔ | gūmǔ | jiùmǔ] [祖母 | 姑母 | 舅母] [grandmother | aunt (father's sister) | aunt (mother's brother's wife)] **2** *adj* (of a species) female; [mǔláng | mǔxiàng | mǔmāo] [母狼 | 母象 | 母猫] female [wolf | elephant | cat]

mǔqīn 母亲 *n* mother

mǔ 亩 *n* (unit for measuring land area) 0.0667 hectares, 1/6 of an acre

mù 木 **1** *n* tree, timber; wood **2** *adj* wooden, made out of wood; (of body or mind) numb, insensitive, dull

mùtou 木头 *n* wood, log, timber

mùbiāo 目标 *n* goal, aim, target

mùdì 目的 *n* aim, objective, purpose

mùqián 目前 *adv* currently, at present, at this moment

mùmín 牧民 *n* herdsman

mù 墓 *n* grave, tomb, mausoleum

mù 幕 *n* curtain, screen; (of a dramatic performance) act

Nn

ná 拿 1 vb (in one's hands) take, take hold of, carry; (with qù 去 and lái 来 to mean take and bring respectively) **náqù** 拿去 take (it) away; **nálái** 拿来 bring here; take...as/for; **tā méi ná wǒ dāng kèrén** 他没拿我当客人 he didn't treat me as a guest 2 prep with; **ná kuàizi chī** 拿筷子吃 eat with chopsticks; **ná...láishuō** 拿... 来说 speaking of..., take... as an example; **ná...zuò...** 拿...做... take...as...; **tā ná wǒ zuò xiǎo háizi kàn** 他拿我做小孩子看 he treats me like a child

nǎ 哪 1 det which? what?; **nǐ yào nǎkuài biǎo?** 你要哪块表? which watch would you like?; (used with dōu 都) any, whatever, whichever; **nǐ yào nǎkuài biǎo dōu kěyǐ** 你要哪块表都可以 you can have any watch you want 2 adv (used in a rhetorical question) how is it possible that...?; **wǒ nǎ zhīdào tāde míngzi?** 我哪知道他的名字? how could I know his name?

nǎge 哪个 det which? which one?; **nǎge rén?** 哪个人? which person?

nǎli 哪里, **nǎr** 哪儿 1 adv (in a question) where?; **nǐde chē zài nǎli?** 你的车在哪里? where is your car?; (with dōu 都 in a statement) anywhere, wherever, everywhere; **fàng zài nǎli dōu kěyǐ** 放在哪里都可以 you can put it anywhere 2 adv (used to form a rhetorical question) how can it be that...?; **wǒ nǎli mǎi de qǐ qìchē?** 我哪里买得起汽车? how could I possibly afford to buy a car?; **nǎli** you're welcome, don't mention it; **'xièxie nǐ de bāngzhù.'—'nǎli, nǎli'** '谢谢你的帮助。'—'哪里，哪里' 'thanks for your help.'—'don't mention it'.

nǎpà 哪怕 conj even, even if, no matter how; **nǎpà...yě...** 哪怕... 也... even if, even though; **nǎpà nǐ bù tóngyì, wǒ yě yào qù** 哪怕你不同意，我也要去 I'll still go even if you don't agree

nǎxiē 哪些 1 pron (plural form) which? which ones? what?; **nǎxiē shì xīn de?** 哪些是新的? which ones are new? 2 det which; **nǎxiē shū shì nǐde? 哪些书是你的?** which books are yours?

nà 那 1 *pron* that; **nà shì tāde shū 那是他的书** that is his book **2** *det* (before a number plus a measure word) that, those; **nà sānzhāng zhuōzi dōu hěn guì 那三张桌子都很贵** those three tables are all very expensive **3** *conj* then, in that case; **nà wǒ yě yào mǎi yíge 那我也要买一个** in that case I want to buy one too

nà biān 那边 *adv* that side, over there

nàge 那个 *det* that; **nàge wèntí 那个问题** that problem

nàli 那里, nàr 那儿 *adv* there, that place, over there

nàme 那么 *adv* that way, like that, so; **nǐ wèishénme nàme zuò? 你为什么那么做?** why do you do it like that?; in that case, then; **nàme zánmen yíkuàir qù ba 那么咱们一块儿去吧** then let's go together

nàxiē 那些 1 *pron* (*plural form*) those, that quantity of **2** *det* those

nàyàng 那样 *adv* like that, so, in that way; **nǐ bié nàyàng zuò 你别那样做** don't do it that way

na 哪 *pt* (when expressing appreciation or confirmation, or when giving advice or encouragement) **kuài lái na! 快来哪!** hurry up!

nǎi 奶 *n* milk

nǎinai 奶奶 *n* paternal grandmother

nàifán 耐烦 *adj* patient

nàixīn 耐心 1 *adj* patient **2** *adv* patiently **3** *n* patience

nàiyòng 耐用 *adj* enduring, durable, capable of withstanding heavy use

nán 男 *adj* (refers to humans only) man, male

nánháizi 男孩子 *n* boy

nánpéngyou 男朋友 *n* boyfriend

nánrén 男人 *n* man, husband

nán 南 **1** n south **2** adj south, southern

nánbian 南边 n the south, south side

nánbù 南部 n southern part

nánfāng 南方 n (as a direction) south; southern part of the country

nánjí 南极 n South Pole, Antarctic

nán miàn 南面 ▶ **nán bian** 南边

nán 难 adj difficult, hard; (when it precedes a verb) bad, unpleasant; **nán** [**chī** | **tīng**] 难 [吃 | 听] [bad tasting | unpleasant to the ear]

nándào 难道 adv (in rhetorical questions that end with the particle ma 吗) could it be that...? you don't mean to say that...? is it really true that...?; **nándào nǐ lián yí kuài qián yě méi yǒu ma?** 难道你连一块钱也没有吗? do you mean to say you don't even have one yuan? **!** Note that the speaker doubts or questions the statement that occurs within this pattern.

nánguài 难怪 conj no wonder that

nánguò 难过 **1** adj sad, aggrieved **2** vb have a hard time

nánkàn 难看 adj ugly, unpleasant to look at, disgraceful looking; unhealthy, pale; embarrassing, shameful

nánmiǎn 难免 **1** adj difficult to avoid **2** adv inevitably

nánshòu 难受 adj unbearable, hard to stand; uncomfortable, unwell; unhappy, distressed, miserable

nǎodai 脑袋 n (part of the body) head

nǎojīn 脑筋 n brain, mind

nǎozi 脑子 n (part of the body) brain; (mental capacity) brains, mind, intelligence

nào 闹 **1** vb make a disturbance, make a noise, cause trouble; suffer bad effects from, be troubled by, undergo; **nào jīhuāng** 闹饥荒 suffer from famine; (when talking about something disruptive or troublesome) cause to happen, do, undertake; **nǐ bǎ zhè shì nào fùzá le** 你把这事闹复杂了 you made this matter complicated; (when speaking of emotions like anger or resentment) give vent to; **nào qíngxù** 闹情绪 be moody **2** adj noisy, loud

nàozhōng 闹钟 n alarm clock

ne 呢 pt (for questions on a subject under consideration) 'nǐ hǎo ma?'—'hǎo, nǐ ne?' '你好吗?'—'好, 你呢?' 'how are you?'—'fine, and you?'; (to indicate continued action) tā zài nàr zuòzhe ne 他在那儿坐着呢 he is sitting there; (to indicate emphasis or suspense) hái yǒu shí fēnzhōng ne 还有十分钟呢 there are still ten minutes left; (to introduce a topic) as for, with regard to; zhège wèntí ne, wǒmen kěyǐ yǐhòu zài tǎolùn 这个问题呢, 我们可以以后再讨论 as for this problem, we can talk about it later; where?; wǒde gāngbǐ ne? 我的钢笔呢? where is my pen?

nèi 内 **1** prep (when referring to time, place, scope or limits) within, in, inside; yì liǎng tiān nèi 一两天内 within one or two days **2** adj inner, internal

nèibù 内部 adj internal, interior, on the inside ! This term sometimes refers to something that is for officials only, meaning that it is restricted or exclusive; **nèibù wénjiàn** 内部文件 restricted document

nèikē 内科 n (department of) internal medicine

nèiróng 内容 n content, contents, the inner part

néng 能 **1** vb can, be able to; tā néng shuō wǔzhǒng wàiyǔ 他能说五种外语 he can speak five foreign languages **2** n ability, skill; (in science) energy

nénggàn 能干 adj capable, able, competent

nénggòu 能够 vb can, be able to, be capable of

nénglì 能力 n capability, potentiality, ability

néngyuán 能源 n (in the power industry) energy source, energy

ní 泥 n mud, clay, mire; puréed/mashed vegetable/fruit

nǐ 你 pron (singular) you

nǐmen 你们 pron (plural) you

nián 年 *n* year; New Year; person's age; every year, annual, yearly

niándài 年代 *n* era, period, age; decade; **qīshí niándài** 七十年代 the seventies

niánjí 年级 *n* (in school or university) year, form, grade

niánjì 年纪, **niánlíng** 年龄 *n* (when speaking of a person) age

niánqīng 年轻, **niánqīng** 年青 *adj* young

nián 粘 ▸**zhān** 粘

niàn 念 *vb* (a course or subject) study; read, read aloud

niànshū 念书 *vb* study, read books

niáng 娘 *n* mother, ma, mum

niǎo 鸟 *n* bird

nín 您 *pron* (polite form of nǐ 你) you

nìngkě 宁可, **nìngkěn** 宁肯, **nìngyuàn** 宁愿 *adv* would rather, better

niú 牛 *n* ox, cow, cattle

niúnǎi 牛奶 *n* cow's milk

niúròu 牛肉 *n* beef

niǔ 扭 *vb* turn, rotate, turn round; twist, wrench, sprain; grapple, wrestle; swing back and forth, sway from side to side

Niǔyuē 纽约 *n* New York

nóng 农 *n* farming, agriculture

nóngchǎng 农场 *n* farm

nóngcūn 农村 *n* village, rural area, countryside

nónglì 农历 *n* traditional Chinese lunar calendar

nóngmín 农民 *n* farmer, farming population, peasant

nóngyè 农业 *n* agriculture, farming

nóng 浓 *adj* (when talking about tea, smoke, colour, atmosphere, fog, etc.) dense, concentrated, thick; **nóng chá**

浓茶 strong tea; (*when speaking of degree or extent*) great, rich, strong

nòng 弄 *vb* do, make, cause; **nòng** [huài | cuò | qīngchu] 弄 [坏 | 错 | 清楚] [ruin | make a mistake | clear up]; handle, manage; obtain, get hold of; **zhèzhǒng yào hěn nán nòngdào** 这种药很难弄到 this type of medicine is very difficult to obtain; play with, fiddle with, do for amusement

nǔlì 努力 **1** *vb* work hard, make a strenuous effort, exert oneself **2** *adj* hardworking, studious, diligent **3** *adv* studiously, diligently

nù 怒 **1** *adj* angry, furious, indignant **2** *n* anger, passion, rage

nǔ 女 *adj* female, woman

nǔ'ér 女儿 *n* daughter, girl

nǔháizi 女孩子 *n* girl

nǔpéngyou 女朋友 *n* girlfriend

nǔrén 女人 *n* (*less polite than* nǔshì 女士) woman

nǔshì 女士 *n* (*polite form of address or reference*) lady, miss

nuǎn 暖 **1** *adj* warm, genial **2** *vb* warm up, make warm

nuǎnhuo 暖和 **1** *adj* warm, comfortably warm **2** *vb* warm up, make warm

nuǎnqì 暖气 *n* warm air, heating, central heating

....

Oo

ó 哦 *exc* (*connoting a sense of doubt:* really? *or* is that really so?) Oh!

ò 哦 *exc* (*showing understanding or realization*) Oh!

ōuyuán 欧元 *n* euro

Ōuzhōu 欧洲 *n* Europe

ǒurán 偶然 *adv* by chance, accidentally

Pp

pá 爬 *vb* crawl, creep; climb

pà 怕 *vb* fear, be afraid; be worried/concerned about; (*especially when anticipating a negative reaction*) think, suppose; **wǒ pà tā bú huì lái 我怕他不会来** I'm afraid he won't come

pāi 拍 *vb* beat, clap, tap; take, send, shoot; **pāi [zhào | diànyǐng | diànbào] 拍 [照 | 电影 | 电报]** [take a picture | make a film | send a telegram]

pāi(zi) 拍(子) *n* (*used in some games*) raquet, bat

pái 排 **1** *n* row, line **2** *mw* ▶ 213 (*for things grouped or set in rows*) row **3** *vb* set in a row, line up, arrange in order; (*for drama performances, etc.*) rehearse

páiduì 排队 *vb* queue (up), line up, form a line

páiqiú 排球 *n* volleyball

pái 牌 *n* sign, signboard; trademark, brand; cards, dominoes; **dǎ pái 打牌** play cards

pài 派 **1** *vb* send, dispatch, appoint **2** *n* school of thought, sect; clique, group, faction

pán 盘 **1** *n* plate, dish, tray; (*used in some games*) board; **qípán 棋盘** chessboard **2** *mw* ▶ 213 (*for flat things*); (*for board games*)

pánzi 盘子 *n* dish, plate, tray

pànduàn 判断 **1** *vb* decide, judge, assess **2** *n* judgement, assessment, decision

pàn(wàng) 盼(望) *vb* hope for, yearn for

páng 旁 **1** *n* side; **lù páng 路旁** roadside; (*part of a Chinese character*) radical **2** *adj* side, on the side; other, else

pángbiān 旁边 **1** *n* side, nearby position **2** *adv* beside, alongside, nearby

pàng 胖 *adj* fat, obese

pāoqì 抛弃 *vb* abandon, forsake, discard

pǎo 跑 *vb* run, run away, escape; do errands, run around busily; *(after a verb, indicating quick movement away)* **gǎnpǎo le** 赶跑了 drive away

pǎobù 跑步 **1** *vb* run, jog **2** *n* jogging, running

pào 炮 *n* artillery, cannon

péi(tóng) 陪(同) *vb* accompany, be in the accompany of, keep company with

péiyǎng 培养 *vb* train, foster, develop

péiyù 培育 *vb* cultivate, nurture, breed

péi 赔 *vb* lose money, sustain a financial loss; reimburse, compensate, indemnify

pèi 配 *vb* deserve, be worthy of, be qualified; fit; match; blend, mix, compound; *(when talking about animals)* mate

pèihé 配合 *vb* co-ordinate, co-operate

pēn 喷 *vb* gush, spurt, spray

pén 盆 *n* basin, pot, tub

péngyou 朋友 *n* friend

pěng 捧 *vb* carry in the hands; flatter, praise excessively

pèng 碰 *vb* touch, knock against, collide; encounter, meet, run into; try one's luck

pèngjiàn 碰见 *vb* encounter, meet unexpectedly, run into

pèngqiǎo 碰巧 *adv* coincidentally, by chance, happen to

pī 批 **1** *mw* ▶ **213** *(for people or goods)* group, batch, lot **2** *vb* *(written work, etc.)* correct, mark; criticise

pīpàn 批判 **1** *vb* criticise **2** *n* critique, criticism

pīpíng 批评 **1** *vb* criticise **2** *n* comment, criticism

pīzhǔn 批准 *vb* approve, grant (a request), ratify

pī 披 *vb* wear over the shoulders, wrap round

pí 皮 *n* skin, hide, leather; bark, peel, outer covering

píbāo 皮包 *n* leather handbag, briefcase, portfolio

pífū 皮肤 *n* skin

píjuàn 疲倦 *adj* tired, fatigued, weary

píláo 疲劳 *adj* tired, exhausted

píjiǔ 啤酒 *n* beer

píqi 脾气 *n* temperament, disposition; **fā píqi** 发脾气 get angry, lose one's temper

pǐ 匹 *mw* ▶ **213** (for horses, mules)

pìrú 譬如 *adv* for example, for instance, such as

piān 偏 ▶ *See also* **piānpiān** 偏偏. **1** *adv* (*contrary to expectation*) deliberately, insistently, stubbornly; **nǐ piān yào gēn tā láiwǎng** 你偏要跟他来往 you insist on having dealings with him **2** *adj* slanted, inclined, leaning; favouring one side, partial, biased

piānjiàn 偏见 *n* prejudice, bias

piānpiān 偏偏 *adv* deliberately, stubbornly, insistently; (*contrary to expectation*) **yǒu yíjiàn hěn jǐnjí de shìqíng yào tā zuò, piānpiān tā bìng le** 有一件很紧急的事情要他做, 偏偏他病了 there is a very urgent matter for him to deal with, but he has unexpectedly fallen ill

piān 篇 *mw* ▶ **213** (for papers, articles, written versions of a speech)

piányi 便宜 ! *Note that in other uses* pián 便 *is pronounced* biàn. **1** *adj* cheap, inexpensive **2** *n* advantages, gain

piàn 片 *mw* ▶ **213** (for flat, thin things or things in slices); (for expanses or stretches of ocean, desert, mist, fog, etc.); (for atmospheres, moods, etc.)

piànmiàn 片面 *adj* partial, incomplete, one-sided

piàn 骗 *vb* cheat, swindle, deceive

piāo 漂 *vb* (*when talking about something in the water*) float, drift

piāo 飘 *vb* float in the air, be borne by the wind

piāoyáng 飘扬 *vb (when talking about something in the wind)* fly, flutter, wave

piào 票 *n* ticket, ballot

piàoliang 漂亮 *adj* pretty, good-looking, beautiful

pīnmìng 拼命 **1** *vb* give one's all, risk one's life **2** *adv* to the death, with all one's effort

pīnyīn 拼音 *n* Chinese phonetic alphabet; combined sounds in syllables

pínkǔ 贫苦 *adj* poor, poverty-stricken

pínqióng 贫穷 *adj* poor, impoverished

pǐndé 品德 *n* moral character, morality

pǐngé 品格 *n (when talking about a person)* character, morality; *(when talking about literary or artistic works)* quality, style

pǐnzhì 品质 *n* character, quality

pǐnzhǒng 品种 *n* breed, strain, variety

pīngpāngqiú 乒乓球 *n* table tennis, ping-pong

píng 平 **1** *adj* flat, level, equal; ordinary, average, common; peaceful, calm, balanced; fair, objective, impartial **2** *vb* even out, level, make even; pacify, bring peace to, calm down; *(in a game, match, race, etc.)* draw, tie

píng'ān 平安 **1** *adj* peaceful **2** *n* peace

píngcháng 平常 **1** *adj* ordinary, usual, common **2** *adv* ordinarily, usually

píngděng 平等 **1** *adj* equal **2** *n* equality

píngfán 平凡 *adj* ordinary, common

píngfāng 平方 *n (in measuring area)* square; **yì píngfāng gōnglǐ** 一平方公里 a square kilometre

píngjìng 平静 *adj* quiet, peaceful, calm

píngjūn 平均 **1** *adj* average, mean **2** *adv* equally

píngshí 平时 *adv* ordinarily, usually, normally

píngyuán 平原 *n* plain, flatlands

pínglùn 评论 **1** *vb* comment on, discuss **2** *n* commentary, comment, review

píngguǒ 苹果 *n* apple

píng 凭 *vb* go by, take as the basis, base on; rely on, depend on

píng(zi) 瓶(子) *n* bottle, jar, vase

pō 坡 *n* slope, incline, bank

pòqiè 迫切 **1** *adj* urgent, pressing **2** *adv* urgently

pò 破 **1** *vb* break, cut, destroy **2** *adj* broken, damaged, in ruins; torn, worn-out

pòhuài 破坏 *vb* break, destroy, spoil

pū 扑 *vb* rush toward, assault, pounce on; devote all one's energies to; tā zhěngtiān pū zài xuéxí shang 他整天扑在学习上 he devotes all his time to his studies

pū 铺 *vb* spread out, extend, unfold; spread over, cover; pave, lay; pū [chuáng | lù | tiěguǐ] 铺[床 | 路 | 铁轨] [make the bed | pave a road | lay a railway track]

pǔshí 朴实 *adj* simple, plain; down-to-earth, sincere and honest, guileless

pǔsù 朴素 *adj* simple, plain

pǔbiàn 普遍 *adj* general, common, universal

pǔtōng 普通 *adj* general, common

pǔtōnghuà 普通话 *n* common spoken Chinese, Mandarin

Qq

qī 七 *num* seven

qīyuè 七月 *n* July

qī 期 **1** *n* period of time, date, term; due date, deadline, scheduled time; dào qī 到期 be due; (of a project, etc.) stage, phase **2** *mw* ▶ 213 (for issues of periodicals, magazines, journals, etc.) issue

qīdài 期待 *vb* hope, expect, look forward to

qījiān 期间 *n* period of time, course of time

qīwàng 期望 **1** *vb* hope, anticipate, expect **2** *n* hope, anticipation, expectation

qīpiàn 欺骗 *vb* cheat, deceive

qīzi 妻子 *n* wife

qí 齐 **1** *adj* neat, tidy, in good order; complete, ready; similar, alike; together **2** *adv* together, simultaneously, in unison

qícì 其次 *adv* (in order or importance) next, secondly, secondarily

qíshí 其实 *adv* in fact, actually

qítā 其他 **1** *pron* the others **2** *adj* other, else

qíyú 其余 *n* the rest, the remaining

qízhōng 其中 *adv* (a group or situation) in which, among whom

qíguài 奇怪 *adj* strange, peculiar, surprising

qíjī 奇迹 *n* miracle, wonder

qí 骑 *vb* (a horse or cycle) ride; **qí chē** 骑车 ride a bicycle

qí 棋 *n* chess, board game

qízi 旗子 *n* flag, banner

qǐqiú 乞求 *vb* beg, supplicate

qǐtú 企图 **1** *vb* try, seek, attempt **2** *n* try, attempt

qǐyè 企业 *n* enterprise, business

qǐfā 启发 **1** *vb* inspire, stimulate, open the mind **2** *n* inspiration, stimulation

qǐ 起 *vb* rise, get up, arise; raise, grow; begin, start; (after another verb, to indicate upward movement) up; [**ná** | **tí**] **qǐ** [**拿** | **提**] 起 [take | lift] up; (after another verb, to indicate the beginning of an action) start, begin; **cóng tóu shuō qǐ** 从头说起 tell it from the beginning; (after another verb that is followed by de 得 or bu 不, to mean can or cannot attain a certain standard) **mǎi** [**de** | **bù**] **qǐ** 买 [**得** | **不**] 起 [can | cannot] afford

qǐchuáng 起床 *vb* get up, get out of bed

qǐdiǎn 起点 *n* starting point

qǐfēi 起飞 *vb* take off (as an airplane)

qǐlai 起来 *vb* get up, rise, get out of bed; stand up; (*in opposition, rebellion, etc.*) arise, rise up, stand up against; (*after a verb, to indicate upward direction*) raise, lift; (*after a verb, indicate the beginning of an action*) start, begin; (*after a verb, to indicate an accomplishment*) **xiǎngqǐlai...** 想起来... think of..., remember...; (*after a verb, to indicate one's impression in the midst of an activity*) **tīngqǐlai...** 听起来... it sounds...; **kànqǐlai...** 看起来... it looks...

qì 气 **1** *vb* become angry, become enraged, fume; make angry, anger, enrage **2** *n* air, gas, fumes; breath; **chuī yìkǒu qì** 吹一口气 blow out a puff of air; smell, odour

qìfēn 气氛 *n* atmosphere, ambience

qìhòu 气候 *n* climate, weather; situation, atmosphere

qìwēn 气温 *n* air temperature

qìxiàng 气象 *n* weather, climatic/atmospheric phenomena

qì 汽 *n* steam, vapour

qìchē 汽车 *n* car, automobile, vehicle; bus; **qìchēzhàn** 汽车站 bus station, bus stop

qìshuǐ 汽水 *n* carbonated drink, soft drink, pop

qìyóu 汽油 *n* petrol, gasoline

qì 器 *n* implement, utensil, instrument, machine; **yuèqì** 乐器 musical instrument

qiàdàng 恰当 *adj* appropriate, suitable, fitting

qiàhǎo 恰好 *adv* it so happened that, luckily; **qiàhǎo tā yě zài nàr** 恰好她也在那儿 it just so happened that she was there too

qiān 千 *num* thousand; a large number of

qiānwàn 千万 **1** *adv* (*in a warning*) please do...at all costs; **qiānwàn yào jìzhù!** 千万要记住! please do remember! **2** *num* ten million, millions upon millions

qiān 牵 *vb* lead by the hand, pull

qiānbǐ 铅笔 *n* pencil

qiānxū 谦虚 *adj* modest, self-effacing

qiāndìng 签订 *vb* (*as an agreement, etc.*) sign, put one's signature on

qiānmíng 签名 *vb* sign name, autograph

qiānzì 签字 *vb* sign, affix signature

qián 前 **1** *n* front, the front, ahead **2** *adj* preceding, former; front, first, top **3** *adv* forward, ahead, ago **4** *prep* in front of, ahead of; (*sometimes preceded by* yǐ 以) before

qiánbiān 前边, **qiántou** 前头 *adv* in front, ahead

qiánjìn 前进 *vb* advance, go forward, move ahead

qiánmiàn 前面 *adv* in front, ahead; (*referring to something mentioned before*) above, the above, preceding

qiánnián 前年 *n* the year before last, two years ago

qiántiān 前天 *n* the day before yesterday

qiántú 前途 *n* the future, future prospects, the road ahead

qiánxī 前夕 *n* eve

qián 钱 *n* money; coins; (*when talking about cost*) money, cost; píngguǒ duōshǎo qián? 苹果多少钱? how much are the apples?; táng yì máo qián 糖一毛钱 the sweets cost 10 cents

qiánbāo 钱包 *n* purse, wallet

qiǎn 浅 *adj* shallow; superficial, not profound; elementary, simple, easy; (*of colour*) light; qiǎn lǜ 浅绿 light green

qiàn 欠 *vb* (debt, gratitude, *etc.*) owe; need, be short of, lacking

qiāng 枪 *n* gun, rifle, pistol

qiáng 强 *adj* strong, powerful; better

qiángdà 强大 *adj* strong, powerful

qiángdào 强盗 *n* robber, bandit

qiángdiào 强调 **1** *vb* emphasise, stress **2** *n* emphasis, stress

qiángdù 强度 *n* degree of strength, degree of intensity

qiángliè 强烈 *adj* strong, intense, fervent

qiángpò 强迫 *vb* compel, coerce, force

qiáng 墙 *n* wall

qiǎng 抢 *vb* rob, snatch, loot; vie for; (*in an emergency*) rush, seize the moment; **qiǎng gòu shípǐn** 抢购食品 rush to buy food

qiāoqiāo 悄悄 *adv* silently, quietly, stealthily

qiāo 敲 *vb* (*a door, etc.*) knock, tap; (*a drum, gong, etc.*) beat, strike

qiáo(liáng) 桥(梁) *n* bridge

qiáo 瞧 *vb* see, look at; **qiáo [de | bù] qǐ** 瞧[得|不]起 look [up to | down on]

qiǎo 巧 **1** *adj* skilful, clever, ingenious; artful, cunning, deceiving; by coincidence, fortuitous, lucky **2** *adv* cleverly; fortuitously, coincidentally

qiǎomiào 巧妙 *adj* (*of methods, skills, etc.*) brilliant, ingenious, clever

qiē 切 *vb* (*as meat, fruit, vegetables, etc.*) cut, slice

qīnlüè 侵略 **1** *vb* invade, encroach **2** *n* invasion, aggression

qīn 亲 **1** *n* parent; blood relation, next of kin, relative; marriage, match **2** *adj* close, intimate, dear **3** *adv* in person, oneself **4** *vb* kiss

qīn'ài 亲爱 *adj* dear, darling, beloved

qīnjìn 亲近 *vb* be close to, be on intimate terms with

qīnmì 亲密 *adj* close, intimate

qīnqi 亲戚 *n* relative(s), relation(s), kin

qīnqiè 亲切 *adj* warm, kind, cordial

qīnrè 亲热 *adj* affectionate, intimate, warmhearted

qīnzì 亲自 *adv* in person, personally, oneself

qín 琴 *n* (*general name for stringed musical instruments*)
    xiǎotíqín 小提琴 violin

qīng 青 *adj* blue, green

qīngnián 青年 *n* youth, young person

qīngshàonián 青少年 *n* teenager, youngster

qīng 轻 **1** *adj* (in weight or importance) light; (in degree or age) small; (when talking about one's work or job) easy **2** *adv* lightly, softly, gently

qīngsōng 轻松 *adj* light, relaxed

qīngxiàng 倾向 **1** *n* tendency, trend, inclination **2** *vb* be inclined to, prefer

qīng 清 **1** *adj* clear, distinct **2** *vb* (an account, etc.) clear up, settle

qīngchu 清楚 **1** *adj* clear, distinct **2** *vb* understand, know, have a clear understanding of

qīngjié 清洁 *adj* clean

qīngjìng 清静 *adj* quiet, peaceful, undisturbed

qíngjié 情节 *n* (when talking about literature) plot; qíngjié jǐncòu 情节紧凑 a tightly constructed plot; circumstances

qíngjǐng 情景 *n* scene, sight; situation, circumstances

qíngkuàng 情况 *n* situation, condition, circumstance

qíngxíng 情形 *n* situation, condition, circumstance

qíngxù 情绪 *n* state of mind, mood, morale

qíng 晴 *adj* (referring to the sky or weather) clear, fair, fine

qínglǎng 晴朗 *adj* fine, sunny

qǐng 请 *vb* (word used in polite requests) please; qǐng [zuò | jìn | chīfàn] 请[坐 | 进 | 吃饭] please [sit down | come in | start eating]; invite, ask, request

qǐngjià 请假 *vb* ask for time off, ask for leave of absence

qǐngjiào 请教 *vb* ask for advice, consult

qǐngkè 请客 *vb* invite someone to dinner, treat, entertain guests

qīngqiú 请求 **1** vb ask, request **2** n request

qǐngwèn 请问 vb (polite way of asking a question) may I ask...,

qìnghè 庆贺 vb congratulate, celebrate

qìngzhù 庆祝 **1** vb celebrate **2** n celebration

qióng 穷 adj poor, impoverished

qiū(tiān) 秋(天) n autumn, fall

qiú 求 vb seek, request, strive for

qiú 球 n ball, game played with a ball; sphere, globe, earth

qiúchǎng 球场 n playing field, court, diamond

qiúmí 球迷 n (someone fond of games played with a ball) fan; **zúqiúmí** 足球迷 football fan

qū 区 n area, region, zone; district, precinct, administrative division

qūbié 区别 **1** n difference **2** vb discriminate, distinguish

qūfēn 区分 vb differentiate, distinguish

qūshì 趋势 n trend, tendency

qūxiàng 趋向 **1** n trend, tendency, direction **2** vb tend to, incline to

qú 渠 n drain, ditch, channel

qǔzi 曲子 n song, tune, melody

qǔ 取 vb take, fetch, obtain; (money from a bank, etc.) withdraw, draw out, take out; (as a candidate) accept, admit, select; (as a course of action) aim for, choose

qǔdé 取得 vb obtain, achieve, gain

qǔxiāo 取消 vb cancel, abolish, call off

qù 去 vb go; leave, depart; (after a verb, indicating action directed away from the speaker) (move) away; **náqù** 拿去 take away; (expressing purpose or reason for an action) to, in order to; **ná yìdiǎnr qián qù mǎi dōngxi** 拿一点儿钱去买东西 take some money and go shopping; remove, get rid of, discard

qùshì 去世 *vb* die, pass away

qùnián 去年 *n* last year

qùwèi 趣味 *n* interest, delight; taste, liking, preference

quān 圈 **1** *n* circle, ring; enclosure **2** *vb* enclose, fence in, encircle

quán 全 **1** *adj* whole, entire; complete **2** *adv* completely, entirely, all

quánbù 全部 **1** *adj* whole, complete, all **2** *adv* wholly, completely

quánmiàn 全面 *adj* overall, all-round, comprehensive

quántǐ 全体 **1** *n* as a whole, whole body/group **2** *adj* all, entire, whole

quán 权 *n* right; power, authority

quánlì 权力 *n* power, authority

quán 泉 *n* spring; **wēnquán** 温泉 hot spring

quán(tou) 拳(头) *n* fist

quán 鬈 *adj (when describing hair)* curly, wavy

quàn 劝 *vb* persuade, advise, urge

quàngào 劝告 *vb* advise, urge, exhort

quē 缺 *vb* lack, be short of

quēdiǎn 缺点 *n* defect, shortcoming, deficiency

quēfá 缺乏 **1** *vb* lack, be short of **2** *n* lack, deficiency

quēshǎo 缺少 *vb* lack, be short of

què 却 *conj* however, but, yet

quèdìng 确定 **1** *vb* settle on, determine, fix **2** *adj* settled, definite, sure

quèshí 确实 **1** *adj* certain, true, reliable **2** *adv* certainly, really, indeed

qúnzi 裙子 *n* skirt

qún 群 **1** *mw* ▶**213** (*for a group of, many*) group, herd, flock **2** *n* group, crowd, herd

qúnzhòng 群众 *n* the masses, the public; **qúnzhòng yùndong** 群众运动 mass movement

Rr

rán'ér 然而 *conj* but, however, nevertheless

ránhòu 然后 *adv* thereafter, afterwards, subsequently

ránshāo 燃烧 *vb* burn

rǎn 染 *vb* dye; (*when talking about a disease, etc.*) contract, become infected with; (*when talking about a bad habit, etc.*) acquire

rǎng 嚷 *vb* yell, shout

ràng 让 **1** *vb* let, allow, permit; **ràng tā qù ba** 让她去吧 let her go; make, cause; **zhèjiàn shì ràng tā hěn gāoxing** 这件事让她很高兴 this matter made her very happy; yield, give way, concede; **ràng zuò** 让座 give up one's seat **2** *prep* (*when used to introduce the agent in a passive construction*) by; **tā zuò de cài ràng gǒu chī le** 他做的菜让狗吃了 the food he made was eaten by the dog

ràngbù 让步 *vb* make concessions

ráo 饶 *vb* forgive, pardon

rǎoluàn 扰乱 *vb* disturb, create confusion, harass

rào 绕 *vb* move around, encircle, coil; **rào dìqiú yì zhōu** 绕地球一周 go round the world once; bypass, go round; **ràoguo zhàng'ài** 绕过障碍 bypass an obstacle

rě 惹 *vb* provoke, annoy, tease; (*when talking about trouble, nuisance, attention, etc.*) stir up, incite, attract

rè 热 **1** *adj* (of weather, temperature, etc.) hot **2** *vb* heat up, warm up **3** *n* heat; temperature, fever; **fā rè** 发热 have a high temperature; rush, craze; [chūguó | jīng shāng | wǎngqiú] rè [出国 | 经商 | 网球] 热 a craze for [going abroad | business | tennis]

rè'ài 热爱 *vb* love, feel warm affection for

rèliè 热烈 *adj* enthusiastic, passionate, fervent

rènao 热闹 **1** *adj* bustling, lively, boisterous **2** *vb* liven up, have a jolly time **3** *n* excitement, fun

rèqíng 热情 **1** *adj* warm-hearted, enthusiastic, zealous **2** *n* passionate feelings, love, ardour

rèxīn 热心 *adj* earnest, warm-hearted, enthusiastic

rén 人 *n* person, people, humanity; others, other people; **tā duì rén bú kèqi** 他对人不客气 he is impolite to others; **rénrén** 人人 everyone, everybody

réncái 人才 *n* talent, talented person

réngōng 人工 **1** *adj* artificial, man-made **2** *n* manual work; labour; **nàr de réngōng hěn guì** 那儿的人工很贵 labour there is very expensive

rénjiā 人家 *n* household, family

rénjia 人家 *pron* others, other people; (when referring indirectly to a certain person or people) 'they', someone; **nǐ yàoshi xiǎng qǐng tā chī fàn, nǐ zuìhǎo zǎo diǎn gàosu rénjia** 你要是想请他吃饭，你最好早点告诉人家 if you want to invite him to a meal, you had better tell him ahead of time; (when referring indirectly to the speaker) someone, one; **wǒ cuò le, rénjia xiàng nǐ dàoqiàn hái bù xíng ma?** 我错了，人家向你道歉还不行吗? I was wrong and I apologize to you; won't that do?

rénkǒu 人口 *n* population; family members, number of family members

rénlèi 人类 *n* humankind, humanity; **rénlèixué** 人类学 anthropology

rénmen 人们 *n* people, men

rénmín 人民 n people, the people

Rénmínbì 人民币 n (official currency of the People's Republic of China) Renminbi (RMB)

rénquán 人权 n human rights

rénshēng 人生 n life, human life

rénwù 人物 n personage, figure; (in a literary work) character

rényuán 人员 n staff members, personnel

rénzào 人造 adj man-made, artificial

rěn 忍 vb endure, tolerate, be patient

rěnnài 忍耐 vb be patient, endure, restrain oneself

rěnshòu 忍受 vb bear, endure

rěnxīn 忍心 vb be hard-hearted, be callous

rèn 认 vb (when speaking of a person, object, etc.) recognize, know, identify; (when speaking of a fact, fault, problem, etc.) admit, acknowledge, recognize; **rèn...zuò...** 认... 作... regard...as..., take...for...

rènde 认得 vb be acquainted with, know, recognize

rènshi 认识 1 vb (when speaking of a person) be acquainted with, know, recognize; (when speaking of a fact, reason, error, etc.) realize, understand 2 n understanding, knowledge

rènwéi 认为 vb consider that, think that, take it that

rènzhēn 认真 adj serious, earnest, conscientious

rèn 任 vb appoint, assign, be responsible for; let, allow; **rèn(píng)** 任 (凭) no matter (who, what, how); **rènpíng tā zěnme hǎnjiào, méi yǒu rén lǐ tā** 任凭他怎么喊叫, 没有人理他 no matter how much he shouted, no one paid attention to him

rènhé 任何 det any, whatever; **tā bú rènshi rènhé rén** 她不认识任何人 she doesn't know anyone

rènmìng 任命 vb employ, appoint

rènwu 任务 n assigned duty, task, responsibility

rēng 扔 *vb* throw, throw away, cast aside

réngjiù 仍旧 *adv* as before, still, yet

réng(rán) 仍(然) *adv* still, yet, as before

rì 日 *n* sun; day, daytime; (*in general*) time; every day, day by day

rìbào 日报 *n* daily paper, daily

Rìběn 日本 *n* Japan

rìcháng 日常 *adj* daily, day to day, everyday

rìchéng 日程 *n* daily schedule, agenda, programme

rìchū 日出 *n* sunrise

rìjì 日记 *n* diary

rìlì 日历 *n* calendar

rìluò 日落 *n* sunset

rìqī 日期 *n* date

Rìwén 日文 *n* Japanese language (usually written)

rìyì 日益 *adv* increasingly, day by day

rìyòngpǐn 日用品 *n* daily necessities, basic commodities

Rìyǔ 日语 *n* Japanese language (usually spoken)

rìyuán 日元 *n* Japanese yen

rìzi 日子 day, date; a period of time, days; way of life, livelihood

róng 容 *vb* allow, let, permit; tolerate; hold, contain

róngnà 容纳 *vb* hold, have the capacity of

róngrěn 容忍 *vb* tolerate, put up with

róngxǔ 容许 *vb* allow, permit

róngyì 容易 *adj* easy; likely, apt; **xiàtiān niúnǎi hěn róngyì huài** 夏天牛奶很容易坏 in the summer milk goes bad easily

ròu 肉 *n* (*of an animal*) meat, flesh; (*of a person*) muscle, flesh; (*of fruit or vegetable*) pulp, flesh

rú 如 **1** *vb* be like, be as, be similar to; (*when used with a negative*) ▶ See also **bùrú** 不如. **2** *prep* in accordance with, according to **3** *conj* if, supposing; **rú** 如下雨, 我们就不去了 if it rains, we just won't go **4 rú** 如 such as, for example; **Běijīng yǒu hěn duō míngshèng, rú Chángchéng, Gùgōng, děngděng** 北京有很多名胜, 如长城, 故宫, 等等 Beijing has many famous places, such as the Great Wall, the Forbidden City, etc.

rúcǐ 如此 *adv* so, such, in this way

rúguǒ 如果 *conj* if, supposing that, in case

rúhé 如何 *adv* (*in a question or a statement*) how, what; **nǐde kǎoshì rúhé?** 你的考试如何? how was your examination?; **tā bù zhīdào rúhé wánchéng zhèxiàng rènwu** 他不知道如何完成这项任务 he doesn't know how to finish this task

rújīn 如今 *adv* these days, nowadays, at the present time

rúyì 如意 *adj* ideal, as one wishes

rù 入 *vb* enter, come in, go in; join, be admitted to, become a member of

ruǎn 软 *adj* soft, gentle, flexible; (*when referring to physical weakness*) weak, feeble; (*when speaking about a person*) easily moved/influenced

ruògān 若干 *det* a certain number of, several

ruòshì 若是 *conj* if

ruò 弱 *adj* weak, feeble; inferior, not up to standard

ruòdiǎn 弱点 *n* weakness, weak point

Ss

sā 撒 *vb* let go, let out, cast

sǎ 洒 *vb* sprinkle, spill, spray

sài 赛 **1** *vb* compete, race; rival, overtake, surpass **2** *n* competition, race, match

sān 三 *num* three

sānyuè 三月 *n* March

sǎn 伞 *n* umbrella, parasol, sunshade

sànbù 散步 *vb* take a stroll, go for a walk

sǎngzi 嗓子 *n* throat, larynx, voice

sǎo 扫 *vb* sweep, clean

sǎozi 嫂子 *n* sister-in-law, elder brother's wife

sàozhou 扫帚 *n* broom

sè 色 *n* colour, look, quality; expression, countenance; sex, physical attraction, sexual passion

sēnlín 森林 *n* forest

shā 杀 *vb* kill, put to death; weaken, reduce

shāfā 沙发 *n* sofa

shāmò 沙漠 *n* desert

shāzi 沙子 *n* sand, grains of sand; small grains, pellets, grit

shǎ 傻 *adj* foolish, stupid, silly

shài 晒 *vb* (*when speaking about the sun*) shine upon; (*when speaking about people*) sunbathe, dry in the sun; **shài tàiyáng** 晒太阳 sunbathe

shān 山 *n* mountain, hill

shānmài 山脉 *n* mountain range

shānqū 山区 *n* mountainous region

shǎn 闪 *vb* evade, dodge, duck; (*as a light, lightning, inspiration, etc.*) flash; **dǎ shǎn** 打闪 lightning flashes

shànyú 善于 *vb* be good at

shāng 伤 **1** *vb* (*physically, emotionally, etc.*) wound, injure, hurt **2** *n* wound, harm, injury

shāngxīn 伤心 *adj* sad, broken-hearted

shāngchǎng 商场 *n* market

shāngdiàn 商店 *n* shop, store

shāngliang 商量 *vb* talk over, consult, discuss

shāngpǐn 商品 *n* goods, commodities, merchandise

shāngyè 商业 *n* commerce, business, trade

shàng 上 **1** *vb* go up, ascend; **shàng lóu** 上楼 go upstairs; (*when talking about getting on or into a vehicle, mode of transport, stage or platform*) mount, board, get on; **shàng** [gōnggòng qìchē | chuán | fēijī] 上 [公共汽车 | 船 | 飞机] board [the bus | the boat | the plane] go, come **2** *adv* (*after a verb to indicate an upward direction or accomplishment*) up; [guān | dēng | chuān] shang 上 [关 | 登 | 穿] 上 [close up | climb up to, reach | put on]; (*to indicate the beginning and continuity of an action*) tāmen zhùshangle xīn fángzi 他们住上了新房子 they now live in a new house **3** *adj* up, upper, high; (*in grade or quality*) first, top; first, preceding, previous; **shàng...qù** 上... 去 qù...; **nǐ shàng nǎr qù?** 你上那儿去? where are you going?; **shàng...** [qù | lái] 上... [去 | 来] [go | come]; **wǒ shàng xuéxiào qù** 我上学校去 I am going to the school

shàngbān 上班 *vb* go to the office, start work

shàngbian 上边 **1** *n* top, above, higher parts; the top of, the surface of; the higher authorities, the higher-ups; aspect, respect, regard; tā bú yòng zài zhè shàngbian huā hěn duō shíjiān 他不用在这上边花很多时间 he does not need to spend much time on this **2** *adj* above-mentioned, aforesaid, foregoing

shàngdàng 上当 *vb* be swindled, be taken in, fall into a trap

Shàngdì 上帝 *n* God

Shànghǎi 上海 *n* Shanghai city

shàngjí 上级 *n* upper grade, higher level; higher authority

shàngkè 上课 *vb* go to class, attend a lecture; teach a class

shànglai 上来 *vb* come up; (*after a verb to indicate a direction up and toward the speaker*) ...up; **náshànglai** 拿上来 bring up; (*after a verb to indicate accomplishment*) **tā dá bú shànglai zhège wèntí** 他答不上来这个问题 he is unable to answer this question

shàngmian 上面 ▶ **shàngbian** 上边

shàngqu 上去 *vb* go up; (*after a verb to indicate a direction up and away from the speaker*) up; **náshàngqu** 拿上去 take up

shàngtou 上头 ▶ **shàngbian** 上边

shàngwǔ 上午 *n* morning, a.m., forenoon

shàngxué 上学 *vb* attend school, go to school

shàngyī 上衣 *n* outer garment (worn on the upper half of the body), jacket

shāo 烧 **1** *vb* burn; heat, cook; bake, stew, roast; have a temperature, have a fever **2** *n* temperature, fever

shāo 稍, **shāowěi** 稍微 *adv* a little, somewhat, slightly

sháozi 勺子 *n* spoon, ladle

shǎo 少 ! Can also be pronounced **shào** with a different meaning. **1** *adj* few, little, scarce; (*in comparisons*) less **2** *adv* seldom, hardly ever, scarcely ever **3** *vb* be short of, lack, be missing; (*used in imperative sentences*) stop, quit, reduce; **nǐ shǎo guǎn xiánshì** 你少管闲事 stop meddling in other people's affairs

shǎoshù 少数 *n* minority; **shǎoshù mínzú** 少数民族 ethnic minority, minority peoples

shàonián 少年 *n* (*a time of life*) youth; (*a person*) youth, young person

shétou 舌头 *n* tongue

shé 蛇 *n* snake, serpent

shèbèi 设备 *n* equipment

shèjì 设计 **1** *vb* design, plan, draw up plans **2** *n* design, plan, project

shèhuì 社会 *n* society, community

shè 射 *vb* shoot; emit, radiate, send out

shei 谁 *pron* ! Also pronounced **shuí**; who?; **nǐ shì shéi?** 你是谁? who are you?; anybody?; **yǒu shéi yuànyì qù?** 有谁愿意去?

would anyone like to go?; (*used with* **dōu** 都) everybody; **shéi dōu xǐhuan kàn shū** 谁都喜欢看书 everybody likes to read books; (*used with* **dōu** 都 *in the negative*) nobody; **shéi dōu méi qián** 谁都没钱 nobody has any money

shēn 伸 *vb* stretch, extend

shēn 身 *n* body; life; oneself, personally, itself

shēnbiān 身边 1 *n* one's side, one's person 2 *adv* at/by one's side, to hand, nearby

shēntǐ 身体 *n* body; health

shēn 深 1 *adj* (*of water, thought, etc.*) deep, profound; (*of understanding, etc.*) thorough, penetrating; (*of friendships, relationships, etc.*) close, intimate; (*of forests, mysteries, etc.*) hidden, inaccessible, obscure; (*of colours*) dark, deep; (*of night, season, etc.*) late 2 *adv* profoundly, greatly, deeply

shēnhòu 深厚 *adj* (*of friendships, foundations, etc.*) deep, profound, solid

shēnkè 深刻 *adj* (*of impressions, etc.*) deep, profound

shēnrù 深入 1 *vb* penetrate deeply into, go deeply into 2 *adj* deep, thorough, penetrating

shénme 什么 1 *pron* what? what kind of? **nǐ xué shénme?** 你学什么? what do you study?; something; **wǒ xiǎng jìn chéng mǎi diǎnr shénme** 我想进城买点儿什么 I want to go into town to buy something; (*when it comes before* **dōu** 都) everything; **tā shénme dōu chī** 她什么都吃 she eats everything; (*when used in the negative before* **yě** 也 *or* **dōu** 都) nothing, not anything; **tā shénme yě bù zhīdào** 他什么也不知道 he doesn't know anything; (*when enumerating things*) etc., ...and what not; **shénme yīfu a, shípǐn a, wánjù a, nàge shāngdiàn dōu mài** 什么衣服啊, 食品啊, 玩具啊, 那个商店都卖 that shop sells clothes, food, toys, and what not 2 *exc* (*to indicate surprise or displeasure*) what? 3 *det* what; **xiànzài shì shénme shíhòu?** 现在是什么时候? what time is it (now)?; **...shénme...shénme ...** 什么... 什么 whatever; **nǐ yào shénme jiù mǎi shénme** 你要什么就买什么 buy whatever you want

shénmede 什么的 *pron* and so forth, etc.

shén 神 **1** *n* spirit, god, deity; spirit, mind; expression, look **2** *adj* spiritual, supernatural, magical

shénjīng 神经 *n* (of the body) nerve

shènzhì(yú) 甚至(于) *adv* even, so much so that, so far as to

shēng 升 **1** *vb* rise, ascend, move upward; (in position or rank) promote **2** *n* (unit for measuring liquids) litre

shēng 生 **1** *vb* be born, give birth to, give rise to; grow; become **2** *adj* living, alive, live; unripe, green, raw; unprocessed, unrefined; unfamiliar, strange **3** *n* life, existence; living, livelihood; lifetime

shēngchǎn 生产 **1** *vb* produce, make, manufacture; give birth **2** *n* production

shēngcí 生词 *n* new word, new vocabulary

shēngdòng 生动 *adj* moving, vivid, lively

shēnghuó 生活 **1** *n* life; living, livelihood **2** *vb* live

shēngmìng 生命 *n* (biological existence) life

shēngrì 生日 *n* birthday

shēngqì 生气 *adj* angry

shēngwù 生物 *n* living beings, organisms; **shēngwùxué** 生物学 biology

shēngyi 生意 *n* business, trade; **zuò shēngyi** 做生意 do business

shēngzhǎng 生长 *vb*; grow, develop; grow up, be brought up

shēng 声 **1** *n* voice, sound; (as in the linguistic tone of a Chinese word) tone; **sìshēng** 四声 the four tones of Chinese **2** *mw* ▶ 213 (for counting cries, shouts, or other utterances)

shēngdiào 声调 *n* (of words, sentences, speaking) tone, intonation; (of a Chinese character) tone; melody

shēngyīn 声音 *n* sound, voice, noise

shéngzi 绳子 *n* cord, string, rope

shěng 省 **1** n province **2** vb (when talking about time or money) economize, save, spare; omit, leave out

Shèngdàn(jié) 圣诞(节) n Christmas (Day)

shèng 胜 **1** n victory, success **2** vb conquer, win, defeat; excel, surpass, be better than

shènglì 胜利 **1** vb be victorious, be successful, win **2** n victory **3** adv victoriously, successfully

shèngxia 剩下 vb; remain, be left over, have...left over; leave behind; **shèngxia(lai)** 剩下(来) remain, be left over

shībài 失败 **1** vb fail, be defeated **2** n failure, defeat

shīqù 失去 vb (when talking about objects, opportunities, friends, etc.) lose

shīwàng 失望 **1** adj disappointed **2** vb lose hope, lose confidence

shīyè 失业 **1** vb be unemployed, lose one's job **2** n unemployment

shīfu 师傅 n master worker, teacher, instructor; a polite term of address to people who have skill or specialized knowledge

shī 诗 n poetry, poem, verse; **shīrén** 诗人 poet

shīzi 狮子 n lion

shīgōng 施工 vb be under construction, engage in construction

shī 湿 adj damp, humid, wet

shīrùn 湿润 adj humid, moist

shí 十 num ten, tens, multiples of ten

shíyuè 十月 n October

shí'èr 十二 num twelve

shí'èryuè 十二月 n December

shífēn 十分 adv completely, fully, utterly

shíyī 十一 num eleven

shíyīyuè 十一月 *n* November

shízì lùkǒu 十字路口 *n* crossroads

shí 石, **shítou** 石头 *n* rock, stone, pebble

shíyóu 石油 *n* petroleum, oil

shídài 时代 *n* time, period, age

shíhou 时候 **1** *n* time, length of time; (*when speaking of time on the clock*) time, moment in time, point in time; tā shì shénme shíhòu zǒu de? 他是什么时候走的? what time did he leave? **2** *conj* ...de shíhòu ...的时候 when..., during..., while...; dāng...shíhòu 当... 时候 when..., while...

shíjiān 时间 *n* (*as an abstract concept*) time; (*a set period of time*) time, duration; (*point of time*) time; nǐ shénme shíjiān dào de? 你什么时间到的? what time did you arrive?; time zone; Běijīng shíjiān 北京时间 Beijing time; **shíjiānbiǎo** 时间表 timetable, schedule

shíkè 时刻 **1** *n* time, hour **2** *adv* every moment, constantly, always

shíqī 时期 *n* time period

shíjì 实际 *n* reality, fact **1** *adj* realistic, practical; **shíjìshang** 实际上 actually, in fact, in reality

shíjiàn 实践 **1** *vb* put into practice, carry out **2** *n* practice

shíshì 实事 *n* fact, facts; **shíshì qiúshì** 实事求是 seek truth from facts, be realistic

shíxiàn 实现 *vb* (*as a hope, dream, plan*) realise, come true, actualise

shíxíng 实行 *vb* implement, put into practice, carry out

shíyàn 实验 **1** *vb* experiment **2** *n* experiment; **shíyànshì** 实验室 laboratory

shíyòng 实用 *adj* practical, functional, applied

shízài 实在 **1** *adj* true, real, honest **2** *adv* actually, really

shí 拾 *vb* pick up, gather, collect

shípǐn 食品 *n* food, provisions

shítáng 食堂 *n* dining hall, cafeteria

shíwù 食物 *n* food

shǐ 使 *vb* use, employ, apply; enable, cause, make

shǐyòng 使用 **1** *vb* utilise, make use of, apply **2** *n* use, deployment

shǐzhōng 始终 *adv* from beginning to end, all along

shìjì 世纪 *n* century

shìjiè 世界 *n* world

shì 市 *n* municipality, city; market, fair; (*pertaining to the Chinese system of weights and measures*) **yí shìjīn** 一市斤 1/2 kilo

shìchǎng 市场 *n* market, bazaar

shìyàng 式样 *n* style, type, model

shì 事 *n* affair, matter, event; trouble, accident; work, job; **zuòshì** 做事 work at a job

shìgù 事故 *n* accident

shìjiàn 事件 *n* incident, event

shìqing 事情 *n* thing, matter, affair

shìshí 事实 *n* reality, fact; **shìshíshang** 事实上 in fact, as a matter of fact, in reality

shìwù 事务 *n* affairs, matters; work, routine, duties

shìwù 事物 *n* thing, object, matter

shìxiān 事先 *adv* prior to, in advance, beforehand

shìyè 事业 *n* profession, career, cause; enterprise, undertaking

shì 试 **1** *vb* try, try out, test **2** *n* test, examination; **shìshì kàn** 试试看 try and see

shìjuàn 试卷 *n* examination paper, answer booklet, script

shìyàn 试验 **1** *vb* test, experiment **2** *n* experiment, test, trial

shì 是 1 *vb* (*the verb to be*) am, is, are; certainly, indeed; **wǒ shì méi qù** 我是没去 I certainly did not go 2 *adj* right, correct; (*used to answer the affirmative*) yes, right; **shì, nǐ shuō de duì** 是，你说得对 yes, what you said is correct 3 (*used in certain patterns*) **bú shì...ér shì...** 不是...而是... it's not...but...; **yào bú shì...jiù shì...** 要不是...就是... if it's not..., it's...; **shì...de** 是...的; (*for emphasis*) **tā shì hěn yònggōng de** 她是很用功的 she studies hard; (*when giving the details about someone or something, its origin, manufacture, provenence, etc.*) **zhèliàng qìchē shì Rìběn zào de** 这辆汽车是日本造的 this car was made in Japan; **shì bú shì?** 是不是? is it?; **shì...háishi...** 是...还是... ...or..., whether...or...; **nǐ shì zǒulù lái de, háishi qí chē lái de?** 你是走路来的，还是骑车来的? did you walk or come by bicycle?; (*here* shì 是 *is used in a clause of concession*) yes, it is..., but..., although..., yet...; **zhèbù diànyǐng hǎo shì hǎo, kěshì tài cháng le** 这部电影好是好，可是太长了 although this movie is good, it's too long

shìdàng 适当 *adj* suitable, appropriate, proper

shìhé 适合 *vb* fit, suit, be appropriate

shìyìng 适应 *vb* adapt, suit, fit

shìyòng 适用 *adj* suitable, applicable, appropriate

shì 室 *n* room

shōu 收 *vb* receive, accept; collect, gather, harvest; **shōuhuílai** 收回来 recover, get back; **shōuqǐlai** 收起来 put away, store away

shōuhuò 收获 1 *vb* harvest, gather in the crops, reap 2 *n* (*of hard work, study, etc.*) results, harvest, gains

shōurù 收入 1 *vb* receive, take in 2 *n* income, revenue

shōushi 收拾 *vb* put in order, straighten up, tidy; repair, fix, mend

shōuyīnjī 收音机 *n* radio

shóu 熟 ▶ **shú** 熟

shǒu 手 1 *n* hand 2 *adv* by hand

shǒubiǎo 手表 *n* watch, wristwatch

shǒuduàn 手段 *n* method, means

shǒugōng 手工 **1** *n* handicraft, handiwork **2** *adj* manual, handmade **3** *adv* by hand

shǒujuàn 手绢 *n* handkerchief

shǒushù 手术 *n* surgical operation

shǒutào 手套 *n* gloves

shǒuxù 手续 *n* procedures, formalities, process

shǒuzhǐ 手指 *n* finger; **shǒuzhǐjiǎ** 手指甲 fingernail

shǒu 首 **1** *n* (*part of the body*) head; (*a person*) leader, chief, head **2** *mw* ▶ **213** (*for songs, poems, music*) **3** *adj* first, beginning, most important

shǒudū 首都 *n* (*of a country*) capital

shǒuxiān 首先 *adv* first, in the first place, above all

shòu 受 *vb* receive, accept; suffer, be subjected to; stand, endure, bear; (*used to express the passive voice*) receive, be subject to

shòuhuòyuán 售货员 *n* shop assistant

shòupiàoyuán 售票员 *n* (*on a bus*) conductor; (*at a train station*) booking-office clerk; (*at a cinema or theatre*) box-office clerk

shòu 瘦 *adj* (*of people*) thin, emaciated; (*of meat*) lean; (*of clothing*) tight

shū 书 *n* book; letter

shūbāo 书包 *n* satchel, book bag, school bag

shūdiàn 书店 *n* bookshop, bookstore

shūfǎ 书法 *n* calligraphy

shūjì 书记 *n* (*of a political party or a political organization*) secretary

shūjià 书架 *n* bookcase, bookshelf

shūzhuō 书桌 *n* desk

shūshu 叔叔 *n* uncle, father's younger brother; (*a man in one's father's generation*) uncle

shūfu 舒服 *adj* comfortable, feeling well

shūshì 舒适 *adj* comfortable, cosy

shū 输 *vb* transport, transmit, convey; (*when speaking about a game, a gamble*) lose, be defeated

shūcài 蔬菜 *n* vegetables

shú 熟 ! *Can also be pronounced* shóu. **1** *adj* (*of fruit, etc.*) ripe, mature; (*of food*) cooked, done, processed; (*of people*) familiar, well-acquainted; (*in a subject, a type of work, etc.*) skilled, trained, experienced **2** *adv* (*of sleep*) deeply, soundly; **shúrén** 熟人 acquaintance

shúliàn 熟练 *adj* expert, adept, proficient

shúxī 熟悉 *vb* know well, be familiar with

shǔjià 暑假 *n* summer holidays, summer vacation

shǔyú 属于 *vb* belong to, pertain to, be part of; Xiānggǎng shǔyú Zhōngguó 香港属于中国 Hong Kong belongs to China

shǔ 数 *vb* ▶ *See also* shù 数. count, enumerate, list; count as, be counted as, be notable for; **shǔ de shàng** 数得上 qualify, count, be counted; **shǔ bù qīng** 数不清 unable to count exactly, countless; **shǔ bú guòlai** 数不过来 too many to count

shǔ 鼠 *n* mouse, rat

shù 束 *mw* ▶ **213** bunch

shù 树 **1** *n* tree **2** *vb* establish, set up

shùlín 树林 *n* woods

shù 数 ▶ *See also* shǔ 数. **1** *n* number, figure **2** *det* several, a few

shùliàng 数量 *n* number, quantity, amount

shùxué 数学 *n* mathematics

shùzì 数字 *n* number, figure, digit

shuā 刷 *vb* brush, scrub; paint, whitewash, paste up

shuāi 摔 *vb* fall, stumble; **tā shuāile yìjiāo** 她摔了一交 she tripped over something and fell; break, smash; **shuāiduàn** 摔断 break; throw down, cast

shuǎi 甩 *vb* swing, move back and forth; fling, cast away, throw

shuài 率, **shuàilǐng** 率领 *vb* lead, head, command

shuāng 双 **1** *mw* ▶213 *(for things that come in twos, such as shoes, socks, chopsticks, etc.)* pair **2** *adj* double, twin, dual; **shuāng shǒu** 双手 both hands; *(when talking about numbers)* even; **shuāng shù** 双数 even numbers

shuāngfāng 双方 *n* both sides

shuí 谁 ▶ **shéi** 谁

shuǐ 水 *n* water, juice, liquid

shuǐdào 水稻 *n* rice grown in a paddy field

shuǐguǒ 水果 *n* fruit, fresh fruit

shuǐní 水泥 *n* cement

shuǐpíng 水平 *n* standard, level

shuì 睡 *vb* sleep; **shuìzháo** 睡着 go to sleep, fall asleep, be sleeping

shuìjiào 睡觉 *vb* sleep

shùn 顺 **1** *prep* along, in the direction of **2** *vb* obey, submit to; follow, accord with, go with **3** *adj* favourable, successful; smooth, fluent; **shùnzhe** 顺着 along, following

shùnbiàn 顺便 *adv* along the way, in passing

shùnlì 顺利 **1** *adj* smooth, successful, with no obstacles **2** *adv* smoothly, successfully, well

shuō 说 *vb* say, speak, talk; explain; scold, rebuke

shuōmíng 说明 **1** *vb* make clear, explain **2** *n* instructions, explanation, directions; **shuōmíngshū** 说明书 directions, instructions, synopsis

sījī 司机 *n* driver, chauffeur

sī 丝 *n* silk; fine thread; slight amount, trace

sī 私 **1** *adj* private, secret, confidential; selfish; illegal, underhanded **2** *adv* privately, confidentially, secretly

sīrén 私人 *adj* private, personal

sīxiǎng 思想 *n* thought, philosophy, ideas

sī 撕 *vb* tear, rip, shred

sǐ 死 **1** *vb* die, pass away **2** *adj* dead; stagnant, inflexible **3** *adv* (when it comes before a verb) to the death; **sǐ shǒu** 死守 defend to the death; (when it comes after a verb) die of, to death; [dòng | yān | è] **sǐ** [冻 | 淹 | 饿] 死 [freeze | drown | starve] to death; (when it comes after an adjective) extremely; [lè | qì | lèi] **sǐ le** [乐 | 气 | 累] 死了 extremely [happy | angry | tired]

sì 四 *num* four

sìyuè 四月 *n* April

sìhū 似乎 **1** *adv* seemingly, apparently **2** *vb* seem, appear, seem to be; **sìhū tài wǎn le** 似乎太晚了 it seems too late

sōng 松 **1** *n* pine tree, fir tree **2** *adj* loose, lax, slack **3** *vb* relax, loosen, slacken

sòng 送 *vb* (as a gift) give, present; **sòng gěi tā yíjiàn lǐwù** 送给她一件礼物 give her a present; deliver, take, bring; see off, accompany

sòngxíng 送行 *vb* see off, send off, wish someone a safe journey

sōu 艘 *mw* ▶213 (for ships)

sùjìng 肃静 *adj* solemn and silent

sùdù 速度 *n* speed, velocity

sùshè 宿舍 *n* dormitory

sùliào 塑料 *n* plastic, plastics

suān 酸 **1** *adj* sour tasting; sad, distressed, sorrowful; (muscles, back, etc.) sore, aching **2** *n* acid

suàn 算 *vb* figure, count, calculate; include, count in; be counted as, be considered as, be regarded as; **tā suàn shì wǒmen de hǎo péngyou** 他算是我们的好朋友 he can be considered our good friend; carry weight, count; **suànshang** 算上 count in, include; **suànle** 算了 forget it, let it be, let's drop the matter

suīrán 虽然 *conj* although, though; **suīrán...kěshi/dànshì...** 虽然... 可是/但是... although..., (still, yet)...

suí 随 **1** *prep* along with; **tā suí(zhe) wēndù ér biànhuà** 它随(着)温度而变化 it varies with the temperature **2** *vb* follow, go along with; *(whatever one wishes or finds convenient)* **mǎi bù mǎi suí nǐ** 买不买随你 it's up to you whether you buy it or not

suíbiàn 随便 **1** *adj* casual, informal, random; careless, thoughtless, cursory **2** *adv* following one's convenience, as one pleases, freely; carelessly, in a cursory manner, randomly **3** *conj* no matter whether, whatever, in whatever way

suíshí 随时 *adv* at any time

suì 岁 *n* year of age, year old; **tāde érzi wǔ suì** 他的儿子五岁 his son is five years old

suì 碎 **1** *adj* broken, shattered, fragmentary **2** *vb* break, break in pieces, smash to bits

sūnnǚ 孙女 *n* granddaughter

sūnzi 孙子 *n* grandson

sǔnshī 损失 **1** *vb* lose, damage, harm **2** *n* loss, damage

suō 缩 *vb* *(in size)* shrink, reduce, contract; *(in movement)* shrink back, withdraw

suǒ 所 **1** *mw* ▶213 *(for buildings, houses, schools, etc.)* **2** *n* place, site, station; office, bureau, institute **3** *pt* *(used with* **wéi** 为 *or* **bèi** 被 *to indicate the passive voice)* **bèi dàjiā suǒ chēngzàn** 被大家所称赞 be praised by everyone; *(when it precedes a verb)* what, whatever; **wǒ suǒ [shuō de | xǐhuan de | zuò de]** 我所[说的 | 喜欢的 | 做的] [what I said | what I like | what I do/did]

suǒwèi 所谓 *adj* so-called, what is called

suǒyǐ 所以 *conj* therefore, thus, as a result; **tā bìng le, suǒyǐ méi lái** 他病了，所以没来 he is ill, so he didn't come; *(when* *giving a cause or reason)* the reason why...; **tā zhī suǒyǐ shēngbìng shì yīnwèi nàtiān chūqù méi chuān dàyī** 他之所以生病是因为那天出去没穿大衣 the reason why he became ill is that he went out that day without a coat

suǒyǒu 所有 **1** *det* all **2** *n* possession

Tt

tā 他 *pron* he, him; another, other, some other; **tārén** 他人 other people

tāmen 他们 *pron* they, them

tā 它 *pron (neuter, for animals and things)* it

tāmen 它们 *pron (neuter, for animals and things)* they, them

tā 她 *pron* she, her

tāmen 她们 *pron (when referring to females)* they

tā 塔 *n* pagoda, tower

tà 踏 *vb* step on, tread, set foot on

tái 台 **1** *n* terrace, raised platform, stage; stand, support; broadcasting station **2** *mw* ▶ 213 *(for stage performances, machines, equipment, etc.)*

táifēng 台风 *n* typhoon

Táiwān 台湾 *n* Taiwan

tái 抬 *vb* lift, raise, carry

tài 太 *adv* too, excessively; extremely; *(in the negative)* (not) very; **bú tài gāo** 不太高 not very tall

tàijíquán 太极拳 *n* Taijiquan, traditional Chinese shadow boxing

tàikōng 太空 *n* outer space

Tàipíngyáng 太平洋 *n* the Pacific Ocean

tàitai 太太 *n* married woman, wife; Mrs., Madam

tàiyáng 太阳 *n* sun, sunshine, sunlight

tàidu 态度 *n* attitude, manner, bearing

tān 摊 *n* (for selling things) stand, booth, stall

tán 谈 *vb* talk, discuss, chat

tánhuà 谈话 **1** *vb* talk, chat, carry on a conversation **2** *n* conversation, discussion

tánlùn 谈论 *vb* talk about, discuss

tánpàn 谈判 **1** *vb* negotiate, talk, discuss **2** *n* negotiation, talk

tán 弹 **!** Can also be pronounced **dàn** 弹 with a different meaning; shoot, send forth; (as fingers, ashes off a cigarette, etc.) flick, flip, snap; (a stringed instrument, piano, etc.) play, pluck

tǎnzi 毯子 *n* rug, carpet, blanket

tànqì 叹气 *vb* sigh

tàn 探 *vb* search out, seek, explore; visit, pay a call on

tāng 汤 *n* soup, broth

táng 堂 **1** *n* hall **2** *mw* ▶ **213** (for classes or periods at school or university) period, class

táng 糖 *n* sugar, sweets, candy

tǎng 躺 *vb* lie, recline, be lying

tàng 烫 **1** *vb* scald, burn; (clothes) iron; (using heat on the hair) curl, set, perm; heat up, warm **2** *adj* hot to the touch, scalding

tàng 趟 *mw* ▶ **213** (for scheduled services of public transportation); (for trips, journeys, visits, etc.) time, trip

tāo 掏 *vb* (with the hand as from a pocket) take out, fish out, extract

táo 逃 *vb* escape, run away, evade

táo(zi) 桃(子) *n* peach

tǎolùn 讨论 **1** *vb* discuss, debate, talk over **2** *n* discussion, debate

tǎoyàn 讨厌 **1** *adj* disgusting, objectionable; troublesome, annoying, a nuisance **2** *vb* dislike, be disgusted with

tào 套 **1** *mw* ▶ 213 (*for sets of books, clothing, tools, furniture, etc.*) set, suit, suite **2** *n* cover, sheath, case

tè 特 *adv* specially, particularly, exceptionally

tèbié 特别 **1** *adj* special, distinctive, unique **2** *adv* especially, specially

tècǐ 特此 *adv* hereby

tèdiǎn 特点 *n* special characteristic, special feature

tèsè 特色 *n* unique feature

tèshū 特殊 *adj* special, particular, exceptional

téng 疼 *vb* ache, hurt, be painful; love, be fond of, have affection for

tī 踢 *vb* kick; (*when talking about football or other games requiring kicking*) play

tí 提 *vb* lift, raise, carry; (*when talking about a subject*) bring up, mention; (*when talking about money in a bank*) draw out, take out, withdraw; (*when talking about a suggestion, an objection, etc.*) put forward, bring up, raise

tíchàng 提倡 *vb* advocate, promote

tíchū 提出 *vb* put forward, raise, advance

tígāo 提高 *vb* raise, elevate, increase; enhance, improve

tígōng 提供 *vb* offer, make available to, provide

tíqián 提前 **1** *vb* (*when speaking of an appointment or deadline*) bring forward, advance, change to an earlier time/date **2** *adv* in advance, ahead of time, beforehand

tíxǐng 提醒 *vb* remind, warn

tíyì 提议 **1** *vb* propose, suggest **2** *n* proposal, suggestion, motion

tí 题 **1** n subject, topic, title **2** vb (on a poem, painting, fan, etc.) inscribe

tímù 题目 n (of a lecture, discussion, essay, etc.) subject, title, topic

tǐhuì 体会 **1** vb sense, realize, understand **2** n sense, feeling, understanding

tǐjī 体积 n bulk, physical volume

tǐxì 体系 n system

tǐyàn 体验 vb learn through practice/experience

tǐyù 体育 n sports, physical education, training

tǐyùchǎng 体育场 n stadium, arena

tǐyùguǎn 体育馆 n gymnasium, gym

tì 替 **1** vb substitute for, take the place of, replace **2** prep for, on behalf of

tiān 天 n sky, heaven; God, Heaven; weather; day; season; nature, world of nature; **tiāntiān** 天天 every day

Tiān'ānmén 天安门 n Tian An Men, the Gate of Heavenly Peace

tiāncái 天才 n talent, gift, genius

Tiānjīn 天津 n Tianjin (City)

tiānkōng 天空 n the sky, the heavens

tiānqì 天气 n weather

tiānrán 天然 adj natural

tiānxià 天下 **1** n all under heaven, the whole world, the whole of China **2** adv everywhere under heaven, all over the world, all over China

tiānzhēn 天真 adj innocent, naive, pure

tiān 添 vb add, supplement with, replenish

tián 田 n farm, field

tiányě 田野 n field, open country

tián 甜 *adj* (in flavour, love, dreams, music) sweet; (when referring to sleep) sound

tián 填 *vb* (a hole, a blank space) fill up, fill in

tiāo 挑 *vb* **!** Can also be pronounced tiǎo with a different meaning; choose, select; (with a pole on the shoulders) carry; tiāo shuǐ 挑水 carry water; (as heavy responsibilities) shoulder, carry

tiáo 条 **1** *mw* ▶ **213** (for long, narrow things); (for items of news, laws, ideas, views); (for limbs of the human body); (for human lives) four lives sìtiáo rénmìng 四条人命 **2** *n* strip, slip; slip of paper, short note, message; (in a treaty, constitution, law, contract, or other written document) item, clause, article

tiáojiàn 条件 *n* (of an agreement) condition, term, stipulation; requirement, qualification, condition

tiáoyuē 条约 *n* treaty, agreement, pact

tiáo 调 *vb* ▶ See also **diào** 调. mix, adjust, mediate

tiáopí 调皮 *adj* naughty, mischievous, unruly

tiáozhěng 调整 **1** *vb* adjust, reorganize, revise **2** *n* adjustment, revision

tiǎozhàn 挑战 *n* **!** The character tiǎo 挑 can also be pronounced tiāo with a different meaning. **1** *vb* challenge, challenge to a contest, challenge to battle **2** *n* challenge

tiào 跳 *vb* jump, hop, leap; (as a heart, etc.) beat; skip, skip over, miss out

tiàowǔ 跳舞 *vb* dance

tiē 贴 *vb* paste, stick on; stay next to, nestle close to

tiě 铁 *n* iron

tiělù 铁路, **tiědào** 铁道 *n* railway, railroad

tīng 厅 *n* hall; office, department

tīng 听 *vb* listen to, hear; obey, heed; allow, let

tīnghuà 听话 *adj* obedient

tīngjian 听见 *vb* hear, perceive by hearing

tīngjiǎng 听讲 *vb* listen to a talk, attend a lecture

tīngshuō 听说 *vb* hear, it is said, hear it said that

tīngxiě 听写 *vb* dictate **2** *n* dictation

tíng 停 *vb* stop, cease, halt; stay, stop over; (*of cars*) park; (*of ships*) anchor, lie at anchor

tíngzhǐ 停止 *vb* stop, cease

tǐng 挺 *adv* rather, quite, very

tōng 通 **1** *vb* go through, pass through; communicate with, get through; **wǒ cháng hé tā tōngxìn** 我常和他通信 I often communicate with him by letter; lead to, go to **2** *adj* open, passable; (*of writing, arguments*) logical, coherent, grammatical **3** *n* authority, expert; **Zhōngguó tōng** 中国通 China expert, old China hand

tōngcháng 通常 **1** *adv* usually, normally, generally **2** *adj* usual, normal, general

tōngguò 通过 **1** *prep* by means of, by way of, via **2** *vb* pass through; (*by voting*) pass, carry, adopt

tōngxùn 通讯 *n* communication; news report, news despatch, newsletter

tōngzhī 通知 **1** *vb* notify, inform **2** *n* notice, notification

tóng 同 **1** *adj* same, identical, similar **2** *adv* together, in the same way **3** *prep* with

tóngbàn 同伴 *n* companion

tóngqíng 同情 **1** *vb* sympathize with, be sympathetic toward, share feelings with **2** *n* sympathy, compassion

tóngshí 同时 *adv* at the same time, simultaneously, meanwhile; moreover, besides

tóngshì 同事 *n* colleague, fellow worker

tóngwū 同屋 *n* roommate

tóngxué 同学 *n* classmate, schoolmate, fellow student

tóngyàng 同样 **1** *adj* same, alike, similar **2** *adv* in the same way, equally

tóngyì 同意 *vb* agree

tóngzhì 同志 *n* comrade

tóng 铜 *n* copper, bronze, brass

tóngnián 童年 *n* childhood

tǒngjì 统计 **1** *n* statistics **2** *vb* count, add up

tǒngyī 统一 **1** *vb* unify, unite **2** *adj* unified

tǒngzhì 统治 *vb* control, rule, govern

tǒng 桶 *n* bucket, barrel, keg

tòng 痛 **1** *vb* hurt, ache, pain **2** *n* pain, sorrow **3** *adv* thoroughly, extremely, deeply; (*when speaking of unpleasant actions*) severely, bitterly

tòngkǔ 痛苦 **1** *adj* bitter, painful **2** *n* suffering, agony, pain

tòngkuài 痛快 **1** *adj* happy, delighted, refreshed; frank, outspoken, forthright **2** *adv* frankly, outspokenly; to one's heart's content, with abandon, to one's great satisfaction

tōu 偷 **1** *vb* steal, attack **2** *adv* stealthily, secretly, illegally

tōutōu 偷偷 *adv* stealthily, secretly, on the sly

tóu 头 **1** *n* head; top, beginning; terminus, end; chief, head **2** *mw* ▶ **213** (*for certain animals*); (*for garlic bulbs*) **3** *adj* first, leading, the first

tóufa 头发 *n* (*on a person's head*) hair

tóunǎo 头脑 *n* brains, mind

tóu 投 *vb* throw in/at, put in, drop; (*when voting*) cast; (*when talking about suicide, in a river, sea, etc.*) throw oneself into

tóurù 投入 *vb* throw into, put into

tóuxiáng 投降 *vb* surrender, capitulate

tóuzī 投资 **1** *vb* invest **2** *n* investment

tòu 透 **1** *vb* penetrate, pass through, seep through **2** *adj* thorough, complete **3** *adv* fully, thoroughly, completely

tūchū 突出 **1** vb stress, highlight, give prominence to **2** adj protruding, projecting; prominent, outstanding **3** adv conspicuously

tūjī 突击 **1** vb attack suddenly, assault, take by surprise; attack a job to get it done, go all out to finish a task **2** n attack, sudden attack

tūrán 突然 **1** adj sudden, abrupt, unexpected **2** adv suddenly, abruptly

tú 图 n picture, map, diagram; plan, scheme **2** vb seek, pursue

túshūguǎn 图书馆 n library

tú 涂 vb smear, spread on, apply; scribble, scrawl, disfigure by marking; delete, blot out, cross out

tǔ 土 **1** n earth, soil, dust; land, territory, ground **2** adj local, native, locally produced; earthen, made of earth; rustic, crude, unenlightened

tǔdì 土地 n land, territory

tǔdòu 土豆 n potato

tǔ 吐 vb ▶ See also **tù** 吐. spit, spit out; (as in releasing one's emotions) speak out, pour out, say

tù 吐 vb ▶ See also **tǔ** 吐. vomit, disgorge, regurgitate

tùzi 兔子 n rabbit, hare

tuán 团 **1** n group of people, organization; lump, round mass **2** mw ▶**213** (for certain round things) **3** vb unite, round up

tuánjié 团结 **1** vb unite, band together, rally **2** n unity

tuántǐ 团体 n organization, group, team

tuányuán 团圆 n (of a family) reunion

tuī 推 vb push, shove; push forward, promote, advance; promote, elect, recommend; (as a responsibility) decline, refuse, shirk; put off, postpone

tuīchí 推迟 vb put off, postpone, defer

tuīdòng 推动 vb prod, promote, push forward

tuīguǎng 推广 *vb* spread, extend; promote, popularise

tuījiàn 推荐 **1** *vb* recommend **2** *n* recommendation

tuǐ 腿 *n* leg, thigh

tuì 退 *vb* retreat, withdraw, step back; return, give back; decline, recede, subside; resign, quit, retire; cancel, break off, quit

tuìbù 退步 **1** *vb* regress, slip back, fall behind **2** *n* retrogression

tuìxiū 退休 **1** *vb* retire (from work)

tuō 托 *vb* (on the palm of one's hand) support from underneath, hold up, hold; entrust, rely on; make excuses, give as a pretext **2** *n* tray, stand

tuō'érsuǒ 托儿所 *n* nursery, child-care centre

tuō 拖 *vb* pull, haul, drag; procrastinate, delay

tuō 脱 *vb* (when talking about clothes, shoes, etc.) take off, remove, cast off; (when talking about difficult situations, danger, etc.) free oneself from, get away from, escape from

tuōlí 脱离 *vb* leave, break away from, escape from; separate from, divorce, break off

tuǒdàng 妥当 **1** *adj* proper, appropriate **2** *adv* properly, appropriately

Ww

wā 挖 *vb* dig, excavate

wàzi 袜子 *n* socks

wāi 歪 *adj* crooked, askew, awry; devious, dishonest, immoral

wài 外 **1** *n* out, outside; foreign country/countries; **duì wài màoyì** 对外贸易 foreign trade **2** *adj* outside, other; foreign, external; (referring to relatives of one's mother, sister, or daughter) **wài zǔfù** 外祖父 maternal grandfather **3** prep out of, outside, beyond

wàibian 外边 n outside, out

wàidì 外地 n (beyond one's home area or place of residence) outside area, external region, other parts of the country

wàiguó 外国 n foreign country; **wàiguórén** 外国人 foreigner

wàihuì 外汇 n foreign currency, foreign exchange

wàijiāo 外交 n foreign affairs, diplomacy; **Wàijiāobù** 外交部 Ministry of Foreign Affairs

wàikē 外科 n surgical department

wàimian 外面 ▶ **wàibian** 外边

wàitou 外头 ▶ **wàibian** 外边

wàiwén 外文 n (referring primarily to a written language) foreign language

wàiyǔ 外语 n (referring primarily to a spoken language) foreign language

wān 弯 **1** vb bend, flex **2** n bend, curve, corner; **guǎi wānr** 拐弯儿 go round a bend, turn a corner **3** adj bent, curved, crooked

wán 完 vb finish, complete; (after a verb to indicate completing an action) finish..., use up, run out of; **wǒ chīwán le** 我吃完了 I've finished eating

wánchéng 完成 vb complete, finish, accomplish

wánquán 完全 **1** adj complete, whole **2** adv completely, fully

wánzhěng 完整 **1** adj complete, perfect, whole **2** n wholeness, integrity

wánjù 玩具 n toy, plaything

wánr 玩儿 vb play, play with, have fun; (for sports and other recreational activities) play, engage in

wánxiào 玩笑 *n* joke, jest; (gēn mǒurén) kāi wánxiào (跟某人)开玩笑 play a joke (on someone)

wǎn 晚 **1** *adj* late, late in the day, late in life **2** *adv* late **3** *n* evening, night

wǎnfàn 晚饭 *n* supper, dinner

wǎnhuì 晚会 *n* evening party, soirée

wǎnshang 晚上 *n* evening, night, night time

wǎn 碗 *n* bowl

wàn 万 *num* ten thousand; a very great number

wànsuì 万岁 *vb* long live...!

wànyī 万一 **1** *conj* just in case, if by any chance **2** *n* contingency, eventuality

wǎng 网 *n* net, web, network

wǎngqiú 网球 *n* tennis; tennis ball

wǎng 往 ▶ See also **wàng** 往. **1** *vb* go **2** *adj* past, previous **3** *prep* towards, in the direction of

wǎngwǎng 往往 *adv* often, frequently

wàng 忘, **wàngjì** 忘记 *vb* forget

wàng 往 *prep* ▶ See also **wǎng** 往. to, towards, in the direction of

wàng 望 *vb* look up, gaze; hope, expect

wēihài 危害 **1** *vb* endanger, harm, damage **2** *n* danger, harm

wēijī 危机 *n* crisis

wēixiǎn 危险 **1** *adj* dangerous, critical **2** *n* danger

wēixiào 微笑 **1** *vb* smile (slightly) **2** *n* (slight) smile

wéi 为 ▶ See also **wèi** 为. **1** *vb* be, equal; do, act; act as, serve as **2** *prep* (used with suǒ 所 in passive sentences) by; wéi rénmín suǒ hèn 为人民所恨 be hated by the people

wéinán 为难 **1** *adj* embarrassed, awkward **2** *vb* make things difficult for

wéifǎn 违反 *vb* violate, go against

wéi 围 *vb* surround, enclose

wéijīn 围巾 *n* scarf

wéirào 围绕 *vb* surround, circulate, revolve around

wéiyī 唯一, **wéiyī** 惟一 *adj* only, sole

wéihù 维护 *vb* protect, guard, defend

wěidà 伟大 *adj* great, remarkable

wěi 尾 *n* tail, end

wěiba 尾巴 *n* ! *This word is sometimes pronounced* yǐba; tail

wěiyuán 委员 *n* committee member, designated/appointed official

wèishēng 卫生 **1** *adj* clean, good for health, hygienic **2** *n* sanitation, health, hygiene

wèixīng 卫星 *n* satellite

wèi 为 *prep* ▶ *See also* **wéi** 为. (*indicating who will benefit*) for, on account of, for the sake of; **wèi tā mǔqīn mǎi yào** 为她母亲买药 buy medicine for her mother; (*indicating the reason or purpose for an action*) for the sake of, out of concern for, in order to; **wèi shěng qián** 为省钱 in order to save money; **wèi...ér...** 为...而... ...for the sake of...; **wèi hépíng ér fèndòu** 为和平而奋斗 struggle for peace

wèile 为了 *prep* for the sake of, for the purpose of, in order to

wèishénme 为什么 *adv* why, for what reason

wèi 未 *adv* not, not yet

wèilái 未来 *n* future, time to come

wèi 位 *mw* ▶ **213** (*a polite measure word for people*)

wèiyú 位于 *vb* be situated in, be located in, lie in

wèizhi 位置 *n* position, place, post

wèizi 位子 *n* seat, place

wèi(dao) 味(道) *n* flavour, taste

wèi 胃 *n* stomach

wèi 喂 **1** *vb* (when talking about a person or animal) feed, give food to **2** *exc* (as a greeting or to attract attention) hello!, hey!

wēndù 温度 *n* temperature

wēnnuǎn 温暖 *adj* warm

wénhuà 文化 *n* civilisation, culture; education, schooling, literacy

wénjiàn 文件 *n* document, paper

wénkē 文科 *n* (a branch of learning) liberal arts

wénmíng 文明 **1** *n* civilisation, culture, enlightenment **2** *adj* enlightened, civilised

wénwù 文物 *n* relic, antique

wénxué 文学 *n* literature; **wénxuéjiā** 文学家 writer of literary works

wényì 文艺 *n* literature and the arts, art and literature

wénzhāng 文章 *n* essay, article, literary composition

wénzì 文字 *n* written language, characters, script

wén 闻 *vb* hear; smell

wénmíng 闻名 *adj* well-known, famous, renowned

wénzi 蚊子 *n* mosquito

wěn 稳 *adj* stable, steady, sure

wěndìng 稳定 **1** *adj* firm, stable **2** *vb* stabilize

wèn 问 *vb* ask, inquire, question

wènhǎo 问好 *vb* send one's regards to, ask after; **xiàng tāmen wènhǎo** 向他们问好 send my regards to them

wènhòu 问候 *vb* send one's respects to, extend greetings to

wèntí 问题 *n* question, problem, issue; trouble, mishap; **tāde qìchē chū wèntí le** 他的汽车出问题了 he had trouble with his car; examination question

wǒ 我 *pron* I, me, self

wǒmen 我们 *pron* we, us

wòpù 卧铺 *n* sleeping compartment, berth

wòshì 卧室 *n* bedroom

wò 握 *vb* grasp, hold fast to

wòshǒu 握手 *vb* shake hands, clasp hands

wūrǎn 污染 **1** *vb* pollute, contaminate **2** *n* pollution

wū 屋 *n* house, room

wūzi 屋子 *n* room

wú 无 **1** *vb* have not, there is not **2** *n* nothing, void **3** *adj* no **4** *adv* not

wúliáo 无聊 *adj* boring; bored; silly, stupid, senseless

wúlùn 无论 *conj* no matter what/how, regardless, whether (or not); **wúlùn rúhé** 无论如何 whatever happens, in any case

wúshù 无数 *adj* countless, innumerable

wúsuǒwèi 无所谓 **1** *adj* indifferent **2** *vb* be indifferent, not matter; cannot be taken as, cannot be designated as

wúxiàn 无限 **1** *adj* infinite, boundless, unlimited **2** *adv* infinitely, without bounds

wǔ 五 *num* five

wǔyuè 五月 *n* May

wǔfàn 午饭 *n* lunch, midday meal

wǔqì 武器 *n* weapon, armament, arms

wǔshù 武术 *n* martial arts

wǔ 舞, **wǔdǎo** 舞蹈 *n* dance

wǔtái 舞台 *n* stage, arena

wù 勿 *adv* (when indicating prohibition) not, don't

wù 物 *n* thing, matter

wùjià 物价 *n* price

wùlǐ 物理 *n* physics

wùzhì 物质 **1** *n* matter, material, substance **2** *adj* (*of resources, etc.*) physical, material

wùhuì 误会 **1** *vb* misunderstand **2** *n* misunderstanding

wù 雾 *n* fog, mist

Xx

xī 西 **1** *n* west **2** *adj* west, western

Xībānyá 西班牙 *n* Spain; **Xībānyárén** 西班牙人 Spaniard; **Xībānyáwén** 西班牙文, **Xībānyáyǔ** 西班牙语 (*the language*) Spanish

xīběi 西北 **1** *n* northwest **2** *adj* northwest, northwestern

xībian 西边 *n* western side

xīcān 西餐 *n* Western food

xīfāng 西方 **1** *n* (*a direction*) the west; (*part of the world*) the West **2** *adj* western

xīfú 西服 *n* Western-style clothes

xīguā 西瓜 *n* watermelon

xīhóngshì 西红柿 *n* tomato

xīnán 西南 **1** *n* southwest **2** *adj* southwestern

xīmian 西面 ▶ xībian 西边

xīzhuāng 西装 ▶ xīfú 西服

Xīzàng 西藏 *n* Tibet

xī 吸 *vb* inhale, breathe; attract, absorb

xīshōu 吸收 *vb* absorb, take in, assimilate; recruit, enrol, admit

xīyān 吸烟 *vb* smoke cigarettes, smoke

xīyǐn 吸引 *vb* attract, draw

xīwàng 希望 **1** vb hope, wish **2** n hope, expectation

xīshēng 牺牲 vb sacrifice

xíguàn 习惯 **1** n habit, custom **2** vb be accustomed to, get used to

xǐ 洗 vb wash, clean

xǐyījī 洗衣机 n washing machine

xǐzǎo 洗澡 vb have a bath/shower

xǐ 喜 **1** adj happy, pleased, delighted **2** n happiness, happy event

xǐhuan 喜欢 vb be pleased with, like, prefer; **tā xǐhuan kàn shū** 他喜欢看书 he likes to read

xì 戏 n play, opera, drama

xìjù 戏剧 n play, drama

xì 系 n department in a university/college, faculty

xìtǒng 系统 n system

xì 细 **1** adj fine, thin, delicate; careful, meticulous, detailed **2** adv attentively, carefully, in detail

xìjūn 细菌 n bacteria, germs

xìxīn 细心 **1** adj attentive, careful, meticulous **2** adv attentively, with concentration

xiā 虾 n shrimp; **duìxiā** 对虾 prawn

xiā 瞎 adj blind

xià 下 **1** vb descend, go down from, get off; (when referring to weather) fall; **xià** [**yǔ** | **xuě** | **báozi**] **le** 下 [雨 | 雪 | 雹子] 了 it is [raining | snowing | hailing]; (as an order) issue, give, proclaim; (in making or sending down a decision) decide, determine; **xià** [**juéxīn** | **jiélùn** | **dìngyì**] 下 [决心 | 结论 | 定义] [make up one's mind | draw a conclusion | give a definition]; (when speaking of animals or eggs) give birth to, lay **2** adv (after a verb to indicate downward movement) down; **zuòxia** 坐下 sit down; (after a verb to indicate having space for something) **zhèlǐ fàng bú xia** 这里放不下 there's no room to put (it) here; (after a verb to indicate completion or result) **dìngxia kāihuì de shíjiān** 定下开会的时间 fix a time for the meeting **3** adj next; **xiàge yuè** 下个月 next month; lower, inferior **4** prep under, below; **chuáng xià** 床下 under the bed **5** mw ▶213 (for brief actions) time

xiàbān 下班 vb go off duty, get out of work

xiàbian 下边 **1** n the bottom, below **2** adj next, following **3** prep below, under, underneath

xiàkè 下课 vb class is over, dismiss class

xiàlai 下来 vb come down; (after a verb to indicate downward movement) **tiàoxiàlai** 跳下来 jump down; (after a verb to indicate movement away) **bǎ yǎnjìng zhāixiàlai** 把眼镜摘下来 take off your glasses; (after a verb to indicate completion or result of an action) **wǒ bǎ nǐde dìzhǐ jìxiàlai le** 我把你的地址记下来了 I noted down your address

xiàmian 下面 ▶ **xiàbian** 下边

xiàqu 下去 vb go down, descend; (when referring to the future) continue, go on; (used after a verb to express the continuation of an action) **shuōxiàqu** 说下去 keep on speaking

xiàtou 下头 ▶ **xiàbian** 下边

xiàwǔ 下午 n afternoon, p.m.

xià 吓 vb frighten, scare; be frightened; intimidate, threaten

xiàtiān 夏天 n summer, summer season

xiān 先 adv first, before, in advance; **xiān...zài...** 先...再... first...and then...; **xiān chīfàn zài xiūxi** 先吃饭再休息 first eat, then rest; **xiān...cái...** 先...才... not...until..., must first...before...; **nǐ děi xiān gěi wǒ jiěshì yíxià, wǒ cái néng qù bàn** 你得先给我解释一下，我才能去办 I can't do it until you explain it to me

xiānhòu 先后 **1** n order of precedence, priority **2** adv successively, one after another

xiānjìn 先进 adj (as in techniques, experience, etc.) advanced

xiānsheng 先生 n Mr.; husband; (courteous address to scholars, elders) sir

xiānwéi 纤维 *n* fibre, fibrous tissue

xiān 掀 *vb (as a cover, etc.)* raise, lift

xiān 鲜 *adj (as in food or air)* fresh; tasty, delicious; bright, colourful

xiānhuā 鲜花 *n* fresh flowers

xián 闲 **1** *adj (as a person, a room, etc.)* idle, unoccupied, free; *(when referring to time)* free, leisure **2** *adv* leisurely, freely

xiǎnde 显得 *vb* appear, seem

xiǎnrán 显然 **1** *adj* obvious, clear **2** *adv* obviously, evidently, clearly

xiǎnshì 显示 *vb* display, show, manifest

xiǎnzhù 显著 *adj* distinct, prominent, marked

xiàn 县 *n* district, county

xiàndài 现代 **1** *n* contemporary era, modern age **2** *adj* modern, contemporary

xiàndàihuà 现代化 **1** *adj* modernized **2** *n* modernization

xiànshí 现实 **1** *n* reality **2** *adj* practical, realistic; **xiànshí zhǔyì** 现实主义 realism

xiànxiàng 现象 *n* phenomenon

xiànzài 现在 **1** *n* present, now **2** *adv* now, at present, currently

xiànzhì 限制 **1** *vb* control, restrict, limit **2** *n* control, restriction, limit

xiàn 线 *n* thread, string, wire; line

xiànmù 羡慕 *vb* admire; envy

xiàn 献 *vb* offer up, present; donate, dedicate

xiāng 乡 *n* country, countryside, village; native place, home

xiāngxia 乡下 *n* country, countryside, village

xiāng 相 *adv* ! Can also be pronounced xiàng *with a different meaning*; mutually, reciprocally, each other

xiāngdāng 相当 **1** *adj* suitable, appropriate **2** *adv* fairly, quite, rather

xiāngfǎn 相反 **1** *adj* opposite, contrary **2** *adv* on the contrary

xiānghù 相互 **1** *adj* mutual, reciprocal **2** *adv* mutually, each other

xiāngsì 相似 **1** *adj* similar to, like **2** *vb* resemble, be alike

xiāngtóng 相同 *adj* alike, the same, similar

xiāngxìn 相信 *vb* believe, believe in, trust

xiāng 香 **1** *adj* (*of flowers, etc.*) fragrant, scented, pleasant smelling; (*of food*) delicious, appetizing **2** *n* fragrance, aroma; perfume, incense, joss stick

xiāngcháng 香肠 *n* sausage

Xiānggǎng 香港 *n* Hong Kong

xiāngjiāo 香蕉 *n* banana

xiāngzào 香皂 *n* perfumed soap, toilet soap

xiāngzi 箱子 *n* trunk, box, case

xiángxì 详细 **1** *adj* careful, meticulous, in detail **2** *adv* carefully, thoroughly, meticulously

xiǎngshòu 享受 **1** *vb* enjoy **2** *n* enjoyment

xiǎng 响 **1** *adj* (*as a sound or noise*) loud, noisy **2** *vb* make a sound **3** *n* sound, noise

xiǎngyìng 响应 **1** *vb* respond, answer **2** *n* response, answer

xiǎng 想 *vb* think, consider, ponder; think about, miss, long for; want to, intend to, plan to

xiǎngfa 想法 *n* viewpoint, opinion, way of thinking

xiǎngniàn 想念 *vb* remember, long for, miss

xiǎngxiàng 想象 **1** *vb* imagine **2** *n* imagination

xiàng 向 **1** *prep* towards, facing **2** *vb* face; incline towards, side with **3** *n* direction, trend

xiàng 巷 *n* lane, alley

xiàngpiàn 相片 *n* photograph, picture

xiàng 项 *mw* ▶ 213 (for work, projects, tasks, requirements, etc.); (for decisions or announcements)

xiàngmù 项目 *n* item, project

xiàng 象 1 *n* elephant 2 *vb* be like, look as if

xiàngzhēng 象征 1 *n* symbol, emblem 2 *vb* symbolize, signify, stand for

xiàng 像 1 *vb* be like, resemble, look like 2 *adj* similar, alike 3 *n* portrait, picture, image; **xiàng...yíyàng/yìbān** 像...一样/一般 resemble..., be like...

xiàngpí 橡皮 *n* rubber, eraser

xiāofèi 消费 *vb* consume; **xiāofèipǐn** 消费品 consumer goods

xiāohuà 消化 1 *vb* digest 2 *n* digestion

xiāomiè 消灭 *vb* wipe out, extinguish, destroy

xiāoshī 消失 *vb* vanish, disappear

xiāoxi 消息 *n* news, information

xiǎo 小 *adj* small, little; young; unimportant, trifling

xiǎochī 小吃 *n* snack, refreshments

xiǎoháir 小孩儿 *n* child, children

xiǎohuǒzi 小伙子 *n* young man, lad

xiǎojie 小姐 *n* young lady, Miss, daughter

xiǎomài 小麦 *n* wheat

xiǎomàibù 小卖部 *n* small shop, snack bar

xiǎopéngyǒu 小朋友 *n* child, children

xiǎoqì 小气 *adj* mean, stingy, petty

xiǎoshí 小时 *n* hour

xiǎoshuō 小说 *n* fiction, short story, novel

xiǎotōu 小偷 *n* petty thief, sneak thief, pilferer

xiǎoxīn 小心 **1** *adj* careful, cautious **2** *vb* be careful, look out, take care

xiǎoxué 小学 *n* elementary/primary school

xiǎozǔ 小组 *n* group

xiǎode 晓得 *vb* know

xiàoyuán 校园 *n* school yard, campus

xiàozhǎng 校长 *n* (*of a school, college, or university*) headmaster, principal, president

xiào 笑 *vb* smile, laugh; laugh at, make fun of, ridicule

xiàohua 笑话 **1** *n* joke, funny story **2** *vb* laugh at, ridicule, make fun of

xiàoguǒ 效果 *n* effect, result

xiàolǜ 效率 *n* efficiency

xiē 些 **1** *det* some, a few; **ná xiē shuǐguǒ lái** 拿些水果来 bring some fruit **2** *adv* a little, a bit

xiē 歇 *vb* rest, have a rest

xiéhuì 协会 *n* association, society

xié 斜 *adj* slanting, inclined, askew

xié 鞋 *n* shoes; **xiézi** 鞋子 shoes

xiě 写 *vb* write, compose

xiězuò 写作 *n* writing

xiě 血 ▶ **xuè** 血

xièxie 谢谢 *vb* thank you, thanks

xīn 心 *n* heart; mind, feeling; middle, centre

xīndé 心得 *n* insight, understanding

xīnqíng 心情 *n* feelings, mood, state of mind

xīnzàng 心脏 *n* (*the organ in the body*) heart; **xīnzàng bìng** 心脏病 heart disease

xīnkǔ 辛苦 **1** *adj* laborious, hard, hard-working **2** *adv* with great difficulty and effort, laboriously **3** *vb* work very hard, undergo many hardships, take trouble **4** *n* hardship, laborious work

xīnshǎng 欣赏 *vb* enjoy, appreciate

xīn 新 **1** *adj* new, fresh, recent; up-to-date, modern **2** *adv* newly, recently, freshly

xīnláng 新郎 *n* bridegroom

xīnnián 新年 *n* New Year

xīnniáng 新娘 *n* bride

xīnwén 新闻 *vb* news; **xīnwénjiè** 新闻界 the press

xīnxiān 新鲜 *adj* fresh, new

xìn 信 **1** *n* letter, mail, correspondence; message, information **2** *vb* believe, believe in

xìnfēng 信封 *n* envelope

xìnrèn 信任 **1** *n* trust, confidence **2** *vb* trust, have confidence in

xìnxī 信息 *n* information, news, message

xìnxīn 信心 *n* confidence, faith

xīngfèn 兴奋 *adj* excited

xīngqī 星期 *n* week; **xīngqī** [yī | èr | sān | sì | wǔ | liù] 星期[一 | 二 | 三 | 四 | 五 | 六] [Monday | Tuesday | Wednesday | Thursday | Friday | Saturday]

xīngqīrì 星期日, **xīngqītiān** 星期天 *n* Sunday

xīngxing 星星 *n* star

xíng 行 ! *Can also be pronounced* háng *with a different meaning.* **1** *vb* go, walk, travel; do, carry out, practise **2** *adj* satisfactory, all right, OK; **zhèyàng zuò xíng bù xíng?** 这样做行不行? is it all right to do (it) this way?; capable, proficient, competent **3** *n* trip, journey; conduct, behaviour, actions

xíngdòng 行动 **1** *vb* move, act, take action **2** *n* movement, physical movement, action

xíngli 行李 *n* luggage, baggage

xíngrén 行人 *n* pedestrian

xíngshǐ 行驶 *vb* (when talking about buses, trains, ships, etc.) travel, go, run

xíngwéi 行为 *n* behaviour, action, conduct

xíngchéng 形成 *vb* take shape, take form, form into; develop, evolve, form

xíngróng 形容 *vb* describe

xíngshì 形式 *n* form

xíngshì 形势 *n* situation, circumstances; terrain, lie of the land

xíngxiàng 形象 *n* form, appearance, image

xíngzhuàng 形状 *n* shape, form, appearance

xǐng 醒 *vb* wake up, awaken, be awakened; regain consciousness, sober up

xìngqù 兴趣 *n* interest, interest in; tā duì lìshǐ yǒu/gǎn xìngqù 她对历史有/感兴趣 she is interested in history

xìngfú 幸福 **1** *adj* happy **2** *n* happiness, well-being

xìnghǎo 幸好 ▶xìngkuī 幸亏

xìngkuī 幸亏 *adv* fortunately, luckily

xìngyùn 幸运 **1** *adj* fortunate, lucky **2** *n* good luck, good fortune

xìng 性 *n* quality, nature, character; (used at the end of many words to make them nouns) -ity, -ness; kěnéngxìng 可能性 probability; chuàngzàoxìng 创造性 creativity; sex, gender; [nán | nǚ] xìng [男 | 女] 性 the [male | female] sex

xìngbié 性别 *n* sex, gender

xìnggé 性格 *n* personality, character, temperament

xìngzhì 性质 *n* quality, nature

xìng 姓 **1** *vb* be surnamed; tā xìng Zhào 他姓赵 his surname is Zhao **2** *n* surname, family name

xìngmíng 姓名 *n* surname and given name, full name

xiōngdì 兄弟 *n* brothers; **xiōngdì jiěmèi** 兄弟姐妹 brothers and sisters, siblings

xiōng 胸 *n* chest, thorax, breast

xióng 雄 *adj* (when referring to animals) male; (in reference to humans) strong, powerful, virile

xióngwěi 雄伟 *adj* magnificent, imposing, grand

xióng 熊 *n* bear

xióngmāo 熊猫 *n* panda

xiūxi 休息 *vb* rest, take a rest

xiū 修 *vb* repair, mend, maintain; build, construct; study, cultivate a knowledge of

xiūgǎi 修改 1 *vb* correct, revise, amend 2 *n* revision, modification

xiūlǐ 修理 *vb* repair, mend

xiù(zi) 袖(子) *n* sleeve

xūxīn 虚心 1 *adj* humble, modest 2 *adv* humbly, with humility

xūyào 需要 1 *vb* need, require 2 *n* need, demand

xǔ 许 *vb* allow, permit, give consent; promise, pledge

xǔduō 许多 *det* a lot of, many, much

xùshù 叙述 *vb* narrate, recount

xuānbù 宣布 1 *vb* declare, proclaim 2 *n* declaration, proclamation

xuānchuán 宣传 1 *vb* propagate, propagandize 2 *n* propaganda, dissemination

xuǎn 选 1 *vb* choose, select; elect 2 *n* selection, election

xuǎnjǔ 选举 1 *vb* elect, vote 2 *n* election; **xuǎnjǔ quán** 选举权 the right to vote

xuǎnzé 选择 1 *vb* choose, pick out, select 2 *n* selection, choice

xué 学 1 *vb* study, learn; imitate 2 *n* school, institution of learning, level of schooling; [xiǎo | zhōng | dà] xué [小 | 中 | 大] 学 [primary or elementary school | secondary or high school | college or university]; *(added to fields of study, similar to the English ending* -ology) study of, field of: [wén | shù | rénlèi] xué [文 | 数 | 人类] 学 [literature | mathematics | anthropology]; learning, knowledge

xuéfèi 学费 *n* school fees, tuition

xuéqī 学期 *n* term, semester

xuésheng 学生 *n* student, pupil

xuéshù 学术 1 *n* learning, scholarship, academic research 2 *adj* academic, learned; **xuéshùjiè** 学术界 academic circles

xuéwen 学问 *n* scholarship, learning

xuéxí 学习 *vb* study, learn

xuéxiào 学校 *n* school

xuéyuàn 学院 *n* academic institution, college, institute

xuézhě 学者 *n* scholar, learned person

xuě 雪 *n* snow; **xià xuě le** 下雪了 it's snowing

xuěhuā 雪花 *n* snowflake

xuè 血 ! *Can also be pronounced* xiě; blood

xuèyè 血液 *n* blood

xúnzhǎo 寻找 *vb* look for, seek, search for

xúnwèn 询问 *vb* inquire, ask about

xùnliàn 训练 *vb* instruct, train, drill

xùnsù 迅速 1 *adj* fast, rapid 2 *adv* fast, rapidly, at high speed

Yy

yā 压 **1** vb press down, apply pressure, crush; (when speaking of emotions, disorder, rebellion, etc.) control, suppress **2** n pressure

yālì 压力 n pressure

yāpò 压迫 **1** vb oppress, repress, constrict **2** n oppression, repression

yā 呀 exc ! Can also be pronounced ya 呀 in a neutral tone with a different meaning; (indicating surprise) ah! oh!

yā(zi) 鸭(子) n duck

yá 牙 n tooth, teeth

yáshuā 牙刷 n toothbrush

Yàzhōu 亚洲 n Asia

yān 烟 n smoke; cigarette, tobacco

yángé 严格 **1** adj stern, strict, rigorous **2** adv strictly, rigidly

yánsù 严肃 adj solemn, serious, earnest

yánzhòng 严重 adj (when talking about a situation, a condition, health, etc.) serious, grave, critical

yáncháng 延长 **1** vb extend, prolong, lengthen **2** n prolongation, extension

yán 沿 prep along, alongside

yánjiū 研究 **1** vb study, do research; (for problems, suggestions, applications) consider, discuss **2** n research, study; **yánjiūhuì** 研究会 research association; **yánjiūshēng** 研究生 research student, postgraduate student; **yánjiūsuǒ** 研究所 research institute; **yánjiūyuán** 研究员 research fellow; **yánjiūyuàn** 研究院 research institute, academy

yán 盐 n salt

yánsè 颜色 *n* colour

yǎn 眼 *n* eye; hole, opening

yǎnjing 眼睛 *n* eye, eyes

yǎnjìng 眼镜 *n* glasses, spectacles

yǎnlèi 眼泪 *n* tears

yǎnqián 眼前 *adv* in front of one's eyes, before one's eyes; at the present moment, momentarily

yǎn 演 *vb* (*when speaking of a play, film, show*) perform, act, show

yǎnchū 演出 **1** *vb* (*when talking about a play, film, show*) perform, show, put on **2** *n* performance, production

yǎnyuán 演员 *n* actor, actress, performer

yàn 咽 *vb* swallow

yànhuì 宴会 *n* banquet, feast

yáng 羊 *n* sheep, goat

yángròu 羊肉 *n* mutton, lamb

yángguāng 阳光 *n* sunlight, sunshine

yǎng 仰 *vb* look up, face upward; look up to, admire, respect

yǎng 养 **1** *vb* (*as dependents*) nurture, support, provide for; (*as animals, flowers, etc.*) raise, keep, grow; give birth to **2** *adj* (*as a foster parent, etc.*) foster

yàng 样 **1** *mw* ▶213 (*for things in general*) kind, sort, type **2** *n* way, manner; form, appearance, shape; pattern, model, sample

yàngzi 样子 *n* form, appearance, shape; pattern, sample, model; (*describing how something or someone looks*) **tā xiàng shì bìngle de yàngzi** 她象是病了的样子 she has the appearance of being ill; manner, air

yāoqiú 要求 ! *The word yāo 要 can also be pronounced yào with a different meaning.* **1** *vb* demand, request, ask for **2** *n* demand, request, need

yāo 腰 *n* (*of a person or a garment*) waist; (*of a person*) back, small of the back

yāoqǐng 邀请 **1** vb (formal word) invite **2** n invitation

yáo 摇 vb shake, wag, wave; sway back and forth, rock; (when talking about a boat) row; (when talking about a bell) ring

yǎo 咬 vb bite, snap at

yào 药 n medicine, drug, certain chemicals

yào 要 **1** vb want, wish, desire; need, must; (when talking about an amount of time) need, take; **dào Lúndūn qù yào yíge xiǎoshí** 到伦敦去要一个小时 it takes an hour to get to London; demand, request; beg; need to, must, should; **nǐ yào xiǎoxīn** 你要小心 you must be careful; (when talking about what one expects will happen) will, be going to; **tiān kuài yào hēi le** 天快要黑了 it's going to get dark soon **2** conj (short for yàoshi) **yào shi** 要是 if; **nǐ yào bú qù, tā huì hěn shīwàng** 你要不去，她会很失望 if you don't go, she'll be very disappointed **3** adj important

yàobu(rán) 要不(然) conj if not, or else, otherwise

yàobushì 要不是 conj if it were not for, but for

yàojǐn 要紧 adj important; (as an illness) critical, serious

yàoshi 要是 conj if, suppose, in case; **yàoshi...jiù...(le)** 要是... 就... (了) if...then...; **yàoshi kāichē qù jiù kěyǐ fāngbiàn yìxiē** 要是开车去就可以方便一些 if you drive it is slightly more convenient

yàoshi 钥匙 adv (to a lock) key

yéye 爷爷 n paternal grandfather, grandpa; (a polite and respectful way of addressing an old man, used by children) grandpa

yě 也 adv also, too; (indicating concession) still; **nǐ gěi wǒ qián, wǒ yě bú qù** 你给我钱，我也不去 I won't go even if you give me money; **yě bù** 也不 neither, neither; **tā bú huì tán qín, yě bú huì chànggē** 他不会弹琴，也不会唱歌 he can neither play the piano nor sing

yěxǔ 也许 adv maybe, perhaps, possibly

yěcān 野餐 n picnic

yèwù 业务 *n* business affairs, professional work

yèyú 业余 **1** *adj* extracurricular, done outside business hours; **yèyú huódòng** 业余活动 extracurricular activities; amateur **2** *adv* in one's spare time

yèzi 叶子 *n* (of a plant) leaf, leaves

yè 页 *n* (in a book) page, leaf

yè 夜 *n* night, evening

yèli 夜里 *adv* at night, during the night, in the night

yèwǎn 夜晚 *n* night, evening

yī 一 ! *The tone on* yī 一 *changes, depending on the tone of the word that follows it. It is pronounced* yì *before words in first, second, and third tone, but* yí *before the fourth tone. When used to count numbers,* yī 一 *has the first tone. Because the tone changes for* yī 一 *do not indicate any difference in meaning, but only in pronunciation, combinations beginning with* yī 一 *are listed in alphabetical order below, regardless of tone.* ▸**xiii** **1** *num* one **2** *det* a, an; each, per **3** *adj* single, alone, only one; the same, together; whole, all, throughout; **yī yè** the whole night **4** *adv* (indicating a brief action or one taken lightly) briefly; **qǐng nǐ kàn yí kàn** 请你看一看 please take a look **5** *conj* once; as soon as; **tā yí kàn jiù xiào le** 他一看就笑了 he laughed as soon as he saw it; **yī...jiù...** 一...就... as soon as; **yī...yě...** 一...也... (used with the negative particle bù 不 or méi 没) (not) slightly, (not) at all; **tā yíge Hànzì yě bú rènshi** 他一个汉字也不认识 he doesn't know a single Chinese character

yìbān 一般 **1** *adj* alike, the same, just as; general, common, ordinary; so so **2** *adv* the same as, similarly; **yí yàng** **tā hé tā gēge yìbān gāo** 她和她哥哥一般高 she is as tall as her elder brother; generally, in general, ordinarily

yíbàn 一半 *n* half, one-half

yíbèizi 一辈子 **1** *adv* throughout one's life, all one's life **2** *n* lifetime

yìbiān 一边 *n* one side; **yìbiān...yìbiān...** 一边...一边... (indicating two simultaneous actions) at the same time,

simultaneously; **háizimen yìbiān zǒulù, yìbiān chànggē** 孩子们
一边走路，一边唱歌 the children are singing while they are
walking

yídào 一道 *adv* together, side by side, alongside

yìdiǎnr 一点儿 **1** *adv* a bit, a little; **wǒ yìdiǎnr dōu bù zhīdào**
我一点儿都不知道 I have not the faintest idea **2** *pron* a little;
zhǐ shèngxia zhème yìdiǎnr, gòu yòng ma? 只剩下这么一点
儿，够用吗? there's so little left, is it enough for the present
purposes? **3** *det* a little, some; **yìdiǎnr fàn** 一点儿饭 a little rice

yídìng 一定 **1** *adj* certain, given, particular; fixed, definite,
specified; proper, fair, due **2** *adv* certainly, definitely, surely

yì fāngmiàn 一方面 *n* one side

yì fāngmiàn... (lìng) yì fāngmiàn... 一方面...
（另）一方面... *adv* on the one hand...on the other hand...; for
one thing...for another...

yígòng 一共 *adv* altogether, in all, in total

yíhuìr 一会儿 *adv* in a moment, for a little while, shortly;
yíhuìr...yíhuìr... 一会儿...一会儿... one moment..., the next...

yíkuàir 一块儿 *adv* together

yílù 一路 *adv* all the way, on the journey; **yílù píng'ān** 一路
平安 have a pleasant journey, have a good trip; **yílù shùnfēng**
一路顺风 have a pleasant journey, have a good trip

yìqí 一齐 *adv* together, at the same time, sumultaneously

yìqǐ 一起 *adv* together, in the same place

yíqiè 一切 **1** *det* all, every, whole **2** *pron* all, everything, the
whole thing

yìshēng 一生 *n* all one's life, one's whole life

yìshí 一时 *adv* for a period of time; for the moment, for a short
while, temporarily; by chance, accidentally, it just so happened
that; **yìshí...yìshí...** 一时...一时... now... now..., ...one moment
and...the next

yìtóng 一同 *adv* together, at the same time and place

yì tiān dào wǎn 一天到晚 *adv* all day long, from morning till night, from dawn to dusk

yíxià(r) 一下(儿) *adv* (*indicating short duration*) once, a bit, for a short while; (*indicating a sudden change*) all at once, all of a sudden, suddenly

yíxiàzi 一下子 *adv* suddenly, all at once

yìxiē 一些 *det* some, a few, a little

yíyàng 一样 **1** *adj* alike, the same, similar **2** *adv* equally, similarly

yīyuè 一月 *n* January

yìzhí 一直 *adv* continuously, consistently, all the time; straight, straight on; **yìzhí méi...guo** 一直没... 过 have never...

yízhì 一致 **1** *adj* consistent, the same, identical **2** *adv* consistently, unanimously

yīfu 衣服 *n* clothes, clothing, dress

yīguì 衣柜 *n* wardrobe

yīkào 依靠 **1** *vb* depend upon, rely on **2** *n* dependence, support

yīrán 依然 *adv* still, as before

yīzhào 依照 *prep* in accordance with, in the light of

yīshēng 医生 *n* doctor, physician

yīwùshì 医务室, **yīwùsuǒ** 医务所 *n* clinic

yīxué 医学 *n* (*as a field of study*) medicine

yīyuàn 医院 *n* hospital

yíqì 仪器 *n* (*usually for scientific use*) apparatus, equipment, instrument

yí 姨 *n* aunt on one's mother's side, mother's sister

yí 移 *vb* change position, move, shift; change, alter

yídòng 移动 *vb* move, shift

yíhàn 遗憾 **1** *vb* regret **2** *n* regret, pity

yíwèn 疑问 *n* question, doubt, query

yǐ(jīng) 已 (经) *adv* already

yǐ 以 **1** *prep* according to; (*indicating implement, instrument, etc.*) with, using **2** *adv* (*indicating purpose*) in order to, so as to **3** *vb* use, take; take, consider; **yǐ...wéi...** 以... 为... take...as..., consider...as...

yǐbiàn 以便 *conj* in order that, so that, in order to

yǐhòu 以后 **1** *prep* after **2** *adv* later, hereafter, afterwards **3** *conj* after

yǐjí 以及 *conj* and, as well as, along with

yǐlái 以来 *prep* (*sometimes the time-word or cut-off point is preceded by* zì 自 *or* zìcóng 自从, *meaning* from) since, after, until now; (*when it follows a quantity of time*) during the past..., in the past..., for the past...; jǐ qiān nián yǐlái 几千年以来 for several thousand years

yǐnèi 以内 *prep* within, less than

yǐqián 以前 **1** *prep* before, prior to **2** *adv* previously, formerly, ago **3** *conj* before

yǐshàng 以上 **1** *prep* over, above **2** *adv* above

yǐwài 以外 *prep* outside, beyond; (*when used in the pattern* chú(le)...yǐwài, ...dōu... 除 (了)...以外, ...都..) except, except for; chú(le) tā yǐwài, wǒmen dōu bú huì zuò 除了他以外, 我们都不会做 none of us can do it except him; (*when used in the pattern* chú(le)...yǐwài, ...hái... 除(了)...以外, ... 还...) besides, apart from, in addition to; chú(le) Běijīng yǐwài, wǒmen hái qùle Shànghǎi 除了北京以外, 我们还去了上海 apart from Beijing, we also went to Shanghai

yǐwéi 以为 *vb* think, regard, consider; thought, used to think **!** Note that in this use, yǐwéi 以为 means that one originally thought something was true, but later found it to be false.

yǐxià 以下 **1** *prep* below, under **2** *adv* below

yǐzhì 以致 *conj* (*when indicating an unpleasant consequence*) so that, with the result that, consequently

yǐzi 椅子 *n* chair

yì 亿 *num* hundred million, 100,000,000; **shíyì** 十亿 one billion

yìshù 艺术 **1** *n* art; skill, technique, craft **2** *adj* artistic, in good taste; **yìshùpǐn** 艺术品 work of art, art object; **yìshùjiā** 艺术家 artist

yìlùn 议论 **1** *vb* discuss, comment, talk **2** *n* opinion, discussion, comment

yìcháng 异常 **1** *adj* unusual, abnormal, exceptional **2** *adv* unusually, exceedingly, extremely

yìjiàn 意见 *n* idea, opinion, view

yìsi 意思 *n* meaning, idea, theme; opinion, wish, desire; interest, fun; **yǒu yìsi** 有意思 interesting, enjoyable

yìwài 意外 **1** *adj* unexpected, unforeseen, surprising **2** *n* accident, mishap, unexpected development

yìwèizhe 意味着 *vb* signify, mean, imply

yìyì 意义 *n* significance, meaning

yìzhì 意志 *n* will, volition, will power

yīncǐ 因此 *adv* therefore, because of this, for this reason

yīn'ér 因而 *adv* because of this, thus, as a result

yīnsù 因素 *n* element, factor

yīnwèi 因为 *conj* because, since, as

yīn 阴 *adj* cloudy, overcast, shady

yīnyuè 音乐 *n* music; **yīnyuèhuì** 音乐会 concert

yín 银 *n* (the metal or the colour) silver

yínháng 银行 *n* bank

yǐnqǐ 引起 *vb* cause, give rise to, bring about

yǐnliào 饮料 *n* drink, beverage

yìn 印 **1** *vb* print, engrave, replicate **2** *n* imprint, print, mark; stamp, chop, seal

yìnshuā 印刷 *vb* print

yìnxiàng 印象 *n* impression

yīngbàng 英镑 *n* British pound

Yīngguó 英国 *n* Britain, the United Kingdom

Yīngwén 英文 *n* English language (usually written)

yīngxióng 英雄 **1** *n* hero, heroine **2** *adj* heroic

yīngyǒng 英勇 *adj* heroic, brave, valiant

Yīngyǔ 英语 *n* English language (usually spoken)

yīng(dāng) 应(当) *vb* ! The word yīng 应 can also be pronounced yìng with a different meaning; should, ought to

yīnggāi 应该 *vb* should, ought to

yīng'ér 婴儿 *n* baby, infant

yíngjiē 迎接 *vb* welcome, greet, meet

yíngyǎng 营养 *n* nutrition, nourishment

yíngyè 营业 *vb* do business

yíng 赢 *vb* gain, win, beat

yǐngpiàn 影片 *n* film, movie

yǐngxiǎng 影响 **1** *vb* influence, affect; **shòu...yǐngxiǎng** 受...影响 be influenced by... **2** *n* influence

yǐngzi 影子 *n* shadow, reflection

yìngyòng 应用 ! The word yìng 应 can also be pronounced yīng with a different meaning. **1** *vb* apply, use, make use of **2** *adj* applied **3** *n* use, application

yìng 硬 **1** *adj* hard, stiff, tough **2** *adv* by force, stubbornly

yǒngbào 拥抱 *vb* hug, embrace

yǒnghù 拥护 *vb* support, endorse

yǒngjǐ 拥挤 **1** *vb* crowd, push **2** *adj* crowded, packed

yǒngyuǎn 永远 *adv* always, forever

yǒnggǎn 勇敢 *adj* brave, daring, courageous

yǒngqì 勇气 *n* bravery, courage

yòng 用 **1** *vb* use, employ, apply **2** *prep* with, using **3** *n* use, usefulness; [yǒu | méi] yòng [有 | 没] 用 [useful | useless]; **yòng bu zháo** 用不着 no need to, have no use

yòngchu 用处 *n* use, application

yònggōng 用功 *adj* diligent, studious, hard-working

yònglì 用力 **1** *vb* exert one's strength **2** *adv* with all one's strength, with a concentrated effort

yōudiǎn 优点 *n* good point, strong point, merit

yōuliáng 优良 *adj* fine, good

yōuměi 优美 *adj* beautiful, graceful, exquisite

yōuxiù 优秀 *adj* outstanding, excellent

yōujiǔ 悠久 *adj* long, long-standing

yóuqí 尤其 *adv* especially; **yóuqí shì** 尤其是 especially

yóu 由 **1** *prep* from, by, through **2** *vb* follow, obey; let, allow

yóuyú 由于 *prep* because of, due to the fact that, as a result of

yóudìyuán 邮递员 *n* postman, postwoman

yóujú 邮局 *n* post office

yóupiào 邮票 *n* postage stamp

yóuyù 犹豫 **1** *vb* hesitate **2** *adj* hesitant, undecided **3** *n* hesitation

yóu 油 *n* oil, fat, grease

yóuqī 油漆 *n* paint

yóukè 游客 ▶yóurén 游人

yóulǎn 游览 *vb* tour, visit, go sightseeing

yóurén 游人 *n* tourist, sightseer, excursionist

yóuxì 游戏 *n* (for recreation and amusement) game

yóuyǒng 游泳 **1** *vb* swim **2** *n* swimming

yóuyǒngchí 游泳池 *n* swimming pool

yǒuhǎo 友好 *adj* friendly

yǒuyì 友谊 *n* friendship

yǒu 有 **1** *vb* have, possess; there is, there are, exist; (*when making an estimate of age, height, weight, degree, distance, etc.*) be about as much as; **tā yǒu nǐ nàme gāo** 她有你那么高 she is about your height; (*used with a noun to make an adjective*) having..., with...; **yǒu yì** 有意 intentional; have a good deal of, have much; **yǒu xuéwèn** 有学问 learned, knowledgeable; take place, happen, occur; **nàr yǒu hěn dà de biànhuà** 那儿有很大的变化 great changes have taken place there **2** *det* some; **yǒu rén** 有人 some, some people

yǒude 有的 **1** *det* some; **yǒude rén** 有的人 some people **2** *pron* some, some people; **yǒude...yǒude...** 有的..., 有的... some..., others...; **yǒude xǐhuan kāfēi, yǒude xǐhuan chá** 有的喜欢咖啡, 有的喜欢茶 some like coffee, others like tea

yǒu(de) shíhòu 有(的)时候 *adv* sometimes, at times

yǒudeshì 有的是 *vb* have plenty of, there's no lack of; **yǒudeshì shíjiān** 有的是时间 there's plenty of time

yǒu diǎn(r) 有点(儿) **1** *vb* there is a little/some, have a little/some **2** *adv* somewhat, a little, a bit

yǒuguān 有关 **1** *vb* be related to, have something to do with, concern **2** *adj* relevant, concerned

yǒulì 有利 *adj* beneficial, advantageous

yǒulì 有力 *adj* strong, powerful, energetic

yǒumíng 有名 *adj* famous, well-known

yǒuqù 有趣 *adj* interesting, amusing, fascinating

yǒu shí(hòu) 有时(候) ▶ **yǒu(de) shíhòu** 有(的)时候

yǒuxiàn 有限 *adj* limited

yǒuxiào 有效 *adj* effective, efficient, valid

yǒuxiē 有些 **1** *pron* some, a few, several **2** *det* some, a few, several

yǒu yìdiǎn(r) 有一点(儿) ▶ **yǒu diǎn(r)** 有点(儿)

yǒu yìsi 有意思 *adj* interesting, enjoyable, meaningful

yǒu yòng 有用 *adj* useful

yòu 又 *adv* also, in addition; again; however; **wǒ xiǎng gěi tā xiě xìn, kě yòu bù zhīdào tāde dìzhǐ** 我想给她写信, 可又不知道她的地址 I want to write her a letter but I don't know her address; **yòu...yòu...** 又... 又... both...and..., on the one hand... on the other...

yòu 右 **1** *n* right, the right-hand side, the right; (*when speaking of politics*) right-wing **2** *adj* right, right-hand

yòubian 右边 *n* right-hand side, right side

yòu'ér 幼儿 *n* child, infant; **yòu'éryuán** 幼儿园 pre-school, nursery school, kindergarten

yú 于 *prep* in, on, at; from; by; to, than

yúshì 于是 *adv* consequently, thus, as a result

yú 鱼 *n* fish

yúlè 娱乐 *n* entertainment, amusement, recreation

yúkuài 愉快 *adj* happy, pleased, joyful

yǔ 与 **1** *prep* with, to, for **2** *conj* and

yǔmáoqiú 羽毛球 *n* badminton; shuttlecock

yǔ 雨 *n* rain

yǔsǎn 雨伞 *n* umbrella

yǔyī 雨衣 *n* raincoat

yǔdiào 语调 *n* intonation, sentence intonation

yǔfǎ 语法 *n* grammar

yǔqì 语气 *n* tone, tone of voice, manner of speaking

yǔyán 语言 *n* language

yǔyīn 语音 *n* pronunciation

yùmǐ 玉米 *n* maize, corn

yùshì 浴室 *n* bathroom, shower room

yùbào 预报 **1** *n* forecast **2** *vb* forecast

yùbèi 预备 *vb* prepare, get ready

yùfáng 预防 *vb* prevent, take precautions against, guard against

yùxí 预习 *vb* (*usually referring to an academic lesson*) prepare

yù 遇, **yùdào** 遇到 *vb* meet, encounter

yùjiàn 遇见 *vb* meet, meet by chance

yùwàng 欲望 *n* desire, wish, lust

yuán 元 *n* dollar, *yuan*

Yuándàn 元旦 *n* New Year's Day

yuánxiāo 元宵 *n* sweet dumplings made of glutinous rice flour; **Yuánxiāojié** 元宵节 Lantern Festival (the 15th of the first month in the lunar year)

yuán 员 *n* (*of a profession, party, or other organisation*) member, personnel, staff; [dǎng | hǎi | chúshī | shòuhuò] **yuán** [党 | 海 | 炊事 | 售货] 员 [party member | sailor | cook | shop assistant]

yuánlái 原来 **1** *adj* original, former, previous **2** *adv* it turns out that, as a matter of fact; originally, in the first place

yuánliàng 原谅 *vb* forgive, excuse, pardon

yuánliào 原料 *n* raw material, source material

yuányīn 原因 *n* cause, reason

yuánzé 原则 *n* principle; **yuánzé shang** 原则上 in principle

yuán 圆 **1** *adj* round, circular **2** *n* circle; (*a unit of Chinese money*) yuan

yuánzhūbǐ 圆珠笔 *n* biro, ball-point pen

yuán 园 *n* garden, park

yuǎn 远 *adj* far away, distant, remote

yuàn 院 *n* courtyard, compound; (*public facility*) [yī | diànyǐng | bówù] **yuàn** [医 | 电影 | 博物] 院 [hospital | cinema | museum]

yuànzhǎng 院长 *n* (*of an academy or organization*) director, president, chairman

yuànzi 院子 *n* court, yard, compound

yuànwàng 愿望 *n* hope, wish

yuàn(yì) 愿(意) *vb* wish, would like, want; be willing, be ready

yuē 约 **1** *vb* make an appointment, arrange a meeting, set a time to meet **2** *adv* about, approximately **3** *n* agreement, contract, treaty; appointment, date

yuēhuì 约会 *n* engagement, appointment, meeting

yuè 月 *n* moon; month

yuèliang 月亮 *n* moon, moonlight

yuèqiú 月球 *n* (*as an astronomical body*) moon

yuèqì 乐器 *n* musical instrument

yuèdú 阅读 *vb* read

yuèlǎnshì 阅览室 *n* reading room

yuè...yuè... 越...越... *adv* the more...the more...; **xuéxí yuè nǔlì, chéngjī yuè hǎo** 学习越努力, 成绩越好 the harder one studies the better one's marks

yuèlái yuè... 越来越... *adv* getting more and more..., becoming more and more...; **tiānqì yuèlái yuè rè** 天气越来越热 the weather is getting hotter

yún 云 *n* cloud

yǔnxǔ 允许 *vb* allow, permit, give permission to

yùn 运 **1** *vb* transport, ship **2** *n* luck, fate

yùndòng 运动 **1** *vb* move, exercise, engage in sports **2** *n* movement, motion; sports, athletics, exercise; (*social or political*) movement, campaign

yùndònghuì 运动会 *n* sports meet, athletic contest, games

yùndòngyuán 运动员 *n* athlete

yùnqi 运气 *n* fortune, luck

yùnshū 运输 **1** *vb* transport, move, ship **2** *n* transport, transportation, conveyance

yùnyòng 运用 *vb* utilize, wield, apply

Zz

zá 杂 *adj* miscellaneous, mixed, varied

zájì 杂技 *n* acrobatics

zázhì 杂志 *n* magazine

zá 砸 *vb* break, smash; pound, tamp

zāi 灾 *n* disaster, calamity, misfortune

zāihài 灾害 *n* disaster, calamity

zāinàn 灾难 *n* disaster, calamity, suffering

zāi 栽 *vb* plant, grow

zài 再 *adv* again, once more, further; even, still; (*when predicting what will happen if an action continues*) still, continue, keep ...-ing (any) longer; **nǐ zài hēxiàqu huì hēzuì de** 你再喝下去会喝醉的 you will get drunk if you continue to drink any longer; (*when preceded by a negative, to indicate that an action will not continue*) (no) longer, (never) again; **wǒ bú zài shuō le** 我不再说了 I won't ever say it again; (*when one actions follows another*) after, then, only after; **xǐle zǎo zài qù shuìjiào** 洗了澡再去睡觉 go to bed after you've had your bath

zàijiàn 再见 *vb* good-bye, see you again

zàisān 再三 *adv* over and over again, again and again, repeatedly

zàishuō 再说 **1** *adv* furthermore, in addition, besides **2** *vb* postpone until some time later, put aside until

zài 在 **1** *prep* in, at, on **2** *vb* exist, be alive, be present; depend on, be conditional on **3** *adv* just in the midst of, in the process of doing something; **tā zài mǎi cài** 他在买菜 he is shopping for food; **zài...shang** 在... 上; (*referring to a place*) at, above, on top of; (*rhetorically*) in; **zài yuánzé shang** 在原则上 in principle; **zài...xià** 在... 下; (*referring to physical location*) under, underneath; (referring to help, leadership, etc.) with, under; **zài tāde bāngzhù xià** 在她的帮助下 with her help; **zài...hòu** 在...后 after; **zài...lǐ** 在...里 inside; **zài...nèi** 在...内 within, among, in; **zài...qián** 在...前 before; **zài...shí** 在...时 when; **zài...wài** 在...外 out of, outside; **zài...yídài** 在...一带 in the region of; **zài...zhōngjiān** 在...中间 between

zàihu 在乎 vb (usually used in a negative sentence) care about, mind, take seriously

zàiyú 在于 vb lie in, consist in, rest with; be determined by, depend on

zán(men) 咱(们) pron (used to include only the speaker and those directly spoken to) we, the two of us, you and I

zǎn 攒 vb save, accumulate, hoard

zànshí 暂时 1 adj temporary, transient 2 adv temporarily, for the time being

zànchéng 赞成 vb agree, agree with, approve

zànměi 赞美 vb praise, sing the praises of, eulogize

zànyáng 赞扬 vb praise, speak highly of, commend

zāng 脏 adj ! This word is pronounced zàng when it means viscera, organs, as in xīnzàng 心脏; dirty, filthy

zāodào 遭到 vb (usually referring to something unpleasant) meet with, encounter, suffer

zāoshòu 遭受 vb suffer, be subjected to

zāogāo 糟糕 1 adj terrible, disastrous, unfortunate 2 exc too bad, bad luck

zǎo 早 1 adj early 2 adv early; in advance, beforehand; a long time ago 3 n morning; **nǐ zǎo!** 你早! good morning!; **zǎo jiù** 早就 a long while ago; **zǎo yǐ** 早已 long ago, for a long time

zǎochén 早晨 n morning, early morning

zǎofàn 早饭 n breakfast

zǎoshang 早上 n morning, early morning

zào 造 vb make, create, manufacture; build, establish

zàojù 造句 vb make up sentences

zé 则 **1** conj (when talking about cause, effect, or condition) then **2** n rule, regulation

zébèi 责备 vb blame, reproach, reprove

zérèn 责任 n responsibility, duty

zěnme 怎么 adv (in the interrogative) how, in what way, why; (in the positive) however, whatever; **zěnme zuò dōu kěyǐ** 怎么做都可以 any way you do it is fine; (in the negative to indicate inadequacy) (not) very; **bù zěnme hǎo** 不怎么好 not very good; **zěnme le?** 怎么了? what? what's the matter?; **zěnme huí shì?** 怎么回事? how come? how did this happen? what happened?

zěnmeyàng 怎么样 adv (in the interrogative) how, how about; (colloquial greeting) how are you? how's everything? how's it going?; (in the negative) (not) very good/well; **nàbù diànyǐng bù zěnmeyàng** 那部电影不怎么样 that film is not very good

zěnyàng 怎样 adv how, in what way

zēngjiā 增加 **1** vb increase, add **2** n increase

zēngzhǎng 增长 vb increase, grow, become larger

zhā 扎 vb pierce, prick, stick into

zhá 炸 vb ▶ See also **zhà** 炸. deep-fry, fry in deep fat/oil

zhà 炸 vb ▶ See also **zhá** 炸. explode, burst; blow up, bomb, blast

zhāi 摘 vb (for flowers, fruit, etc.) pick, pluck; (for hats, glasses, etc.) take off, remove

zhǎi 窄 adj narrow, tight

zhān 粘 **1** vb stick, paste, glue **2** adj sticky

zhǎnchū 展出 vb show, put on display, exhibit

zhǎnkāi 展开 vb develop, unfold, open up

zhǎnlǎn 展览 **1** vb exhibit, show, put on display **2** n exhibition, display; **zhǎnlǎnguǎn** 展览馆 exhibition centre, exhibition hall; **zhǎnlǎnhuì** 展览会 exhibition; **zhǎnlǎnpǐn** 展览品 item on display, exhibit

zhǎnxīn 崭新 *adj* brand-new, completely new

zhàn 占 *vb* occupy, seize; constitute, make up, hold

zhàndòu 战斗 **1** *vb* fight, struggle **2** *n* fight, struggle

zhànshèng 战胜 *vb* defeat, win in battle/war; overcome

zhànshi 战士 *n* soldier, warrior, fighter

zhànzhēng 战争 *n* war, warfare

zhàn 站 **1** *vb* stand **2** *n* station, depot, stop

zhǎn 盏 *mw* ▶ **213** (for lamps)

zhāng 张 **1** *mw* ▶ **213** (for flat things such as paper, paintings, tables, etc.) **2** *vb* open, stretch, extend

zhāng 章 *n* chapter, section; rules, regulations; stamp, seal

zhǎng 长 ▶ See also **cháng** 长. **1** *vb* grow, develop, form; gain, acquire; increase **2** *n* (often used as a suffix) head, chairman, director; [suǒ | shì | xiào] zhǎng [所 | 市 | 校] 长 [director of an institute | mayor | principal]

zhǎng 涨 *vb* (of water-level, prices, etc.) rise, go up

zhǎngwò 掌握 *vb* grasp, control, master

zhàng 丈 *n* (measure of length) 3.3 metres, 10 Chinese feet

zhàngfu 丈夫 *n* husband

zhāodài 招待 *vb* (of guests, visitors, etc.) entertain, receive, serve

zhāodàihuì 招待会 *n* reception, welcoming party

zhāohu 招呼 *vb* call, notify, tell; hail, greet, say hello to; **xiàng/gēn mǒurén dǎ zhāohu** 向/跟某人打招呼 say hello to someone

zháojí 着急 *adj* worried, anxious

zháo 着 ▶ See also **zhe** 着. touch; (when speaking of an illness) catch, be affected by; **zháoliáng** 着凉 catch cold; burn; **zháohuǒ** 着火 catch fire; (after a verb to indicate

accomplishment or result [zhǎo | diān | shuì] **zháo** [找 | 点 | 睡] 着
[find | succeed in lighting | fall asleep]

zhǎo 找 *vb* look for, seek; give change, return a balance; **tā zhǎo wǒ wǔ kuài qián** 他找我五块钱 he gave me five dollars change; **zhǎodào** 找到 find; **zhǎozháo** 找着 find

zhàokāi 召开 *vb* (*when talking about a conference, meeting, etc.*) hold, convene

zhào 照 **1** *vb* shine on, put a light on, illuminate; reflect, look at one's reflection; take (a photograph) **2** *prep* according to; towards

zhàocháng 照常 *adv* as usual, as normally done

zhàogu 照顾 *vb* take care of, look after, attend to; take into account, consider

zhàokàn 照看 *vb* take care of, look after, attend to; keep an eye on

zhàoliào 照料 *vb* care for, look after, attend to

zhàopiàn 照片 *n* photograph, picture

zhàoxiàng 照相 *vb* take a picture or photograph, have a photograph taken

zhàoxiàngjī 照相机 *n* camera

zhé 折 *vb* bend, fold

zhéxué 哲学 *n* philosophy; **zhéxuéjiā** 哲学家 philosopher, specialist in philosophy

zhè 这 **1** *pron* this **2** *det* this

zhèbiān 这边 *adv* this side, over here

zhège 这个 **1** *pron* this, this one **2** *det* this

zhèr 这儿, **zhèlǐ** 这里 *adv* here

zhème 这么 *adv* by this means, in this way, like this; to this degree, so, such

zhèxiē 这些 **1** *pron* these **2** *det* these

zhèyàng 这样 *adv* in this way, like this, so

zhe 着 *pt* ▶ *See also* **zháo** 着. *(indicating a continuous state or action, often translated by the present participle [-ing] in English)* [zǒu | tīng | chàng] **zhe** [走 | 听 | 唱] 着 [walking | listening | singing]

zhēn 真 **1** *adj* real, genuine, true **2** *adv* really, truly

zhēnlǐ 真理 *n (as an abstract concept)* truth

zhēnshí 真实 *adj* true, real, factual

zhēnzhèng 真正 *adj* genuine, true

zhēn 针 *n* needle, pin; stitch; *(as for medical treatment)* injection

zhēnduì 针对 *vb* point exactly against, be directed against, be aimed at in view of, in the light of, in accordance with

zhěntou 枕头 *n* pillow

zhèn 阵 *mw* ▶ **213** *(for events or states of short duration)*

zhèn 镇 *n* town

zhēngyuè 正月 *n* ! *The character* zhēng 正 *is also pronounced* zhèng *with a different meaning;* first month of the lunar year

zhēng 争 *vb* fight over, compete; argue about, dispute

zhēnglùn 争论 **1** *vb* debate, argue **2** *n* argument, debate

zhēngqǔ 争取 *vb* strive for, gain by fighting, win; win over, persuade

zhēngqiú 征求 *vb (as opinions, advice, etc.)* consult, solicit, seek

zhēng 睁 *vb (used for the eyes)* open

zhěng 整 *adj* whole, entire, complete; *(when talking about the time)* sharp, exact; **bā diǎn zhěng** 八点整 eight o'clock sharp

zhěnggè 整个 *adj* whole, entire

zhěnglǐ 整理 *vb* tidy up, put in order, arrange

zhěngqí 整齐 *adj* in good order, neat, tidy

zhèng 正 ! *Can also be pronounced* zhēng *with a different meaning.* **1** *adj* right, straight, upright; right side up, right side out; chief, main; (of time) punctual, exact, precise **2** adv precisely, exactly; (indicating that an action is in progress) right in the midst of, just now; **tā zhèng xiězhe nàfēng xìn** 他正写着那封信 he is just writing that letter

zhèngcháng 正常 adj normal

zhèngdāng 正当 conj just when, just at the time when

zhèngdàng 正当 adj proper, appropriate, legitimate

zhènghǎo 正好 **1** adj (in time, quantity, etc.) just right **2** adv (referring to time, quantity, etc.) just right; happen to, chance to, as it happens

zhèngqiǎo 正巧 adv it so happens, as it happens, happen to; just in time, just at the right time, in the nick of time

zhèngquè 正确 adj correct, right

zhèngshì 正式 **1** adj formal, regular, official **2** adv formally

zhèngyào 正要 adv about to, on the point of

zhèngzài 正在 adv (indicating an ongoing action or condition) in the midst of; **wǒ zhèngzài kàn tā xiě de shū** 我正在看她写的书 I am just now reading the book she wrote

zhèngmíng 证明 **1** vb certify, prove **2** n proof, documentation, certificate

zhèngcè 政策 n policy

zhèngdǎng 政党 n political party

zhèngfǔ 政府 n government

zhèngquán 政权 n political power, state political power, regime

zhèngzhì 政治 n politics, political affairs; **zhèngzhìjiā** 政治家 politician, statesman

zhèng 挣 vb earn, make

...zhīhòu ...之后 prep after..., behind...

...zhījiān ...之间 prep between..., among...

...zhīqián ...之前 prep before..., prior to..., in front of...

...zhīshàng ...之上 *prep* above..., on top of...

...zhīxià ...之下 *prep* below..., under...

...zhīzhōng ...之中 *prep* amid..., among..., within...

zhī 支 *mw* ▶ **213** (for stick-like things); (for music, songs, or teams)

zhīchí 支持 **1** *vb* support **2** *n* support

zhīyuán 支援 **1** *vb* support, aid, assist **2** *n* support, aid, assistance

zhī 只 *mw* ▶ **213** ▶ See also **zhǐ** 只. (one of a pair); (for some animals); (for boats)

zhīdao 知道 *vb* know, know how, know that

zhīshi 知识 *n* knowledge

zhī 织 *vb* weave, spin, knit

zhī 枝 **1** *n* (of a tree or other plant) branch **2** *mw* ▶ **213** (for stick-like things)

zhíxíng 执行 *vb* carry out, execute, implement

zhí 直 **1** *adj* (as a line, road, etc.) straight; (in expressing opinions, etc.) straightforward, frank **2** *adv* directly, straight; in a straightforward manner, frankly

zhídào 直到 *prep* until, up to

zhíjiē 直接 **1** *adj* direct, straightforward, straight **2** *adv* directly, straightforwardly, frankly

zhíde 值得 *vb* be worthwhile, be worth

zhígōng 职工 *n* workers, staff

zhíyè 职业 *n* profession, occupation

zhíyuán 职员 *n* office worker, member of staff

zhíwù 植物 *n* plant, vegetation, flora

zhǐ 止 **1** *vb* stop **2** *n* end, terminus; **dào xīngqīliù wéizhǐ** 到星期六为止 up to Saturday, until Saturday **3** *adv* only; **bù zhǐ yīcì** 不止一次 not just once

zhǐ 只 *adv* ▶ See also **zhī** 只. only, merely

zhǐhǎo 只好 *adv* have to, can only, the only thing to do is; **yīnwèi tā bú zài, suǒyǐ wǒ zhǐhǎo huí jiā** 因为他不在, 所以我只好回家 since he's not in, I have to go home

zhǐshì 只是 **1** *adv* just, only **2** *conj* but, however

zhǐyào 只要 *conj* so long as, provided; **zhǐyào yǒu hǎo diànyǐng, wǒ jiù qǐng nǐ qù kàn** 只要有好电影, 我就请你去看 as long as there's a good film showing, I'll invite you to see it

zhǐyǒu 只有 **1** *adv* only **2** *conj* only, only if, unless; **zhǐyǒu...cái...** 只有... 才... only...can...; **zhǐyǒu nǔlì xuéxí, cái néng xuéhuì** 只有努力学习, 才能学会 you can master (it) only if you study hard

zhǐ 纸 *n* paper

zhǐ 指 **1** *vb* point at, point to, point toward **2** *n* finger

zhǐchū 指出 *vb* point out, indicate

zhǐdǎo 指导 **1** *vb* guide, direct **2** *n* direction, guidance, advice; **zhǐdǎo lǎoshī** 指导老师 supervisor, advisor

zhǐhuī 指挥 **1** *vb* (for an army, an orchestra, etc.) direct, command, conduct **2** *n* (of an orchestra) conductor

zhǐshì 指示 **1** *n* instructions, directive **2** *vb* point out, indicate; instruct, direct

zhì 至 *prep* to, until

zhìjīn 至今 *adv* until now, so far, up to now

zhìshǎo 至少 *adv* at least

zhìyú 至于 *prep* as for, as to; **bú zhìyú** 不至于 wouldn't go so far as to

zhìliàng 质量 *n* quality

zhì 治 *vb* rule, govern, manage; (water, emotions, etc.) harness, control; heal, cure, treat

zhìliáo 治疗 **1** *n* medical treatment **2** *vb* cure, treat

zhìdìng 制定 *vb* (as a plan, policy, law, etc.) draft, draw up, formulate

zhìdìng 制订 *vb (as a scheme, a solution, etc.)* work out, come up with, formulate

zhìdù 制度 *n* system

zhìzào 制造 *vb* manufacture, make, create; *(as a lie, a rumour, etc.)* make up, fabricate, invent

zhìxù 秩序 *n* order, sequence

zhōng 中 **1** *n* middle, centre; *(short for* Zhōngguó 中国*)* China **2** *prep* in, in the midst of, among **3** *adj* middle, mid-; medium, intermediate; Chinese; Zhōngshì 中式 Chinese style

Zhōngcān 中餐 *n* Chinese food

Zhōngguó 中国 *n* China

Zhōngguóhuà 中国话 *n* Chinese (spoken) language

Zhōngguórén 中国人 *n* Chinese person, Chinese people

Zhōnghuá Mínguó 中华民国 *n* the Republic of China

Zhōnghuá Rénmín Gònghéguó 中华人民共和国 *n* the People's Republic of China

zhōngjiān 中间 **1** *n* middle, centre **2** *prep* amongst, between, in the middle of

Zhōngqiūjié 中秋节 *n* Mid-autumn Festival, Moon Festival (15th of the 8th lunar month)

Zhōngwén 中文 *n* Chinese language (usually written)

zhōngwǔ 中午 *n* noon, midday

zhōngxīn 中心 *n* centre, heart, core

zhōngxué 中学 *n* middle school, secondary school, high school

zhōngyāng 中央 *n* centre, middle

Zhōngyào 中药 *n (as a drug or remedy)* traditional Chinese medicine

Zhōngyī 中医 *n (as a field or department)* traditional Chinese medicine

zhōngyú 终于 *adv* in the end, at last, finally

zhōng 钟 *n* bell; clock; *(for telling time)* **wǔ diǎn zhōng** 五点钟 five o'clock; **wǔ fēn zhōng** 五分钟 five minutes

zhōngbiǎo 钟表 *n* clock, clocks and watches

zhōngtóu 钟头 *n* hour

zhǒng 种 ▶ *See also* **zhòng** 种 **1** *n* seed; breed, species, ethnic group **2** *mw* ▶**213** kind, type, sort

zhǒnglèi 种类 *n* kind, type, sort

zhǒngzi 种子 *n* seed

zhòng 种 *vb* ▶ *See also* **zhǒng** 种. plant, sow, cultivate

zhòng 重 ▶ *See also* **chóng** 重. **1** *adj* heavy; important, weighty, serious **2** *n* weight

zhòngdà 重大 *adj* great, weighty, important

zhòngdiǎn 重点 *n* point of emphasis, main point

zhòngliàng 重量 *n* weight

zhòngshì 重视 *vb* regard as important, take seriously, value

zhòngyào 重要 *adj* important, significant

zhōu 周 *n* all around, circumference, circuit; week

zhōudào 周到 *adj* thoughtful, considerate

zhōumò 周末 *n* weekend

zhōuwéi 周围 *n* circumference, surroundings, environment

zhū 猪 *n* pig, hog

zhūròu 猪肉 *n* pork

zhúzi 竹子 *n* bamboo

zhúbù 逐步 *adv* gradually, step by step

zhújiàn 逐渐 *adv* gradually, bit by bit

zhǔdòng 主动 **1** *n* initiative **2** *vb* hold/take the initiative

zhǔguān 主观 *adj* subjective

zhǔrén 主人 *n* owner; host, hostess

zhǔrèn 主任 *n* director, chairperson, responsible person

zhǔxí 主席 *n* chairperson, chair, chairman

zhǔyào 主要 *adj* main, principal, chief

zhǔyì 主义 *n* doctrine, -ism

zhǔyì 主意 *n* idea, plan, decision

zhǔzhāng 主张 **1** *vb* propose, suggest, advocate **2** *n* proposal, suggestion

zhǔ 煮 *vb* boil, cook

zhù 住 *vb* live, reside, stay; (*after certain verbs to indicate coming to a halt or grasping hold*) [zhuā | zhàn | jì] zhù [抓 | 站 | 记] 住 [hold on to | stop | remember]

zhùyuàn 住院 *vb* be in hospital, be hospitalized

zhùyì 注意 *vb* pay attention to, take notice of, be careful of

zhù 祝 *vb* wish, extend wishes

zhùhè 祝贺 *vb* congratulate

zhùmíng 著名 *adj* famous, prominent, well-known

zhùzuò 著作 *n* writings, works

zhuā 抓 *vb* grasp, seize; catch, arrest; scratch

zhuājǐn 抓紧 *vb* grasp firmly, pay close attention to, make the best use of

zhuānjiā 专家 *n* specialist, expert

zhuānmén 专门 *adj* specialized, special

zhuānxīn 专心 **1** *adj* attentive, with undivided attention, with concentration **2** *adv* attentively

zhuānyè 专业 *n* specialty, specialized field/profession

zhuān 砖 *n* brick

zhuǎn 转 *vb* ▶ See also **zhuàn** 转. turn, change, shift; (*when speaking of a message, phone call, etc.*) transfer, pass on, forward

zhuǎnbiàn 转变 *vb* turn, change, transform

zhuǎngào 转告 *vb* (*as a message*) forward, pass on

zhuàn 转 *vb* ▶ *See also* **zhuǎn** 转. turn, revolve, rotate; walk around, stroll

zhuàn 赚 *vb* (*when talking about money or profit*) make, gain, earn

zhuāngjia 庄稼 *n* crop, crops

zhuāngyán 庄严 *adj* dignified, solemn, stately

zhuāng 装 **1** *vb* install, fit, put in; pack, load; pretend, disguise, play a part **2** *n* clothing, outfit, dress

zhuàngkuàng 状况 *n* state of affairs, situation

zhuàngtài 状态 *n* condition, appearance, state of affairs

zhuàng 撞 *vb* bump/knock against, bump into, collide

zhuī 追 *vb* follow, pursue, chase

zhuīqiú 追求 *vb* seek, go after, pursue; court, woo

zhǔn 准 **1** *adj* accurate **2** *adv* accurately, certainly **3** *vb* permit, allow

zhǔnbèi 准备 **1** *vb* prepare, get ready for, prepare to; plan, intend **2** *n* preparation

zhǔnquè 准确 *adj* accurate, precise, exact

zhǔnshí 准时 *adj* on time, punctual

zhuō 捉 *vb* seize, arrest, catch hold of

zhuōzi 桌子 *n* table, desk

zīliào 资料 *n* information, data

zīyuán 资源 *n* resources, natural resources

zǐnǚ 子女 *n* sons and daughters, children

zǐxì 仔细 **1** *adj* careful of detail, meticulous, attentive **2** *adv* in detail, meticulously, carefully

zǐ 紫 *adj* purple

zì 自 **1** *pron* oneself, one's own **2** *prep* from, since **3** *conj* since

zìcóng 自从 **1** *prep* since, from **2** *conj* since; **zìcóng...yǐhòu** 自从... 以后 from... (that time) on, ever since...; **zìcóng...yǐlái** 自从... 以来 ever since...

zìdòng 自动 **1** *adj* automatic, voluntary, self-motivated **2** *adv* automatically, voluntarily, on one's own initiative

zìfèi 自费 *adj* at one's own expense, self-funded

zìjǐ 自己 *pron* self, oneself

zìjué 自觉 **1** *adj* conscious, aware; conscientious **2** *adv* consciously; conscientiously

zìláishuǐ 自来水 *n* running water, tap water

zìrán 自然 **1** *n* nature, the natural world **2** *adj* natural **3** *adv* of course; naturally

zìsī 自私 *adj* selfish

zìwǒ 自我 *pron* self, self-, oneself

zìxíngchē 自行车 *n* bicycle, bike

zìxué 自学 *vb* self-study, study by oneself, teach oneself

zìyóu 自由 **1** *n* freedom, liberty **2** *adj* free, unrestrained

zìyuàn 自愿 *adj* voluntary, of one's own accord

zì 字 *n* word, written character

zìdiǎn 字典 *n* dictionary

zìmǔ 字母 *n* letters of an alphabet, letter

zōngjiào 宗教 *n* religion

zōnghé 综合 **1** *vb* synthesize, summarize **2** *adj* comprehensive, overall

zǒng 总 **1** *adv* always, in every case, all the time; eventually, sooner or later, inevitably; in any event, anyway, after all **2** *adj* general, total; chief, main, master

zǒngjié 总结 **1** *vb* sum up, summarize **2** *n* summary, report

zǒnglǐ 总理 *n* prime minister, premier

zǒngshì 总是 *adv* always, in every case, all the time

zǒngtǒng 总统 *vb* (of a republic) president

zǒu 走 *vb* walk, go; depart, leave; (for something mechanical) work, tick, go

zǒudào 走道 *n* path, walkway

zǒu hòumén 走后门 *vb* get in by the back door; do business or other things by means of backdoor dealings

zǒuláng 走廊 *n* corridor, passage, passageway

zǒulù 走路 *vb* walk

zū 租 *vb* rent, hire, charter; rent out, let out, lease

zúqiú 足球 *n* football, soccer

zǔzhǐ 阻止 *vb* prevent, stop

zǔ 组 *n* group

zǔzhī 组织 **1** *vb* organize **2** *n* organisation

zǔfù 祖父 *n* grandfather on the father's side

zǔguó 祖国 *n* one's native country, motherland, fatherland

zǔmǔ 祖母 *n* grandmother on the father's side

zǔxiān 祖先 *n* ancestors, forefathers

zuān 钻 *vb* drill, bore, enter

zuānyán 钻研 *vb* study intensively

zuǐ 嘴 *n* mouth

zuì 最 *adv (indicating the superlative)* most, the most

zuìchū 最初 **1** *adj* first, initial **2** *adv* at first, in the beginning, initially

zuìhǎo 最好 **1** *adj* best **2** *adv* had better

zuìhòu 最后 **1** *adj* final, ultimate, last **2** *adv* at last, finally, eventually

zuìjìn 最近 **1** *adj (in the recent past)* last, recent; *(in the near future)* next, coming **2** *adv (in the recent past)* lately, recently; *(in the near future)* soon, in the near future, coming

zuì 罪 *n* crime, guilt; suffering, pain, hardship; **shòu zuì** 受罪 have a hard time, endure suffering, be in pain

zuì 醉 *adj* drunk, intoxicated, inebriated

zūnjìng 尊敬 **1** *vb* respect, honour, esteem **2** *adj* honourable, distinguished

zūnzhòng 尊重 *vb* respect, esteem

zūnshǒu 遵守 *vb* comply with, observe, abide by

zuótiān 昨天 *n* yesterday

zuǒ 左 **1** *n* left, left-hand side, the left; (*when speaking of politics*) left-wing **2** *adj* left, left-hand

zuǒbian 左边 *n* left-hand side, left side

zuǒyòu 左右 *adv* (*after an expression of quantity*) approximately, about, more or less

zuò 作 *vb* do, make; zuò bàogào 作报告 make a report; create, write, compose; zuò qǔ 作曲 compose a piece of music; act as, be, become; regard as, treat as; tā bǎ wǒ dāngzuò qīnshēng nǚ'ér 她把我当作亲生女儿 she treats me like her own daughter

zuòjiā 作家 *n* writer

zuòpǐn 作品 *n* literary/artistic work

zuòwéi 作为 **1** *vb* serve as, function as, use as; regard as **2** *prep* as, being **3** *n* conduct, action, deed; achievement, accomplishment

zuòwén 作文 *n* composition, essay

zuòyè 作业 *n* school assignment

zuòyòng 作用 *n* purpose, function, role; qǐ hěn dà de zuòyòng 起很大的作用 perform an important function; action, effect

zuòzhě 作者 *n* author, writer

zuò 坐 *vb* sit; ride on, go by, travel by; zuò [gōnggòng qìchē | huǒchē | fēijī] 坐 [公共汽车 | 火车 | 飞机] travel by [bus | train | plane]

zuò 座 **1** *mw* ▶ **213** (*for mountains, buildings, structures, etc.*) **2** *n* seat, place to sit

zuòtán 座谈 **1** *vb* discuss **2** *n* discussion; zuòtánhuì 座谈会 discussion, symposium, forum

zuòwèi 座位 *n* seat, place to sit

zuò 做 *vb* do, be engaged in; **zuò shìyàn** 做试验 do experiments; make, create, manufacture; **zuò yīfu** 做衣服 make clothes; cook, prepare (food); **zuò cài** 做菜 cook a meal, prepare a meal; be, act as, take on the role of; **tā kuài zuò māma le** 她快做妈妈了 she is about to become a mother; *(when talking about posts, positions, professions, etc.)* work as, be, become; **tā zuòle sān nián xì zhǔrèn le** 他做了三年系主任了 he has been chairperson of the department for three years; serve as, be used as; **zhège fángjiān kěyǐ zuò wǒde shūfáng** 这个房间可以做我的书房 this room can serve as my study

zuòfǎ 做法 *n* way of doing things, method, practice

zuòkè 做客 *vb* be a guest

zuòmèng 做梦 *vb* dream, have a dream

Basic Chinese measure words

Nominal Measure Words

In Chinese, a numeral cannot quantify a noun by itself. It has to be accompanied by the measure word that is appropriate for the noun that is being used. Each noun has a specific measure word or set of measure words that can be used with it. There is often a link between the measure word and the shape of the object. In expressions of quantification, the numeral comes first, followed by the measure word and the noun. Below is a list of commonly used nominal measure words, along with descriptions of the types of nouns for which they are used, translations (if appropriate), and some examples of their uses. A list of verbal measure words follows this list. Some nominal measure words can also be used as verbal measure words, and these are cross-referenced below.

bǎ 把 (for objects with a handle or with something a person can hold) three [brushes | knives | keys | umbrellas | chairs...] sānbǎ [shuāzi | dāo | yàoshi | yǔsǎn | yǐzi...] 三把 [刷子 | 刀 | 钥匙 | 雨伞 | 椅子...]; (for things that can be grouped in bunches or bundles) bunch; bundle; **a bunch of flowers** yìbǎ* huā 一把*花; **a bundle of chopsticks** yìbǎ kuàizi 一把筷子; handful; **a handful of** [sand | rice | beans...] yìbǎ [shāzi | dàmǐ | dòuzi...] 一把 [沙子 | 大米 | 豆子...]

bān 班 (for scheduled services of public transportation) **this train service to London** qù Lúndūn de zhèbān huǒchē; **the next flight to Beijing** qù Běijīng de xià yìbān fēijī 去北京的下一班飞机

bāo 包 package, packet, bundle; **a packet of cigarettes** yìbāo xiāngyān 一包香烟; **two packages of sweets** liǎngbāo táng 两包糖; **this bundle of clothes** zhèbāo yīfu 这包衣服

běn 本 (for things that are bound, such as books, magazines, etc.) **five books** wǔběn shū 五本书

bǐ 笔 (for sums of money) **that sum of money** nàbǐ qián 那笔钱; (for deals in business or trade) **this deal** zhèbǐ jiāoyì 这笔交易

biàn 遍 ▶ See the list of Verbal Measure Words below.

*less formal

bù 部 (for novels, films, etc.) three [novels | films] sānbù [xiǎoshuō | diànyǐng] 三部[小说 | 电影]

cè 册 (for books or volumes of books) volume, book; this novel has two volumes zhèbù xiǎoshuō yǒu liǎngcè 这部小说有两册; (for copies of books) copy; shíwàncè shū 十万册书 100,000 books

céng 层 storey, floor; a five-storey building yízuò wǔcéng dàlóu 一座五层大楼; (for a layer, coat, sheet) a coat of paint yìcéng yóuqī 一层油漆; a thin sheet of ice yìcéng báo bīng 一层薄冰

chǎng 场 ▶ See also the list of Verbal Measure Words below. (for the whole process of being ill) an illness yìchǎng bìng 一场病; (for a natural disturbance, war, disaster, etc.) a rain shower, a cloudburst yìchǎng yǔ 一场雨; (for a show, performance, game, or debate) [the showing of a film | a performance of Peking Opera | a debate] yìchǎng [diànyǐng | jīngjù | biànlùn] 一场[电影 | 京剧 | 辩论]; two [football matches | basketball games] liǎngchǎng [zúqiú bǐsài | lánqiú bǐsài] 两场[足球比赛 | 篮球比赛]

chuáng 床 (for quilts, blankets, sheets) three [quilts | blankets | sheets] sānchuáng [bèizi | tǎnzi | chuángdān] 三床[被子 | 毯子 | 床单]

cì 次 ▶ See also the list of Verbal Measure Words below. (for events such as examinations, accidents, experiments, etc.) two [examinations | accidents | experiments...] liǎngcì [kǎoshì | shìgù | shíyàn...] 两次[考试 | 事故 | 实验...]

dào 道 (for orders issued by an authority, questions on an examination) an [order | arithmetic question] yídào [mìnglìng | suànshù tí] 一道[命令 | 算数题]; (for things in the shape of a line) a [crack | ray of light | wrinkle] yídào [lièfèng | guāngxiàn | zhòuwén] 一道[裂缝 | 光线 | 皱纹]; (for courses in a meal) a three-course lunch yǒu sāndào cài de wǔfàn 有三道菜的午饭

dī 滴 drop; six drops of blood liùdī xuè 六滴血

diǎn 点 (for suggestions, requirements, ideas, opinions) two [suggestions | requirements | ideas] liǎngdiǎn [jiànyì | yāoqiú | yìjiàn] 两点[建议 | 要求 | 意见]

dǐng 顶 (for hats, caps, or things with a top) a [hat | tent] yìdǐng [màozi | zhàngpeng] 一顶[帽子 | 帐篷]

dòng 栋 (for buildings) ten buildings shídòng lóufáng 十栋楼房

dǔ 堵 (for walls) a wall yìdǔ qiáng 一堵墙

duàn 段 (for lengths of road, cable, etc.) section, segment; a section of highway yíduàn gōnglù 一段公路; (for periods of time) period, length; that period of history nà yíduàn lìshǐ 那一段历史; (for units of writing, articles, speeches, etc.) piece, passage, paragraph; a piece of music yíduàn yīnyuè 一段音乐

duì 对 pair, couple; a (married) couple yíduì fūqī 一对夫妻; a pair of vases yíduì huāpíng 一对花瓶

dùn ▶ See also the list of Verbal Measure Words below. (for meals) three meals every day měitiān sāndùn fàn 每天三顿饭

duǒ 朵 (for flowers, clouds) a few [flowers | clouds] jǐduǒ [huā | yún] 几朵[花 | 云]

fèn 份 portion, share; a portion of food yífèn fàn 一份饭; a gift yífèn lǐwù 一份礼物; (for copies of newspapers, magazines, or manuscripts) two documents liǎngfèn wénjiàn 两份文件

fēng 封 (for letters, telegrams) eight letters bāfēng xìn 八封信

fú 幅 (for paintings, works of calligraphy, maps) a landscape painting yìfú shānshuǐhuà 一幅山水画

fù 服 (for doses of Chinese medicine) four doses of Chinese medicine sìfù zhōngyào 四服中药

fù 副 (for things that come in pairs or sets) set, pair; a set of chess yífù xiàngqí 一副象棋; a pair of [gloves | glasses...] yífù [shǒutào | yǎnjìng...] 一副[手套 | 眼镜...]; (for facial expressions) a [smiling face | serious expression] yífù [xiàoliǎn | yánsù de biǎoqíng] 一副[笑脸 | 严肃的表情]

gè 个 ! This is the most common measure word. It can take the place of many nominal measure words, and is handy to use if one does not know the measure word that is specific to a particular noun. It usually has a neutral tone, but has a fourth tone when stressed. a [person | problem | month | school...] yíge [rén | wèntí | yuè | xuéxiào...] 一个[人 | 问题 | 月 | 学校...]

gēn 根 (for long, thin objects) a [rope | needle | pillar | sausage...] yìgēn [shéngzi | zhēn | zhùzi | xiāngcháng...] 一根[绳子 | 针 | 柱子 | 香肠...]

háng 行 *(for things that form a line)* **two lines of Chinese characters** liǎngháng Hànzì 两行汉字

huí 回 ▶ *See the list of Verbal Measure Words below.*

hù 户 *(for households)* **five Chinese households** wǔhù Zhōngguórén 五户中国人

huǒ 伙 **!** *This measure word usually has a negative connotation:* *(for groups or bands of people)* **a gang of** [people | robbers | hooligans...] yìhuǒ [rén | qiángdào | liúmáng...] 一伙 [人 | 强盗 | 流氓...]

jiā 家 *(for families, enterprises, restaurants, hotels, etc.)* **twelve** [families | factories | banks | shops...] shí'èrjiā [rénjiā | gōngchǎng | yínháng | shāngdiàn...] 十二家 [人家 | 工厂 | 银行 | 商店...]

jià 架 *(for aeroplanes, pianos, cameras, etc.)* **six** [aeroplanes | cameras] liùjià [fēijī | zhàoxiàngjī] 六架 [飞机 | 照相机]

jiān 间 *(for rooms)* **a(n)** [room | office | kitchen] yìjiān [wūzi | bàngōngshì | chúfáng] 一间 [屋子 | 办公室 | 厨房]

jiàn 件 *(for luggage, clothes, furniture, matters, etc.)* **a** [piece of luggage | shirt | matter] yíjiàn [xíngli | chènshān | shì] 一件 [行李 | 衬衫 | 事]

jié 节 *(for sections of things)* **section, length, segment; a section of bamboo** yìjié zhúzi 一节竹子; *(for torch batteries, railway carriages, class periods at school)* **four** [carriages | batteries | periods] sìjié [chēxiāng | diànchí | kè] 四节 [车厢 | 电池 | 课]

jiè 届 *(for regular sessions, conferences, sports tournaments, terms of office, etc.)* **the tenth** [session of the UN General Assembly | Agriculture Conference | presidency] dìshíjiè [Liánhéguó Dàhuì | Nóngyè Huìyì | zǒngtǒng] 第十届 [联合国大会 | 农业会议 | 总统]; *(for students graduating in the same year)* **year, class, grade; the fourth graduating class** dìsìjiè bìyèbān 第四届毕业班

jù 句 *(for lines, sentences, units of speech, poetry, etc.)* **a** [sentence | line of a poem] yíjù [huà | shī] 一句 [话 | 诗]

kē 棵 *(for trees, plants)* **a** [tree | grass | daffodil] yìkē [shù | cǎo | shuǐxiānhuā] 一棵 [树 | 草 | 水仙花]

kē 颗 *(for small, round things such as pearls, teeth and hearts; also for things that appear small such as stars, satellites and* *planets*) **a [pearl | bean | satellite]** yìkē [zhūzi | dòuzi | wèixīng] 一颗 [珠子 | 豆子 | 卫星]; (*for bullets, bombs, etc.*) **a [bullet | bomb]** yìkē [zǐdàn | zhàdàn] 一颗 [子弹 | 炸弹]

kǒu 口 (*for the number of people in a family or village*) **eight people** bākǒu rén 八口人; (*for spoken languages, used with the verb "speak" and with the number one,* yì 一) **to speak Beijing dialect** shuō yìkǒu Běijīng huà 说一口北京话

kuài 块 (*for things that come in chunks or solid pieces*) **three [soaps | sweets | stones]** sānkuài [féizào | táng | shítou] 三块 [肥皂 | 糖 | 石头]; (*for things that are shaped like sheets*) **five [table cloths | wooden boards | handkerchiefs]** wǔkuài [zhuōbù | mùbǎn | shǒujuàn] 五块 [桌布 | 木板 | 手绢]; (*for slices, sections, divisions, etc.*) **four pieces of [cake | cloth | land]** sìkuài [dàngāo | bù | dì] 四块 [蛋糕 | 布 | 地]

lèi 类 **kind of, sort of;** zhèlèi dōngxi 这类东西 **this type of thing, this kind of thing**

lì 粒 (*for very small, round things, such as peas, peanuts, bullets, or grains*) **a grain of [rice | sand]** yìlì [mǐ | shāzi] 一粒 [米 | 沙子]; **three pills/tablets** sānlì yào 三粒药

liàng 辆 (*for vehicles*) **ten [cars | bikes | lorries]** shíliàng [qìchē | zìxíngchē | kǎchē] 十辆 [汽车 | 自行车 | 卡车]

liè 列 (*for trains*) **a train** yíliè huǒchē 一列火车

mén 门 (*for academic courses, subjects or disciplines*) **a [course | science | speciality]** yìmén [kèchéng | kèxué | zhuānyè] 一门 [课程 | 科学 | 专业]

miàn 面 (*for flat, smooth objects, such as mirrors, flags, etc.*) **a [red flag | mirror]** yímiàn [hóngqí | jìngzi] 一面 [红旗 | 镜子]

míng 名 (*for persons with professional or prominent social identities*) **seven [students | doctors | soldiers | workers]** qīmíng [xuésheng | yīshēng | shìbīng | gōngrén] 七名 [学生 | 医生 | 士兵 | 工人]

pái 排 (*for things grouped or seated in rows*) **row; a row of [seats | trees | houses]** yìpái [zuòwèi | shù | fángzi] 一排 [座位 | 树 | 房子]

pán 盘 (*for flat things*) **a video tape** yìpán lùxiàngdài 一盘录像带; (*for board games*) **a game of chess** yìpán qí 一盘棋

pī 批 (for people or goods) group, batch, lot; **a group of people** yìpī rén 一批人; **two batches of goods** liǎngpī huòwù 两批货物

pǐ 匹 (for horses, mules) **three** [horses | mules] sānpǐ [mǎ | luózi] 三匹 [马 | 骡子]

piān 篇 (for papers, articles, written versions of a speech) **an** [essay | diary | editorial | editorial] yìpiān [lùnwén | rìjì | shèlùn] 一篇 [论文 | 日记 | 社论]

piàn 片 (for flat, thin things or things in slices) **three slices of bread** sānpiàn miànbāo 三片面包; **two** [tablets | biscuits] liǎngpiàn [yàopiàn | bǐnggān] 两片 [药片 | 饼干]; (for expanses or stretches of ocean, desert, mist, fog, etc.) **a stretch of sandy beach** yípiàn shātān 一片沙滩; (for atmospheres, moods, etc.) **a scene of great joy** yípiàn huānlè 一片欢乐

qī 期 (for issues of periodicals, magazines, journals, etc.) **the first issue of that magazine** nàběn zázhì de dìyīqī 那本杂志的第一期

qún 群 (for a group, crowd, herd, or flock) group, crowd, flock; **a crowd of football fans** yìqún zúqiúmí 一群足球迷; **a flock of birds** yìqún niǎo 一群鸟

shēng 声 ▶ See the list of Verbal Measure Words below.

shǒu 首 (for songs, poems, music) **six** [songs | poems] liùshǒu [gē | shī] 六首 [歌 | 诗]

shù 束 bunch; **a bunch of flowers** yíshù huā 一束花

shuāng 双 (for things that come in twos, such as shoes, socks, chopsticks, etc.) pair; **a pair of** [shoes | socks | eyes] yìshuāng [xié | wàzi | yǎnjing] 一双 [鞋 | 袜子 | 眼睛]

sōu 艘 (for ships) **three** [ships | oil tankers | warships] sānsōu [chuán | yóulún | jūnjiàn] 三艘 [船 | 油轮 | 军舰]

suǒ 所 (for buildings, houses, schools, etc.) **two** [hospitals | schools | houses] liǎngsuǒ [yīyuàn | xuéxiào | fángzi] 两所 [医院 | 学校 | 房子]

tái 台 (for stage performances, machines, equipment, etc.) **nine** [TV sets | washing machines | computers] jiǔtái [diànshìjī | xǐyījī | jìsuànjī] 九台 [电视机 | 洗衣机 | 计算机]; **a theatrical performance** yìtái xì 一台戏

táng 堂 (for classes or periods at school or university) period, class; **four periods** sìtáng kè 四堂课

tàng 趟 ▶ See also the list of Verbal Measure Words below. (for scheduled services of public transportation) **the next train service to Beijing** qù Běijīng de xià yítàng huǒchē 去北京的下一趟火车

tào 套 (for sets of books, clothing, tools, furniture, etc.) set, suit, suite; **a set of** [stamps | regulations | textbooks] yítào [yóupiào | guīzé | kèběn] 一套 [邮票 | 规则 | 课本]

tiáo 条 (for long, narrow things) a [towel | boat | pair of trousers | skirt | river | road | street | snake | fish | dog] yìtiáo [máojīn | chuán | kùzi | qúnzi | hé | lù | jiē | shé | yú | gǒu] 一条 [毛巾 | 船 | 裤子 | 裙子 | 河 | 路 | 街 | 蛇 | 鱼 | 狗]; (for items of news, laws, ideas, views) **three** [news items | laws | ideas] sāntiáo [xiāoxi | fǎlǜ | yìjiàn] 三条 [消息 | 法律 | 意见]; (for limbs of the human body) **two** [legs | arms] liǎngtiáo [tuǐ | gébó] 两条 [腿 | 胳膊]; (for human lives) **four lives** sìtiáo rénmìng 四条人命

tóu 头 (for certain animals) **five** [cows | pigs | sheep | elephants | lions...] wǔtóu [niú | zhū | yáng | xiàng | shīzi...] 五头 [牛 | 猪 | 羊 | 象 | 狮子...]; (for garlic bulbs) **a bulb of garlic** yìtóu suàn 一头蒜

tuán 团 (for certain round things) **a ball of wool** yìtuán máoxiàn 一团毛线

wèi 位 (a polite measure word for people) a [gentleman | lady | teacher | professor...] yíwèi [xiānsheng | nǚshì | lǎoshī | jiàoshòu...] 一位 [先生 | 女士 | 老师 | 教授...]

xià 下 ▶ See the list of Verbal Measure Words below.

xiàng 项 (for work, projects, tasks, requirements, etc.) a [piece of work | project] yíxiàng [gōngzuò | gōngchéng] 一项 [工作 | 工程]; (for decisions or announcements) a(n) [decision | announcement] yíxiàng [juédìng | shēngmíng] 一项 [决定 | 声明]

yàng 样 (for things in general) kind, sort, type; **three types of tool** sānyàng gōngjù 三样工具

zhǎn 盏 (for lamps) **a lamp** yìzhǎn dēng 一盏灯

zhāng 张 *(for flat things such as paper, paintings, tables, maps, etc.)* a [sheet of paper | newspaper | table | bed | picture | ticket | postage stamp] yìzhāng [zhǐ | bào | zhuōzi | chuáng | huà | piào | yóupiào] 一张 [纸 | 报 | 桌子 | 床 | 画 | 票 | 邮票]

zhèn 阵 *(for events or states of short duration)* a [downpour of rain | gust of wind | fit of coughing] yízhèn [dà yǔ | fēng | késou] 一阵 [大雨 | 风 | 咳嗽]

zhī 支 *(for stick-like things)* a [pen | chopstick | candle | flute] yìzhī [bǐ | kuàizi | làzhú | dízi] 一支 [笔 | 筷子 | 蜡烛 | 笛子]; *(for music, songs, or teams)* a piece of music yìzhī qǔzi 一支曲子

zhī 只 *(one of a pair)* a(n) [shoe | eye | ear | hand | foot] yìzhī [xié | yǎnjing | ěrduo | shǒu | jiǎo] 一只 [鞋 | 眼睛 | 耳朵 | 手 | 脚]; *(for some animals)* a [chicken | sheep | monkey | bird | cat | crab] yìzhī [jī | yáng | hóuzi | niǎo | māo | pángxiè] 一只 [鸡 | 羊 | 猴子 | 鸟 | 猫 | 螃蟹]; *(for boats)* a small boat yìzhī xiǎo chuán 一只小船

zhī 枝 *(for stick-like things)* ▶ See **zhī** 支 above. a rifle yìzhī bùqiāng 一枝步枪; a long-stemmed rose yìzhī méiguìhuā 一枝玫瑰花

zhǒng 种 kind, type, sort; two kinds of [people | plants | clothes | dictionaries] liǎngzhǒng [rén | zhíwù | yīfu | zìdiǎn] 两种 [人 | 植物 | 衣服 | 字典]

zuò 座 *(for mountains, buildings, structures, etc.)* a [mountain | bridge | building | palace | cinema] yízuò [shān | qiáo | lóu | gōngdiàn | diànyǐngyuàn] 一座 [山 | 桥 | 楼 | 宫殿 | 电影院]

Verbal Measure Words

Below is a short list of commonly used verbal measure words. These are generally used to indicate the number of times an action or a state occurs. The numeral and measure word are preceded by the verb and are usually followed by the object if there is one (i.e. if the verb is transitive). Some verbal measure words, such as *shēng* 声 and *xià* 下, imply that the action involved is short and brief. Please note that some verbal measure words can also be used as nominal measure words and therefore also occur in the list of Nominal Measure Words above.

biàn 遍 (to indicate the number of times an action or state occurs) time **!** Note that biàn 遍 is different from cì 次 in that it emphasizes the whole process from the beginning to the end; I've read that book twice nàběn shū wǒ kànle liǎngbiàn 那本书我看了两遍

chǎng 场 ▶ See also the list of Nominal Measure Words above. (to indicate the occasion on which a state or an action occurs) last month she was sick shàngge yuè tā bìngle yìchǎng 上个月她病了一场; I went back to my room and had a cry wǒ huídào wǒde fángjiān kūle yìchǎng 我回到我的房间哭了一场

cì 次 ▶ See also the list of Nominal Measure Words above. (to indicate the number of times an action or state occurs) time; he came three times tā láile sāncì 他来了三次

dùn 顿 ▶ See also the list of Nominal Measure Words above. (for actions that take place in single sessions) he received [some criticism | a reprimand | a beating] tā bèi [pīpíng | màle | dǎle] yídùn 他被 [批评了 | 骂了 | 打了] 一顿

huí 回 (for times, occurrences) **!** Note that huí 回 is colloquial and informal; I'd like to try two more times wǒ yào zài shì liǎnghuí 我要再试两回

shēng 声 (for counting cries, shouts, or other utterances) she called me twice tā hǎnle wǒ liǎngshēng 她喊了我两声; give me a shout before you go nǐ zǒu yǐqián hǎn wǒ yìshēng 你走以前喊我一声

tàng 趟 ▶ See also the list of Nominal Measure Words above. (for trips, journeys, visits, etc.) time, trip; last month I made three trips to Beijing shàngge yuè wǒ qùle sāntàng Běijīng 上个月我去了三趟北京; she came to my room twice yesterday zuótiān tā dào wǒ fángjiān láile liǎngtàng 昨天她到我房间来了两趟

xià 下 (for brief actions) time; I knocked at the door three times wǒ qiàole sānxià mén 我敲了三下门; he nodded his head several times tā diǎnle jǐxià tóu 他点了几下头

a, an *det* ▶ 213 yī 一; a dog yìtiáo gǒu 一条狗; an exhibition yíge zhǎnlǎnhuì 一个展览会; a crowd of people yìqún rén 一群人

able *adj* (used as a modifier) nénggàn de 能干的; an able nurse yíge nénggàn de hùshi 一个能干的护士; (having enough strength, skills or knowledge) néng 能; to be able to [walk | type | translate] néng [zǒu | dǎzì | fānyì] 能 [走 | 打字 | 翻译]

aboard *adv* ! Note that the type of vehicle needs to be specified in Chinese; to go aboard shàng [qìchē | huǒchē | fēijī] 上 [汽车 | 火车 | 飞机]

about ! Often about occurs in combinations with verbs, for example: bring about, run about etc. To find the correct translations for this type of verb, look up the separate dictionary entries at bring, run, etc. **1** prep guānyú 关于; a book about China yìběn guānyú Zhōngguó de shū 一本关于中国的书 **2** adv (pre-modifier) dàyuē 大约; Oxford is about 40 km from here Niújīn lí zhèr dàyuē sìshí gōnglǐ 牛津离这儿大约40公里; (post-modifier) zuǒyòu 左右; he goes to bed at about 11 o'clock tā shíyī diǎn zuǒyòu shuìjiào 他十一点左右睡觉 **3** to be about to jiùyào...le 就要...了, kuàiyào...le 快要...了 ! Note that a sentence-final particle le is needed in Chinese; to be about to [leave | cry | fall asleep] jiùyào [líkāi | kū | shuìzháo] le 就要 [离开 | 哭 | 睡着] 了

above 1 prep zài...shàngbian 在...上边; their office is above a shop tāmende bàngōngshì zài yíge shàngdiàn shàngbian 他们的办公室在一个商店上边 **2** adv zài shàngbian 在上边; his room is just above here tāde fángjiān jiù zài shàngbian 他的房间就在上边 **3** above all shǒuxiān 首先

abroad *adv* guówài 国外; be abroad zài guówài 在国外; return from abroad cóng guówài huílai 从国外回来; go abroad chūguó 出国

absent adj méi lái 没来, méi qù 没去, bú zài 不在: she is absent from work tā méi lái shàngbān 他没来上班; absent from classes quē kè 缺课

accent n kǒuyīn 口音

accept vb jiēshòu 接受

accident n (causing injury or damage) an accident yícì shìgù 一次事故; a car accident yícì chēhuò 一次车祸; (by accident) ǒurán 偶然: I met him by accident wǒ ǒurán yùjiànle tā 我偶然遇见了他

accommodation n zhùchù 住处; look for accommodation zhǎo zhùchù 找住处

accompany vb péitóng 陪同

account n (in a bank) an account yíge zhànghù 一个帐户; there's money in my account wǒde zhànghù lǐ yǒu qián 我的帐户里有钱; (consideration) take travelling expenses into account kǎolǜ lǚxíng de huāfèi 考虑旅行的花费

accountant n an accountant yíge kuàijì 一个会计

accuse vb accuse someone of cheating zhǐzé mǒurén qīpiàn 指责某人欺骗

across prep (to go across the road) guò mǎlù 过马路; to run across the road pǎoguò mǎlù 跑过马路; a journey across the desert chuānguò shāmò de lǚxíng 穿过沙漠的旅行; (on the other side of) zài...de nà yìbiān 在...的那一边: he lives across the street tā zhù zài mǎlù de nà yìbiān 他住在马路的那一边

act vb (to do something) xíngdòng 行动; (to play a role) bànyǎn 扮演

activity n huódòng 活动

actor n an actor yíge nán yǎnyuán 一个男演员

actress n an actress yíge nǚ yǎnyuán 一个女演员

actually adv shíjìshang 实际上, shìshíshang 事实上: actually, she's a very good athlete shíjìshang, tā shì yíge hěn hǎo de yùndòngyuán 实际上, 她是一个很好的运动员

adapt vb shǐ...shìyìng 使...适应: I must adapt myself to the new environment wǒ yídìng yào shǐ zìjǐ shìyìng xīn de huánjìng 我一定要使自己适应新的环境

add vb jiā 加

address n dìzhǐ 地址

admire vb qīnpèi 钦佩, zànshǎng 赞赏

admit vb (to own up or recognize as being true) chéngrèn 承认: he admitted that he was wrong tā chéngrèn tā cuò le 他承认他错了; to be admitted to (the) hospital zhùjìn yīyuàn 住进医院

adolescent n qīngshàonián 青少年

adopt vb cǎiyòng 采用, cǎinà 采纳

adult n chéngniánrén 成年人, dàrén 大人

advantage n (a benefit) hǎochù 好处; (a favouring condition) yǒulì tiáojiàn 有利条件; (superiority over another) yōushì 优势: at the beginning of the game, the advantage was with the blue team bǐsài kāishǐ de shíhou, lán duì zhàn yōushì 比赛开始的时候, 蓝队占优势; to take advantage of... lìyòng... 利用...

adventure n an adventure yícì màoxiǎn 一次冒险

advertise vb wèi...dēng guǎnggào 为...登广告; to advertise goods wèi shāngpǐn dēng guǎnggào 为商品登广告

advertisement n guǎnggào 广告

advice n zhōnggào 忠告, quàngào 劝告

advise vb quàngào 劝告, jiànyì 建议

aerial n tiānxiàn 天线

aerobics n zēngyǎng jiànshēn fǎ 增氧健身法

affect vb yǐngxiǎng 影响

afford vb (to bear the expense) mǎi de qǐ 买得起; he [can | cannot] afford to buy this car tā [mǎi de qǐ | mǎi bù qǐ] zhèliàng chē 他 [买得起 | 买不起] 这辆车; (to have the time) chōu de chū 抽得出; I [can | cannot] afford the time to go to the cinema wǒ [chōu de chū | chōu bù chū] shíjiān qù kàn diànyǐng 我 [抽得出 | 抽不出]

时间去看电影！Note that to negate, de 得 in mǎi de qǐ 买得起 and chōu de chū 抽得出 has to be replaced with the negative particle bù 不。

afraid adj (fearful) hàipà 害怕, pà 怕; she is afraid of dogs tā hàipà gǒu 她害怕狗; she is afraid to lose this opportunity tā pà diūle zhège jīhuì 她怕丢了这个机会; (regretfully thinking) kǒngpà 恐怕！Note that in this usage, if the subject of the main clause is a first-person singular pronoun (I wǒ 我), it has to be phonetically silent and the subject of the embedded clause can often be moved to the main clause; I'm afraid that I won't be able to go kǒngpà bù néng qù le 恐怕我不能去了, wǒ kǒngpà bù néng qù le 我恐怕不能去了; I'm afraid that he has left kǒngpà tā yǐjīng líkāi le 恐怕他已经离开了, tā kǒngpà yǐjīng líkāi le 他恐怕已经离开了

Africa n Fēizhōu 非洲

African 1 adj Fēizhōu de 非洲的 **2** n Fēizhōurén 非洲人

after 1 prep (zài)...yǐhòu (在)...以后; after breakfast zǎofàn yǐhòu 早饭以后; the day after tomorrow hòutiān 后天 **2** conj ...yǐhòu ...以后; after we had eaten, we went for a walk chīle fàn yǐhòu, wǒmen chūqu sànbù 吃了饭以后, 我们出去散步; they went in after the film had started diànyǐng kāishǐ yǐhòu tāmen cái jìnqù 电影开始以后他们才进去 **3** after all bìjìng 毕竟

afternoon n xiàwǔ 下午

afterwards, afterward (US English) adv yǐhòu 以后; (when talking about a past event) hòulái 后来

again adv (when the repetition has already happened) yòu 又; he has come again tā yòu lái le 他又来了; (when the repetition is to happen) zài 再; please try it again qǐng zài shì yícì 请再试一次

against prep (in the sense of being opposed to something) fǎnduì 反对; I am against this plan wǒ fǎnduì zhège jīhuà 我反对这个计划; (to resist the wind) dǐng 顶; the ship is sailing against the wind chuán zhèng dǐngzhe fēng xíngshǐ 船正顶着风行驶; (to resist a water current) nì 逆; she swam against the current tā nì shuǐ yóuyǒng 她逆水游泳; (to put pressure upon) kào 靠, yǐ 倚; I was standing against the wall wǒ kàozhe qiáng zhànzhe 我靠着墙站着

age n suì 岁, niánjì 年纪, niánlíng 年龄

aged adj (advanced in age) lǎo 老; (of the age of) ...suì de ... 岁 的; children aged 10 shí suì de háizi 十岁的孩子

ago adv yǐqián 以前; two weeks ago liǎngge xīngqī yǐqián 两个 星期以前; long ago hěn jiǔ yǐqián 很久以前

agree vb (to have the same opinion) tóngyì 同意, zàntóng 赞同; I don't agree with you wǒ bù tóngyì nǐde yìjian 我不同意你的 意见; (to consent to do) dāying 答应, yīngyún 应允; he agrees to help us tā dāying bāngzhù wǒmen 他答应帮助我们; (to decide jointly) shāngdìng 商定, yuēdìng 约定; we have agreed on the date for the meeting wǒmen shāngdìngle huìyì de rìqī 我们商定了会议的日期

agriculture n nóngyè 农业

ahead adv (location) zài...qiánmian 在...前面; he is ahead of others tā zài biéren qiánmian 他在别人前面; (direction) xiàng qián 向前; look ahead xiàngqián kàn 向前看

Aids n àizībìng 艾滋病

aim 1 n an aim (an object aimed at) yíge mùbiāo 一个目标; (a purpose aimed at) yíge mùdì 一个目的 **2** vb (to be directed at) to be aimed at young people zhēnduì niánqīng rén 针对年 轻人; (when using a weapon) to aim a rifle at someone yòng qiāng miáozhǔn mǒurén 用枪瞄准某人

air n kōngqì 空气; in the air zài kōngzhōng 在空中

air force n kōngjūn 空军

air hostess n (British English) an air hostess yíwèi kōngzhōng xiǎojiě 一位空中小姐

airmail n to send a letter by airmail jì yìfēng hángkōng xìn 寄一封航空信

airport n an airport yíge fēijīchǎng 一个飞机场

alarm clock *n* an alarm clock yíge nàozhōng 闹钟

alcohol *n* (*chemical term*) jiǔjīng 酒精; (*drink containing alcohol*) jiǔ 酒

alive *adj* huózhe 活着

all 1 *det* (*whole*) zhěnggè 整个; I spent all week working wǒ zhěnggè xīngqī dōu gōngzuò 我整个星期都工作; (*every*) suǒyǒu de 所有的, quánbù de 全部的; all the men have left suǒyǒu de nánrén dōu líkāi le 所有的男人都离开了 **2** *pron* (*people*) suǒyǒu de rén 所有的人; all of us wǒmen suǒyǒu de rén 我们所有的人; (*things*) yíqiè 一切; these are all I have zhè shì wǒ yōngyǒu de yíqiè 这是我拥有的一切; that's all wán le 完了 **3** *adv* to be all alone dúzì yì rén 独自一人; he didn't go all along the street tā méiyǒu yìzhí yánzhe mǎlù zǒu 他没有一直沿着马路走

allow *vb* yúnxǔ 允许, zhǔnxǔ 准许; to allow someone to [work | play | leave...] yúnxǔ mǒurén [gōngzuò | wán | líkāi...] 允许某人 [工作 | 玩 | 离开...]; smoking is not allowed jìnzhǐ xīyān 禁止吸烟

all right *adj* (*when giving your opinion*) búcuò 不错, hái kěyǐ 还可以; the film was all right zhèbù diànyǐng búcuò 这部电影不错; (*when talking about health*) are you all right? nǐ hái hǎo ma? 你还好吗?, nǐ hái xíng ma? 你还行吗?; (*when asking someone's agreement*) is it all right if I come later? wǒ wǎn diǎnr lái xíng ma? 我晚点来行吗?; come at about nine, all right? dàyuē jiǔ diǎn lái, xíng ma? 大约九点来, 行吗?; (*when agreeing*) xíng 行, hǎo 好

almond *n* xìngrén 杏仁

almost *adv* jīhū 几乎, chàbùduō 差不多; I almost forgot wǒ jīhū wàng le 我几乎忘了

alone 1 *adj* dāndú 单独, dúzì yìrén 独自一人; to be all alone dúzì yìrén 独自一人; leave me alone! bié guǎn wǒ! 别管我!, bié dòng wǒ! 别动我! **2** *adv* to [work | to live | to travel...] alone dúzì yìrén [gōngzuò | shēnghuó | lǚxíng...] 独自一人 [工作 | 生活 | 旅行...]

along *prep* yánzhe 沿着; there are trees along the river yánzhe hébiān yǒu yìxiē shù 沿着河边有一些树

aloud adv dàshēng de 大声地; to read aloud lǎngdú 朗读

already adv yǐjīng 已经; it's ten o'clock already yǐjīng shí diǎn le 已经十点了

also adv (likewise) yě 也; he also agrees with me tā yě tóngyì wǒde yìjiàn 他也同意我的意见; (in addition) hái 还; I also bought a bottle of wine wǒ hái mǎile yìpíng jiǔ 我还买了一瓶酒

although conj suīrán 虽然, jǐnguǎn 尽管; although she's strict, she's fair suīrán tā hěn yángé, dàn tā hěn gōngpíng 虽然她很严格, 但她很公平

always adv (every time) zǒngshì 总是, lǎoshì 老是; I always go to China in (the) summer wǒ zǒngshì xiàtiān qù Zhōngguó 我总是夏天去中国; (ever) yǒngyuǎn 永远; I'll always remember him wǒ jiāng yǒngyuǎn jìzhù tā 我将永远记住他

amazed adj jīngyà 惊讶, jīngqí 惊奇

amazing adj lìngrén jīngyà 令人惊讶, liǎobuqǐ 了不起

ambition n (aspiration for success or advancement) bàofù 抱负, xióngxīn 雄心; (inordinate desire for power, fame) yěxīn 野心, shēwàng 奢望

ambitious adj (aspiring) yǒu bàofù de 有抱负的, yǒu xióngxīn de 有雄心的; (inordinately longing for power, fame) yǒu yěxīn de 有野心的

ambulance n jiùhùchē 救护车

America n Měiguó 美国

American 1 adj Měiguó de 美国的 **2** n Měiguórén 美国人

among, amongst prep (in the middle of) zài...zhōngjiān 在...中间; she was sitting among the students tā zuò zài xuésheng zhōngjiān 她坐在学生中间; (in a particular group) zài...zhōng 在...中; unemployment among young people zài niánqīng rén zhōng de shīyè qíngkuàng 在年轻人中的失业情况

amount n shùliàng 数量

amusement arcade n diànzǐ yóuxì fáng 电子游戏房

amusement park n yùlè chǎng 娱乐场

an ▶ a

ancestor n zǔzōng 祖宗, zǔxiān 祖先

and conj and hé 和; father and mother bàba hé māma 爸爸和
妈妈; (and is not translated when it is used to connect two verb
phrases or two sentences) she went to the shop and bought
some fruit tā qù shāngdiàn mǎile yìxiē shuǐguǒ 她去商店买了
一些水果; (in numbers, and is not translated) three hundred
and sixty-five sānbǎi liùshí wǔ 三百六十五

anger n fènnù 愤怒, qìfèn 气愤

angry adj to be angry shēngqì 生气; to be angry with someone
duì mǒurén shēngqì 对某人生气

animal n dòngwù 动物; farm animals sìyǎng de dòngwù 饲养
的动物

ankle n huáiguānjié 踝关节, jiǎobózi 脚脖子

announcement n an announcement yíge tōnggào/tōngzhī
一个通告/通知

annoy vb shǐ...shēngqì 使...生气, shǐ...náohuǒ 使...恼火; to
annoy someone shǐ mǒurén shēngqì 使某人生气

annoyed adj to be annoyed with someone duì mǒurén shēngqì
对某人生气

another 1 det another zài...yī 再...一, lìng...yī 另...一; another
cup of coffee? zài hē yìbēi kāfēi? 再喝一杯咖啡?; I'll buy
another ticket for her wǒ gěi tā lìng mǎi yìzhāng piào 我给她另
买一张票; (different) biéde 别的, lìngwài de 另外的; there's
another way of doing it hái yǒu biéde fāngfǎ zuò zhèjiàn shì 还
有别的方法做这件事; he has become another person tā
biànchéngle lìngwài de yíge rén 他变成了另外的一个人
2 pron I don't like [this pen | this book | this coat...], please show me
another wǒ bù xǐhuān [zhèzhī bǐ | zhèběn shū | zhèjiàn shàngyī...], qǐng
ná [lìng yìzhī | lìng yìběn | lìng yìjiàn...] gěi wǒ kànkan 我不喜欢[这支
笔|这本书|这件上衣...], 请拿[另一支|另一本|另一件...]给

我看看! Note that it is necessary to use an appropriate measure word after lìng yī... 另一..., when another is translated as a pronoun.

answer 1 n dáfù 答复, huídá 回答; **did you get an answer?** nǐ dédào dáfù le ma? 你得到答复了吗?; **there's no answer (at the door)** méi rén huídá 没人回答; (solution) dá'àn 答案: **answers to the exercises** liànxí dá'àn 练习答案 **2** vb huídá 回答; **to answer a question** huídá yíge wèntí 回答一个问题; **to answer the phone** jiē diànhuà 接电话

answering machine n an answering machine yìtái lùyīn diànhuà 一台录音电话

ant n an ant yìzhī mǎyǐ 一只蚂蚁

antique n an antique yíjiàn gǔwù 一件古物, yíjiàn gǔdǒng 一件古董

antique shop n an antique shop yìjiā gǔwù shāngdiàn 一家古物商店, yìjiā gǔdǒng diàn 一件古董店

anxious adj (uneasy with fear) dānxīn 担心, jiāolǜ 焦虑; **I'm anxious about her safety** wǒ wèi tāde ānquán dānxīn 我为她的安全担心; (eager) jíqiè 急切, kěwàng 渴望; **she is anxious to go with me** tā jíqiè xiǎng gēn wǒ yíqǐ qù 她急切想跟我一起去

any 1 det (in questions) shénme 什么! Note that it is often unnecessary to translate any in questions; **do you have any questions?** nǐ yǒu (shénme) wèntí ma? 你有(什么)问题吗?; (with the negative) rènhé 任何; **I didn't have any friends** wǒ méi yǒu rènhé péngyou 我没有任何朋友; (whatever) rènhé 任何; **any pen will do** rènhé bǐ dōu xíng 任何笔都行 **2** pron do any of you know his telephone number? nǐmen shéi zhīdao tāde diànhuà hàomǎ ma? 你们谁知道他的电话号码吗?; **do you have any?** nǐ yǒu ma? 你有吗?; **he doesn't have any** tā méi yǒu 他没有! Note that it is often unnecessary to translate any when it is used as a pronoun in an object position.

anyone pron (also **anybody**) rènhé rén 任何人; **did you meet anyone?** nǐ yùjiàn rènhé rén le ma? 你遇见任何人了吗?; **anyone could do it** rènhé rén dōu néng zuò zhèjiàn shì 任何人都能做这件事

anything pron (in questions or with the negative) shénme shì 什么事, rènhé shì 任何事; can I do anything for you? wǒ néng wèi nǐ zuò diǎnr shénme shì ma? 我能为你做点儿什么事吗?; there isn't anything to do here zhèr méi yǒu rènhé shì kě zuò 这儿没有任何事可做; (everything) rènhé shìqíng 任何事情, yíqiè 一切; he is willing to do anything for her tā yuàn wèi tā zuò rènhé shìqíng 他愿为她做任何事情

anyway adv fǎnzhèng 反正; I didn't want to go there anyway fǎnzhèng wǒ běnlái yě bù xiǎng qù nàr 反正我本来也不想去那儿

anywhere adv (in questions or with the negative) nǎr 哪儿, nǎli 哪里; can you see a telephone anywhere? nǐ néng kànjiàn nǎr yǒu diànhuà ma? 你能看见哪儿有电话吗?; you can't go anywhere nǐ nǎr yě bù néng qù 你哪儿也不能去; (any place) zài rènhé dìfang 在任何地方; we can meet anywhere you like wǒmen kěyǐ zài rènhé dìfang jiànmiàn, suí nǐ biàn 我们可以在任何地方见面, 随你便

apart 1 adj they don't like being apart tāmen bú yuànyì fēnkāi 他们不愿意分开 2 apart from chúle...(yǐwài) 除了...(以外); apart from Tom, I don't know anyone there chúle Tāngmǔ (yǐwài), nàr wǒ shéi dōu bú rènshi 除了汤姆(以外), 那儿我谁都不认识

apartment n an apartment yítào gōngyù fángjiān 一套公寓房间

apartment block n an apartment block yìpái gōngyù lóu 一排公寓楼

apologize vb dàoqiàn 道歉; did you apologize to him? nǐ xiàng tā dàoqiàn le ma? 你向他道歉了吗?

apology n dàoqiàn 道歉, rèncuò 认错; to make an apology to him for coming late wèi láiwǎn xiàng tā dàoqiàn 为来晚了向他道歉

appear vb (to seem) kànqǐlai 看起来, hǎoxiàng 好象; (to come into view) chūxiàn 出现, xiǎnlù 显露

appetite n shíyù 食欲, wèikǒu 胃口; to have a good appetite shíyù hǎo 食欲好

apple n an apple yíge píngguǒ 一个苹果

apple juice n píngguǒ zhī 苹果汁

appliance n qìjù 器具; yòngjù 用具; an appliance yíjiàn qìjù 一件器具

application n an application yífèn shēnqǐng 一份申请

apply vb shēnqǐng 申请; to apply for a passport shēnqǐng yìbén hùzhào 申请一本护照

appointment n yuēhuì 约会; to make an appointment with someone gēn mǒurén yuēhuì 跟某人约会

appreciate vb I'd appreciate it if you could let me know rúguǒ nǐ néng gàosu wǒ, wǒ huì fēicháng gǎnxiè 如果你能告诉我, 我会非常感谢

approach vb jiējìn 接近, kàojìn 靠近

approve vb pīzhǔn 批准, tōngguò 通过; to approve of someone zànchéng mǒurén 赞成某人

apricot n an apricot yíge xìng 一个杏

April n sìyuè 四月

architect n an architect yíge jiànzhùshī 一个建筑师

area n (a region) dìqū 地区; an area yíge dìqū 一个地区; (an academic field) lǐngyù 领域; an area yíge lǐngyù 一个领域

area code n (US English) yóuzhèng biānmǎ 邮政编码

argue vb zhēnglùn 争论, biànlùn 辩论; to argue about politics zhēnglùn zhèngzhì 争论政治

argument n an argument yíge lùndiǎn 一个论点, yíge lǐyóu 一个理由; to have an argument with someone gēn mǒurén zhēnglùn 跟某人争论

arm n the arm gēbo 胳膊, bì 臂

armchair n an armchair yíge fúshǒuyǐ 一个扶手椅

armed adj wǔzhuāng de 武装的

arms n wǔqì 武器

army n jūnduì 军队; to join the army cān jūn 参军

around ! *Often around occurs in combinations with verbs, for example:* run around, turn around, *etc. To find the correct translations for this type of verb, look up the separate dictionary entries at* run, turn, *etc.* **1** *prep* zài...zhōuwéi 在...周围; there are trees all around the garden zài huāyuán zhōuwéi dōu shì shù 在花园周围都是树; the people around me were speaking Chinese zài wǒ zhōuwéi de rén shuō Hànyǔ 在我周围的人说汉语; to go around the world zhōuyóu shìjiè 周游世界 **2** *adv* (*nearby*) zhōuwéi 周围; he looked around tā xiàng zhōuwéi kàn le kàn 他向周围看了看; (*approximately*) dàyuē 大约; we'll be there at around four o'clock wǒmen dàyuē sì diǎn zhōng dào nàr 我们大约四点钟到那儿

arrange *vb* (*to make plans in advance*) ānpái 安排; to arrange a break in Italy ānpái zài Yìdàlì xiūxi yíxià 安排在意大利休息一下; to arrange to have lunch together ānpái yìqǐ chī wǔfàn 安排一起吃午饭; (*to put in order*) zhěnglǐ 整理; to arrange his books zhěnglǐ tāde shū 整理他的书

arrest *vb* dàibǔ 逮捕

arrive *vb* dàodá 到达, dào 到; we arrived at the station at noon wǒmen zhōngwǔ dàodá chēzhàn 我们中午到达车站

arrow *n* (*missile*) jiàn 箭; an arrow yìzhī jiàn 一支箭; (*mark or object*) jiàntóu 箭头; an arrow yíge jiàntóu 一个箭头

art *n* yìshù 艺术

art gallery *n* an art gallery yíge měishùguǎn 一个美术馆

artificial *adj* réngōng 人工, rénzào 人造

artist *n* an artist yíge yìshùjiā 一个艺术家

arts *n* arts and humanities rénwén xuékē 人文学科

arts and crafts *n* gōngyì měishù 工艺美术

as 1 *conj* as ànzhào 按照; do as he does ànzhào tāde yàngzi zuò 按照他的样子做; (*at the time when*) ... de shíhou ... 的时候; the phone rang as I was getting out of the bath wǒ zhèng cóng zǎopén chūlái de shíhou, diànhuà líng xiǎng le 我正从澡盆出来的时候电话铃响了; I used to live there as a child wǒ xiǎo de shíhou zhù zài nàr 我小的时候住在那儿; (*because, since*) yīnwèi 因为, yóuyú 由于; **as you were out, I left a note** yīnwèi nǐ chūqu le, suǒyǐ wǒ jiù liúle zhāng tiáo 因为你出去了, 所以我就留了张条; (when used with the same) gēn...yíyàng 跟...一样, hé...yíyàng 和...一样; **my coat is the same as yours** wǒde shàngyī gēn nǐde yíyàng 我的上衣跟你的一样; **2** prep **she's got a job as a teacher** tā zhǎodào le yíge jiàoshī de gōngzuò 她找到了一个教师的工作; **he was dressed as a sailor** tā chuān de xiàng yíge shuǐshǒu 他穿得象一个水手; **3** adv **as** [intelligent | rich | strong...] **as he is** tā yíyàng [cōngming | yǒuqián | qiángzhuàng...] 和他一样 [聪明 | 有钱 | 强壮...]; **go there as fast as you can** nǐ jǐnkuài qù nàr 你尽快去那儿; **I have as much work as you** wǒde gōngzuò hé nǐde yíyàng duō 我的工作和你的一样多; **he plays the piano as well as his younger sister** tā gāngqín tán de hé tā mèimei yíyàng hǎo 他弹钢琴弹得和他妹妹一样好 **4 as usual** xiàng wǎngcháng yíyàng 象往常一样, zhàolì 照例

ashamed adj **to be ashamed** gǎndào cánkuì 感到惭愧, gǎndào hàisào 感到害臊

ashes n huī(jìn) 灰(烬); (of a cigarette) yānhuī 烟灰; (of a dead body) gúhuī 骨灰

ashtray n an ashtray yíge yānhuīgāng 一个烟灰缸

Asia n Yàzhōu 亚洲

Asian 1 adj Yàzhōu de 亚洲的 **2** n Yàzhōurén 亚洲人

ask vb **to ask** wèn 问; **he asked me my name** tā wèn wǒ jiào shénme 他问我叫什么; **I'll ask them if they want to come** wǒ yào wèn tāmen xiǎng bù xiǎng lái 我要问他们想不想来; **to ask a question** wèn wèntí 问问题; (to request) ràng 让, jiào 叫, yāoqiú 要求; **to ask someone to** [phone | come | do the shopping...] ràng mǒurén [dǎ diànhuà | lái | mǎi dōngxi...] 让某人 [打电话 | 来 | 买东西...]; **to ask to speak to someone** yāoqiú gēn mǒurén jiǎnghuà 要求跟某人讲话; **to ask for money** yào qián 要钱; (to invite) yāoqǐng 邀请, qǐng 请; **to ask some friends to dinner** yāoqǐng yìxiē péngyou chī fàn 邀请一些朋友吃饭; (to look for information) xúnwèn 询问; **did you ask about the tickets?** nǐ xúnwèn piào de shìqing le ma? 你询问票的事情了吗?

asleep *adj* to be asleep zài shuìjiào 在睡觉; to fall asleep shuìzháo 睡着

assemble *vb* (*to call together*) jíhé 集合; all the students assembled in the school hall xuéshēng dōu zài xuéxiào lǐtáng lǐ jíhé 学生都在学校礼堂里集合; (*to collect*) shōují 收集; she has assembled some materials tā yǐjīng shōují le yìxiē cáiliào 她已经收集了一些材料; (*to put together the parts of*) zhuāngpèi 装配; to assemble a machine zhuāngpèi jīqì 装配机器

assignment *n* a school assignment xuéxiào zuòyè 学校作业

assistant *n* an assistant yíge zhùshǒu 一个助手; a shop assistant yíge shòuhuòyuán 一个售货员; a teaching assistant yíge zhùjiào 一个助教

at *prep* **!** There are many verbs which involve the use of at, like look at, laugh at, point at, etc. For translations, look up the entries at look, laugh, point, etc.; (*when talking about a position or place*) zài 在; we'll meet at the concert wǒmen zài yīnyuèhuì jiànmiàn 我们在音乐会见面 [zài 在 [at home | at school | at work...] [zài jiā | zài xuéxiào | zài shàngbān...] [在家 | 在学校 | 在上班...]; to be at one's desk zài xuéxí 在学习, zài gōngzuò 在工作; (*when talking about time and age*) zài)...(de shíhou)...(的时候), the film starts at nine o'clock diànyǐng jiǔ diǎn kāiyǎn 电影九点开演; she was able to read at four years of age tā (zài) sì suì (de shíhou) jiù néng kàn shū le 她(在)四岁(的时候)就能看书了; (*when talking about speed and price*) yǐ 以; the car goes at seventy miles an hour qìchē yǐ měi xiǎoshí wǔshí yīnglǐ de sùdù xíngshǐ 汽车以每小时五十英里的速度行驶; at a low price yǐ hěn dī de jiàqián 以很低的价钱

athlete *n* an athlete yíge yùndòngyuán 一个运动员, yìmíng yùndòngyuán 一名运动员

athletics *n* (*in Britain*) tiánjìng yùndòng 田径运动; (*in the US*) tǐyù yùndòng 体育运动

Atlantic *n* the Atlantic Dàxīyáng 大西洋

atmosphere *n* (*the air*) dàqì 大气, kōngqì 空气; (*a mood, a feeling*) qìfēn 气氛

attach vb to be attached to the wall tiē zài qiáng shang 贴在墙上; to attach a basket to the bike bǎ yíge lánzi jì zài zìxíngchē shang 把一个篮子系在自行车上

attack vb gōngjī 攻击, jìngōng 进攻

attempt 1 vb shìtú 试图; to attempt to break the record shìtú dǎpò jìlù 试图打破纪录 2 n chángshì 尝试, shìtú 试图

attend vb (to be present) cānjiā 参加, chūxí 出席; to attend a meeting cānjiā huìyì 参加会议; (to go regularly to) shàng 上; to attend evening classes shàng yèxiào 上夜校

attention n zhùyì 注意; to get someone's attention yǐnqǐ mǒurén de zhùyì 引起某人的注意; to pay attention to the teacher zhùyì tīng lǎoshī jiǎngkè 注意听老师讲课

attic n gélóu 阁楼, fángdǐngshì 房顶室

attitude n tàidu 态度; his attitude toward(s) me tā duì wǒ de tàidu 他对我的态度

attract vb to attract people xīyǐn rén 吸引人; to attract [attention | interest | appreciation] yǐnqǐ [zhùyì | xìngqu | zànshǎng] 引起[注意 | 兴趣 | 赞赏]

attractive adj yǒu xīyǐnlì de 有吸引力的, yòurén de 诱人的

auburn adj jīn zōngsè de 金棕色的

audience n (assembly of hearers) tīngzhòng 听众; (assembly of spectators) guānzhòng 观众

August n bāyuè 八月

aunt n (father's sister) gūmǔ 姑母, gūgu 姑姑; (mother's sister) yímǔ 姨母, yí 姨; (a respectful form of address to an elderly woman) dàmā 大妈, dàniáng 大娘; (a respectful form used by children to address an adult woman) āyí 阿姨

au pair n an au pair yíge bāngshǒu 一个帮手, yíge bānggōng 一个帮工

Australia n Àodàlìyà 澳大利亚

Australian 1 adj Àodàlìyà de 澳大利亚的 2 n Àodàlìyàrén 澳大利亚人

Austria n Àodìlì 奥地利

Austrian 1 adj Àodìlì de 奥地利的 **2** n Àodìlìrén 奥地利人

author n zuòzhě 作者

automatic adj zìdòng 自动

autumn n qiūtiān 秋天, qiūjì 秋季

available adj (obtainable through purchase) néng mǎidào 能买到, mǎi de dào 买得到; **tickets for the concert are still available** yīnyuèhuì de piào hái néng mǎidào 音乐会的票还能买到; (accessible for use) kěyǐ yòng 可以用; **all the books are available to the students** suǒyǒu de shū xuésheng dōu kěyǐ yòng 所有的书学生都可以用

average adj (mean) píngjūn 平均; (ordinary) pǔtōng de 普通的, tōngcháng de 通常的; **the average man** pǔtōng de rén 普通的人

avoid vb (to prevent) bìmiǎn 避免; **to avoid spending money** bìmiǎn huā qián 避免花钱; (to stay away from) duǒkāi 躲开, huíbì 回避

awake adj **to be awake** (having slept) xǐngle 醒了; **to stay awake** shuì bù zháo 睡不着; **to keep someone awake** shǐ mǒurén shuì bù zháo 使某人睡不着

award n **an award** yíge jiǎng(pǐn) 一个奖(品); **she got the award for best actress** tā huòdé zuìjiā nǚ yǎnyuán jiǎng 她获得最佳女演员奖

aware adj **to be aware of the** [problem | danger | difficulty...] yìshídào zhège [wèntí | wēixiǎn | kùnnan...] 意识到这个 [问题 | 危险 | 困难...]

away adv (absent) **to be away** bú zài 不在; **she's away on business** tā chūchāi le 她出差了; (when talking about distances) **to be far away** zài hěn yuǎn 在很远; **London is 40 km away** Lúndūn lí zhèr sìshí gōnglǐ 伦敦离这儿四十公里

awful adj (no good) zāotòu le 糟透了, hěn zāogāo 很糟糕; **I thought the film was awful** wǒ juéde zhège diànyǐng zāotòu le 我觉得这个电影糟透了; (causing shock) kěpà 可怕; **an**

awful accident yígè kěpà de shìgù 一个可怕的事故; I feel awful wǒ gǎndào fēicháng nánshòu 我感到非常难受

awkward *adj (describing a situation, a problem)* jíshǒu 棘手, nán chǔlǐ 难处理; *(embarrassed)* gāngà 尴尬; I feel awkward about telling him gàosu tā wǒ juéde hěn gāngà 告诉他我觉得很尴尬

axe *n* an axe yìbǎ fǔtóu 一把斧头, yìbǎ fǔzi 一把斧子

Bb

baby *n* a baby yígè yīng'ér 一个婴儿

babysit *vb* zhàokàn háizi 照看孩子

back ! *Often back occurs in combinations with verbs, for example: come back, get back, give back, etc. To find the correct translations for this type of verb, look up the separate dictionary entries at come, get, give, etc.* **1** *n (part of the body)* the back bèibù 背部, bèi 背; I've hurt my back wǒ bèibù shòule shāng 我背部受了伤; *(the rear)* hòumian 后面; at the back of the supermarket zài chāojí shìchǎng hòumian 在超级市场后面; to sit in the back of the car zuò zài chē hòumian 坐在车后面 **2** *adv* to be back huílai 回来; I'll be back in five minutes wǒ guò wǔ fēnzhōng huílai 我过五分钟回来

back door *n* the back door hòumén 后门

background *n (previous history of a person)* lǚlì 履历; *(upbringing of a person)* chūshēn 出身; *(of a picture or a story)* the background bèijǐng 背景

backpack *n* a backpack yígè bèibāo 一个背包

back seat *n* the back seat hòumian de zuòwei 后面的坐位

back to front *adv* fǎn 反; to put a sweater on back to front bǎ máoyī chuānfǎn le 把毛衣穿反了

backwards, backward adv xiànghòu 向后

bacon n bacon xián zhūròu 咸猪肉

bad adj bad huài 坏, bù hǎo 不好; a bad idea yíge huài zhǔyì 一个坏主意; a bad film yíge bù hǎo de diànyǐng 一个不好的电影; I have some bad news wǒ yǒu yíge huài xiāoxi 我有一个坏消息; to be bad at [maths | tennis | chess...] bú shàncháng [shùxué | dǎ wǎngqiú | xià qí...] 不善长 [数学 | 打网球 | 下棋...]; it's a bad time to go on holiday zhège shíjiān dùjià bù hǎo 这个时间度假不好; 'was the film good?'—'not bad' 'zhège diànyǐng hǎo ma?'—'bú cuò' '这个电影好吗?'—'不错'; smoking is bad for you xīyān duì nǐ shēntǐ bù hǎo 吸烟对你身体不好; (serious) yánzhòng 严重; a bad accident yíge yánzhòng de shìgù 一个严重的事故; to have a bad cold dé zhòng gǎnmào 得重感冒; (when talking about food) the milk has gone bad niúnǎi huài le 牛奶坏了; (not kind, not honest) bú dàodé, 不道德, huài 坏

badger n a badger yìzhī huān 一只獾

badly adv (not well) bù hǎo 不好; she slept badly tā shuì de bù hǎo 她睡得不好; (seriously) yánzhòng 严重; he was badly injured tā shāng de hěn yánzhòng 他伤得很严重; (naughty) tiáopí 调皮; this child behaves badly zhège háizi hěn tiáopí 这个孩子很调皮

badminton n yǔmáoqiú 羽毛球

bad-tempered adj to be bad-tempered píqì hěn huài 脾气很坏

bag n a bag yíge bāo 一个包

baggage n a piece of baggage yíjiàn xíngli 一件行李

bake vb kǎo 烤

baker n a baker yíge miànbāoshī 一个面包师

bakery n a bakery yìjiā miànbāodiàn 一家面包店

balance n (an instrument for weighing) chèng 称, tiānpíng 天平; (equilibrium) pínghéng 平衡; to lose one's balance shīqù pínghéng 失去平衡

balcony n a balcony yíge yángtái 一个阳台

bald adj tūdǐng 秃顶, tūtóu 秃头

ball n a ball yíge qiú 一个球; to play ball dǎ qiú 打球

ballet n ballet bālěiwǔ 芭蕾舞

balloon n a balloon yíge qìqiú 一个气球

ballpoint (US English) n a ballpoint pen yìzhī yuánzhūbǐ 一支圆珠笔

ban vb jìnzhǐ 禁止

banana n a banana yíge xiāngjiāo 一个香蕉

band n (a flat strip) a band yìgēn dàizi 一根带子; (a body of musicians) yíge yuèduì 一个乐队; (a group) qún 群; a band of football fans yìqún qiúmí 一群球迷

bandage n a bandage yìgēn bēngdài 一根绷带

bang 1 n (a loud noise) a bang pēng de yìshēng 砰的一声; (US English) (fringe) bangs liúhǎir 刘海儿 2 vb (to close with a bang) pēng de guānshang 砰地关上; (to strike with the head or body) měng zhuàng 猛撞; (to beat with the hand) měng qiāo 猛敲; to bang one's fist on the table yòng quántou měng qiāo zhuōzi 用拳头猛敲桌子

bank n (a financial institution) a bank yìjiā yínháng 一家银行; (blood bank) a blood bank yíge xuèkù 一个血库; (of a river) a river bank yíge hé'àn 一个河岸

bank account n a bank account yíge yínháng zhànghù 一个银行帐户

bank holiday n (British English) a bank holiday yíge gōngjiàrì 一个公假日

bar n (a place) a bar yíge jiǔbā 一个酒吧; (made of metal) an iron bar yìgēn tiěbàng 一根铁棒 (on a cage or window) a bar yìgēn zhàlan 一根栅栏; (other uses) a bar of soap yìtiáo féizào 一条肥皂; a bar of chocolate yí dà kuài qiǎokèlì 一大块巧克力

barbecue n a barbecue yícì shāokǎo yěcān 一次烧烤野餐

barely adv miǎnqiǎng 勉强; he was barely able to walk tā miǎnqiǎng nénggòu zǒulù 他勉强能够走路

bargain *n* a bargain yìbǐ jiāoyì 一笔交易

bark 1 *n* (of a tree) shùpí 树皮; (of a dog) the dog's bark gǒu jiào de shēngyīn 狗叫的声音 **2** *vb* the dog is barking gǒu zài jiào 狗在叫

barn *n* a barn yíge gǔcāng 一个谷仓

barrel *n* a barrel of water yìtǒng shuǐ 一桶水

base *vb* (use as a basis for) yǐ ... wéi jīchǔ 以 ... 为基础, yǐ ... wéi gēnjù 以 ... 为根据; to be based on a true story yǐ yíge zhēnshí de gùshì wéi jīchǔ 以一个真实的故事为基础; (of a company or diplomatic mission) to be based in London cháng zhù (zài) Lúndūn 常驻(在)伦敦

baseball *n* baseball bàngqiú 棒球

basement *n* a basement yíge dìxiàshì 一个地下室

basically *adv* jīběnshang 基本上

basin *n* a basin yíge pén 一个盆

basket *n* a basket yíge lánzi 一个篮子

basketball *n* basketball lánqiú 篮球

bat *n* (in cricket or baseball) a bat yìgēn qiúbàng 一根球棒; (an animal) a bat yíge biānfú 一个蝙蝠

bath *n* to have a bath xǐzǎo 洗澡; he's in the bath tā zài xǐzǎo 他在洗澡; (a bathtub) a bath yíge yùpén 一个浴盆

bathroom *n* a bathroom yíge yùshì 一个浴室; (US English) (the toilet) to go to the bathroom shàng cèsuǒ 上厕所

battery *n* a battery (for a torch) yìjié diànchí 一节电池; (for a car) yíge diànchí 一个电池

battle *n* a battle yìchǎng zhàndòu 一场战斗

bay *n* a bay yíge hǎiwān 一个海湾

be *vb* to be shì 是; he is a lawyer tā shì yíge lǜshī 他是一个律师; (in the future tense or in the infinitive) chéngwéi 成为; Tom will be a film star Tāngmǔ jiāng chéngwéi yíge diànyǐng míngxīng 汤姆将成为一个电影明星; my son hopes to be a footballer wǒ érzi xīwàng chéngwéi yíge zúqiú yùndòngyuán

我儿子希望成为一个足球运动员; (when talking about travelling) **I've never been to Japan** wǒ cónglái méi qùguo Rìběn 我从来没去过日本; **have you ever been to Africa?** nǐ qùguo Fēizhōu ma? 你去过非洲吗; (when talking about health) **how are you?** nǐ hǎo ma? 你好吗? **I'm very well** wǒ hěn hǎo 我很好; **how is your mother?** nǐ māma hǎo ma? 你妈妈好吗?

beach n a beach (on a sea) yīge hǎitān 一个海滩; (on a river) yīge hétān 一个河滩; (on a lake) yīge hútān 一个湖滩

beam n (in a building) a beam yìgēn liáng 一根梁; (a ray of light) **a beam of light** yíshù guāng 一束光, yídào guāng 一道光

bean n a bean yíge dòuzi 一个豆子

bear 1 n a bear yìzhī xióng 一只熊 2 vb (to sustain) fùdān 负担, chéngdān 承担; (to endure) rěnshòu 忍受, róngrěn 容忍

beard n húzi 胡子

beat vb (to hit hard) dǎ 打; (in cooking) jiǎobàn 搅拌; (to win against) zhànshèng 战胜, dǎbài 打败; **Scotland beat England two to one** Sūgélán èr bǐ yī zhànshèng le Yīnggélán 苏格兰二比一战胜了英格兰

beautiful adj měilì 美丽, piàoliang 漂亮; **a beautiful garden** yíge měilì de huāyuán 一个美丽的花园; **a beautiful girl** yíge piàoliang de gūniang 一个漂亮的姑娘

beauty n měilì 美丽, měi 美

because 1 conj yīnwèi 因为; **he didn't come because he was ill** yīnwèi tā bìngle, suǒyǐ tā méi lái 因为他病了, 所以他没来 2 **because of** yīnwèi 因为; **we didn't go out because of the rain** yīnwèi xiàyǔ, suǒyǐ wǒmen méi chūqu 因为下雨, 所以我们没出去! Note that the clause or phrase introduced by yīnwèi 因为 usually appears before the main clause. Note also that when yīnwèi 因为 is used, the main clause is often preceded by suǒyǐ 所以 which means therefore.

become vb (followed by a noun) biànchéng 变成, chéngwéi 成为; **he has become an adult** tā biànchéng/chéngwéi dàrén le 他变成/成为大人了; (followed by an adjective) biàn 变, biànde 变得; **it has become cold** tiān biàn lěng le 天变冷了

bed *n* a bed yìzhāng chuáng 一张床; to go to bed shàng chuáng shuìjiào 上床睡觉

bedroom *n* a bedroom yíge wòshì 一个卧室, yíge qǐnshì 一个寝室

bee *n* a bee yìzhī mìfēng 一只蜜蜂

beef *n* niúròu 牛肉; roast beef kǎo niúròu 烤牛肉

beer *n* (the product) beer píjiǔ 啤酒; (a glass of beer) a beer yìbēi píjiǔ 一杯啤酒

beet, beetroot *n* (British English) tiáncài 甜菜

before 1 *prep* (referring to time) zài...yǐqián 在...以前, ...yǐqián ...以前; before 6 o'clock (zài) liù diǎn yǐqián (在)六点以前; the day before yesterday qiántiān 前天; the day before the exam kǎoshì de qián yì tiān 考试的前一天; (in front of) zài...qiánmiàn 在...前面, zài...qiántóu 在...前头; he was before me in the queue tā pái zài wǒ qiánmiàn 他排在我前面 2 *adv* yǐqián 以前; have you been to Beijing before? nǐ yǐqián qùguo Běijīng ma? 你以前去过北京吗? 3 *conj* zài...yǐqián 在...以前, zài...zhīqián 在...之前; I'd like to phone him before he goes (zài) tā zǒu yǐqián wǒ xiǎng gěi tā dǎ ge diànhuà (在)他走以前我想给他打个电话

beg *vb* (for food, money, etc.) beg for yào 要, qǐtǎo 乞讨; (making requests) qǐqiú 乞求, kěnqiú 恳求

beggar *n* a beggar yíge qǐgài 一个乞丐, yíge yào fàn de 一个要饭的

begin *vb* kāishǐ 开始; to begin [working | laughing | raining] kāishǐ [gōngzuò | xiào | xiàyǔ] 开始 [工作 | 笑 | 下雨]

beginner *n* a beginner yíge chūxuézhě 一个初学者

beginning *n* (of an event, of an activity) kāishǐ 开始, kāiduān 开端; a good beginning yíge liánghǎo de kāiduān 一个良好的开端; (of a year, of a month) the beginning of [the month | the year | May] [yuè | nián | wǔyuè] chū [月 | 年 | 五月] 初

behave *vb* (to act, to function) biǎoxiàn 表现; he behaved badly tā biǎoxiàn bù hǎo 他表现不好; (to conduct oneself) *well*) shǒu guījǔ 守规矩; she always behaves (herself) tā zǒngshì hěn shǒu guījǔ 她总是很守规矩; behave yourself! guījǔ diǎn! 规矩点!

behaviour (*British English*), **behavior** (*US English*) *n* xíngwéi 行为, biǎoxiàn 表现

behind 1 *prep* zài...hòumiàn 在...后面, zài...hòubian 在...后边; my house is behind the school wǒde jiā zài xuéxiào hòumiàn 我的家在学校后面 **2** *adv* zài hòumiàn 在后面, zài hòubian 在后边; she is sitting behind tā zuò zài hòumiàn 她坐在后面

Belgian 1 *adj* Bǐlìshí de 比利时的 **2** *n* a Belgian yíge Bǐlìshírén 一个比利时人

Belgium *n* Bǐlìshí 比利时

believe *vb* xiāngxìn 相信; believe in xìnrèn 信任

bell *n* (*in a church*) zhōng 钟; (*on a door or bicycle*) líng 铃

belong *vb* (*to be the property of*) shǔyú 属于; that piece of land belongs to our college nàkuài dì shǔyú wǒmen xuéyuàn 那块地属于我们学院; (*be a member of*) belong to a party shì yíge dǎng de dǎngyuán 是一个党的党员

belongings *n* (*luggage*) xínglǐ 行李; (*things that one owns*) dōngxi 东西; his belongings tāde dōngxi 他的东西

below 1 *prep* (*in space*) zài ... xiàmiàn 在 ... 下面; the kitchen is below my bedroom chúfáng zài wǒde wòshì xiàmiàn 厨房在我的卧室下面; (*in rank, age, degree, etc.*) (zài) ... yǐxià (在) ... 以下; below 60 years old liùshí suì yǐxià 六十岁以下; 10 degrees below zero língxià shí dù zǐng xià shí dù 零下十度 **2** *adj* xiàmiàn de 下面的; please do the exercises below qǐng zuò xiàmiàn de liànxí 请做下面的练习

belt *n* (*worn around the waist*) yāodài 腰带, pídài 皮带; (*in machinery*) jīqì pídài 机器皮带

bench *n* chángdèng 长凳

bend 1 *vb* (*to bend an object*) wān 弯, nòngwān 弄弯; he bent the iron bar with his bare hands tā yòng shǒu bǎ tiěbàng nòngwān le 他用手把铁棒弄弯了; (to bend down or lower one's head) dīxia 低下; to bend down one's head dīxia tóu 低下头; to bend down one's body) wānxia 弯下; he bent down to pick up the coin tā wānxia shēnzi bǎ qián jiǎnqǐlai 他弯下身子把钱捡起来 **2** n zhuǎnwān 转弯, guǎiwān 拐弯; there is a sharp bend in this road zhètiáo lù shang yǒu yíge jí zhuǎnwān 这条路上有一个急转弯

beneath prep zài...xiàmian 在... 下面, zài...dǐxia 在... 底下

beside prep zài...pángbiān 在... 旁边; to sit beside me zuò zài wǒ pángbiān 坐在我旁边; to live beside the sea zhù zài hǎibiān 住在海边

best 1 adj zuì hǎo 最好; my best friend wǒ zuì hǎo de péngyou 我最好的朋友; this is the best hotel in the city zhè shì zhège chéngshì zuì hǎo de lǚguǎn 这是这个城市最好的旅馆 **2** adv zuì hǎo 最好; she sings the best tā chàng de zuì hǎo 她唱得最好; (most) zuì 最; I like tennis best wǒ zuì xǐhuan wǎngqiú 我最喜欢网球 **3** pron the best zuì hǎo de... 最好的...; he's the best in his class tā shì bān lǐ zuì hǎo de xuésheng 他是班里最好的学生; do one's best jìnlì 尽力, jìn zuì dà nǔlì 尽最大努力

bet vb (with money) tóng...dǎdǔ 同... 打赌; (predict) gǎn duàndìng 敢断定; I bet he'll win wǒ gǎn duàndìng tā huì yíng 我敢断定他会赢

better 1 adj gèng hǎo 更好; they will have a better future tāmen huì yǒu yíge gèng hǎo de wèilái 他们会有一个更好的未来; is she better today? tā jīntiān hǎo xiē le ma? 她今天好些了吗?; his Chinese is better than mine tāde Hànyǔ bǐ wǒde hǎo 他的汉语比我的好 **2** adv gèng hǎo de 更好地; he swims better than I do tā yóuyǒng yóu de bǐ wǒ hǎo 他游泳游得比我好; zuì hǎo 最好; we'd better go wǒmen zuì hǎo háishì zǒu ba 我们最好还是走吧; it's better to go by bus zuì hǎo zuò qìchē qù 最好坐汽车去

between prep zài...zhījiān 在... 之间, zài...zhōngjiān 在... 中间; there is a stream between the two gardens zài liǎngge huāyuán zhījiān yǒu yìtiáo xiǎo hé 在两个花园之间有一条

小河; between 2 and 3 o'clock liǎng diǎn dào sān diǎn zhījiān 两点到三点之间

beyond prep (on the further side of) zài...nà bian 在... 那边; **beyond the mountain** zài shān nà bian 在山那边; (out of reach of) chāochū 超出; **beyond my ability** chāochū wǒde nénglì 超出我的能力

bicycle n a bicycle yíliàng zìxíngchē 一辆自行车

big adj (large) dà 大; **a big garden** yíge dà huāyuán 一个大花园; (important) zhòngyào 重要; **a big question** yíge zhòngyào wèntí 一个重要问题; (serious) yánzhòng 严重; **a big mistake** yíge yánzhòng cuòwù 一个严重错误; (heavy, thick) hòu 厚, zhòng 重; **a big book** yìběn hěn hòu de shū 一本很厚的书

bill n (for gas, electricity, telephone) dān 单; [gas | electricity | telephone] bill [méiqì fèi | diàn fèi | diànhuà fèi] dān [煤气费 | 电费 | 电话费] 单; (in a restaurant or hotel) zhàngdān 帐单; **here is your bill** zhè shì nínde zhàngdān 这是您的帐单; **could we have the bill, please?** qǐng gěi wǒmen jié yíxià zhàng hǎo ma? 请给我们结一下帐好吗?; (US English) (money) chāopiào 钞票; **a 10-dollar bill** yìzhāng shí měiyuán de chāopiào 一张十美元的钞票

billiards n billiards táiqiú 台球

bin n (British English) a bin yíge lājītǒng 一个垃圾桶

biology n biology shēngwùxué 生物学

bird n a bird yìzhī niǎo 一只鸟

biro® n (British English) a biro® yìzhī yuánzhūbǐ 一支圆珠笔

birth n a birth chūshēng 出生, dànshēng 诞生; **a place of birth** chūshēng dì 出生地

birthday n shēngri 生日; **happy birthday!** shēngri kuàilè! 生日快乐!

biscuit n (British English) a biscuit yíkuài bǐnggān 一块饼干

bit 1 n a bit of [cheese | bread | paper] yìdiǎnr [nǎilào | miànbāo | zhǐ] 一点儿 [奶酪 | 面包 | 纸] **2 a bit** (British English) **a bit** [early | hot | odd] yǒu diǎnr [zǎo | rè | qíguài] 有点儿 [早 | 热 | 奇怪]

bite *vb* yǎo 咬

bitter *adj* kǔ 苦

black *adj* hēi 黑

blackberry *n* hēiméi 黑莓; a blackberry yíge hēiméi 一个黑莓

blackboard *n* a blackboard yíkuài hēibǎn 一块黑板

blackcurrants *n* blackcurrants hēi pútaogān 黑葡萄干

blade *n* (of a knife, a sword) dāorèn 刀刃, dāokǒu 刀口; a blade of grass yíyè cǎopiàn 一叶草片

blame 1 *vb* zébèi 责备, zéguài 责怪 **2** *n* to take the blame fùzé 负责, shòuguò 受过

blank *adj* (describing a page) kòngbái 空白; (describing a cassette) kōng 空

blanket *n* a blanket yìtiáo tǎnzi 一条毯子

blaze *n* huǒyàn 火焰

bleed *vb* chū xuě/chū xiě 出血; my nose is bleeding wǒde bízi zài chū xuě 我的鼻子在出血

blind 1 *adj* shīmíng 失明, xiā 瞎 **2** *vb* (destroy someone's sight) shǐ ... shīmíng 使 ... 失明; he was blinded in an accident tā zài yícì shìgù zhōng shīmíng le 他在一次事故中失明了; (to dazzle) shǐ ... kànbújiàn 使 ... 看不见 **3** *n* a blind yíge bǎiyèchuāng 一个百叶窗

blink *vb* zhǎ yǎnjīng 眨眼睛

blister *n* a blister yíge pào 一个疱, yíge pào 一个泡

block 1 *n* (a building) a block of apartments yízhuàng gōngyùlóu 一幢公寓楼; (a group of houses) a block of houses yíge jiēqū 一个街区; (a large piece) a block of wood yí dà kuài 一大块, a block of ice yí dà kuài bīng 一大块冰 **2** *vb* zǔsāi 阻塞, dǔsāi 堵塞; to block a road zǔsāi mǎlù 阻塞马路

blond, blonde *adj* jīnsè 金色; he has blond hair tāde tóufa shì jīnsè de 他的头发是金色的

blood *n* xuě/xiě 血

blouse *n* a blouse yíjiàn (nǚshì) chènshān 一件(女式)衬衫

blow 1 *vb* (if it's the wind or a person) chuī 吹; the wind blew the door shut fēng chuī de bǎ mén guānshang le 风吹得把门关上了; to blow a whistle chuī shào 吹哨; to blow one's nose xǐng bízi 擤鼻子 **2** *n* a blow yíge dǎjī 一个打击; **blow away** to be blown away chuīzǒu le 吹走了; **blow down** to be blown down chuīdǎo le 吹倒了; **blow out** chuīmiè 吹灭; to blow out a candle chuīmiè làzhú 吹灭蜡烛; **blow up** (to destroy) zhàhuǐ 炸毁, zhàdiào 炸掉; to blow up a car zhàhuǐ yíliàng qìchē 炸毁一辆汽车; (to put air into) chōng qì 充气

blue *adj* lán 蓝

blush *vb* liǎnhóng 脸红

board 1 *n* (a piece of wood) mùbǎn 木板; a board yíkuài mùbǎn 一块木板; (in chess, draughts, checkers) qípán 棋盘; a board yíkuài qípán 一块棋盘; (a blackboard) a board yíkuài hēibǎn 一块黑板 **2** *vb* to board a ship shàng chuán 上船 **3 on board** [a ship | a train | a plane...] zài [chuán | huǒchē | fēijī...] shang 在[船|火车|飞机...]上

boarding school *n* a boarding school yìsuǒ jìsù xuéxiào 一所寄宿学校

boast *vb* zìwǒ chuīxū 自我吹嘘, zìkuā 自夸, chuīniú 吹牛

boat *n* a boat yìtiáo chuán 一条船

body *n* (the body) shēntǐ 身体; (a dead body) shītǐ 尸体

boil *vb* (an action done by a person) to boil water shāo kāishuǐ 烧开水, zhǔ 煮; to boil an egg zhǔ jīdàn 煮鸡蛋; (referring to water or milk) kāi 开; the water is boiling shuǐ kāi le 水开了

boiled egg *n* a boiled egg yíge zhǔ jīdàn 一个煮鸡蛋

boiler *n* a boiler yíge guōlú 一个锅炉

boiling *adj* (when describing water or milk) fèiténg 沸腾; (when describing the weather) hěn rè 很热

bomb 1 *n* a bomb yìkē zhàdàn 一颗炸弹 **2** *vb* hōngzhà 轰炸

bone *n* a bone (in the body, in meat) yíkuài gǔtou 一块骨头; (in fish) yìgēn yúcì 一根鱼刺

bonnet n (British English) the bonnet (in a car) qìchē yǐnqíng gàizi 汽车引擎盖子

book 1 n a book shū 一本书 **2** vb yùdìng 预订; to book a room yùdìng yíge fángjiān 预订一个房间; the flight is fully booked zhècì hángbān quánbù dìngmǎn le 这次航班全部订满了

booking n a booking yùdìng 预订

bookshop, bookstore n a bookshop, a bookstore yíge shūdiàn 一个书店

boot n (worn on the feet) a boot yìzhī xuēzi 一只靴子; a pair of boots yìshuāng xuēzi 一双靴子; (British English) (of a car) the boot xínglixiāng 行李箱

border n a border yìtiáo biānjiè 一条边界; to cross the border yuèguò biānjiè 越过边界

bore vb shǐ ... yànfán 使 ... 厌烦; her speech bored everyone tāde jiǎnghuà shǐ dàjiā dōu gǎndào yànfán 他的讲话使大家都感到厌烦

bored adj to be bored, to get bored gǎndào yànfán 感到厌烦

boring adj lìng rén yànfán 令人厌烦

born adj to be born chūshēng 出生; he was born in February tā èryuè chūshēng 他二月出生; she was born in Italy tā chūshēng zài Yìdàlì 她出生在意大利

borrow vb jiè 借; to borrow some money from someone xiàng mǒurén jiè qián 向某人借钱

boss n the boss lǎobǎn 老板

both 1 det liǎng ... dōu ... 两 ... 都 ...; both girls have blonde hair liǎngge gūniang dōu shì jīnsè de tóufa 两个姑娘都是金色的头发; both my daughter and my son came wǒde nǚ'ér hé érzi dōu lái le 我的女儿和儿子都来了 **2** pron liǎng ... dōu ... 两 ... 都 ...; you are both wrong, both of you are wrong nǐmen liǎngge rén dōu cuò le 你们两个人都错了

bother vb (to take the trouble); don't bother calling back bú bì huí diànhuà 不必回电话; (to worry, to upset) shǐ ... fánnǎo

使... 烦恼, shǐ ... cāoxīn 使 ... 操心; her health bothers her a lot tāde shēntǐ shǐ tā hěn fánnǎo 她的身体使她很烦恼; (in polite apologies) I'm sorry to bother you duìbuqǐ, dǎrǎo nín 对不起, 打扰您

bottle n a bottle yíge píngzi 一个瓶子; a bottle of [wine | beer | water] yìpíng [jiǔ | píjiǔ | shuǐ...] 一瓶 [酒 | 啤酒 | 水...]

bottle-opener n a bottle-opener yíge píngqǐzi 一个瓶起子

bottom 1 n (the lowest part) dǐ(bù) 底(部); the bottom of a bottle píngzi dǐ(bù) 瓶子底(部); at the bottom [of the lake | of the sea | of the river...] zài [hú | hǎi | hé...] dǐ 在 [湖 | 海 | 河...] 底; (of a mountain) jiǎo 脚; the bottom of the hill shānjiǎo 山脚; (of a page) xiàduān 下端; at the bottom of the page zài nà yíyè de xiàduān 在那一页的下端; (of a garden or street) jìntóu 尽头; at the bottom of the garden zài huāyuán de jìntóu 在花园的尽头; (at the lowest position) zuìhòu yìmíng 最后一名; to be at the bottom of the class quán bān zuìhòu yìmíng 全班最后一名; (part of the body) the bottom pìgu 屁股 **2** adj zuì dīxià de 最底下的; the bottom [shelf | drawer...] zuì dīxià de [yìcéng shūjià | chōutì...] 最底下的 [一层书架 | 抽屉...]

bound: to be bound to vb kěndìng 肯定, bìdìng 必定; it's bound to create problems zhè kěndìng huì zàochéng yìxiē wèntí 这肯定会造成一些问题; she's bound to complain tā kěndìng huì bàoyuàn 她肯定会抱怨

bow¹ n (a knot) a bow yíge húdiéjié (lǐngdài) 一个蝴蝶结(领带); (a weapon) a bow yìbǎ gōngzi 一把弓子; (used for playing a stringed instrument) a bow yìgēn qínggōng 一根琴弓

bow² vb jūgōng 鞠躬; to bow one's head dīxià tóu 低下头

bowl n a bowl yíge wǎn 一个碗

bowling n bowling bǎolíngqiú 保龄球

box n hézi 盒子; xiāngzi 箱子; a box yíge hézi 一个盒子

boxing n quánjī 拳击

boy n a boy yíge nánháir 一个男孩儿

boyfriend n a boyfriend yíge nánpéngyou 一个男朋友

bra n a bra yíge rǔzhào 一个乳罩

bracelet n a bracelet yíge shǒuzhuó 一个手镯

braid n (US English) a braid yìgēn biànzi 一根辫子

brain n nǎozi 脑子

brake n a brake yíge zhá 一个闸, yíge zhìdòngqì 一个制动器, yíge shāchē 一个刹车

branch n a branch (of a tree) yìgēn shùzhī 一根树枝; (of a river) yìtiáo zhīliú 一条支流; (of a bank) yíge fēnháng 一个分行; (of a department store) yíge fēndiàn 一个分店

brand-new adj zhǎnxīn 崭新

brandy n brandy báilándì jiǔ 白兰地酒

brave adj yǒnggǎn 勇敢

Brazil n Brazil Bāxī 巴西

bread n bread miànbāo 面包

break 1 vb (to be damaged) [the window | the teapot | the bowl...] broke [chuānghu | cháhú | wǎn...] pò le [窗户 | 茶壶 | 碗...] 破了; [the leg of the chair | the needle | the rope...] broke [yǐzi tuǐ | zhēn | shéngzi...] duàn le [椅子腿 | 针 | 绳子...] 断了; (to crack, to smash or damage) to break [the window | the teapot | the bowl...] bǎ [chuānghu | cháhú | wǎn...] dǎpò [窗户 | 茶壶 | 碗...] 打破; to break [the leg of the chair | the needle | the rope] bǎ [yǐzi tuǐ | zhēn | shéngzi...] nòngduàn 把 [椅子腿 | 针 | 绳子...] 弄断; (to injure) to break one's arm bǎ gēbo nòngduàn le 把胳膊弄断了; (not to keep) to break a promise wéifǎn nuòyán 违反诺言; to break the rules wéifǎn guīzé 违反规则 **2** n (a short rest) xiūxi 休息; (at school) kèjiān xiūxi 课间休息; (a holiday) xiūjià 休假 **break down** (if it's a TV, a car) huàile 坏了; (to stop, as a negotiation or meeting) tíngzhǐ 停止, zhōngzhǐ 中止; (in health or spirit) kuǎxiàlai 垮下来; (to get upset) **break down crying** nánguò de kū le 难过得哭了; **break into (a house)** chuǎngrù 闯入; **to be broken into by someone** bèi rén pò mén ér rù 被人破门门而入; **break out** (if it's a fire) fāshēng 发生; **a fire broke out** fāshēngle huǒzāi 发生了火灾; (if it's violence) bàofā 爆发; **break up** (to break up a crowd) qūsàn 驱散; (*if it's a couple breaking up by themselves*) fēnshǒu 分手; **to break up with someone** gēn mǒurén duànjué láiwǎng 跟某人断绝来往; (*if it's a third party breaking up a couple*) chāisàn 拆散; (*to end*) jiéshù 结束; **the meeting didn't break up until eight o'clock** huìyì bā diǎn cái jiéshù 会议八点才结束

breakfast n zǎofàn 早饭; **to have breakfast** chī zǎofàn 吃早饭

breast n a breast (*of a female*) yíge rǔfáng 一个乳房; (*of a male or an animal*) yíge xiōngpú 一个胸脯

breath n hūxī 呼吸; **to be out of breath** shàngqì bù jiē xiàqì 上气不接下气; **to hold one's breath** bù chū shēng 不出声, bìngzhù qì 屏住气

breathe vb hūxī 呼吸; **breathe in** xīrù 吸入; **breathe out** hūchū 呼出

breeze n a breeze wēifēng 微风

brick n a brick yíkuài zhuān 一块砖

bride n a bride yíge xīnniáng 一个新娘

bridegroom n a bridegroom yíge xīnláng 一个新郎

bridge n a bridge yízuò qiáo 一座桥

brief adj (*in time*) duǎnzàn 短暂; (*in content*) jiǎnduǎn 简短

bright adj (*describing colours, light*) xiānyàn 鲜艳; **a bright red dress** yíjiàn xiānhóng de yīfu 一件鲜红的衣服; (*having plenty of light, sun*) míngliàng 明亮; **this room is not very bright** zhège fángjiān bú tài míngliàng 这个房间不太明亮; (*intelligent*) cōngming 聪明

brilliant adj (*very intelligent*) zhuóyuè 卓越, cáihuá héngyì 才华横溢; (*British English*) (*informal, for emphasis*) tài hǎo le 太好了, miào jí le 妙极了

bring vb dàilai 带来; **to bring someone a present** gěi mǒurén dàilai yíjiàn lǐwù 给某人带来一件礼物; **it will bring us good luck** tā jiāng gěi wǒmen dàilai hǎo yùnqì 它将给我们带来好运气; **bring about** dàilai 带来, zàochéng 造成; **to bring about a change** dàilai biànhuà 带来变化; **bring back** dàihuílai 带回来; **he brought me back some perfume** tā gěi wǒ dàihuílai yìxiē xiāngshuǐ 他给我带回来一些香水; **bring up** péiyǎngchéng rén 培养成人; to bring up a child bǎ yíge háizi péiyǎngchéng rén 把一个孩子培养成人

Britain n Yīngguó 英国

British 1 adj Yīngguó de 英国的 **2** n the British Yīngguórén 英国人

broad adj (wide) kuān 宽; (covering a wide range) guǎngdà 广大

broadcast vb guǎngbō 广播; to be broadcast live shíkuàng zhíbō 实况直播

brochure n a brochure yìběn xiǎo cèzi 一本小册子

broke adj fēnwén méi yǒu 分文没有, pòchǎn 破产

broken adj (if it's a window, a teapot, or a bowl) pò 破, suì 碎; (if it's a leg, a needle, or a rope) duàn 断; (if it's a car, a machine, or a watch) huài 坏

bronze n qīngtóng 青铜

brother n a brother yíge xiōngdì 一个兄弟; a younger brother yíge dìdi 一个弟弟; an elder brother yíge gēge 一个哥哥

brother-in-law n (the husband of a younger sister) mèifu 妹夫; (the husband of an elder sister) jiěfu 姐夫

brown adj zōngsè de 棕色的, kāfēisè de 咖啡色的

bruise n a bruise yíkuài qīngzhǒng 一块青肿, yíkuài shānghén 一块伤痕

brush 1 n (for clothes, shoes, hair, and for sweeping up) shuāzi 刷子; a brush yìbǎ shuāzi 一把刷子; a toothbrush yìbǎ yáshuā 一把牙刷; (for painting) huàbǐ 画笔; a brush yìzhī huàbǐ 一支画笔; (for writing) máobǐ 毛笔; a writing brush yìzhī máobǐ 一支毛笔 **2** vb shuā 刷; to brush one's teeth shuā yá 刷牙

Brussels n Bùlǔsài'ěr 布鲁塞尔

bubble n a bubble yíge shuǐpào 一个水泡

bucket n a bucket yíge shuǐtǒng 一个水桶

Buddhism n Fójiào 佛教

Buddhist 1 *adj* Fójiào de 佛教的, Fó de 佛 的 **2** *n* a Buddhist yíge Fójiàotú 佛教徒

build *vb* (*to construct as a house or a railway*) jiàn 建, jiànzào 建造; (*to establish as a society or a system*) jiànlì 建立, jiànshè 建设

building *n* a building yíge jiànzhùwù 一个建筑物

bull *n* a bull yìtóu gōngniú 一头公牛

bullet *n* a bullet yìkē zǐdàn 一颗子弹

bulletin *n* a bulletin yíge/fèn gōngbào 一个/份公报; a news bulletin yìtiáo xīnwén bàodǎo 一条新闻报导; a bulletin board yíge gōnggào lán 一个公告栏

bully *vb* qīfu 欺负, qīwǔ 欺侮

bump *vb* zhuàng 撞, pèngzhuàng 碰撞; he bumped his head against the wall tāde tóu zhuàngzàile qiáng shang 他的头撞在了墙上; **bump into** (*to hit*) zhuàng 撞, pèngzhuàng 碰撞; (*to meet*) yùjiàn 遇见, pèngjiàn 碰见

bunch *n* a bunch of flowers yíshù huā 一束花; a bunch of grapes yíchuàn pútáo 一串葡萄; a bunch of keys yíchuàn yàoshi 一串钥匙

burger *n* a burger yíge jiā ròubǐng de miànbāo 一个夹肉饼的面包, yíge hànbǎobāo 一个汉堡包

burglar *n* a burglar yíge qièzéi 一个窃贼

burglar alarm *n* a burglar alarm yíge fángdào jǐngbàoqì 一个防盗警报器

burglary *n* a burglary yìqǐ dàoqiè àn 一起盗窃案

burn 1 *vb* (*to destroy, to get rid of*) shāohuǐ 烧毁, shāodiào 烧掉; to burn rubbish shāodiào lājī 烧掉垃圾; (*to injure by fire*) shāoshāng 烧伤; (*to injure by boiling water or something hot*) tàngshāng 烫伤; (*to be on fire*) ránshāo 燃烧; (*when cooking*) shāojiāo 烧焦; (*in the sun*) shàishāng 晒伤; to burn easily róngyì shàishāng 容易晒伤; **burn down** shāohuǐ 烧毁, shāodiào 烧掉 **2** *n* (*by a fire*) shāoshāng 烧伤; (*by boiling water or something very hot*) tàngshāng 烫伤

burst vb (if it's a balloon) bào 爆; (if it's a water pipe) liè 裂; (if it's a river dam) kuìjué 溃决; **to burst its banks** juékǒu 决口; **burst into** to burst into [tears | laughter] tūrán [kū | xiào] qǐlai 突然 [哭 | 笑] 起来; **burst out** to burst out [laughing | crying] tūrán [xiào | kū] qǐlai 突然 [笑 | 哭] 起来

bury vb (to put in the grave as a dead body) máizàng 埋葬, mái 埋; (to hide in the ground) máicáng 埋藏, mái 埋

bus n a bus yíliàng gōnggòng qìchē 一辆公共汽车

bus conductor n a bus conductor yíge qìchē shòupiàoyuán 一个汽车售票员

bus driver n a bus driver yíge gōnggòng qìchē sījī 一个公共汽车司机

bush n a bush yíge guànmùcóng 一个灌木丛

business n (commercial activities) shāngyè 商业, shēngyi 生意; **to go to London on business** qù Lúndūn chūchāi 去伦敦出差; (a company) a business yìjiā shāngdiàn 一家商店, yíge gōngsī 一个公司; (when protecting one's privacy) **that's my business** nà shì wǒde shì 那是我的事; **it's none of your business** nǐ shǎo guǎn xiánshì 你少管闲事

businessman, businesswoman n a businessman, a businesswoman yíge shāngrén 一个商人

bus station n a bus station, a bus stop yíge (gōnggòng) qìchē zhàn 一个(公共)汽车站

busy adj máng 忙, fánmáng 繁忙; **to be busy working** mángzhe gōngzuò 忙着工作; **a busy day** fánmáng de yì tiān 繁忙的一天; **to lead a busy life** guòzhe mánglù de shēnghuó 过着忙碌的生活

but conj dànshì 但是, kěshì 可是; **he can read Chinese but he doesn't speak it** tā néng kàndǒng Zhōngwén, dànshì tā bú huì shuō 他能看懂中文, 但是他不会说

butcher n a butcher (one selling meat) yíge mài ròu de 一个卖肉的; (one whose business is to slaughter animals for food) yíge túzǎi gōngrén 一个屠宰工人; (one who delights in bloody deeds) yíge guìzishǒu 一个刽子手

butter n butter huángyóu 黄油

butterfly n a butterfly yìzhī húdié 一只蝴蝶

button n a button; (on clothes) yíge niǔkòu 一个钮扣; (on a machine) yíge diànniǔ 一个电钮

buy vb mǎi 买; to buy a present for someone gěi mǒurén mǎi yíjiàn lǐwù 给某人买一件礼物; she bought herself a new coat tā gěi zìjǐ mǎile yíjiàn xīn wàitào 她给自己买了一件新外套

buzz vb fāchū wēngwēng shēng 发出嗡嗡声

by prep (by means of) to travel by bus | train | plane | boat zuò [qìchē | huǒchē | fēijī | chuán] lǚxíng 坐 [汽车 | 火车 | 飞机 | 船] 旅行; we went there by bicycle wǒmen qí zìxíngchē qù nàr 我们骑自行车去那儿; to pay by cheque yòng zhīpiào fù qián 用支票付钱; to book by phone dǎ diànhuà yùdìng 打电话预订; to come in by the back door cóng hòumén jìnlái 从后门进来; he succeeded by working hard tā tōngguò nǔlì gōngzuò chénggōng le 他通过努力工作成功了; (beside) zài ... (páng)biān 在 ... (旁)边; by the sea zài hǎi biān 在海边; by the side of the road zài lù (páng)biān 在路(旁)边; (along a route passing) jīngguò 经过; to go by the post office jīngguò yóujú 经过邮局; (indicating an author or painter) a book by Dickens Dígèngsī xiě de shū 获更斯写的书; a painting by his father tā bàba huà de huà 他爸爸画的画; (in the passive voice) bèi 被, jiào 叫, ràng 让; he was bitten by a dog tā jiào yìtiáo gǒu yǎo le 他叫一条狗咬了; the house was burnt down by a fire nàzhuàng fángzi bèi yìchǎng huǒ shāohuǐ le 那幢房子被一场火烧毁了; (when talking about time) by next Thursday xiàge xīngqīsì yǐqián 下个星期四以前; he should be here by now xiànzài tā yīnggāi lái le 现在他应该来了; (when talking about figures, rates) to increase by 20% zēngjiā bǎifēn zhī èrshí 增加百分之二十; to be paid by the hour àn xiǎoshí fù qián 按小时付钱; 8 metres by 4 metres bā mǐ chéng sì mǐ 八米乘四米; (set phrases) by accident ǒurán 偶然, pèngqiǎo 碰巧; by chance ǒurán 偶然, pèngqiǎo 碰巧; [take... | see... | write...] by mistake [ná | kàn | xiě] cuò... [拿 | 看 | 写] 错...; one by one yíge yíge 一个接一个; by and large dàtǐshang 大体上; by oneself dāndú 单独

Cc

cab *n* a cab yíliàng chūzūchē 一辆出租车

cabbage *n* juǎnxīncài 卷心菜; Chinese cabbage dà báicài 大白菜

cable car *n* a cable car yíliàng lǎnchē 一辆缆车

café *n* a café yìjiā kāfēiguǎn 一家咖啡馆

cake *n* a cake yíge dàngāo 一个蛋糕; a piece of cake yíkuài dàngāo 一块蛋糕

calculator *n* a calculator yíge jìsuànqì 一个计算器

calendar *n* a calendar yíge rìlì 一个日历

calf *n* (*the animal*) a calf yìtóu xiǎoniú 一头小牛; (*part of the leg*) the calf xiǎotuǐ 小腿

call *vb* (*to name*) jiào 叫; he's called Mark tā jiào Mǎkè 他叫马克; it's called 'chá' in Chinese Zhōngwén zhège jiào 'chá' 中文这个叫茶; we call him 'Xiǎo Lǐ' wǒmen jiào tā 'Xiǎo Lǐ' 我们叫他‘小李’; (*to describe as*) to call someone a coward rènwéi mǒurén shì ge dǎnxiǎoguǐ 认为某人是个胆小鬼; (*to cry aloud*) hǎn 喊; the teacher is calling us at the window lǎoshī zài chuānghu nàr hǎn wǒmen 老师在窗户那儿喊我们; (*to phone*) dǎ diànhuà 打电话; he'll call me this evening tā jīntiān wǎnshang gěi wǒ dǎ diànhuà 他今天晚上给我打电话; (*to get to come*) qǐng 请; to call the doctor qǐng dàifu 请大夫; (*to wake*) jiàoxǐng 叫醒; (*to pay a visit*) bàifǎng 拜访; I called at his house yesterday wǒ zuótiān qù tā jiā bàifǎng 我昨天去他家拜访; **call back** (*to command to return*) jiào huílái 叫回来; (*to phone back*) huí diànhuà 回电话; **call off** qǔxiāo 取消; **call on** they called on him to make a speech at the meeting tāmen qǐngqiú tā zài huì shang jiǎnghuà 他们请求他在会上讲话; **call out** to call out the numbers for the lottery dàshēng hǎn zhòngjiǎng hàomǎ 大声喊中奖号码

calm 1 adj (when talking about the weather, the sea) píngjìng 平静; (when talking about people) zhènjìng 镇静 **2** vb píngjìng 平静, zhènjìng 镇静; **calm down** píngjìng xiàlai 平静下来, zhènjìng xiàlai 镇静下来

camcorder n a camcorder yíjià shèxiàngjī 一架摄像机

camel n a camel yìtóu luòtuo 一头骆驼

camera n a camera (for taking photos) yíjià zhàoxiàngjī 一架照相机; (in a studio, for videos) yíjià shèyǐngjī 一架摄影机

camp 1 n a yěyíng 野营; a summer camp yíge xiàlìngyíng 一个夏令营 **2** vb yěyíng 野营; to go camping qù yěyíng 去野营

campsite n a campsite yíge yíngdì 一个营地

campus n a campus yíge xiàoyuán 一个校园

can¹ vb (to have the possibility) néng 能; can he come? tā néng lái ma? 他能来吗?; where can I buy stamps? wǒ zài nǎr néng mǎidào yóupiào 我在哪儿能买到邮票?; (to know how to) huì 会, néng 能; she can swim tā huì yóuyǒng 她会游泳; he can't drive yet tā hái bú huì kāi chē 他还不会开车; can/do you speak Chinese? nǐ huì shuō Hànyǔ ma? 你会说汉语吗? ! Note that when talking about the ability to speak a language, whether or not can is used in English, huì 会 is required in Chinese; (to be allowed to) kěyǐ 可以 ! Note that to negate, you have to use bù néng 不能 rather than bù kěyǐ 不可以; can I smoke? wǒ kěyǐ xīyān ma? 我可以吸烟吗?; sorry, you can't smoke here duìbuqǐ, nǐ bù néng zài zhèr xīyān 对不起, 你不能在这儿吸烟; we can't turn right here wǒmen zài zhèr bù néng xiàng yòu guǎi 我们在这儿不能向右拐; can/may I help you? xūyào wǒ bāngmáng ma? 需要我帮忙吗?; (when asked by a shop assistant) nín yào mǎi shénme dōngxi ma? 您要买什么东西吗?

can² n a can yìtīng guàntou 一听罐头

Canada n Canada Jiānádà 加拿大

Canadian 1 adj Jiānádà de 加拿大的 **2** n Jiānádàrén 加拿大人

canal n a canal yìtiáo yùnhé 一条运河

cancel *vb* qǔxiāo 取消; he cancelled his room reservation tā qǔxiāole yùdìng de fángjiān 他取消了预订的房间

cancer *n* cancer áizhèng 癌. áizhèng 癌症

candle *n* a candle yìzhī làzhú 一支蜡烛

candy *n* (US English) candy tángguǒ 糖果; (a sweet) a candy yíkuài táng 一块糖

canoe *n* a canoe yìtiáo dúmùzhōu 一条独木舟

canoeing *n* canoeing huá dúmùzhōu yùndòng 划独木舟运动

can-opener *n* a can-opener yíge guàntou qǐzi 一个罐头起子

canteen *n* a canteen; (a dining hall) yíge shítáng 一个食堂; (a container of water) yíge shuǐhú 一个水壶

Cantonese 1 *adj* Guǎngdōng de 广东的 **2** *n* (the people) Guǎngdōngrén 广东人; (the dialect) Guǎngdōnghuà 广东话

cap *n* a cap yìdǐng màozi 一顶帽子; a baseball cap yìdǐng bàngqiú mào 一顶棒球帽

capable *adj* yǒu nénglì 有能力; a very capable nurse yíge hěn yǒu nénglì de hùshi 一个很有能力的护士; to be capable of looking after oneself yǒu nénglì zhàogù zìjǐ 有能力照顾自己

capital 1 *n* shǒudū 首都; Beijing is the capital of China Běijīng shì Zhōngguó de shǒudū 北京是中国的首都 **2** *adj* dà xiě de 大写的; capital P dà xiě de P 大写的P

captain *n* (of a ship) chuánzhǎng 船长; (of a team) duìzhǎng 队长

car *n* (a vehicle driven on a road) qìchē 汽车, jiàochē 轿车; a car yíliàng qìchē 一辆汽车; (a vehicle for railway travelling) chēxiāng 车厢; a sleeping car yìjié wòpù chēxiāng 一节卧铺车厢; a dining car yìjié cānchē 一节餐车

caravan *n* (British English) a caravan yíliàng sùyíng chē 一辆宿营车

card n (for sending to someone) xiǎopiàn 卡片; a card yìzhāng kǎpiàn 一张卡片; (for playing games) zhǐpái 纸牌; a card yìzhāng zhǐpái 一张纸牌; to play cards dǎ púkèpái 打扑克牌

cardphone n a cardphone yíge cíkǎ diànhuà 一个磁卡电话

care 1 n (watchfulness) xiǎoxīn 小心; he takes great care crossing the street tā guò mǎlù hěn xiǎoxīn 他过马路很小心; (charge) zhàoguǎn 照管; to take care of someone zhàoguǎn mǒurén 照管某人 **2** vb (to be concerned) guānxīn 关心; to care about the environment guānxīn huánjìng wèntí 关心环境问题; (to look after) zhàogù 照顾, guānhuái 关怀; to care for the students zhàogù xuésheng 照顾学生; (to mind) zàihu 在乎; I don't care wǒ bú zàihu 我不在乎

career n (progress through life) shēngyá 生涯; (profession or occupation) zhíyè 职业

careful adj xiǎoxīn 小心, zǐxì 仔细; he is very careful crossing the street tā guò mǎlù hěn xiǎoxīn 他过马路很小心; to make a careful study of the problem duì zhège wèntí jìnxíng zǐxì de yánjiū 对这个问题进行仔细的研究

careless adj cūxīn 粗心, shūhu 疏忽

car ferry n a car ferry yìsōu qìchē dùlún 一艘汽车渡轮

carnival n (British English) (a festival) a carnival yíge kuánghuānjié 一个狂欢节; (US English) (a fair) a carnival yíge yóuyì yúlè huì 一个游艺娱乐会

car park n (British English) a car park yíge tíngchēchǎng 一个停车场

carpet n a carpet dìtǎn 地毯

car phone n a car phone yíge chēyòng diànhuà 一个车用电话

carrot n a carrot yíge húluóbo 一个胡萝卜

carry vb (with one's hand) tí 提; she was carrying a handbag tā tízhe yíge shǒutíbāo 他提着一个手提包; (on one's shoulder) káng 扛; he was carrying a box on his shoulder tā kángzhe yíge xiāngzi 他扛着一个箱子; (in one's arms) bào 抱; she was carrying her daughter in her arms tā bàozhe tāde nǚ'ér 她抱着

她的女儿: (on one's back) bēi 背; she was carrying her daughter on her back tā bēizhe tāde nǚ'ér 她背着她的女儿; to carry a bookbag on one's back bēi shūbāo 背书包; carry on jìxù 继续

cartoon *n* a cartoon (a comic strip) yìzhāng mànhuà 一张漫画; (a film) yíbù dònghuàpiàn 一部动画片

case¹: in case *conj* (in the event that) jiǎshǐ 假使, jiǎrú 假如; in case you can't come, please phone me jiǎshǐ nǐ bù néng lái, qǐng gěi wǒ dǎ diànhuà 假使你不能来, 请给我打电话; (lest) miǎnde 免得, yǐfáng 以防; I'll remind him again in case he forgets wǒ yào zài tíxǐng tā yíxià, miǎnde tā wàng le 我要再提醒他一下, 免得他忘了

case² *n* a case, (a box) yíge hézi 一个盒子; (luggage) yíge xiāngzi 一个箱子

cash **1** *n* cash xiànjīn 现金, xiànkuǎn 现款; to pay in cash yòng xiànjīn fù kuǎn 用现金付款 **2** *vb* duìhuànchéng xiànjīn 兑换成现金

cash dispenser *n* a cash dispenser yíge zìdòng qǔkuǎnjī 一个自动取款机

cassette *n* a cassette yíge hézi 一个盒子, yíge lùyīndài hé 一个录音带盒

cassette player *n* a cassette player yítái lùyīndài bōfàngjī 一台录音带播放机

castle *n* a castle yízuò chéngbǎo 一座城堡

cat *n* a cat yìzhī māo 一只猫

catch *vb* (to capture) zhuō 捉; to catch a fish zhuō yìtiáo yú 捉一条鱼; (to take hold of) zhuāzhù 抓住; catch my hand zhuāzhù wǒde shǒu 抓住我的手; (to take hold of something in motion) jiēzhù 接住; he didn't catch the ball tā méi jiēzhù nàge qiú 他没接住那个球; (to pinch, to stick) he caught his finger in the door tāde shǒuzhǐ bèi mén jiāzhù le 他的手指被门夹住了; my shirt got caught by a nail wǒde chènshān bèi yíge dīngzi guàzhù le 我的衬衫被一个钉子挂住了; (to be in time for) gǎn 赶; he was running to catch the train tā pǎozhe qù gǎn huǒchē 他跑着去赶火车; (to take by surprise, to come upon) to catch someone stealing fāxiàn mǒurén tōu dōngxi 发现某人偷东西; (to become ill with) dé 得; he caught flu tā déle liúgǎn 他得了流感; to catch fire zháohuǒ 着火; catch up gǎnshàng 赶上; to catch up with someone gǎnshàng mǒurén 赶上某人

cathedral n a cathedral yízuò dà jiàotáng 一座大教堂

cauliflower n càihuā 菜花

cause vb to cause damage zàochéng sǔnhuài 造成损坏; to cause someone a lot of problems gěi mǒurén dàilai hěn duō wèntí 给某人带来很多问题; to cause one to be suspicious yǐnqǐ mǒurén de huáiyí 引起某人的怀疑

cautious adj xiǎoxīn 小心

cave n a cave yíge shāndòng 一个山洞

CD, compact disk n a CD yìzhāng guāngpán 一张光盘

CD player n a CD player yìtái guāngpán bōfàngjī 一台光盘播放机

ceiling n the ceiling tiānhuābǎn 天花板

celebrate vb qìngzhù 庆祝; to celebrate someone's birthday qìngzhù mǒurén de shēngri 庆祝某人的生日

celery n qíncài 芹菜

cell n (a unit of living matter) xìbāo 细胞; a cell yíge xìbāo 一个细胞; (a small room) xiǎo wū 小屋; a cell yìjiān xiǎo wū 一间小屋

cellar n a cellar yíge dìjiào 一个地窖

'cello n a 'cello yìbǎ dàtíqín 一把大提琴

cement n shuǐní 水泥

cemetery n a cemetery yíge gōngmù 一个公墓

centimetre (British English), **centimeter** (US English) n a centimetre yì gōngfēn 一公分, yì límǐ 一厘米

central heating n jízhōng gòngrè 集中供热

centre (British English), **center** (US English) n zhōngxīn 中心; a leisure centre yíge yúlè zhōngxīn 一个娱乐中心; near the centre of London kàojìn Lúndūn shì zhōngxīn 靠近伦敦市中心

century n a century yíge shìjì 一个世纪

certain adj (sure) yídìng 一定; (some) mǒu 某; a certain person mǒu yíge rén 某一个人

certainly adv yídìng 一定, kěndìng 肯定

chain n a chain yìtiáo liànzi 一条链子

chair n a chair yìbǎ yǐzi 一把椅子

chalk n fěnbǐ 粉笔

champagne n xiāngbīnjiǔ 香槟酒

champion n a champion yíge guànjūn 一个冠军; a tennis champion yíge wǎngqiú guànjūn 一个网球冠军

chance n (a possibility) kěnéng 可能; there is a chance that she'll have a job in Beijing yǒu kěnéng tā huì zài Běijīng zhǎodào gōngzuò 有可能她会在北京找到工作; (an opportunity) jīhuì 机会; to have a chance to meet him yǒu jīhuì jiàndào tā 有机会见到他; by chance ǒurán 偶然

change 1 n a change yíge biànhuà 一个变化; a change of temperature wēndù de biànhuà 温度的变化; (cash) língqián 零钱; have you got change for 50 pence? nǐ yǒu wǔshí biànshì língqián ma? 你有五十便士零钱吗? **2** vb (to become different) biànhuà 变化; this city has changed a lot zhège chéngshì biànhuà hěn dà 这个城市变化很大; (to make different) gǎibiàn 改变; I've changed my mind wǒ yǐjīng gǎibiànle zhǔyì 我已经改变了主意; (to replace, exchange, switch) huàn 换; to change a wheel huàn lúnzi 换轮子; to change a shirt for a smaller size huàn yíjiàn xiǎo yìdiǎn de chènshān 换一件小一点的衬衫; to change places with someone gēn mǒurén huàn dìfāng 跟某人换地方; to change channels huàn píndào 换频道; to get changed huàn yīfu 换衣服; to change trains huàn chē 换车; to change dollars into pounds bǎ měiyuán (duì)huànchéng yīngbàng 把美元(兑)换成英镑

changing room n a changing room yìjiān gēngyīshì 一间更衣室

channel n a TV channel yíge diànshì píndào 一个电视频道

Channel n the (English) Channel Yīngjílì Hǎixiá 英吉利海峡

chapter n a chapter yìzhāng 一章

charge 1 vb that hotel charged him 10 pounds for the night nàjiā lǚguǎn yíyè shōule tā shí bàng 那家旅馆一夜收了他十镑; they'll charge you for the electricity tāmen huì xiàng nǐ shōu diànfèi 他们会向你收电费 **2** n (a fee, a price) fèiyòng 费用, jiàqián 价钱; there is no charge miǎnfèi 免费 **3** in charge fùzé 负责, zhǎngguǎn 掌管, zhǔguǎn 主管; to be in charge of the money zhǎngguǎn qián 掌管钱

charming adj mírén 迷人, kě'ài 可爱

chase vb zhuīgǎn 追赶; **chase away** qūzhú 驱逐, qūgǎn 驱赶

chat 1 vb liáotiān 聊天, xiántán 闲谈 **2** n a chat liáotiān 聊天, xiántán 闲谈; **chat up** (British English) hōngpiàn 哄骗

cheap adj (not expensive) piányi 便宜; it's cheap zhè hěn piányi 这很便宜; (of poor quality) dīliè 低劣

cheat vb piàn 骗, qīpiàn 欺骗

check 1 vb jiǎnchá 检查; you should check whether it's true nǐ yīnggāi jiǎnchá yíxià zhè shìfǒu shì zhēn de 你应该检查一下这是否是真的; they didn't even check our passports tāmen shènzhì méiyǒu jiǎnchá wǒmende hùzhào 他们甚至没有检查我们的护照 **2** n (US English) (a bill) zhàngdān 帐单; a check yìzhāng zhàngdān 一张帐单; (US English) (a cheque) zhīpiào 支票; a check yìzhāng zhīpiào 一张支票; **check in** dēngjì 登记; **check out** jiézhàng líkāi 结帐离开

checkbook n (US English) a checkbook yìběn zhīpiàobù 一本支票簿

checkers n (US English) tiàoqí 跳棋

check-in n (at an airport) bànlǐ dēngjī shǒuxù 办理登机手续; (at a hotel) bànlǐ zhùdiàn shǒuxù 办理住店手续

checkout n (at a hotel) bànlǐ lídiàn shǒuxù 办理离店手续

cheek n miànjiá 面颊

cheeky adj wúlǐ 无礼, hòuliǎnpí 厚脸皮

cheerful adj kuàihuo 快活, gāoxìng 高兴

cheese n nǎilào 奶酪, rǔlào 乳酪

chef n chúshī 厨师

chemist n (in a shop) a chemist yíge yàojìshī 一个药剂师; (in a laboratory) a chemist yíge huàxuéjiā 一个化学家, yíge huàxué gōngzuòzhě 一个化学工作者

chemistry n huàxué 化学

cheque n (British English) a cheque yìzhāng zhīpiào 一张支票; to write a cheque for £50 xiě yìzhāng wǔshí yīngbàng de zhīpiào 写一张五十英镑的支票

cheque book n (British English) a cheque book yìběn zhīpiàobù 一本支票簿

cherry n a cherry yíge yīngtáo 一个樱桃

chess n xiàngqí 象棋

chest n (of the human body) xiōng 胸, xiōngqiāng 胸腔; (furniture) guìzi 柜子; a chest yíge guìzi 一个柜子

chestnut 1 n a chestnut yíge lìzi 一个栗子 **2** adj zǎohóngsè 枣红色; she has chestnut hair tā shì zǎohóngsè de tóufa 她是枣红色的头发

chew vb jiáo 嚼

chewing gum n kǒuxiāngtáng 口香糖

chicken n (the bird) a chicken yìzhī jī 一只鸡; (the meat) jīròu 鸡肉

child n a child yíge xiǎoháir 一个小孩儿

chilly adj hánlěng 寒冷

chimney n a chimney yíge yāncōng 一个烟囱

chin n xiàba(kěr) 下巴(颏儿)

China n Zhōngguó 中国

Chinese 1 adj Zhōngguó de 中国的 **2** n (the people) Zhōngguórén 中国人; (the language) Zhōngwén 中文, Zhōngguóhuà 中国话; (Hànyǔ) 汉语

Chinese New Year n Chūnjié 春节, Zhōngguó Xīnnián 中国新年

Chinese New Year's Eve n chúxī 除夕

chips n (British English) (fries, French fries) tǔdòutiáo 土豆条, shǔtiáo 薯条; (US English) (crisps) tǔdòupiàn 土豆片

chocolate n qiǎokèlì 巧克力; a box of chocolates yìhé qiǎokèlì 一盒巧克力

choice n xuǎnzé 选择; he made a wrong choice tā zuòle yíge cuòwù de xuǎnzé 他做了一个错误的选择

choir n (in a church) chàngshībān 唱诗班; (a chorus of singers) gēyǒngduì 歌咏队, héchàngduì 合唱队

choke vb he choked on a fish bone tā bèi yìgēn yúcì qiǎzhùle hóulóng 他被一根鱼刺卡住了喉咙; he choked her to death tā bǎ tā qiāsǐ le 他把她掐死了

choose vb xuǎnzé 选择, tiāoxuǎn 挑选

chopsticks n kuàizi 筷子; a pair of chopsticks yìshuāng kuàizi 一双筷子

chore n jiāwù 家务; to do the chores zuò jiāwù 做家务

Christian 1 n Jīdūjiàotú 基督教徒 **2** adj Jīdūjiào de 基督教的

Christian name n a Christian name yíge jiàomíng 一个教名

Christmas n Christmas (Day) Shèngdàn(jié) 圣诞(节); Merry Christmas!, Happy Christmas! Shèngdàn kuàilè! 圣诞快乐!

Christmas carol n a Christmas carol yìshǒu Shèngdàn sònggē 一首圣诞颂歌

Christmas cracker n (British English) a Christmas cracker yíge Shèngdàn cǎisè bàozhú 一个圣诞彩色爆竹

Christmas Eve n Christmas Eve Shèngdàn qiányè 圣诞前夜

Christmas tree n a Christmas tree yìkē Shèngdàn shù 一棵圣诞树

church n (building) a church yízuò jiàotáng 一座教堂; (a group of people) a church yíge jiàohuì 一个教会

cider n guǒjiǔ 果酒

cigar n a cigar yìzhī xuějiā(yān) 一支雪茄(烟)

cigarette n a cigarette yìzhī xiāngyān 一支香烟

cigarette lighter n a cigarette lighter yíge dǎhuǒjī 一个打火机

cinema n (British English) a cinema yíge diànyǐngyuàn 一个电影院

circle n a circle yíge yuánquān 一个圆圈; we were sitting in a circle wǒmen zuòchéng yíge yuánquān 我们坐成一个圆圈

circus n a circus yíge mǎxìtuán 一个马戏团

citizen n (of a country) a citizen yíge gōngmín 一个公民; (of a city or town) a citizen yíge shìmín 一个市民, yíge jūmín 一个居民

city n a city yízuò chéngshì 一座城市

city centre (British English), **city center** (US English) n the city centre shì zhōngxīn 市中心

civilized adj wénmíng 文明

civil servant n a civil servant yíge gōngwùyuán 一个公务员

clap vb (to pat) pāi 拍; (to applaud) gǔzhǎng 鼓掌

clarinet n a clarinet yíge dānhuángguǎn 一个单簧管

class n (a group of students) a class yíge bān 一个班; (a lesson) a class yìjié kè 一节课; a history class yìjié lìshǐ kè 一节历史课; (a social group) a (social) class yíge (shèhuì) jiējí 一个(社会)阶级

classical music n classical music gǔdiǎn yīnyuè 古典音乐

classmate n a classmate yíge tóngxué 一个同学

classroom n a classroom yìjiān jiàoshì 一间教室

clean 1 adj gānjìng 干净, qīngjié 清洁; my hands are clean wǒde shǒu hěn gānjìng 我的手很干净; to keep the room clean bǎochí fángjiān gānjìng 保持房间清洁 **2** vb bǎ...nòng gānjìng 把...弄干净 ! Note that the verb nòng 弄 can be replaced by another verb, such as xǐ 洗 (= to wash) or cā 擦 (= to wipe), depending on the way the object is cleaned; to have the clothes cleaned bǎ yīfu xǐgānjìng 把衣服洗干净; I have cleaned the windows wǒ bǎ chuānghu cāgānjìng le 我把窗户擦干净了

clear 1 adj (easy to understand, see, or hear) qīngchu 清楚; is that clear? qīngchu ma? 清楚吗?; his voice isn't clear tāde shēngyīn bù qīngchu 他的声音不清楚; your writing must be very clear nǐ bìxū xiě de hěn qīngchu 你必须写得很清楚; (obvious) xiǎnrán 显然, míngxiǎn 明显; it is clear that he is unhappy xiǎnrán tā bù gāoxìng 显然他不高兴; (with no rain or cloud) qínglǎng 晴朗; a clear day yíge qíng tiān 一个晴天 **2** vb (to empty, to remove from) to clear the table shōushi zhuōzi 收拾桌子; to clear the house of everything in it qīngchú fángzi lǐ suǒyǒude dōngxi 清除房子里所有的东西; to clear the snow off the road qīngsǎo lù shang de xuě 清扫路上的雪; (about the sky or the weather) biànqíng 变晴

clever adj cōngming 聪明; she is a clever girl tā shì yíge cōngming de gūniang 她是一个聪明的姑娘; clever at shàncháng 擅长; to be clever at mathematics shàncháng shùxué 擅长数学

cliff n a cliff yíge xuányá 一个悬崖, yíge qiàobì 一个峭壁

climate n qìhòu 气候

climb vb (to ascend by clutching with hands and feet) pá 爬; to climb (up) a tree pá shù 爬树; to climb a mountain pá shān 爬山; to climb over a wall fānguò qiáng 翻过墙; (to rise higher) xiàng shàng pá 向上爬

climbing n pāndēng 攀登

clinic n a clinic yíge ménzhěnsuǒ 一个门诊所, yíge yīwùshì 一个医务室

cloakroom n a cloakroom yíge xǐshǒujiān 一个洗手间, yíge yīmàojiān 一个衣帽间

clock n (on a building, in a room, or as an ornament) zhōng 钟; (in sporting events) miǎobiǎo 秒表

close¹ 1 adj (near) jìn 近; the station is quite close chēzhàn bǐjiào jìn 车站比较近; is the house close to the school? fángzi lí xuéxiào jìn ma? 房子离学校近吗?; (as a relative) jìn 近; a close relative yíge jìnqīn 一个近亲; (as a friend) qīnmì 亲密; a close friend yíge qīnmì de péngyou 一个亲密的朋友 **2** adv to live close (by) zhù zài fùjìn 住在附近; to follow close behind someone jǐn gēn zài mǒurén hòumian 紧跟在某人后面

close² vb (if it's a door or a window) guān 关; to close the window guān chuāng 关窗; the door closed suddenly mén tūrán guānshang le 门突然关上了; (if it's the eye or the mouth) bì 闭; close your eyes bìshang nǐde yǎnjing 闭上你的眼睛; (if it's a shop or a bank) guānmén 关门; the shop closes at noon zhèjiā shāngdiàn zhōngwǔ guānmén 这家商店中午关门; **close down** guānbì 关闭, dǎobì 倒闭; the factory has closed down zhèjiā gōngchǎng guānbì le le zhèjiā gōngchǎng guānbì le 这家工厂关闭了

closed adj guānbì 关闭, guānmén 关门

cloth n (material) bù 布; a cloth (for dusting) yíkuài mābù 一块抹布; a table cloth yíkuài zhuōbù 一块桌布; a cloth (for dishes) yíkuài shuā wǎn bù 一块刷碗布; (for the floor) yíkuài cā dìbǎn bù 一块擦地板布

clothes n yīfu 衣服; to put on one's clothes chuānshang yīfu 穿上衣服; to take off one's clothes tuōxia yīfu 脱下衣服; to have no clothes on méi chuān yīfu 没穿衣服

cloud n a cloud yìduǒ yún 一朵云

clown n a clown yíge xiǎochǒu 一个小丑

club n a club yíge jùlèbù 一个俱乐部; a tennis club yíge wǎngqiú jùlèbù 一个网球俱乐部; (a nightclub) a club yíge yèzǒnghuì 一个夜总会

clue n a clue yìtiáo xiànsuǒ 一条线索

clumsy adj bènzhuō 笨拙

coach 1 n (British English) (a bus) a coach yíliàng chángtú qìchē 一辆长途汽车; (of a train) (British English); a coach yìjié chēxiāng 一节车厢; (a trainer in sports) a coach yíge jiàoliàn 一个教练; (a private tutor) a coach yíge sīrén jiàoshī 一个私人教师 **2** vb (in sports) xùnliàn 训练; (in academic studies) fúdǎo 辅导

coach station n a coach station yíge chángtú qìchē zhàn 一个长途汽车站

coal n méi 煤

coast n hǎi'àn 海岸

coat n a coat yíjiàn wàitào 一件外套; (of an animal) pímáo 皮毛

coat hanger n a coat hanger yíge yījià 一个衣架

cobweb n a cobweb yíge zhīzhūwǎng 一个蜘蛛网

cock n a cock yìzhī gōngjī 一只公鸡

cocoa n (the drink) kěkě chá 可可茶; (the product) kěkě fěn 可可粉

coconut n a coconut yíge yēzi 一个椰子

cod n xuěyú 鳕鱼

coffee n (the product) kāfēi 咖啡; (a cup of coffee) a coffee yìbēi kāfēi 一杯咖啡

coffee machine n a coffee machine (an appliance) yíge kāfēiqì 一个咖啡器; (a machine) yìtái kāfēijī 一台咖啡机

coin n a coin yíge yìngbì 一个硬币; a ten-pence coin yíge shí biànshì de yìngbì 一个十便士的硬币

coincidence n a coincidence yíge qiǎohé 一个巧合

cold 1 adj lěng 冷; I'm very cold wǒ hěn lěng 我很冷; it's cold in the classroom jiàoshì lǐ hěn lěng 教室里很冷; a cold meal yídùn liáng fàn 一顿凉饭 **2** n (the lack of heat) hánlěng 寒冷; (a common illness) gǎnmào 感冒

collapse vb (if it's a building, a wall) dǎotā 倒塌; (in health) kuǎ 垮; (when talking about a person falling down physically) dǎoxià 倒下

collar n (on a shirt or jacket) a collar yíge lǐngzi 一个领子; (for a pet) a collar yíge jǐngquān 一个颈圈

colleague n a colleague yíge tóngshì 一个同事

collect vb (to gather) jí 集, shōují 收集; to collect materials shōují cáiliào 收集材料; he collects stamps tā jíyóu 他集邮; (to pick up or meet a person) jiē 接; she is going to collect her son tā yào qù jiē tā érzi 她要去接她儿子; (to collect money or rubbish) shōu 收; to collect taxes shōu shuì 收税; to collect my post qǔ wǒde xìnjiàn 取我的信件

collection n (a set) shōují 收集; she has a great collection of posters tā shōují le hěn duō zhāotiēhuà 她收集了很多招贴画; (money collected) shōu de qián 收的钱

college n a college yíge xuéyuàn 一个学院; to go to college shàng dàxué 上大学; to be at college zài dàxué shàngxué 在大学上学

colour (British English), **color** (US English) 1 n a colour yìzhǒng yánsè 一种颜色; what colour is the car? chē shì shénme yánsè de? 车是什么颜色的? 2 vb gěi...zhuósè 给...着色; to colour the drawings (in...) (yòng...) gěi huà zhuósè (用...)给画着色

colourful (British English), **colorful** (US English) adj yànlì 艳丽, sècǎi fēngfù 色彩丰富; a colourful shirt yíjiàn yànlì de chènshān 一件艳丽的衬衫

colour television (British English), **color television** (US English) n a colour television yìtái cǎisè diànshìjī 一台彩色电视机

comb 1 n a comb yìbǎ shūzi 一把梳子 2 vb to comb one's hair shū tóufa 梳头发

come vb to come lái 来; she's coming today tā jīntiān lái 她今天来; we'll come by bike wǒmen qí zìxíngchē lái 我们骑自行车来; I'm coming wǒ zhè jiù lái 我这就来; is the bus coming? chē lái le ma? 车来了吗?; be careful when you come down the stairs tā lóutī de shíhou yào xiǎoxīn 下楼梯的时候要小心; to come through the city centre chuānguò shì zhōngxīn 穿过市

中心; (to happen) fāshēng 发生; whatever comes, I won't change my mind bùguǎn fāshēng shénme shì, wǒ dōu bú huì gǎibiàn zhǔyì 不管发生什么事，我都不会改变主意; (to reach) dào 到; turn left when you come to the traffic lights nǐ dàole jiāotōng dēng de shíhou xiàng zuǒ guǎi 你到了交通灯的时候向左拐; (to attend) cānjiā 参加; will you be able to come to the meeting? nǐ néng cānjiā huìyì ma? 你能参加会议吗?; (to be a native or a product of) láizì 来自; she comes from Japan tā láizì Rìběn 他来自日本; the strawberries all come from Spain zhèxiē cǎoméi quánbù láizì Xībānyá 这些草莓全部来自西班牙; (in a contest) dé 得; to come first dé diyī 得第一; **come around ▶ come round; come back** huílái 回来; when will you come back? nǐ shénme shíhou huílái? 你什么时候回来?; to come back home huí jiā 回家; **come in** (to enter) jìnlái 进来; (if it's a plane, a train) dàodá 到达; the tide's coming in zhèngzài zhǎngcháo 正在涨潮; **come off** diào diào 掉掉; a button came off my shirt wǒde chènshān diàole yíge kòuzi 我的衬衫掉了一个扣子; **come on** (to start) kāishǐ 开始; (if it's heating) kāishǐ rè 开始热; (if it's a light) kāishǐ liàng 开始亮; (when encouraging someone) kuài 快, déla 得啦; come on, hurry up! kuài, gǎnjǐn! 快，赶紧!; come on, you can do better than that! déla, nǐ néng zuò de bǐ nà gèng hǎo! 得啦，你能做得比那更好; **come out** (to leave a place) chūlái 出来; I saw him as I was coming out of the shop wǒ cóng shāngdiàn chūlái de shíhou kànjiànle tā 我从商店出来的时候看见了他; (to become available) (if it's a film) shàngyǎn 上演; (if it's a book) chūbǎn 出版; (to wash out) xǐdiào 洗掉; (if it's a photo) the photo didn't come out zhèzhāng zhàopiàn méi zhàohǎo 这张照片没照好; (if it's smoke, fire) màochūlái 冒出来; there are flames coming out of the windows yǒu yìxiē huǒmiáo cóng chuānghu lǐ màochūlái 有一些火苗从窗户里冒出来; **come round** (to visit) lái 来; (after a faint) sūxǐngguòlái 苏醒过来; **come to** (to total) gòngjì 共计; the meal came to 75 pounds fàn fèi gòngjì qīshíwǔ bàng 饭费共计七十五镑; how much does it come to? gòngjì duōshǎo qián 共计多少钱; **come up** (to be discussed) tíchūlái 提出来; has this question come up? zhège wèntí tíchūlái le ma? 这个问题提出来了吗?; (if it's the sun) chūlái 出来

comfortable adj shūfu 舒服, shūshì 舒适; do you feel comfortable? nǐ gǎnjué shūfu ma? 你感觉舒服吗?

comforter n (US English) a comforter; (if it's a person) yíge ānwèizhě 一个安慰者; (if it's a blanket) yìtiáo tǎnzi 一条毯子

comic strip n a comic strip yítào liánhuán mànhuà 一套连环漫画

commercial 1 adj shāngyè 商业, shāngwù 商务 **2** n a commercial (on TV or radio) yíge guǎnggào jiémù 一个广告节目

commit vb to commit [a crime | a mistake | a murder] fàn [zuì | cuò | móushā zuì] 犯 [罪 | 错 | 谋杀罪]

common adj (public) gòngyǒu de 共有的, gòngtóng de 共同的; (ordinary) pǔtōng de 普通的, tōngcháng de 通常的

communicate vb (to pass, to impart) chuándá 传达, chuánsòng 传送; (to have communication) liánxì 联系, liánluò 联络; to communicate with someone by [letter | telephone | fax] yǔ mǒurén tōngguò [xìnjiàn | diànhuà | chuánzhēn] liánxì 与某人通过 [信件 | 电话 | 传真] 联系

community n a community yíge shètuán 一个社团, yíge tuántǐ 一个团体

company n (a business) gōngsī 公司; a company yíge gōngsī 一个公司; (a group of actors) jùtuán 剧团; a theatre company yíge jùtuán 一个剧团; (other people) péibàn 陪伴; to keep someone company péibàn mǒurén 陪伴某人; to part company with someone gēn mǒurén fēnshǒu 跟某人分手

compare vb bǐjiào 比较; to compare China with Japan ná Rìběn gēn Zhōngguó bǐjiào 拿日本跟中国比较; she compares herself to her older sister tā ná zìjǐ gēn tā jiějie bǐjiào 她拿自己跟她姐姐比较

compass n a compass yíge zhǐnánzhēn 一个指南针

competition n jìngzhēng 竞争; there's a lot of competition between the schools zài gè xuéxiào zhījiān yǒu hěn duō jìngzhēng 在各学校之间有很多竞争; (a contest) bǐsài 比赛; a drawing competition yícì huìhuà bǐsài 一次绘画比赛

competitive adj jùyǒu jìngzhēng xìng de 具有竞争性的

complain vb bàoyuàn 抱怨; to complain about the food bàoyuàn fàn bù hǎo 抱怨饭不好

complete 1 adj (entire) wánquán 完全; it was a complete disaster zhè wánquán shì yīchǎng zāinàn 这完全是一场灾难; this is a complete waste of time zhè wánquán shì làngfèi shíjiān 这完全是浪费时间; (finished) wánchéng 完成; the work must be complete by 10 o'clock zhège gōngzuò shí diǎn yǐqián bìxū wánchéng 这个工作十点以前必须完成 **2** vb wánchéng 完成; the project has not been completed yet zhèxiàng gōngchéng hái méiyǒu wánchéng 这项工程还没有完成

completely adv wánquán 完全

complicate vb shǐ...fùzá 使...复杂; this has further complicated the situation zhè shǐ xíngshì gèng fùzá le 这使形势更复杂了

complicated adj fùzá 复杂

compliment 1 n a compliment zànyáng 赞扬, zànměi de huà 赞美的话 **2** vb chēngzàn 称赞, zànměi 赞美; to compliment someone chēngzàn mǒurén 称赞某人

compulsory adj (if it's education or military service) yìwù 义务; (if it's a school subject) bìxiū 必修; (if it's a way of handling something) qiángzhì 强制, qiángpò 强迫

computer n a computer yītái jìsuànjī 一台计算机, yītái diànnǎo 一台电脑

computer game n a computer game yīge jìsuànjī yóuxì 一个计算机游戏

computer programme n a computer programme yīge jìsuànjī chéngxù 一个计算机程序

computer programmer n a computer programmer yīge biān jìsuànjī chéngxù de rén 一个编计算机程序的人

computer scientist n a computer scientist yīge jìsuànjī kēxuéjiā 一个计算机科学家

computer studies n jìsuànjīxué 计算机学

concentrate vb (to bring towards a centre) jízhōng 集中; (to direct one's thoughts towards one object) jízhōng jīnglì 集中精力

concert n a concert yìchǎng yīnyuèhuì 一场音乐会

concert hall n a concert hall yíge yīnyuètīng 一个音乐厅

concrete n hùnníngtǔ 混凝土

condemn vb (to censure or blame) qiǎnzé 谴责; (to sentence) pànchǔ 判处; to condemn someone to death pànchǔ mǒurén sǐxíng 判处某人死刑

condition n (prerequisite) tiáojiàn 条件; conditions of success chénggōng de tiáojiàn 成功的条件; (a state) zhuàngkuàng 状况; the car is in good condition chē de zhuàngkuàng hěn hǎo 车的状况很好; on condition that rúguǒ 如果; you can go on condition that her parents drive you home rúguǒ tā fùmǔ kāi chē sòng nǐ huí jiā, nǐ jiù kěyǐ qù 如果她父母开车送你回家, 你就可以去! Note that the conditional clause precedes the main clause in Chinese.

condom n a condom yíge bìyùntào 一个避孕套

conductor n (in an orchestra or a choir) a conductor yíge yuèduì zhǐhuī 一个乐队指挥; (in a bus) a conductor yíge shòupiàoyuán 一个售票员; (in a train) a conductor yíge lièchēyuán 一个列车员

conference n a conference yícì huìyì 一次会议

confidence n xìnxīn 信心; (trust) xìnrèn 信任; to have confidence in someone xìnrèn mǒurén 信任某人

confident adj yǒu xìnxīn 有信心

confidential adj (given in confidence) mìmì de 秘密的, jīmì de 机密的; (admitted into confidence) cānyù jīmì de 参与机密的; a confidential secretary yíge jīyào mìshū 一个机要秘书

confiscate vb mòshōu 没收

conflict n chōngtū 冲突

Confucian 1 adj Kǒngzǐ de 孔子的, Rújiā de 儒家的 **2** n Rújiā 儒家, Kǒngzǐ de méntú 孔子的门徒

confused adj hútu 糊涂

congratulate vb zhùhè 祝贺

congratulations n (also exc) zhùhè 祝贺; congratulations! zhùhè nǐ! 祝贺你!

connection n guānxi 关系; it has no connection with the strike zhè yǔ bàgōng méi yǒu guānxi 这与罢工没有关系

conscientious adj rènzhēn 认真

conscious adj (aware) yìshìdào 意识到; (after an operation) shénzhì qīngxǐng 神志清醒

construct vb jiànzào 建造, jiànshè 建设

consult vb (to discuss) shāngliang 商量; to consult with him gēn tā shāngliang 跟他商量; (to ask advice of) qīngjiào 请教; to consult the teacher qīngjiào lǎoshī 请教老师; (to look up for information) chá 查; to consult a dictionary chá zìdiǎn 查字典

contact 1 n to be in contact with someone gēn mǒurén yǒu liánxì 跟某人有联系; to lose contact shīqù liánxì 失去联系 **2** vb to contact someone gēn mǒurén liánxì 跟某人联系

contact lens n yǐnxíng yǎnjìng 隐形眼镜

contain vb (if it's a substance) hányǒu 含有; sea water contains salt hǎishuǐ hányǒu yán 海水含有盐; (if it's a container) zhuāng 装; this box contains apples zhège xiāngzi zhuāngzhe píngguǒ 这个箱子装着苹果; (if it's a room or a hall) róngnà 容纳; this room can contain 20 people zhège fángjiān néng róngnà èrshíge rén 这个房间能容纳二十个人

content adj (satisfied) mǎnyì 满意; (not wanting more) mǎnzú 满足

contest n bǐsài 比赛, jìngsài 竞赛

continent n (a large mass of land) a continent yíge dàlù 一个大陆; (British English) (Europe) the Continent Ōuzhōu dàlù 欧洲大陆

continue vb jìxù 继续; to continue to talk, to continue talking jìxù tánhuà 继续谈话

continuous adj chíxù 持续, búduàn 不断; a continuous noise chíxù de zàoyīn 持续的噪音

contraception n bìyùn 避孕

contract n a contract yíge hétong 一个合同; to have a two-year contract huòdé yíge liǎng nián de hétong 获得一个两年的合同

contradict vb (to oppose by words) fǎnbó 反驳; (to deny) fǒurèn 否认; (to be contrary to) yǔ...xiāng máodùn 与...相矛盾; this document contradicts that one zhège wénjiàn yǔ nàge wénjiàn xiāng máodùn 这个文件与那个文件相矛盾

contradiction n a contradiction yíge máodùn 一个矛盾

contrast n duìbǐ 对比, duìzhào 对照

contribute vb (to give money) juān(xiàn) 捐(献); to contribute one's share gòngxiàn zìjǐ de yífèn lìliàng 贡献自己的一份力量

control 1 n kòngzhì 控制; to take control of a situation kòngzhì júshì 控制局势; to lose control of a car duì chē shīqù kòngzhì 对车失去控制 **2** vb kòngzhì 控制; to control a region kòngzhì yíge dìqū 控制一个地区; to control traffic guǎnlǐ jiāotōng 管理交通

convenient adj fāngbiàn 方便; it's more convenient to take the bus zuò qìchē gèng fāngbiàn 坐汽车更方便; it's not convenient for me zhè duì wǒ bù fāngbiàn 这对我不方便

conversation n tánhuà 谈话; to have a conversation with someone yǔ mǒurén tánhuà 与某人谈话

convince vb (to persuade) shuōfú/shuìfú 说服; (to satisfy as to the truth of something) shǐ...xìnfú 使...信服, shǐ...quèxìn 使...确信; he convinced me of his innocence tā shǐ wǒ quèxìn tā shì qīngbái de 他使我确信他是清白的

cook 1 vb zuò fàn 做饭; to cook a meal zuò fàn 做饭 **2** n a cook yíge chúshī 一个厨师, yíge chuīshìyuán 一个炊事员

cooker n (British English) a cooker yíge lúzào 一个炉灶

cookie n (US English) a cookie yíkuài bǐnggān 一块饼干, yíge xiǎo tiánbǐng 一个小甜饼

cooking n pēngtiáo 烹调, pēngrèn 烹饪; to do the cooking zuò fàn 做饭

cool adj (fresh, not hot) liáng 凉, liángkuai 凉快; a cool drink yíge lěngyǐn 一个冷饮; it's much cooler today jīntiān liángkuai duō le 今天凉快多了; (calm) lěngjìng 冷静; (fashionable) kù 酷*; **cool down** (to get colder) biàn liáng 变凉; (to calm down) píngjìng xiàlai 平静下来

cooperate vb hézuò 合作; to cooperate with someone yǔ mǒurén hézuò 与某人合作

cope vb yìngfu 应付, duìfu 对付; can he cope with this work? tā néng yìngfu zhège gōngzuò ma? 他能应付这个工作吗?

copper n tóng 铜

copy 1 n a copy yíge fùzhìpǐn 一个复制品, (if it's photocopy) yíge fùyìnjiàn 一个复印件, yíge yǐngyìnjiàn 一个影印件 **2** vb (to photocopy) fùyìn 复印, yǐngyìn 影印; (to reproduce a painting, a videotape, an antique) fùzhì 复制; (to plagiarize) chāoxí 抄袭; (to imitate) mófǎng 模仿

cork n a cork yíge ruǎnmù sāi 一个软木塞; cork ruǎnmù 软木

corkscrew n a corkscrew yìbǎ kāisāizuān 一把开塞钻

corner n (of a street) guǎijiǎo 拐角; (of a table, a room) jiǎo 角; the corner of a table zhuōzi jiǎo 桌子角; (in football, hockey) jiǎoqiú 角球; a corner yícì jiǎoqiú 一次角球

correct 1 adj zhèngquè 正确 **2** vb to correct a mistake gǎizhèng cuòwù 改正错误; to correct an essay xiūgǎi wénzhāng 修改文章

correction n gǎizhèng 改正, xiūgǎi 修改

corridor n a corridor yíge zǒuláng 一个走廊

cost 1 *n* fèiyòng 费用 **2** *vb* how much does it cost? zhège duōshǎo qián? 这个多少钱?; it will cost a lot of money zhè yào huā hěn duō qián 这要花很多钱

costume *n* a costume yìzhǒng zhuāngshù 一种装束

cosy (British English), **cozy** (US English) *adj* a cosy room yíge wēnnuǎn shūshì de fángjiān 一个温暖舒适的房间

cot *n* (British English) a cot yìzhāng értóng chuáng 一张儿童床

cottage *n* a cottage yìsuǒ xiǎo biéshù 一所小别墅, yìsuǒ cūnshè 一所村舍

cotton *n* (the material) miánhuā 棉花; (the thread) mián xiàn 棉线

cotton wool *n* (British English) tuōzhīmián 脱脂棉, yàomián 药棉

couch *n* a couch yíge cháng shāfā 一个长沙发

cough *vb* késou 咳嗽

could *vb* (knew how to) néng 能; she could read at the age of three tā sān suì jiù néng kàn shū 她三岁就能看书; he couldn't type tā bú huì dǎzì 他不会打字 **!** Note that here in the negative sentence, bú huì 不会 should be used instead of bù néng 不能; (when talking about speaking or writing in a foreign language) huì 会; he could speak Japanese but I couldn't tā huì shuō Rìyǔ kěshì wǒ bú huì 他会说日语可是我不会; (in the negative sentence when talking about seeing, hearing, understanding, could is not translated) I couldn't see those words wǒ kàn bú jiàn nàxiē zì 我看不见那些字; he couldn't hear me tā tīng bú jiàn wǒde shēngyīn 他听不见我的声音; they couldn't understand English tāmen bù dǒng Yīngyǔ 他们不懂英语; (when implying that something did not happen) she could have become a doctor tā běnlái kěyǐ chéngwéi yíge yīshēng 他本来可以成为一个医生; you could have apologized! nǐ dāngshí yīnggāi dàoqiàn! 你当时应该道歉!; (when indicating a possibility) kěnéng 可能; they could be wrong tāmen kěnéng cuò le 他们可能错了; it could be very cold in Shanghai Shànghǎi kěnéng hěn lěng 上海可能很冷;

(*when making a request or suggestion*) **could you tell me his address, please?** qǐng nín gàosu wǒ tāde dìzhǐ hǎo ma? 请您告诉我他的地址好吗?; **we could go back by bus** wǒmen kěyǐ zuò chē huíqù 我们可以坐车回去

count *vb* shǔ 数; **count on** to count on someone yīkào mǒurén 依靠某人

counter *n* (*a surface for putting things on*) **a counter** yíge guìtái 一个柜台; (*a device that counts*) **a counter** yíge jìshùqì 一个计数器

country *n* (*a state*) **a country** yíge guójiā 一个国家; (*the countryside*) nóngcūn 农村, xiāngxia 乡下; **to live in the country** zhù zài nóngcūn 住在农村

countryside *n* the countryside nóngcūn 农村, xiāngxia 乡下

couple *n* (*husband and wife*) fūfù 夫妇, fūqī 夫妻; **a couple** yíduì fūfù 一对夫妇; (*when talking about the approximate number*) liǎngsān 两三; **a couple of days** liǎngsān tiān 两三天; **a couple of books** liǎngsānběn shū 两三本书; (*two, a pair*) duì 对; **a couple of players** yíduì xuǎnshǒu 一对选手

courage *n* yǒngqì 勇气

courageous *adj* yǒnggǎn 勇敢

course 1 *n* (*a series of lessons or lectures*) kèchéng 课程; **a course** yìmén kèchéng 一门课程; **a language course** yìmén yǔyán kèchéng 一门语言课程; (*part of a meal*) **a course** cài 一道菜; **what's the main course?** zhǔ cài shì shénme? 主菜是什么? **2 of course** dāngrán 当然

court *n* (*of law*) fǎyuàn 法院, fǎtíng 法庭; **a court** yíge fǎyuàn 一个法院; **to go to court** qǐsù 起诉; (*for playing sports*) chǎng 场; **a tennis court** yíge wǎngqiú chǎng 一个网球场; **a basketball court** yíge lánqiú chǎng 一个篮球场

court case *n* a court case yíge fǎtíng ànjiàn 一个法庭案件

cousin *n* (*a male cousin, older than oneself*) **a cousin** yíge biǎogē 一个表哥; (*a male cousin younger than oneself*) **a cousin** yíge biǎodì 一个表弟; (*a female cousin older than* *oneself*) **a cousin** yíge biǎojiě 一个 表姐; (*a female cousin younger than oneself*) **a cousin** yíge biǎomèi 一个 表妹

cover 1 *vb* gài 盖, fùgài 覆盖; **he covered his daughter with his overcoat** tā bǎ dàyī gài zài tāde nǚ'ér shēn shang 他把大衣 盖在女儿身上; (*to cover a table, a bed*) pū 铺; **he covered the bed with a white sheet** tā bǎ yìtiáo bái chuángdān pū zài chuáng shang 他把一条白床单铺在床上; **the table was covered with a blue cloth** zhuōzi shang pūzhe yíkuài lán zhuōbù 桌子上铺 着一块蓝桌布 **2** *n* (*a lid*) **a cover** yíge gàizi 一个 盖子; (*for a cushion, a quilt*) **a cover** yíge tàozi 一个 套子; (*on a book, a magazine, an exercise book*) **the front cover** fēngmiàn 封面; **the back cover** fēngdǐ 封底

cow *n* **a cow** yìtóu mǔniú 一头 母牛

coward *n* **a coward** yíge dǎnxiǎoguǐ 一个 胆小鬼

cowboy *n* **a cowboy** yíge mùtóng 一个 牧童, yíge niúzǎi 一个 牛仔

cozy ▶ **cosy**

crab *n* **a crab** yìzhī xiè 一只 蟹

crack *vb* (*to fracture with the parts remaining in contact*) nòngliè 弄裂; **the accident has cracked the walls of the house** zhècì shìgù bǎ fángzi de qiáng nòngliè le 这次事故把房子的墙弄 裂了; (*to be fractured with the parts remaining in contact*) liè 裂; **the bottle cracked** píngzi liè le 瓶子裂了; (*to break partially and suddenly*) dǎpò 打破; **the ball cracked the window** qiú bǎ chuānghu dǎpò le 球把窗户打破了

cradle *n* **a cradle** yíge yáolán 一个 摇篮

cramp *n* **a cramp** chōujīnr 抽筋儿, jīngluán 痉挛

crash 1 *n* pèngzhuàng 碰撞; **a car crash** yícì zhuàng chē shìgù 一次撞车事故; **to crash into a tree** zhuàng zài shù shang 撞在树上; **the plane crashed** fēijī zhuìhuǐ le 飞机坠毁了

crayon *n* **a crayon** yìzhī cǎi bǐ 一支 彩笔

crazy *adj* fāfēng 发疯, fākuáng 发狂

cream *n* nǎiyóu 奶油

create vb chuàngzào 创造; to create employment chuàngzào jiùyè jīhuì 创造就业机会

credit 1 n (honour, glory) shēngwàng 声望; a scholar of the highest credit yígè jí yǒu shēngwàng de xuézhě 一个极有声望的学者; (financial reliability and reputation) xìnyù 信誉; (belief, trust) xiāngxìn 相信, xìnrèn 信任; do you give credit to this report? nǐ xiāngxìn zhètiáo bàodào ma? 你相信这条报道吗?; (merit) gōngláo 功劳, gōngjì 功绩; she deserves all the credit for this zhèjiàn shì suǒyǒu de gōngláo dōu yīnggāi guī tā 这件事所有的功劳都应该归她 **2** vb (to believe) xiāngxìn 相信; I don't credit his words wǒ bù xiāngxìn tāde huà 我不相信他的话; (to add to a bank account or financial statement) to credit the money to someone's account bǎ qián jìrù mǒurén de zhàng 把钱记入某人的账

credit card n a credit card yìzhāng xìnyòng kǎ 一张信用卡

cricket n bǎnqiú 板球

crime n zuì 罪, zuìxíng 罪行

criminal 1 n a criminal yígè zuìfàn 一个罪犯 **2** adj fànzuì de 犯罪的

crisis n a crisis yícì wēijī 一次危机

crisps n (British English) yóuzhá tǔdòupiàn 油炸土豆片

critical adj (relating to criticism) pīpíng de 批评的; (relating to a turning point or a crisis) guānjiànxìng de 关键性的, wēijí 危急

criticize vb pīpíng 批评

crocodile n a crocodile yìtiáo èyú 一条鳄鱼

crooked adj (bent like a crook) wān 弯, wānqū 弯曲; a crooked line yìtiáo wānqū de xiàn 一条弯曲的线; (deviating from a right position) wāi 歪; the picture is crooked zhàopiàn wāi le 照片歪了

cross 1 vb (to go across) to cross the road (chuān)guò mǎlù (穿)过马路; to cross the Channel dùguò Yīngjílì Hǎixiá 渡过英吉利海峡; to cross the border yuèguò biānjiè 越过边界;

(other uses) to cross one's legs pántuǐ 盘腿; our letters crossed wǒmende xìn hùxiāng cuòguò le 我们的信互相错过了 **2** *n (a mark)* a cross yíge shízì (biāojì) 一个十字 (标记); *(of a church or as a religious symbol)* a cross yíge shízìjià 一个十字架; *(to get cross with someone)* duì mǒurén fā píqì 对某人发脾气; cross out huádiào 划掉

crossroad *n* a crossroad yíge shízì lùkǒu 一个十字路口

crossword puzzle *n* a crossword puzzle yíge zònghéng zìmí 一个纵横字迷

crow *n* a crow yìzhī wūyā 一只乌鸦

crowd *n (a large number of people)* a crowd yìqún rén 一群人; crowds of people xǔduō rén 许多人; *(watching a game)* the crowd guānzhòng 观众

crown *n (on a king's head)* wángguān 王冠; a crown yìdǐng wángguān 一顶王冠; *(on a queen's head)* huángguān 皇冠; a crown yìdǐng huángguān 一顶皇冠

cruel *adj* cánkù 残酷

cruelty *n* cánkù 残酷

cruise *n* xúnyóu 巡游

crush *vb (to squeeze together)* zhà zhà 榨; *(if it's an object!)* yāsuì 压碎; *(if it's a person)* yādǎo 压倒

crutch *n* a crutch yìgēn guǎizhàng 一根拐杖

cry 1 *vb (to weep)* kū 哭; *(to utter loudly)* hǎn 喊 **2** *n (a sound of weeping)* kūshēng 哭声; *(a shout)* hǎnshēng 喊声

cub *n* a cub yìzhī yòuzǎi 一只幼仔

cuckoo *n* a cuckoo yìzhī bùgǔniǎo 一只布谷鸟

cucumber *n* a cucumber yìgēn huángguā 一根黄瓜

cuddle *n* yōngbào 拥抱; to give someone a cuddle yōngbào mǒurén 拥抱某人

culprit *n* a culprit yíge fànrén 一个犯人

cultural *adj* wénhuà 文化

culture *n* wénhuà 文化

cunning *adj* (*describing a person*) jiǎohuá 狡猾; (*describing a plan*) qiǎomiào 巧妙

cup *n* a cup yíge bēizi 一个杯子; a cup of coffee yìbēi kāfēi 一杯咖啡; (*in sport*) a cup yíge jiǎngbēi 一个奖杯

cupboard *n* a cupboard yíge wǎnchú 一个碗橱

curb *n* the curb lùbiān xiāngbiānshí 路边镶边石

cure 1 *vb* zhìhǎo 治好, zhìyù 治愈 **2** *n* zhìhǎo 治好

curious *adj* hàoqí 好奇

curly *adj* juǎnqū 卷曲; curly hair juǎnqū de tóufa 卷曲的头发

currency *n* a currency yìzhǒng huòbì 一种货币; foreign currency wàibì 外币, wàihuì 外汇

curry *n* a curry gālí 咖喱

curtain *n* a curtain yíge chuānglián 一个窗帘; to draw the curtains lā chuánglián 拉窗帘

cushion *n* a cushion yíge diànzi 一个垫子

custard *n* niúnǎi dànhú 牛奶蛋糊

custom *n* a custom yìzhǒng xíguàn 一种习惯

customer *n* a customer yíge gùkè 一个顾客

customs *n* hǎiguān 海关; to go through customs tōngguò hǎiguān 通过海关

customs officer *n* a customs officer yíge hǎiguān guānyuán 一个海关官员

cut 1 *vb* (*if it's an object*) qiē 切, gē 割; to cut an apple in half bǎ píngguǒ qiēchéng liǎng bàn 把苹果切成两半; (*if it's part of the body*) gēpò 割破; to cut [one's fingers | one's knee | one's foot...] gēpò [shǒuzhǐ | xīgài | jiǎo...] 割破 [手指 | 膝盖 | 脚...]; (*to cut with scissors*) jiǎn 剪; to cut cloth jiǎn bù 剪布; she got her hair cut tā jiǎn tóufa le 她剪头发了; he got his hair cut tā lǐfà le 他理发了 **2** *n* (*of the body*) shāngkǒu 伤口; (*in finance, expense*) xuējiǎn 削减; (*in a film, a book*) shānjié 删节; **cut down** (*to bring down by cutting*) kǎndǎo 砍倒; (*to reduce, curtail*) xuējiǎn

削减; **cut out** to cut a photo out of a magazine cóng zázhì shang jiǎnxià yìzhāng zhàopiàn 从杂志上剪下一张照片; **cut up** qiēsuì 切碎

cute adj kě'ài 可爱, dòu rén xǐ'ài 逗人喜爱

CV n a CV yìfēn jiǎnlì 一份简历

cycle vb qí zìxíngchē 骑自行车; to cycle to school qí zìxíngchē shàngxué 骑自行车上学; to go cycling qù qí zìxíngchē 去骑自行车

cycle lane, cycle path n a cycle lane yìtiáo zìxíngchē dào 一条自行车道

cycling n cycling zìxíngchē yùndòng 自行车运动

cyclist n a cyclist yíge qí zìxíngchē de rén 一个骑自行车的人

cynical adj wán shì bù gōng 玩世不恭, lěngcháo rèfēng 冷嘲热讽

....

Dd

....

dad, Dad n bàba 爸爸

daffodil n a daffodil yìkē shuǐxiānhuā 一棵水仙花

daisy n a daisy yìkē chújú 一棵雏菊

damage 1 vb (to damage) huǐhuài 毁坏; the building was damaged by the fire fángzi bèi dàhuǒ huǐhuài le 房子被大火毁坏了; (to harm) sǔnhài 损害; it can damage your health zhè huì sǔnhài nǐde jiànkāng 这会损害你的健康 **2** n (loss) sǔnshī 损失; (harm) sǔnhài 损害

damp adj cháoshī 潮湿

dance 1 vb tiàowǔ 跳舞 **2** n a dance yíge wǔdǎo 一个舞蹈

dancer n a dancer yíge wǔdǎo yǎnyuán 一个舞蹈演员

dancing n tiàowǔ 跳舞

danger n wēixiǎn 危险; to be in danger zài wēixiǎn zhōng 在危险中

dangerous adj wēixiǎn 危险

Danish 1 adj Dānmài de 丹麦的 **2** n Dānmàiyǔ 丹麦语

dare vb (to have the courage) gǎn 敢; (when testing someone) I dare you to criticise her wǒ gǎn shuō nǐ bù gǎn pīpíng tā 我敢说你不敢批评她; (when expressing anger) don't dare speak to me like that! nǐ zěnme gǎn zhèyàng gēn wǒ jiǎnghuà! 你怎么敢这样跟我讲话!

dark 1 adj (lacking light) àn 暗, hēi'àn 黑暗; it's getting dark tiān hēixiàlai le 天黑下来了; (black) hēi 黑; he's got dark hair tā shì hēi tóufa 他是黑头发; (darkish) shēn 深; a dark blue dress yíjiàn shēn lánsè de yīfu 一件深蓝色的衣服 **2** n (if it's a colour) hēisè 黑色, ànsè 暗色; (absence of light) hēi'àn 黑暗

darts n fēibiāo 飞镖; a game of darts fēibiāo yóuxì 飞镖游戏

date n (in a calendar) a date yíge rìqī 一个日期; what date is today? jīntiān jǐ hào? 今天几号? yuēhuì 约会; to go out on a date with someone gēn mǒurén chūqu yuēhuì 跟某人出去约会

daughter n a daughter yíge nǚ'ér 一个女儿

daughter-in-law n a daughter-in-law yíge érxífu 一个儿媳妇

dawn n límíng 黎明; at dawn límíng shí 黎明时

day n a day yì tiān 一天; what day is it today? jīntiān xīngqíjǐ? 今天星期几?; during the day zài báitiān 在白天; we had a very nice day wǒmen dùguòle měihǎo de yì tiān 我们度过了美好的一天; the next day, the day after dì'èr tiān 第二天; the day before yíqián yì tiān 前一天; the day after tomorrow hòutiān 后天; the day before yesterday qiántiān 前天; New Year's Day Yuándàn 元旦, Xīnnián 新年; Christmas Day Shèngdànjié 圣诞节

daylight n rìguāng 日光; before daylight tiān liàng qián 天亮前

dead *adj* sǐ 死; he is dead tā sǐ le 他死了; *(more polite form)* qùshì 去世, shìshì 逝世; he is dead tā qùshì le 他去世了

deaf *adj* lóng 聋

deal 1 *n* a deal *(in business)* yībǐ mǎimai 一笔买卖; *(with a friend)* yíge yuēdìng 一个约定; a great deal of [money | time | energy] dàliàng de [qián | shíjiān | jīnglì] 大量的[钱 | 时间 | 精力] 2 *vb* to deal the cards fā pái 发牌; deal with chǔlǐ 处理, duìfu 对付; to deal with a problem chǔlǐ yíge wèntí 处理一个问题

dear 1 *adj (in letters)* qīn'ài de 亲爱的; Dear Anne and Paul Qīn'ài de Ānnī he Bǎoluó 亲爱的安妮和保罗; *(expensive)* guì 贵 2 *exc* oh dear! A! Tiān na! 啊! 天哪!

death *n* sǐ 死, sǐwáng 死亡

death penalty *n* sǐxíng 死刑

debate *n* a debate yícì biànlùn 一次辩论

debt *n* a debt yībǐ zhài 一笔债; to be in debt qiàn zhài 欠债

decade *n* a decade shí nián 十年

decaffeinated *adj* chúqù kāfēiyīn de 除去咖啡因的

deceive *vb* qīpiàn 欺骗

December *n* shí'èryuè 十二月

decide *vb* juédìng 决定; he decided [to accept | to go | to get married...] tā juédìng [jiēshòu | qù | jiēhūn...] 他决定[接受 | 去 | 结婚...]

decision *n* a decision yíxiàng juédìng 一项决定; to make a decision zuò yíge juédìng 做一个决定

deck *n* jiǎbǎn 甲板; on deck zài jiǎbǎn shang 在甲板上

deckchair *n* a deckchair yìbǎ zhédiéshì tǎngyǐ 一把折叠式躺椅

decorate *vb* zhuāngshì 装饰

decoration *n* zhuāngshì 装饰

deep *adj* shēn 深; how deep is the lake? zhège hú yǒu duō shēn? 这个湖有多深?; the hole is three metres deep zhège dòng yǒu sān mǐ shēn 这个洞有三米深

deer *n* a deer yìtóu lù 一头鹿

defeat 1 *vb* to defeat an enemy zhànshèng dírén 战胜敌人; the team was defeated zhège duì bèi dǎbài le 这个队被打败了 **2** *n* a defeat yícì shībài 一次失败

defence (*British English*), **defense** (*US English*) *n* (*protection*) bǎohù 保护; (*guarding against attack*) bǎowèi 保卫

defend *vb* (*to protect*) bǎohù 保护; (*to maintain against attack*) bǎowèi 保卫

definite *adj* (*describing an answer, a decision, a plan*) míngquè 明确; (*fixed*) quèdìng 确定; nothing is definite shénme dōu méi quèdìng 什么都没确定; (*obvious, visible*) míngxiǎn 明显; a definite improvement míngxiǎn de gǎijìn 明显的改进

definitely *adv* kěndìng 肯定; they're definitely lying tāmen kěndìng zài shuōhuǎng 他们肯定在说谎; I'm definitely coming wǒ kěndìng lái 我肯定来

defy *vb* mièshì 蔑视

degree *n* (*from a university*) a degree yíge xuéwèi 一个学位; (*in measurements*) dù 度; 5 degrees wǔ dù 五度

delay 1 *vb* yánwù 延误, dānwù 耽误 **2** *n* yánwù 延误, dānwù 耽误

deliberate *adj* gùyì 故意

deliberately *adv* gùyì de 故意地

delicious *adj* hǎochī 好吃

delighted *adj* gāoxìng 高兴; to be delighted with a present shōudào lǐwù hěn gāoxìng 收到礼物很高兴

deliver *vb* (*if it's something heavy*) (yùn)sòng (运)送; to deliver goods (yùn)sòng huòwù (运)送货物; (*if it's mail*) tóudì 投递; to deliver mail tóudì xìnjiàn 投递信件

demand 1 *vb* yāoqiú 要求 **2** *n* yāoqiú 要求

demolish *vb* chāihuǐ 拆毁

demonstration *n* (*a practical show or exhibition*) shìfàn 示范; a demonstration yícì shìfàn 一次示范; (*a public procession or movement*) shìwēi 示威; a demonstration yícì shìwēi 一次示威

denim jacket *n* a denim jacket yíjiàn láodòngbù jiákèshān
·件劳动布夹克衫

Denmark *n* Dānmài 丹麦

dentist *n* a dentist yíge yáyī 一个牙医

deny *vb* fǒurèn 否认

department *n* a department; (*in a firm*) yíge bùmén 一个部门;
(*in a university*) yíge xì 一个系; (*in a large store*) a [food | clothes |
furniture] department yíge [shípǐn | fúzhuāng | jiājù] bù 一个 [食品 |
服装 | 家具] 部

department store *n* a department store yíge bǎihuò
shāngdiàn 一个百货商店

depend *vb* (*to rely*) yīkào 依靠, to depend on someone yīkào
mǒurén 依靠某人; (*to be determined*) it depends on you zhè
yào qǔjué yú nǐ 这要取决于你; it depends zhè děi kàn
qíngkuàng (ér dìng) 这得看情况(而定)

depressed *adj* jǔsàng 沮丧, xiāochén 消沉

depressing *adj* lìng rén jǔsàng 令人沮丧, lìng rén xiāochén
令人消沉

deprive *vb* bōduó 剥夺

depth *n* shēnchù 深处, shēndù 深度

describe *vb* (*in writing*) miáoxiě 描写; (*in speaking*) miáoshù
描述

description *n* (*in writing*) miáoxiě 描写; (*in speaking*)
miáoshù 描述

desert *n* a desert yíge shāmò 一个沙漠

deserve *vb* yīnggāi shòudào 应该受到; he deserves to be
punished tā yīnggāi shòudào chéngfá 他应该受到惩罚

design 1 *vb* (*to contrive*) shèjì 设计; to design clothes shèjì
fúzhuāng 设计服装; that bridge was designed by him nàzuò
qiáo shì tā shèjì de 那座桥是他设计的; (*to plan*) cèhuà 策划,
jìhuà 计划; she designed the art exhibition zhècì yìshù
zhǎnlǎnhuì shì tā cèhuà de 这次艺术展览会是她策划的 **2** *n*

(drawing or sketching) shèjì 设计; **fashion design** fúzhuāng shèjì 服装设计; *(a pattern)* tú'àn 图案; **a design** yíge tú'àn 一个图案

desk *n* **a desk** yìzhāng shūzhuō 一张书桌

desperate *adj (in a state of despair)* juéwàng 绝望; *(despairingly reckless)* búgù yíqiè 不顾一切

dessert *n* tiánshí 甜食

destroy *vb* cuīhuǐ 摧毁, huǐhuài 毁坏

detail *n* **a detail** yíge xìjié 一个细节; **to go into detail** xiángxì xùshù 详细叙述

detective *n* **a detective** yíge zhēntàn 一个侦探; **a private detective** yíge sìjiā zhēntàn 一个私家侦探

detective story *n* **a detective story** yíge zhēntàn gùshi 一个侦探故事

determined *adj* jiānjué 坚决, yǒu juéxīn de 有决心的; **to be determined to go** juéxīn yào qù 决心要去

develop *vb (to evolve)* fāzhǎn 发展; **to develop a friendly relationship** fāzhǎn yǒuhǎo guānxi 发展友好关系; *(to bring out what is latent or potential in)* kāifā 开发; **to develop a new market** kāifā xīn shìchǎng 开发新市场

development *n* **the rapid development of computer science** jìsuànjī kēxué de xùnsù fāzhǎn 计算机科学的迅速发展; **the development of natural resources** zìrán zīyuán de kāifā 自然资源的开发

diagram *n* **a diagram** yìzhāng túbiǎo 一张图表

dial *vb* **to dial a number** bō yíge hàomǎ 拨一个号码

dialling code *n (British English)* **a dialling code** yíge bōhào 一个拨号

dialling tone *(British English)*, **dial tone** *(US English) n* **a dialling tone** yíge bōhào yīn 一个拨号音

diamond *n* **a diamond** yíkuài zuànshí 一块钻石

diary *n* **a diary** yìběn rìjì 一本日记

dice n a pair of dice yíduì tóuzi 一对骰子

dictionary n a dictionary yìběn cídiǎn 一本词典, yìběn zìdiǎn 一本字典

die vb (to die) sǐ 死; he died in the war tā zài zhànzhēng zhōng sǐ le 他在战争中死了; she is dying of cancer tā yīn déle áizhèng kuàiyào sǐ le 她因得了癌症快要死了; (to indicate extreme desire) I'm dying to go on holiday wǒ kěwàng qù dùjià 我渴望去度假

diet n yīnshí 饮食; to go on a diet jié shí 节食

difference n chābié 差别; I can't tell the difference wǒ kàn bù chū yǒu shénme chābié 我看不出有什么差别; it won't make any difference zhè bú huì yǒu shénme guānxì 这不会有什么关系; what difference does it make? zhè yǒu shénme guānxì? 这有什么关系?

different adj bùtóng 不同

difficult adj nán 难; Chinese is not difficult to learn Zhōngwén bù nán xué 中文不难学; it is difficult to get along with someone gēn mǒurén hěn nán xiāngchǔ 跟某人很难相处

difficulty n a difficulty yíge kùnnan 一个困难; to have difficulty concentrating hěn nán jízhōng jīnglì 很难集中精力

dig vb wā 挖; dig up (when gardening) wāchūlai 挖出来; (to find what was buried) wājué chūlai 挖掘出来

dim adj (describing a light) àndàn 暗淡; (describing a room) hūn'àn 昏暗

diner (US English) n a diner yíge kuàicāndiàn 一个快餐店

dining room n a dining room yíge fàntīng 一个饭厅

dinner n a dinner (the chief meal of the day) yídùn zhèngcān 一顿正餐; (a feast) yícì yànhuì 一次宴会

dip vb zhàn 蘸

direct 1 adj zhíjiē 直接 **2** vb (when talking about direction) could you direct me to the station? nǐ néng gàosu wǒ qù chēzhàn zěnme zǒu ma? 你能告诉我去车站怎么走吗? (in cinema or theatre) dǎoyǎn 导演; to direct [a film | a play] dǎoyǎn [yíbù diànyǐng | yìchǎng xì] 导演 [一部电影 | 一出戏]

direction n a direction yígè fāngxiàng 一个方向; is this the right direction? zhège fāngxiàng duì ma? 这个方向对吗?; they were walking in the other direction tāmen zài cháo lìngyígè fāngxiàng zǒu 他们在朝另一个方向走

directions n zhǐshì 指示; to give someone directions xiàng mǒurén fāchū zhǐshì 向某人发出指示; to ask someone for directions xiàng mǒurén qǐng(qiú zhǐ)shì 向某人请(求指)示; (directions for use) shǐyòng shuōmíng 使用说明

director n (of a film or play) dǎoyǎn 导演; a director yígè dǎoyǎn 一个导演; a director (of a research institute or department) yígè suǒzhǎng 一个所长, yígè zhǔrèn 一个主任; (of a factory) yígè chǎngzhǎng 一个厂长; (of a company) yígè zǒngcái 一个总裁

dirt n zāng dōngxi 脏东西

dirty 1 adj zāng 脏 **2** vb nòngzāng 弄脏

disabled adj shāngcán 伤残,..cánjí 残疾

disadvantage n a disadvantage yígè búlì tiáojiàn 一个不利条件

disagree vb bù tóngyì 不同意; I disagree with you wǒ bù tóngyì nǐde yìjiàn 我不同意你的意见

disappear vb bújiàn 不见, xiāoshī 消失

disappoint vb to disappoint someone shǐ mǒurén shīwàng 使某人失望

disappointed adj shīwàng 失望

disappointing adj lìng rén shīwàng 令人失望

disappointment n shīwàng 失望

disapprove vb to disapprove of someone bú zànchéng mǒurén 不赞成某人

disaster n a disaster yìchǎng zāinàn 一场灾难

discipline n jìlǜ 纪律

disco n (a party) dísīkē wǔhuì 迪斯科舞会; a disco yígè dísīkē wǔhuì 一个迪斯科舞会; (the dance) dísīkē(wǔ) 迪斯科(舞)

disconnect vb (to cut off) qiēduàn 切断; (to separate) chāikāi 拆开

discourage vb (dishearten) xièqì 泄气; to discourage someone shǐ mǒurén xièqì 使某人泄气; he was discouraged by the difficulties he met tā yīnwèi yùdào kùnnan ér xièqì 他因为遇到困难而泄气; (oppose by showing disfavour) zǔzhǐ 阻止, quànzǔ 劝阻; to discourage someone zǔzhǐ mǒurén 阻止某人

discover vb fāxiàn 发现

discovery n a discovery yíge fāxiàn 一个发现

discreet adj jǐnshèn 谨慎

discrimination n (distinction) qūbié 区别; (different treatment of a group of people) qíshì 歧视

discuss vb tǎolùn 讨论; to discuss politics tǎolùn zhèngzhì 讨论政治

discussion n a discussion yícì tǎolùn 一次讨论

disease n a disease yìzhǒng (jí)bìng 一种(疾)病

disguise 1 n wěizhuāng 伪装 2 vb to disguise oneself as a woman bǎ zìjǐ zhuāngbànchéng nǚ de 把自己装扮成女的

disgusting adj lìng rén ěxīn 令人恶心

dish n (food) a dish yìpán cài 一盘菜; (object on which to place food for eating) yíge pánzi 一个盘子; to wash the dishes xǐ pánzi 洗盘子

dishonest adj bù chéngshí 不诚实

dishwasher n a dishwasher yìtái xǐwǎnjī 一台洗碗机

dislike vb bù xǐhuan 不喜欢; I dislike him wǒ bù xǐhuan tā 我不喜欢他

dismiss vb (to remove from office) chè...de zhí 撤...的职; to dismiss someone from his post chè mǒurén de zhí 撤某人的职; he was dismissed tā bèi chèzhí le 他被撤职了; (to remove from employment) jiěgù 解雇; to dismiss a worker jiěgù yíge gōngrén 解雇一个工人; (to send away) the teacher didn't dismiss the class until 6 o'clock lǎoshī liù diǎn cái xiàkè 老师六点才下课

disobedient adj bù fúcóng de 不服从的; (*when talking about children*) bù tīnghuà de 不听话的; a disobedient child yíge bù tīnghuà de háizi 一个不听话的孩子

disobey vb wéikàng 违抗, bù fúcóng 不服从; to disobey someone wéikàng mǒurén 违抗某人

display n zhǎnlǎn 展览, chénliè 陈列; a window display yíge chúchuāng zhǎnlǎn 一个橱窗展览

dispute n (*an argument or a debate*) zhēnglùn 争论, biànlùn 辩论; a dispute yícì zhēnglùn 一次争论; (*a quarrel*) jiūfēn 纠纷, zhēngduān 争端; a dispute yícì jiūfēn 一次纠纷

disqualify vb to disqualify someone qǔxiāo mǒurén de zīgé 取消某人的资格

disrupt vb (*to break up*) fēnliè 分裂; to disrupt a country fēnliè yíge guójiā 分裂一个国家; (*to interrupt*) dǎluàn 打乱, rǎoluàn 扰乱; to disrupt the traffic rǎoluàn jiāotōng 扰乱交通

dissatisfied adj bù mǎnyì 不满意

distance n jùlí 距离; in the distance zài yuǎnchù 在远处; to keep one's distance bǎochí shūyuǎn 保持疏远

distinct adj (*distinguished*) dútè 独特; (*clear*) qīngchu 清楚

distinguish vb qūbié 区别; to distinguish between truth and lies qūbié zhēnlǐ yú huǎngyán 区别真理与谎言

distract vb fēnsàn...de zhùyìlì 分散...的注意力; to distract someone from working fēnsàn mǒurén de zhùyìlì shǐ tā bù néng gōngzuò 分散某人的注意力使他不能工作

distressed adj kǔnǎo 苦恼, tòngkǔ 痛苦

distribute vb (*to divide and deal out among several*) fēn 分; (*to spread out*) sànfā 散发

disturb vb dǎrǎo 打扰

disturbing adj lìng rén bù ān 令人不安

dive vb tiàoshuǐ 跳水; to go diving qù tiàoshuǐ 去跳水

divide vb (*in arithmetic*) chú 除; (*to share*) fēn 分

diving board n a diving board yíge tiào(shuǐ) tái 一个跳(水)台

divorce 1 n líhūn 离婚 **2** vb she divorced him tā gēn tā líhūn le 她跟他离婚了

DIY, Do-It-Yourself n (British English) zìjǐ zhìzuò 自己 制作

dizzy adj tóuyūn 头晕; to feel dizzy gǎndào tóuyūn 感到头晕

do vb (to do) zuò 做, gàn 干; to do the cooking zuò fàn 做饭; to do one's homework zuò zuòyè 做作业; what is he doing? tā zài gàn shénme? 他在干什么?; do as I told you ànzhào wǒ gàosu nǐ de nàyàng zuò 按照我告诉你的那样做; (in questions, negatives) ! Note that in Chinese questions and negatives, there is no auxiliary like the word do in English; when did you come? nǐ shénme shíhou lái de? 你什么时候来的?; do you like cats? nǐ xǐhuan māo ma? 你喜欢猫吗?; I didn't go wǒ méi qù 我没去; she doesn't live in Beijing tā bú zhù zài Běijīng 他不住在北京; don't shout! bié hǎn! 别喊!; don't shut the door bié guān mén 别关门; do come on time yídìng yào zhǔnshí lái 一定要准时来; (in emphatic uses) quèshí quèshí 确实, díquè díquè 的确; I do like your dress wǒ quèshí xǐhuan nǐde yīfu 我确实喜欢你的衣服; I do think you should go wǒ quèshí rènwéi nǐ yīnggāi qù 我确实认为你应该去; (in short answers) ! Note that when do is used in English to refer to a previous verb, in Chinese the previous verb is normally repeated in short answers; 'Do you like strawberries?' — 'Yes, I do' Nǐ xǐhuan cǎoméi ma?'—'(Duì, wǒ) xǐhuan' '你喜欢草莓吗?'—'(对, 我) 喜欢'; 'I never said I liked him' — 'Yes, you did' 'Wǒ cónglái méi shuōguo wǒ xǐhuan tā'—'Bù, nǐ shuōguo' '我从来没说过我喜欢他.'—'不, 你说过'; 'I love chocolate' — 'So do I' 'Wǒ xǐhuan qiǎokèlì' — 'Wǒ yě xǐhuan' '我喜欢巧克力.'—'我也喜欢'; 'May I sit here?' — 'Of course, please do' 'Wǒ kěyǐ zuò zài zhèr ma?'—'Dāngrán kěyǐ, qǐng zuò' '我可以坐在这儿吗?'—'当然可以. 请坐'; 'Who wrote it?' — 'I did' 'Shéi xiě de?'—'Wǒ xiě de' '谁写的?'—'我写的'; (in tag questions) ! Note that tag questions in English are usually translated as shì bú shì 是不是 or duì bú duì 对不对 in Chinese; he lives in London, doesn't he? tā zhù zài Lúndūn, shì bú shì? 他住在伦敦, 是不是?; you didn't phone, did you? nǐ méi dǎ diànhuà, duì bú duì? 你没打电话. 对不对?; (to be enough) ten pounds will do shí bàng jiù gòu le 10镑就够 了; *that box will do* nàge hézi jiù xíng 那个盒子就行; *(to perform)* *(when talking about a task, a project)* gàn 干; *he did well* tā gàn de hěn hǎo 他干得很好; *he did badly* tā gàn de bù hǎo 他干得不好; *(when talking about an exam)* kǎo 考; *you did well* nǐ kǎo de hěn hǎo 你考得很好; *(when talking about a performance, a show)* yǎn 演; *she did well* tā yǎn de hěn hǎo 她演得很好; *do up* to do up one's buttons bǎ kòuzi kòuhǎo 把扣子扣好; *to do up a house* zhěngxiū fángzi 整修房子; *do with* it's got something to do with computers zhè yǔ jìsuànjī yǒuguān 这与计算机有关; *do without* méi yǒu...yě xíng 没有...也行; *I can do without a television* wǒ méi yǒu diànshìjī yě xíng 我没有电视机也行

dock *n* a dock yíge mǎtou 一个码头, yíge chuánwù 一个船坞

doctor *n* a doctor *(of medicine)* yíge yīshēng 一个医生, yíge dàifu 一个大夫; *(Ph.D.)* yíge bóshì 一个博士

document *n* a document yífèn wénjiàn 一份文件

documentary *n* a documentary yíbù jìlùpiàn 一部纪录片

dog *n* a dog yìtiáo gǒu 一条狗

doll *n* a doll yíge (yáng)wáwa 一个(洋)娃娃

dollar *n* a [US | Canadian | Hong Kong] dollar yíkuài [měiyuán | jiāyuán | gǎngbì] 一块[美元 | 加元 | 港币]

dolphin *n* a dolphin yìtiáo hǎitún 一条海豚

dominoes *n* duōmǐnuò gǔpái 多米诺骨牌

donkey *n* a donkey yìtóu lǘ 一头驴

door *n* a door yíge mén 一个门

doorbell *n* a doorbell yíge ménlíng 一个门铃

dormitory *n* a dormitory yíge sùshè 一个宿舍

dose *n* a dose of medicine yíjì yào 一剂药; a dose of Chinese medicine yífù zhōngyào 一服中药

double 1 *adj* *(for two people)* shuāngrén 双人; a double bed yìzhāng shuāngrén chuáng 一张双人床; a double room yíge shuāngrén fángjiān 一个双人房间; *(twice as much)* shuāngbèi de 双倍的, liǎngbèi de 两倍的; **to pay double the money** fù shuāngbèi de qián 付双倍的钱; (*when spelling or giving a number*) **a double 'n'** liǎngge 'n' 两个 'n'; **three double five** (*British English*) sān wǔ wǔ 三五五 **2** vb zēngjiā yíbèi 增加一倍; **the number of students has been doubled** xuéshēng rénshù zēngjiāle yíbèi 学生人数增加了一倍

double bass n **a double bass** yìbǎ dīyīn tíqín 一把低音提琴

double-decker n **a double-decker** yíliàng shuāngcéng qìchē 一辆双层汽车

doubt 1 n huáiyí 怀疑, yíwèn 疑问; **I have some doubt that it's true** wǒ huáiyí zhè shì zhēn de 我怀疑这是真的; **there is no doubt that he is innocent** háowú yíwèn tā shì wúgū de 毫无疑问他是无辜的 **2** vb huáiyí 怀疑; **I doubt if she'll come** wǒ huáiyí tā huì lái 我怀疑她会来

dough n shēngmiàntuán 生面团

doughnut, donut (*US English*) n **a doughnut** yíge zhá miànbǐngquānr 一个炸面饼圈儿

down ! *Often* down *occurs in combination with verbs. For example:* calm down, let down, slow down, *etc. To find the correct translations for this type of verb, look up the separate dictionary entries at* calm, let, slow, *etc.* **1** prep **to go down the street** yánzhe mǎlù wǎng xià zǒu 沿着马路往下走; **he walked down the corridor** tā yánzhe zǒuláng zǒuqu 他沿着走廊走去; **he ran down the hill** tā pǎo xià shān qu 他跑下山去; **the kitchen is down those stairs** chúfáng zài lóutī xiàmian 厨房在楼梯下面 **2** adv **she's down in the cellar** tā zài xiàmian dìjiào li 她在下面地窖里; **to go down** xiàjiàng 下降; **to fall down** dǎoxia 倒下; **down there** zài xiàmian nàr 在下面那儿

downstairs adv lóuxià 楼下; **to go downstairs** xià lóu 下楼; **to bring the boxes downstairs** bǎ hézi nádào lóuxià lai 把盒子拿到楼下来

dozen n **a dozen** yìdá 一打; **a dozen eggs** yìdá jīdàn 一打鸡蛋; **dozens of people** jǐshíge rén 几十个人

draft n a draft (a preliminary sketch, version, plan) yìfèn cǎogǎo 一份草稿; (an order for the payment of money) yìzhāng huìpiào 一张汇票

drag vb tuō 拖

drain vb (to discharge) páidiào 排掉; to drain away the water bǎ shuǐ páidiào 把水排掉; (to drink dry) hēwán 喝完; he drained his glass of wine tā bǎ tā nàbēi jiǔ hēwán le 他把他那杯酒喝完了

drama n (a play) xì 戏; a drama yìchū xì 一出戏; (theatre) xìjù 戏剧

dramatic (belonging to the drama) xìjù de 戏剧的; (with the force and vividness of the drama) xìjùxìng de 戏剧性的

drapes n (US English) bùlián 布帘, chuānglián 窗帘

draught n (British English) a draught chuāntáng fēng 穿堂风

draughts n (British English) tiàoqí 跳棋

draw 1 vb (with a pen or pencil) huà 画; to draw a rabbit huà yìzhī tùzi 画一只兔子; to draw a line huà yìtiáo xiàn 画一条线 (to pull) lā 拉; to draw the curtains lā chuānglián 拉窗帘; (to take out) to draw a knife chōuchū yìbǎ dāo 抽出一把刀; to draw a nail from the door cóng mén shàng báchū yíge dīngzi 从门上拔出一个钉子; (in a lottery) chōu 抽; to draw a ticket chōu yìzhāng cǎipiào 抽一张彩票; (to attract) xīyǐn 吸引; the circus drew a large crowd mǎxìtuán xīyǐnle hěn duō rén 马戏团吸引了很多人; (in sports) (British English) sàichéng píngjú 赛成平局; Christmas is drawing near Shèngdànjié kuài dào le 圣诞节快到了 2 n (in sports) píngjú 平局; (in a lottery) chōujiǎng 抽奖; **draw aside** to draw someone aside bǎ mǒurén lādào pángbiān 把某人拉到旁边; **draw back** to draw back the curtain bǎ chuānglián lāhuílái 把窗帘拉回来; **draw up** to draw up a list lièchū yíge míngdān 列出一个名单

drawer n a drawer yíge chōutì 一个抽屉

drawing n huàr 画儿

dread vb jùpà 惧怕

dreadful adj (producing great fear) kěpà 可怕, hàipà 害怕; (very bad, unpleasant) jíhuài de 极坏的, zāotòu de 糟透的

dream 1 n a dream yíge mèng 一个梦; to have a dream zuò yíge mèng 做一个梦 **2** vb to dream of going to Japan zuò mèng qù Rìběn 做梦去日本

dress 1 n a dress yíjiàn nǚzhuāng 一件女装 **2** vb (to put one's own clothes on) chuān yīfu 穿衣服; to dress someone gěi mǒurén chuān yīfu 给某人穿衣服; **dress up** (in good clothes) dǎbàn 打扮; (in a disguise) zhuāngbàn 装扮

dressing gown n a dressing gown yíjiàn chényī 一件晨衣

drill 1 n (a training exercise) cāoliàn 操练; a drill yícì cāoliàn 一次操练; (an instrument for boring hard substances) zuàntóu 钻头; a drill yíge zuàntóu 一个钻头 **2** vb to drill a hole zuān yíge kǒng 钻一个孔; to drill through the wall zuāntòu qiáng 钻透墙

drink 1 vb hē 喝 **2** n yǐnliào 饮料; give me a drink of water gěi wǒ yìxiē shuǐ 给我一些水喝

drive 1 vb (in a car) kāi chē 开车; to learn to drive xué kāi chē 学开车; he drives to work tā kāi chē qù shàngbān 他开车去上班; to drive someone home kāi chē sòng mǒurén huí jiā 开车送某人回家; (to make) shǐ 使; to drive someone mad shǐ mǒurén qì de fāfēng 使某人气得发疯 **2** n to go for a drive qù kāi chē wányiwán 去开车玩一玩, qù dòufēng 去兜风; **drive away** (in a car) kāi chē líkāi 开车离开; (to chase away) gǎnzǒu 赶走; **drive back** kāi chē huílái 开车回来

driver n a driver yíge sījī 一个司机, yíge jiàshǐyuán 一个驾驶员

driver's license (US English), **driving licence** (British English) n a driver's license yíge jiàshǐ zhízhào 一个驾驶执照

drizzle vb xià xiǎo yǔ 下小雨, xià máomaoyǔ 下毛毛雨

drop 1 vb (to come down) xiàjiàng 下降; the temperature has dropped wēndù xiàjiàng le 温度下降了; (to let fall) rēngxia 扔下; she dropped her suitcase tā rēngxia xiāngzi 她扔下箱子; (to fall) diàoxia 掉下, luòxia 落下; the paper has dropped zhǐ diàoxiàlai le 纸掉下来了; (to fall in drops) dīxia 滴下 **2** n (*a fall*) xiàjiàng 下降: a drop in temperature wēndù xiàjiàng 温度下降; (*of liquid*) a drop yīdī 一滴; **drop in** shùnbiàn fǎngwèn 顺便访问; he dropped in on me tā shùnbiàn lái kànkan wǒ 他顺便来看看我; **drop off** bǎ...fàngxià 把...放下; could you drop me off at the railway station? zài huǒchē zhàn bǎ wǒ fàngxià, hǎo ma? 在火车站把我放下，好吗? **drop out** tuìchū 退出; to drop out of school tuìxué 退学; to drop out of a race tuìchū bǐsài 退出比赛

drought *n* a drought yīchǎng gānhàn 一场干旱

drown *vb* yānsǐ 淹死

drug **1** *n* dúpǐn 毒品; to be on drugs xīdú 吸毒; (*for medical use*) yào 药, yàopǐn 药品 **2** *vb* to drug someone shǐ mǒurén xīdú 使某人吸毒! *Note that Chinese uses the verb xī 吸, specifying the method by which the drugs are ingested, i.e. by smoking. However, xīdú 吸毒 generally means to take drugs, whether by smoking, injecting, or taking them as a pill.*

drug addict *n* a drug addict yíge xīdú chéngyǐn de rén 一个吸毒成瘾的人

drum *n* a drum yíge gǔ 一个鼓; to play drums dǎ gǔ 打鼓, qiāo gǔ 敲鼓

drunk *adj* (hē)zuì (喝)醉

dry **1** *adj* gān 干, gānzào 干燥; the clothes are not dry yet yīfu hái bù gān 衣服还不干; a dry climate gānzào de qìhòu 干燥的气候 **2** *vb* (*to dry in the sun*) shàigān 晒干; (*to dry by a heater or fire*) kǎogān 烤干; (*to dry with a towel or cloth*) cāgān 擦干

duck *n* a duck yìzhī yāzi 一只鸭子; a Peking roast duck yìzhī Běijīng kǎoyā 一只北京烤鸭

due **1** due to yīnwèi 因为, yóuyú 由于; the game was cancelled due to bad weather yóuyú tiānqì bù hǎo, bǐsài qǔxiāo le yóuyú tiānqì bù hǎo, 比赛取消了! *Note that the phrase introduced by yóuyú 由于 or yīnwèi 因为 comes at the beginning of the sentence in Chinese.* **2** *adj* (*expected*) to be due (*in*) at two o'clock huǒchē yùdìng liǎng diǎn dào 火车预定两点到; (*that ought to be paid or done*) the amount of money due to

someone yīnggāi fùgěi mǒurén de qián 应该付给某的人钱；
the rent is due tomorrow míngtiān yīnggāi jiāo fángzū le 明天应该交房租了；*(proper)* **in due time** zài shìdàng de shíhòu 在适当的时候；**to pay due attention** jǐyǔ yīngyǒu de zhùyì 给予应有的注意

dull *adj (describing a person)* chídùn 迟钝, dāibèn 呆笨; **a dull mind** chídùn de tóunǎo 迟钝的头脑; *(describing a colour)* àndàn 暗淡; *(describing the weather or a landscape)* yīnchén 阴沉; *(not interesting, boring)* dāndiào fáwèi 单调乏味

dumb *adj (unable to speak)* yǎ 哑; *(stupid)* bèn 笨

dump 1 *vb (to unload)* qīngdào 倾倒; *(to get rid of)* pāoqì 抛弃; *(to sell at excessively low prices)* qīngxiāo 倾销 **2** *n* **a dump** *(a rubbish heap)* yíge lājīduī 一个垃圾堆; *(an untidy place)* *(US English)* **her room is a dump** tāde fángjiān luànqībāzāo 她的房间乱七八糟

during *prep* zài...qījiān 在...期间, zài...de shíhòu 在...的时候; **during the examination** zài kǎoshì qījiān 在考试期间

dust 1 *n* huīchén 灰尘 **2** *vb* qùdiào...shang de huīchén 去掉...上的灰尘; **to dust off one's clothes** qùdiào yīfu shang de huīchén 去掉衣服上的灰尘

dustbin *n (British English)* **a dustbin** yíge lājītǒng 一个垃圾桶

dustman *n (British English)* **a dustman** yíge qīngjiégōng 一个清洁工

dustpan *n* **a dustpan** yíge bòji 一个簸箕, yíge běnjī 一个畚箕

Dutch 1 *n* **1** *adj* Hélán de 荷兰的 **2** *n* **1** *(the language)* Hélányǔ 荷兰语 **2** *(the people)* Hélánrén 荷兰人

duty *n (a task, part of one's job)* zhízé 职责; **a duty** yíxiàng zhízé 一项职责; **what are your duties?** nǐde zhízé shì shénme? 你的职责是什么; *(what one must do)* yìwù 义务, zérèn 责任; **it is our duty to protect the environment** bǎohù huánjìng shì wǒmende yìwù 保护环境是我们的义务; *(a tax)* shuì 税; **customs duties** guānshuì 关税; **duty-free** miǎnshuì 免税

dye *n* rǎn 染; **to dye one's hair** rǎn tóufa 染头发

Ee

each 1 *det* měi 每; **each time I see him** měicì wǒ kànjiàn tā 每次我看见他 **2** *pron* ！ Note that when the pronoun **each** is translated into Chinese, it functions as a modifier rather than a pronoun; **each of the boys** měi (yí)ge nánháir 每（一）个男孩儿; **I wrote to each of them** wǒ gěi tāmen měi (yí)ge rén dōu xiěle xìn 我给他们每（一）个人都写了信; **each of the books** měi (yì)běn shū 每（一）本书

each other hùxiāng 互相, xiānghù 相互; **they know each other already** tāmen hùxiāng yǐjīng rènshi le 他们互相已经认识了; **we write to each other every year** wǒmen měi nián dōu hùxiāng tōng xìn 我们每年都互相通信

eager *adj* kěwàng 渴望

ear *n* **an ear** yìzhī ěrduo 一只耳朵

early *adv* zǎo 早; **to get up early** zǎo qǐchuáng 早起床; **early in the afternoon** xiàwǔ zǎoxiē shíhou 下午早些时候; **early** [last month | next month | last year | next year | this year] [shànggè yuè | xiàgè yuè | qùnián | míngnián | jīnnián] chū [上个月｜下个月｜去年｜明年｜今年] 初

earn *vb* zhèng 挣, zhuàn 赚; **to earn lots of money** zhèng hěn duō qián 挣很多钱

earring *n* **an earring** yíge ěrhuán 一个耳环

earth *n* (*the planet*) dìqiú 地球; (*soil*) tǔ 土; (*land as opposed to sea*) lùdì 陆地, dìmiàn 地面

easily *adv* róngyì de 容易地

east 1 *n* (*the eastern part of the heavens*) dōngfāng 东方; **the sun rises in the east** tàiyáng cóng dōngfāng shēngqǐ 太阳从东方升起; **the Far East** Yuǎndōng 远东; (*the eastern part of a region*) dōngbù 东部; **in the east of Asia** zài Yàzhōu dōngbù 在亚洲东部 **2** *adv* **to go east** wǎng dōng qù 往东去; **to live**

east of Beijing zhù zài Běijīng dōngmian 住在北京东面 **3** *adj* dōng 东; to work in east London zài dōng Lúndūn gōngzuò 在东伦敦工作

Easter *n* Fùhuó jié 复活节; Happy Easter! Fùhuó jié kuàilè! 复活节快乐!

Easter egg *n* an Easter egg yíge Fùhuó jié cǎidàn 一个复活节彩蛋

easy *adj* róngyì 容易; it's easy to fix hěn róngyì xiūlǐ 很容易修理; it's not easy to find work there zài nàr zhǎo gōngzuò bù róngyì 在那儿找工作不容易

eat *vb* chī 吃; eat out shàng fàndiàn chīfàn 上饭店吃饭

EC *n* European Community; the EC Ōuzhōu Gòngtóngtǐ 欧洲共同体

echo *n* an echo yíge huíshēng 一个回声, yíge huíyīn 一个回音

economic *adj* jīngjì 经济

economics *n* jīngjìxué 经济学

economy *n* jīngjì 经济

edge *n* (of a road, table, forest, an object) biān 边; the edge of the lake húbiān 湖边; at the edge of the town zài chéngbiān 在城边; (of a blade or knife) dāokǒu 刀口, dāorèn 刀刃

educate *vb* jiàoyù 教育; he was educated in America tā shì zài Měiguó shòu de jiàoyù 他是在美国受的教育

education *n* jiàoyù 教育

effect *n* jiéguǒ 结果, xiàoguǒ 效果; an effect yíge jiéguǒ 一个结果

effective *adj* yǒuxiào 有效

efficient *adj* gāo xiàolù de 高效率的

effort *n* nǔlì 努力; to make an effort zuòchū nǔlì 作出努力

egg *n* an egg (a hen's egg) yíge jīdàn 一个鸡蛋

eggcup *n* an eggcup yíge dànbēi 一个蛋杯

eight *num* bā 八; eight apples bāge píngguǒ 八个苹果

eighteen num shíbā 十八

eighteenth num (in a series) dìshíbā 第十八; (in dates) the eighteenth of August bāyuè shíbā hào 八月十八号

eighth num (in a series) dìbā 第八; (in dates) the eighth of August bāyuè bā hào 八月八号

eighty num bāshí 八十

either 1 conj either...or...; (in the affirmative) huòzhě...huòzhě... 或者...或者..., yàome...yàome... 要么...要么...; they're coming on either Tuesday or Wednesday tāmen yàome xīngqī'èr lái, yàome xīngqīsān lái 他们要么星期二来, 要么星期三来; (in the negative) (yě)...yě... (也)...也...! Note that in the negative, the translation of either is sometimes optional and or is translated as yě 也; He didn't contact either Helen or Paul tā (yě) méi gēn Hǎilún liánxì yě méi gēn Bǎoluó liánxì 他(也)没跟海伦联系也没跟保罗联系 **2** pron (in the affirmative) rènhé yī... 任何一...; you can borrow either of the books zhè liǎngběn shū nǐ jiè rènhé yìběn dōu xíng 这两本书你借任何一本都行; (in the negative) dōu bù 都不; I don't know either of them tāmen liǎngge rén wǒ dōu bú rènshi 他们两个人我都不认识 **3** det (in the affirmative) rènhé yī... 任何一...; you can take either road nǐ kěyǐ zǒu rènhé yìtiáo lù 你可以走任何一条路; (in the negative) dōu bù 都不; I don't want to live in either country zhè liǎngge guójiā wǒ dōu bù xiǎng zhù 这两个国家我都不想住 **4** adv yě 也; she can't come either tā yě bù néng lái 她也不能来

elbow n gébozhǒu 胳膊肘

elder adj niánlíng jiào dà de 年龄较大的; his [elder brother | elder sister] tā [gēge | jiějie] 他[哥哥 | 姐姐]

elderly adj shàngle niánjì de 上了年纪的, lǎo 老

eldest adj zuì niánzhǎng de 最年长的; the eldest [daughter | son | granddaughter | grandson] tā [nǚ'ér | érzi | sūnnǚ | sūnzi] 大[女儿 | 儿子 | 孙女 | 孙子]

elect vb xuǎnjǔ 选举

election n an election yícì xuǎnjǔ 一次选举; to win an election xuǎnjǔ zhōng huòshèng 选举中获胜

electric *adj* diàn 电

electrician *n* an electrician yíge diàngōng 一个电工

electricity *n* diàn 电

electronic *adj* diànzǐ 电子

elegant *adj* yǎzhì 雅致, yōuyǎ 优雅

elephant *n* yìtóu dàxiàng 一头大象

elevator *n* an elevator yíge diàntī 一个电梯

eleven *num* shíyī 十一; eleven apples shíyīge píngguǒ 十一个苹果

eleventh *num* (in a series) dìshíyī 第十一; (in dates) the eleventh of May wǔyuè shíyī hào 五月十一号

else *adj* biéde 别的, qítā de 其他的; someone else bié(de) rén 别(的)人; there is nothing else méi yǒu biéde dōngxi 没有别的东西; what else did you say? nǐ hái shuō shénme le? 你还说什么了?; something else biéde dōngxi 别的东西; everything else qítā de suǒyǒu dōngxi 其他的所有东西; or else fǒuzé 否则, yàobù 要不; be quiet or else I'll get angry ānjìng yìdiǎnr, fǒuzé wǒ huì shēngqì de 安静一点儿, 否则我会生气的

elsewhere *adv* biéde dìfang 别的地方

e-mail *n* an e-mail yíge diànzǐ yóujiàn 一个电子邮件

embarrassed *adj* nánwéiqíng 难为情, bùhǎoyìsi 不好意思

embarrassing *adj* lìng rén nánwéiqíng 令人难为情

embassy *n* an embassy yíge dàshǐguǎn 一个大使馆

emergency *n* an emergency yíge jǐnjí qíngkuàng 一个紧急情况

emergency exit *n* an emergency exit yíge jǐnjí chūkǒu 一个紧急出口

emigrate *vb* yíjū 移居

emotion *n* jīdòng 激动

emotional *adj* (describing a scene or moment) dòngrén de 动人的; (describing a person) jīdòng de 激动的

emperor n an emperor yíge huángdì 一个皇帝

employ vb (to give work to) gùyòng 雇用, gù 雇; (to use as a means) yòng 用, shǐyòng 使用

employed adj to be employed by someone shòu gù yú mǒurén 受雇于某人

employee n an employee yíge gùyuán 一个雇员

employer n an employer yíge gùzhǔ 一个雇主

employment n (the act of employing) gùyòng 雇用; (occupation) gōngzuò 工作, zhíyè 职业

empty 1 adj kōng 空 2 vb to empty the dustbin bǎ lājītǒng dàokōng 把垃圾桶倒空; they emptied three bottles of wine tāmen hēguāngle sānpíng jiǔ 他们喝光了三瓶酒

encourage vb gǔlì 鼓励

end 1 n (of a novel, film, play, speech) jiéwěi 结尾; the end of the book shū de jiéwěi 书的结尾; (of a month, year) dǐ 底; the end of next year míngnián dǐ 明年底; in the end zuìhòu 最后, zhōngyú 终于; (the furthest part) jìntóu 尽头; at the end of the street zài mǎlù jìntóu 在马路尽头 2 vb (to come to an end) jiéshù 结束; (to put an end to, to finish) jiéshù 结束; to end the war jiéshù zhànzhēng 结束战争; to end a concert jiéshù yīnyuèhuì 结束音乐会

end up vb he ended up in London tā zuìhòu dāizàile Lúndūn 他最后呆在了伦敦; to end up going abroad zuìhòu qùle guówài 最后去了国外

ending n jiéjú 结局, jiéwěi 结尾

enemy n an enemy yíge dírén 一个敌人

energetic adj jīnglì wàngshèng de 精力旺盛的

energy n (vigour) jīnglì 精力; (the power of doing work) néngliàng 能量

engaged adj (to be married) dìnghūn 订婚; to be engaged (to someone) (yǔ mǒurén) dìnghūn (与某人) 订婚; (occupied) she is engaged in writing a new novel tā zhèng mángzhe xiě yíbù xīn xiǎoshuō 她正忙着写一部新小说; (British English) (describing a phone, a toilet) the line is engaged diànhuà zhànxiàn 电话占线; the toilet is engaged cèsuǒ yǒu rén 厕所有人

engine n an engine yìtái fādòngjī 一台发动机

engineer n an engineer yíge gōngchéngshī 一个工程师

England n Yīnggélán 英格兰

English 1 adj Yīnggélán de 英格兰的 **2** n (the people) Yīnggélánrén 英格兰人; (the language) Yīngyǔ 英语

enjoy vb (to like) xǐhuan 喜欢, xǐ'ài 喜爱: he enjoys fishing tā xǐhuan diàoyú 他喜欢钓鱼; did you enjoy your holiday? nǐ jiàqí guò de hǎo ma? 你假期过得好吗?; (to use with delight) xiǎngshòu 享受; to enjoy social benefits xiǎngshòu shèhuì fúlì 享受社会福利; (to have a good time) enjoy yourself! zhù nǐ wánr de kuàihuo! 祝你玩儿得快活!

enjoyable adj yúkuài 愉快, kuàilè 快乐

enormous adj jùdà 巨大, pángdà 庞大

enough 1 adj zúgòu 足够: I don't have enough [money | time | friends...] wǒ méi yǒu zúgòu de [qián | shíjiān | péngyou...] 我没有足够的[钱 | 时间 | 朋友...]; there is enough wine for everyone yǒu zúgòu de jiǔ gòng dàjiā hē 有足够的酒供大家喝 **2** adv zúgòu 足够, zúgòu 足够: is it big enough? zhè gòu dà ma? 这够大吗?; you are not old enough nǐde niánlíng hái bú gòu dà 你的年龄还不够大 **3** pron we have enough to eat wǒmen yǒu zúgòu de dōngxi chī 我们有足够的东西吃; I've had enough wǒ yǐjīng shòu gòu le 我已经受够了; that's enough zúgòu le 足够了

enquire vb xúnwèn 询问: I'll enquire about the price wǒ xúnwèn yíxià jiàqián 我询问一下价钱

enter vb (to go into) jìnrù 进入; (to take part in) cānjiā 参加; to enter a competition cānjiā bǐsài 参加比赛

entertain vb (to treat hospitably) kuǎndài 款待, zhāodài 招待; (to amuse) shǐ...gāoxìng 使...高兴, shǐ...yúlè 使...娱乐; his performance entertained everyone tāde biǎoyǎn shǐ dàjiā dōu hěn gāoxìng 他的表演使大家都很高兴

entertaining *adj* yǒuqù 有趣

entertainment *n (the act of entertaining guests)* kuǎndài 款待, zhāodài 招待; *(amusement)* yúlè 娱乐, lèqù 乐趣

enthusiasm *n* rèqíng 热情

enthusiastic *adj* rèqíng 热情

entrance *n* an entrance yíge rùkǒu 一个入口; the entrance to the castle chéngbǎo de rùkǒu 城堡的入口

envelope *n* an envelope yíge xìnfēng 一个信封

environment *n* huánjìng 环境

envy 1 *n (a feeling of chagrin at the fortune of another)* jìdù 忌妒, dùjì 妒忌; *(a person or an object being envied)* jìdù de duìxiàng 忌妒的对象, jìdù de mùbiāo 忌妒的目标 2 *vb* jìdù 忌妒, dùjì 妒忌

episode *n* an episode *(an event or an incident in a story, a novel, a film)* yíge qíngjié 一个情节; *(an event)* yíge shìjiàn 一个事件

equal 1 *adj (identical in quality, value, proportion, etc)* xiāngděng 相等, jūnděng 均等; *(in social status)* píngděng 平等; to fight for equal rights wèi píngděng quánlì ér dòuzhēng 为平等权利而斗争 2 *vb* děngyú 等于; six plus four equal ten liù jiā sì děngyú shí 六加四等于十

equality *n* píngděng 平等, tóngděng 同等

equator *n* chìdào 赤道

equipment *n (in a factory, laboratory, or office)* shèbèi 设备; *(in military forces)* zhuāngbèi 装备

eraser *n (for a blackboard)* an eraser yíge hēibǎn cā 一个黑板擦; *(a pencil rubber)* (US English) an eraser yíkuài xiàngpí 一块橡皮

escalator *n* an escalator yíge diàndòng fútī 一个电动扶梯

escape *vb (to get away)* táopǎo 逃跑; he escaped from prison tā cóng jiānyù li táopǎo le 他从监狱里逃跑了; *(to avoid)* táobì 逃避, táotuō 逃脱; to escape punishment táobì chéngfá 逃避惩罚

especially adv tèbié 特别, yóuqí 尤其

essay n an essay yīpiān wénzhāng 一篇文章

essential adj (relating to the essence) shízhí de 实质的, běnzhì de 本质的; (indispensable) bìyào 必要, bìbùkěshǎo 必不可少

ethnic adj zhǒngzú de 种族的

EU, European Union n Ōuzhōu Liánméng 欧洲联盟

euro n ōuyuán 欧元

Europe n Ōuzhōu 欧洲

European adj Ōuzhōu de 欧洲的

evacuate vb (to withdraw) chèlí 撤离; (to clear out inhabitants from) shūsàn 疏散

even¹ 1 adv (when expressing surprise) shènzhì 甚至, lián...yě... 连...也...; he didn't even believe his mother tā shènzhì bù xiāngxìn tāde māma 他甚至不相信他的妈妈; she even works on weekends tā lián zhōumò yě gōngzuò 她连周末也工作; (in comparison) gèng 更, hái 还; it's even colder today jīntiān gèng lěng 今天更冷; (when used with the conjunction if or though) even if/though jíshǐ 即使, jíbiàn 即便; even if it rains tomorrow, you still have to go jíshǐ míngtiān xià yǔ, nǐ yě děi qù 即使明天下雨, 你也得去

even² adj (flat, smooth) píng de 平的, píngtǎn de 平坦的; (when talking about numbers) an even number yīgè shuāng shù 一个双数, yīgè ǒu shù 一个偶数

evening n an evening yīgè wǎnshang 一个晚上; at eight o'clock in the evening (zài) wǎnshang bā diǎn (在)晚上八点

event n (an incident) shìjiàn 事件; an event yīgè shìjiàn 一个事件; (in a sports programme) xiàngmu 项目; an event yīgè xiàngmu 一个项目

eventually adv zhōngyú 终于, zuìhòu 最后

ever adv (at any time) nothing ever happens here zhèr cónglái bù fāshēng shénme shì 这儿从来不发生什么事; have you

ever been to Thailand? nǐ qùguo Tàiguó ma? 你去过泰国吗?;
I hardly ever go there wǒ jīhū cónglái bú qù nàr 我几乎从来
不去那儿; for ever yǒngyuǎn 永远; we'll remember him for
ever wǒmen jiāng yǒngyuǎn jìzhù tā 我们将永远记住他

every det měi 每; every time I meet her měi cì wǒ jiàndào tā
每次我见到她; every [day | week | month | year] měi [tiān | zhōu |
yuè | nián] 每[天 | 周 | 月 | 年]; every other [day | week | month |
year] měi gé [yì tiān | yì zhōu | yíge yuè | yì nián] 每隔 [一天 | 一周 |
一个月 | 一年]; two out of every three people are men měi
sānge rén zhōng yǒu liǎngge shì nánrén 每三个人中有两个
是男人,

everyone, everybody pron měi ge rén 每个人, dàjiā 大家;
everyone else suǒyǒu qítā de rén 所有其他的人

everything pron (every single matter) měi jiàn shì 每件事,
suǒyǒu de shì 所有的事; (every single thing) měi jiàn dōngxi
每件东西, suǒyǒu de dōngxi 所有的东西

everywhere adv dàochù 到处; there are flowers everywhere
dàochù dōu shì xiānhuā 到处都是鲜花; (when used to
introduce a clause) everywhere I went, I would buy some
souvenirs wǒ měi dào yíge dìfang dōu yào mǎi yìxiē jìniànpǐn
我每到一个地方都要买一些纪念品

evidence n (support for a belief) zhèngjù 证据; a piece of
evidence yíge zhèngjù 一个证据; (indications or signs) jìxiàng 迹象

evil n xié'è 邪恶, zuì'è 罪恶

exact adj quèqiè 确切, jīngquè 精确

exactly adv quèqiè de 确切地, jīngquè de 精确地

exaggerate vb kuādà 夸大, kuāzhāng 夸张

exam n an exam yícì kǎoshì 一次考试; to pass an exam kǎoshì
jígé 考试及格; to take an exam cānjiā kǎoshì 参加考试

examine vb (to check) jiǎnchá 检查; (to test in schools or
universities) kǎo 考, kǎochá 考查

example n an example yíge lìzi 一个例子; for example lìrú
例如, bǐrú 比如

excellent adj yōuxiù 优秀, jiéchū 杰出; (in an exclamation) excellent! hǎo jíle! 好极了!

except prep chúle...(yǐwài)...dōu 除了...(以外)...都

exchange vb to exchange [books | students | gifts] jiāohuàn [书 | 学生 | 礼物] 交换 [书 | 学生 | 礼物]; to exchange [foreign currency | US dollars | British pounds] duìhuàn [外币 | 美元 | 英镑] 兑换 [外币 | 美元 | 英镑]; to exchange seats diàohuàn zuòwei 调换座位

exchange rate n duìhuàn huìlǜ 兑换汇率

excited adj jīdòng 激动, xīngfèn 兴奋

exciting adj lìng rén jīdòng 令人激动, lìng rén xīngfèn 令人兴奋

exclude vb (hinder from participation) I excluded him from the meeting wǒ méiyǒu ràng tā cānjiā zhège huì 我没有让他参加这个会; (to rule out) páichú 排除; I cannot exclude this possibility wǒ bù néng páichú zhèzhǒng kěnéngxìng 我不能排除这种可能性

excuse 1 n an excuse yíge jièkǒu 一个借口; to make excuses zhìzào jièkǒu 制造借口 **2** vb yuánliàng 原谅; excuse me! duìbuqǐ! 对不起!, láojià! 劳驾!

exercise n (physical exercise) duànliàn 锻炼; to take exercise, to do exercise jìnxíng duànliàn 进行锻炼; (a piece of work) an exercise yíge liànxí 一个练习

exercise book n an exercise book yìběn liànxí běn 一本练习本

exhausted adj (tired out) jīnpílìjìn 筋疲力尽; (consumed) yòngwán 用完, hàojìn 耗尽

exhibition n an exhibition yíge zhǎnlǎnhuì 一个展览会

exit n an exit yíge chūkǒu 一个出口

expect vb (to be prepared for) qīdài 期待; to expect bad news qīdài huài xiāoxi 期待坏消息; they expect to win tāmen qīdàizhe yíng 他们期待着赢; (to wait for) děngdài 等待, děng 等; (to want) pànwàng 盼望, qīwàng 期望; they expect us to do the work tāmen qīwàng wǒmen zuò zhège gōngzuò 他们期望我们做这个工作

expenses *n* huāfèi 花费, zhīchū 支出

expensive *adj* guì 贵, ángguì 昂贵

experience *n* (passing through an event or events) jīnglì 经历; an experience yícì jīnglì 一次经历; (practical acquaintance with any matter) jīngyàn 经验

experienced *adj* yǒu jīngyàn de 有经验的

experiment **1** *n* an experiment yícì shíyàn 一次实验, yícì shìyàn 一次试验 **2** *vb* shíyàn 实验, shìyàn 试验

expert *n* an expert yíge zhuānjiā 一个专家

explain *vb* jiěshì 解释, shuōmíng 说明; to explain a rule to someone xiàng mǒurén jiěshì yíge guīzé 向某人解释一个规则

explanation *n* an explanation yíge jiěshì 一个解释, yíge shuōmíng 一个说明

explode *vb* (if it's a bomb) bàozhà 爆炸; (in personal emotion or feeling) to explode with laughter hōngtáng dàxiào 哄堂大笑

exploit *vb* (to turn to use) kāifā 开发, kāicǎi 开采; (to make gain at the expense of) bōxuē 剥削

explosion *n* an explosion yícì bàozhà 一次爆炸

export *vb* chūkǒu 出口, shūchū 输出

express **1** *vb* biǎoshì 表示, biǎodá 表达 **2** *adj* tèkuài 特快; an express train yítàng kuài chē 一趟快车; an express letter yìfēng kuài xìn 一封快信

expression *n* a happy expression yífù gāoxìng de biǎoqíng 一副高兴的表情; the expression of different opinions bùtóng yìjiàn de biǎodá 不同意见的表达

extinct *adj* (describing an animal or a plant) juézhǒng de 绝种的, mièjué de 灭绝的; (describing a volcano) xīmiè de 熄灭的, sǐ 死

extra **1** *adj* (beyond or more than the usual) éwài 额外; to pay an extra ten pounds éwài duō fù shí bàng qián 额外多付十镑

钱; (additional) wàijiā 外加: **an extra bed** yìzhāng jiā chuáng 一张加床 **2** adv **to pay extra for wine** jiǔ qián lìng fù 酒钱另付

extraordinary adj tèbié 特别, fēicháng 非常

extreme adj (most remote) jìntóu de 尽头的; (highest in degree) jíduān 极端; (extraordinary in opinions or behaviour) jījìn 激进, piānjī 偏激

extremely adv jíduān 极端, fēicháng 非常

eye n **an eye** yìzhī yǎnjing 一只眼睛

eyebrow n méimao 眉毛

eyelash n jiémáo 睫毛

eyelid n yǎnjiǎn 眼睑, yǎnpí 眼皮

eye shadow n yǎnyǐng 眼影

eyesight n shìlì 视力

Ff

face 1 n **the face** liǎn 脸, miànkǒng 面孔; **to make a face** zuò guǐliǎnr 做鬼脸儿 **2** vb (to be opposite) miànduì 面对; **she was facing me** tā miànduìzhe wǒ 面对着我 (to have to deal with) zhèngshì 正视, duìfu 对付; **we have to face these difficulties** wǒmen bìxū zhèngshì zhèxiē kùnnan 我们必须正视这些困难; (to look toward(s)) cháo 朝, miànxiàng 面向; **my room faces the sea** wǒde fángjiān cháo hǎi 我的房间朝海; **face up to** yǒnggǎn de duìfu 勇敢地对付

fact 1 n **a fact** yíge shìshí 一个事实 **2 in fact** qíshí 其实, shíjìshang 实际上

factory n **a factory** yíge gōngchǎng 一个工厂

fade vb (if it's a flower or tree leaf) kūwěi 枯萎, diāoxiè 凋谢; (if it's a colour) tuìsè 褪色

fail vb (in an examination) bù jígé 不及格; to fail an exam kǎoshì bù jígé 考试不及格; (miss an achievement) shībài 失败; his plan failed tāde jìhuà shībài le 他的计划失败了; (to prove deficient) the plane failed to arrive on time fēijī méiyǒu zhǔnshí dàodá 飞机没有准时到达; she never fails to remember my birthday tā cónglái méi wàngjì wǒde shēngrì 她从来没忘记我的生日; (in health, sight or hearing) shuāituì 衰退, shuāiruò 衰弱

failure n a failure (an event, an attempt) yícì shībài 一次失败; (a person in an exam) bù jígé 不及格

faint vb hūndǎo 昏倒, yūndǎo 晕倒

fair 1 adj (just) gōngpíng 公平, gōngzhèng 公正; it's not fair zhè bù gōngpíng 这不公平; (in colour) fair hair jīnhuángsè de tóufa 金黄色的头发; fair skin báinèn de pífū 白嫩的皮肤 **2** n (British English) (a funfair) a fair yíge yóulèhuì 一个游乐会; (a display of goods) a (trade) fair yíge shāngpǐn jiāoyìhuì 一个商品交易会

fairly adv (justly) gōngpíng de 公平地, gōngzhèng de 公正地; (quite) xiāngdāng 相当

faith n (trust or confidence) xìnrèn 信任, xiāngxìn 相信; to have faith in someone xìnrèn mǒurén 信任某人; (in religion) xìnyǎng 信仰

faithful adj zhōngchéng 忠诚, zhōngshí 忠实

fall 1 vb (if it's a person) shuāidǎo 摔倒, diēdǎo 跌倒; she fell to the ground tā shuāidǎo zài dì shang 她摔倒在地上; (to drop) luò 落, diào 掉; an apple fell onto his head yíge píngguǒ diào zài tāde tóu shang 一个苹果掉在他的头上; (in price, temperature) xiàjiàng 下降, jiàngdī 降低; (other uses) to fall asleep shuìzháo 睡着; to fall ill bìng le 病了; to fall in love with someone àishang mǒurén 爱上某人 **2** n (in price, temperature) xiàjiàng 下降, jiàngdī 降低; (US English) (autumn) qiūtiān 秋天; **fall down** (if it's a person) dǎoxia 倒下, shuāidǎo 摔倒; (if it's a building) dǎotā 倒塌, tāntā 坍塌; **fall off** to fall off a chair cóng yǐzi shang diēxiàlai 从椅子上跌下来; **fall out** (from somewhere) diàochūlai 掉出来; the letter fell out of his pocket xìn cóng tā kǒudài li diàochūlai 信从他口袋里掉出来: (to quarrel) chǎojià 吵架; nàofān 闹翻; **fall over** diējiāo 跌跤; diēdǎo 跌倒; **fall through** shībài 失败

false adj (untrue, not real) jiǎ 假; (wrong, erroneous) cuòwù de 错误的, miùwù de 谬误的

familiar adj shúxī 熟悉

family n a family yíge jiātíng 一个家庭

famous adj zhùmíng 著名, yǒumíng 有名

fan n (of a pop star, an actor, a sport) mí 迷; a football fan yíge zúqiú mí 一个足球迷; (for cooling) a fan (electric) yìtái (diàn)fēngshàn 一台(电)风扇; (hand-held) yìbǎ shànzi 一把扇子

fancy dress party n (British English) a fancy dress party yíge huàzhuāng wǔhuì 一个化妆舞会

fantastic adj (fanciful) huànxiǎng de 幻想的; (weird, odd) qíyì 奇异, gǔguài 古怪; fantastic! tài hǎo le! 太好了!

far 1 adv far (away) yuǎn 远; how far is it to London? dào Lúndūn yǒu duō yuǎn? 到伦敦有多远? how far is Oxford from London? Niújīn lí Lúndūn yǒu duō yuǎn? 牛津离伦敦有多远? we went as far as the coast wǒmen yìzhí zǒudàole hǎibiān 我们一直走到了海边; (in time) as far back as 1950 yuǎn zài yījiǔwǔlíng nián 远在1950年; (very much) you're eating far too much bread miànbāo nǐ chī de tài duō le 面包你吃得太多了; far [better | colder | earlier...] [hǎo | lěng | zǎo...] de duō [好 | 冷 | 早...] 得多 **2** adj (farther) nàyìbiān 那一边, at the far side of the room zài fángjiān de nàyìbiān 在房间的那一边; the Far East Yuǎndōng 远东 **3** so far dào mùqián wéizhǐ 到目前为止

fare n the fare (on a bus, train, or underground) chēfèi 车费; (on a boat) chuánfèi 船费

farm n a farm (for cultivation) yíge nóngchǎng 一个农场; (for pasture) yíge xùmùchǎng 一个畜牧场

farmer n a farmer yíge nóngchǎngzhǔ 一个农场主

fascinating adj mírén 迷人

fashion n (form or pattern) yàngzi 样子; (prevailing mode or shape of dress) liúxíng shìyàng 流行式样; to be in fashion zhèng shíxíng 正时兴; to go out of fashion guòshí 过时, bù shíxíng 不时兴

fashionable adj shímáo 时髦, liúxíng 流行

fast 1 adj (rapid) kuài 快, xùnsù 迅速; (as a clock or watch) kuài 快; my watch is ten minutes fast wǒde shǒubiǎo kuài shí fēnzhōng 我的手表快十分钟 **2** adv kuài 快, xùnsù 迅速

fasten vb jìláo 系牢, jìhǎo 系好; to fasten a seatbelt jìhǎo ānquándài 系好安全带

fast-forward vb to fast-forward a cassette kuàisù xiàngqián zhuàn cídài 快速向前转磁带

fat adj (describing a person) pàng 胖; (describing animals or meat) féi 肥

fatal adj (causing death) zhìmìng de 致命的; (decided by fate) mìngzhōng zhùdìng de 命中注定的; (determining fate) juédìng 决定; a fatal decision for me juédìng wǒ mìngyùn de juédìng 决定我命运的决定

father n a father yíge bàba 一个爸爸, yíge fùqin 一个父亲

Father Christmas n (British English) Father Christmas Shèngdàn Lǎorén 圣诞老人

father-in-law n (husband's father) gōnggong 公公; (wife's father) yuèfù 岳父

faucet n (US English) a faucet yíge shuǐlóngtóu 一个水龙头

fault n a fault (a mistake made by someone) yíge guòcuò 一个过错; (in a mechanical, electrical or electronic system) yíge gùzhàng 一个故障

favour (British English), **favor** (US English) **1** n to do someone a favour bāng mǒurén yíge máng 帮某人一个忙; to ask someone a favour qǐng mǒurén bāng ge máng 请某人帮个忙 **2 in favour of** to be in favour of the new law zànchéng xīn de fǎlǜ 赞成新的法律

favourite (*British English*), **favorite** (*US English*) *adj* tèbié xǐhuan de 特别喜欢的; it's my favourite film zhè shì wǒ tèbié xǐhuan de diànyǐng 这是我特别喜欢的电影

fax *n* a fax yífèn chuánzhēn 一份传真

fear *n* hàipà 害怕, kǒngjù 恐惧

feather *n* a feather yìgēn yǔmáo 一根羽毛

February *n* èryuè 二月

fed up *adj* be fed up fēicháng yànjuàn 非常厌倦

fee *n* (*for attending an event, a show*) fèi 费; (*for joining a club, a union*) huìfèi 会费

feeble *adj* xūruò 虚弱, wúlì 无力

feed *vb* (*if it's a person*) wèi 喂; (*if it's an animal*) sìyǎng 饲养, wèi(yǎng) 喂(养)

feel *vb* (*referring to an emotion, an impression, or a physical feeling*) juéde 觉得, gǎndào 感到; to feel happy gǎndào gāoxìng 感到高兴; he's feeling uncomfortable tā juéde bù shūfu 他觉得不舒服; to feel afraid juéde hàipà 觉得害怕; I feel as if I'm being followed wǒ gǎndào hǎoxiàng yǒu rén gēnzhe wǒ 我感到好像有人跟着我; to feel [hot | cold | sleepy] juéde [rè | lěng | kùn] 觉得[热 | 冷 | 困]; I don't feel a thing wǒ shénme dōu gǎnjué bú dào 我什么都感觉不到; (*describing how something seems*) the box felt very heavy nàge hézi náqǐlai hěn zhòng 那个盒子拿起来很重; the room feels very cold zhège fángjiān ràng rén juéde hěn lěng 这个房间让人觉得很冷; (*to touch*) mō 摸; the doctor felt her head dàifu mōle yíxià tāde tóu 大夫摸了一下她的头; to feel like [going out | eating | dancing...] xiǎngyào [chūqu | chī dōngxi | tiàowǔ...] 想要 [出去 | 吃东西 | 跳舞...]; I don't like it (*if it's about going out*) wǒ bù xiǎng (chū)qù 我不想(出)去; (*if it's about eating something*) wǒ bù xiǎng chī 我不想吃; (*if it's about doing something*) wǒ bù xiǎng zuò 我不想做

feeling *n* (*emotional*) gǎnqíng 感情; a feeling yìzhǒng gǎnqíng 一种感情; to hurt someone's feelings shānghài mǒurén de gǎnqíng 伤害某人的感情; (*physical*) gǎnjué 感觉; a feeling yìzhǒng gǎnjué 一种感觉; I have a feeling he's right wǒ juéde tā shì duì de 我觉得他是对的

felt-tip pen n a felt-tip pen yìzhī zhāntóubǐ 一支毡头笔

female adj (in biology) cíxìng de 雌性的; (relating to women) nǚ 女, nǚxìng de 女性的; (relating to animals) mǔ 母

feminine adj (female) nǚxìng de 女性的; (effeminate) nǚzǐqì de 女子气的, jiāoróu de 娇柔的

fence n a fence yíge líba 一个篱笆, yíge wéilán 一个围栏

fencing n jíjiàn 击剑

festival n a festival day yíge jié(rì) 一个节(日)

fetch vb ná 拿, qǔ 取; go and fetch some water qù ná diǎn shuǐ lai 去拿点水来; fetch a doctor qǐng ge dàifu lai 请个大夫来

fever n to have a fever fāshāo 发烧, fārè 发热

few 1 a few yìxiē 一些, jǐge 几个; a few [people | houses | books...] yìxiē [rén | fángzi | shū...] 一些 [人 | 房子 | 书...]; a few of them speak Cantonese tāmen dāngzhōng de jǐge rén huì shuō Guǎngdōnghuà 他们当中的几个人会说广东话 2 det (not many) jīhū méi yǒu 几乎没有, hěn shǎo 很少; few [people | letters | cars...] jīhū méi yǒu [rén | xìn | chē...] 几乎没有 [人 | 信 | 车...]; (several) jǐge 几个; the first few weeks kāishǐ de jǐge xīngqī 开始的几个星期 3 pron few of us succeeded wǒmen dāngzhōng jīhū méi yǒu rén chénggōng 我们当中几乎没有人成功

field n (open country in general) tiányě 田野, tiándì 田地; a field yíkuài tiándì 一块田地; (a piece of ground enclosed for sports, construction, entertainment, etc.) a field yíge chǎngdì 一个场地; (an area of knowledge or speciality) lǐngyù 领域; a field yíge lǐngyù 一个领域

fifteen num shíwǔ 十五

fifteenth num (in a series) dìshíwǔ 第十五; (in dates) the fifteenth of May wǔyuè shíwǔ hào 五月十五号

fifth num (in a series) dìwǔ 第五; (in dates) the fifth of June liùyuè wǔ hào 六月五号

fifty num wǔshí 五十

fight 1 vb to fight (against) prejudice yǔ piānjiàn zuò dòuzhēng 与偏见作斗争; to fight for justice wèi zhèngyì ér fèndòu 为正义而奋斗; (in war) yǔ...zhàndòu 与...战斗, yǔ...zuòzhàn 与...作战; to fight (against) the enemy yǔ dírén zhàndòu 与敌人战斗; (physically) yǔ...dǎzhàng 与...打仗; (to quarrel) yǔ...zhēngchǎo 与...争吵 **2** n (a campaign) dòuzhēng 斗争; a fight yìchǎng dòuzhēng 一场斗争; (physical) a fight yìchǎng zhàndòu 一场战斗, yìchǎng bódòu 一场搏斗; fight back huánjī 还击

figure n (a number) shùzì 数字; a figure yíge shùzì 一个数字; to have a good figure yǒu yíge hǎo de tǐxíng 有一个好的体型

file n (for documents) yíge ànjuàn 一个案卷, yíge juànzǒng 一个卷宗; (in a computer) yíge wénjiàn 一个文件

fill vb (to fill a container) zhuāngmǎn 装满; (if it's people filling a room or a hall) jǐmǎn 挤满; (if it's a form) tiánxiě 填写; (if it's a hole or a sunken place) tián 填; **fill in** tián 填; (if it's a form) tiánxiě 填写; (if it's a hole or a sunken place) tián 填

film 1 n (in a cinema or on TV) a film yíbù diànyǐng 一部电影; (for a camera) a film yíge jiāojuǎn 一个胶卷 **2** vb pāishè 拍摄

filthy adj āngzāng 肮脏

final 1 adj zuìhòu 最后, zuìzhōng 最终 **2** n a final (in sports) yícì juésài 一次决赛; (an examination) zuìhòu dàkǎo 最后大考

finally adv zuìhòu 最后, zuìzhōng 最终

find vb (to reach the thing or person one has looked for) zhǎodào 找到; (to discover) fāxiàn 发现; (to come to perceive) fājué 发觉, gǎnjué 感觉; **find out** to find out the truth chámíng zhēnxiàng 查明真相; if he ever finds out he'll be furious rúguǒ tā fāxiànle, tā huì dà fā léitíng 如果他发现了, 他会大发雷霆

fine 1 adj (describing a person's character) yōuliáng 优良, yōuxiù 优秀; (describing the weather) qínglǎng 晴朗, búcuò 不错; (describing the appearance of a person, a building, or a scene) hǎokàn 好看, piàoliang 漂亮; (in good health) I feel fine wǒ gǎnjué hěn hǎo 我感觉很好; (expressing agreement) (that's) fine xíng 行 **2** n a fine yìfēn fákuǎn 一份罚款

finger n shǒuzhǐ 手指

finish 1 vb (to complete) wánchéng 完成; to finish one's [homework | task | experiment] wánchéng [zuòyè | rènwù | shíyàn] 完成 [作业 | 任务 | 实验]; (used after a verb to indicate a result of an action) wán 完; to finish [cooking | eating] supper [zuò | chī] wán wǎnfàn [做 | 吃] 完晚饭; (to come to an end) jiéshù 结束; the film finishes at 8:00 diànyǐng bā diǎn jiéshù 电影八点结束 **2** n the finish (the last part in a film, a race, or a certain process) zuìhòu yíduàn 最后一段

fire 1 n huǒ 火; a fire (for heat) lúhuǒ 炉火; (causing damage) yìchǎng huǒzāi 一场火灾; to catch fire zháohuǒ 着火, qǐhuǒ 起火; to be on fire zháohuǒ 着火, qǐhuǒ 起火 **2** vb (to shoot) kāiqiāng 开枪; (to dismiss) jiěgù 解雇, kāichú 开除

fire alarm n a fire alarm yíge huǒjǐng bàojǐngqì 一个火警报警器

fire brigade (British English), **fire department** (US English) n xiāofángduì 消防队

fire engine n a fire engine yíliàng xiāofángchē 一辆消防车

fireman n a fireman yíge xiāofáng duìyuán 一个消防队员

fire station n a fire station yíge xiāofángzhàn 一个消防站

fireworks display n a fireworks display yìchǎng yānhuǒ wǎnhuì 一场烟火晚会

firm 1 n a firm yíge gōngsī 一个公司 **2** adj (when describing a structure, foundation, or frame) jiēshi 结实, láogù 牢固; (when describing one's attitude, position) jiāndìng 坚定, jiānjué 坚决

first 1 adj the first [time | lesson | day] dìyī [cì | kè | tiān] 第一 [次 | 课 | 天]; the first [three weeks | two months | few days] tóu [sān zhōu | liǎngge yuè | jǐ tiān] 头 [三周 | 两个月 | 几天] **2** adv (to begin with) shǒuxiān 首先; first of all shǒuxiān 首先; (for the first time) dìyīcì 第一次; to arrive first dìyīge dàodá 第一个到达 **3** n (in a series or group) the first dìyīge 第一个; he was the first to congratulate us tā shì dìyīge zhùhè wǒmen de rén 他是第一个祝贺我们的人; (in dates) the first of June liùyuè yī hào 六月一号 **4** at first qǐchū 起初, kāishǐ de shíhou 开始的时候

first aid n jíjiù 急救

first class adv to travel first class (in a boat or a plane) zuò tóuděng cāng lǚxíng 坐头等舱旅行; (in a train) zuò tóuděng chēxiāng lǚxíng 坐头等车厢旅行

first floor n (in Britain) èrlóu 二楼; (in the US) yīlóu 一楼

first name n jiàomíng 教名, míng 名

fish 1 n a fish yìtiáo yú 一条鱼 2 vb to go fishing (with a rod) qù diàoyú 去钓鱼; (with a net) qù bǔ yú 去捕鱼

fisherman n a fisherman yíge yúmín 一个渔民

fishing n (with a rod) diàoyú 钓鱼; (with a net) bǔ yú 捕鱼

fishing rod n a fishing rod yìgēn diàoyú gǎnr 一根钓鱼杆儿

fist n quántou 拳头

fit 1 vb the shoes don't fit me zhèshuāng xié wǒ chuān bù héshì 这双鞋我穿不合适; the photo won't fit into the envelope zhèzhāng zhàopiàn zhuāng bú jìn zhège xìnfēng lǐ qu 这张照片装不进这个信封里去; will the table fit here? zhèzhāng zhuōzi fàng zài zhèr héshì ma? 这张桌子放在这儿合适吗? 2 adj (suitable) héshì 合适, shìhé 适合; the house isn't fit to live in zhè(zhuàng) fángzi bú shìhé jūzhù 这(幢)房子不适合居住; to be fit to drive shìhé kāi chē 适合开车; he is not fit to be a leader tā bù héshì zuò lǐngdǎo 他不合适做领导; (healthy) to be fit jiànkāng 健康; **fit in !** Note that the translation varies with the context, which determines the verb that is used; (in a car) can you all fit in? nǐmen dōu néng zuòjìnqu ma? 你们都能坐进去吗?; (in a group or team) can he fit in? tā néng gēn qítā rén hé de lái ma? 他能跟其他人合得来吗?

fitness n (physical) fitness (shēntǐ) jiànkāng (身体)健康

five num wǔ 五; five apples wǔge píngguǒ 五个苹果

fix vb (to decide on) quèdìng 确定, juédìng 决定; (to fasten or attach) gùdìng 固定, ānzhuāng 安装; (to repair) xiūlǐ 修理; (to prepare) zhǔnbèi 准备

flag n a flag yímiàn qí 一面旗

flame n huǒyàn 火焰

flash 1 n a flash (for a camera) yíge shǎnguāngdēng 一个闪光灯 **2** vb to flash (on and off) shǎnliàng 闪亮, shǎnguāng 闪光

flashlight n a flashlight yíge shǎnguāngdēng 一个闪光灯

flat 1 n (British English) a flat yíge tàofáng 一个套房, yítào dānyuán fángjiān 一套单元房间 **2** adj (smooth and level) píng 平, píngtǎn 平坦; to have a flat tyre chētāi biě le 车胎瘪了

flavour (British English), **flavor** (US English) n a flavour yìzhǒng wèidào 一种味道

flea n a flea yíge tiàozǎo 一个跳蚤

flight n a flight (a regular air journey, numbered and at a fixed time) yíge hángbān 一个航班, yíge bānjī 一个班机; (the act of flying) fēi 飞, fēixíng 飞行

flight attendant n a flight attendant yìmíng jīshàng fúwùyuán 一名机上服务员

float vb (in the air) piāo 飘; to float up into the air piāodào kōng zhōng qu 飘到空中去; (in the water) piāo 漂; to float in the river zài hé li piāo 在河里漂

flock n a flock of [sheep | geese | birds...] yìqún [yáng | é | niǎo...] 一群 [羊 | 鹅 | 鸟...]

flood n a flood yícì hóngshuǐ 一次洪水, yícì shuǐzāi 一次水灾

floor n (a surface) a floor dìbǎn 地板; to sit on the floor zuò zài dìbǎn shang 坐在地板上; (a storey) céng 层, lóu 楼; the ground floor (British English) yìcéng 一层, yìlóu 一楼

florist n a florist yíge mài huā de rén 一个卖花的人, yíge huāshāng 一个花商

flour n miàn 面, miànfěn 面粉

flow vb liú 流, liúdòng 流动

flower 1 n a flower (if it's a single flower) yìzhī huā 一枝花; (if it's a plant) yìkē huā 一棵花 **2** vb kāihuā 开花

flu n liúxíngxìng gǎnmào 流行性感冒, liúgǎn 流感

fluently adv liúlì de 流利地

flush vb to flush the toilet chōng cèsuǒ 冲厕所

flute n a flute yìgēn chángdí 一根长笛

fly 1 n a fly yìzhī cāngying 一只苍蝇 **2** vb (if it's a bird, plane) fēi 飞; to fly from London to Beijing cóng Lúndūn fēidào Běijīng 从伦敦飞到北京; to fly a plane jiàshǐ yìjià fēijī 驾驶一架飞机; (if it's a flag) piāoyáng 飘扬; **fly away** fēizǒu 飞走

fog n wù 雾

fold vb (if it's a chair, bed, or table) zhédié 折叠; (if it's clothes, a handkerchief, a bed sheet) dié 叠; to fold one's arms bǎ shuāngbì zài xiōngqián jiāochālái 把双臂在胸前交叉起来

folder n a folder yíge wénjiànjiā 一个文件夹

follow vb (to go or come after) gēnsuí 跟随; (to pursue) zhuīgǎn 追赶, zhuīzōng 追踪; (to understand) dǒng/lǐjiě...de yìsi 懂/理解...的意思; (to obey) tīngcóng 听从, zūnxún 遵循; (to imitate) fǎngxiào 仿效; (to keep an eye fixed on) zhùshì 注视; (to keep one's hearing fixed on) qīngtīng 倾听; (to keep one's attention fixed on) zhùyì 注意

following adj the following (below) xiàmian 下面; the following paragraph xiàmian yíduàn 下面一段; the following names xiàliè míngzi 下列名字; (when talking about the day, the week, the month, the year) dì'èr 第二; the following day dì'èr tiān 第二天

fond adj I'm very fond of you wǒ hěn xǐhuan nǐ 我很喜欢你

food n shíwù 食物, shípǐn 食品

fool 1 vb qīpiàn 欺骗, yúnòng 愚弄 **2** n a fool yíge shǎzi 一个傻子, yíge shǎguā 一个傻瓜

foot n (part of the leg) jiǎo 脚; on foot bùxíng 步行; (in measurements) a foot yì yīngchǐ 一英尺

football n (soccer) zúqiú 足球; (American football) gǎnlǎnqiú 橄榄球; (a ball) a football yíge zúqiú 一个足球

footballer (British English), **football player** (US English) n a footballer yíge zúqiú yùndòngyuán 一个足球运动员

footprint *n* a footprint yíge jiǎoyìn 一个脚印

footstep *n* a footstep yíge jiǎobù 一个脚步

for *prep* (*indicating the purpose of*) wèile 为了, wèi 为; to fight for national interests wèile guójiā lìyì ér dòuzhēng 为了国家利益而斗争; (*indicating the beneficiary*) wèi 为, gěi 给; to work for a company tā wèi yíge gōngsī gōngzuò 为一个公司工作; he cooked dinner for us tā gěi wǒmen zuò fàn 他给我们做饭; (*indicating time and distance*) ! Note that when indicating time and distance, for is not translated into Chinese; we've been living here for two years wǒmen zài zhèr zhùle liǎng nián le 我们在这儿住了两年了; he's going to Shanghai for a year tā yào qù Shànghǎi yì nián 他要去上海一年; we drove for 80 kilometres wǒmen kāile bāshí gōnglǐ 我们开了80公里; (*indicating the price of a purchase*) huā 花; he bought the bag for £50 tā huā wǔshí yīngbàng mǎile zhège bāo 他花50英镑买了这个包; (*indicating the selling price*) yǐ 以; he sold his bike for £40 tā yǐ sìshí yīngbàng mǎile tāde zìxíngchē 他以40英镑卖了他的自行车; (*in favour of*) zànchéng 赞成, yōnghù 拥护; are you for or against his suggestion? nǐ zànchéng háishì fǎnduì tāde jiànyì? 你赞成还是反对他的建议?; (*indicating to whom or what something or somebody is intended or destined*) ! Note that in this use for is usually not translated into Chinese; a letter for you nǐde xìn 你的信; the Minister for Education Jiàoyù Bùzhǎng 教育部长; the money is for buying a new car zhè qián shì mǎi xīn chē yòng de 这钱是买新车用的; (*on behalf of, in place of*) tì 替, dài 代; let me do it for you ràng wǒ tì nǐ zuò ba 让我替你做吧; say hello to her for me dài wǒ xiàng tā wèn hǎo 代我向她问好; (*indicating the direction or the destination*) the plane for Beijing fēi wǎng Běijīng de fēijī 飞往北京的飞机; [the train | the bus | the boat] for London kāi wǎng Lúndūn de [huǒchē | qìchē | chuán] 开往伦敦的 [火车 | 汽车 | 船]; (*other uses*) a cheque for £20 yì zhāng èrshí yīngbàng de zhīpiào 一张20英镑的支票; what is the Chinese for 'badger'? Hànyǔ 'badger' zěnme shuō? 汉语 'badger' 怎么说?; we went [for a swim | for a run | for a walk...] wǒmen qù [yóuyǒng | pǎobù | sànbù...] 我们去 [游泳 | 跑步 | 散步...]

forbid vb jìnzhǐ 禁止, bùxǔ 不许; to forbid someone to go out bùxǔ mǒurén chūqu 不许某人出去; smoking is forbidden jìnzhǐ xīyān 禁止吸烟

force 1 vb qiángpò 强迫, bī 逼; to force someone to leave qiángpò mǒurén líkāi 强迫某人离开 **2** n (strength) lì 力, lìliang 力量; (influence) shìlì 势力; by force tōngguò wǔlì 通过武力; [police | air] force [jǐngchá | kōngjūn] [警察 | 空军]

forecast n yùbào 预报; the forecast is for rain yùbào shuō yǒu yǔ 预报说有雨

forehead n qián'é 前额

foreign adj wàiguó de 外国的

foreigner n a foreigner yíge wàiguórén 一个外国人

forest n a forest yíge sēnlín 一个森林

forever, for ever adv yǒngyuǎn 永远

forget vb wàng 忘, wàngjì 忘记; to forget about someone wàngle mǒurén 忘了某人; to forget [to do the shopping | to eat | to call...] wàngle [mǎi dōngxi | chī fàn | dǎ diànhuà...] 忘了 [买东西 | 吃饭 | 打电话...]

forgive vb yuánliàng 原谅

fork n a fork yìbǎ chāzi 一把叉子

form 1 n a form (a shape) yìzhǒng xíngzhuàng/yàngzi 一种形状/样子; (a style) yìzhǒng xíngshì/fāngshì 一种形式/方式; (a document) yìzhāng biǎogé 一张表格; (referring to mood or fitness) to be in good form zhuàngtài liánghǎo 状态良好; (British English) (a year in a school) a form yíge niánjí 一个年级; to be in the sixth form zài (zhōngxué) liù niánjí 在(中学)六年级 **2** vb (to create, to make) xíngchéng 形成, gòuchéng 构成; to form a circle yíge yuánquān 形成一个圆圈; (to establish, set up) zǔchéng 组成, jiànlì 建立

formal adj (describing language) guīfàn 规范; to wear formal clothes (for the evening) chuān wǎnlǐfú 穿晚礼服; (official) zhèngshì 正式

former adj (before in time, past) yǐqián de 以前的, cóngqián de 从前的; (the first of the two mentioned) qiánzhě 前者

fortnight n (British English) a fortnight liǎngge xīngqī 两个星期

fortunately adv xìngyùn de shì 幸运的是, xìngkuī 幸亏

fortune n a fortune yìbǐ cáichǎn 一笔财产; to make a fortune fā yìbǐ cái 发一笔财; to tell someone's fortune gěi mǒurén suàn mìng 给某人算命

forty num forty sìshí 四十

forward 1 adv xiàngqián 向前; to step forward xiàngqián zǒu 向前走 **2** vb to forward a letter to someone bǎ yìfēng xìn zhuǎn gěi mǒurén 把一封信转给某人

found vb (to found an organisation, a system, an institution) jiànlì 建立, chuànglì 创立; (to found a building, a city) jiànshè 建设, jiànzhù 建筑

fountain n a fountain yíge pēnquán 一个喷泉

four num sì 四

fourteen num shísì 十四

fourteenth num (in a series) dìshísì 第十四; (in dates) the fourteenth of July qīyuè shísì hào 七月十四号

fourth num (in a series) dìsì 第四; (in dates) the fourth of July qīyuè sì hào 七月四号

fox n a fox yìzhī húli 一只狐狸

fragile adj (easily broken) yìsuì 易碎; (delicate, frail) cuìruò 脆弱

frame n a frame (a structure) yíge gòujià 一个构架, yíge jiégòu 一个结构; (a case made to enclose, border, or support something) yíge kuàngzi 一个框子, yíge kuàngjià 一个框架; (the body) yíge shēnqū 一个身躯

France n Fǎguó 法国

frank adj tǎnshuài 坦率, zhíshuài 直率

freckle n a freckle yíge quèbān 一个雀斑

free 1 adj (costing nothing) miǎnfèi 免费; he gets free medical treatment tā jiēshòu miǎnfèi zhìliáo 他接受免费治疗; (independent, not bound by rules) zìyóu 自由; free trade zìyóu màoyì 自由贸易; he is free to do what he likes tā kěyǐ zuò rènhé tā xiǎng zuò de shì 他可以做任何他想做的事; (not occupied, available) yǒu kòngr 有空儿; kòngzixián 空闲; are you free on Monday? nǐ xīngqīyī yǒu kòngr ma? 你星期一有空儿吗? **2** vb to free the prisoners shìfàng qiúfàn 释放囚犯

freedom n zìyóu 自由

freeway n (US English) a freeway yìtiáo (gāosù)gōnglù 一条 (高速)公路

freeze vb (if it is water, river) jiébīng 结冰; the river froze hé jiébīng le 河结冰了; (to freeze something) dòng 冻; to freeze the chicken in the freezer bǎ jī fàng zài bīngxiāng li dòngqǐlai 把鸡放在冰箱里冻起来; the ground was frozen hard dì dòng de hěn yìng 地冻得很硬; (to stop as if by cold) dòngjié 冻结; to freeze the prices dòngjié wùjià 冻结物价; to freeze to death dòngsǐ 冻死

freezer n a freezer yíge lěngdòngguì 一个冷冻柜, yíge lěngcángguì 一个冷藏柜

freezing adj hěn lěng 很冷, jí lěng 极冷; it's freezing tiānqì hěn lěng 天气很冷

French 1 adj Fǎguó de 法国的 **2** n (the people) Fǎguórén 法国人; (the language) Fǎyǔ 法语, Fǎwén 法文

French fries n (US English) yóuzhá tǔdòutiáo 油炸土豆条

fresh adj (when describing food, vegetables, fruits, fish) xīnxiān 新鲜; (new) xīn 新; fresh paint xīn (shuā) de yóuqī 新(刷)的 油漆

Friday n Friday xīngqīwǔ 星期五

fridge n a fridge yíge bīngxiāng 一个冰箱

fried adj yóujiān de 油煎的, yóuzhá de 油炸的

fried egg n a fried egg yíge jiān jīdàn 一个煎鸡蛋

friend n a friend yíge péngyou 一个朋友; to make friends with someone hé mǒurén jiāo péngyou 和某人交朋友

friendly adj yǒuhǎo 友好

fright n to get a fright chī yìjīng 吃一惊, xià yítiào 吓一跳;
to give someone a fright xià mǒurén yítiào 吓某人一跳, shǐ
mǒurén chī yìjīng 使某人吃一惊

frightened adj to be frightened hàipà 害怕

fringe n (of the hair) (British English) liúhǎir 刘海儿; (border)
biānyuán 边缘, biānyán 边沿

frog n a frog yìzhī qīngwā 一只青蛙

from prep ! There are many verbs which involve the use of from,
like borrow from, escape from, etc. For translations, look up the
entries at borrow, escape, etc.; (indicating a location, a place, a
time, etc., which is the starting point of an activity, journey,
period of time, etc.) cóng 从; the boy from London cóng Lúndūn
lái de nánháir 从伦敦来的男孩儿; where did she come from?
tā cóng nǎr lái? 她从哪儿来?; to come back from the office
cóng bàngōngshì huílai 从办公室回来; the shop is open from
eight to six zhège shāngdiàn cóng bā diǎn dào liù diǎn kāimén
这个商店从八点到六点开门; from Monday to Saturday
cóng xīngqīyī dào xīngqīliù 从星期一到星期六; from April on
cóng sìyuè qǐ 从四月起; (indicating a location, a place, an
object from which distance is stated) lí 离; we live ten minutes
from the city centre wǒmen zhù de dìfang lí shì zhōngxīn yǒu
shí fēnzhōng de lù 我们住的地方离市中心有十分钟的路;
my house is not very far from the seaside wǒ jiā lí hǎibiān bú
tài yuǎn 我家离海边不太远; (indicating a basis on which a
point of view, an assumption, an idea is formed) gēnjù 根据;
from this information, I think we should let him go gēnjù zhège
xìnxī, wǒ rènwéi wǒmen yīnggāi ràng tā qù 根据这个信息,
我认为我们应该让他去; from his point of view gēnjù tāde
guāndiǎn 根据他的观点

front 1 n (of a building) qiánmian 前面, zhèngmiàn 正面; my
room is at the front of the house wǒde fángjiān zài fángzi de
zhèngmian 我的房间在房子的正面; (of a car, a train or
queue) qiánmian 前面; at the front of the bus zài qìchē
qiánmian 在汽车前面 **2 in front of** zài...qiánmian 在...前面

front door n qián mén 前门

front page n (of a newspaper) tóubǎn 头版; (of a book) biāotí yè 标题页

front seat n qiánpái zuòwèi 前排座位

frost n shuāngdòng 霜冻, shuāng 霜

frozen adj (turned solid by fall of temperature) bīngdòng de 冰冻了的; (stopped as if by cold) dòngjié de 冻结的

fruit n a piece of fruit yíkuài shuǐguǒ 一块水果; he likes fruit tā xǐhuan shuǐguǒ 他喜欢水果

frustrated adj huīxīn 灰心; huīxīn sàngqì 灰心丧气

fry vb (yóu)jiān (油)煎, (yóu)zhá (油)炸

frying pan n a frying pan yíge jiānguō 一个煎锅

full adj (of people) jǐmǎn 挤满: the streets were full of people jiē shang jǐmǎnle rén 街上挤满了人; (describing a flight, a hotel, or maximum possible marks in an examination) mǎn 满; to get full marks dé mǎn fēn 得满分; (unable to eat any more) bǎo 饱; I'm full wǒ bǎo le 我饱了, wǒ chībǎo le 我吃饱了; (complete) quán 全; to pay the full fare fù quán fèi 付全费; his full name tāde quán míng 他的全名; at full speed quán sù 全速

full-time 1 adj zhuānzhí 专职, quánrì 全日; a full-time job yíge zhuānzhí gōngzuò 一个专职工作 **2** adv to work full-time quánrì gōngzuò 全日工作

fumes n (smoke) yān 烟; (of wine, chemicals) qì 气, qìwèi 气味

fun n (amusement) hǎowánr 好玩儿, yǒuqù 有趣; it's fun zhè zhēn hǎowánr 这真好玩儿; skiing is fun huáxuě hěn yǒuqù 滑雪很有趣; she is fun tā hěn yǒuqù 她很有趣; to have fun wán de tòngkuai 玩得痛快

function 1 n (the role played by a part in a system) yíge gōngnéng 一个功能, yíge zuòyòng 一个作用; (duty peculiar to any office) yíxiàng zhínéng 一项职能, yíxiàng zhízé 一项职责 **2** vb (to work) gōngzuò 工作; (to perform a function) qǐ zuòyòng 起作用

funeral n a funeral yíge zànglǐ 一个葬礼

funfair n (British English) a funfair yíge yóulèhuì 一个游乐会

funny adj (amusing) hǎowánr 好玩儿, yǒuqù 有趣; (odd) gǔguài 古怪, qíguài 奇怪

fur n (on an animal's coat) pímáo 皮毛; (on a garment) máopí 毛皮, pízi 皮子

furious adj (describing a person) dànù 大怒, kuángnù 狂怒; (violent) měngliè 猛烈, jùliè 剧烈

furniture n jiājù 家具; a piece of furniture yíjiàn jiājù 一件家具

further adv (when talking about distance) gèng yuǎn 更远; he lives further away from the school tā zhù de lí xuéxiào gèng yuǎn 他住的离学校更远; (in addition, to a greater degree) jìn yíbù de 进一步地; to improve quality further jìn yíbù de tígāo zhìliàng 进一步地提高质量

fuss n to make a fuss about something yīnwèi mǒushì dàjīng-xiǎoguài 因为某事大惊小怪

future 1 n (prospects) qiántú 前途; (time to come) jiānglái 将来, jìnhòu 今后; in (the) future jiānglái 将来, jìnhòu 今后 2 adj jiānglái de 将来的, wèilái de 未来的; my future wife wǒ wèilái de tàitai 我未来的太太

....

Gg

....

gallery n (a building for displaying works of art) a gallery yíge měishùguǎn 一个美术馆, yíge huàláng 一个画廊; (a long passage) a gallery yìtiáo chángláng 一条长廊

game n (a contest for recreation) yóuxì 游戏; a game yíge yóuxì 一个游戏; (in sport) bǐsài 比赛; a game yìchǎng bǐsài 一场比赛; a game of [football | tennis] yìchǎng [zúqiú | wǎngqiú] bǐsài 一场 [足球 | 网球] 比赛

games n yùndònghuì 运动会; the Olympic Games Àolínpǐkè Yùndònghuì 奥林匹克运动会

gang *n* a gang (a group of friends, young people) yìhuǒ 一伙; (of criminals) yìbāng 一帮

gap *n* a gap (in a fence or hedge) yíge quēkǒu 一个缺口, yíge huōkǒu 一个豁口; (between buildings, cars) yíduàn jiàngé 一段间隔, yíduàn jùlí 一段距离; (a period of time) yíduàn jiàngé 一段间隔

garage *n* a garage (for keeping a car) yíge chēkù 一个车库; (for fixing a car) yíge qìchē xiūlǐchǎng 一个汽车修理厂

garbage *n* (US English) lājī 垃圾

garden 1 *n* a garden yíge huāyuán 一个花园 **2** *vb* cóngshì yuányì 从事园艺

gardener *n* a gardener yíge yuánlín gōngrén 一个园林工人

gardening *n* yuányì 园艺

garlic *n* suàn 蒜, dàsuàn 大蒜

gas *n* (for cooking, heating) méiqì 煤气; (US English) (gasoline) qìyóu 汽油

gas station *n* (US English) a gas station yíge jiāyóuzhàn 一个加油站

gate *n* a gate yíge mén 一个门, yíge dàmén 一个大门

gather *vb* (to come together) jíhé 集合, jùjí 聚集; (to collect) sōují 搜集, shōují 收集; (to pick up) cǎijí 采集; to gather information sōují zīliào 搜集资料; (to pick up) cǎijí 采集; to gather fruit cǎijí shuǐguǒ 采集水果

gay *adj* tóngxìngliàn 同性恋

gear *n* (in a car or bus, on a bike) a gear yíge dǎng 一个挡; (equipment) yòngjù 用具; fishing gear diàoyú yòngjù 钓鱼用具; (clothes) my football gear wǒde zúqiú fú 我的足球服; your swimming gear nǐde yóuyǒng yī 你的游泳衣

general 1 *n* a general yíge jiāngjūn 一个将军 **2** *adj* (common, not special) yìbān 一般, pǔtōng 普通; general knowledge yìbān zhīshi 一般知识, chángshí 常识; (whole or all) quántǐ 全体; a general meeting yícì quántǐ dàhuì 一次全体大会

(*vague*) dàtǐ 大体, lóngtǒng 笼统; **a general idea** yíge dàtǐ de xiǎngfǎ 一个大体的想法; (*widespread*) pǔbiàn 普遍; **a matter of general concern** yíge pǔbiàn guānxīn de wèntí 一个普遍关心的问题 **3 in general** dàtǐshang 大体上, yībān shuōlái 一般说来

generation *n* **a generation** yídài rén 一代人

generous *adj* kāngkǎi 慷慨, dàfāng 大方

Geneva *n* Geneva Rìnèiwǎ 日内瓦

genius *n* **a genius** yíge tiāncái 一个天才

gentle *adj* (*when describing manners or actions*) wényǎ 文雅, wēnróu 温柔; (*when describing a person's disposition*) wēnróu 温柔; (*amiable*) yǒushàn 友善

gentleman *n* (*a polite term used for men in general*) **a gentleman** yíwèi xiānsheng 一位先生; (*a man of refined manners*) **a gentleman** yíwèi shēnshì 一位绅士

geography *n* dìlǐ 地理

germ *n* xìjūn 细菌

German 1 *adj* Déguó de 德国的 **2** *n* (*the people*) Déguórén 德国人; (*the language*) Déyǔ 德语, Déwén 德文

Germany *n* Déguó 德国

get *vb* **get away** (*to escape*) táotuō 逃脱; **he won't get away with it** tā zuò de zhèjiàn shì kěndìng huì bèi fājué 他做的这件事肯定会被发觉; **get back** (*to come back*) huílái 回来; (*to go back*) huíqù 回去; (*to have back after being stolen*) zhǎohuílái 找回来; **I got my bike back** wǒ bǎ zìxíngchē zhǎohuílái le 我把自行车找回来了; (*to have back after being borrowed*) huánhuílái 还回来; **he's got his book back** tāde shū huánhuílái le 他的书还回来了; **get down** (*to go down*) xiàqù 下去; **can you get down from the tree?** nǐ néng cóng shù shang xiàlái ma? 你能从树上下来吗?; (*to take down*) náxiàlái 拿下来; **I got the box down from the shelf** wǒ bǎ hézi cóng jiàzi shang náxiàlái 我把盒子从架子上拿下来; (*to be depressed over something*) shǐ...jǔsàng 使...

沮丧; it gets him down 这使他很沮丧; **get in** (to enter) jìnrù 进入; (to arrive) dàodá 到达; **get off** (to leave a bus or train) xià chē 下车; I'm getting off at the next stop wǒ xià yí zhàn xià chē 我下一站下车; he fell as he was getting off the train tā xià huǒchē de shíhou shuāidǎo le 他下火车的时候摔倒了; (to remove) bǎ...nòngxiàlai 把...弄下来; to get a stain off bǎ wūdiǎn nòngxiàlai 把污点弄下来; **get on** (to climb on board a bus or train) shàng chē 上车; to get on the bus shàng qìchē 上汽车; to get on well xiāngchǔ de hěn hǎo 相处得很好; I get on well with her wǒ gēn tā xiāngchǔ de hěn hǎo 我跟她相处得很好; (in polite enquiries) how did you get on? nǐ guò de zěnmeyàng? 你过得怎么样?; how is she getting on at school? tā zài xuéxiào zěnmeyàng? 她在学校怎么样?; **get out** she got out of the building 她从大楼里出来; to get out of the building tā cóng dàlóu li chūlai 她从大楼里出来; to get the furniture out of the house bǎ jiājù cóng fángzi li náchūlai 把家具从房子里拿出来; **get over** to get over a shock cóng zhènjīng zhōng huīfùguòlai 从震惊中恢复过来; **get through** to to get through to someone chuándào mǒurén 传到某人; **get together** jùjí 聚集, jùhuì 聚会; **get up** when do you get up? nǐ shénme shíhou qǐchuáng? 你什么时候起床?

ghost n a ghost yíge guǐ 一个鬼

gift n (a present) yíge lǐwù 一个礼物; (an ability) a gift tiānfù 天赋; to have a gift for languages yǒu yǔyán tiānfù 有语言天赋

ginger 1 n (a vegetable used for spices) jiāng 姜 **2** adj jiānghuángsè de 姜黄色的; ginger hair (British English) jiānghuángsè de tóufa 姜黄色的头发

girl n a girl yíge nǚhái(zi) 一个女孩(子); yíge gūniang 一个姑娘

girlfriend n a girlfriend yíge nǚpéngyou 一个女朋友

give vb ! For translations of expressions like to give someone a lift, to give someone an injection, to give someone a fright, etc, look up the entries lift, injection, fright; to give someone a book gěi mǒurén yìběn shū 给某人一本书; I gave him the photos wǒ bǎ nàxiē zhàopiàn gěile tā 我把那些照片给了他; (to offer as a gift) sònggěi 送给; to give someone a present sònggěi mǒurén yíge lǐwù 送给某人一个礼物; **to give someone a message** (chuán)gěi mǒurén yíge kǒuxìn (传)给某人一个口信; **give away** (to make a present of ...) sònggěi biéren ... 送给别人...; **to give away a secret** xièlòu mìmì 泄漏秘密; **give back** huándìng 还给; **give in** ràngbù 让步, qūfú 屈服; **give off** to give off fumes màochū yān lai 冒出烟来; **give out** to give out the exercise books fēnfā liànxíběn 分发练习本; **give up** (to stop) to give up smoking jiè yān 戒烟 **to give up the idea of working abroad** fàngqì qù guówài gōngzuò de xiǎngfǎ 放弃去国外工作的想法; **to give oneself up to the police** xiàng jīngchá zìshǒu 向警察自首

glad adj gāoxìng 高兴

glass n a glass of water yìbēi shuǐ 一杯水; **a glass of water** yìbēi shuǐ 一杯水

glasses n yǎnjìng 眼镜

glove n a pair of gloves yìfù shǒutào 一副手套

glow vb fāguāng 发光

glue 1 n jiāo 胶 2 vb zhān 粘

go vb **go across** chuānguò 穿过; **go after** (physically) zhuī 追; (when talking about pursuing an abstract goal) zhuīqiú 追求; **go ahead** (if it's an event) zhàocháng jìnxíng 照常进行; **the concert's going ahead** yīnyuèhuì jiāng zhàocháng jìnxíng 音乐会将照常进行; (if it's a person) **go ahead** (when about to do something) gàn ba 干吧; (when about to say something) shuō ba 说吧; (when about to walk somewhere) zǒu ba 走吧; **go around go round; go around with go round with; go away** zǒu ba, líkāi 离开; **go away!** nǐ zǒukāi! 你走开! gǔn! 滚!; **go back** huí 回, huíqù 回去; **Gary went back to London** Jiālì huí Lúndūn le 加里回伦敦了; **to go back to school** huíqù shàngxué 回去上学; **to go back to work** huíqù gōngzuò 回去工作; **go by** guòqu 过去; **go by...** lùguò... 路过; **go down** (if it's quality, a price, a salary) xiàjiàng 下降; (if it's a person) she went down to have a look tā xiàqu kànkan 她下去看看; they went down the hill tāmen xià shān le 他们下山了; (if it's the sun or moon) luòxià 落下; (if it's a computer) huài le 坏了; **go in** jìnqu 进去; he didn't go in tā méi jìnqù 他没进去; **go off** (to explode) bàozhà 爆炸; (to ring) xiǎng 响; (to leave) líqù 离去, zǒudiào 走掉; (when talking about food becoming bad) biànhuài 变坏; the milk will go off niúnǎi huì biànhuài le 牛奶会变坏; (to be switched off) guāndiào 关掉, tíngdiào 停掉; **go on** (to continue) jìxù 继续; to go on talking jìxù jiǎnghuà 继续讲话; (to happen) what's going on? fāshēngle shénme shì? 发生了什么事?; (to keep talking) he goes on (and on) about his work tā yígejìnr de tán tāde gōngzuò 他一个劲儿地谈他的工作; (to be switched on) dǎkāi 打开; **go out** (to leave the house) chūqu 出去; are you going out this evening? jīntiān wǎnshang nǐ chūqu ma? 今天晚上你出去吗?; (as with a boyfriend, a girlfriend) chūqu tán péngyou 出去谈朋友; to go out with someone gēn mǒurén chūqu tán péngyou 跟某人出去谈朋友; (to be switched off as a fire, to stop burning) xīmiè 熄灭; **go over** (to check) jiǎnchá 检查; to go over some grammar jiǎnchá yìxiē yǔfǎ 检查一些语法; (to revise) fùxí 复习; **go round** (British English) (to call on) shùnbiàn qù 顺便去; to go round to see someone shùnbiàn qù kànwàng mǒurén 顺便去看望某人; (to walk around, to visit) guàng 逛; to go round the museums guàng bówùguǎn 逛博物馆; to go round the shops guàng shāngdiàn 逛商店; is there enough bread to go round? miànbāo gòu fēn de ma? 面包够分的吗?; **go round with** (British English) (to spend time with) to go round with someone gēn mǒurén jiāowǎng 跟某人交往; **go through** (to have, to live through) to go through a difficult time jīnglì yíduàn kùnnan shíqī 经历一段困难时期; (to search) sōuchá 搜查; (to check) jiǎnchá 检查; **go together** xiāngpèi 相配; the skirt and blouse go well together qúnzi hé chènshān hěn xiāngpèi 裙子和衬衫很相配; **go up** (if it's a person) shàng 上; he went up the stairs tā shàng lóu le 他上楼了; to go up to the top of the hill shàng shāndǐng 上山顶; (if it's a price, a salary) zhǎng 涨; **go with** yǔ...xiāngpèi 与...相配; the trousers don't really go with the jacket kùzi yǔ jiákè bù xiāngpèi 裤子与夹克不相配

goal n (an end or aim) yíge mùdì 一个目的, yíge mùbiāo 一个目标; (a score in some ball games) yìfēn 一分; (in a football field) qiúmén 球门

goalkeeper n a goalkeeper yíge shǒuményuán 一个守门员

goat n a goat yìzhī shānyáng 一只山羊

god n a god yíge shén 一个神; God Shàngdì 上帝

goddaughter n a goddaughter yíge jiàonǚ 一个教女

godfather n a godfather yíge jiàofù 一个教父

godmother n a godmother yíge jiàomǔ 一个教母

godson n a godson yíge jiàozǐ 一个教子

going: to be going to zhǔnbèi 准备, dǎsuàn 打算; I'm going to [leave | go to Ireland | learn to drive...] wǒ zhǔnbèi [líkāi | qù Ài'ěrlán | xué kāi chē...] 我准备 [离开 | 去爱尔兰 | 学开车...]

gold 1 n gold jīn 金, huángjīn 黄金 **2** adj jīn de 金的; a gold ring yíge jīn jièzhi 一个金戒指

goldfish n a goldfish yìtiáo jīnyú 一条金鱼

golf n gāo'ěrfūqiú 高尔夫球

golf course n a golf course yíge gāo'ěrfūqiú chǎng 一个高尔夫球场

good 1 adj good hǎo 好; a good book yìběn hǎo shū 一本好书; to be good at [chemistry | drawing | chess...] shàncháng [huàxué | huà huà | xià qí...] 擅长 [化学 | 画画 | 下棋...]; (beneficial) yǒuyì 有益, yǒu hǎochù 有好处; exercise is good for you duànliàn duì nǐ yǒuyì 锻炼对你有益; (pleasant) I had a good time wǒ guò de hěn yúkuài 我过得很愉快; (healthy) to look good kànshangqu shēntǐ hěn hǎo 看上去身体很好; I don't feel too good wǒ gǎnjué shēntǐ bù tài hǎo 我感觉身体不太好; (talking about food) hǎochī 好吃; (obedient) tīnghuà 听话; (when expressing gratitude) it's very good of you to let me know xièxie nǐ gàosu wǒ 谢谢你告诉我 **2** n it's no good [shouting | crying | going there...] [hǎn | kū | qù nàr...] méi yòu yòng [喊 | 哭 | 去哪儿...] 没有用 he is no good at Latin tāde Lādīngyǔ hěn zāogāo 他的拉丁语很糟糕; the change will do you good zhège biànhuà huì duì nǐ yǒu hǎochù 这个变化会你有好处 **3** *exc* Good heavens! tiān a! 天啊!; Good for you! gàn de hǎo! 干得好! **4** for good yǒngjiǔ 永久, yǒngyuǎn 永远

good afternoon *n* (also *exc*) (when meeting) xiàwǔ hǎo 下午好; (when leaving) zàijiàn 再见

goodbye *n* (also *exc*) zàijiàn 再见

good evening *n* (also *exc*) wǎnshang hǎo 晚上好

good-looking *adj* hǎokàn 好看

good morning *n* (also *exc*) (when meeting) zǎoshang hǎo 早上好; (when leaving) zàijiàn 再见

goodnight *n* (also *exc*) wǎn'ān 晚安

goods *n* huòwù 货物

goose *n* a goose yìzhī é 一只鹅

gooseberry *n* a gooseberry yíge cùlì 一个醋栗

gorilla *n* a gorilla yíge dà xīngxing 一个大猩猩

gossip *vb* (to chat) xiánliáo 闲聊; (to talk in a harmful way) sànbù liúyán fēiyǔ 散布流言蜚语

got: to have got *vb* (to have) yǒu 有; I've got work to do wǒ yǒu gōngzuò yào zuò 我有工作要做; have you got a cold? nǐ gǎnmào le ma? 你感冒了吗? (to be obliged to) to have got to bìxū 必须, děi 得; I've got to [go | work | buy a new computer...] wǒ bìxū [zǒu | gōngzuò | mǎi yítái xīn jìsuànjī...] 我必须 [走 | 工作 | 买一台新计算机...]

government *n* a government yíge zhèngfǔ 一个政府

GP, General Practitioner (medicine) *n* a GP yíge jiātíng yīshēng 一个家庭医生

grab *vb* to grab someone by the arm zhuāzhù mǒurén de gēbo 抓住某人的胳膊; he tried to grab my handbag tā shìtú qiǎng wǒde shǒutíbāo 他试图抢我的手提包

grade *n* (a mark on an examination or in a class or course of study) a grade yíge fēnshù 一个分数; (US English) (a class in school) a grade yíge niánjí 一个年级; he's in the eighth grade tā zài bā niánjí 他在八年级

grade school n (US English) a grade school yìsuǒ xiǎoxué 一所小学

gradually adv zhújiàn 逐渐, jiànjiàn 渐渐

gram(me) n a gram yí kè 一克

grammar n yǔfǎ 语法

grandchild n a grandchild (a son's son) yíge sūnzi 一个孙子; (a son's daughter) yíge sūnnǚ 一个孙女; (a daughter's son) yíge wàisūn 一个外孙; (a daughter's daughter) yíge wàisūnnǚ 一个外孙女

granddaughter n a granddaughter (a son's daughter) yíge sūnnǚ 一个孙女; (a daughter's daughter) yíge wàisūnnǚ 一个外孙女

grandfather n (father's father) yéye 爷爷, zǔfù 祖父; (mother's father) wàigōng 外公, lǎoyé 姥爷, wàizǔfù 外祖父
! Note that zǔfù 祖父, wàizǔfù 外祖父 cannot be used in direct address.

grandmother n (father's mother) nǎinai 奶奶, zǔmǔ 祖母; (mother's mother) wàipó 外婆, lǎolao 姥姥, wàizǔmǔ 外祖母
! Note that zǔmǔ 祖母, wàizǔmǔ 外祖母 cannot be used in direct address.

grandparents n (father's parents) yéye (he) nǎinai 爷爷(和)奶奶; (mother's parents) lǎolao (he) lǎoyé 姥姥(和)姥爷, wàigōng (he) wàipó 外公(和)外婆

grandson n a grandson (a son's son) yíge sūnzi 一个孙子; (a daughter's son) yíge wàisūn 一个外孙

grapefruit n pútaoyòu 葡萄柚; a grapefruit yíge pútaoyòu 一个葡萄柚

grapes n pútao 葡萄; a bunch of grapes yíchuàn pútao 一串葡萄

grass n cǎo 草; to cut the grass gē cǎo 割草

grasshopper n a grasshopper yìzhī zhàměng 一只蚱蜢

grateful adj gǎnjī 感激, gǎnxiè 感谢; I would be grateful if you could let me know rúguǒ nǐ néng gàosu wǒ, wǒ huì hěn gǎnjī 如果你能告诉我, 我会很感激

grave n a grave yíge fénmù 一个坟墓

gray (US English) ▶ **grey**

grease n yóuzhī 油脂

greasy adj (yǒu) yóuzhī de (有)油脂的

great adj (stressing size, amount) dà 大; a great improvement yíge hěn dà de tígāo 一个很大的提高; to have great difficulty reading yuèdú yǒu hěn dà de kùnnan 阅读有很大的困难; (when describing a country or an outstanding person) wěidà 伟大; your great country nǐmen wěidà de guójiā 你们伟大的国家; (showing enthusiasm) that's great! hǎo jíle! 好极了!; I had a great time wǒ wán de fēicháng yúkuài 我玩得非常愉快

Great Britain n Dàbùlièdiān 大不列颠

great grandfather n (if it's on the father's side) zēngzǔfù 曾祖父; (if it's on the mother's side) wàizēngzǔfù 外曾祖父

great grandmother n (if it's on the father's side) zēngzǔmǔ 曾祖母; (if it's on the mother's side) wàizēngzǔmǔ 外曾祖母

Greece n Xīlà 希腊

greedy adj (having a voracious appetite) tānchī 贪吃, tānzuǐ 贪嘴; (inordinately desirous of increasing one's own share) tānlán 贪婪, tānxīn 贪心

Greek 1 adj Xīlà de 希腊的 **2** n (the people) Xīlàrén 希腊人; (the language) Xīlàyǔ 希腊语, Xīlàwén 希腊文

green adj lǜ 绿, lǜsè de 绿色的

greenhouse n a greenhouse yíge wēnshì 一个温室

grey (British English), **gray** (US English) adj huī 灰, huīsè de 灰色的; grey hair bái tóufa 白头发

grill vb zài kǎojià shang kǎo 在烤架上烤

grin vb liěkāi zuǐ xiào 咧开嘴笑

grocer n a grocer yíge záhuòshāng 一个杂货商

grocery n a grocery yíge záhuòdiàn 一个杂货店

ground n dì 地; the ground is hard in winter dōngtiān dì hěn yìng 冬天地很硬; (land used for sports) a sports ground yíge yùndòngchǎng 一个运动场

ground floor n (British English) the ground floor yīlóu 一楼, yīcéng 一层

group n (a number of persons or things put together in a certain way) zǔ 组; we are divided into 3 groups wǒmen bèi fēnchéng sān zǔ 我们被分成三组; (a crowd) qún 群; a group of children yìqún háizi 一群孩子; (a band) a rock group yíge yáogǔnyuèduì 一个摇滚乐队

grow vb (to get big, strong, long, tall) zhǎng 长, chéngzhǎng 成长; the tree grows fast shù zhǎng de hěn kuài 树长得很快; (as a gardener, a farmer) zhòng 种; to grow vegetables zhòng cài 种菜; (to let grow); to grow a beard liú húzi 留胡子; (to become) biàn de 变得! Note that it's often unnecessary to translate grow here; she's grown more cynical tā (biàn de) gèngjiā wán shì bù gōng 她(变得)更加玩世不恭; he has grown old tā lǎo le 他老了; (to increase) zēngzhǎng 增长; the population will grow rénkǒu jiānghuì zēngzhǎng 人口将会增长; (to develop) fāzhǎn 发展; that place is growing into a city nàge dìfang zhèngzài fāzhǎn chéngwéi yíge chéngshì 那个地方正在发展成为一个城市; grow up zhǎngdà 长大; when I grow up, I want to be a doctor wǒ zhǎngdà le yào dāng yīshēng 我长大了要当医生

grumble vb bàoyuàn 抱怨, fā láosāo 发牢骚

guard n a guard (in a prison) yíge kānshǒu(yuán) 一个看守(员); (in a bank or important institution) yíge bǎowèi rényuán 一个保卫人员; (in the army) yíge wèibīng 一个卫兵; to be on guard zhàngǎng 站岗

guard dog n a guard dog yìtiáo jǐngquǎn 一条警犬

guess vb cāi 猜

guest n a guest yíwèi kèren 一位客人

guesthouse n a guesthouse yíge zhāodàisuǒ 一个招待所

guide 1 *n* a guide (*for tourists*) yíge dǎoyóu 一个导游; (*for travellers, mountaineers*) yíge xiàngdǎo 一个向导 **2** *vb* yǐndǎo 引导

guide book *n* a guide book yìběn lǚxíng zhǐnán 一本旅行指南

guided tour *n* a guided tour yícì yǒu dǎoyóu de lǚxíng 一次有导游的旅行

guilty *adj* (*having broken the law*) yǒu zuì de 有罪的; to feel guilty gǎndào nèijiù 感到内疚

guitar *n* a guitar yìbǎ jítā 一把吉它

gum *n* (*part of the mouth*) chǐyín 齿龈, yáchuáng 牙床; (*for chewing*) kǒuxiāngtáng 口香糖

gun *n* a gun yìzhī qiāng 一支枪

gym, gymnasium *n* a gym/gymnasium yíge tǐyùguǎn 一个体育馆

gymnastics *n* tǐcāo 体操

Hh

habit *n* a habit yíge xíguàn 一个习惯

hail *n* bīngbáo 冰雹

hair *n* (*on the head*) tóufa 头发; (*on the body*) máo 毛

hairbrush *n* a hairbrush yìbǎ tóufashuā 一把头发刷

hairdresser *n* a hairdresser yíge lǐfàshī 一个理发师

hairdryer *n* a hairdryer yíge chuīfàjī 一个吹发机

hairstyle *n* a hairstyle yìzhǒng fàxíng 一种发型

half 1 *n* a half yí bàn 一半; to cut a melon in half bǎ guā qiēchéng liǎng bàn 把瓜切成两半; (*in a game*) the first half shàng bàn chǎng 上半场 **2** adj bàn 半; **a half-litre of milk, half a litre of milk** bàn shēng niúnǎi 半升牛奶 **3** pron (when talking about quantities, numbers) yí bàn 一半; **to spend half of one's pocket money** huā yí bàn de línghuāqián 花一半的零花钱; **half the pupils speak Japanese** yí bàn de xuésheng shuō Rìyǔ 一半的学生说日语; (when talking about time, age) bàn 半; **an hour and a half** yíge bàn xiǎoshí 一个半小时; **he's three and a half** tā sān suì bàn 他三岁半; **it's half (past) three** sān diǎn bàn 三点半 **4** adv **Sam's half Chinese and half English** Sàmǔ shì yí bàn Zhōngguó xuètǒng yí bàn Yīngguó xuètǒng 萨姆是一半中国血统一半英国血统

half hour n **a half hour** bàng xiǎoshí 半个小时

half term n (British English) qīzhōng jià 期中假

hall n (in a house, an apartment) **a hall** yíge tīng 一个厅; (for public events) **a hall** yíge dàtīng 一个大厅, yíge lǐtáng 一个礼堂

ham n huǒtuǐ 火腿

hamburger n **a hamburger** yíge Hànbǎobāo 一个汉堡包

hammer n **a hammer** yìbǎ chuízi 一把锤子

hamster n **a hamster** yìzhī cāngshǔ 一只仓鼠

hand 1 n (the part of the body) shǒu 手; **he had a pencil in his hand** tā shǒu lǐ názhe yìzhī qiānbǐ 他手里拿着一支铅笔; **to hold someone's hand** lāzhe mǒurén de shǒu 拉着某人的手; (help) **a hand** bāngzhù 帮助; (on a clock or watch) **a hand** yìgēn zhǐzhēn 一根指针; (when judging a situation or subject) **on the one hand..., on the other...** yì fāngmiàn..., lìng yì fāngmiàn... 一方面..., 另一方面... **2** vb (to pass with the hand) dì 递, gěi 给

handbag n **a handbag** yíge shǒutíbāo 一个手提包

handball n shǒuqiú 手球

handicapped adj cánjí 残疾

handkerchief n **a handkerchief** yìtiáo shǒujuàn(r) 一条手绢 (儿)

handle *n* a handle yíge bǎshǒu 一个把手

handsome *adj* piàoliang 漂亮, yīngjùn 英俊; a handsome young man yíge yīngjùn de niánqīngrén 一个英俊的年轻人

handwriting *n* shūxiě 书写, bǐjì 笔迹

handy *adj* (*convenient*) fāngbiàn 方便; (*near*) jìnbiàn 近便

hang *vb* (*on a hook, a coat hanger, a line*) guà 挂; to hang clothes (up) in a wardrobe bǎ yīfu guà zài yīguì li 把衣服挂在衣柜里; (*for drying*) liàng 晾; to hang clothes on a line bǎ yīfu liàng zài shéngzi shang 把衣服晾在绳子上; (*to suspend*) diào 吊; to hang the light above the table bǎ dēng diào zài zhuōzi shàng fāng 把灯吊在桌子上方; (*to kill*) diàosǐ 吊死, jiǎosǐ 绞死; **hang around** (*walking around doing nothing*) xiánguàng 闲逛; (*stay around out of affection or respect*) jù zài...pángbiān 聚在... 旁边; the children hung around the old man háizimen jù zài lǎorén pángbiān 孩子们聚在老人身边; **hang on to** jǐnjǐn wòzhù 紧紧握住; she was hanging on to the rope tā jǐnjǐn wòzhù shéngzi 她紧紧握住绳子; **hang up** (*on a hook, a coat hanger, a line*) guà 挂; to hang up one's coat guà yīfu 挂衣服; your coat's hanging up in the hall nǐde wàiyī guà zài tīng li 你的外衣挂在厅里; (*for drying*) liàng 晾; drying clothes liàng yīfu 晾衣服; (*when phoning*) guàduàn 挂断

happen *vb* (*to occur*) fāshēng 发生; what happened? fāshēng shénme shì le? 发生什么事了?; the accident happened last week zhège shìgù shì shàng xīngqī fāshēng de 这个事故是上星期发生的; (*to affect someone*) what happened to you? nǐ zěnme le? 你怎么了?; something odd happened to me wǒ yùdàole yíjiàn qíguài de shì 我遇到了一件奇怪的事; (*to chance*) pèngqiǎo 碰巧; I happened to be out when he came tā lái de shíhou, wǒ pèngqiǎo chūqu le 他来的时候, 我碰巧出去了

happy *adj* (*delighted*) gāoxìng 高兴; to make someone happy shǐ mǒurén gāoxìng 使某人高兴; they were happy to receive your letter tāmen hěn gāoxìng shōudào nǐde xìn 他们很高兴收到你的信; (*content*) mǎnyì 满意; he's happy with the language course tā duì yǔyán kè hěn mǎnyì 他对语言课程很

满意; (in greetings) kuàilè 快乐; **Happy Birthday!** Shēngrì kuàilè! 生日快乐!; **Happy New Year!** Xīnnián kuàilè! 新年快乐!

hard 1 adj (firm, stiff) yìng 硬; **the ground is hard** dì hěn yìng 地很硬; (difficult) nán 难; **a hard question** yíge hěn nán de wèntí 一个很难的问题; **it's hard to explain this problem** hěn nán jiěshì zhège wèntí 很难解释这个问题; **we were having a hard time during the war** zhànzhēng qījiān wǒmen guòzhe jiānnán de rìzi 战争期间我们过着艰难的日子; (severe) **it's a hard blow to her** zhè duì tā shì ge chénzhòng de dǎjī 这对她是个沉重的打击 **2** adv (diligently) nǔlì 努力; **to work hard** nǔlì gōngzuò 努力工作; (severely) **it's raining hard** yǔ xià de hěn dà 雨下得很大

hardly adv (not quite) bú tài 不太; **I hardly know them** wǒ bú tài rènshi tāmen 我不太认识他们; (scarcely) jīhū...bù 几乎...不, jiǎnzhí...bù 简直...不; **she could hardly recognize me** tā jīhū rèn bù chū wǒ lái le 她几乎认不出我来了

hardware n hardware (for computers) (jìsuànjī) yìngjiàn (计算机)硬件

hard-working adj qínfèn 勤奋, nǔlì 努力

hare n a hare yìzhī yětù 一只野兔

harm vb to harm someone shānghài mǒurén 伤害某人; to harm the environment sǔnhài huánjìng 损害环境

harmful adj yǒuhài 有害

harmless adj wúhài 无害

harp n a harp yíjià shùqín 一架竖琴

harvest n shōuhuò 收获, shōuchéng 收成

hat n a hat yìdǐng màozi 一顶帽子

hate vb (to feel a strong dislike for) bù xǐhuan 不喜欢; **she hates pork** tā bù xǐhuān zhūròu 她不喜欢猪肉; (to feel hatred for) hèn 恨; **to hate somebody** hèn mǒurén 恨某人

hatred n (zēng)hèn (憎)恨

have 1 vb (to possess or be in a special relation to) yǒu 有; **she doesn't have much money** tā méi yǒu hěn duō qián 她没有

很多钱; they have three children tāmen yǒu sānge háizi 他们
有三个孩子; (to eat) chī 吃; to have a sandwich chī yíkuài
sānmíngzhì 吃一块三明治; to have dinner chī fàn 吃饭;
(to drink) hē 喝; to have a glass of wine hē yìbēi jiǔ 喝一杯酒;
(to get) I had a letter from Bob yesterday wǒ zuótiān shōudàole
Bàobó de yìfēng xìn 我昨天收到了鲍勃的一封信; I'll let
you have the money soon wǒ huì hěn kuài ràng nǐ nádào qián
我会很快让你拿到钱; (to hold or organize) jǔxíng 举行;
to have a party jǔxíng yíge jùhuì 举行一个聚会; to have a
competition jǔxíng yícì bǐsài 举行一次比赛; (to spend) we
had a nice day at the beach wǒmen zài hǎibiān dùguòle yúkuài
de yì tiān 我们在海边度过了愉快的一天; I'll have a good
time in Beijing wǒ huì zài Běijīng guò de hěn yúkuài 我会在
北京过得很愉快; (to suffer) tā [a headache | a toothache |
a stomach ache...] tā [tóuténg | yáténg | dùzi téng...] 他 [头疼 | 牙疼 | 肚子
疼...]; Note that in this case, have is not translated in Chinese;
(to catch a disease) dé 得; to have [flu | cancer | heart disease...]
dé [liúgǎn | áizhèng | xīnzàng bìng...] 得 [流感 | 癌症 | 心脏病...];
(to get something done) to have the house painted shuà fángzi
刷房子; she had her hair cut tā jiǎn tóufa le 她剪头发了
2 aux vb you've seen her, haven't you? nǐ jiànguò tā. shì ba?
你见过她, 是吧?; they've already left, haven't they? tāmen
yǐjīng zǒu le, shì ba? 他们已经走了, 是吧? **3** to have to
bùdébù 不得不, bìxū 必须; I have to [study hard | go home |
go to see a doctor] wǒ bùdébù [nǔlì xuéxí | huí jiā | qù kàn yīshēng] 我不
得不 [努力学习 | 回家 | 去看医生]; you have to come nǐ bìxū lái
你必须来

hay n gāncǎo 干草

hazel adj dàn hèsè de 淡褐色的

hazelnut n a hazelnut yíge zhēnzi 一个榛子

he pron tā 他

head 1 n (the part of the body) tóu 头; (the mind) nǎozi 脑子;
he's got lots of ideas in his head tā nǎozi lǐ zhǔyi hěn duō 他脑
子里主意很多; a head of cabbage yìkē juǎnxīn cài 一棵卷心
菜; a head of lettuce yìkē shēngcài 一棵生菜; (the person in

charge) the head of a delegation dàibiǎotuán tuánzhǎng 代表团团长; the head of the Chinese Department Zhōngwén xì xìzhǔrèn 中文系系主任; a head of State yíwèi guójiā yuánshǒu 一位国家元首 **2** *vb* (*to be in charge of*) to head a team shuàilǐng yígè duì 率领一个队; (*in soccer*) to head the ball (yòng tóu) dǐng qiú (用头)顶球; **head for...** xiàng...qu 向...去; the car headed for the city centre qìchē xiàng shì zhōngxīn shǐqu 汽车向市中心驶去

headache *n* he has a headache tā tóuténg 他头疼
! *Note that in* have a headache, have *is not translated into Chinese*; my headache's gone wǒde tóuténg hǎo le 我的头疼好了

headlamp, headlight *n* a headlamp yígè qiándēng 一个前灯

headline *n* a headline yígè biāotí 一个标题; to hit the headlines chéngwéi tóutiáo xīnwén 成为头条新闻; the news headlines xīnwén tíyào 新闻提要

headquarters *n* (*of a company, an organization*) zǒngbù 总部; (*of an army*) sīlìngbù 司令部

headteacher *n* a headteacher yígè xiàozhǎng 一个校长

health *n* jiànkāng 健康

healthy *adj* (*in good health*) jiànkāng 健康; (*good for the health*) yǒuyìyú jiànkāng de 有益于健康的

hear *vb* to hear tīngjiàn 听见; he can't hear anything tā tīng bú jiàn rènhé shēngyīn 他听不见任何声音; I heard someone coming in wǒ tīngjiàn yǒu rén jìnlai 我听见有人进来; you can hear him practising the piano nǐ néng tīngjiàn tā liànxí gāngqín de shēngyīn 你能听见他练习钢琴的声音; (*to learn, to discover*) to hear the news tīngdào zhège xiāoxi 听到这个消息; I've heard about that school wǒ tīngshuōguo nàge xuéxiào 我听说过那个学校; (*to listen to*) tīng 听; he'd like to hear our opinions tā xiǎng tīng wǒmende yìjian 他想听我们的意见; **hear from...** shōudào...de xìn 收到...的信; have you heard from her? nǐ shōudàoguo tāde xìn ma? 你收到过她的信吗?;

hear of tīngshuōguo 听说过; I've never heard of the place wǒ cónglái méi tīngshuōguo nàge dìfang 我从来没听说过那个地方

heart n (part of the body) xīnzàng 心脏; (the centre) zhōngxīn 中心; right in the heart of London jiù zài Lúndūn zhōngxīn 就在伦敦中心; to learn...by heart jìzhù... 记住..., bèixialai... 背下来...

heart attack n a heart attack yícì xīnzàngbìng fāzuò 一次心脏病发作

heat 1 vb bǎ...jiārè 把... 加热; to heat the water bǎ shuǐ jiārè 把水加热 **2** n (a high temperature, or hotness) gāowēn 高温, rè 热; I can't stand the heat in Hong Kong wǒ shòu bù liǎo Xiānggǎng de rè 我受不了香港的热; (a degree of hotness) rèdù 热度; the heat in the oven kǎoxiāng de rèdù 烤箱的热度; (in a sporting contest) a heat yícì jìngsài 一次竞赛; **heat up** (to cook) shāorè 烧热; (to warm up again) chóngxīn jiārè 重新加热

heater n a heater yìtái fārèqì 一台发热器

heating n (a system) gòng nuǎn xìtǒng 供暖系统; (providing the heat) gòng rè 供热

heatwave n a heatwave yìgǔ rèlàng 一股热浪

heaven n tiāntáng 天堂

heavy adj (in weight) zhòng 重; (in quantity, intensity) the traffic is very heavy jiāotōng hěn yōngjǐ 交通很拥挤; a heavy smoker yíge chōuyān hěn duō de rén 一个抽烟很多的人; to have a heavy cold dé zhòng gǎnmào 得重感冒; (describing food) nán xiāohuà de 难消化的; it's very heavy today jīntiān tiānqì hěn chénmèn 今天天气很闷沉; the air is heavy kōngqì hěn chénmèn 空气很沉闷

hedge n a hedge yìpái shùlí 一排树篱

hedgehog n a hedgehog yìzhī cìwei 一只刺猬

heel n (part of the foot) jiǎohòugēn 脚后跟; (part of the shoe) hòugēn 后跟

height n (of a person) shēngāo 身高; (of a building, a tree) gāodù 高度, gāo 高; **to be afraid of heights** hàipà dēng gāo 害怕登高

helicopter n a helicopter yíjià zhíshēngfēijī 一架直升飞机

hell n dìyù 地狱

hello n (also exc) hello!; (when greeting someone) nǐ hǎo! 你好!; (on the phone) wèi! 喂!

helmet n a helmet yíge tóukuī 一个头盔

help 1 vb to help bāngzhù 帮助; **to help someone** [study | do the housework | escape...] bāngzhù mǒurén [xuéxí | zuò jiāwù | táopǎo...] 帮助某人 [学习 | 做家务 | 逃跑...]; **to help each other** hùxiāng bāngzhù 互相帮助; (to remedy) **the medicine helps to cure the illness** zhèzhǒng yào zhìliáo zhèzhǒng bìng 这种药治疗这种病; (at a meal) **help yourselves!** qǐng suíbiàn chī! 请随便吃!; **I couldn't help laughing** wǒ jìnbúzhù xiàole qǐlai 我禁不住笑了起来 **2** exc **help!** (when the speaker is in danger) jiùmìng a! 救命啊!; (when someone else is in danger) jiù rén a! 救人啊! **3** n (assistance) bāngzhù 帮助; **to ask someone for help** qǐng mǒurén bāngzhù 请某人帮助; (one who assists) bāngshǒu 帮手, zhùshǒu 助手; **she is quite a help to me** tā shì wǒde yíge hǎo bāngshǒu 她是我的一个好帮手; **help out help someone out** bāngzhù mǒurén bǎituō kùnjìng 帮助某人摆脱困境

helpful adj (giving help) yǒu bāngzhù de 有帮助的; (useful) yǒu yòng de 有用的

helping n a helping of food yífèn fàn 一份饭

helpless adj (having no one to help) méi yǒu rén bāngzhù de 没有人帮助的; **she was left helpless** tā bèi rēng zài nàr méi yǒu rén bāngzhù 他被扔在那儿没有人帮助; (because of weakness, ill health) gūruò de 孤弱的

hen n a hen yìzhī mǔjī 一只母鸡

her 1 pron tā 她; **I know her** wǒ rènshi tā 我认识她 **2** det tāde 她的; **I don't like her dog** wǒ bù xǐhuan tāde gǒu 我不喜欢她的狗

herd *n* a herd of cattle yìqún niú 一群牛

here *adv (when talking about location)* zhèr 这儿, zhèlǐ 这里; is your house far from here? nǐde jiā lí zhèr yuǎn ma? 你的家离这儿远吗? he doesn't live here tā bú zài zhèlǐ zhù 他不在这里住; *(when drawing attention)* here's the post office zhè jiùshì yóujú 这就是邮局; here they are tāmen lái le 他们来了; here comes the train huǒchē lái le 火车来了; here's my telephone number zhè shì wǒde diànhuà hàomǎ 这是我的电话号码

hers *pron* tāde 她的; the green pen is hers nàzhī lǜ bǐ shì tāde 那支绿笔是她的; my room is smaller than hers wǒde fángjiān bǐ tāde xiǎo 我的房间比她的小

herself *pron (when used as a reflexive pronoun)* (tā) zìjǐ (她)自己; she's cut herself with a knife tā yòng dāo gēshāngle zìjǐ 她用刀割伤了自己; will she forgive herself? tā huì yuánliàng zìjǐ ma? 她会原谅自己吗? *(when used for emphasis)* she said it herself tā qīnzì shuō de zhèjiàn shì 她亲自说的这件事; she did it all by herself zhè dōu shì tā yígè rén zuò de 这都是她一个人做的

hesitate *vb* yóuyù 犹豫

hi *exc* hi! nǐ hǎo! 你好!

hiccups *n* to have hiccups dǎgér 打嗝儿

hidden *adj* yǐncáng de 隐藏的

hide *vb* (yīn)cáng (隐)藏; she hid the money in her shoes tā bǎ qián cáng zài xié lǐ 她把钱藏在鞋里

hi-fi *n* a hi-fi yítào zǔhé yīnxiǎng 一套组合音响

high 1 *adj* gāo 高; [the mountain | the price | the speed...] is high [shān | jiàgé | sùdù...] hěn gāo [山|价格|速度...] 很高; to get high grades dé gāo fēn 得高分 **2** *adv* don't go any higher bié wǎng shàng qù le 别往上去了

high rise block *n* a high rise block yízuò duōcéng gāolóu 一座多层高楼

high school *n* a high school; *(in the US)* yìsuǒ zhōngxué 一所中学; *(in Britain)* yìsuǒ gāozhōng 一所高中

hijack vb jiéchí 劫持

hike vb to go hiking qù túbù lǚxíng 去徒步旅行

hiking n túbù lǚxíng 徒步旅行

hill n a hill yīzuò xiǎo shān 一座小山; (a rise in the road) yīge xiépō 一个斜坡

him pron tā 他; I know him wǒ rènshi tā 我认识他

himself pron (when used as a reflexive pronoun) (tā) zìjǐ (他)自己; he's cut himself with a knife tā yòng dāo gēshāng le (tā) zìjǐ 他用刀割伤了(他自己); will he forgive himself? tā huì yuánliàng (tā) zìjǐ ma? 他会原谅(他)自己吗?; (when used for emphasis) he said it himself tā qīnzì shuō de zhèjiàn shì 他亲自说的这件事; he did it all by himself zhè dōu shì tā yíge rén zuò de 这都是他一个人做的

hip n túnbù 臀部

hire vb (to employ) gù 雇; (British English) (to rent) zū 租; to hire a car zū yīliàng chē 租一辆车; (to lend for a fee) chūzū 出租; they hire (out) bikes tāmen chūzū zìxíngchē 他们出租自行车

his 1 det tāde 他的; I don't like his dog wǒ bù xǐhuan tāde gǒu 我不喜欢他的狗 2 pron tāde 他的; the blue pen is his lán de bǐ shì tāde 蓝的笔是他的

history n lìshǐ 历史

hit 1 vb (to strike on purpose) dǎ 打; to hit someone on the head dǎ mǒurén de tóu 打某人的头; (to strike accidentally) pèng 碰; she hit her head on a chair tā de tóu pèng zài yìbǎ yǐzi shang 她的头碰在一把椅子上; (to crash into) zhuàng 撞; to hit a wall zhuàngdào qiáng shang 撞到墙上 2 n a hit (a song) yìshǒu liúxíng gēqǔ 一首流行歌曲; (a film or a play) yíbù fēngxíng yìshí de zuòpǐn 一部风行一时的作品; (in baseball) dé fēn 得分; hit back huíjī 回击; to hit someone back huíjī mǒurén 回击某人

hitchhike vb (to have a free lift in a vehicle) miǎnfèi dā tārén de chē 免费搭他人的车; (to request a free lift in a vehicle) yāoqiú miǎnfèi dā chē 要求免费搭车

hitchhiker n a hitchhiker yíge yāoqiú miǎnfèi dā chē de rén
一个要求免费搭车的人

hoarse adj sīyǎ 嘶哑

hobby n a hobby yíge shìhào 一个嗜好

hockey n qūgùnqiú 曲棍球

hold 1 vb to hold názhe 拿着; he held some keys in his hand
tā shǒu lǐ názhe yìxiē yàoshi 他手里拿着一些钥匙; to hold
someone's hand wòzhe mǒurén de shǒu 握着某人的手;
(when used to mean to have meetings, competitions, parties)
jǔxíng 举行; to hold a competition jǔxíng bǐsài 举行比赛; the
party will be held in the school jùhuì jiāng zài xuéxiào jǔxíng
聚会将在学校举行; (to detain) kòuliú 扣留; hold someone
hostage kòuliú mǒurén zuò rénzhí 扣留某人作人质; (to keep
back) (bǎo)liú (保)留; to hold a seat for someone wèi mǒurén
(bǎo)liú yíge zuòwèi 为某人(保)留一个座位; (other uses) to
hold the world record bǎochí shìjiè jìlù 保持世界纪录; to
hold someone responsible yào mǒurén fùzé 要某人负责; please
hold the line! qǐng bié guàduàn (diànhuà)! 请别挂断(电话)!
2 n to get hold of the ball zhuāzhù qiú 抓住球; to get hold of
someone zhǎodào mǒurén 找到某人; hold on (to wait)
děngyíděng 等一等; hold on tight! jǐnjǐn zhuāzhù! 紧紧抓住!;
hold on to the rope zhuāzhù shéngzi 抓住绳子; hold up (to
raise) jǔqǐ 举起; to hold up one's hand jǔqǐ shǒu lai 举起手来;
(to delay) to hold someone up tuōzhù mǒurén 拖住某人; to
hold up the traffic zǔsè jiāotōng 阻塞交通; (to rob) qiǎngjié
抢劫

hole n a hole (if it's a pit in the ground) yíge kēng 一个坑; (if it's
a round-shaped gap) yíge kǒng 一个孔, yíge dòng 一个洞;
(in a wall, clothes) yíge kūlong 一个窟窿

holiday n (British English) (a vacation) a holiday yíge jiàqī 一个
假期; to go on holiday qù dù jià 去度假; (a national or religious
festival) jiàrì 假日; a (public) holiday yíge (gōngxiū)jiàrì 一个
(公休)假日; (British English) (time taken off work) jià 假; to take
two weeks' holiday xiū liǎngge xīngqī de jià 休两个星期的假

Holland n Hélán 荷兰

home 1 n a home (a place to live) yíge jiā 一个家; (a house) yíge zhùzhái 一个住宅; to leave home líkāi jiā 离开家; to work from home zài jiā shàngbān 在家上班; a home for elderly people yìsuǒ yǎnglǎoyuàn 一所养老院; a home for handicapped children yíge cánjí értóng zhī jiā 一个残疾儿童之家 **2** adv to go home (to one's house) huí jiā 回家; (to one's home country) huí guó 回国; on my way home zài wǒ huí jiā de lù shang 在我回家的路上; to be home (from school, work) dào jiā 到家; I can take you home wǒ kěyǐ sòng nǐ huí jiā 我可以送你回家 **3** at home (in one's house) zài jiā 在家; she's working at home tā zài jiā gōngzuò 她在家工作; he lives at home tā zài jiā zhù 他在家住; to feel at home wú jūshù 无拘束; make yourselves at home bú yào jūshù 不要拘束; (when talking about a sports team) zài běndì 在本地

homeless adj wú jiā kě guī 无家可归

homesick adj xiǎng jiā 想家

homework n zuòyè 作业

homosexual n a homosexual yíge tóngxìngliànzhě 一个同性恋者

honest adj chéngshí 诚实; (frank, sincere) tǎnshuài 坦率; to be honest, I'd rather stay here tǎnshuài de shuō, wǒ nìngyuàn dāi zài zhèr 坦率地说, 我宁愿呆在这儿

honestly adv chéngshí de 诚实地

honey n fēngmì 蜂蜜

honeymoon n mìyuè 蜜月

Hong Kong n Xiānggǎng 香港

hood n (to cover the head) a hood yìdǐng dōumào 一顶兜帽; (US English) (of a car) the hood chēpéng 车篷

hoof n a hoof yìzhī tízi 一只蹄子

hook n (for hanging clothes, pictures) a hook yíge gōu(zi) 一个钩(子); (for fishing) a hook yíge diàoyúgōu 一个钓鱼钩

hooligan n a hooligan yíge liúmáng 一个流氓

hoover vb (British English) to hoover the house gěi fángzi xī chén 给房子吸尘

hop vb tiào 跳

hope 1 vb xīwàng 希望; I hope you don't mind wǒ xīwàng nǐ bú jièyì 我希望你不介意; I hope so wǒ xīwàng rúcǐ 我希望如此 **2** n xīwàng 希望; she is my only hope tā shì wǒde wéiyī xīwàng 她是我的唯一希望

hopeless adj (without hope of success) méi yǒu xīwàng 没有希望; (without any ability) méi yǒu zàojiù 没有造就; to be hopeless at cooking zài zuò fàn fāngmiàn méi yǒu zàojiù 在做饭方面没有造就

horn n (on a car, a bus) lǎbā 喇叭; to blow a horn àn lǎbā 按喇叭; (of an animal) a horn yìzhī jiǎo 一只角; (an instrument) a horn yígè hào 一个号

horoscope n xīngzhàn 星占

horrible adj (exciting horror) kěpà 可怕, kǒngbù 恐怖; (very bad) zāogāo 糟糕, huài 坏

horror film n a horror film yíbù kǒngbù diànyǐng 一部恐怖电影

horse n a horse yìpǐ mǎ 一匹马

horseracing n sài mǎ 赛马

horseriding n qí mǎ 骑马

hospital n a hospital yìjiā yīyuàn 一家医院; he's still in (the) hospital tā hái zài yīyuàn lǐ 他还在医院里; to be taken to (the) hospital bèi sòngjìn yīyuàn 被送进医院

host n a host yígè zhǔrén 一个主人

hostage n a hostage yìmíng rénzhì 一名人质

hostel n a hostel yígè zhāodàisuǒ 一个招待所

hostess n a hostess (a female host) yígè nǚ zhǔrén 一个女主人; (in a plane) yígè kōngzhōng xiǎojie 一个空中小姐

hot adj (very warm) rè 热; I'm very hot wǒ hěn rè 我很热; a hot meal yídùn rè cān 一顿热餐; (strong, with a lot of spices) là 辣; a very hot dish yídào hěn là de cài 一道很辣的菜

hot air balloon *n* a hot air balloon yíge rè qìqiú 一个热气球

hot dog *n* a hot dog yíge hóngcháng miànbāo 一个红肠面包

hotel *n* a hotel yìjiā lǚguǎn 一家旅馆

hour *n* an hour yíge xiǎoshí 一个小时, yíge zhōngtóu 一个钟头; I earn two pounds an hour wǒ yíge xiǎoshí zhèng liǎng bàng qián 我一个小时挣两镑钱

house *n* (*a building*) fángzi 房子; a house yízuò fángzi 一座房子; (*a dwelling place*) jiā 家; to go to someone's house qù mǒurén de jiā 去某人的家; the bike is at my house zìxíngchē zài wǒ jiā lǐ 自行车在我家里

housewife *n* a housewife yíge jiātíng fùnǚ 一个家庭妇女

housework *n* jiāwùhuór 家务活儿; to do the housework zuò jiāwùhuór 做家务活儿

housing estate (*British English*), **housing development** (*US English*) *n* a housing estate yíge zhùzhái qū 一个住宅区

hovercraft *n* a hovercraft yìsōu qìdiànchuán 一艘气垫船

how *adv* (*in what way*) zěnme 怎么, zěnyàng 怎样; how did you find us? nǐ zěnme zhǎodào de wǒmen? 你怎么找到的我们?; I know how [to swim | to ride a horse | to cook a curry...] wǒ zhīdào zěnyàng [yóuyǒng | qí mǎ | zuò gālí cài...] 我知道怎样 [游泳 | 骑马 | 做咖喱菜...]; (*in polite questions*) how are you? nǐ hǎo ma? 你好吗?; how is your mother? nǐ māma hǎo ma? 你妈妈好吗?; how was your holiday? nǐ jiàqī wánr de hǎo ma? 你假期玩儿得好吗?; (*in questions requiring specific information*) how long will it take? zhè yào huā duō cháng shíjiān? 这要花多长时间?; how tall are you? nǐ yǒu duō gāo? 你有多高?; how old is he? tā duōshǎo suì? 他多少岁?; (*when making a suggestion*) how would you like to eat out? chūqù chī fàn zěnmeyàng? 出去吃饭怎么样?

however *adv* (*nevertheless*) kěshì 可是, búguò 不过; however hard I try, I can't understand grammar bùguǎn zěnme nǔlì, wǒ yě nòng bù dǒng yǔfǎ 不管怎么努力, 我也弄不懂语法

how many 1 *pron* duōshǎo 多少; how many do you want? nǐ yào duōshǎo? 你要多少?; how many of you are there? nǐmen yǒu duōshǎo rén? 你们有多少人? **2** *det* duōshǎo 多少; how many children are going on the trip? yǒu duōshǎo háizi qù lǚxíng? 有多少孩子去旅行?

how much 1 *pron* duōshǎo 多少; how much does it come to? yígòng duōshǎo? 一共多少?; **2** *det* duōshǎo 多少; how much money do you have left? nǐ hái shèng duōshǎo qián? 你还剩多少钱?

huge *adj* jùdà 巨大

human being *n* rén 人

humour (British English), **humor** (US English) *n* yōumò 幽默; to have a sense of humour yǒu yōumò gǎn 有幽默感

hundred *num* one hundred, a hundred yìbǎi 一百; three hundred sānbǎi 三百; five hundred and fifty dollars wǔbǎi wǔshí měiyuán 五百五十美元; about a hundred people dàyuē yìbǎi rén 大约一百人

hungry *adj* è 饿; I'm very hungry wǒ hěn è 我很饿

hunt *vb* dǎliè 打猎; to go hunting qù dǎliè 去打猎

hurdles *n* kuàlán 跨栏

hurrah, hurray *n* (also *exc*) hurrah! hǎo wa! 好哇!

hurry 1 *vb* gǎnjǐn 赶紧; hurry home! gǎnjǐn huí jiā! 赶紧回家!; to hurry someone cuī mǒurén 催某人 **2** *n* be in a hurry hěn cōngmáng 很匆忙; there's no hurry bú yòng zháojí 不用着急; hurry up gǎnjǐn 赶紧

hurt *vb* (to injure) I hurt myself wǒ shòule shāng 我受了伤; she hurt her leg tāde tuǐ shòule shāng 她的腿受了伤; (to be painful) téng 疼; my throat hurts wǒde sǎngzi téng 我的嗓子疼; that hurts nà hěn téng 那很疼; (to upset) shānghài 伤害; to hurt someone's feelings shānghài mǒurén de gǎnqíng 伤害某人的感情

husband *n* zhàngfu 丈夫

li

I *pron* wǒ 我: Mr. Li and I are going to Hong Kong tomorrow wǒ hé Lǐ xiānsheng míngtiān qù Xiānggǎng 我和李先生明天去香港

ice *n* bīng 冰

ice cream *n* an ice cream yíge bīngqílín 一个冰淇淋

ice hockey *n* bīngqiú 冰球

ice rink *n* an ice rink yíge huábīngchǎng 一个滑冰场

ice-skate *n* a pair of ice-skates yìshuāng bīngxié 一双冰鞋

ice-skating *n* huábīng 滑冰

icing *n* tángshuāng 糖霜

ID, identity card *n* an identity card yíge shēnfènzhèng 一个身份证

idea *n* an idea (*a thought*) yìzhǒng sīxiǎng 一种思想; (*a view*) yìzhǒng kànfǎ 一种看法; (*a plan*) yíge zhǔyì 一个主意; **what a good idea!** duōme hǎo de zhǔyì a! 多么好的主意啊! **I've got no idea how much it costs** wǒ bù zhīdào zhè yào duōshǎo qián 我不知道这要多少钱

idiot *n* an idiot yíge báichī 一个白痴, yíge shǎzi 一个傻子

if *conj* (*on condition that*) rúguǒ 如果; **you'll get good marks if you study hard** rúguǒ nǐ nǔlì xuéxí, nǐ huì qǔdé hǎo chéngjì 如果你努力学习, 你会取得好成绩; (*in case that*) yàoshì 要是; **we won't go if it rains** yàoshì xiàyǔ, wǒmen jiù bú qù 要是下雨, 我们就不去; (*supposing that*) jiǎrú 假如, yàoshì 要是; **I would travel if I were rich** jiǎrú wǒ hěn yǒuqián, wǒ huì qù lǚxíng 假如我很有钱, 我会去旅行; **I'd refuse if I were you** yàoshì wǒ shì nǐ, wǒ jiù jùjué 要是我是你, 我就拒绝! Note that the conditional clause introduced by *if* precedes the main clause in

Chinese; (whether) shìfǒu 是否: **I don't know if they'll come** wǒ bù zhīdào tāmen shìfǒu huì lái 我不知道他们是否会来 **!** *Note that* shìfǒu 是否 *appears after the subject of the subordinate clause in Chinese.*

ignore *vb* **to ignore someone** bù lǐ mǒurén 不理某人; **to ignore a problem** hūshì yīge wèntí 忽视一个问题

ill *adj* bìng 病, yǒu bìng 有病; **she is ill** tā bìng le 她病了

illegal *adj* fēifǎ 非法

illness *n* **an illness** yīzhǒng (jí)bìng 一种(疾)病

imagination *n* (*the act of imagining*) xiǎngxiàng 想象; **this is only my imagination** zhè zhǐ shì wǒde xiǎngxiàng 这只是我的想象; (*the ability to imagine*) xiǎngxiànglì 想象力; **he has no imagination** tā méi yǒu xiǎngxiànglì 他没有想象力

imagine *vb* (*to form an image in one's mind*) xiǎngxiàng 想象; (*to think vainly or falsely*) shèxiǎng 设想

imitate *vb* mófǎng 模仿, fǎngxiào 仿效

immediately *adv* lìjí 立即, mǎshàng 马上

impatient *adj* bú nàifán 不耐烦; **to get impatient** biànde bú nàifán 变得不耐烦

import *vb* jìnkǒu 进口

important *adj* zhòngyào 重要; **it is important to keep fit** bǎochí jiànkāng hěn zhòngyào 保持健康很重要

impossible *adj* bù kěnéng 不可能; **it's impossible to change this plan** gǎibiàn zhège jìhuà shì bù kěnéng de 改变这个计划是不可能的

impress *vb* **I'm impressed by his speech** tāde jiǎnghuà gěi wǒ liúxià hěn shēn de yìnxiàng 他的讲话给我留下很深的印象

impression *n* **she made a good impression on me** tā gěi wǒ liúxià hěn hǎo de yìnxiàng 她给我留下很好的印象

improve *vb* (*to make better*) tígāo 提高, gǎishàn 改善; **to improve living conditions** gǎishàn shēnghuó tiáojiàn 改善生活

条件; to improve one's spoken Chinese tígāo zìjǐde Hànyǔ kǒuyǔ shuǐpíng 提高自己的汉语口语水平; (to get better) hǎozhuǎn 好转; the economic situation is improving jīngjì xíngshì zhèngzài hǎozhuǎn 经济形势正在好转

improvement n gǎijìn 改进, gǎishàn 改善

in ! Often in occurs in combination with verbs, for example: drop in, fit in, move in, etc. To find the correct translations for this type of verb, look up the separate dictionary entries at **drop, fit, move,** etc. **1** prep (inside) zài...lǐ 在...里; in the house zài fángzi lǐ 在房子里; there is a letter in the envelope (zài) xìnfēng li yǒu yìfēng xìn (在)信封里有一封信; (when talking about being in print) zài...shang 在...上; the woman in the photograph (zài) zhàopiàn shang de nǚrén (在)照片上的女人; I saw your picture in the newspaper wǒ zài bàozhǐ shang kàndào le nǐde zhàopiàn 我在报纸上看到了你的照片; in the world zài shìjiè shang 在世界上 **!** Note that when zài 在 appears at the beginning of a sentence or when a phrase introduced by zài 在 is used to modify a noun phrase, the use of zài 在 is optional; (at) zài 在; I am learning Japanese in school wǒ zài xuéxiào xuéxí Rìyǔ 我在学校学习日语; in the countryside zài nóngcūn 在农村; (when talking about countries or cities) zài 在 to live in [America | Japan | Shanghai...] zhù zài [Měiguó | Rìběn | Shànghǎi...] 住在 [美国 | 日本 | 上海...]; (dressed in) chuānzhe 穿着; in a skirt chuānzhe qúnzi 穿着裙子; to be dressed in black chuānzhe hēisè de yīfu 穿着黑色的衣服; (showing the way in which something is done) yòng 用; to write a letter in Chinese yòng Zhōngwén xiě xìn 用中文写信; we paid in cash wǒmen yòng xiànjīn fù qián 我们用现金付钱; in ink yòng mòshuǐ(r) 用墨水 (儿); (during) zài 在; in October zài shíyuè 在十月; in the night zài yèlǐ 在夜里; in the morning zài zǎochén 在早晨; (within) guò 过, zài...zhīnèi 在...之内; I'll be ready in ten minutes wǒ zài shí fēnzhōng zhīnèi huì zhǔnbèihǎo 我在十分钟之内会准备好; she'll be back in half an hour tā guò bàn xiǎoshí huílái 她过半小时回来; (other uses) to stay in the rain dāi zài yǔ zhōng 呆在雨中; she is in her twenties tā èrshíjǐ suì 她二十几岁; one in ten shíge dāngzhōng yǒu yíge 十个当中有一个; to cut an apple in two bǎ yíge píngguǒ qiēchéng liǎng bàn 把一个苹果切成两半 **2** adv (at home) zài jiā 在家; (available) zài 在; tell her I'm not in gàosu tā wǒ bú zài 告诉她 我不在; (arrived) the train is in huǒchē dào le 火车到了

inch n an inch yì yīngcùn 一英寸 ! Note that an inch = 2.54 cm.

include vb bāokuò 包括; service is included in the bill zhàngdān li bāokuò fúwùfèi 帐单里包括服务费

including prep bāokuò 包括: they were all invited, including the children tāmen dōu shòudào yāoqǐng, bāokuò háizi 他们都 受到邀请, 包括孩子

income n an income yífèn shōurù 一份收入

income tax n suǒdéshuì 所得税

inconvenient adj bù fāngbiàn 不方便

increase 1 vb zēngjiā 增加: to increase by 10% zēngjiā bǎifēn zhī shí 增加百分之十 **2** n zēngjiā 增加

incredible adj nányǐzhìxìn 难以置信

independent adj dúlì de 独立的

India n Yìndù 印度

Indian 1 adj Yìndù de 印度的 **2** n (the people from India) Yìndùrén 印度人; (the indigenous people of America) Yìndì'ānrén 印地安人

indicate vb (to show) biǎoshì 表示; (to point out) zhǐchū 指出

indifferent adj (unconcerned) bú zàihu 不在乎, bù guānxīn 不关心; (of a middle quality) zhíliàng bù gāo 质量不高

indigestion n to have indigestion xiāohuà bùliáng 消化 不良

individual 1 adj (pertaining to one only or to each one separately) gèrén de 个人的; (separate) gèbié de 个别的 **2** n an individual yígè rén 一个人

indoor adj shìnèi 室内; an indoor swimming pool yíge shìnèi yóuyǒngchí 一个室内游泳池

indoors adv zài wū li 在屋里; go indoors jìn wū li 进屋里

industrial adj gōngyè de 工业的

industry n gōngyè 工业

inevitable adj bùkě bìmiǎn de 不可避免的

infant school n (British English); an infant school yíge xuéqiánbān 一个学前班

infection n (the act of tainting) gǎnrǎn 感染; (the act of imparting some disease) chuánrǎn 传染; (an infectious disease) chuánrǎnbìng 传染病

influence 1 n an influence yìzhǒng yǐngxiǎng 一种影响; to have influence over duì... yǒu yǐngxiǎng 对... 有影响 **2** vb yǐngxiǎng 影响; to influence someone yǐngxiǎng mǒurén 影响某人; to be influenced by someone shòudào mǒurén de yǐngxiǎng 受到某人的影响

inform vb (to tell) gàosu 告诉; to inform them of the news gàosu tāmen zhège xiāoxi 告诉他们这个消息; (to impart knowledge) tōngzhī 通知; to inform the police of the accident bǎ zhège shìgù tōngzhī gěi jǐngchá 把这个事故通知给警察; to keep someone informed suíshí xiàng mǒurén bàogào 随时向某人报告

informal adj (describing a person, a person's manner) suíbiàn 随便; (describing a word, a language) rìcháng shǐyòng de 日常使用的; (describing a discussion or an interview) fēi zhèngshì de 非正式的

information n a piece of information yìtiáo xiāoxi 一条消息; thank you for your information xièxie nǐ gàosu wǒ zhètiáo xìnxī 谢谢你告诉我这条信息

information desk n wènxùn chù 问讯处

information technology n xìnxī jìshù 信息技术

ingredient n an ingredient yìzhǒng pèiliào 一种配料

inhabitant n an inhabitant yíge jūmín 一个居民

injection n an injection yìzhī zhùshèjì 一支注射剂; to give someone an injection gěi mǒurén dǎ yìzhēn 给某人打一针

injured adj shòushāng 受伤

injury n sǔnshāng 损伤, shāng 伤

ink n mòshuǐ(r) 墨水(儿)

innocent adj (not legally guilty) wúzuì 无罪; (harmless) wúhài 无害; (naïve) tiānzhēn 天真; (ignorant of evil) yòuzhì 幼稚

inquiry n (a question) xúnwèn 询问, dǎtīng 打听; (an investigation) diàochá 调查; (a search for knowledge) tànjiū 探究

insect n an insect yíge kūnchóng 一个昆虫

inside 1 prep zài...lǐmiàn 在...里面; inside the house zài fángzi lǐmiàn 在房子里面 2 adv lǐmiàn 里面; he's inside tā zài lǐmiàn 他在里面; I looked inside wǒ xiàng lǐmiàn kàn 我向里面看; let's bring the chairs inside wǒmen bǎ yǐzi nádào lǐmiàn qu ba 我们把椅子拿到里面去吧 3 n lǐmiàn 里面; the inside of the house fángzi lǐmiàn 房子里面 4 adj lǐmiàn de 里面的 5 inside out to put one's shirt on inside out bǎ chènshān chuān fǎn le 把衬衫穿反了

inspect vb (to examine) jiǎnchá 检查; (to look at officially) shìchá 视察; (to look at ceremonially) jiǎnyuè 检阅; the president inspected the guard of honour zǒngtǒng jiǎnyuèle yízhàngduì 总统检阅了仪仗队

inspector n an inspector (an examining officer) yíge jiǎncháyuán 一个检察员; (one who inspects officially) yíge shìcházhě 一个视察者; (one who inspects ceremonially) yíge jiǎnyuèzhě 一个检阅者

instantly adv lìjí 立即

instead 1 instead of (rather than) ér bùshì 而不是; he hired a van instead of a car tā zūle yíliàng huòchē ér bùshì yíliàng jiàochē 他租了一辆货车而不是一辆轿车; instead of working he watched TV tā kàn diànshì ér bùshì gōngzuò 他看电视而不是工作; (in place of) dàitì 代替; use oil instead of butter yòng yóu dàitì huángyóu 用油代替黄油; his wife came instead of him tā tàitai dàitì tā lái le 他太太代替他来了 2 adv I don't feel like going to the cinema—let's stay at home instead wǒ bù xiǎng qù kàn diànyǐng—zánmen dāi zài jiālǐ ba 我不想去看电影—咱们呆在家里吧

instruction n an instruction yíxiàng zhǐshì 一项指示, yíxiàng mìnglìng 一项命令; to give someone instructions to check the baggage zhǐshì mǒurén jiǎnchá xínglǐ 指示某人检查行李; instructions for use shǐyòng shuōmíng 使用说明

instrument n an instrument (an indicating device) yíge yíqì 一个仪器; (a tool) yíjiàn gōngjù 一件工具; (for hospital operations) yíjiàn qìxiè 一件器械; (for playing music) yíjiàn yuèqì 一件乐器

insult vb wǔrǔ 侮辱

insurance n bǎoxiǎn 保险

insure vb bǎoxiǎn 保险; is your car insured? nǐde qìchē bǎoxiǎn le ma? 你的汽车保险了吗?

intelligent adj cōngming 聪明

intend n he intends to [leave | learn Cantonese | travel abroad...] tā dǎsuàn [zǒu | xué Guǎngdōnghuà | qù guówài lǚxíng...] 他打算[走|学广东话|去国外旅行...]

intense adj (when describing a pain) jùliè 剧烈; (when describing feelings) qiángliè 强烈; (when describing an earnestly or deeply emotional person or manner) rèqiè 热切

intensive care n to be in intensive care jiēshòu tèbié jiānhù 接受特别监护

interest 1 n (enthusiasm) xìngqù 兴趣; to have an interest in music duì yīnyuè gǎn xìngqù 对音乐感兴趣; (premium paid for money borrowed from or saved in a bank) lìxī 利息; (benefit) lìyì 利益 2 vb to interest somebody shǐ mǒurén gǎn xìngqù 使某人感兴趣

interested adj gǎn xìngqù 感兴趣; to be interested in [politics | sports | painting...] duì [zhèngzhì | tǐyù | huì huà...] gǎn xìngqù 对[政治|体育|绘画...]感兴趣; are you interested? nǐ gǎn xìngqù ma? 你感兴趣吗?

interesting adj yǒuqù 有趣, yǒu yìsi 有意思

interfere vb (to get involved in) gānshè 干涉; to interfere in someone's business; gānshè mǒurén de shì 干涉某人的事

(*to have a bad effect on*) fáng'ài 妨碍; it's going to interfere with his work zhè yào fáng'ài tāde gōngzuò 这要妨碍他的工作

intermission n jiànxiē 间歇, xiūxi 休息

international adj guójì 国际

internet n the internet hùliánwǎng 互联网, yīntèwǎng 因特网

interpreter n an interpreter yíge fānyì 一个翻译, yíge kǒuyì 一个口译

interrupt vb (*to break in upon someone's action, speech, etc.*) dǎduàn 打断; (*to disturb by breaking in upon*) dǎrǎo 打扰; (*to stop continuity in*) zhōngduàn 中断

interval n (*in time*) jiàngé 间隔; at regular intervals měi gé yídìng shíjiān 每隔一定时间; (*at a location*) jiàngé 间隔; at regular intervals měi gé yídìng jùlí 每隔一定距离; (*British English*) (*during a play, a show*) mùjiān xiūxi 幕间休息

interview 1 n an interview (*for a job*) yícì miànshì 一次面试; (*with a journalist*) yícì cǎifǎng 一次采访 **2** vb to interview someone (*if it's an employer*) miànshì mǒurén 面试某人; (*if it's a journalist*) cǎifǎng mǒurén 采访某人; (*if it's the police*) shěnwèn mǒurén 审问某人

intimidate vb dònghè 恫吓, kǒnghè 恐吓

into prep (*when talking about a location*) zǒu jìn huāyuán 走进花园; to get into a car jìndào qìchē li 进到汽车里; to get into bed shàngchuáng 上床; (*indicating a change*) chéng 成; to translate a letter into French bǎ yìfēng xìn fānyìchéng Fǎwén 把一封信翻译成法文; to turn someone into a frog bǎ mǒurén biànchéng yìzhī qīngwā 把某人变成一只青蛙

introduce vb (*to bring in*) to introduce a new technique yǐnjìn yíxiàng xīn jìshù 引进一项新技术; (*when people meet, or on radio or television*) jièshào 介绍; he introduced me to Peter tā bǎ wǒ jièshào gěi Bǐdé 他把我介绍给彼得; to introduce a programme jièshào yíge jiémù 介绍一个节目

invade vb qīnfàn 侵犯, qīnrù 侵入

invent vb fāmíng 发明

invention *n* an invention yíxiàng fāmíng 一项发明

investigate *vb* diàochá 调查

investigation *n* an investigation yíxiàng diàochá 一项调查

invisible *adj* kàn bú jiàn de 看不见的

invitation *n* (*the act of inviting*) yāoqǐng 邀请; (*a written form*) qǐngtiě 请帖, qǐngjiǎn 请柬; an invitation yífèn qǐngtiě 一份请帖, yìfēn qǐngjiǎn 一份请柬

invite *vb* yāoqǐng 邀请; to invite someone to dinner yāoqǐng mǒurén chīfàn 邀请某人吃饭

involve *vb* to be involved in an accident juǎnrù yícì shìgù 卷入一次事故; this activity involves both teachers and students zhèxiàng huódòng bāokuò lǎoshī hé xuésheng 这项活动包括老师和学生

Ireland *n* Ài'ěrlán 爱尔兰

Irish 1 *adj* Ài'ěrlán de 爱尔兰的 **2** *n* (*the people*) Ài'ěrlánrén 爱尔兰人; (*the language*) Ài'ěrlányǔ 爱尔兰语

iron 1 *n* iron tiě 铁; an iron yíge yùndǒu 一个熨斗 **2** *vb* yùn 熨

island *n* an island yíge dǎo(yǔ) 一个岛(屿)

it *pron* where is it? zài nǎr? 在哪儿?; who is it? shéi (a)? 谁(啊)?; it's me (shi) wǒ (a) (是)我(啊); it's a large school zhè shì yíge hěn dà de xuéxiào 这是一个很大的学校; it is [difficult | easy | interesting...] to learn Chinese xuéxí Zhōngwén [hěn nán | hěn róngyì | hěn yǒu yìsi...] 学习中文 [很难 | 很容易 | 很有意思...]; it doesn't matter méi guānxi 没关系; it's [cold | warm | mild...] (tiān qì) [hěn lěng | hěn rè | hěn nuǎnhuo...] (天气) [很冷 | 很热 | 很暖和...]; I've heard about it wǒ tīngshuōle zhèjiàn shì 我听说了这件事

Italian 1 *adj* Yìdàlì de 意大利的 **2** *n* (*the people*) Yìdàlìrén 意大利人; (*the language*) Yìdàlìyǔ 意大利语, Yìdàlìwén 意大利文

Italy *n* Yìdàlì 意大利

itchy *adj* my leg is itchy wǒde tuǐ fāyǎng 我的腿发痒

its det tāde 它的; **its** [nose | tail | eyes] tāde [bízi | wěiba | yǎnjīng] 它的[鼻子 | 尾巴 | 眼睛]

itself pron (when used as a reflexive pronoun) (tā)zìjǐ (它)自己; the dog is going to wash itself zhèzhǐ gǒu yào gěi (tā)zìjǐ xǐzǎo 这只狗要给(它)自己洗澡; (when used for emphasis) the car itself was not damaged chē běnshēn méiyǒu sǔnhuài 车本身没有损坏; the heating comes on by itself nuǎnqì zìdòng kāi le 暖气自动开了

Jj

jacket n a jacket yíjiàn duǎn shàngyī 一件短上衣; (gathered at the waist) yíjiàn jiákè 一件夹克

jail n a jail yìsuǒ jiānyù 一所监狱

jam n jam guǒjiàng 果酱

January n January yīyuè 一月

Japan n Rìběn 日本

Japanese 1 adj Rìběn de 日本的 **2** n (the people) Rìběnrén 日本人; (the language) Rìyǔ 日语, Rìwén 日文

jaw n è 颚

jazz n juéshìyuè 爵士乐

jealous adj jídù 忌妒, dùjì 妒忌; he is jealous of her tā jídù tā 他妒忌她

jeans n niúzǎikù 牛仔裤

jeer vb to jeer someone cháoxiào mǒurén 嘲笑某人

jelly n (US English) (jam) guǒjiàng 果酱; (a gelatinized dessert) guǒzidòng 果子冻

Jesus n Yēsū 耶稣

jet n a jet (an aircraft) yíjià pēnqìshì fēijī 一架喷气式飞机

jewellery (British English), **jewelry** (US English) n zhūbǎo 珠宝; a piece of jewellery yíjiàn zhūbǎo 一件珠宝

Jewish adj Yóutàirén de 犹太人的

jigsaw puzzle n a jigsaw puzzle yíge pīnbǎn wánjù 一个拼板玩具

job n (work) gōngzuò 工作; a job yíge gōngzuò 一个工作; to look for a job zhǎo gōngzuò 找工作; (a task) rènwù 任务; a job yíxiàng rènwù 一项任务

jogging n mànpǎo 慢跑

join vb (become a member of) cānjiā 参加, jiārù 加入; to join a club cānjiā yíge jùlèbù 参加一个俱乐部; to join a company jiārù yíge gōngsī 加入一个公司; (meet up with) I'll join you for lunch tomorrow míngtiān wǒ hé nǐmen yìqǐ chī wǔfàn 明天我和你们一起吃午饭; to join the army cānjūn 参军; join in to join in a game cānjiā bǐsài 参加比赛

joke 1 n a joke yíge wánxiào 一个玩笑, yíge xiàohua 一个笑话 **2** vb kāi wánxiào 开玩笑

journalist n a journalist yíge jìzhě 一个记者

journey n a journey yícì lǚxíng 一次旅行; to go on a journey qù lǚxíng 去旅行

joy n huānlè 欢乐, lèqù 乐趣

judge 1 n a judge (in a court) yíge fǎguān 一个法官; (in competitions) yíge cáipàn 一个裁判 **2** vb (in a court) shěnpàn 审判; (in competitions) píngpàn 评判; (to determine the truth) duàndìng 断定

judo n róudào 柔道

jug n a jug yíge guànzi 一个罐子

juice n zhī 汁; fruit juice guǒzhī 果汁

July n qīyuè 七月

jump vb tiào 跳; the children were jumping on the bed háizimen zài chuáng shang tiào 孩子们在床上跳; to jump across the stream tiàoguò xiǎo hé 跳过小河; to jump a rope tiào shéng 跳绳; to jump out of the window tiàodào chuāng wài qu 跳到窗外去; to jump the queue (British English) chāduì 插队

jumper n (British English) a jumper yíjiàn tàotóushān 一件套头衫

June n liùyuè 六月; **junior high school** n (US English) a junior high school yìsuǒ chūjí zhōngxué 一所初级中学

junior school n (British English) a junior school yìsuǒ xiǎoxué 一所小学

jury n (in a court) péishěntuán 陪审团; (in a competition) píngjiǎngtuán 评奖团

just¹ adv (very recently) gāng 刚; I have just [arrived | seen her | received the letter...] wǒ gāng [dào | kànjiàn tā | shōudào xìn...] 我刚 [到 | 看见她 | 收到信...]; I had just turned on the TV wǒ gāng dǎkāi diànshìjī 我刚打开电视机; (at this or that very moment) zhènghǎo 正好; I was just about to phone you wǒ zhènghǎo yào gěi nǐ dǎ diànhuà 我正好要给你打电话; I arrived just as he was leaving tā zhènghǎo yào zǒu de shíhou, wǒ dào le 他正好要走的时候, 我到了; (only) jǐnjǐn 仅仅, zhǐbúguò 只不过; just two days ago jǐnjǐn liǎng tiān yǐqián 仅仅两天以前; he's just a child tā zhǐbúguò shì ge háizi 他只不过是个孩子; (barely) I got there just in time wǒ chàyìdiǎnr méi ànshí dào nàr 我差一点儿没按时到那儿; she's just 18 tā gānggāng shíbā suì 她刚刚十八岁; (when comparing) she is just as intelligent as he is tā hé tā yíyàng cōngming 她和他一样聪明; (immediately) jiù 就; just before the weekend jiù zài zhōumò yǐqián 就在周末以前

just² adj (righteous) zhèngyì 正义; (impartial, fair) gōngzhèng 公正, gōngpíng 公平

justice n (rightness) zhèngyì 正义; (impartiality) gōngzhèng 公正, gōngpíng 公平

Kk

kangaroo *n* a kangaroo yìzhī dàishǔ 一只袋鼠

karate *n* Rìběn kōngshǒudào 日本空手道

keen *adj* a keen teacher yíwèi rèxīn de lǎoshī 一位热心的老师; to be keen on swimming xǐhuan yóuyǒng 喜欢游泳

keep *vb* (to maintain) bǎochí 保持; to keep a speed of 30 miles an hour bǎochí měi xiǎoshí sānshí yīnglǐ de sùdù 保持每小时三十英里的速度; (to reserve) bǎoliú 保留; could you keep this seat for me? qǐng nǐ gěi wǒ bǎoliú zhège zuòwèi, hǎo ma? 请你给我保留这个座位好吗?; (to restrain from departure) liú 留; to keep someone in (the) hospital bǎ mǒurén liú zài yīyuàn 把某人留在医院; (to preserve) (bǎo)cún (保)存; we keep the wine in the cellar wǒmen bǎ jiǔ cún zài dìjiào li 我们把酒存在地窖里; (to cause to remain in a state or position) this sweater will keep you warm zhèjiàn máoyī huì shǐ nǐ nuǎnhuo 这件毛衣会使你暖和; to keep someone waiting ràng mǒurén děnghòu 让某人等候; (to delay) dāngē 耽搁; I won't keep you long wǒ bú huì dāngē nǐ hěn jiǔ 我不会耽搁你很久; what kept you? shénme shì dāngele nǐ? 什么事耽搁了你?; (to put away) fàng 放; where do you keep the cups? nǐ bǎ chábēi fàng zài nǎr? 你把茶杯放在哪儿?; (not to break, not to reveal) to keep a promise lǚxíng nuòyán 履行诺言; to keep a secret bǎoshǒu mìmì 保守秘密; (to continue) **keep (on)** bù tíng de 不停地; to keep (on) [walking | talking | running...] bù tíng de [zǒu | jiǎng | pǎo...] 不停地 [走 | 讲 | 跑...]; **keep away** bié kàojìn 别靠近; keep away from the fire! bié kàojìn huǒ! 别靠近火!; **keep back** liúxià 留下; he kept the children back after school fàngxué yǐhòu tā bǎ háizimen liúxià 放学以后他把孩子们留下; **keep out** to keep out of the sun búyào jiēchù yángguāng 不要接触阳光; to keep the rain out bú ràng yǔshuǐ liújìnlai 不让雨水流进来; **keep up** gǎnshàng

赶上; to keep up with the other pupils gǎnshàng biéde xuésheng 赶上别的学生

kerb (British English) n lùbiān xiāngbiānshí 路边镶边石

kettle n a kettle yíge shuǐhú 一个水壶

key n a key (of a lock) yìbǎ yàoshi 一把钥匙; (of a keyboard) yíge jiàn 一个键

keyhole n a keyhole yíge yàoshikǒng 一个钥匙孔

kick vb tī 踢; to kick someone tī mǒurén 踢某人; he didn't kick the ball tā méi tī qiú 他没踢球; **kick off** (in a football match) kāiqiú 开球; **kick out** to kick someone out bǎ mǒurén gǎnchūqu 把某人赶出去

kid n (a child) a kid yíge xiǎoháir 一个小孩儿; (a young goat) a kid yìtóu xiǎo shānyáng 一头小山羊

kidnap vb bǎngjià 绑架

kill vb shāsǐ 杀死; kill [someone | a pig | a chicken...] shāsǐ [mǒurén | yìtóu zhū | yìzhī jī...] 杀死 [某人 | 一头猪 | 一只鸡...]; (to kill in a certain way) ...sǐ ...死; the poison killed lots of animals dúyào dúsǐle xǔduō dòngwù 毒药毒死了许多动物; the frost tonight will kill those plants jīn yè de yánshuāng huì dòngsǐ nàxiē zhíwù 今夜的严霜会冻死那些植物; (to kill oneself) zìshā 自杀

kilo, kilogram(me) n a kilo yì gōngjīn 一公斤

kilometre (British English), **kilometer** (US English) n a kilometre yì gōnglǐ 一公里

kind 1 n zhǒng 种; it's a kind of [fish | novel | hotel...] zhè shì yìzhǒng [yú | xiǎoshuō | lǚguǎn...] 这是一种 [鱼 | 小说 | 旅馆...]; this kind of film zhèzhǒng diànyǐng 这种电影 **2** adj shànliáng 善良, hé'ǎi 和蔼

king n a king yíge guówáng 一个国王

kingdom n a kingdom yíge wángguó 一个王国

kiss 1 vb wěn 吻; to kiss someone wěn mǒurén 吻某人 **2** n wěn 吻, jiēwěn 接吻

kitchen n a kitchen yíge chúfáng 一个厨房

kite n a kite yìzhī fēngzheng 一只风筝

kitten *n* a kitten yìzhī xiǎomāo 一只小猫

knee *n* xīgài 膝盖

kneel down *vb* guìxia 跪下

knife *n* a knife yìbǎ dāo 一把刀

knit *vb* to knit a sweater out of wool zhī máoyī 织毛衣

knock 1 *vb* qiāo 敲; to knock on the door qiāo mén 敲门 **2** *n* to get a knock on the head tóu bèi qiāole yíxià 头被敲了一下; **knock down** (in an accident) zhuàngdǎo 撞倒; (to demolish) chāichú 拆除; **knock out** (to make unconscious) dǎhūn 打昏; (in a contest) táotài 淘汰; **knock over** zhuàngdǎo 撞倒

knot *n* a knot (of a cord, a piece of ribbon or lace) yíge jié 一个结; (of wood) yíge jiébā 一个节疤

know *vb* (to be acquainted with) rènshi 认识; do you know her? nǐ rènshi tā ma? 你认识她吗?; (when talking about languages) dǒng 懂, huì 会; he knows five languages tā dǒng wǔzhǒng yǔyán 他懂五种语言; (to have the knowledge of) zhīdao 知道; I know why he phoned wǒ zhīdao tā wèishénme dǎ diànhuà 我知道他为什么打电话; does he know about the party? tā zhīdao zhège jùhuì ma? 他知道这个聚会吗?; he knows how to [swim | ride a bike | play chess...] tā huì [yóuyǒng | qí zìxíngchē | xià qí...] 他会[游泳 | 骑自行车 | 下棋...]; please let me know qǐng gàosu wǒ 请告诉我

knowledge *n* (learning) zhīshi 知识; (that which is known) zhīdào 知道, liǎojiě 了解

Ll

laboratory *n* a laboratory yíge shíyànshì 一个实验室

lace *n* (the material) huābiānr 花边儿; (for tying shoes) xiédài 鞋带; to tie one's laces jì xiédài 系鞋带

lack 1 n a lack of [food | money | air...] quēshǎo [shípǐn | qián | kōngqì...] 缺少[食品 | 钱 | 空气...] **2** vb quēshǎo 缺少, quēfá 缺乏; he lacks confidence tā quēshǎo xìnxīn 他缺少信心

ladder n a ladder yíge tīzi 一个梯子

lady n a lady yíwèi nǚshì 一位女士

lake n a lake yíge hú 一个湖

lamb n a lamb yìzhī xiǎo yáng 一只小羊

lamp n a lamp yìzhǎn dēng 一盏灯

lampshade n a lampshade yíge dēngzhào 一个灯罩

land 1 n (as opposed to the sea) lùdì 陆地; (for farming) tiándì 田地; (property) tǔdì 土地; a piece of land yíkuài tǔdì 一块土地; to own land yōngyǒu tǔdì 拥有土地 **2** vb (to fall) luò 落; (if it's a plane) jiàngluò 降落, zhuólù 着陆; (to set on shore) shàng àn 上岸

landscape n (scenery) fēngjǐng 风景, jǐngsè 景色; (a painting) fēngjǐnghuà 风景画

language n a language yìzhǒng yǔyán 一种语言; foreign languages wàiyǔ 外语; bad language cūhuà 粗话, zānghuà 脏话

language laboratory n a language laboratory yíge yǔyán shíyànshì 一个语言实验室

large adj dà 大; a large garden yíge dà huāyuán 一个大花园; a large sum of money yí dà bǐ qián 一大笔钱; a large population rénkǒu hěn duō 人口很多

last 1 adj (final) zuìhòu 最后; the last month of the year yì nián de zuìhòu yíge yuè 一年的最后一个月; the last person to leave zuìhòu líkāi de nàge rén 最后离开的那个人; that's the last time I saw her nà shì wǒ zuìhòu yícì kànjiàn tā 那是我最后一次看见她; (the most recent) last [time | week | month] shàng [yícì | ge xīngqī | ge yuè] 上 [一次 | 个星期 | 个月]; last year qùnián 去年 **2** adv (most recently) shàng yícì 上一次; when I was last here wǒ shàng yícì lái zhèr de shíhou 我上一次来这儿的时候; (at the end) zuìhòu 最后; I'll do the Chinese homework last

(of all) wǒ zuìhòu zuò Zhōngwén zuòyè 我最后做中文作业;
he came last in the race tā bǐsài dé zuìhòu yìmíng 他比赛得最
后一名 **3** *pron* they were the last to arrive tāmen shì zuìhòu
dào de 他们是最后到的; [the night | the day | the year] before last
qián [tiān wǎnshang | tiān | nián] 前 [天晚上 | 天 | 年]; [the week |
the month] before last dà shàngge [xīngqī | yuè] 大上个 [星期 | 月]
4 *vb* chíxù 持续; the film lasts two hours diànyǐng chíxùle
liǎngge xiǎoshí 电影持续了两个小时

late 1 *adv* (far into the day or night); late in the afternoon xiàwǔ
wǎn xiē shíhou 下午晚些时候; late in the night shēnyè 深夜;
(not on time) **2** *adj* wǎn 晚, chídào 迟到; to arrive half an hour late wǎn dào
bàngge xiǎoshí 晚到半个小时 **2** *adj* wǎn 晚, chídào 迟到; to
be late for work shàngbān chídào 上班迟到; the train was two
hours late huǒchē wǎnle liǎngge xiǎoshí 火车晚了两个小时;
to make someone late shǐ mǒurén chídào 使某人迟到

later *adv* I'll tell you later wǒ yǐhòu zài gàosu nǐ 我以后再告诉
你; see you later huítóu jiàn 回头见, zàijiàn 再见

latest *adj* (the most up-to-date) zuì xīn 最新; the latest news
zuì xīn xiāoxi 最新消息; at the latest zuì chí 最迟

Latin *n* Lādīngyǔ 拉丁语, Lādīngwén 拉丁文

laugh 1 *vb* xiào 笑; they laughed loudly tāmen dàshēng de xiào
他们大声地笑; to laugh at somebody xiàohua mǒurén 笑话
某人 **2** *n* xiào 笑

laundry *n* (when referring to the place) xǐyīfáng 洗衣房; clean
laundry xǐhǎo de yīfu 洗好的衣服; to do the laundry xǐ yīfu
洗衣服

law *n* (a set of rules in a country) fǎlǜ 法律; to obey the law
zūnshǒu fǎlǜ 遵守法律; it's against the law zhè shì wéifàn fǎlǜ
de 这是违犯法律的; (physical or scientific law) dìnglǜ 定律;
a law yìtiáo dìnglǜ 一条定律; (as a subject) fǎxué 法学

lawn *n* a lawn yíkuài cǎodì 一块草地

lawnmower *n* a lawnmower yíge gēcǎojī 一个割草机

lawyer *n* a lawyer yíge lǜshī 一个律师

lay vb (to put) fàng 放; to lay some newspapers on the floor bǎ yìxiē bàozhǐ fàng zài dì shang 把一些报纸放在地上; (when talking about setting the table for dinner) bǎi 摆; to lay the table bǎihǎo cānjù 摆好餐具; (of a chicken) xià 下; to lay an egg xià yíge jīdàn 下一个鸡蛋; **lay down** fàngxia 放下; he laid the tray down gently tā bǎ pánzi qīngqīng fàngxia 他把盘子轻轻放下; **lay off** jiěgù 解雇

lazy adj lǎn 懒, lǎnduò 懒惰

lead¹ vb (to act as a head) lǐngdǎo 领导; to lead a political party lǐngdǎo yíge zhèngdǎng 领导一个政党; (to guide) he led us through the forest tā dàilǐng wǒmen chuānguò sēnlín 他带领我们穿过森林; (in a match or race) lǐngxiān 领先; (to live) guò 过; to lead a busy life guò fánmáng de shēnghuó 过繁忙的生活; (to have as a result) dǎozhì 导致; to lead to an accident dǎozhì yìchǎng shìgù 导致一场事故

lead² n qiān 铅

leader n a leader (of a political party) yíge lǐngxiù 一个领袖; (of a state) yíge lǐngdǎorén 一个领导人

leaf n a leaf yípiàn yèzi 一片叶子

leak vb lòu 漏; the pipe leaks guǎnzi lòule 管子漏了

lean 1 vb (to rest sideways against) kào 靠; to lean against the wall kào zài qiáng shang 靠在墙上; to lean a bicycle against the wall bǎ zìxíngchē kào zài qiáng shang 把自行车靠在墙上; to lean out of the window bǎ shēnzi tànchū chuāng wài 把身子探出窗外 **2** adj (not fat) shòu 瘦; **lean on** yīkào 依靠

learn vb xué 学, xuéxí 学习; to learn how to drive xué kāichē 学开车

least 1 adj zuì shǎo 最少; they have the least money tāmende qián zuì shǎo 他们的钱最少 **2** pron it was the least I could do! wǒ qǐmǎ kěyǐ zuò zhèjiàn shì! 我起码可以做这件事! **3** adv ! Note that when the least is used to modify an adjective, the opposite of that adjective is used in Chinese, along with the word zuì 最 (= the most); the least expensive shop zuì piányi de shāngdiàn 最便宜的商店; the least difficult question zuì róngyì de wèntí 最容易的问题 **4 at least** zhìshǎo 至少; he's at least thirty tā zhìshǎo sānshí suì 他至少三十岁

leather vb pí 皮、pígé 皮革

leave vb (to depart or go away from) líkāi 离开; she left the room tā líkāile fángjiān 她离开了房间; (to allow to remain) leave your coat here bǎ wàiyī fàng zài zhèr 把外衣放在这儿; she left the window open tā ràng chuānghu kāizhe 她让窗户开着; (to put, to give) liúxià 留下; he didn't leave a message tā méi liúxià shénme huà 他没留下什么话; he left him some money tā gěi tā liúxià yìxiē qián 她给他留下一些钱; (to put off) leave the work until tomorrow děngdào míngtiān zài zuò zhège gōngzuò 等到明天再做这个工作; (to forget) wàng 忘; I left my bag on the train wǒ bǎ wǒde bāo wàng zài huǒchē shang le 我把我的包忘在火车上了; (to remain) shèngxia 剩下; there's nothing left shénme yě méi shèngxia 什么也没剩下; we've got only ten minutes left wǒmen zhǐ shèngxia shí fēnzhōng le 我们只剩下十分钟了; (to let) ràng 让; I left them to clean the room wǒ ràng tāmen dǎsǎo fángjiān 我让他们打扫房间; **leave behind** liúxià 留下; he left his belongings behind tā bǎ xínglǐ liúxià le 他把行李留下了; **leave me alone** bié guǎn wǒ 别管我; **leave out** (not to show or talk about) (by accident) lòudiào 漏掉; (deliberately) shěngqù 省去, lüèqù 略去; (to exclude) páichú 排除; to leave out this possibility páichú zhège kěnéngxìng 排除这个可能性; **leave over** shèngxia 剩下; there is some food left over shèngxia yìxiē fàn 剩下一些饭

lecture n a lecture (as part of the curriculum) yìtáng kè 一堂课; (specially arranged) yíge jiǎngzuò 一个讲座

left **1** n (when referring to the direction) zuǒ 左; to turn to the left xiàng zuǒ zhuǎnwān 向左转弯; (when referring to the side) zuǒbian 左边; she sat on my left tā zuò zài wǒde zuǒbian 她坐在我的左边 **2** adj zuǒ 左; his left hand tāde zuǒ shǒu 他的左手 **3** adv xiàng zuǒ 向左; to turn left xiàng zuǒ guǎi 向左拐

leg n noun tuǐ 腿

legal adj (pertaining to law) fǎlǜ de 法律的; (lawful) héfǎ 合法

leisure n kòngxián 空闲

leisure centre n a leisure centre yíge yùlè zhōngxīn 一个娱乐中心

lemon n a lemon yíge níngméng 一个柠檬

lemonade n níngméngshuǐ 柠檬水

lend vb jiègěi 借给; to lend someone money jiègěi mǒurén qián 借给某人钱

length n (in measurements) chángdù 长度; (of a book, a film, a list, an event) cháng 长

leopard n a leopard yìzhī bào 一只豹

less 1 det shǎo 少; drink less coffee shǎo hē kāfēi 少喝咖啡; I have less work than he does wǒde gōngzuò bǐ tāde shǎo 我的工作比他的少 **2** pron shǎo 少; to pay less shǎo fù qián 少付钱; he has less than you tāde bǐ nǐde shǎo 他的比你的少 **3** adv we travel less in winter wǒmen dōngtiān lǚxíng bǐjiào shǎo 我们冬天旅行比较少 **4** prep (minus) jiǎnqù 减去 **5** less and less less and less often yuèláiyuè yuè bù jīngcháng 越来越 不经常 **6** less than bú dào 不到; less than half an hour bú dào bànge xiǎoshí 不到半个小时

lesson n a lesson yìjié kè 一节课; an English lesson yìjié Yīngyǔ kè 一节英语课

let vb (when making suggestions) let's go home zánmen huí jiā ba 咱们回家吧; let's go! zánmen zǒu ba! 咱们走吧!; (to rent out) (British English) chūzū 出租; (to allow) ràng 让; he let me help him tā ràng wǒ bāngzhù tā 他让我帮助他; I let him use my computer wǒ ràng tā yòng wǒde jìsuànjī 我让他用我的计算机; she wouldn't let me go tā bú ràng wǒ zǒu 她不让我走; **let down** (to someone down) shǐ mǒurén shīwàng 使某人失望; **let go** (to stop holding) fàngkāi 放开; he let go of me tā fàngkāile wǒ 他放开了我; (to release) shìfàng 释放; he let the prisoners go tā shìfàngle nàxiē fànrén 他释放了那些犯人; **let in** (to a room or house) he didn't let me in tā méi ràng wǒ jìn 他没让我进; to let in the rain lòu yǔ 漏雨; **let out** (to allow to go out) fàng (...) chūqù 放(...)出去; let me out! fàng wǒ chūqù! 放我出去!

放我出去! to let out a scream fāchū yìshēng jiānjiào 发出一
声尖叫; **let through** to let someone through ràng mǒurén
guòqu 让某人过去

letter *n* a letter yìfēng xìn 一封信

letter box *n* a letter box yíge xìnxiāng 一个信箱

lettuce *n* a head of lettuce yìkē shēngcài 一棵生菜

level 1 *n* (a horizontal position) shuǐpíng 水平; (a horizontal
plane) shuǐpíng miàn 水平面; (a horizontal line) shuǐpíng xiàn
水平线 **2** *adj* píng 平

library *n* a library yíge túshūguǎn 一个图书馆

licence (British English), **license** (US English) *n* a licence
yíge zhízhào 一个执照

license plate (US English) *n* a license plate yíge qìchē
páizhào 一个汽车牌照

lick *vb* tiǎn 舔

lid *n* a lid yíge gàizi 一个盖子

lie 1 *vb* (on the ground, on a bed) tǎng 躺; he lay down on the
sofa tā tǎngdào shāfā shang 他躺到沙发上; he was lying on
the sofa tā tǎng zài shāfā shang 他躺在沙发上; (to be
situated) wèiyú 位于; (not to tell the truth) shuōhuǎng 说谎
sāhuǎng 撒谎 **2** *n* huǎnghuà 谎话; to tell a lie shuō huǎnghuà
说谎话; **lie around** he always leaves his keys lying around tā
zǒngshì bǎ tāde yàoshi diàochù luàn diū 他总是把他的钥匙到
处乱丢; **lie down** tǎngxia 躺下

life *n* (a living being) shēngmìng 生命; (the stretch of time
between birth and death) shòumìng 寿命; (manner of living)
shēnghuó 生活

lifestyle *n* a lifestyle yìzhǒng shēnghuó fāngshì 一种生活方式

lift 1 *vb* to lift one's arm táiqǐ gēbo 抬起胳膊; to lift a suitcase
tíqǐ yíge xiāngzi 提起一个箱子 **2** *n* (British English) (an
elevator) a lift yíge diàntī 一个电梯; (in a car) can you give me
a lift to the station? wǒ néng dā nǐde chē qù chēzhàn ma? 我能
搭你的车去车站吗?

light 1 n *(from the sun, moon)* guāng 光; *(in a room, on a machine)* to switch on the light dǎkāi dēng 打开灯; **traffic lights** jiāotōng dēng 交通灯, hónglǜdēng 红绿灯; **have you got a light?** nǐ yǒu huǒ ma? 你有火吗? **2** adj *(not dark in colour)* qiǎn 浅; **a light blue dress** yíjiàn qiǎn lánsè de yīfu 一件浅蓝色的衣服; *(bright)* míngliàng 明亮; **a light room** yìjiān míngliàng de fángjiān 一间明亮的房间; *(not heavy)* qīng 轻 **3** vb *(to set fire to)* diǎn 点, diǎnrán 点燃; **he lit a cigarette** tā diǎn yān 他点烟; **to light a fire** diǎnhuǒ 点火; *(to give light to)* zhàoliàng 照亮; **the lamp lit the room** dēng zhàoliàng le fángjiān 灯照亮了房间

light bulb n **a light bulb** yíge dēngpào 一个灯泡

lighthouse n **a lighthouse** yízuò dēngtǎ 一座灯塔

lightning n **a lightning** yíge shǎndiàn 一个闪电

like¹ prep *(with a resemblance to)* xiàng 像; **he looks like a foreigner** tā kànshangqu xiàng ge wàiguórén 他看上去像个外国人; *(in the same manner as)* xiàng...yíyàng 像... 一样; **all his sons work like him** tāde érzimen dōu xiàng tā yíyàng gōngzuò 他的儿子们都像他一样工作

like² vb *(when expressing an interest)* xǐhuan 喜欢; **I like [swimming | reading | dancing...]** wǒ xǐhuan [yóuyǒng | kàn shū | tiàowǔ...] 我喜欢[游泳 | 看书 | 跳舞...]; **how do you like America?** nǐ juéde Měiguó zěnmeyàng? 你觉得美国怎么样?; *(when expressing a wish)* xiǎng 想, xīwàng 希望; **I'd like coffee** wǒ xiǎng hē kāfēi 我想喝咖啡; **I'd like to live here** wǒ xīwàng zhù zài zhèr 我希望住在这儿

limit n *(boundary)* jièxiàn 界限; *(that which may not be passed)* xiàndù 限度; *(restriction)* xiànzhì 限制

line n xiàn 线; **a line** *(a thread, string, cord)* yìgēn xiàn 一根线; *(a long, narrow mark)* yìtiáo xiàn 一条线; **a straight line** yìtiáo zhí xiàn 一条直线; *(US English)* *(a queue)* **to stand in line** páiduì 排队; *(a row)* pái 排; **the line is engaged** diànhuà zhàn xiàn 电话占线

link vb *(physically)* liánjiē 连接; **to link London to Paris** bǎ Lúndūn gēn Bālí liánjiēqǐlai 把伦敦跟巴黎连接起来; *(to* *relate to)* liánxì 联系; **the two murders are linked** zhè liǎngcì móushā shì yǒu liánxì de 这两次谋杀是有联系的

lion *n* a lion yìtóu shīzi 一头狮子

lip *n* chún 唇, zuǐchún 嘴唇

lipstick *n* kǒuhóng 口红

list *n* a list *(a catalogue)* yíge mùlù 一个目录; *(an enumeration)* yìzhāng biǎo 一张表, yìlánbiǎo 一览表; **a list of names** yífèn míngdān 一份名单

listen *vb* tīng 听; **to listen to music** tīng yīnyuè 听音乐

litre *(British English)*, **liter** *(US English)* *n* a litre yì shēng 一升

little 1 *adj (in quantity)* **little** [food | wine | money...] méi yǒu duōshǎo [fàn | jiǔ | qián...] 没有多少 [饭 | 酒 | 钱...]; **there is very little time** méi yǒu duōshǎo shíjiān le 没有多少时间了; *(in size, age)* xiǎo 小; **a little girl** yíge xiǎo nǚhái 一个小女孩; **the little finger** xiǎo shǒuzhǐ 小手指 **2** *pron* a little yìdiǎnr 一点儿; **I only ate a little** wǒ zhǐ chīle yìdiǎnr 我只吃了一点儿 **3** *adv* **he is little known** hěn shǎo yǒu rén zhīdào tā 很少有人知道他 **4** a little *(bit)* yìxiē 一些, yìdiǎnr 一点儿; **to add a little (bit) of sugar** jiā yìxiē táng 加一些糖; **I can speak a little (bit) of Chinese** wǒ huì shuō yìdiǎnr Hànyǔ 我会说一点儿汉语 **5** little by little yìdiǎn yìdiǎn de 一点一点地, zhújiàn de 逐渐地

live¹ *vb (to have one's home)* zhù 住; **he lives in Beijing** tā zhù zài Běijīng 他住在北京; *(to be alive)* huó 活; **to live to be a hundred** huódào yìbǎi suì 活到一百岁; *(to spend or pass)* guò 过; **to live a happy life** guò xìngfú de shēnghuó 过幸福的生活

live² *adj (alive)* huó 活; *(of a broadcast)* shíkuàng 实况, xiànchǎng 现场

lively *adj (active)* huóyuè 活跃; *(vital)* chōngmǎn huólì 充满活力; *(vivacious)* huópō 活泼; *(vivid)* shēngdòng 生动

living room *n* a living room yìjiān qǐjūshì 一间起居室

load *n (burden)* fùdān 负担; *(weight that can be carried)* zhuāngzàiliàng 装载量; **loads of money** dàliàng de qián 大量的钱

loaf n a loaf (of bread) yìtiáo (miànbāo) 一条(面包)

loan n (money lent) dàikuǎn 贷款; a loan yìbǐ dàikuǎn 一笔贷款; **on loan** on loan the book is on loan zhèběn shū jièchūqu le 这本书借出去了

lobster n a lobster yìzhī lóngxiā 一只龙虾

local adj dāngdì 当地, běndì 本地; a local newspaper yífèn dāngdì bàozhǐ 一份当地报纸; the local people běndì rén 本地人

lock 1 vb suǒ 锁; she locked the door tā suǒshangle mén 她锁上了门 **2** n a lock yìbǎ suǒ 一把锁; **lock in**; to lock someone in bǎ mǒurén suǒ zài lǐmian 把某人锁在里面; to lock oneself in bǎ zìjǐ guān zài lǐmian 把自己关在里面

locker n a locker yíge yǒu suǒ de xiǎo chú 一个有锁的小橱

logical adj fúhé luójí de 符合逻辑的

London n Lúndūn 伦敦

lonely adj gūdú 孤独

long 1 adj cháng 长; a long letter yìfēng cháng xìn 一封长信; long hair cháng tóufa 长头发; the film is two hours long zhèbù diànyǐng yǒu liǎngge xiǎoshí cháng 这部电影有两个小时长; I haven't seen him for a long time wǒ hěn cháng shíjiān méi kànjiàn tā le 我很长时间没看见他了 **2** adv jiǔ 久; long ago hěn jiǔ yǐqián 很久以前; you can stay as long as you like nǐ yuànyì dāi duō jiǔ jiù dāi duō jiǔ 你愿意呆多久就呆多久 **3 as long as** zhǐyào 只要; as long as the weather is nice zhǐyào tiānqì hǎo 只要天气好

look 1 vb kàn 看; to look at a photograph kàn zhàopiàn 看照片; to look out of the window kàn chuāng wài 看窗外; (to appear) kànshangqu 看上去; to look tired kànshangqu hěn lèi 看上去很累; to look well kànshangqu hěn hǎo 看上去很好; he looks young tā kànshangqu hěn niánqīng 他看上去很年青; she looks like her mother tā kànshangqu xiàng tā māma 她看上去像她妈妈; what does he look like? tā (kànshangqu) shénmeyang? 他(看上去)什么样? **2** n have a look kàn (yi) kàn 看(一)看; let me have a look ràng wǒ kàn (yi) kàn 让我看(一

看; **look after** zhàogù 照顾, zhàoliào 照料; to look after a child zhàogù yíge háizi 照顾一个孩子; **look down on** kànbuqǐ 看不起; to look down on someone kànbuqǐ mǒurén 看不起某人; **look for** zhǎo 找; he is looking for a job tā zài zhǎo gōngzuò 他在找工作; **look forward to** qīdài 期待, pànwàng 盼望; I am looking forward to meeting her wǒ qīdàizhe gēn tā jiànmiàn 我期待着跟她见面; **look into** diàochá 调查; he has looked into this problem tā diàochále zhège wèntí 他调查了这个问题; **look out!** dāngxīn! 当心!, xiǎoxīn! 小心!; **look through** to look through a book cháyuè yìběn shū 查阅一本书; **look up** to look up a word in a dictionary zài cídiǎn lǐ chá yíge cí 在词典里查一个词

loose adj (describing clothes) kuānsōng 宽松; (describing a screw, a tooth) sōng 松

lorry n (British English) a lorry yíliàng kǎchē 一辆卡车

lose vb (when talking about a thing) diū(shī) 丢(失); to lose [a pen | a key | a bag...] diūshī [yìzhī bǐ | yìbǎ yàoshi | yíge bāo...] 丢失 [一支笔 | 一把钥匙 | 一个包...]; (when talking about friendship or a psychological state) shīqù 失去; to lose [friends | interest | confidence] shīqù [péngyou | xìngqù | xìnxīn] 失去 [朋友 | 兴趣 | 信心]; (be defeated in) shū 输; we lost the game wǒmen shūle zhèchǎng bǐsài 我们输了这场比赛; to lose face diū liǎn 丢脸, diū miànzi 丢面子; to lose one's temper fā píqì 发脾气

lost adj to get lost mílù 迷路

lot pron a lot hěn duō 很多; he eats a lot tā chī de hěn duō 他吃得很多; a lot of [money | time | books...] hěn duō [qián | shíjiān | shū...] 很多 [钱 | 时间 | 书...]; there is not a lot left shèngxia de bù duō le 剩下的不多了

lottery n cǎijiǎng 彩奖; a lottery ticket yìzhāng cǎipiào 一张彩票

loud adj dàshēng de 大声的; to talk in a loud voice dàshēng de jiǎnghuà 大声地讲话

loudspeaker n a loudspeaker yíge lǎba 一个喇叭

lounge n a lounge yìjiān xiūxishì 一间休息室

love 1 vb (when talking about people) ài 爱; do you love her? nǐ ài tā ma? 你爱她吗?; (when talking about things, activities) àihào 爱好, xǐhuan 喜欢 **2** n to be in love zài tán liàn'ài 在谈恋爱; to make love zuò ài 做爱

lovely adj (beautiful) měilì 美丽; a beautiful view měilì de jǐngsè 美丽的景色; you've got lovely eyes nǐ yǒu yìshuāng měilì de yǎnjing 你有一双美丽的眼睛; (very nice) (lìng rén) yúkuài de (令人)愉快的; a lovely weekend yíge (lìng rén) yúkuài de zhōumò 一个(令人)愉快的周末

low adj (when talking about temperature, voice, position) dī 低; to speak in a low voice dī shēng shuōhuà 低声说话; (when talking about heights) ǎi 矮; a low wall yìdǔ ǎi qiáng 一堵矮墙

lower vb to lower a flag bǎ qí qiāngxiàlai 把旗降下来; to lower the price jiàng/jiǎn jià 降/减价

loyal adj zhōngchéng 忠诚, zhōngshí 忠实

luck n yùnqì 运气; good luck! zhù nǐ hǎo yùnqì! 祝你好运气!; to bring someone (good) luck gěi mǒurén dàilái hǎo yùnqì 给某人带来好运气; to have bad luck bù zǒuyùn 不走运

lucky adj xìngyùn 幸运, yùnqì hǎo 运气好; he is lucky tā hěn xìngyùn 他很幸运

lunch n wǔfàn 午饭

Luxembourg n Lúsēnbǎo 卢森堡

luxury 1 n shēchǐ 奢侈 **2** adj a luxury hotel yìjiā háohuá lǚguǎn 一家豪华旅馆

Mm

machine n a machine yìtái jīqì 一台机器

mad adj (insane) fēng 疯; the dog went mad zhètiáo gǒu fēng le 这条狗疯了; (infatuated) to be mad about [something | somebody] kuángrè de míliàn [mǒushì | mǒurén] 狂热地迷恋[某事|某人]; (very angry) fēicháng shēngqì 非常生气

magazine *n* a magazine yìběn zázhì 一本杂志

magic 1 *adj* yǒu mólì de 有魔力的 **2** *n* (*referring to the magical arts*) móshù 魔术, xìfǎ 戏法

maiden name *n* niángjiā de xìng 娘家的姓

mail 1 *n* (*the postal system*) yóudì 邮递, yóuzhèng xìtǒng 邮政系统; (*letters*) xìnjiàn 信件 **2** *vb* (*US English*) to mail a letter to someone gěi mǒurén jì yìfēng xìn 给某人寄一封信

mailbox *n* (*US English*) a mailbox yíge xìnxiāng 一个信箱

mailman *n* (*US English*) a mailman yíge yóudìyuán 一个邮递员

main *adj* zhǔyào 主要

main course *n* a main course yídào zhǔ cài 一道主菜

major 1 *adj* zhǔyào 主要; major industries zhǔyào gōngyè 主要工业 **2** *n* (*a military rank*) yíge shàoxiào 一个少校; (*in university or college*) yìmén zhuānyè 一门专业; my major is mathematics wǒde zhuānyè shì shùxué 我的专业是数学

majority *n* duōshù 多数, dàduōshù 大多数

make *vb* ! *Note that the word* **make** *can be translated by* zuò 做, zào 造, *or* shǐ 使, *etc., depending on the meaning to be expressed. Very often the translation of the word* **make** *is decided by other words with which it is collocated, such as* make a phone call *or* make friends. *To find translations for other expressions like* to make a mess, to make a mistake, to make sure, *etc., look up the entries at* mess, mistake, sure, *etc*; zuò 做; to make [breakfast | furniture | a dress...] zuò [zǎofàn | jiājù | yíjiàn yīfu...] 做 [早饭 | 家具 | 一件衣服...]; (*to produce*) zào 造; to be made of [gold | metal | wood...] yíge [jīnzi | jīnshǔ | mùtou...] zào de 是 [金子 | 金属 | 木头...] 造的; (*to cause a particular reaction*) shǐ 使; to make someone [happy | angry | jealous...] shǐ mǒurén [gāoxìng | shēngqì | jìdù...] 使某人 [高兴 | 生气 | 嫉妒...]; to make someone wait ràng mǒurén děnghòu 让某人等候; to make a bed pū chuáng 铺床; to make a film shèzhì yíbù diànyǐng 摄制一部电影; to make coffee chōng kāfēi 冲咖啡; to make room téngchū dìfang 腾出地方; to make a phone call dǎ yíge diànhuà 打一个电话; to make friends jiāo péngyou 交朋友; (*to earn*) to make a lot of money zhuàn hěn duō qián 赚很多钱; to make a living wéichí shēnghuó 维持生活; to make a profit huò(dé) lì(rùn) 获(得)利(润); **make do** còuhe 凑合; **make out** to make out a list of names liè yìzhāng míngdān 列一张名单; to make a cheque out to someone gěi mǒurén kāi yìzhāng zhīpiào 给某人开一张支票; **make up** (to be friends again) héhǎo 和好, héjiě 和解; to make up an excuse biānzào yíge jièkǒu 编造一个借口; to make up a parcel bāochéng yíge bāoguǒ 包成一个包裹; to make up for lost time bǔshàng sǔnshī de shíjiān 补上损失的时间

make-up n huàzhuāng 化妆; she wears make-up tā huàzhe zhuāng 她化着妆

male adj (in biology) xióng 雄; (relating to men) nán 男

man n a man yíge nánrén 一个男人; (humankind) rénlèi 人类

manage vb (to run) guǎnlǐ 管理; to manage [a school | a hospital | a factory] guǎnlǐ [yíge xuéxiào | yíge yīyuàn | yíge gōngchǎng] 管理 [一个学校 | 一个医院 | 一个工厂]; to manage to finish one's homework shèfǎ zuòwán zuòyè 设法做完作业

manager n a manager yíge jīnglǐ 一个经理

mandarin n (standard Chinese) Hànyǔ pǔtōnghuà 汉语普通话; (the fruit) gānjú 柑橘; a mandarin yíge gānjú 一个柑橘

manner n (the way in which something is done) yìzhǒng fāngshì 一种方式; (method) yìzhǒng fāngfǎ 一种方法; (personal style of acting) yìzhǒng fēngdù 一种风度

manners n (good behaviour) lǐmào 礼貌; she has no manners tā méi yǒu lǐmào 她没有礼貌; (social conduct) guīju 规矩

manufacture vb zhìzào 制造

many 1 det (a lot of) xǔduō 许多, hěn duō 很多; were there many shops? yǒu xǔduō shāngdiàn ma? 有许多商店吗?; there weren't many people there tā méi yǒu hěn duō rén 那儿没有很多人; (when used with how, and the anticipated number is above nine) how many? duōshǎo? 多少?; how many dictionaries do you have? nǐ yǒu duōshǎoběn cídiǎn? 你有多少本词典?; (when used with how, and the anticipated number is below ten) how many? jǐ 儿; how many elder brothers do you

map 385 **mask**

have? nǐ yǒu jǐge gēge? 你有几个哥哥?; **too many** tài duō 太多; **so many** zhème duō 这么多, nàme duō 那么多; **as many as** hé...yíyàng duō 和...一样多 **2** *pron* are there many left? shèngxia hěn duō ma? 剩下很多吗?; I've got too many wǒde tài duō le 我的太多了; take as many as you like nǐ yuànyì ná duōshǎo jiù ná duōshǎo 你愿意拿多少就拿多少; **many of them speak English** tāmen xǔduō rén huì shuō Yīngyǔ 他们许多人会说英语

map *n* a map yìzhāng dìtú 一张地图

marble *n* (*a kind of stone*) dàlǐshí 大理石; (*a toy*) dànzi 弹子; a marble yíge dànzi 一个弹子

march *vb* xíngjìn 行进

March *n* sānyuè 三月

margarine *n* rénzào huángyóu 人造黄油

mark 1 *n* a mark (*a symbol*) yíge biāojì 一个标记, yíge jìhào 一个记号; (*British English*) (*a grade*) chéngjì 成绩, fēnshù 分数; to get good marks dé hǎo chéngjì 得好成绩 **2** *vb* to mark homework pàn zuòyè 判作业; (*to indicate*) biāomíng 标明

marker *n* a marker (*an examiner*) yíge kǎoguān 一个考官; (*a pen*) yìzhī zhāntóubǐ 一支毡头笔; (*a bookmark*) yíge shūqiān 一个书签

market *n* shìchǎng 市场; a market yíge shìchǎng 一个市场; a flea market yíge tiàozǎo shìchǎng 一个跳蚤市场; the job market láowù shìchǎng 劳务市场

marmalade *n* júzi jiàng 橘子酱, guǒjiàng 果酱

marriage *n* hūnyīn 婚姻, jiéhūn 结婚

married *adj* jiéle hūn de 结了婚的, yǐ hūn de 已婚的; to be married to someone gēn mǒurén jiéhūn 跟某人结婚

marry *vb* to marry someone gēn mǒurén jiéhūn 跟某人结婚

marsh *n* a marsh yíkuài zhǎozédì 一块沼泽地

mashed potatoes *n* tǔdòu ní 土豆泥

mask *n* a mask yíge miànjù 一个面具

mat n a mat yíge diànzi 一个垫子

match 1 n (a game) **a match** yìchǎng bǐsài 一场比赛; **a football match** (British English) yìchǎng zúqiú bǐsài 一场足球比赛; (a matchstick) **a match** yìgēn huǒchái 一根火柴 **2** vb **the shoes match the belt** xié hé pídài hěn xiāngpèi 鞋和皮带很相配

mate n a mate (a friend, good buddy, pal) (British English) yíge péngyou 一个朋友, yíge huǒbàn 一个伙伴; (a partner, husband, or wife) yíge duìxiàng 一个对象, yíge bànlǚ 一个伴侣; (for animals) dòngwù de pèiduì 动物的配对

material n a material (for making things) yìzhǒng cáiliào 一种材料; (in written form) yífèn cáiliào 一份材料

math (US English), **maths** (British English) n shùxué 数学

mathematics n shùxué 数学

matter 1 n **what's the matter (with her)?** (tā) zěnme le? (她)怎么了? **2** vb **does it really matter?** zhè zhēn de hěn yàojǐn ma? 这真的很要紧吗?; **it doesn't matter** méi guānxi 没关系, bú yàojǐn 不要紧

maximum 1 adj (the highest) zuì gāo 最高; **the maximum price** zuì gāo jiàgé 最高价格; **a maximum temperature** zuìgāo wēndù 最高温度; (greatest in quantity) zuì dà 最大, zuì duō 最多; **the maximum amount of work** zuì dà de gōngzuò liàng 最大的工作量 **2** n **the maximum** (of quantity) zuì dà liàng 最大量; (of space) zuì dà kōngjiān 最大空间; (of speed) zuì gāo sùdù 最高速度 ! Note that the expression the maximum is translated into Chinese as a modifier, which differs according to the noun it modifies.

may vb (when talking about a possibility) kěnéng 可能, yěxǔ 也许; **this may be true** zhè kěnéng shì zhēn de 这可能是真的; **he may have got lost** tā yěxǔ mílù le 他也许迷路了; (when asking for or giving permission) kěyǐ 可以; **may I come in?** wǒ kěyǐ jìnlai ma? 我可以进来吗?; **you may sit down** nǐ kěyǐ zuòxia 你可以坐下

May n wǔyuè 五月

maybe adv dàgài 大概, yěxǔ 也许

mayor n a mayor yíge shìzhǎng 一个市长

me pron wǒ 我; they know me tāmen rènshi wǒ 他们认识我

meal n a meal yídùn fàn 一顿饭

mean 1 vb to mean shì...yìsi 是...意思; what does it mean? zhè shì shénme yìsi? 这是什么意思?; what does this word mean? zhège cí shì shénme yìsi? 这个词是什么意思?; what do you mean? nǐ shì shénme yìsi? 你是什么意思?; (to have as a result) yìwèizhe 意味着; it means giving up my job zhè yìwèizhe fàngqì wǒde gōngzuò 这意味着放弃我的工作; (to intend) I meant to buy a new car wǒ yuánlái dǎsuàn mǎi yíliàng xīn qìchē 我原来打算买一辆新汽车; she didn't mean to upset you tā bú shì gùyì ràng nǐ bù gāoxìng 她不是故意让你不高兴; (to be of much/little importance) her work means a lot to her tāde gōngzuò duì tā hěn zhòngyào 她的工作对她很重要; money doesn't mean much to him qián duì tā bìng bú zhòngyào 钱对他并不重要 **2** adj (British English) (not generous) lìnsè 吝啬, xiǎoqì 小气; (unfriendly) to be mean to someone duì mǒurén bù yǒuhǎo 对某人不友好

meaning n a meaning yìzhǒng yìsi 一种意思, yìzhǒng hányì 一种含义

means n (an instrument) gōngjù 工具; a means of transport yìzhǒng yùnshū gōngjù 一种运输工具; (a way to an end) fāngfǎ 方法; a means of earning money yìzhǒng zhuàn qián de fāngfǎ 一种赚钱的方法

meanwhile adv tóngshí 同时

measles n mázhěn 麻疹

measure vb liàng 量, cèliáng 测量

meat n ròu 肉

mechanic n a mechanic yíge jìgōng 一个技工

medal n a medal yíge jiǎngzhāng 一个奖章, yíge jiǎngpái 一个奖牌; a gold medal yíkuài jīn pái 一块金牌, yíkuài jīnzhì jiǎngzhāng 一块金质奖章

media *n* the media xīnwén méijiè 新闻媒介

medical *adj* yīxué de 医学的; a medical college yíge yīxuéyuàn 一个医学院; to have medical treatment jiēshòu zhìliáo 接受治疗

medicine *n* (*the study*) yīxué 医学; (*a drug*) yào 药; a type of Chinese medicine yìzhǒng zhōngyào 一种中药

Mediterranean *n* Dìzhōnghǎi 地中海

medium *adj* zhōngděng 中等

meet *vb* (*by accident*) yùjiàn 遇见, pèngshang 碰上; she met him on the street tā zài jiē shang yùjiànle tā 她在街上遇见了他; (*by appointment*) jiànmiàn 见面; can we meet next week? wǒmen xià xīngqī jiànmiàn, hǎo ma? 我们下星期见面, 好吗?; (*to become acquainted with*) rènshi 认识, jiéshí 结识; she met him at a wedding tā zài yí hūnlǐ shang rènshile tā 她在一次婚礼上认识了他; (*to come face to face with*) jiàn 见; have you met Tom? nǐ jiànguo Tāngmǔ ma? 你见过汤姆吗?; (*to fetch*) jiē 接; I can come to the station to meet you wǒ kěyǐ lái chēzhàn jiē nǐ 我可以来车站接你; (*to satisfy*) mǎnzú 满足; can this meet your requirements? zhè néng mǎnzú nǐde yāoqiú ma? 这能满足你的要求吗?; (*to have a meeting*) kāihuì 开会; the whole school will meet in the hall this afternoon jīntiān xiàwǔ quán xiào zài lǐtáng kāihuì 今天下午全校在礼堂开会

meeting *n* a meeting yícì huì(yì) 一次会(议)

melon *n* a melon yíge guā 一个瓜

melt *vb* rónghuà 融化; the snow is starting to melt xuě kāishǐ rónghuà le 雪开始融化了; (*cause to melt*) rónghuà 溶化; the salt will melt the ice yán huì shǐ bīng rónghuà 盐会使冰溶化

member *n* a member (*of a party*) yíge dǎngyuán 一个党员; (*of a team*) yíge duìyuán 一个队员; (*of an association*) yíge huìyuán 一个会员; (*of the Congress, Parliament*) yíge yìyuán 一个议员; a member of staff (*in a school*) yíge jiàoyuán 一个教员; (*in a bank, a firm*) yíge zhíyuán 一个职员

memory *n* jìyìlì 记忆力; he's got a good memory tāde jìyìlì hěn hǎo 他的记忆力很好; (*of a person, a place, or time*) huíyì

回忆; a memory of one's childhood duì tóngnián de huíyì 对童年的回忆

mend *vb (to fix)* xiūlǐ 修理; *(by sewing)* féngbǔ 缝补

mental *adj (pertaining to the mind)* jīngshén de 精神的; *(done in the mind)* nǎolì de 脑力的; *mental labour* nǎolì láodòng 脑力劳动; *(relating to a disease of the mind)* jīngshénbìng de 精神病的; *a mental patient* yíge jīngshénbìngrén 一个精神病人; *a mental hospital* yíge jīngshénbìngyuàn 一个精神病院

menu *n a menu* yífèn càidān 一份菜单, yífèn càipǔ 一份菜谱

mess *n a mess* yìtuánzāo 一团糟, luànqībāzāo 乱七八糟; *your room is (in) a mess* nǐde fángjiān luànqībāzāo 你的房间乱七八糟; *to make a mess in the kitchen* bǎ chúfáng nòng de yìtuánzāo 把厨房弄得一团糟

message *n a message (if it's verbal)* yíge kǒuxìn 一个口信; *(if it's written on a piece of paper)* yìzhāng tiáo 一张条; *(a piece of information)* yìtiáo xiāoxi 一条消息

metal *n a type of metal* yìzhǒng jīnshǔ 一种金属

method *n a method* yìzhǒng fāngfǎ 一种方法

metre *(British English)*, **meter** *(US English)* *n a metre* yì mǐ 一米

Mexico *n* Mòxīgē 墨西哥

microphone *n a microphone* yíge màikèfēng 一个麦克风

microwave *n a microwave* yíge wēibōlú 一个微波炉

midday *n* zhèngwǔ 正午, zhōngwǔ 中午; *at midday* zài zhèngwǔ 在正午

middle *n* zhōngjiān 中间; *in the middle of the road* zài mǎlù zhōngjiān 在马路中间; *to be in the middle of cooking a meal* zhèngzài zuò fàn 正在做饭

middle-aged *adj* zhōngnián 中年

midnight *n* wǔyè 午夜; *at midnight* zài wǔyè 在午夜

might *vb (when talking about a possibility)* yěxǔ 也许, kěnéng 可能; *she might be right* tā yěxǔ shì duì de 她也许是对的; *he*

said he might not come tā shuō tā kěnéng bù lái 他说他可能
不来; (when implying something didn't happen) you might have
been late nǐ běnlái huì chídào de 你本来会迟到的; she might
have told us tā běnlái kěyǐ gàosu wǒmen 她本来可以告诉
我们; (when making suggestions) you might like to phone him
nǐ yěxǔ kěyǐ gěi tā dǎ ge diànhuà 你也许可以给他打个电话;
it might be better to wait zuìhǎo děng yi děng 最好等一等

mild adj (in temper and disposition) wēnhé 温和; (of weather)
wēnnuǎn 温暖, nuǎnhuo 暖和; the weather's mild, it's mild
tiānqì hěn nuǎnhuo 天气很暖和

mile n a mile yì yīnglǐ 一英里 ! Note that one mile is 1609
metres.

military adj jūnshì de 军事的

milk 1 n (of a cow) niúnǎi 牛奶; (of a mother) mǔnǎi 母奶 **2** vb
jǐnǎi 挤奶

milkman n a milkman yíge sòng niúnǎi de ren 一个送牛奶的
人

million num one million, a million yìbǎiwàn 一百万; three
million American dollars sānbǎiwàn měiyuán 三百万美元; a
million inhabitants yìbǎiwàn jūmín 一百万居民

mind 1 n tóunǎo 头脑; to have a logical mind yǒu luójí tóunǎo
有逻辑头脑; to make up one's mind to change jobs xià juéxīn
huàn gōngzuò 下决心换工作; to change one's mind gǎibiàn
zhǔyi 改变主意 **2** vb (when expressing an opinion) 'where
shall we go?'—'I don't mind' 'wǒmen qù nǎr?'—'wǒ wúsuǒwèi'
'我们去哪儿?'—'我无所谓'; she doesn't mind the heat tā bù
zàihu rè 她不在乎热; (in polite questions or requests) do you
mind if I smoke? wǒ chōu yān nǐ jièyi ma? 我抽烟你介意吗?;
would you mind turning on the light? qǐng nǐ dǎkāi dēng, hǎo
ma? 请你开灯,好吗?; (to be careful) xiǎoxīn 小心, dāngxīn
当心; mind the steps xiǎoxīn lóutī 小心楼梯; mind you don't
break the plates bié dǎpò pánzi 别打破盘子; (to take care of)
zhàoliào 照料, zhàokàn 照看; to mind a few children zhàoliào
jǐge háizi 照料几个孩子; never mind, she'll
get the next train méiguānxi, tā huì zuò xià yítàng huǒchē 没
关系, 她会坐下一趟火车

mine¹ pron wǒde 我的: the green pen is mine nàzhī lǜ de bǐ shì wǒde 那支绿的笔是我的

mine² n (for extracting minerals from the ground) yíge kuàng 一个矿

miner n a miner yíge kuànggōng 一个矿工

mineral water n a bottle of mineral water yìpíng kuàngquánshuǐ 一瓶矿泉水

minimum 1 adj (lowest) zuì dī 最低; the minimum price zuì dī jiàgé 最低价格; (smallest in quantity) zuì xiǎo 最小, zuì shǎo 最少; the minimum amount of work zuì xiǎo gōngzuò liàng 最小工作量 **2** n the minimum (of quantity) zuì xiǎo liàng 最小量, zuì shǎo liàng 最少量; (of space) zuì xiǎo kōngjiān 最小空间; (of speed) zuì dī sùdù 最低速度 ! Note that the expression the minimum is translated into Chinese as a modifier, which differs according to the noun it modifies.

minister n (in government) bùzhǎng 部长; a minister yíge bùzhǎng 一个部长; the minister for education jiàoyù bùzhǎng 教育部长; (in religion) mùshī 牧师; a minister yíge mùshī 一个牧师

minor adj (small) xiǎo 小; a minor operation yíge xiǎo shǒushù 一个小手术; (not serious) qīng 轻; a minor injury yícì qīng shāng 一次轻伤

minority n (the smaller number) shǎoshù 少数; (in a population) shǎoshù mínzú 少数民族; a minority yíge shǎoshù mínzú 一个少数民族

minus prep (in temperature) língxià 零下; it's minus four outside wàimiàn língxià sì dù 外面零下四度; (in calculation) jiǎn 减; 10 minus 5 is 5 shí jiǎn wǔ děngyú wǔ 十减五等于五

minute n (a minute) yì fēnzhōng 一分钟; wait a minute, please qǐng děng yíhuìr 请等一会儿

mirror n a mirror yímiàn jìngzi 一面镜子

miserable adj (extremely unhappy) tòngkǔ 痛苦; to feel miserable gǎndào tòngkǔ 感到痛苦; (extremely poor) pínkùn 贫困; to have a miserable life guò pínkùn de shēnghuó 过贫困的生活

miss vb (to fail to hit) méi dǎzhòng 没打中; (to fail to see) you can't miss it nǐ bú huì kàn bú dào de 你不会看不到的; (to fail to take) cuòguò 错过; to miss an opportunity cuòguò yíge jīhuì 错过一个机会; (to feel sad not to see) xiǎng(niàn) 想(念); I miss you wǒ xiǎng nǐ 我想你; (other uses) don't miss this film bié cuòguò zhège diànyǐng 别错过这个电影; she missed her plane tā wùle fēijī 她误过了飞机; to miss school quēkè 缺课

Miss n xiǎojie 小姐

missing adj (not to be found) shīzōng 失踪; missing soldiers shīzōng de shìbīng 失踪的士兵; (lacking) quē(shǎo) 缺(少); a dictionary with two pages missing yìběn quēle liǎngyè de cídiǎn 一本缺了两页的词典

mist n wù 雾, wùqì 雾气

mistake n a mistake yíge cuòwù 一个错误; to make a mistake fàn cuòwù 犯错误

mix vb (to put together) hùn 混, huò 和; to mix blue paint with yellow paint bǎ lán yóuqī hé huáng yóuqī hùn zài yìqǐ 把蓝油漆和黄油漆混在一起; he mixed flour and water tā bǎ miàn hé shuǐ huò zài yìqǐ 他把面和水和在一起; (to associate) láiwǎng 来往; to mix with the other students hé biéde xuésheng láiwǎng 和别的学生来往; **mix up** gǎohùn 搞混; to get the two languages mixed up bǎ liǎngzhǒng yǔyán gǎohùn le 把两种语言搞混了; I'm always mixing him up with his brother wǒ zǒngshì bǎ tā hé tā gēge gǎohùn 我总是把他和他哥哥搞混

mixture n a mixture yìzhǒng hùnhéwù 一种混合物

model n (of a train, a car, a building) móxíng 模型; a model yíge móxíng 一个模型; (a fashion) model yíge (shízhuāng) mótèr 一个(时装)模特儿

modern adj xiàndài 现代

mole n a mole (if it's a small and round mark) yíge hēizhì 一个黑痣; (if it's a large mark) yíkuài hēizhì 一块黑痣

moment n a moment yíhuìr 一会儿; please wait a moment qǐng děng yíhuìr 请等一会儿; there's no-one there at the moment xiànzài nàr méi yǒu rén 现在那儿没有人

Monday *n* xīngqīyī 星期一, lǐbàiyī 礼拜一

money *n* qián 钱

monkey *n* a monkey yìzhī hóuzi 一只猴子

month *n* a month yíge yuè 一个月; he'll be back in two months' time tā liǎngge yuè yǐhòu huílai 他两个月以后回来

monument *n* a monument (if it's a pillar, a stone) yízuò jìniànbēi 一座纪念碑; (if it's an object) yíge jìniànwù 一个纪念物

mood *n* (state of emotions) xīnqíng 心情, qíngxù 情绪; to be in a good mood qíngxù hěn hǎo 情绪很好; I'm in a very bad mood wǒde qíngxù bú tài hǎo 我的情绪不太好

moon *n* (the earth's satellite) yuèliàng 月亮; a moon cake yíkuài yuèbǐng 一块月饼; the Moon Festival Zhōngqiūjié 中秋节

moonlight *n* yuèguāng 月光

moral *adj* (conforming to the right or the virtuous) yǒu dàodé de 有道德的; (relating to ethics) dàodéshang de 道德上的

more 1 *det* gèng duō de 更多的; to have more [friends | money | time] yǒu gèng duō de [péngyou | qián | shíjiān] 有更多的 [朋友 | 钱 | 时间]; more...than someone ...bǐ mǒurén duō... 比某人多; I have more work than he does wǒde gōngzuò bǐ tā duō 我的工作比他多; he bought more books than I did tā mǎi de shū bǐ wǒ duō 他买的书比我多; there's no more [bread | milk | money] méi yǒu [miànbāo | niúnǎi | qián] le 没有 [面包 | 牛奶 | 钱] 了; there's more [bread | milk | money] hái yǒu [miànbāo | niúnǎi | qián] 还有 [面包 | 牛奶 | 钱]; would you like more [coffee | wine | vegetables]? nǐ hái yào [kāfēi | jiǔ | cài] ma? 你还要 [咖啡 | 酒 | 菜] 吗？; he bought two more tickets tā yòu mǎile liǎngzhāng piào 他又买了两张票 **2** *pron* please give me a little more qǐng zài gěi wǒ yìxiē 请再给我一些; to cost more gèng guì 更贵; I did more than you wǒ zuò de bǐ nǐ duō 我做的比你多; she spends more of her time studying Chinese now xiànzài tā huā gèng duō de shíjiān xuéxí Hànyǔ 现在她花更多的时间学习汉语

3 adv (when comparing) gèng 更: it's more complicated than that zhè bǐ nàge gèng fùzá 这比那个更复杂; (when talking about time) not...any more búzài... 不再...; he doesn't smoke any more tā búzài chōu yān le 他不再抽烟了 **4 more and more** yuèlái yuè 越来越; more and more people can afford to buy cars yuèlái yuè duō de rén mǎi de qǐ qìchē le 越来越多的人买得起汽车了; more and more expensive yuèlái yuè guì 越来越贵 **5 more or less** huò duō huò shǎo 或多或少 **6 more than** duō 多; there were more than 20 people there nàr yǒu èrshí duō ge rén 那儿有二十多个人

morning n a morning (between dawn and 8 or 9 am) yíge zǎochén 一个早晨; (between dawn and 12:00 noon) yíge shàngwǔ 一个上午; at three o'clock in the morning língchén sān diǎn zhōng 凌晨三点钟

mosquito n a mosquito yíge wénzi 一个蚊子

most 1 det (the majority of) dàduōshù 大多数, dàbùfen 大部分: most schools start next week dàduōshù xuéxiào xiàge xīngqī kāixué 大多数学校下个星期开学; (in quantity) zuì duō 最多; who has the most money? shéide qián zuì duō 谁的钱最多? (in degree) zuì 最; who has the most need of help? shéi zuì xūyào bāngzhù? 谁最需要帮助? **2** pron dàduōshù 大多数, dàbùfen 大部分; most of them are Chinese tāmen dāngzhōng dàduōshù shì Zhōngguórén 他们当中大多数是中国人; he did the most he could tā jìnle zuì dà de nǔlì 他尽了最大的努力 **3** adv zuì 最: the most expensive shop in London Lúndūn zuì guì de shāngdiàn 伦敦最贵的商店; the most beautiful city in China Zhōngguó zuì měilì de chéngshì 中国最美丽的城市 **4 at (the) most** zhìduō 至多, zuì duō 最多

mostly adv dàbùfen 大部分, duōbàn 多半

mother n a mother yíge māma 一个妈妈; (more formal) yíwèi mǔqīn 一位母亲

mother-in-law n (wife's mother) yuèmǔ 岳母; (husband's mother) pópo 婆婆

motor n a motor (a machine) yìtái fādòngjī 一台发动机; (a motor-car) yíliàng jīdòngchē 一辆机动车

motorbike *n* a motorbike yíliàng mótuōchē 一辆摩托车

motorcyclist *n* a motorcyclist yíge qí mótuōchē de rén 一个骑摩托车的人

motorist *n* a motorist yíge kāi qìchē de rén 一个开汽车的人

motor racing *n* qìchē bǐsài 汽车比赛

motorway *n* a motorway yìtiáo gāosù gōnglù 一条高速公路

mountain *n* a mountain yízuò shān 一座山

mountain bike *n* a mountain bike yíliàng shāndì zìxíngchē 一辆山地自行车

mountain climbing *n* dēngshān 登山

mouse *n* a mouse yìzhī lǎoshǔ 一只老鼠, yìzhī hàozi 一只耗子

moustache, mustache *n* a moustache yízuò bāzìhú 一撮八字胡

mouth *n* (of a person or an animal) zuǐ 嘴, kǒu 口; **open your mouth** bǎ kǒu zhāngkāi 把口张开; **it has a big mouth** tāde zuǐ hěn dà 它的嘴很大; (of a river or a volcano) kǒu 口; **the mouth of** [a river | a volcano] [hé | huǒshān] kǒu [河 | 火山] 口

move *vb* (to make a movement) **don't move!** bié dòng! 别动! **the train's starting to move** huǒchē kāishǐ kāidòng 火车开始开动; (to make a movement with) **to move the car** yídòng qìchē 移动汽车; **to move the chair (out of the way)** bǎ yǐzi bānkāi 把椅子搬开; **don't move the camera** bié dòng zhàoxiàngjī 别动照相机; **to move (house)** bānjiā 搬家; **move away** (to live elsewhere) bānzǒu 搬走; (to make a movement away) líkāi 离开; **to move away from the window** líkāi chuānghu 离开窗户; **move back** (in house-moving) bānhuí 搬回; (to step back) hòutuì 后退; **move forward** qiánjìn 前进; **move in** bānjìn 搬进; **he moved in yesterday** tā zuótiān bānjìnqù le 他昨天搬进去了; **move out** bānchū 搬出

moved *adj* **moved to tears** gǎndòng de liú lèi 感动得流泪

movement *n* (a current of action) yùndòng 运动; **a students' movement** yícì xuéshēng yùndòng 一次学生运动; (an act of moving) yídòng 移动, huódòng 活动

movie (*US English*) *n* a movie yíbù diànyǐng 一部电影

movies (*US English*) *n* the movies diànyǐng 电影

movie theatre (*US English*) *n* a movie theatre yíge diànyǐngyuàn 一个电影院

moving *adj (affecting the feelings)* dòngrén 动人, lìng rén gǎndòng 令人感动; *(changing position)* huódòng 活动

mow *vb* gē 割; to mow the grass gē cǎo 割草; to mow the lawn xiūjiǎn cǎopíng 修剪草坪

MP, Member of Parliament *n* an MP yíge yìyuán 一个议员

Mr *n* xiānsheng 先生

Mrs *n* fūrén 夫人, tàitai 太太

much 1 *adv (in comparison)* ...duō ... 多; he is much taller than you tā bǐ nǐ gāo duō le 他比你高多了; her work is much more tiring tāde gōngzuò lèi duō le 她的工作累多了; *(often)* chángcháng 常常, jīngcháng 经常; they don't go out much tāmen bù chángcháng chūqu 他们不常常出去; *(when used with very or so)* hěn 很, fēicháng 非常; he misses her very much tā hěn xiǎngniàn tā 他很想念她 **2** *pron (in questions)* hěn duō 很多; is there much to be done? yǒu hěn duō shì yào zuò ma? 有很多事要做吗?; *(in negative statements)* duō 多; he doesn't eat much tā chī de bù duō 他吃得不多 **3** *det (a lot of)* hěn duō 很多; do you have much work? nǐ yǒu hěn duō gōngzuò ma? 你有很多工作吗?; *(in questions)* hěn duō 很多; we haven't got much time wǒmende shíjiān bù duō le 我们的时间不多了; *(when used with how, very, too, so, or as)* how much money have you got? nǐ yǒu duōshǎo qián? 你有多少钱?; she doesn't eat very much meat tā chī ròu chī de bù duō 她吃肉吃得不多; I spent too much money wǒ huā qián huā de tài duō le 我花钱花得太多了; don't drink so much wine bié hē zhème duō jiǔ 别喝这么多酒; she has as much work as I do tāde gōngzuò hé wǒde yíyàng duō 她的工作和我的一样多

mud *n* ní 泥

mug n a mug yíge bēizi 一个杯子

multiply vb (in arithmetic) chéng 乘; multiply three by five sān chéng wǔ 三乘五; (to increase) zēngjiā 增加; the population has multiplied there nàr rénkǒu zēngjiāle hěn duō 那儿人口增加了很多

mum, Mum (British English) n māma 妈妈

murder 1 n a murder yìqǐ móushā àn 一起谋杀案 **2** vb móushā 谋杀

murderer n a murderer yíge shārénfàn 一个杀人犯

muscle n a muscle yíkuài jīròu 一块肌肉

museum n a museum yíge bówùguǎn 一个博物馆

mushroom n a mushroom yíge mógu 一个蘑菇

music n yīnyuè 音乐

musical instrument n a musical instrument yíjiàn yuèqì 一件乐器

musician n a musician (a person who works with music) yíge yīnyuè gōngzuòzhě 一个音乐工作者; (a person who is famed for working with music) yíge yīnyuèjiā 一个音乐家

Muslim adj Mùsīlín 穆斯林

mussel n a mussel yíge gébèi 一个蛤贝

must vb (when indicating obligation) bìxū 必须, yídìng děi 一定得; you must come on time nǐ yídìng děi zhǔnshí lái 你一定得准时来; she must take the exam in June tā bìxū cānjiā liùyuè de kǎoshì 她必须参加六月的考试; (when indicating necessity) yídìng yào 一定要; you must go to the doctor nǐ yídìng yào qù kàn yīshēng 你一定要去看医生; we mustn't tell anyone wǒmen yídìng bú yào gàosu rènhé rén 我们一定不要告诉任何人; (when assuming something is true) yídìng 一定, hěn kěnéng 很可能; he must be kidding tā yídìng shì zài kāi wánxiào 他一定是在开玩笑; they must have left tāmen hěn kěnéng yǐjīng zǒu le 他们很可能已经走了; (when indicating prohibition, with 'not') bùzhǔn 不准, jìnzhǐ 禁止; cars mustn't be parked in front of the gate mén qián bùzhǔn tíng chē 门前不准停车

mustard *n* jièmo 芥末

mutton *n* yángròu 羊肉

my *det* wǒde 我的; **this is my car** zhè shì wǒde chē 这是我的车; **I broke my leg** wǒ bǎ tuǐ shuāiduàn le 我把腿摔断了! *Note that when talking about parts of the body,* wǒde 我的 *is not used.*

myself *pron (when used as a reflexive pronoun)* zìjǐ 自己; **I didn't hurt myself** wǒ méiyǒu shāngzhe zìjǐ 我没有伤着自己; **I bought myself a new watch** wǒ gěi zìjǐ mǎile yíkuài xīn shǒubiǎo 我给自己买了一块新手表; *(when used for emphasis)* **I told them myself** shì wǒ qīnzì gàosu tāmen de 是我亲自告诉他们的; **I did it all by myself** zhè dōu shì wǒ yíge rén zuò de 这都是我一个人做的

mystery *n* **a mystery** yíge mí 一个迷

Nn

nail *n (for use in attaching, repairing)* dīngzi 钉子; **a nail** yìkē dīngzi 一颗钉子; *(on the fingers or toes)* zhǐjiǎ 指甲; **a nail** yíge zhǐjiǎ 一个指甲

nail polish *n* zhǐjiǎyóu 指甲油

naked *adj (when describing the body)* luǒtǐ de 裸体的, guāngzhe 光着; **naked trees** guāngtūtū de shù 光秃秃的树; **a naked light** yìzhǎn méi yǒu zhào de dēng 一盏没有罩的灯

name *n* **a name** yíge míngzi 一个名字; **what's your name?** nǐ jiào shénme míngzi? 你叫什么名字?; **my name is Louis** wǒ(de) míngzi jiào Lùyìsī 我(的)名字叫路易斯

narrow *adj* zhǎi 窄, xiázhǎi 狭窄

nasty *adj (when referring to a smell)* nánwén 难闻, chòu 臭; *(threatening, dangerous)* xiōngxiǎn 凶险; *(ill natured)* bēibǐ 卑鄙; **nasty weather** huài tiānqì 坏天气

national adj (of a country) guójiā de 国家的; the national team guójiā duì 国家队; (nation-wide) quánguóxìng de 全国性的; a national newspaper quánguóxìng de bàozhǐ 全国性的报纸; national income guómín shōurù 国民收入; national economy guómín jīngjì 国民经济; national anthem guógē 国歌; (referring to a group of people marked by common descent, language, culture, or historical tradition) mínzú de 民族的; national costume mínzú fúzhuāng 民族服装

native adj a native language yìzhǒng mǔyǔ 一种母语; a native Chinese speaker mǔyǔ shì Hànyǔ de rén 母语是汉语的人

natural adj (not made by humans) natural gas tiānránqì 天然气; natural resources zìrán zīyuán 自然资源; (happening in the usual course of things) zìrán 自然; a natural voice shēngyīn zìrán 声音自然; (normal) zhèngcháng 正常; a natural death zhèngcháng sǐwáng 正常死亡

naturally adv (in a natural manner) zìrán 自然; she acted very naturally tā biǎoyǎn de hěn zìrán 她表演得很自然; (of course) dāngrán 当然; he'll naturally be sad when he hears the news tā tīngdào xiāoxi hòu dāngrán huì nánguò 他听到消息后当然会难过

nature n (the external world untouched by human beings) zìránjiè 自然界; dàzìrán 大自然; (inborn mind) běnxìng 本性; (disposition of a person) gèxìng 个性; (kind, sort) zhǒng, lèi 类; mistakes of this nature zhèzhǒng cuòwù 这种错误; (character of a certain matter) xìngzhì 性质; this incident is quite serious in nature zhèjiàn shì de xìngzhì xiāngdāng yánzhòng 这件事的性质相当严重; the two questions are different in nature zhè liǎngge wèntí de xìngzhì bù tóng 这两个问题的性质不同

naughty adj táoqì 淘气, tiáopí 调皮

navy n hǎijūn 海军

navy blue adj zàngqīngsè 藏青色, hǎijūn lán 海军蓝

near 1 prep (in proximity) he lives near us tā zhù zài wǒmen fùjìn 他住在我们附近; (with respect to a goal) the new house is near completion zhèzuò xīn fángzi jiùyào wángóng le 这座新

房子就要完工了 2 adv (close by) jìn 近；they live quite near tāmen zhù de hěn jìn 他们住得很近；(in time) Christmas is drawing near Shèngdànjié kuài dào le 圣诞节快到了 3 adj (close) jìn 近；the school is quite near xuéxiào hěn jìn 学校很近；a near relative yígè jìnqīn 一个近亲；in the near future bùjiǔ 不久, bùjiǔ de jiānglái 不久的将来

nearby adv zài fùjìn 在附近

nearly adv chàbùduō 差不多, jīhū 几乎；I nearly [forgot | gave up | fell asleep] wǒ jīhū [wàng le | fàngqì le | shuìzháo le] 我几乎 [忘了 | 放弃了 | 睡着了]；we're nearly there wǒmen kuài dào nàr le 我们快到那儿了

neat adj (when describing a room, someone's clothing) zhěngjié 整洁；(when describing someone's handwriting) gōngzhěng 工整；(when describing objects that have been arranged) zhěngqí 整齐

necessary adj (when referring to something that must be or happen) bìxū 必须, yǒu bìyào 有必要；it's necessary to tell him immediately bìxū lìjí gàosù tā 必须立即告诉他；(when used with not) búbì 不必；it is not necessary for you to come nǐ búbì lái 你不必来；(indispensable) bìxū 必需；I'll only take the necessary tools wǒ zhǐ dài nàxiē bìxū de gōngjù 我只带那些必需的工具；(unavoidable) bìrán 必然；a necessary outcome yígè bìrán jiéguǒ 一个必然结果；if necessary rúguǒ yǒu bìyào (de huà) 如果有必要(的话)；I'll phone you if necessary rúguǒ yǒu bìyào, wǒ huì gěi nǐ dǎ diànhuà, 如果有必要, 我会给你打电话

neck n bózi 脖子

necklace n a necklace yìtiáo xiàngliàn 一条项链

need vb (used with not to mean not have to) búbì 不必, bù xūyào 不需要；you don't need to ask him nǐ búbì wèn tā 你不必问他；the house doesn't need to be sold zhèzuò fángzi bù xūyào mài 这座房子不需要卖；(to have to or want) xūyào 需要；they'll need to come early tāmen xūyào zǎo lái 他们需要早来；they need [money | help | friends...] tāmen xūyào [qián | bāngzhù | péngyou...] 他们需要 [钱 | 帮助 | 朋友...]；we need to see the doctor wǒmen xūyào kàn yīshēng 我们需要看医生

needle *n* a needle yìgēn zhēn 一根针

negative 1 *adj* (*expressing denial, refusal, or prohibition*) fǒudìng de 否定的; **a negative answer** yíge fǒudìng de huídá 一个否定的回答; (*unconstructive*) xiāojí 消极; (*in mathematics and when referring to an electrical charge*) fù 负 **2** *n* (*a word that expresses denial*) fǒudìngcí 否定词; **a negative** yíge fǒudìngcí 一个否定词; (*in photography*) dǐpiàn 底片; **a negative** yìzhāng dǐpiàn 一张底片

neighbour (*British English*), **neighbor** (*US English*) *n* a neighbour yíge línjū 一个邻居

neither 1 *conj* (*in* neither... *nor* sentences) jì bù... yě bù 既不…也不, jì méi...yě méi 既没…也没; **she speaks neither Chinese nor Japanese** tā jì bú huì shuō Hànyǔ yě bú huì shuō Rìyǔ 她既不会说汉语也不会说日语; **I have neither the time nor the energy to argue with him** wǒ jì méi yǒu shíjiān yě méi yǒu jīnglì gēn tā zhēnglùn 我既没有时间也没有精力跟他争论; **I bought neither fruits nor vegetables** wǒ jì méi mǎi shuǐguǒ yě méi mǎi qīngcài 我既没买水果也没买青菜; (*nor*) yě bù 也不, yě méi 也没: 'I don't agree'—'neither do I' 'wǒ bù tóngyì'—'wǒ yě bù tóngyì' '我不同意'—'我也不同意'; 'I didn't come'—'neither did she' 'wǒ méi lái'—'tā yě méi lái' '我没来'—'她也没来' ! *Note that in sentences using the verb* yǒu 有 *or sentences indicating past events,* (neither*...*) nor*... is translated as* (jì méi*...*) *... 既没…) 也没…2 det* liǎng... dōu bù/méi 两…都 不/没: **neither book is mine** liǎngběn shū dōu bú shì wǒde 两本书都不是我的; **neither girl came** liǎngge nǚháir dōu méi lái 两个女孩儿都没来 **3** *pron* liǎng... dōu bù 两…都不, liǎng... dōu méi 两…都没: **neither of them is coming** tāmen liǎngge dōu bù lái 他们两个都不来; **neither of us has met her** wǒmen liǎngge dōu méi jiànguo tā 我们两个都没见过她 ! *Note that in sentences with the verb* yǒu 有 *or sentences indicating past events, the determiner* neither *and the pronoun* neither *are translated as* liǎng... dōu méi 两…都没

nephew *n* (*brother's son*) zhízi 侄子; **a nephew** yíge zhízi 一个侄子; (*sister's son*) wàisheng 外甥; **a nephew** yíge wàisheng 一个外甥

nerves n shénjīng 神经: to get on someone's nerves shǐ mǒurén xīnfán 使某人心烦

nervous adj (frightened) hàipà 害怕; (anxious) jīnzhāng 紧张; to feel nervous gǎndào jīnzhāng 感到紧张

nest n a nest (for birds) yíge cháo 一个巢, yíge wō 一个窝; (for mice, wasps) yíge wō 一个窝

net n (for fishing) yúwǎng 鱼网; a net yìzhāng yúwǎng 一张鱼网; (in sports) wǎng 网

Netherlands n Hélán 荷兰

network n wǎng 网; a [radio | TV | railway...] network yíge [guǎngbō | diànshì | tiělù...] wǎng 一个 [广播 | 电视 | 铁路...] 网

neutral adj (not siding with either party) zhōnglì 中立; a neutral nation yíge zhōnglì guó 一个中立国; (belonging to neither of two opposites in chemistry or electronics) zhōngxìng 中性

never adv (for future events or actions) jué bù 决不, yǒngyuǎn bù 永远不; I'll never go back again wǒ jué bú huì zài huíqu 我决不会再回去; she'll never forget that day tā yǒngyuǎn bú huì wàngjì nà yì tiān 她永远不会忘记那一天; (for habitual events or actions) cónglái bù 从来不; they never come to see us tāmen cónglái bù lái kàn wǒmen 他们从来不来看我们; (for past events or actions) cónglái méi (yǒu) 从来没(有); she's never been to China tā cónglái méi(yǒu) qùguo Zhōngguó 她从来没(有)去过中国; never in my life have I read such a good novel wǒ cónglái méi(yǒu) kànguo zhème hǎo de xiǎoshuō 我从来没(有)看过这么好的小说

nevertheless adv rán'ér 然而, búguò 不过

new adj xīn 新; a new bike yíliàng xīn zìxíngchē 一辆新自行车

newborn baby n a newborn baby yíge xīnshēng yīng'ér 一个新生婴儿

news n a piece of news yìtiáo xiāoxi 一条消息; have you heard the news? nǐ tīngdào zhètiáo xiāoxi le ma? 你听到这条消息了吗?; (on radio, TV) xīnwén 新闻

newsagent's n (British English) a newsagent's yìjiā bàokān xiāoshòudiàn 一家报刊销售店

newspaper n a newspaper (a sheet) yìzhāng bàozhǐ 一张报纸; (if it consists of more than one sheet) yífèn bàozhǐ 一份报纸

New Year n Xīnnián 新年; **Happy New Year!** Xīnnián Kuàilè! 新年快乐!

New Year's Day, New Year's (US English) n Yuándàn 元旦

New Year's Eve n Xīnnián chúxì 新年除夕

New Zealand n Xīnxīlán 新西兰

next 1 adj (when talking about what is still to come or what followed) xià 下; **I'll take the next train to London** wǒ zuò xià (yi)bān huǒchē qù Lúndūn 我坐下(一)班火车去伦敦; **we chatted while waiting for the next bus** wǒmen yìbiān liáotiān yìbiān děng xià (yi)tàng qìchē 我们一边聊天一边等下(一)趟汽车; **'who's next?'—'I'm next'** 'shéi shì xià yìge?'—'wǒ shì xià yìge' '谁是下一个?'—'我是下一个'; (when talking about future time) **next** [week | month | term] xià [xīngqī | yuè | xuéqī] 下个 [星期 | 月 | 学期]; **next year** míngnián 明年; **next time** xià yìcì 下一次; (when talking about the past) dì'èr 第二; **the next** [day | week | month | year], **we went to Shanghai** dì'èr [tiān | ge xīngqī | ge yuè | nián], wǒmen qùle Shànghǎi 第二 [天 | 个星期 | 个月 | 年], 我们去了上海 **2** adv (in the past) ránhòu 然后, jiēzhe 接着; **what happened next?** ránhòu fāshēngle shénme shì? 然后发生了什么事?; (now) xiàmian 下面, jiēxiàlai 接下来; **what'll we do next?** wǒmen xiàmian zuò shénme? 我们下面做什么?; (in the future) xià (yi)cì 下(一)次; **when will you go to China next?** nǐ xià (yi)cì shénme shíhou qù Zhōngguó? 你下(一)次什么时候去中国? **3 next to** (adjacent to) jǐn'ái 紧挨, jǐnkào 紧靠; (in rank) jǐn cìyú 仅次于

next door adv gébì 隔壁

nice adj (when talking about the weather) hǎo 好; **it's a nice day today** jīntiān tiānqì hěn hǎo 今天天气很好; (kind, friendly) hǎo 好; **a nice girl** yíge hǎo gūniang 一个好姑娘; **to be nice to someone** duì mǒurén hěn hǎo 对某人很好; (pleasant, delightful) lìng rén yúkuài 令人愉快; **we had a nice holiday** wǒmen dùguòle yíge lìng rén yúkuài de jiàqī 我们度过了一个令人愉快的假期

nickname n a nickname (given in contempt) yíge wàihào 一个外号, yíge chuòhào 一个绰号; (given to express affection) yíge àichēng 一个爱称

niece n a niece (brother's daughter) yíge zhínǚ 一个侄女; (sister's daughter) yíge wàishēngnǚ 一个外甥女

night n (as opposed to day) yè 夜; a night yí yè 一夜; I didn't sleep last night wǒ zuótiān yí yè méi shuì 我昨天一夜没睡; he stayed out all night tā yì zhěng yè dōu zài wàimian 他一整夜都在外面; (evening) wǎnshang 晚上; a night yíge wǎnshang 一个晚上; last night zuótiān wǎnshang 昨天晚上; at night zài yè li 在夜里; late at night zài shēnyè 在深夜

nightclub n a nightclub yíge yèzǒnghuì 一个夜总会

nightdress (British English), **nightgown** (US English) n a nightdress yíjiàn shuìyī 一件睡衣

nightmare n a nightmare yíge èmèng 一个恶梦; to have a nightmare zuò yíge èmèng 做一个恶梦

nil n líng 零

nine num jiǔ 九

nineteen num shíjiǔ 十九

nineteenth num (in a series) dìshíjiǔ 第十九; (in dates) the nineteenth of July qīyuè shíjiǔ rì 七月十九日

ninety num jiǔshí 九十

ninth num (in a series) dìjiǔ 第九; (in dates) the ninth of December Shí'èryuè jiǔ rì 十二月九日

no 1 adv (in negative answers) bù 不; 'do you like it?'—'no, I don't' 'nǐ xǐhuan ma?'—'bù, wǒ bù xǐhuan' '你喜欢吗?'—'不, 我不喜欢'; (in a negative response to a negative statement or question) shìde 是的, duì 对; 'is he not coming?'—'no, he is not' 'tā bù lái ma?'—'shìde, tā bù lái' '他不来吗?'—'是的, 他不来'; 'you didn't go, did you?'—'no, I didn't' 'nǐ méi qù, duì ma?'—'duì, wǒ méi qù' '你没去, 对吗?'—'对, 我没去'; no longer bú zài 不再; he no longer smokes tā bú zài chōu yān le 他不再抽烟了 **2** det (not any) méi yǒu 没有; we have no money wǒmen méi yǒu qián 我们没有钱; there are no trains méi yǒu huǒchē 没有火车; it's no problem méi yǒu wèntí 没有问题; (when refusing permission) bùxǔ 不许,jìnzhǐ 禁止; no smoking jìnzhǐ xīyān 禁止吸烟; no talking! bùxǔ jiǎnghuà! 不许讲话!

nobody ▶ no-one

noise n (sound of any kind) xiǎngshēng 响声; (excessively loud or disturbing sound) zàoyīn 噪音

noisy adj cáozá 嘈杂, zàoshēng dà 噪声大

none pron none of yíge yě bù 一个也不, dōu bù 都不; none of [us | you | them...] can speak German [wǒmen | nǐmen | tāmen...] yíge yě bú huì shuō Déyǔ [我们 | 你们 | 他们...] 一个也不会说德语; none of the [books | gifts | clothes...] is mine zhèxiē [shū | lǐwù | yīfu...] dōu bú shì wǒde 这些 [书 | 礼物 | 衣服...] 都不是我的; (when used in sentences with the verb yǒu 有, or in sentences indicating past events or actions) yíge yě méi yǒu 一个也没有, dōu méi yǒu 都没有; none of the girls went to the class nǚháizi yíge yě méiyǒu qù shàngkè 女孩子一个也没有去上课; none of us has his telephone number wǒmen dōu méi yǒu tāde diànhuà hàomǎ 我们都没有他的电话号码; (when referring to something uncountable) yìdiǎnr yě méi yǒu 一点儿也没有; I wanted some bread but there was none left in the house wǒ xiǎng chī miànbāo, kěshì jiā lǐ yìdiǎnr yě méi yǒu le 我想吃面包, 可是家里一点儿也没有了! Note that the measure word gè 个 in yíge yě bù 一个也不 and yíge yě méi yǒu 一个也没有 is replaced by a different measure word, such as jiàn 件 and běn 本, when certain nouns, such as yīfu 衣服 and shū 书, are used.

noodles n miàntiáo 面条

nonsense n húshuō 胡说, fèihuà 废话

noon n zhōngwǔ 中午

no-one pron (also **nobody**)! Note that in sentences with the verb yǒu 有, or in sentences describing past events or actions, the negative méi 没 is used instead of bù 不: (when used as a subject) shéi yě bù 谁也不, méi yǒu rén 没有人; no-one has a

Japanese dictionary shéi yě méi yǒu Rìwén cídiǎn 谁也没有日文词典; no-one tells me anything shéi yě bú gàosu wǒ rènhé shìqing 谁也不告诉我任何事情; no-one saw him méi yǒu rén kànjian tā 没有人看见他; (when used as an object) shéi yě bù 谁也不; I know no-one wǒ shéi yě bú rènshi 我谁也不认识; I saw no-one wǒ shéi yě méi kànjian 我谁也没看见

nor conj ! For translations of nor when used in combination with neither, look at the entry for neither in this dictionary; yě bù 也不; 'I don't like him'—'nor do I' 'wǒ bù xǐhuan tā'—'wǒ yě bù xǐhuan tā' '我不喜欢他'—'我也不喜欢他'; (when used with the verb yǒu 有 or to describe past events or actions) yě méi (yǒu) 也没(有); I don't have any money and nor does he wǒ méi yǒu qián, tā yě méi yǒu qián 我没有钱, 他也没有钱; he didn't come and nor did his wife tā méi(yǒu) lái, tā tàitai yě méi(yǒu) lái 他没(有)来, 他太太也没(有)来

normal adj zhèngcháng 正常

normally adv yìbān 一般, tōngcháng 通常

north 1 n (when talking about the direction) běi 北; (when talking about the region) běifāng 北方, běibù 北部; in the north of China zài Zhōngguó de běifāng 在中国的北方 **2** adv (when talking about the direction) xiàng běi 向北, wǎng běi 往北; to drive north xiàng běi kāi chē 向北开; (when talking about the region) zài...běibiānr 在...北边儿; to live north of Beijing zhù zài Běijīng běibiānr 住在北京北边儿 **3** adj běi 北; to work in north London zài běi Lúndūn gōngzuò 在北伦敦工作

North America n North America Běi Měizhōu 北美洲

northeast n dōngběi 东北

Northern Ireland n Northern Ireland Běi Ài'ěrlán 北爱尔兰

northwest n the northwest xīběi 西北

Norway n Nuówēi 挪威

Norwegian 1 adj Nuówēide 挪威的 **2** n the Norwegians Nuówēirén 挪威人

nose n bízi 鼻子

not 1 *adv* bù 不; **this film is not bad** zhèbù diànyǐng búcuò 这部电影不错; **we are going to go out whether it rains or not** bùguǎn xià bú xià yǔ, wǒmen dōu yào chūqu 不管下不下雨, 我们都要出去; **hasn't he phoned you?** tā hái méi gěi nǐ dǎ diànhuà ma? 他还没给你打电话吗? **2 not at all** (*in no way*) yìdiǎn yě bù 一点也不; **he's not at all worried** tā yìdiǎn yě bù dānxīn 他一点儿也不担心; **'thanks a lot'—'not at all'** 'fēicháng gǎnxiè'—'bú kèqi' '非常感谢'—'不客气'

note 1 *n* (*to remind oneself*) bǐjì 笔记, jìlù 记录: (*a message*) biàntiáo 便条; **a note** yìzhāng biàntiáo 一张便条; **I left you a note** wǒ gěi nǐ liúle yìzhāng biàntiáo 我给你留了一张便条; (*an explanation attached to a text*) zhùshì 注释; **a note** yìtiáo zhùshì 一条注释; (*British English*) (*money*) chāopiào 钞票, zhǐbì 纸币; **a note** yìzhāng chāopiào 一张钞票; **a 50-pound note** yìzhāng wǔshí yīngbàng de zhǐbì 一张五十英镑的纸币 **2** *vb* (*to make a note of*) jìlù 记录. jìxia 记下; (*to notice*) zhùyì 注意

notebook *n* **a notebook** yìběn bǐjìběn 一本笔记本

nothing *pron* **!** *Note that* shénme 什么 *often appears at the beginning of the sentence or after the subject;* shénme (...) yě méiyǒu 什么(...)也没有: **nothing has changed** shénme yě méiyǒu biàn 什么也没有变; **there's nothing left** shénme yě méi le 什么也没有了; **she said nothing** tā shénme yě méiyǒu shuō 她什么也没有说; (*when used with verbs indicating the current state*) shénme... yě bù 什么... 也不; **I know nothing** wǒ shénme yě bù zhīdào 我什么也不知道; **she is interested in nothing** xiàndài de dōngxi tā shénme yě bù gǎn xìngqu 现代的东西她什么也不感兴趣; **he likes nothing** tā shénme yě bù xǐhuan 他什么也不喜欢; **to have nothing to do with** hé...wú guān 和...无关; **to have nothing to do with it** wǒ hé zhèjiàn shì wú guān 我和这件事无关; **it's nothing to do with us** zhèjiàn shì hé wǒmen wú guān 这件事和我们无关

notice 1 *vb* (*to observe*) zhùyì 注意; (*to write or publish a notice of*) tōngzhī 通知 **2** *n* (*an announcement circulated internally*) tōngzhī 通知; **a notice** yífèn tōngzhī 一份通知;

(an announcement to the public) tōnggào 通告, bùgào 布告;
a notice yìzhāng tōnggào 一张通告; (a warning) (yùxiān) ...
tōngzhī (预先) ... 通知; **my landlord gave me a month's notice
to move out** wǒde fángdōng yùxiān yíge yuè tōngzhī wǒ
bānchūqu 我的房东预先一个月通知我搬出去; **the meeting
was cancelled at short notice** huìyì línshí tōngzhī qǔxiāo le
会议临时通知取消了; **don't take any notice of this matter**
bié lǐhuì zhèjiàn shì 别理会这件事

novel n a novel yìběn xiǎoshuō 一本小说

November n shíyīyuè 十一月

now 1 adv (at the present time) xiànzài 现在; **he is in his office
now** tā xiànzài zài bàngōngshì li 他现在在办公室里; **from
now on** cóng xiànzài qǐ 从现在起; (immediately) mǎshàng
马上, lìkè 立刻; **we have to do it now** wǒmen bìxū mǎshàng
zuò zhèjiàn shì 我们必须马上做这件事; **do it right now**
xiànzài mǎshàng zuò 现在马上做 **2 now and again, now
and then** shícháng 时常, chángcháng 常常

nowhere 1 adv (not to any place) nǎr dōu bù 哪儿都不, rènhé
dìfang dōu bù 任何地方都不; **I go nowhere without my dog**
méi yǒu wǒde gǒu wǒ nǎr dōu bú qù 没有我的狗我哪儿都
不去; (in sentences describing past actions) nǎr dōu méi 哪儿
都没 **she went nowhere**
tā rènhé dìfang dōu méi qù 她任何地方都没去 **2** n méi yǒu
dìfang 没有地方; **there is nowhere to sit** méi yǒu dìfang zuò
没有地方坐

nuclear adj (central) héxīn de 核心的, zhōngxīn de 中心的;
(pertaining to the nucleus of an atom) **a nuclear bomb** yìkē
yuánzǐdàn 一颗原子弹; **a nuclear power-station** yízuò
hédiànzhàn 一座核电站; **a nuclear war** yìchǎng hézhànzhēng
一场核战争; **nuclear weapons** héwǔqì 核武器

nuisance n **these flies are a nuisance** zhèxiē cāngying zhēn
tǎoyàn 这些苍蝇真讨厌; **it's a nuisance having to pay in cash**
zhēn máfan, hái děi fù xiànjīn 真麻烦, 还得付现金

numb adj mámù 麻木; **my hands are numb** wǒde shǒu mámù le
我的手麻木了; (anaesthetized) shīqù gǎnjué 失去感觉

number 1 n a number (a figure) yīge shù(zì) 一个数(字); (of a house, a bus, a telephone, a passport) yíge hàomǎ 一个号码; (when talking about quantities) **a number of** yìxiē 一些; **a number of people** yìxiē rén 一些人; **a small number of tourists** wéishǔ bù duō de lǚyóuzhě 为数不多的旅游者; **a large number of new products** dàliàng de xīn chǎnpǐn 大量的新产品 **2** vb (to give a number to) gěi...biānhào 给...编号; **to number the documents** gěi wénjiàn biānhào 给文件编号; (to amount to) zǒngjì 总计

number plate n (British English) a number plate yíge hàomǎpái 一个号码牌

nun n a nun (Christian) yíge xiūnǚ 一个修女; (Buddhist) yíge nígū 一个尼姑

nurse n a nurse yíge hùshi 一个护士

nursery n a nursery yíge tuō'érsuǒ 一个托儿所

nursery school n a nursery school yíge yòu'éryuán 一个幼儿园

nut n a nut (a walnut) yíge hútáo 一个胡桃; (a chestnut) yíge lìzi 一个栗子

nylon n nílóng 尼龙

Oo

oak n (a tree) xiàngshù 橡树; **an oak** yìkē xiàngshù 一棵橡树; (for making furniture, etc.) zuòmù 柞木, xiàngmù 橡木

oar n an oar yìgēn jiǎng 一根桨

obedient adj shùncóng 顺从, gōngshùn 恭顺

obey vb fúcóng 服从, tīngcóng 听从; **to obey someone** fúcóng mǒurén 服从某人; **to obey the law** zūnshǒu fǎlǜ 遵守法律

object 1 n an object (a thing) yíge dōngxi 一个东西; (something on which attention, interest, or emotion is fixed) yíge duìxiàng 一个对象; (an end or goal) yíge mùdì 一个目的; (part of a sentence) yíge bīnyǔ 一个宾语 **2** vb fǎnduì 反对, bú zànchéng 不赞成; **I object to this plan** wǒ fǎnduì zhège jìhuà 我反对这个计划

oblige vb **to be obliged to leave** bèipò líkāi 被迫离开; **to oblige someone to apologize** qiángpò mǒurén dàoqiàn 强迫某人道歉

obtain vb dédào 得到, huòdé 获得

observe vb (to watch attentively) guānchá 观察, kàn 看; (to notice) zhùyì 注意; (to act according to) zūnshǒu 遵守

obvious adj míngxiǎn 明显, xiǎn'éryìjiàn 显而易见

obviously adv xiǎnrán 显然

occasion n (an event) yíge chǎnghé 一个场合; **on special occasions** zài tèshū chǎnghé xia 在特殊场合下; (an opportunity) yíge jīhuì 一个机会

occasionally adv ǒu'ěr 偶尔, ǒurán 偶然

occupy vb (when talking about taking over a piece of land or a place) zhànlǐng 占领, zhànjù 占据; (when talking about taking up space or time) zhànyòng 占用, zhàn 占; **she is occupied in writing a novel** tā zhèng máng yú xiě xiǎoshuō 她正忙于写小说

occur vb (to happen) fāshēng 发生; **a traffic accident has occurred** fāshēngle yíqǐ jiāotōng shìgù 发生了一起交通事故; (to come to mind) **a good idea occurred to me** wǒ xiǎngchūle yíge hǎo zhǔyì 我想出了一个好主意; **it suddenly occurred to him that he had to phone his wife** tā tūrán xiǎngdào tā děi gěi tā tàitai dǎ diànhuà 他突然想到他得给他太太打电话

ocean n hǎiyáng 海洋

o'clock adv diǎn (zhōng) 点(钟); **it's five o'clock now** xiànzài wǔ diǎn (zhōng) 现在五点(钟)

October n shíyuè 十月

octopus n **an octopus** yìtiáo zhāngyú 一条章鱼

oculist n **an oculist** (an eye doctor) yíge yǎnkē yīshēng 一个眼科医生

odd *adj (strange)* qíguài 奇怪, gǔguài 古怪 de 单只的, bù chéngduì de 不成对的; *(when talking about numbers)* **an odd number** yíge jīshù 一个奇数; *(of a house, cinema seat or room)* yíge dānhào 一个单号

odour *(British English)*, **odor** *(US English)* n wèir 味儿; **an odour** yìzhǒng wèir 一种味儿

of *prep* de 的; **the sound of an engine** fādòngjī de shēngyīn 发动机的声音; **in the centre of Beijing** zài Běijīng de shì zhōngxīn 在北京的市中心; **the names of the pupils** xuéshēng de míngzi 学生的名字; *(when talking about quantities)* **!** *Of is usually not translated in this use;* **a kilo of potatoes** yì gōngjīn tǔdòu 一公斤土豆; **a bottle of mineral water** yì píng kuàngquánshuǐ 一瓶矿泉水; *(when talking about a smaller number out of a larger whole)* **six of them** tāmen dāngzhōng de liùge rén 他们当中的六个人; **only three of the students came** xuéshēng zhǐ láile sānge 学生只来了三个; *(when the number or group mentioned is the entire whole)* **!** *Of is usually not translated in this use;* **there were six of them** tāmen yígòng liùge rén 他们一共六个人; **all of us agree** wǒmen dōu tóngyì 我们都同意; *(when talking about cause)* **he died of cancer** tā sǐ yú áizhèng 他死于癌症; *(when talking about the material or substance used)* **the bottle is made of plastic** zhège píngzi shì sùliào zuò de 这个瓶子是塑料做的

off **!** *Frequently off occurs in combinations with verbs, for example: get off, go off, take off, etc. To find the correct translations for this type of verb, look up the separate dictionary entries at get, go, take, etc.* **1** *adv (leaving)* zǒu 走; **I'm off** wǒ yào zǒu le 我要走了; *(going)* qù 去; **they are off to Japan tomorrow** tāmen míngtiān yào qù Rìběn 他们明天要去日本; **where are you off to?** nǐ qù nǎr? 你去哪儿? *(away)* **the coast is a long way off** hǎibiān lí zhèr hěn yuǎn 海边离这儿很远; **Christmas is only a month off** lí Shèngdànjié zhǐyǒu yíge yuè le 离圣诞节只有一个月了; *(free)* **to take a day off** xiūjià yìtiān 休假一天; **today's her day off** jīntiān tā xiūxi 今天她休息; *(not working, switched off)* **the lights are all off** diàndēng quán miè le 电灯全灭了 **2** *adj* **the milk is off** niúnǎi huài le 牛奶坏了

offence (*British English*), **offense** (*US English*) *n* (*a crime*) fànzuì 犯罪, fànfǎ xíngwéi 犯法行为; an offence yìzhǒng fànzuì 一种犯罪; to take offence shēngqì 生气

offend *vb* (*to displease, to make angry*) dézuì 得罪, chùnù 触怒; offend against wéifǎn 违犯; did he offend against the law? tā wéifǎn fǎlǜ le ma? 他违犯法律了吗?

offer *vb* (*if what is offered is money, a job, an opportunity, a glass of wine, etc.*) tígōng 提供, gěi 给; to offer someone a job gěi mǒurén tígōng yíge gōngzuò jīhuì 给某人提供一个工作机会; to offer someone a cup of coffee gěi mǒurén yìbēi kāfēi 给某人一杯咖啡; (*if what is offered is an opinion, an idea, a suggestion, a resignation, etc.*) tíchū 提出; to offer a suggestion tíchū yìtiáo jiànyì 提出一条建议; (*to propose a price*) chūjià 出价; he offered 1000 pounds for the car tā chūjià yìqiān bàng mǎi zhèliàng qìchē 他出价一千镑买这辆汽车; (*to express willingness*) biǎoshì yuànyì 表示愿意; to offer to help the children biǎoshì yuànyì bāngzhù háizi 表示愿意帮助孩子

office *n* an office (*a room*) yíge bàngōngshì 一个办公室; (*a department*) yíge bànshìchù 一个办事处

office block *n* (*British English*) an office block yízuò bàngōnglóu 一座办公楼

officer *n* an officer (*in the government*) yíge guānyuán 一个官员; (*in the army or navy*) yíge jūnguān 一个军官; (*in the police force*) yíge jǐngguān 一个警官

office worker *n* an office worker yíge kēshì rényuán 一个科室人员

official *adj* (*issued or authorized by a public authority*) guānfāng 官方; an official explanation guānfāng de jiěshì 官方的解释; (*pertaining to an office*) official duties gōngwù 公务

often *adv* jīngcháng 经常, chángcháng 常常

oil *n* (*in general*) yóu 油; (*from a mineral deposit*) shíyóu 石油

okay, OK 1 *adj* (*when asking or giving opinions*) kěyǐ 可以; is it okay if I come later? wǒ wǎndiǎnr lái kěyǐ ma? 我晚点儿来

可以吗?; it's okay to invite them kěyǐ yāoqǐng tāmen 可以邀请他们; (when talking about health) to feel okay gǎnjué búcuò 感觉不错; are you okay? nǐ méi shìr ba? 你没事儿吧? **2** adv okay hǎo 好, xíng 行; 'please tell me'—'ok, I'll tell you' 'qǐng gàosu wǒ'—'hǎo, wǒ gàosu nǐ' '请告诉我'—'好, 我告诉你'

old adj (not new) jiù 旧; old clothes jiù yīfu 旧衣服; (not young) lǎo 老; old people lǎo rén 老人; (with a long history) gǔlǎo 古老, lìshǐ yōujiǔ 历史悠久; an old church yízuò gǔlǎo de jiàotáng 一座古老的教堂; (when talking about a person's age) how old are you? (to a child) nǐ jǐsuì le 你几岁了?; (to an older person) nǐ duōdà niánjì le 你多大年纪了?; (to others) nǐ duōshǎo suì le 你多少岁了?; a three-year old girl yíge sān suì de nǚháir 一个三岁的女孩儿; I'm as old as he is wǒ hé tā yíyàng dà 我和他一样大; she's eight years older than her brother tā bǐ tā dìdi dà bā suì 她比她弟弟大八岁; he is the oldest tāde niánlíng zuì dà 他的年龄最大; (previous) that's my old address nà shì wǒ yǐqián de dìzhǐ 那是我以前的地址; in the old days zài guòqù 在过去

old-fashioned adj (when describing attitudes, ideas, clothes) guòshí de 过时的; (when describing people) shǒujiù de 守旧的

olive 1 n an olive yíge gǎnlǎn 一个橄榄 **2** adj gǎnlǎnsè de 橄榄色的

olive oil n gǎnlǎn yóu 橄榄油

Olympics n Àolínpǐkè 奥林匹克

omelette n an omelette yíge jiāndànbǐng 一个煎蛋饼

on ! Frequently on occurs in combinations with verbs, for example: count on, get on, keep on, keep on going, etc. To find the correct translations for this type of verb, look up the separate dictionary entries for count, get, keep, etc. **1** prep (when the prepositional phrase specifies a location) (zài)...shang (在)... 上! Note that when zài...shang 在... 上 occurs at the beginning of the sentence zài 在 is often omitted; the book is on the table shū zài zhuōzi shang 书在桌子上; the hat is on top of the wardrobe màozi zài yīguì dǐng shang 帽子在衣柜顶上; on the shelf there are lots of dictionaries (zài) shūjià shang yǒu hěnduō cídiǎn (在) 书架上有很多词典; **you've got a spot on your nose** (zài) nǐ bízi shang yǒu ge hēidiǎnr (在) 你鼻子上有个黑点儿; *(when the prepositional phrase is a modifier indicating a location)* ...shang ...上; **I like the picture on the wall** wǒ xǐhuan qiáng shang de nàzhāng huà 我喜欢墙上的那张画; **the pen on the desk is not mine** shūzhuō shang de gāngbǐ bú shì wǒde 书桌上的钢笔不是我的; *(when followed by the name of a street)* zài 在; **to live on Park Avenue** zhù zài Gōngyuán Dàjiē 住在公园大街; *(when talking about transport)*; **to travel on the bus** zuò gōnggòng qìchē lǚxíng 坐公共汽车旅行; **I'm on my bike today** wǒ jīntiān qí zìxíngchē 我今天骑自行车; *(about)* guānyú 关于; **it's a book on Africa** zhè shì yìběn guānyú Fēizhōu de shū 这是一本关于非洲的书; **a TV programme on primary school pupils** yíge guānyú xiǎoxuéshēng de diànshì jiémù 一个关于小学生的电视节目; *(when talking about time)*! Note that **on** is usually not translated in this use; **she was born on the sixth of December** tā shí'èryuè liù hào chūshēng 她十二月六号出生; **I'll go there on Saturday** wǒ xīngqīliù qù nàr 我星期六去那儿; *(when talking about the media)* **on television** zài diànshì shang 在电视上; **I saw you on the news** wǒ zài xīnwén jiémù li kànjiànle nǐ 我在新闻节目里看见了你; *(when talking about an ongoing activity)* zài 在; **the workers are on strike** gōngrénmen zài bàgōng 工人们在罢工; **they are on holiday at the moment** tāmen mùqián zài dùjià 他们目前在度假 **2** *adv (when talking about what one wears)* **to have a sweater on** chuānshang yíjiàn máoyī 穿上一件毛衣; **she has make-up on** tā huàle zhuāng 她化了妆; *(working, switched on)* kāizhe 开着; **why are all the lights on?** wèishénme suǒyǒu de dēng dōu kāizhe? 为什么所有的灯都开着?; **the radio was on all evening** zhěngge wǎnshang shōuyīnjī yìzhí kāizhe 整个晚上收音机一直开着; *(showing)* yǎn 演; **what's on?** *(on TV)* diànshì shang yǎn shénme? 电视上演什么?; *(in the cinema)* diànyǐngyuàn yǎn shénme? 电影院演什么?; *(when talking about a starting point)* qǐ 起, kāishǐ 开始; **from Tuesday on** cóng xīngqī'èr qǐ 从星期二起; *(continuously)* **go on** jìxù xiàqu 继续下去; **I kept on asking questions** wǒ búduàn de wèn wèntí 我不断地问问题

once 1 adv (one time) yícì 一次; once a day yì tiān yícì 一天一次; (formerly) cóngqián 从前, céngjīng 曾经; I once studied Japanese wǒ cóngqián xuéguo Rìyǔ 我从前学过日语 **2** conj yídàn...jiù 一旦...就; life will be easier once I've found a job wǒ yídàn zhǎodào gōngzuò, shēnghuó jiù róngyi le 我一旦找到工作, 生活就容易了 **3** at once líkè 立刻, mǎshàng 马上

one 1 num yī 一; one child yíge háizi 一个孩子; one of my colleagues wǒde yíge tóngshì 我的一个同事; one hundred yìbǎi 一百 **2** det (the only) wéiyī 唯一; she's the one person who can help you tā shì wéiyī néngóu bāngzhù nǐ de rén 她是唯一能够帮助你的人; it's the one thing that annoys me zhè shì wéiyī shǐ wǒ fánnǎo de shì 这是唯一使我烦恼的事; (the same) tóngyī 同一; the two birds are flying in one direction liǎngzhī niǎo zài cháo tóngyī fāngxiàng fēi 两只鸟在朝同一方向飞; (a certain) mǒuyī 某一; one [day | evening | morning] mǒuyì [tiān | tiān wǎnshang | tiān shàngwǔ] 某一[天 | 天晚上 | 天上午] **3** pron (when referring to something generally) **!** Note that when one refers to something generally, it is often not translated; I need an umbrella—have you got one? wǒ xūyào yìbǎ yǔsǎn, nǐ yǒu ma? 我需要一把雨伞, 你有吗?; (when referring to a specific person or thing) **!** Note that when the one refers to a specific person or thing, the definite article the is often translated as zhè(yì) 这 (一) or nà(yì) 那 (一) followed by an appropriate measure word. One is often either not translated or a translation used as the noun it refers to; I like this new house but she prefers that old one wǒ xǐhuan zhèzuò xīn fángzi, kěshì tā xǐhuan nàzuò jiù de 我喜欢这座新房子, 可是她喜欢那座旧的; he's the one who helped me tā jiù shì bāngzhù wǒ de nàge rén 他就是帮助我的那个人; which one? (referring to a [book | bus | table]) nǎ [yìběn | yíliàng | yìzhāng] 哪 [一本 | 一辆 | 一张]?; this one (referring to a [book | bus | table]) zhè [yìběn | yíliàng | yìzhāng] 这 [一本 | 一辆 | 一张]; (when used to mean you or people) one must be honest yíge rén yídìng yào chéngshí 一个人一定要诚实; in the room, one can see the sea zài fángjiān li, nǐ kěyǐ kàndào dàhǎi 在房间里, 你可以看到大海 **4** one by one yíge yíge de 一个一个地

one another *pron* hùxiāng 互相, bǐcǐ 彼此; to help one another hùxiāng bāngzhù 互相帮助

oneself *pron* zìjǐ 自己; to hurt oneself shānghài zìjǐ 伤害自己

onion *n* an onion yíge yángcōng 一个洋葱; a spring onion yìkē cōng 一棵葱

only 1 *adv* (merely) búguò 不过, jǐnjǐn 仅仅; it's only a game zhè búguò shì yìchǎng bǐsài 这不过是一场比赛; (not more than) zhǐ 只, cái 才; they've only met once tāmen zhǐ jiànguo yícì(miàn) 他们只见过一次(面) 2 *adj* wéiyī 唯一; she was the only one who didn't speak French tā shì wéiyī bú huì jiǎng Fǎyǔ de rén 她是唯一不会讲法语的人; an only daughter yíge dúshēngnǚ 一个独生女 3 *only just* I've only just [arrived | heard the news | moved house...] wǒ gānggāng [dào | tīngdào zhège xiāoxi | bānjiā...] 我刚刚[到 | 听到这个消息 | 搬家...]

onto *prep* dào...shang 到...上; to jump onto the table tiàodào zhuōzi shang 跳到桌子上

open 1 *vb* to open dǎkāi 开开; to open a letter dǎkāi yìfēng xìn 打开一封信; the door opens very easily mén hěn róngyì dǎkāi 门很容易打开; (when talking about the eyes) zhēngkāi 睁开; to open one's eyes zhēngkāi yǎnjing 睁开眼睛; (when talking about starting business for the day) kāi mén 开门; what time do you open? nǐmen jǐ diǎn kāi mén 你们几点开门; (when talking about beginning a film, a play) kāiyǎn 开演; (when talking about starting a new business) kāi 开; she opened a Chinese restaurant here tā zài zhèr kāile yìjiā Zhōngguó cānguǎn 她在这儿开了一家中国餐馆 2 *adj* (not closed) kāizhe 开着; leave the door open ràng mén kāizhe 让门开着; an open window kāizhe de chuāng 开着的窗; (when talking about the eyes) zhēngzhe 睁着; with open eyes zhēngzhe yǎnjing 睁着眼睛; (public) gōngkāi 公开; an open letter yìfēng gōngkāi xìn 一封公开信; (frank) tǎnshuài 坦率 3 *n* in the open (outside the room) zài shìwài 在室外; (outside in the country or in a field) zài yěwài 在野外

opener *n* an opener yìbǎ qǐzi 一把起子

open-minded adj (free from prejudice) méi yǒu piānjiàn 没有偏见; (ready to receive and consider new ideas) sīxiǎng kāifàng 思想开放

opera n an opera yìbù gējù 一部歌剧

operate vb (to make something work) cāozuò 操作, kāidòng 开动; (to carry out an operation) zuò shǒushù 做手术; **to operate on someone** gěi mǒurén zuò shǒushù 给某人做手术

operation n (when talking about a person running a machine) cāozuò 操作; (when talking about the machine working) yùnzhuǎn 运转; (when talking about a surgical procedure) shǒushù 手术; **an operation** yíge shǒushù 一个手术; **to have an operation** zuò shǒushù 做手术. kāidāo 开刀

operator n an operator (a person running a machine) yíge cāozuò rényuán 一个操作人员; (a person employed to connect calls) yíge diànhuà jiēxiànyuán 一个电话接线员

opinion n an opinion yìzhǒng kànfa 一种看法; (when stating one's view) in my opinion yī wǒ kàn 依我看, wǒ rènwéi 我认为; in my opinion, they're lying wǒ rènwéi tāmen zài sāhuǎng 我认为他们在撒谎

opponent n an opponent (in a physical game or contest) yíge duìshǒu 一个对手; (in an argument or debate) yíge fǎnduìzhě 一个反对者

opportunity n an opportunity yíge jīhuì 一个机会; **take the opportunity** jiè zhège jīhuì 借这个机会, chèn zhège jīhuì 趁这个机会; **to take the opportunity to visit Beijing** jiè cǐ jīhuì fāngwèn Běijīng 借此机会访问北京

oppose vb fǎnduì 反对; **to oppose a plan** fǎnduì yíge jìhuà 反对一个计划; **to be opposed to nuclear weapons** fǎnduì héwǔqì 反对核武器

opposite 1 prep zài...duìmiàn 在... 对面; **she was sitting opposite me** tā zuò zài wǒ duìmiàn 她坐在我对面 2 adj (directly contrary) xiāngfǎn de fāngxiàng 相反的方向; **the opposite direction** xiāngfǎn de fāngxiàng 相反的方向; **my answer is just opposite** wǒde dá'àn zhènghǎo xiāngfǎn 我的答案正好相反; (facing, on the other side) duìmiàn 对面; **he was on the opposite side**

of the street tā zài mǎlù de duìmiàn 他在马路的对面; the opposite sex yì xìng 异性 **4** n (that which is contrary) xiāngfǎn 相反; his view is completely the opposite tāde guāndiǎn wánquán xiāngfǎn 他的观点完全相反; (a word with an opposite meaning) fǎnyìcí 反义词; what is the opposite of 'big'? 'dà' de fǎnyìcí shì shénme? '大'的反义词是什么?

optician n an optician (one who sells glasses) yíge yǎnjìng shāng 一个眼镜商; (one who makes glasses) yíge yǎnjìng zhìzhàozhě 一个眼镜制造者

optimist n an optimist yíge lèguānzhǔyìzhě 一个乐观主义者

optimistic adj lèguān 乐观, lèguānzhǔyì de 乐观主义的

or conj huò(zhě) 或(者), huò(zhě) liǎngcì 一个星期一次或(者)两次; (when offering alternatives) háishì 还是: would you like tea or coffee? nǐ xiǎng hē chá háishì kāfēi? 你想喝茶还是咖啡?; either...or... huòzhě...huòzhě... 或者..., yàome...yàome... 要么...要么...; I'll come either on Saturday or on Sunday wǒ huòzhě xīngqīliù huòzhě xīngqītiān lái 我或者星期六或者星期天来; (otherwise) fǒuzé 否则, bùrán 不然; you have to come or she'll be angry nǐ yídìng děi lái, bùrán tā huì shēngqì 你一定得来, 不然她会生气

oral adj (spoken, not written) kǒutóu de 口头的; (relating to the mouth) kǒubù de 口部的; (taken by mouth) kǒufú de 口服的

orange 1 n an orange yíge júzi 一个橘子, yíge chéngzi 一个橙子 **2** adj júsè 橘色, chéngsè 橙色

orange juice n júzhī 橘汁, chéngzhī 橙汁

orchard n an orchard yíge guǒyuán 一个果园

orchestra n an orchestra yíge guǎnxián yuèduì 一个管弦乐队

order 1 vb (to command) mìnglìng 命令; to order someone to leave mìnglìng mǒurén líkāi 命令某人离开; (to request the supply of) dìnggòu 定购; to order goods from a shop xiàng yíge shāngdiàn dìnggòu huòwù 向一个商店定购货物; (to ask for food in a restaurant) diǎn cài 点菜 **2** n (a command) mìnglìng 命令; an order yíxiàng mìnglìng 一项命令; to give orders xià mìnglìng 下命令; (a sequence) shùnxù 顺序; in the right order àn zhèngquè shùnxù 按正确顺序 **3 in order to** (when used at the beginning of a sentence) wèile 为了; **in order to get a good seat, he arrived very early** wèile dédào yíge hǎo zuòwei, tā hěn zǎo jiù dào le 为了得到一个好座位，他很早就到了; (when used in mid-sentence) yǐbiàn 以便; **he arrived very early in order to get a good seat** tā hěn zǎo jiù dào le, yǐbiàn dédào yíge hǎo zuòwei 他很早就到了，以便得到一个好座位

ordinary adj pǔtōng 普通, yìbān 一般; **an ordinary family** yíge pǔtōng de jiātíng 一个普通的家庭

organ n (the musical instrument) fēngqín 风琴; **an organ** yíjià fēngqín 一架风琴; (a part of the body) qìguān 器官; **an organ** yíge qìguān 一个器官

organization n **an organization** yíge zǔzhī 一个组织

organize vb (to form into a whole) zǔzhī 组织; (to arrange) ānpái 安排

original adj (first) zuìchū de 最初的, zuì zǎo de 最早的; (not copied or derived) yuán(lái) 原(来); **an original manuscript** yífèn yuángǎo 一份原稿; (new, fresh) xīnyíng 新颖, yǒu dúdào jiànjiě de 有独到见解的

ornament n **an ornament** yíge zhuāngshìpǐn 一个装饰品

orphan n **an orphan** yíge gū'ér 一个孤儿

other 1 adj lìng(wài) 另(外), qítā 其他, bié bié 别! Note that qítā 其他 and bié 别 are used with plural nouns, and that lìng(wài) 另(外) can be used with both plural and singular nouns; **not that dress, the other one** búshì nàjiàn yīfu, shì lìng(wài) yíjiàn 不是那件衣服, 是另(外)一件; **they sold the other two cars** tāmen bǎ lìng(wài) sānliàng chē mài le 他们把另(外)三辆车卖了; **to help the other pupils** bāngzhù qítā de xuéshēng 帮助其他的学生; **every other day** měi gé yìtiān 每隔一天 **2** pron **he makes others angry** tā shǐ biéren shēngqì 他使别人生气; **this book is mine, the others are his** zhèběn shū shì wǒde, lìngwài de shū dōu shì tāde 这本书是我的, 另外的书都是他的; **they came in one after the other** tāmen yíge jiē yíge de jìnlai 他们一个接一个地进来

otherwise conj fǒuzé 否则, bùrán 不然; it's not dangerous, otherwise I wouldn't go zhè bù wēixiǎn, fǒuzé wǒ bú huì qù 这不危险, 否则我不会去

otter n an otter yíge (shuǐ)tǎ 一个水獭

ought vb (when saying what should be done or what may happen) yīngdāng 应当, yīnggāi 应该; you ought not to say things like that nǐ bù yīngdāng nàme jiǎnghuà 你不应当那么讲话; they ought to arrive tomorrow tāmen yīnggāi míngtiān dào 他们应该明天到; (when saying that something didn't happen) běn yīng(gāi) 本应(该), běn gāi 本该; he ought to have gone with them tā běn yīng(gāi) gēn tāmen yìqǐ qù 他本应该跟他们一起去

our det wǒmende 我们的; what do you think of our house? nǐ juéde wǒmende fángzi zěnmeyàng? 你觉得我们的房子怎么样?

ours pron wǒmende 我们的; the grey car is ours nàliàng huī chē shì wǒmende 那辆灰车是我们的

ourselves pron (when used as a reflexive pronoun) (wǒmen) zìjǐ (我们)自己; we didn't hurt ourselves wǒmen méiyǒu shānghe zìjǐ 我们没有伤害自己; (when used for emphasis) we will go to buy the train tickets ourselves wǒmen zìjǐ qù mǎi huǒchē piào 我们自己去买火车票; he wants us to solve the problem by ourselves tā yào wǒmen zìjǐ jiějué zhège wèntí 他要我们自己解决这个问题

out ! Often out occurs in combinations with verbs, for example: blow out, come out, find out, give out, etc. To find the correct translations for this type of verb, look up the separate dictionary entries at blow, come, find, give, etc. **1** adv (outside) zài wàibian 在外边; to stay out in the rain dāi zài wàibian yǔ li 呆在外边雨里; she is out in the garden tā zài wàibian huāyuán li 她在外边花园里; (away from the inside) chūqu 出去; to go out chūqu 出去; to come out chūlai 出来; (absent) bú zài 不在, chūqu 出去; he is out tā bú zài 他不在; someone phoned you while you were out nǐ chūqu de shíhou, yǒu rén gěi nǐ dǎ diànhuà 你出去的时候, 有人给你打电话; (not lit, switched off) (xī)miè 灭; all the lights were out suǒyǒu de dēng dōu (xī)miè le 所有的灯都(熄)灭了 **2 out of** to walk out of the building cóng dàlóu li zǒuchūlai 从大楼里走出来; please get out of this room qǐng líkāi zhège fángjiān 请离开这个房间

outdoor *adj* shìwài 室外; an outdoor swimming pool yíge shìwài yóuyǒngchí 一个室外游泳池

outdoors *adv* (*outside the house or building*) zài shìwài 在室外; (*out in the field*) zài yěwài 在野外

outer space *n* wàicéng kōngjiān 外层空间

outside **1** *prep* zài...wàibian 在...外边; to wait outside the school zài xuéxiào wàibian děng 在学校外边等 **2** *adv* let's go outside zánmen chūqu ba 咱们出去吧 **3** *n* the outside wàibian 外边, wàimiàn 外面; the outside of the building dàlóu de wàibian 大楼的外边 **4** *adj* wàibù de 外部的

oven *n* an oven yíge kǎoxiāng 一个烤箱

over ! *Often over occurs in combinations with verbs, for example: get over, move over, etc. To find the correct translations for this type of verb, look up the separate dictionary entries at get, move, etc.* **1** *prep* (*on*) zài...shang 在... 上; to spread a cloth over the table bǎ yíkuài táibù pū zài zhuōzi shang 把一块台布铺在桌子上; (*from one side to the other*) guò 过; to climb over a wall páguò yìdǔ qiáng 爬过一堵墙; come over here guòlai 过来; (*above*) shàngfāng 上方; the picture is over the piano huà zài gāngqín de shàngfāng 画在钢琴的上方; (*above in age, value, quantity, number*) ...yǐshàng ...以上; young people over 18 shíbā suì yǐshàng de niánqīngrén 十八岁以上的年青人; over 20 kilograms èrshí gōngjīn yǐshàng 二十公斤以上; (*during*) we saw them over the weekend wǒmen zhōumò kànjiàn tāmen le 我们周末看见他们了; (*everywhere*) I've looked all over the house for my keys wǒ zài zhèzuò fángzi li, wǒ dàochù dōu zhǎoguo wǒde yàoshi 在这座房子里, 我到处都找过我的钥匙; all over the world shìjiè gèdì 世界各地 **2** *adv* (*finished*) jiéshù 结束, wán 完; the term is over xuéqī jiéshù le 学期结束了; is the film over? diànyǐng wán le ma? 电影完了吗?; (*to one's home*) to ask someone over qǐng mǒurén dào jiā li lái 请某人到家里来; to start all over again chóngxīn kāishǐ 重新开始

overdose n guòliàng yòng yào 过量用药

overtake vb (when talking about driving) chāo chē 超车; (to catch up with) gǎnshàng 赶上

overweight adj chāozhòng 超重

owe vb (to be indebted to) qiàn 欠; to owe money to someone qiàn mǒurén qián 欠某人钱

owl n an owl yìzhī māotóuyīng 一只猫头鹰

own 1 adj zìjǐ de 自己的; your own room nǐ zìjǐ de fángjiān 你自己的房间 **2** pron zìjǐ de 自己的; I didn't use his pencil—I've got my own wǒ méi yòng tāde qiānbǐ—wǒ yǒu wǒ zìjǐ de 我没用他的铅笔—我有我自己的; they have a house of their own tāmen yǒu tāmen zìjǐ de fángzi 他们有他们自己的房子 **3** vb (to possess) yǒu 有, yǒngyǒu 拥有; he owns a shop in town tā zài chénglǐ yǒu yìjiā shāngdiàn 他在城里有一家商店 **4** on one's own dúzì de 独自地, dúlì de 独立地; own up tǎnbái 坦白, chéngrèn 承认; he owned up that he was wrong tā chéngrèn tā cuò le 他承认他错了

owner n an owner yíge zhǔrén 一个主人

ox n an ox yìtóu gōngniú 一头公牛

oxygen n yǎngqì 氧气

oyster n an oyster yíge mǔlì 一个牡蛎

Pp

Pacific n the Pacific Ocean Tàipíngyáng 太平洋

pack 1 vb (to fill a space or container) zhuāng 装; he's packing his clothes into the suitcase tā zhèngzài bǎ tāde yīfu zhuāngjìn xiāngzi li 他正在把他的衣服装进箱子里; I've got to pack my suitcase wǒ děi zhuāng xiāngzi 我得装箱子; (to wrap up and bundle together) bāozhuāng 包装; to pack the china bāozhuāng cíqì 包装瓷器; (to get one's things together and ready to move) **to pack up one's belongings** shōushi zìjǐ de xíngli 收拾自己的行李 **2** n a pack yībāo 一包, yìhé 一盒; **a pack of cigarettes** yìbāo xiāngyān 一包香烟; **a pack of cards** yíhé pūkèpái 一盒扑克牌

package n a package (a bundle) yīkǔn 一捆; (a parcel) yíjiàn bāoguǒ 一件包裹; (a packet) yìbāo 一包

packed adj (with people) jǐmǎn 挤满; **the classroom was packed with students** jiàoshì li jǐmǎnle xuéshēng 教室里挤满了学生; (with things) zhuāngmǎn 装满; **the box is packed with old newspapers** hézi li zhuāngmǎnle jiù bàozhǐ 盒子里装满了旧报纸

packet n a packet yìbāo 一包

page n a page yíyè 一页; **on page six** zài dìliùyè 在第六页

pain n téng 疼; **I've got a pain in my back** wǒ hòubèi téng 我后背疼; **to be in pain** tòngkǔ 痛苦

painful adj (full of pain) téngtòng 疼痛; (distressing) tòngkǔ 痛苦

paint 1 n (for furniture, doors, windows, etc.) yóuqī 油漆 **2** vb (to produce a picture) huà 画; (to apply paint to furniture, doors, windows, etc.) yóu 油

paintbrush n a paintbrush (for producing a picture) yìzhī huàbǐ 一支画笔; (for painting surfaces) yìbǎ shuāzi 一把刷子

painter n a painter (an artist) yíge huàjiā 一个画家; (one whose job is painting surfaces) yíge yóuqījiàng 一个油漆匠

painting n (a picture) huà 画; **a painting** yìfú huà 一幅画; (the activity of painting pictures) huìhuà 绘画

pair n a pair of shoes yìshuāng xié 一双鞋; **a pair of spectacles** yífù yǎnjìng 一副眼镜; **a pair of vases** yíduì huāpíng 一对花瓶

pajamas ▶ pyjamas

Pakistan n Bājīsītǎn 巴基斯坦

palace n gōngdiàn 宫殿, gōng 宫; a palace yíge gōngdiàn 一个宫殿

pale adj (when describing the face) cāngbái 苍白; (when describing the moon) àndàn 暗淡

pancake n a pancake yíge báojiānbǐng 一个薄煎饼

panic vb kōnghuāng 恐慌, jīnghuāng 惊慌

pants n (underwear) (British English) yìtiáo nèikù 一条内裤; (trousers) (US English) yìtiáo kùzi 一条裤子

pantyhose n (US English) jǐnshēnkù 紧身裤

paper n (for writing or drawing on) zhǐ 纸; a piece of paper yìzhāng zhǐ 一张纸; (a newspaper) bàozhǐ 报纸; (a sheet) yìzhāng bàozhǐ 一张报纸; (consisting of more than one sheet) yífèn bàozhǐ 一份报纸

parachuting n tiàosǎn 跳伞

parade n a parade yícì yóuxíng 一次游行

paralysed (British English), **paralyzed** (US English) adj tānhuàn 瘫痪

parcel n a parcel yíge bāoguǒ 一个包裹

parents n fùmǔ 父母

Paris n Paris Bālí 巴黎

park 1 n a park yíge gōngyuán 一个公园 2 vb to park a car tíngchē 停车; to park near the office zài bàngōngshì fùjìn tíngchē 在办公室附近停车

parking lot n (US English) a parking lot yíge tíngchēchǎng 一个停车场

parking meter n a parking meter yíge tíngchē jìshíqì 一个停车计时器

parliament n guóhuì 国会, yìhuì 议会

parrot n a parrot yìzhī yīngwǔ 一只鹦鹉

part a part yíbùfen 一部分; part of the [book | programme | job] [shū | jiémù | gōngzuò] de yíbùfen [书 | 节目 | 工作] 的一部分; (region, area) dìqū 地区; in this part of China zài Zhōngguó de zhè yì dìqū 在中国的这一地区; (for a machine, a car, etc.) língjiàn 零件, bùjiàn 部件; **a part** yíge língjiàn 一个零件; (a role) juésè 角色; **to play the part of Tom** bànyǎn Tāngmǔ de juésè 扮演汤姆的角色

participate vb cānjiā 参加; **to participate in the discussion** cānjiā tǎolùn 参加讨论

particular 1 adj tèbié 特别, tèshū 特殊 **2 in particular** tèbié 特别, yóuqí 尤其

partner n (in a love relationship) yíge bànlǚ 一个伴侣; (in dancing) yíge wǔbàn 一个舞伴; (in sports and games) yíge dádàng 一个搭档; (in business) yíge hézuòzhě 一个合作者

part-time adv fēi quánrì 非全日; **to work part-time** fēi quánrì gōngzuò 非全日工作

party n (a social event) jùhuì 聚会; **a party** yícì jùhuì 一次聚会; (held in the evening) wǎnhuì 晚会; **a birthday party** yícì shēngri wǎnhuì 一次生日晚会; **a political party** yíge zhèngdǎng 一个政党

pass vb (to go through) guò 过, tōngguò 通过; **to let someone pass** ràng mǒurén guòqu 让某人过去; (to go by) lùguò 路过, jīngguò 经过; **to pass the school** lùguò xuéxiào 路过学校; (to overtake) chāoguò 超过, chāoyuè 超越; **to pass a car** chāoguò yíliàng chē 超过一辆车; (to hand) dì 递; **pass me the salt, please** qǐng bǎ yán dìgěi wǒ 请把盐递给我; (to transfer to another person) chuán 传; **to pass the ball to him** bǎ qiú chuángěi tā 把球传给他; **please pass the word to my mother** qǐng bǎ zhège huà chuángěi wǒ māma 请把这个话传给我妈妈; (to spend) yòng 用; **I pass my time** [reading | painting | listening to the radio ...] wǒ bǎ wǒde shíjiān yòng lái [dú shū | huà huà | tīng shōuyīnjī...] 我把我的时间用来 [读书 | 画画 | 听收音机 ...]; (to succeed in an exam) tōngguò 通过; **to pass an exam** tōngguò yícì kǎoshì 通过一次考试; (to succeed in an exam, just barely, and without honours) jígé 及格; **he narrowly passed the test** tā kǎoshì miǎnqiǎng jígé 他考试勉强及格; (to approve) tōngguò 通过, pīzhǔn 批准; **the parliament has passed a new law** yìhuì tōngguòle yíxiàng xīnde fǎlǜ 议会通过了一项新的法律

passage n (a way or a route for going through) tōngdào 通道; a passage yìtiáo tōngdào 一条通道; (a piece of writing) duàn 段; a passage in a book shū zhōng de yíduàn 书中的一段

passenger n a passenger yíge chéngkè 一个乘客

passport n a passport yìběn hùzhào 一本护照

past 1 (in the past guòqù 过去; in the past zài guòqù 在过去 **2** adj guòqù 过去; the past few days guòqù jǐtiān 过去几天 **3** prep (when talking about time) guò 过 **!** Note that when past means after the hour of, it is often not translated: **it's five past four** xiànzài sì diǎn (guò) wǔ fēn 现在四点(过)五分; **it's past midnight** yìjīng guòle wǔyè le 已经过了午夜了; (by) to go past someone cóng mǒurén pángbiān guòqù 从某人旁边过去; **she ran past me** tā cóng wǒ pángbiān pǎoguòqù 她从我旁边跑过去; (beyond) zài ... nàbian 在...那边; **it's just past the traffic lights** jiù zài hónglùdēng nàbian 就在红绿灯那边 **4** adv to go past guòqù 过去; to walk past zǒuguòqù 走过去; to run past pǎoguòqù 跑过去

pasta n pasta Yìdàlì fěn 意大利粉

pastry n (for baking) miànhú 面糊; (a cake) gāodiǎn 糕点; a pastry yíkuài gāodiǎn 一块糕点

patch n (on a garment or a tyre) bǔdīng 补丁; a patch yíkuài bǔdīng 一块补丁; (a plaster for a cut or sore) gāoyào 膏药; a patch yíkuài gāoyào 一块膏药

path n (a narrow way for pedestrians) xiǎodào 小道, lù 路; a path yìtiáo xiǎodào 一条小道; (a route for a thing to move along) guǐdào 轨道; a path yìtiáo guǐdào 一条轨道

patience n nàixīn 耐心; to lose patience with someone duì mǒurén shīqù nàixīn 对某人失去耐心

patient 1 n a patient yíge bìngrén 一个病人 **2** adj nàixīn 耐心

patrol vb xúnluó 巡逻

patrol car n a patrol car yíliàng xúnluó chē 一辆巡逻车

pattern n a pattern (a thing to be copied as in dressmaking, carpentry, etc.) yíge yàngbǎn 一个样板; (a decorative design) yíge shìyàng 一个式样; (a particular disposition of forms and colours) yíge tú'àn 一个图案

pavement n (British English) the pavement rénxíngdào 人行道; (US English) the pavement (a paved road) pūguo de lùmiàn 铺过的路面, pūguo de dàolù 铺过的道路; (a paved surface) pūguo de dìmiàn 铺过的地面

paw n a paw yìzhī zhuǎzi 一只爪子

pay 1 vb to pay fù 付; to pay the bills fù zhàng 付帐; how much did you pay him? nǐ fùgěi tā duōshǎo qián? 你付给他多少钱?; to pay for; to pay for my meal fù wǒde fàn qián 付我的饭钱; my father paid for her education wǒ bàba gòng tā shàngxué 我爸爸供她上学; (when talking about wages) the work doesn't pay very well zhège gōngzuò gōngzī bù gāo 这个工作工资不高; I'm paid eight pounds an hour wǒ měige xiǎoshí zhèng bā bàng qián 我每个小时挣八镑钱; (to give) to pay attention to the teacher zhùyì lǎoshī 注意老师; to pay someone a visit bàifǎng mǒurén 拜访某人; to pay someone a compliment zànyáng mǒurén 赞扬某人 ! Note that when to pay means to give, it is usually not translated. In most cases, the object, such as attention, visit, or compliment, is translated by the verb in Chinese. **2** n gōngzī 工资, xīnshuǐ 薪水; the pay is very good gōngzī hěn hǎo 工资很好; **pay back** (when in debt) chánghuán 偿还; (in gratitude) bàodá 报答

PE, physical education n tǐyù kè 体育课

pea n a pea yìlì wāndòu 一粒豌豆; green peas qīngdòu 青豆

peace n (freedom from war) hépíng 和平; (a state of quiet) píngjìng 平静; (freedom from disturbance) ān'níng 安宁

peach n a peach yíge táozi 一个桃子

peacock n a peacock yìzhī kǒngquè 一只孔雀

peanut n a peanut yílì huāshēng 一粒花生

pear n a pear yíge lí 一个梨

pearl n a pearl yìkē zhēnzhū 一颗珍珠

pebble n a pebble yíge shízi 一个石子, yíge é'luǎnshí 一个鹅卵石

pedestrian n a pedestrian yíge xíngrén 一个行人

pedestrian crossing n a pedestrian crossing yìtiáo rénxíng héngdào 一条人行横道

peel vb (to use one's hands to strip off an outer covering) bāo...pí 剥... 皮; to peel an orange bāo júzi pí 剥橘子皮; (to use a knife to strip off an outer covering) xiāo...pí 削... 皮; to peel an apple xiāo píngguǒ pí 削苹果皮

pen n a pen yìzhī gāngbǐ 一只钢笔

penalty n (punishment) chǔfá 处罚, chéngfá 惩罚; a penalty yíge chǔfá 一个处罚; (in football) diǎnqiú 点球; a penalty yícì diǎnqiú 一次点球

pencil n a pencil yìzhī qiānbǐ 一只铅笔

pencil case n a pencil case yíge qiānbǐhé 一个铅笔盒

pencil sharpener n a pencil sharpener yíge qiānbǐ dāo 一个铅笔刀

penfriend (British English), **penpal** (US English) n a penfriend yíge bǐyǒu 一个笔友

penguin n a penguin yìzhī qǐ'é 一只企鹅

penknife n a penknife yìbǎ xiāobǐdāo 一把削笔刀

pensioner n (a retired person entitled to a pension) yíge tuìxiū de rén 一个退休的人; (a person receiving an allowance for being disabled, widowed, orphaned, etc.) yíge língqǔ fǔxùjīn de rén 一个领取抚恤金的人

people n (in general) rén 人; we met some very nice people wǒmen yùjiànle yìxiē hěn hǎo de rén 我们遇见了一些很好的人; most people don't know what's happened dàduōshù rén bù zhīdào fāshēngle shénme shì 大多数人不知道发生了什么事; (those from a city, from a nation, or of the world) rénmín 人民; the people of the world shìjiè rénmín 世界人民; (a nation, race, tribe, or ethnic group) mínzú 民族; a people yíge mínzú 一个民族

pepper n (the spice) hújiāo 胡椒; (the general term for the vegetable, usually green) qīngjiāo 青椒; (when the colour is *specified*) a [green | red | yellow] **pepper** yíge [qīng | hóng | huáng] jiāo 一个[青 | 红 | 黄]椒

per *prep* měi 每; **per** [person | hour | week...] měi ge [rén | xiǎoshí | xīngqī...] 每个[人 | 小时 | 星期...]

per cent *n* bǎifēn zhī 百分之, %; **30%** bǎifēn zhī sānshí 百分之三十

perfect *adj* (*extremely good*) jí hǎo de 极好的; **to speak perfect Chinese** jiǎng yìkǒu jí hǎo de Hànyǔ 讲一口极好的汉语; (*flawless*) wánměi de 完美的, wúxiá de 无瑕的; **nothing is perfect** méi yǒu dōngxi shì wánměi (wúxiá) de 没有东西是完美(无瑕)的

perform *vb* (*to do*) **to perform an operation** zuò yíge shǒushù 做一个手术; **to perform a task** wánchéng yíxiàng rènwù 完成一项任务; (*to play an instrument in a performance*) yǎnzòu 演奏; **to perform a piece of music** yǎnzòu yìzhī qǔzi 演奏一支曲子; (*to act*) biǎoyǎn 表演; **to perform for the children** wèi háizimen biǎoyǎn 为孩子们表演

perfume *n* (*if it's a liquid*) xiāngshuǐ 香水; **to spray perfume** pēn xiāngshuǐ 喷香水; (*if it's a fragrance*) xiāng wèir 香味儿

perhaps *adv* kěnéng 可能, yěxǔ 也许

period *n* **a period of time** yíduàn shíjiān 一段时间; (*a stage or phase in history*) shíqī 时期; **the period of the Cold War** lěng zhàn shíqī 冷战时期; (*in the course of an event*) qījiān 期间; **in the period of the experiment** zài shíyàn qījiān 在实验期间; (*a full stop*) jùhào 句号; **a period** yíge jùhào 一个句号; (*for women*) yuèjīngqī 月经期; **a period** yícì yuèjīngqī 一次月经期; (*a school lesson*) kè 课; **a period** yìjié kè 一节课

permanent *adj* yǒngjiǔ 永久

permission *n* xǔkě 许可, yǔnxǔ 允许; **to get permission to leave the hospital** dédào chū yuàn de xǔkě 得到出院的许可

person *n* **a person** yíge rén 一个人

personal *adj* (*one's own*) gèrén de 个人的; (*of private concerns*) sīrén de 私人的

personality n (distinctive character) xìnggé 性格, gèxìng 个性; a person with a strong personality yíge xìnggé hěn qiáng de rén 一个性格很强的人

perspire vb chūhàn 出汗

persuade vb quàn 劝, shuōfú 说服; to persuade someone to buy a car quàn mǒurén mǎi yíliàng chē 劝某人买一辆车

pessimist n a pessimist yíge bēiguānzhě 一个悲观者, yíge bēiguānzhǔyìzhě 一个悲观主义者

pessimistic adj bēiguān 悲观, bēiguānzhǔyì de 悲观主义的

pet n a pet yíge chǒngwù 一个宠物

petrol n (British English) qìyóu 汽油; to run out of petrol qìyóu yòngwán le 汽油用完了

petrol station n (British English) a petrol station yíge jiāyóuzhàn 一个加油站

pet shop n a pet shop yíge chǒngwù shāngdiàn 一个宠物商店

phone 1 n a phone yìtái diànhuà 一台电话; the phone's ringing diànhuà xiǎng le 电话响了; to answer the phone jiē diànhuà 接电话; he's on the phone tā zài dǎ diànhuà 他在打电话 **2** vb dǎ diànhuà 打电话; to phone someone gěi mǒurén dǎ diànhuà 给某人打电话

phone book n a phone book yìběn diànhuàbù 一本电话簿

phone booth n a phone booth yíge diànhuàtíng 一个电话亭

phone call n a phone call yíge diànhuà 一个电话; to receive a phone call jiēdào yíge diànhuà 接到一个电话

phone card n a phone card yìzhāng diànhuà cíkǎ 一张电话磁卡

phone number n a phone number yíge diànhuà hàomǎ 一个电话号码

photo n a photo yìzhāng zhàopiàn 一张照片, yìzhāng xiàngpiàn 一张相片

photocopier n a photocopier yìtái fùyìnjī 一台复印机

photocopy 1 *n* a photocopy yífèn fùyìnjiàn 一份复印件
2 *vb* fùyìn

photograph *n* a photograph yìzhāng zhàopiàn 一张照片,
yìzhāng xiàngpiàn 一张相片; to take a photograph of
someone gěi mǒurén zhào yìzhāng xiàng 给某人照一张相

photographer *n* a photographer yíge shèyǐngshī 一个摄影师

physical *adj* (*material*) wùzhì de 物质的; the physical world
wùzhì shìjiè 物质世界; (*pertaining to natural science*) wùlǐ de
物理的; physical changes wùlǐ biànhuà 物理变化; (*bodily*)
shēntǐ de 身体的; physical examinations shēntǐ jiǎnchá 身体
检查

physics *n* wùlǐxué 物理学, wùlǐ 物理

piano *n* a piano yìjià gāngqín 一架钢琴

pick *vb* (*to choose*) tiāoxuǎn 挑选, xuǎnzé 选择; to pick a
number tiāoxuǎn yíge hàomǎ 挑选一个号码; (*to collect*) zhāi
摘, cǎi 采; to pick blackberries zhāi hēiméi 摘黑莓; (*to take*)
ná 拿; to pick a book off the shelf cóng shūjià shang náxia yìběn
shū 从书架上拿下一本书; **pick on** (*to find fault with*) tiāotì
挑剔; (*to single out for something unpleasant*) tiāochūlai pīpíng
挑出来批评; he's always picking on me tā zǒngshì bǎ wǒ
tiāochūlai pīpíng 他总是把我挑出来批评; **pick out** (*to
select*) tiāoxuǎnchu 挑选出; (*to make out, to distinguish*)
biànbiéchu 辨别出; **pick up** (*to lift*) shíqǐ 拾起, jiǎnqǐ 捡起;
to pick the clothes up off the floor bǎ yīfu cóng dì shang
jiǎnqǐlai 把衣服从地上捡起来; to pick a baby up bǎ yíge
háizi bàoqǐlai 把一个孩子抱起来; to pick up the phone náqǐ
diànhuà lai 拿起电话来; (*to collect*) jiē 接; to pick up
passengers jiē chéngkè 接乘客; he's coming to pick me up tā
lái jiē wǒ 他来接我; (*to buy*) mǎi 买; I stopped to pick up some
milk wǒ tíngxiàlai mǎi diǎnr niúnǎi 我停下来买点儿牛奶;
(*to learn*) xuéhuì 学会; to pick up a little German xuéhuì yìdiǎnr
Déyǔ 学会一点儿德语

picnic *n* a picnic yícì yěcān 一次野餐; to go on a picnic qù
yěcān 去野餐

picture n a picture (a painting or a drawing) yìfú huà 一幅画; (a photograph) yìzhāng zhàopiàn 一张照片, yìzhāng xiàngpiàn 一张相片; (an image on a television screen) yíge túxiàng 一个图象; the pictures (cinema) diànyǐng 电影

piece n a piece of paper yìzhāng zhǐ 一张纸; a piece of cheese yíkuài nǎilào 一块奶酪; a piece of string yìgēn xiànshéng 一根线绳; a piece of furniture yíjiàn jiājù 一件家具; a piece of [news | information ...] yìtiáo [xiāoxi | xìnxī ...] 一条 [消息 | 信息...]; a part of a machine) bùjiàn 部件; (a coin) yìngbì 硬币; a 50-pence piece yíge wǔshí biànshì de yìngbì 一个五十便士的硬币; (broken fragments of something thin) suìpiàn 碎片; pieces of broken glass yìxiē suì bōli piàn 一些碎玻璃片; (portion of a solid object) kuài 块; to cut an apple into four pieces bǎ píngguǒ qiēchéng sìkuài 把苹果切成四块

pierce vb (to make a hole through) chuānkǒng 穿孔, chuāndòng 穿洞; (to thrust) cìchuān 刺穿, cìpò 刺破

pig n a pig yìtóu zhū 一头猪

pigeon n a pigeon yìzhī gēzi 一只鸽子

pile n a pile (in a somewhat regular shape) yìluǒ 一摞; a pile of books yìluǒ shū 一摞书; (a heap) yìduī 一堆; a pile of logs yìduī mùtou 一堆木头; (a large amount, lots) xǔduō 许多, dàliàng 大量; piles of [toys | records | money] xǔduō [wánjù | chàngpiàn | qián] 许多 [玩具 | 唱片 | 钱]

pill n (a tablet) a pill yípiàn yào 一片药; (a method of contraception) the pill bìyùnyào 避孕药

pillow n a pillow yíge zhěntou 一个枕头

pilot n a pilot (of an aircraft) yìmíng fēixíngyuán 一名飞行员, yìmíng fēijī jiàshǐyuán 一名飞机驾驶员; (of a ship) yìmíng línghángyuán 一名领航员

pin 1 n a pin yìgēn biézhēn 一根别针, yìgēn dàtóuzhēn 一根大头针 **2** vb yòng zhēn bié 用针别, yòng zhēn dīng 用针钉; to pin the flower to the dress bǎ huā yòng zhēn bié zài yīfu shang 把花用针别在衣服上

pinch vb to pinch níng 拧, niē 捏; he pinched my arm, he

pinched me on the arm tā níng wǒde gēbo 他拧我的胳膊;
(to hurt ... by being too tight) jǐ...tòng 挤...痛; my shoes are
pinching wǒde xié jǐ de wǒ jiǎo tòng 我的鞋挤得我脚痛

pineapple n a pineapple yíge bōluó 一个菠萝

pine tree n a pine tree yìkē sōngshù 一棵松树

pink adj fěnhóngsè de 粉红色的

pint n (the quantity) a pint yì pǐntuō 一品脱! Note that a pint
0.57 l in Britain and 0.47 l in the US; a pint of milk yì pǐntuō
niúnǎi 一品脱牛奶; (British English) (a drink) to go for a pint
qù hē yìbēi (jiǔ) 去喝一杯(酒)

pipe n (for gas, water) guǎnzi 管子; a pipe yìgēn guǎnzi 一根管
子; (for smoking) yāndǒu 烟斗; a pipe yíge yāndǒu 一个烟斗

pirate 1 n a pirate (on the high seas) yíge hǎidào 一个海盗
2 vb (print or publish illegally) dàoyìn 盗印; a pirated edition
yíge dàobǎn 一个盗版

pitch 1 n (British English) a pitch yíge chǎngdì 一个场地; a
football pitch yíge zúqiú chǎng 一个足球场 2 vb (in baseball)
tóuzhì qiú 投掷球

pity 1 n liánmǐn 怜悯, tóngqíng 同情; (when expressing regret)
yíhàn 遗憾, kěxī 可惜; what a pity! zhēn yíhàn! 真遗憾! it's a
pity you can't come kěxī nǐ bù néng lái 可惜你不能来 2 vb
tóngqíng 同情, kělián 可怜

pizza n a pizza yíge (Yìdàlì) bǐsàbǐng 一个(意大利)比萨饼

place 1 n a place yíge dìfang 一个地方; Oxford is a nice place
Niújīn shì yíge hěn hǎo de dìfang 牛津是一个很好的地方;
this place is dirty zhège dìfang hěn zāng 这个地方很脏; (a
home) jiā 家; at Alison's place zài Àilìsēn de jiā 在艾利森的
家; I'd like a place of my own wǒ xiǎng yǒu yíge zìjǐ de jiā 我想
有一个自己的家; (on a bus, at a table) wèizi 位子, zuòwèi
座位; a place yíge zuòwèi 一个座位; is this place free? zhège
wèizi yǒu rén ma? 这个位子有人吗? to take someone's place
zhànle mǒurén de zuòwèi 占了某人的座位; (in a car park, in a
queue) dìfang 地方, wèizhi 位置; a place yíge wèizhi 一个位
置; to find a place to park zhǎo yíge wèizhi tíng chē 找一个位
置停车; (as an employee in a firm, university, hospital) zhíwèi

职位, gōngzuò 工作; **a place** yíge zhíwèi 一个职位; **to get a place at the university** zài dàxué zhǎodào yíge zhíwèi 在大学找到一个职位; (on a course, a team) wèizi 位子; **a place** yíge wèizi 一个位子; **to get a place in a Chinese course** dédào yíge shàng Zhōngwén kè de wèizi 得到一个上中文课的位子; (in a contest) **a place** yíge míngcì 一个名次; **to win first place** dé dìyīmíng 得第一名 **2** vb (to put) fàng 放; (to arrange) ānzhì 安置, ānfàng 安放

plain 1 adj (simple) jiǎndān 简单, pǔsù 朴素; **a plain dress** yíjiàn pǔsù de yīfu 一件朴素的衣服; (not good-looking) bù hǎo kàn 不好看; (ordinary) pǔtōng 普通, píngcháng 平常 **2** n **a plain** yíge píngyuán 一个平原

plait n (British English) **a plait** yìgēn biànzi 一根辫子

plan 1 n (what one intends to do) jìhuà 计划, dǎsuàn 打算; **a plan** yíge jìhuà 一个计划; **we need a plan** wǒmen xūyào yíge jìhuà 我们需要一个计划; (what one has arranged to do) ānpái 安排; **a plan** yíge ānpái 一个安排; **I don't have any plans for tonight** wǒ jīntiān wǎnshang méi yǒu shénme ānpái 我今天晚上没有什么安排 **2** vb (to prepare, to organize) ānpái 安排; **to plan** [a trip | a timetable | a meeting] ānpái [yícì lǚxíng | yíge shíjiānbiǎo | yícì huìyì] 安排 [一次旅行 | 一个时间表 | 一次会议]; (to intend) jìhuà 计划, dǎsuàn 打算; **I'm planning to visit Scotland** wǒ jìhuà fǎngwèn Sūgélán 我计划访问苏格兰

plane n (aeroplane) fēijī 飞机; **a plane** yíjià fēijī 一架飞机; (flat or level surface) píngmiàn 平面; **a plane** yíge píngmiàn 一个平面

planet n **a planet** yíge xíngxīng 一个行星

plant 1 n (member of the vegetable kingdom) zhíwù 植物; **a plant** yìkē zhíwù 一棵植物; (factory) gōngchǎng 工厂; **a plant** yíge gōngchǎng 一个工厂 **2** vb (to put into the ground for growth) zhòng 种, zāi 栽; (to insert) chā 插, ānchā 安插

plaster n (British English) **a plaster** yìtiē gāoyào 一贴膏药

plastic 1 n sùliào 塑料 **2** adj (made of plastic) sùliào de 塑料的; (flexible and malleable) kěsù de 可塑的, yǒu sùxìng de 有塑性的

plate 435 **pleased**

plate *n* a plate yíge pánzi 一个盘子

platform *n* a platform (at a train station) yíge zhàntái 一个站台; on platform 4 zài sìhào zhàntái 在四号站台; (a raised floor for speakers) yíge jiǎngtái 一个讲台; (a raised floor for singers, dancers, musicians) yíge wǔtái 一个舞台

play 1 *vb* (to have fun) wán'r 玩儿; to play with friends gēn péngyoumen yìqǐ wán'r 跟朋友们一起玩儿; to play a trick on someone zhuōnòng mǒurén 捉弄某人; (when talking about sports) to play [football | cricket | basketball | tennis | cards | chess...] [tī zúqiú | dǎ bǎnqiú | dǎ lánqiú | dǎ wǎngqiú | dǎ púkè | xià qí...] [踢足球 | 打板球 | 打篮球 | 打网球 | 打扑克 | 下棋...]; England is playing (against) America Yīnggélán duì zài gēn Měiguó duì bǐsài 英格兰队在跟美国队比赛; (when talking about music) [to play the piano | to play the violin | to play drums] [tán gāngqín | chuī dízi | lā xiǎotíqín | qiāo gǔ...] [弹钢琴 | 吹笛子 | 拉小提琴 | 敲鼓...]; (to put on music, etc.) (bō)fàng (播)放; to play [a video | a CD | a record] [lùxiàng | guāngpán | chàngpiàn] 放 [录相 | 光盘 | 唱片]; (to act in a role, a part, etc.) bànyǎn 扮演; to play the role of someone bànyǎn mǒurén 扮演某人; (to be in a show in the theatre, cinema, etc.) shàngyǎn 上演; the film will soon be playing at this cinema zhèbù diànyǐng jiāng hěn kuài zài zhèjiā diànyǐngyuàn shàngyǎn 这部电影将很快在这家电影院上演 **2** *n* (a drama, a dramatic performance) yìchū xì 一出戏, yìchū jù 一出剧; (a script of a play) yíge jùběn 一个剧本; **play back** to play back a tape dào cídài 倒磁带

player *n* a player (in sports) yíge yùndòngyuán 一个运动员; (in a musical performance) yíge yǎnzòuzhě 一个演奏者, yíge yǎnyuán 一个演员

playground *n* a playground (for children to play in) yíge yóuxì chǎngdì 一个游戏场地; (a field at a school) yíge cāochǎng 一个操场

please *adv* qǐng 请; please come in qǐng jìn 请进; 'more cake?'—'yes please' nǐ hái yào dàngāo ma?'—'hǎo, qǐng zài gěi wǒ yìdiǎnr' '你还要蛋糕吗?'—'好, 请再给我一点儿'

pleased *adj* (happy, delighted) gāoxìng 高兴, yúkuài 愉快; pleased to meet you hěn gāoxìng jiàndào nǐ 很高兴见到你;

(*content, satisfied*) mǎnyì 满意: I was very pleased with myself wǒ duì zìjǐ hěn mǎnyì 我对自己很满意

plenty *pron* to have plenty of [time | money | friends...] yǒu hěn duō [shíjiān | qián | péngyou...] 有很多 [时间 | 钱 | 朋友...]

plot *n* (*a secret plan*) mìmì jìhuà 秘密计划, yīnmóu 阴谋: a plot yíge yīnmóu 一个阴谋; (*the story in a film, a novel, a play*) qíngjié 情节: a plot yíge qíngjié 一个情节

plug *n* a plug (*on an appliance*) yíge chātóu 一个插头; (*in a sink or bath*) yíge sāizi 一个塞子; **plug in** bǎ chātóu chāshang 把插头插上

plum *n* a plum yíge lǐzi 一个李子

plumber *n* a plumber yíge guǎnzigōng 一个管子工

plus *prep* jiā 加: three plus three are six sān jiā sān děngyú liù 三加三等于六

pocket *n* a pocket yíge kǒudài 一个口袋, yíge yīdōu 一个衣兜

pocketbook *n* (*US English*) a pocketbook (*for keeping money*) yíge qiánbāo 一个钱包; (*for taking notes*) yíge xiǎo bǐjìběn 一个小笔记本

pocket money *n* pocket money línghuāqián 零花钱, língyòngqián 零用钱

poem *n* a poem yìshǒu shī 一首诗

point 1 *n* (*a statement in a discussion*) lùndiǎn 论点: a point yíge lùndiǎn 一个论点; to make a point zhèngmíng yíge lùndiǎn 证明一个论点; (*the most important idea*) yàodiǎn 要点: that's not the point nà bú shì yàodiǎn 那不是要点; (*use, purpose*) yòng 用: there's no point in shouting hǎn méi yǒu yòng 喊没有用; (*when talking about time*) to be on the point of [moving | leaving | selling the house] zhèngyào [dòngshēn | líkāi | mài fángzi] de shíhou 正要 [动身 | 离开 | 卖房子] 的时候; (*the sharp end*) jiān 尖: the point of a pencil qiānbǐ jiān 铅笔尖; (*in a contest, a game*) fēn 分: a point yì fēn 一分 **2** *vb* (*to indicate*) zhǐ 指; to point (*one's finger*) at someone (yòng shǒu) zhǐzhe mǒurén (用手) 指着某人; to point at a house zhǐ xiàng yízuò fángzi 指向一座房子; to point the way to the station zhǐdiǎn qù chēzhàn de lù 指点去车站的路; (to aim) to point a gun at someone bǎ qiāng duìzhǔn mǒurén 把枪对准某人; **point out** zhǐchū 指出; to point out his mistakes zhǐchū tāde cuòwù 指出他的错误

poison 1 n (drug) dúyào 毒药; (substance) dúwù 毒物 **2** vb (to kill with poison) dúsǐ 毒死; (to injure with poison) shǐ...zhòngdú 使.. 中毒; to poison someone shǐ mǒurén zhòngdú 使某人中毒; she got food-poisoning tā shíwù zhòngdú 她食物中毒; (to corrupt) dúhài 毒害; to poison young people's minds dúhài niánqīng rén de sīxiǎng 毒害年轻人的思想

pole n a pole yìgēn gān 一根杆

police n the police jǐngchá 警察

policeman n a policeman yíge jǐngchá 一个警察

police station n a police station yíge jǐngchájú 一个警察局

policewoman n a policewoman yíge nǚ jǐngchá 一个女警察

polish vb to polish [shoes | the car | the furniture...] cā [xié | qìchē | jiājù...] 擦 [鞋 | 汽车 | 家具...]

polite adj yǒu lǐmào 有礼貌, kèqi 客气

political adj zhèngzhì de 政治的, zhèngzhì shang de 政治上的

politician n a politician (in a neutral sense) yíge zhèngzhìjiā 一个政治家; (in a negative sense) yíge zhèngkè 一个政客

politics n politics zhèngzhì 政治

pollute vb wūrǎn 污染

pollution n wūrǎn 污染

pond n a pond yíge chítáng 一个池塘

pony n a pony yìpǐ xiǎomǎ 一匹小马

ponytail n a ponytail yìzhǒng mǎwěi fàxíng 一种马尾发型

pool n (a swimming pool) a pool yíge yóuyǒngchí 一个游泳池; (on the ground, the floor) a pool of water yìtān shuǐ 一滩水; (the game) dànzǐxì 弹子戏

poor adj (not wealthy) qióng 穷, pínqióng 贫穷; (not satisfactory) chà 差, bù hǎo 不好; a poor memory bù hǎo de jìyìlì 不好的记忆力; (expressing sympathy) kělián 可怜; the poor boy is very ill zhè kělián de háizi bìng de hěn lìhài 这可怜的孩子病得很厉害

popular adj (prevailing among the people) liúxíng 流行; a popular hobby yìzhǒng hěn liúxíng de shìhào 一种很流行的嗜好; a popular song yìshǒu liúxíng gēqǔ 一首流行歌曲; (enjoying the favour of) shòu...huānyíng 受... 欢迎, shòu...xīhuan 受... 喜欢; a popular writer yíge shòu (rén) huānyíng de zuòjiā 一个受(人)欢迎的作家; to be popular with the girls shòu nǚháizi xīhuan 受女孩子喜欢

population n rénkǒu 人口 ! Note that rénkǒu 人口 is uncountable and does not have a measure word; a population of one million yìbǎiwàn rénkǒu 一百万人口

pork n zhūròu 猪肉

port n a port yíge gǎngkǒu 一个港口

portrait n a portrait yìzhāng huàxiàng 一张画像, yìzhāng xiàoxiàng 一张肖像

Portugal n Pútáoyá 葡萄牙

Portuguese 1 adj Pútáoyá de 葡萄牙的 **2** n (the people) Pútáoyárén 葡萄牙人; (the language) Pútáoyáyǔ 葡萄牙语, Pútáoyáwén 葡萄牙文

position n a position (place occupied) yíge wèizhi 一个位置, yíge fāngwèi 一个方位; (status or place in society) yíge dìwèi 一个地位, yìzhǒng shēnfèn 一种身份; (post or appointment) yíge zhíwèi 一个职位, yíge zhíwù 一个职务; (attitude or ground taken in an argument) yìzhǒng tàidù 一种态度; (situation) yìzhǒng xíngshì 一种形势, yìzhǒng zhuàngkuàng 一种状况; (posture) yìzhǒng zīshì 一种姿势

positive adj (definitely and explicitly laid down) míngquè 明确, quèshí 确实; (beyond possibility of doubt) kěndìng 肯定; (fully convinced) quèxìn 确信; (having a good and constructive attitude) jījí 积极, jiànshèxìng de 建设性的

possibility n a possibility yìzhǒng kěnéng(xìng) 一种可能(性)

possible adj kěnéng 可能; it's possible that it'll rain tomorrow míngtiān kěnéng xiàyǔ 明天可能下雨; as quickly as possible jìn kuài 尽快; please come as quickly as possible qǐng jìn kuài lái 请尽快来

post (British English) **1** n the post (the system) yóuzhèng 邮政; (the letters) yóujiàn 邮件; has the post come yet? yóujiàn lái le ma? 邮件来了吗? **2** vb jì 寄, yóujì 邮寄; to post a letter jì yìfēng xìn 寄一封信

postbox n (British English) a postbox yíge xìnxiāng 一个信箱

postcard n a postcard yìzhāng míngxìnpiàn 一张明信片

postcode n (British English) a postcode yíge yóuzhèng biānmǎ 一个邮政编码

poster n a poster (giving information) yìzhāng zhāotiē 一张招贴, yìzhāng guǎnggào 一张广告; (used as a picture) yìzhāng zhāotiē huà 一张招贴画

postman n (British English) a postman yíge yóudìyuán 一个邮递员

post office n a post office yíge yóujú 一个邮局

postpone vb tuīchí 推迟, yánqī 延期; let's postpone the party until next week zánmen bǎ jùhuì tuīchídào xiàge xīngqī ba 咱们把聚会推迟到下个星期吧; the concert has been postponed yīnyuèhuì yánqī le 音乐会延期了

pot n (a container for making coffee or tea) hú 壶; a pot yíge hú 一个壶; (a container for preserving something) guàn(zi) 罐(子); a pot yíge guànzi 一个罐子; (a saucepan) guō 锅; a pot yíge guō 一个锅

potato n a potato yíge tǔdòu 一个土豆

pottery n táoqì 陶器

pound n (the currency) yīngbàng 英镑; a pound yì (yīng)bàng 一(英)镑; (in weight) bàng 磅; a pound yí bàng 一磅; two pounds of apples liǎng bàng píngguǒ 两磅苹果

pour vb (from a container) dào 倒; to pour milk into a bowl bǎ niúnǎi dàojìn wǎn li 把牛奶倒进碗里; to pour wine for someone gěi mǒurén dào jiǔ 给某人倒酒; (to flow) liú 流, tǎng 淌; the water was pouring into the kitchen shuǐ liújìnle chúfáng 水流进了厨房; (to escape) mào 冒; there is smoke pouring out of the window yǒu yìxiē yān cóng chuānghu li màochūlai 有一些烟从窗户里冒出来; (to rain) xià dà yǔ 下大雨; it's pouring (with rain) zhèngzài xià dà yǔ 正在下大雨; (to enter in large numbers) yǒngjìn 涌进; to pour into the city yǒngjìn chéngshì 涌进城市; (to leave in large numbers) yǒngchū 涌出; to pour out of the stadium yǒngchū tǐyùchǎng 涌出体育场

powder n fěn 粉

power n (control) quánlì 权力; to be in power zhí zhèng 执政, zhǎng quán 掌权; (influence) shìlì 势力; to have great power yǒu hěn dà de shìlì 有很大的势力; (electricity) diàn 电

practical adj (given to action rather than theory) shíjiàn de 实践的; (relating to real existence or action) shíjì de 实际的; (workable) kěxíng de 可行的; (useful) shíyòng de 实用的

practically adv shíjìshang 实际上, shìshíshang 事实上

practise (British English), **practice** (US English) vb (to work at improving a skill) liànxí 练习; to practise [the piano | one's Chinese | a song | playing basketball...] liànxí [gāngqín | Zhōngwén | yìshǒu gē | dǎ lánqiú...] 练习 [钢琴 | 中文 | 一首歌 | 打篮球...]; (to carry out) shíxíng 实行, shíshī 实施; to practise economy shíxíng jiéyuē 实行节约

praise vb biǎoyáng 表扬, zànyáng 赞扬; to praise someone biǎoyáng mǒurén 表扬某人

prawn n (British English) a prawn yìzhī duìxiā 一只对虾

pray vb (in a religious sense) qídǎo 祈祷, dǎogào 祷告; (to hope) (yīnqiè) pànwàng (殷切) 盼望, qíqiú 祈求; they are praying for rain tāmen pànwàngzhe xiàyǔ 他们盼望着下雨

prayer n dǎowén 祷文, dǎogào 祷告

precaution n a precaution yíxiàng yùfáng cuòshī 一项预防措施

precious *adj* bǎoguì 宝贵, zhēnguì 珍贵

precise *adj* jīngquè 精确, zhǔnquè 准确

predict *vb* yùyán 预言, yùgào 预告

prediction *n* yùyán 预言, yùgào 预告

prefer *vb* xǐhuan 喜欢, yuànyì 愿意; to prefer Chinese food to English food xǐhuan Zhōngguó fàn, bù xǐhuan Yīngguó fàn 喜欢中国饭, 不喜欢英国饭 ! Note that in stating a preference for one thing over another, the thing that is less preferred is expressed in a negative phrase in Chinese, as in bù xǐhuan Yīngguó fàn 不喜欢英国饭 above; I'd prefer to phone wǒ yuànyì dǎ diànhuà 我愿意打电话

pregnant *adj* huáiyùn 怀孕; she's become pregnant tā huáiyùn le 她怀孕了

prejudice *n* a prejudice (against someone or something) yìzhǒng piānjiàn 一种偏见; (in favour of someone or something) yìzhǒng piān'ài 一种偏爱; he has [a prejudice against | a prejudice in favour of] Japanese wine tā duì Rìběn jiǔ yǒu [yìzhǒng piānjiàn | yìzhǒng piān'ài] 对日本酒有 [一种偏见 | 一种偏爱]

prepare *vb* (to get something or someone ready) shǐ...zuòhǎo zhǔnbèi 使...做好准备; to prepare pupils for an exam shǐ xuéshēng wèi kǎoshì zuòhǎo zhǔnbèi 使学生为考试做好准备, (to get ready) zhǔnbèi 准备; to prepare for [an exam | a trip | a party...] zhǔnbèi [yícì kǎoshì | yícì lǚxíng | yícì jùhuì...] 准备 [一次考试 | 一次旅行 | 一次聚会...]

prepared *adj* (willing) yuànyì 愿意; to be prepared to wait yuànyì děng 愿意等; (ready) zuòhǎo zhǔnbèi 做好准备; to be prepared for an exam wèi kǎoshì zuòhǎo zhǔnbèi 为考试做好准备

prescription *n* a prescription yíge chùfāng 一个处方, yíge yàofāng 一个药方

present 1 *n* (a gift) lǐwù 礼物, lǐpǐn 礼品; a present yíge lǐwù 一个礼物; to give someone a present sònggěi mǒurén yíge lǐwù 送给某人一个礼物; (now) the present xiànzài 现在, mùqián 目前; I'm staying here at present mùqián wǒ dāi zài zhèr 目前我呆在这儿 **2** adj (in a place) to be present (at a formal event) chūxí 出席, dàochǎng 到场; to be present at the meeting chūxí huìyì 出席会议; (in an informal situation) he was not present then dāngshí tā bú zài 当时他不在; (now under consideration) mùqián de 目前的, xiànzài de 现在的; the present situation mùqián de xíngshì 目前的形势 **3** vb (to give as a gift) zèngsòng 赠送; to give a book to him zèngsòng gěi tā yìběn shū 赠送给他一本书; (to give as an award) fāgěi 发给, jǐyǔ 给予; to present a gold medal to someone fāgěi mǒurén yíkuài jīnzhì jiǎngpái 发给某人一块金质奖牌; (to give to someone who is one's senior) xiàngěi 献给; a girl presented the hero with a bunch of flowers yíge gūniang xiàngěi nàge yīngxióng yìshù huā 一个姑娘献给那个英雄一束花; (to introduce formally or to introduce on radio or TV) jièshào 介绍; may I present Mr.Wang to you? qǐng yúnxǔ wǒ bǎ Wáng xiānsheng jièshào gěi nín 请允许我把王先生介绍给您; (to hand something to someone formally) dìjiāo 递交; to present a programme jièshào yíge jiémù 介绍一个节目; (to hand something to someone formally) dìjiāo 递交; to present a report to the committee xiàng wěiyuánhuì dìjiāo yífèn bàogào 向委员会递交一份报告; (to put forward) tíchū 提出; to present a proposal to the government xiàng zhèngfǔ tíchū yíge jiànyì 向政府提出一个建议; (to put on a drama, a play) shàngyǎn 上演; when will the play be presented? zhège huàjù shénme shíhou shàngyǎn? 这个话剧什么时候上演?

president n a president (of a country) yíge zǒngtǒng 一个总统; (of an association or a board) yíge huìzhǎng 一个会长; (of a university) yíge xiàozhǎng 一个校长; (of a college) yíge yuànzhǎng 一个院长

press 1 vb (with the hand) àn 按; to press the button àn diànniǔ 按电钮; (to compress) yā 压; (to urge strongly) dūncù 敦促; to press him to change his mind dūncù tā gǎibiàn zhǔyì 敦促他改变主意 **2** n the press xīnwénjiè 新闻界

pressure n yālì 压力; to put pressure on someone xiàng mǒurén shījiā yālì 向某人施加压力

pretend vb jiǎzhuāng 假装; he's pretending to be annoyed tā jiǎzhuāng shēngqì le 他假装生气了

pretty 1 adj piàoliang 漂亮, měilì 美丽; (when talking about music or voice) yōuměi 优美, hǎotīng 好听 **2** adv xiāngdāng 相当, tǐng 挺; that's pretty good nà xiāngdāng hǎo 那相当好

prevent vb (to keep from happening) fángzhǐ 防止, bìmiǎn 避免; to prevent a war fángzhǐ zhànzhēng 防止战争; (to stop or hinder) zǔzhǐ, zhìzhǐ 阻止, 制止; to prevent someone from [working | smoking | going out...] zǔzhǐ mǒurén [gōngzuò | xīyān | chūqù...] 阻止某人 [工作 | 吸烟 | 出去...]; (make unable) shǐ...bù néng 使...不能; the noise prevented him from sleeping zàoyīn shǐ tā bù néng shuìjiào 噪音使他不能睡觉

previous adj the previous [night | year | headmaster] qián [yíge wǎnshang | yìnián | yíge xiàozhǎng] 前 [一个晚上 | 一年 | 一个校长]; previous problems yǐqián de wèntí 以前的问题

price n (the amount for which a thing is bought or sold) jiàqián 价钱, jiàgé 价格; (the cost one suffers in order to gain something) dàijià 代价

pride n jiāo'ào 骄傲, zìháo 自豪; (self-respect) zìzūnxīn 自尊心

priest n a priest (protestant) yíge mùshī 一个牧师; (Roman Catholic) yíge shénfù 一个神父

primary school n a primary school yìsuǒ xiǎoxué 一所小学

primary school teacher n a primary school teacher yíge xiǎoxué jiàoshī 一个小学教师

prime minister n a prime minister yíwèi shǒuxiàng 一位首相

prince n a prince yíge wángzǐ 一个王子

princess n a princess yíge gōngzhǔ 一个公主

principal n a principal yíge xiàozhǎng 一个校长

print 1 vb (to impress) yìn 印, yìnshuā 印刷; to print a book yìn yìběn shū 印一本书; (from a photographic negative) xǐ 洗, xǐyìn 洗印; to print photographs xǐ zhàopiàn 洗照片 **2** n (of a photo) a print yìzhāng zhàopiàn 一张照片; (of a finger) a print yíge shǒuyìn 一个手印; (of a foot) a print yíge jiǎoyìn 一个脚印

priority n a priority (something given special attention) yíge zhòngdiǎn 一个重点; (the privilege of preferential treatment) yíge yōuxiānquán 一个优先权

prison n a prison yísuǒ jiānyù 一所监狱; to put someone in prison bǎ mǒurén guānjìn jiānyù 把某人关进监狱

prisoner n a prisoner (one confined in prison) yíge fànrén 一个犯人; (a captive) yíge qiúfàn 一个囚犯; (a captive) yíge fúlǔ 一个俘虏; to be taken prisoner bèi fúlǔ le 被俘虏了

private 1 adj (personal) sīrén de 私人的, gèrén de 个人的; my private life wǒde sīrén shēnghuó 我的私人生活; (independent) sīlì 私立; a private school yísuǒ sīlì xuéxiào 一所私立学校; (not owned by the state) sīyǒu 私有; private property sīyǒu cáichǎn 私有财产; (not run by the state) sīyíng 私营; private industry sīyíng gōngyè 私营工业 2 in private sīxià 私下, mìmì 秘密

prize n a prize yíge jiǎng(pǐn) 一个奖(品)

probably adv hěn kěnéng 可能, dàgài 大概

problem n a problem yíge wèntí 一个问题

process n a process yíge guòchéng 一个过程; to be in the process of writing a letter zhèngzài xiě yìfēng xìn 正在写一封信

produce 1 vb (to make) shēngchǎn 生产, zhìzào 制造; (to bring about) chǎnshēng 产生, yǐnqǐ 引起; to produce good results chǎnshēng hǎo de jiéguǒ 产生好的结果; (to create) to produce a film shèzhì yíbù diànyǐng 摄制一部电影; to produce a play páiyǎn yìchū xì 排演一出戏 2 n produce chǎnpǐn 产品

product n a product (a thing produced) yíge chǎnpǐn 一个产品; (a result) yíge jiéguǒ 一个结果

production n (of food, cars, clothes, etc.) shēngchǎn 生产; (of a film) shèzhì 摄制, pāishè 拍摄; (of a play) yǎnchū 演出

profession n a profession yìzhǒng zhíyè 一种职业

professional adj (pertaining to a profession) zhuānyè de 专业的; professional knowledge zhuānyè zhīshi 专业知识; (not *amateur*) zhíyè de 职业的; **a professional athlete** yíge zhíyè yùndòngyuán 一个职业运动员

professor n a professor yíwèi jiàoshòu 一位教授

profit n a profit (*benefit*) yíge yìchù 一个益处; (*advantage*) yíge hǎochù 一个好处; (*capital gain*) yìfēn lìrùn 一份利润

program 1 n (*for a computer*) chéngxù 程序; **a program** yíge chéngxù 一个程序; (*US English*) ▶ **programme** 2 vb (*a computer*) biān chéngxù 编程序; (*a concert, a show, a radio or TV broadcast*) ānpái jiémù 安排节目

programme (*British English*), **program** (*US English*) n (*on radio, TV*) jiémù 节目; **a programme** yíge jiémù 一个节目; **a programme about China** yíge guānyú Zhōngguó de jiémù 一个关于中国的节目; (*for a play, a concert*) jiémùdān 节目单; **a programme** yìzhāng jiémùdān 一张节目单; (*for a conference, a course*) ānpái 安排; **the programme of the conference** huìyì de ānpái 会议的安排

progress n (*forward movement*) qiánjìn 前进; (*advance to something better or higher in development*) jìnbù 进步; **to make progress** jìnbù 进步

project n a project (*for study or research*) yíge kètí 一个课题; (*in construction*) yíxiàng gōngchéng 一项工程; (*a scheme*) yíxiàng guīhuà 一项规划, yíge jìhuà 一个计划

promise 1 vb dāyìng 答应, yǔnnuò 允诺; **to promise to** [come | repay a loan | say nothing] dāyìng [lái | huán dàikuǎn | shénme yě bù shuō] 答应[来 | 还贷款 | 什么也不说] 2 n a promise yíge nuòyán 一个诺言, yíge yǔnnuò 一个允诺; [to keep | to break] one's promise [zūnshǒu | bù zūnshǒu] nuòyán [遵守 | 不遵守] 诺言

pronounce vb (*to articulate*) fā...de yīn 发...的音, niàn 念; **how do you pronounce this character?** nǐ zěnme fā zhège zì de yīn? 你怎么发这个字的音?

proof n zhèngmíng 证明, zhèngjù 证据

properly adv (*in an appropriate manner*) shìdàng de 适当地, qiàdàng de 恰当地; (*strictly*) yángé de 严格地

property n (something that is owned) cáichǎn 财产; (house that is owned) fángchǎn 房产; (land that is owned) dìchǎn 地产

protect vb (to guard) bǎohù 保护; to protect oneself bǎohù zìjǐ 保护自己; (to defend) bǎowèi 保卫

protest vb (to make a declaration against) kàngyì 抗议, fǎnduì 反对; (assert formally) duànyán 断言, biǎoshì 表示; he protested his innocence tā duànyán zìjǐ wúzuì 他断言自己 无罪

protester n a protester yíge kàngyìzhě 一个抗议者

proud adj jiāo'ào 骄傲, zìháo 自豪; she's proud of herself tā wèi zìjǐ gǎndào jiāo'ào 她为自己感到骄傲

prove vb zhèngmíng 证明, zhèngshí 证实

provide vb tígòng 提供; to provide meals tígòng fàn 提供饭; to provide a transport service tígòng jiāotōng fúwù 提供交通 服务

provided conj jiǎrú 假如; I'll lend you my car provided you pay me jiǎrú nǐ fù gěi wǒ qián, wǒ jiù bǎ chē jiè gěi nǐ 假如你 付给我钱, 我就把车借给你 ! Note that the clause introduced by jiǎrú 假如 comes before the main clause and jiù 就 is often used after the subject in the main clause.

psychiatrist n a psychiatrist yíge jīngshénbìng yīshēng 一个 精神病医生

psychologist n a psychologist (one who does research) yíge xīnlǐxuéjiā 一个心理学家; (one who sees patients) yíge xīnlǐ yīshēng 一个心理医生

pub n (British English) a pub yíge jiǔguǎn(r) 一个酒馆(儿)

public 1 n the public gōngzhòng 公众, mínzhòng 民众 **2** adj (open to all) gōngkāi 公开; a public library yíge gōnggòng túshūguǎn 一个公共图书馆; (used by all) gōngyòng 公用; a public telephone yíge gōngyòng diànhuà 一个公用电话; (known to all) gōngkāi 公开; to make their relationship public bǎ tāmende guānxi gōngkāi 把他们的关系公开 **3 in public** gōngkāi 公开, dāngzhòng 当众

public holiday *n* a public holiday yíge gōngdìng jiàrì 一个公定假日

public transport *n* gōnggòng jiāotōng 公共交通

pudding *n* a pudding yíge bùdīng 一个布丁; *(general term for a dessert)* *(British English)* yíge tiánshí 一个甜食

puddle *n* a puddle yíge xiǎo shuǐkēng 一个小水坑

pull *vb* *(to move something toward oneself)* lā 拉; to pull on a rope lā yìgēn shéngzi 拉一根绳子; *(if there is a means to facilitate the action, such as wheels or rollers, or if it's a person walking)* lā 拉; to pull the piano into the sitting room bǎ gāngqín lā dào kètīng li 把钢琴拉到客厅里; to pull someone away from the door bǎ mǒurén cóng ménkǒu lāzǒu 把某人从门口拉走; *(if there is no means to facilitate the pulling action)* tuō 拖; to pull the dead body out of the river bǎ shītǐ cóng hé li tuōchūlái 把尸体从河里拖出来; the demonstrators were pulled away by the policeman shìwēizhě bèi jǐngchá tuōzǒu le 示威者被警察拖走了; *(to extract something that is fixed)* bá 拔; to pull [a tooth | a nail | the weeds] bá [yìkē yá | yíge dīngzi | cǎo] 拔[一颗牙 | 一个钉子 | 草]; to pull a face *(British English)* zuò guǐliǎnr 做鬼脸儿; **pull down** *(to knock down)* chāidiào 拆掉; *(to lower)* jiàngdī 降低; **pull out** to pull out a tooth báchū yìkē yá 拔出一棵牙; **pull up** *(to stop)* tíngxià 停下; *(to remove)* to pull up the weeds bá cǎo 拔草; to pull up one's socks bǎ wàzi lāqǐlái 把袜子拉起来

pullover *n* a pullover yíjiàn tàoshān 一件套衫

pump *n* *(for moving or raising fluids)* bèng 泵; a pump yíge bèng 一个泵; *(for transferring air)* a bicycle pump yíge dǎqìtǒng 一个打气筒; **pump up** dǎ qì 打气

pumpkin *n* a pumpkin yíge nánguā 一个南瓜

punch *vb* yòng quán dǎ 用拳打; she punched him in the face tā yòng quán dǎ tāde liǎn 她用拳打他的脸

puncture *n* a puncture yíge cìkǒng 一个刺孔

punish *vb* chǔfá 处罚, chéngfá 惩罚

pupil *n* a pupil yíge xuésheng 一个学生

puppet n a puppet yīgè mù'ǒu 一个木偶

puppy n a puppy yìzhī xiǎogǒu 一只小狗

pure adj (unmixed and untainted) chún 纯; pure gold chún jīn 纯金; (clean) chúnjìng 纯净, jiéjìng 洁净; pure air chúnjìng de kōngqì 纯净的空气; (free from bad taste, bad ideas, evil thinking) chúnjié 纯洁; pure love chúnjié de àiqíng 纯洁的爱情; (sheer) wánquán 完全 chúncuì 纯粹; it's pure nonsense zhè wánquán shì húshuōbādào 这完全是胡说八道; (when talking about the use of a language) chúnzhèng 纯正; a pure Beijing accent chúnzhèng de Běijīng kǒuyīn 纯正的北京口音

purple adj zǐsè de 紫色的

purpose 1 n a purpose (intention) yīgè yìtú 一个意图; (aim) yīgè mùdì 一个目的; (a useful function) yīgè yòngchù 一个用处 2 on purpose gùyì 故意; you did it on purpose! nǐ shì gùyì zhèyàng zuò de! 你是故意这样做的!

purse n (for money) qiánbāo 钱包; a purse yīgè qiánbāo 一个钱包; (US English) (a handbag) shǒutíbāo 手提包; a purse yīgè shǒutíbāo 一个手提包

push vb (press or move forward by pressure) tuī 推; to push a car tuī chē 推车; to push someone down the stairs bǎ mǒurén tuīxià lóutī 把某人推下楼梯; don't push her too hard bié cuī tā tài jǐn 别催她太紧; (sell) fànmài 贩卖; to push drugs fànmài dúpǐn 贩卖毒品

pushchair n (British English) a pushchair yīgè yīnghái tuīchē 一个婴孩推车

pusher n a pusher (a drug seller) yīgè fàn dú de rén 一个贩毒的人

put vb (to place or to add) fàng 放; to put the book on the table bǎ shū fàng zài zhuōzi shang 把书放在桌子上; don't put sugar in my coffee bié wǎng wǒde kāfēi li fàng táng 别往我的咖啡里放糖; (to raise) tíchū 提出; to put a question to him xiàng tā tíchū yīgè wèntí 向他提出一个问题; (to cause to be in a position or state) to put someone in prison bǎ mǒurén guānjìn jiānyù 把某人关进监狱; to put someone in a bad mood shǐ mǒurén xīnqíng bù hǎo 使某人心情不好; **put away** (to pack up) shōuqǐlai 收起来; put your tools away bǎ nǐde gōngjù shōuqǐlai 把你的工具收起来; (to put into a proper or desirable place) fànghǎo 放好; to put the money away bǎ qián fànghǎo 把钱放好; **put back** (to return to its place) fànghuí 放回; to put the book back on the shelf bǎ shū fànghuí shūjià 把书放回书架; (to change the time) to put the clock back bǎ zhōngbiǎo wǎng huí bō 把钟表往回拨; **put down** (to lay down) fàngxia 放下; put the knife down! bǎ dāo fàngxià! 把刀放下; (when phoning) guàduàn 挂断; to put the phone down guàduàn diànhuà 挂断电话; (British English) (to give a lethal injection) to gěi...zhùshè yàopǐn shǐ tā ānlè sǐqù 给…注射药品使它安乐死去; our dog had to be put down zhǐhǎo gěi wǒmende gǒu zhùshè yàopǐn shǐ tā ānlè sǐqù 只好给我们的狗注射药品使它安乐死去; (to write down) xiěxia 写下; please put your name down on this paper qǐng zài zhèzhāng zhǐ shang xiěxia nǐde míngzi 请在这张纸上写下你的名字; **put forward** (to propose) tíchū 提出; to put forward a suggestion tíchū yíge jiànyì 提出一个建议; (to change the time) to put the clocks forward bǎ biǎo wǎng qián bō 把表往前拨; **put off** (to delay) tuīchí 推迟; to put off the meeting till next week bǎ huìyì tuīchí dào xiàge xīngqī 把会议推迟到下个星期; (to switch off) guānshang 关上; **put on** (if it's clothes, shoes, socks) chuānshang 穿上; to put jeans on chuānshang niúzǎikù 穿上牛仔裤; (if it's a hat, gloves, glasses, a scarf) dàishang 戴上; to put on one's watch dàishang shǒubiǎo 戴上手表; (to switch on) dǎkāi 打开; to put the heating on bǎ nuǎnqì dǎkāi 把暖气打开; to put a CD on fàngqǐ yìzhāng guāngpán 放上一张光盘; to put on weight zēngjiā tǐzhòng 增加体重; (to organize, to produce) shàngyǎn 上演; to put on a play shàngyǎn yìchū xì 上演一出戏; **put out** (to extinguish) xīmiè 熄灭; to put out a cigarette mièdiào yānjuǎnr 灭掉烟卷儿; (to switch off) guāndiào 关掉; to put out the lights bǎ dēng guāndiào 把灯关掉; **put up** (to raise) jǔqǐ 举起; táiqǐ 抬起; to put up one's hand jǔqǐ shǒu 举起手; to put a sign up guàqǐ yíge zhāopái 挂起一个招牌; (to erect) dāqǐ 搭起; to put up a tent dāqǐ yíge zhàngpeng 搭起一个帐篷; (British English) (to raise) tígāo 提高; to put the rent up tígāo fángzū 提高房租;

(to give someone a place to stay) to put someone up gěi mǒurén tígōng zhùchù 给某人提供住处; put up with rěnshòu 忍受, róngrěn 容忍

puzzle *n* a puzzle *(a riddle)* yíge míyǔ 一个谜语; *(a question)* yíge nántí 一个难题; *(a bewildering situation)* yíge mí 一个谜 *(a jigsaw puzzle)* yíge pīnbǎn wánjù 一个拼板玩具

pyjamas *n* shuìyī 睡衣; *(if it's trousers only)* shuìkù 睡裤

Qq

qualified *adj (having the right qualifications)* yǒu zīgé de 有资格的; *(competent and fit)* shèngrèn 胜任

quality *n (grade of goodness)* zhìliàng 质量; *(attribute)* pǐnzhì 品质; *(characteristic)* tèxìng 特性

quantity *n* liàng 量, shùliàng 数量; a [small | large] quantity of oil [shǎo | dà] liàng de yóu [少 | 大] 量的油; large quantity of bananas dà liàng de xiāngjiāo 大量的香蕉

quarrel 1 *n* a quarrel yícì zhēngchǎo 一次争吵, yícì chǎojià 一次吵架; **2** *vb* zhēngchǎo 争吵, chǎojià 吵架; to quarrel with someone gēn mǒurén zhēngchǎo 跟某人争吵

quarter 1 *n* a quarter of an hour yí kè zhōng 一刻钟; to divide the tomatoes in quarters bǎ xīhóngshì fēnchéng sì fēn 把西红柿分成四份 **2** *pron (when talking about quantities, numbers)* a quarter sìfēn zhī yī 四分之一; a quarter of the population can't read sìfēn zhī yí de rénkǒu bù shí zì 四分之一的人口不识字; *(when talking about time)* a quarter yí kè (zhōng) 一刻(钟), shíwǔ fēn (zhōng) 十五分(钟); an hour and a quarter yì xiǎoshí (líng) yí kè zhōng 一小时(零)一刻钟; it's a quarter past five wǔ diǎn shíwǔ (fēn) 五点十五(分)
! *Note that when talking about a point of time, zhong 钟 is not used.*

quay *n* a quay yíge mǎtou 一个码头

queen *n* a queen yíge nǚwáng 一个女王

question 1 *n* a question yíge wèntí 一个问题; to ask someone a question wèn mǒurén yíge wèntí 问某一个问题; to answer a question huídá yíge wèntí 回答一个问题 **2** *vb* (to put questions to) xúnwèn 询问, xùnwèn 讯问; (when handling a suspect or a criminal) shěnwèn 审问

queue (British English) **1** *n* a queue yìtiáo duì 一条队; to join the queue cānjiā pái duì 参加排队; to jump the queue chāduì 插队, bú àn cìxù pái duì 不按次序排队, jiāsāir 加塞儿 **2** *vb* pái duì 排队

quick *adj* kuài 快, xùnsù 迅速; a quick answer yíge hěn kuài de dáfù 一个很快的答复; it's quicker to go by train zuò huǒchē qù gèng kuài 坐火车去更快; it's the quickest way [to get to London | to save money | to make friends] zhè shì [qù Lúndūn | shěng qián | jiāo péngyou] de zuì kuài fāngfǎ 这是 [去伦敦 | 省钱 | 交朋友] 的最快方法

quickly *adv* kuài 快, hěn kuài de 很快地

quiet 1 *adj* (silent) jìng 静, ānjìng 安静; to keep quiet bǎochí ānjìng 保持安静; be quiet! ānjìng! 安静!; (not talkative) wénjìng 文静; (calm) píngjìng 平静, níngjìng 宁静; a quiet little village yíge níngjìng de xiǎo cūnzhuāng 一个宁静的小村庄 **2** *n* ānjìng 安静, píngjìng 平静; quiet please! qǐng ānjìng! 请安静!

quietly *adv* to speak quietly qīngshēng de jiǎnghuà 轻声地讲话; [to sit there | to read newspapers | to drink tea] quietly jìngjìng de [zuò zài nàr | kàn bào | hē chá] 静静地 [坐在那儿 | 看报 | 喝茶]

quit *vb* (to resign) cí zhí 辞职, (US English) (to give up) to quit [smoking | drinking | taking drugs] jiè [yān | jiǔ | dú] 戒 [烟 | 酒 | 毒]; to quit school tuìxué 退学

quite *adv* (rather) xiāngdāng 相当, tǐng 挺; I quite like Chinese food wǒ tǐng xǐhuan Zhōngguó fàn 我挺喜欢中国饭; she earns quite a lot of money tā zhèng de qián xiāngdāng duō 她挣的钱相当多; (completely) wánquán 完全, shífēn 十分; I'm

not quite ready yet wǒ hái méi wánquán zhǔnbèihǎo 我还没
完全准备好; you're quite right nǐ wánquán duì 你完全对;
I'm not quite sure what he does wǒ bù shífēn qīngchu tā zuò
shénme 我不十分清楚他做什么

quiz *n* a quiz yícì wèndá bǐsài 一次问答比赛

Rr

rabbit *n* a rabbit yìzhī tùzi 一只兔子

rabies *n* kuángquǎnbìng 狂犬病

race 1 *n* (a contest) bǐsài 比赛; a race yícì bǐsài 一次比赛; to
have a race jìnxíng yícì bǐsài 进行一次比赛; (for horse-racing)
the races sàimǎ 赛马; (a group of people) rénzhǒng 人种,
zhǒngzú 种族; a race yígè rénzhǒng 一个人种 **2** *vb* (to
compete with) gēn...bǐsài 跟...比赛; to race (against) someone
gēn mǒurén bǐsài 跟某人比赛; I'll race you to the car wǒ gēn
nǐ pǎo dào nàliàng qìchē 我跟你比赛, 看谁
先跑到那辆汽车; (to take part in a contest) cānjiā bǐsài 参加
比赛

racehorse *n* a racehorse yìpǐ bǐsài yòng de mǎ 一匹比赛用
的马

racetrack *n* a racetrack yìtiáo pǎodào 一条跑道 (for cars)
yìtiáo (sài)chēdào 一条(赛)车道

racism *n* zhǒngzú zhǔyì 种族主义, zhǒngzú qíshì 种族歧视

racket, racquet *n* a racket yígè pāizi 一个拍子, yígè qiúpāi
一个球拍

radiator *n* a radiator (for heating) yígè nuǎnqì 一个暖气

radio *n* a radio yìtái shōuyīnjī 一台收音机; on the radio zài
guǎngbō li 在广播里

radio station *n* a radio station yígè (guǎngbō) diàntái 一个
(广播)电台

rage n kuángnù 狂怒, dànù 大怒; to fly into a rage bórán dànù 勃然大怒

raid vb xíjī 袭击; to raid a bank xíjī yìjiā yínháng 袭击一家银行; the police raided the building jǐngchá xíjīle nàzuò dàlóu 警察袭击了那座大楼

rail n (for holding on to) fúshǒu 扶手, lángān 栏杆; a rail yíge fúshǒu 一个扶手; (for trains) rails tiěguǐ 铁轨, tiělù 铁路

railway (British English), **railroad** (US English) n (a track) tiělù 铁路, tiědào 铁道; a railway yìtiáo tiělù 一条铁路; (the rail system) the railway tiělù xìtǒng 铁路系统

railway line n (British English) a railway line yìtiáo tiělùxiàn 一条铁路线

railway station n (British English) a railway station yíge huǒchēzhàn 一个火车站

rain 1 n yǔ 雨; to stand in the rain zhàn zài yǔ zhōng 站在雨中
2 vb xiàyǔ 下雨; it's raining zhèngzài xiàyǔ 正在下雨

rainbow n a rainbow yídào cǎihóng 一道彩虹

raincoat n a raincoat yíjiàn yǔyī 一件雨衣

raise vb (to lift) jǔqǐ 举起, táiqǐ 抬起; (to increase) tígāo 提高; to raise prices tígāo jiàqián 提高价钱; to raise one's voice tígāo shēngyīn 提高声音; (to bring up, as an issue or question) tíchū 提出; to raise a question tíchū yíge wèntí 提出一个问题; (to bring up, as a child) fúyǎng 抚养; to raise children fúyǎng háizi 抚养孩子

range n (variation between limits) fúdù 幅度; a range yíge fúdù 一个幅度; the range of increase in temperature qìwēn shēnggāo de fúdù 气温升高的幅度; (scope) fànwéi 范围; a range yíge fànwéi 一个范围; your range of choices nǐ kěyǐ xuǎnzé de fànwéi 你可以选择的范围; (of mountains) shānmài 山脉; a mountain range yíge shānmài 一个山脉; (for cooking) a range yíge lúzào 一个炉灶

rare adj (not common) hǎnjiàn 罕见, xīyǒu 稀有; (very slightly cooked) bàn shú de 半熟的

rarely adv hěn shǎo 很少, nándé 难得

rasher n (British English) a rasher (of bacon) yípiàn xiánròu 一片咸肉

raspberry n a raspberry yíge mùméi 一个木莓

rat n a rat yìzhī lǎoshǔ 一只老鼠, yìzhī hàozi 一只耗子

rather adv (when saying what one would prefer) I'd rather [leave | stay here | read the paper...] wǒ níngyuàn [zǒu | dāizài zhèr | kàn bàozhǐ...] 我宁愿 [走 | 呆在这儿 | 看报纸...]; I'd rather you go with me wǒ dào xiwàng nǐ hé wǒ yíqǐ qù 我倒希望你和我一起去; I'd rather go than stay here wǒ xiǎng zǒu, bù xiǎng dāi zài zhèr 我想走, 不想呆在这儿; (quite) xiāngdāng 相当, tǐng 挺; I think he's rather nice wǒ rènwéi tā xiāngdāng hǎo 我认为他相当好

raw adj (uncooked) shēng 生; raw fish shēng yú 生鱼; (not manufactured) raw materials yuán cáiliào 原材料

razor n a razor yìbǎ guāliǎndāo 一把刮脸刀, yìbǎ guāhúdāo 一把刮胡刀

razor blade n a razor blade yíge dāopiàn 一个刀片

reach vb (to arrive at) dàodá 到达; they reached the school at midnight tāmen bànyè dàodá xuéxiào 他们半夜到达学校; (to be delivered to) the letter never reached me wǒ cónglái jiù méi shōudào nàfēng xìn 我从来就没收到那封信; (by stretching) gòu 够; I can't reach the shelf wǒ gòu bù zháo shūjià 我够不着书架; (to come to) to reach an agreement dáchéng yíge xiéyì 达成一个协议; (to contact) gēn...liánxì 跟... 联系; you can reach me at this number nǐ kěyǐ dǎ zhège diànhuà hàomǎ gēn wǒ liánxì 你可以打这个电话号码跟我联系; **reach out** shēnchū 伸出; to reach out one's hand shēnchū shǒu 伸出手

react vb fǎnyìng 反应; the audience reacted warmly to his speech tīngzhòng duì tāde jiǎnghuà fǎnyìng rèliè 听众对他的讲话反应热烈

read vb (to look at and comprehend) kàn 看, dú 读; to read the newspaper kàn bào 看报; (to read aloud) niàn 念, dú 读; she is reading a story to her children tā zài gěi tāde háizi niàn yíge gùshi 她在给她的孩子念一个故事; (to study) xuéxí 学习; she's reading medicine at a university tā zài yìsuǒ dàxué xuéxí yīxué 她在一所大学学习医学; (understand by reading) kàndǒng 看懂; can you read Chinese? nǐ kàn de dǒng Zhōngwén ma? 你看得懂中文吗? read out to read out the names niàn míngzi 念名字; read through tōngdú 通读, cóng tóu dú dào wěi 从头读到尾

reading n (the action of reading) yuèdú 阅读, dúshū 读书; (material for reading) yuèdú cáiliào 阅读材料

ready adj (prepared) zhǔnbèihǎo 准备好; are you ready? nǐ zhǔnbèihǎo le ma? 你准备好了吗?; to get the meal ready bǎ fàn zhǔnbèihǎo 把饭准备好; (happy) lèyì 乐意, yuànyì 愿意; I'm happy to help you wǒ hěn lèyì bāngzhù nǐ 我很乐意帮助你

real adj (genuine) zhēn 真, zhēnzhèng 真正; real diamonds zhēn zuànshí 真钻石; (actual) xiànshí 现实, zhēnshí 真实; real life xiànshí shēnghuó 现实生活; it's a real shame zhè zhēn kěxī 这真可惜

reality n xiànshí 现实, shíjì cúnzài 实际存在

realize vb (make real) shíxiàn 实现; he has realized his goal tā shíxiànle tāde mùbiāo 他实现了他的目标; (to comprehend completely) rènshidào 认识到; he didn't realize that he was wrong tā méiyǒu rènshidào tā cuò le 他没有认识到他错了

really adv (truly, actually) quèshí 确实; it's really easy to make zhè quèshí hěn róngyì zuò 这确实很容易做; really? zhēn de ma? 真的吗?

rear 1 n (back part) hòubù 后部, hòumiàn 后面 **2** vb (to care for and educate) fǔyǎng 抚养, yǎngyù 养育; to rear the children fǔyǎng háizi 抚养孩子; (to breed) sìyǎng 饲养; to rear pigs sìyǎng zhū 饲养猪

reason n (ground or cause) yuányīn 原因, lǐyóu 理由; a reason yíge yuányīn 一个原因; the reason for being late chídào de yuányīn 迟到的原因; (sensible or logical thought or view) dàolǐ 道理; there is reason in what he said tā shuō de yǒu dàolǐ 他说的有道理

reassure vb the policeman reassured me about my daughter's safety jǐngchá ràng wǒ bú yào wèi wǒ nǚ'ér de ānquán dānyōu 警察让我不要为我女儿的安全担忧; this letter reassured me zhèfēng xìn shǐ wǒ fàngxīn le 这封信使我放心了

receipt n a receipt yìzhāng shōujù 一张收据

receive vb (to obtain from someone by delivery) shōudào 收到, jiēdào 接到; we received a letter from the teacher wǒmen shōudào lǎoshī de yìfēng xìn 我们收到了老师的一封信; (to get) dédào 得到; to receive help from someone dédào mǒurén de bāngzhù 得到某人的帮助; (meet and welcome) jiēdài 接待; the delegation was well received dàibiǎotuán shòudàole hěn hǎo de jiēdài 代表团受到了很好的接待

recent adj zuìjìn de 最近的, jìnlái de 近来的

recently adv zuìjìn 最近, jìnlái 近来

reception n (in a hotel, a hospital, a company) the reception (area) jiēdàichù 接待处; ask at reception zài jiēdàichù xúnwèn 在接待处询问; (a formal event) a reception yíge zhāodàihuì 一个招待会; (the act of receiving or being received) jiēdài 接待

receptionist n a receptionist yíge jiēdàiyuán 一个接待员

recipe n a recipe (instructions for cooking a dish) yìzhǒng pēngtiáo fāngfǎ 一种烹调方法; (medical prescription) yíge yàofāng 一个药方

recognize vb (to identify as known) rènchū 认出; (to acknowledge) chéngrèn 承认

recommend vb (to command or introduce as suitable) tuījiàn 推荐; (to advise) quàngào 劝告, jiànyì 建议

record 1 n (details about a fact or proceeding) jìlù 记录; (information about a person's past) lǚlì 履历, jīnglì 经历; (the best recorded achievement) a record yíxiàng jìlù 一项记录; to break the world record dǎpò shìjiè jìlù 打破世界记录; (for playing music) a record yìzhāng chàngpiàn 一张唱片 **2** vb (to put in writing) jìlù 记录; (to make a recording of music, speech, etc.) lùyīn 录音

recorder n a recorder (a musical instrument) yìzhī dízi 一支笛子; (a machine for recording sounds) yìtái lùyīnjī 一台录音机

record player n a record player yìtái diànchàngjī 一台电唱机, yìtái liúshēngjī 一台留声机

recover vb (to regain one's health) huīfù 恢复; the patient has completely recovered from his illness bìngrén yǐjīng wánquán huīfù le 病人已经完全恢复了; (get back or find again) zhǎohuí 找回; I have recovered the money I lost wǒ bǎ wǒ diū de qián zhǎohuílai le 我把我丢的钱找回来了

recycle vb (to reprocess and reuse) huíshōu chǔlǐ 回收处理, xúnhuán shǐyòng 循环使用; to recycle newspapers huíshōu chǔlǐ bàozhǐ 回收处理报纸; to recycle these bottles xúnhuán shǐyòng zhèxiē píngzi 循环使用这些瓶子

red adj hóng 红, hóngsè de 红色的; to go red, to turn red biàn hóng 变红

red-haired adj hóng tóufa de 红头发的

reduce vb (to lower) jiǎn 减, jiǎnshǎo 减少; to reduce prices jiǎn jià 减价; (to diminish in weight, pressure) jiǎnqīng 减轻; to reduce one's weight jiǎnqīng tǐzhòng 减轻体重; (to slow down) jiǎndī 减低, jiǎnmàn 减慢; to reduce speed jiǎndī sùdù 减低速度

reduction n jiǎnshǎo 减少, suōjiǎn 缩减

redundant adj (British English) (of worker, no longer needed and therefore dismissed) bèi cáijiǎn de 被裁减的; to be made redundant bèi cáijiǎn 被裁减; (superfluous) guòshèng 过剩, duōyú 多余

referee n a referee (in matches and games) yìmíng cáipàn 一名裁判; (one who testifies to someone's character, knowledge, etc.) yìmíng jiàndìngrén 一名鉴定人, yìmíng shēnchárén 一名审查人; (an arbitrator) yìmíng zhòngcáirén 一名仲裁人

reflection n a reflection (a conscious thought) yìzhǒng xiǎngfa 一种想法, yìzhǒng jiànjiě 一种见解; (an image reflected in water, etc.) yíge dàoyǐng 一个倒影; (an expression) yìzhǒng fǎnyìng 一种反映, yìzhǒng biǎoxiàn 一种表现; a reflection of the living standards in this country zhège guójiā shēnghuó shuǐpíng de yìzhǒng fǎnyìng 这个国家生活水平的一种反映

refreshing adj (pleasantly cooling) qīngshuǎng 清爽, liángshuǎng 凉爽; (invigorating) shǐ rén zhènzuò de 使人振作的

refrigerator n a refrigerator yìtái (diàn)bīngxiāng 一台(电)冰箱

refugee n a refugee yíge bìnánzhě 一个避难者, yíge nànmín 一个难民

refuse[1] vb jùjué 拒绝, bùkěn 不肯; to refuse [to listen | to accept a gift | to pay the money...] jùjué [tīng | jiēshòu lǐwù | fù qián...] 拒绝[听 | 接受礼物 | 付钱...]

refuse[2] n lājī 垃圾, fèiwù 废物

regards n wènhòu 问候, zhìyì 致意; give her my regards dài wǒ xiàng tā wènhòu 代我向她问候

region n a region (area, district) yíge dìqū 一个地区; (part of the body) yíge bùwèi 一个部位

regional adj dìqū de 地区的, júbù de 局部的

register n a register (a written record regularly kept) yìběn dēngjìbù 一本登记簿; to take the register dēngjì 登记

regret vb (to wish something had not happened) hòuhuǐ 后悔, àohuǐ 懊悔; I regret changing my mind wǒ hòuhuǐ gǎibiànle zhǔyì 我后悔改变了主意; (feel sorry) yíhàn 遗憾; he regrets that he can't come tā hěn yíhàn tā bù néng lái 他很遗憾他不能来

regular adj (habitual or according to rule) yǒu guīlǜ de 有规律的, guīzé de 规则的; (periodical) dìngqī 定期; (normal) zhèngcháng 正常

regularly adv (habitually, by rule) yǒu guīlǜ de 有规律地, guīzé de 规则地; (periodically) dìngqī 定期地

rehearsal n a rehearsal (a trial or practise performance) yícì páiliàn 一次排练, yícì páiyǎn 一次排演

rehearse vb (to perform privately for trial or practice) páiliàn 排练, páiyǎn 排演

reject vb (to refuse to accept) jùjué (jiēshòu) 拒绝(接受); to reject someone's advice jùjué (jiēshòu) mǒurén de quàngào 拒绝(接受)某人的劝告; (to refuse to pass, as a bill, proposal, etc.) fǒujué 否决; to reject a candidate fǒujué yìmíng hòuxuǎnrén 否决一名候选人

relationship n guānxi 关系; she has a good relationship with her parents tā gēn tāde fùmǔ guānxi hěn hǎo 她跟她的父母关系很好! Note that the indefinite article a in this sentence is not translated.

relative n a relative yíge qīnqi 一个亲戚

relax vb (to make less rigid or strict) fàngkuān 放宽, fàngsōng 放松; to relax a rule fàngkuān yíxiàng guīdìng 放宽一项规定; (to make less tense) fàngsōng 放松; to relax [one's grip | one's muscles | one's efforts] [sōngshǒu | fàngsōng jīròu | sōng jìn(r)] [松手 | 放松肌肉 | 松劲(儿)]; (to become loose or slack) fàngsōng 放松; you can relax now nǐ xiànzài kěyǐ fàngsōng le 你现在可以放松了; (to become less tense) sōngxiè 松懈, fàngsōng 放松; their efforts have started to relax tāmende nǔlì kāishǐ sōngxiè le 他们的努力开始松懈了; (to have a rest) xiūxi 休息; let's stop and relax for a while zánmen tíngxiàlái xiūxi yíhuir ba 咱们停下来休息一会儿吧

relaxed adj (loosened, slackened) fàngsōng de 放松的; (becoming less tense, severe) huǎnhé de 缓和的

relay race vb a relay race yíxiàng jiēlì bǐsài 一项接力比赛

release vb (to set free) shìfàng 释放; he was released tā bèi shìfàng le 他被释放了; (to relieve) jiěchú 解除; to release him from his pain jiěchú tāde téngtòng 解除他的疼痛; (to make available or known widely); (if it's a film, a CD, a video) fāxíng 发行; (if it's an announcement, a piece of news) fābiǎo 发表, fābù 发布; the government is going to release a piece of important news zhèngfǔ zhǔnbèi fābù yìtiáo zhòngyào xiāoxi 政府准备发布一条重要消息; to release a Chinese film fāxíng yíbù Zhōngguó diànyǐng 发行一部中国电影

reliable adj (dependable) kěkào 可靠; is this news reliable? zhè xiāoxi kěkào ma? 这消息可靠吗?; (trustworthy) kěyǐ xìnlài de 可以信赖的; a reliable lawyer yíwèi kěyǐ xìnlài de lǜshī 一位可以信赖的律师

relieved adj kuānwèi 宽慰; my mother was relieved to receive my letter wǒ māma shōudào wǒde xìn gǎndào hěn kuānwèi 我妈妈收到我的信感到很宽慰

religion n zōngjiào 宗教

religious education, RE (British English) n zōngjiào kè 宗教课

rely vb (to lean on as a support) yīkào 依靠; (to count on) yīlài 依赖, zhǐwàng 指望; can we rely on you? wǒmén kěyǐ yīlài nǐ ma? 我们可以依赖你吗?

remain vb (to stay or be left behind) liúxià 留下; only I remained zhǐyǒu wǒ yíge rén liúxià le 只有我一个人留下了; (to be left over) shèngxia 剩下; you can take all those things that remain nǐ kěyǐ bǎ shèngxia de dōngxi dōu názǒu 你可以把剩下的东西都拿走; (to continue in the same place) hái zài 还在, réngrán cúnzài 仍然存在; that old building remains nàzuò gǔlǎo jiànzhù hái zài 那座古老建筑还在; (to dwell or abide) dāi 呆/待, dòuliú 逗留; I'll remain in Shanghai for a week wǒ yào zài Shànghǎi dāi yíge xīngqí 我要在上海呆一个星期; (to continue to be) réngrán 仍然; she remained unhappy tā réngrán bù gāoxìng 她仍然不高兴

remark n a remark (a comment) yíge pínglùn 一个评论; (a statement) yíduàn chénshù 一段陈述; (something said on a subject) yíduàn huà 一段话

remarkable adj fēifán 非凡, zhuóyuè 卓越

remember vb (to have in mind) jìde 记得; do you remember her? nǐ jìde tā ma? 你记得她吗?; (to recall) xiǎngqǐ 想起; now I remember xiànzài wǒ xiǎngqǐlai le 现在我想起来了; (to retain in one's memory) jìzhù 记住; to remember to turn off the lights jìzhù bǎ dēng guānshang 记住把灯关上

remind vb (to put in mind of) tíxǐng 提醒; to remind someone to buy milk tíxǐng mǒurén mǎi niúnǎi 提醒某人买牛奶; (to *cause to remember)* shǐ...xiǎngqǐ 使... 想起; **she reminds me of my younger sister** tā shǐ wǒ xiǎngqǐ wǒde mèimei 她使我想起我的妹妹

remote control *n* **a remote control** yíge yáokòngqì 一个遥控器

remove *vb (to take or put away by hand)* nákāi 拿开, bānzǒu 搬走; **to remove these books** bǎ zhèxiē shū nákāi 把这些书拿开; *(to clean off)* qùdiào 去掉, nòngdiào 弄掉; **to remove stains from a carpet** bǎ wūjì cóng dìtǎn shang nòngdiào 把污迹从地毯上弄掉; **to remove someone from his post** chèdiào mǒurén de zhíwù 撤掉某人的职务; **to remove this wall** bǎ zhèdǔ qiáng chāichú 把这堵墙拆除

rent 1 *vb* zū 租, zūyòng 租用; **to rent a house** zū yídòng fángzi 租一栋房子 **2** *n* **a rental payment** yìfēn zūjīn 一份租金; **rent out** chūzū 出租

repair *vb (if it's something mechanical, electrical, electronic, or a piece of furniture)* xiūlǐ 修理; **to repair** [a bicycle | a TV set | a bed...] xiūlǐ [yíliàng zìxíngchē | yìtái diànshìjī | yìzhāng chuáng...] 修理 [一辆自行车 | 一台电视机 | 一张床...]; *(to patch)* bǔ 补, xiūbǔ 修补; **to repair the damage** míbǔ sǔnshī 弥补损失

repeat *vb (to say again)* chóngfù 重复, chóngshuō 重说; *(to do again)* chóngzuò 重做; **don't repeat this mistake** bié zài fàn zhège cuòwù le 别再犯这个错误了

replace *vb (put back)* fànghuí yuánchù 放回原处; **please replace the magazine after reading** zázhì kànwán hòu qǐng fànghuí yuánchù 杂志看完后请放回原处; *(substitute for)* dàitì 代替, tìhuàn 替换; **can computers replace human beings?** jìsuànjī néng dàitì rén ma? 计算机能代替人吗?; **they replaced the fence with a wall** tāmen bǎ líba chāi le, jiànle yìdǔ qiáng 他们把篱笆拆了, 建了一堵墙

reply 1 *vb* huídá 回答; **to reply to** [someone | a question] huídá [mǒurén | yíge wèntí] 回答 [某人 | 一个问题]; **to reply to** [a letter | a fax] huí [xìn | chuánzhēn] 回 [信 | 传真] **2** *n* **a reply** yíge huídá 一个回答, yíge dáfù 一个答复

report 1 vb (to tell about) bàogào 报告; to report an accident bàogào yícì shìgù 报告 一次事故; (in the news) bàodào 报导; to report on a demonstration bàodào yícì shìwēi yóuxíng 报导 一次示威游行; (to lay a charge against) gàofā 告发, jiēfā 揭发; to report someone to the police xiàng jǐngchá gàofā mǒurén 向警察告发某人 **2** n (in the news) yìtiáo bàodào 一条报道; (an official document) a report yífèn bàogào 一份报告; (British English) (from school) a (school) report yífèn xuéxiào chéngjì bàogào 一份学校成绩报告

report card n (US English) a report card yífèn xuésheng chéngjì bàogào 一份学生成绩报告

reporter n a reporter (a journalist) yíge jìzhě 一个记者; (a person who reports) yíge bàogàorén 一个报告人

represent vb (to act on behalf of) dàibiǎo 代表; would you like her to represent you? nǐ yuànyì tā dàibiǎo nǐ ma? 你愿意她代表你吗?; (stand for, symbolize) biǎoshì 表示, xiàngzhēng 象征; this gift represents our friendship zhège lǐwù biǎoshì wǒmende yǒuyì 这个礼物表示我们的友谊

republic n a republic yíge gònghéguó 一个共和国

request n a request yíge qǐngqiú 一个请求

rescue vb (from danger) yuánjiù 援救, yíngjiù 营救

resemble vb xiàng 象; the two brothers resemble each other xiōngdì liǎ zhǎngde hěn xiàng 兄弟俩长得很象

resent vb duì...bùmǎn 对...不满, duì...bù gāoxìng 对...不高兴; to resent someone duì mǒurén bùmǎn 对某人不满; he resents her for winning tā duì wǒ yíng le bù gāoxìng 他对我赢了不高兴

reservation n a reservation (a booking at a restaurant, theatre, etc.) yùdìng 预订; to make a reservation for two people yùdìng liǎngge rén de zuòwèi 预订两个人的座位; (an uncertainty about something) yíge bǎoliú yìjiàn 一个保留意见; yìzhǒng bǎoliú tàidù 一种保留态度; I have serious reservations about this contract wǒ duì zhège hétong chí yánsù de bǎoliú yìjiàn 我对这个合同持严肃的保留意见; (limiting condition) yíxiàng bǎoliú 一项保留: we accept your proposal with some reservations wǒmen yǒu bǎoliú de jiēshòu nǐde tíyì 我们有保留地接受你的提议

reserve vb (to book) dìng 订; yùdìng 预订: I've reserved rooms for my whole family in that hotel wǒ yǐjīng zài nàjiā lǚguǎn wèi wǒ quán jiā yùdìngle fángjiān 我已经在那家旅馆为我全家预订了房间; (to hold back or set aside) bǎoliú 保留, liúchū 留出: we've reserved ten seats for the delegation wǒmen wèi dàibiǎotuán liúchūle shíge zuòwèi 我们为代表团留出了十个座位; (to save up for a future occasion) chǔbèi 储备, chǔcún 储存

resign vb (to give up) cíqù 辞去: I've resigned my position as head of department wǒ yǐjīng cíqùle xì zhǔrèn de gōngzuò 我已经辞去了系主任的工作; (to give up office, employment) cízhí 辞职: are you going to resign? nǐ yào cízhí ma? 你要辞职吗?

resist vb (to strive against) dǐkàng 抵抗, fǎnkàng 反抗; to resist violence fǎnkàng bàolì 反抗暴力; (to withstand) kàng 抗, nài 耐: does this kind of material resist heat? zhèzhǒng cáiliào nài rè ma? 这种材料耐热吗?; (to hinder the action of) rěnzhù 忍住! Note that the negative form of rěnzhù 忍住 is rěn bú zhù 忍不住; she could not resist laughing tā rěn bú zhù xiào le 她忍不住笑了

respect 1 vb zūnzhòng 尊重, zūnjìng 尊敬 **2** n (deferential esteem) zūnzhòng 尊重, zūnjìng 尊敬; out of respect chūyú zūnzhòng 出于尊重; (point, aspect) fāngmiàn 方面; in this respect zài zhège fāngmiàn 在这个方面

responsibility n (a duty on a job, a task) zhízé 职责; (obligation) zérèn 责任

responsible adj (personally accountable for) fùzé 负责; to be responsible for the damage duì zàochéng de sǔnhuài fùzé 对造成的损坏负责; (in charge) fùzé 负责; to be responsible for organizing a trip fùzé zǔzhī lǚxíng 负责组织旅行

rest 1 n (a break, time to recover) xiūxi 休息; to need rest xūyào xiūxi 需要休息; to have a rest xiūxi yíhuir 休息一会儿; (what *is left)* the rest shèngxia de 剩下的, qíyú de 其余的; we spent the rest of the day in the garden zhè yì tiān shèngxia de shíjiān wǒmen shì zài huāyuán lǐ dùguo de 这一天剩下的时间我们是在花园里度过的 **2** *vb* xiūxi 休息

restaurant *n* a restaurant yìjiā fànguǎnr 一家饭馆儿, yìjiā fàndiàn 一家饭店

result *n* (*effect, consequence*) jiéguǒ 结果: a good result yíge hǎo de jiéguǒ 一个好的结果; (*outcome of an exam, a race, a competition*) chéngjì 成绩, fēnshù 分数; the results of the competition bǐsài chéngjì 比赛成绩; the examination results kǎoshì fēnshù 考试分数; as a result of an accident yīnwèi yícì shìgù 因为一次事故, yóuyú yícì shìgù 由于一次事故

résumé *n* (*US English*) a résumé yìfèn jiǎnlì 一份简历

retire *vb* (*to give up office or work because of old age*) tuìxiū 退休: my father retired at the age of 60 wǒ bàba liùshí suì tuìxiū 我爸爸六十岁退休; (*to go away*) líkāi 离开; after dinner, all the ladies retired chīwán fàn hòu, nǚshìmen dōu líkāi le 吃完饭后, 女士们都离开了; (*to go to bed*) shuìjiào 睡觉, jiùqǐn 就寝

return *vb* (*to go back*) huí 回, huíqù 回去; (*to come back*) huí 回, huílái 回来; (*from abroad, to one's home country*) huí guó 回国; (*to give back*) huán 还: can you return my book? nǐ bǎ wǒde shū huángěi wǒ hǎo ma? 你把我的书还给我好吗? (*to send back*) tuìhuán 退还; to return goods tuìhuán huòwù 退还货物; (*to start again*) to return to work huífù gōngzuò 恢复工作; to return to school fù kè 复课

return ticket *n* (*British English*) a return ticket yìzhāng wǎngfǎn piào 一张往返票, yìzhāng láihuí piào 一张来回票

reveal *vb* to reveal a secret xièlù yíge mìmì 泄露一个秘密

revenge *n* bàochóu 报仇, bàofù 报复; to have one's revenge on someone for something wèi mǒushì xiàng mǒurén bàochóu 为某事向某人报仇

revolution *n* a revolution yìchǎng gémìng 一场革命

reward **1** *n* a reward yìbǐ chóujīn 一笔酬金, yìbǐ bàochóu 一笔报酬 **2** *vb* (*to give a reward in return for a deed or service*) *rendered*) chóuxiè 酬谢; (*to give as a reward*) jiǎngshǎng 奖赏, jiǎnglì 奖励

rewind *vb* (*for video/audio tapes*) dào(zhuàn) (cí)dài 倒(转)(磁)带

rhythm *n* jiézòu 节奏, jiépāi 节拍

rib *n* a rib (*in the human body*) yìgēn lèigǔ 一根肋骨; (*as in spare rib*) yìgēn páigǔ 一根排骨

rice *n* (*raw*) dàmǐ 大米; (*cooked*) mǐfàn 米饭

rich *adj* fù 富, fùyù 富裕, yǒuqián 有钱; to get rich fùqǐlái 富起来, zhìfù 致富

rid: to get rid of *vb* qùdiào 去掉, chúqù 除去

ride 1 *vb* (*on a horse or a bicycle*) qí 骑; to ride a horse qí mǎ 骑马; to go riding qù qí mǎ 去骑马; he is riding a bike tā zài qí zìxíngchē 他在骑自行车; (*in a plane, on a train, or on a bus*) chéng 乘, zuò 坐; to ride [on a train | in a plane | on a bus] zuò [huǒchē | fēijī | qìchē] 坐 [火车 | 飞机 | 汽车] **2** *n* to go for a ride (*in a car*) qù kāi yíhuìr chē 去开一会儿车, qù dōufēng 去兜风; (*on a bike*) qù qí yíhuìr zìxíngchē 去骑一会儿自行车; (*on a horse*) qù qí yíhuìr mǎ 去骑一会儿马

ridiculous *adj* huāngmiù 荒谬, huāngtáng 荒唐

rifle *n* a rifle yìzhī bùqiāng 一枝步枪

right 1 *adj* (*not left*) yòu 右, yòubian de 右边的; his right hand tāde yòu shǒu 他的右手; (*proper*) héshì 合适, qiàdàng 恰当; is she the right person for this job? tā zuò zhège gōngzuò héshì ma? 她做这个工作合适吗？; (*correct*) duì 对, zhèngquè 正确; the right answer zhèngquè de dá'àn 正确的答案; is this the right direction? zhège fāngxiàng duì ma? 这个方向对吗？; what's the right time? xiànzài zhǔnquè de shíjiān shì jǐ diǎn? 现在准确的时间是几点？; you're right nǐ shì duì de 你是对的; that's right duì 对 **2** *n* (*the direction*) the right yòu 右, yòubian 右边; the first road on the right yòubian dìyītiáo mǎlù 右边第一条马路; (*what one is entitled to*) a right yīge quánlì 一个权力; to have a right to education yǒu quánlì shòu jiàoyù 有权力受教育; human rights rénquán 人权 **3** *adv* (*correctly*) duì 对;

did I do it right? wǒ zuò de duì ma? 我做得对吗?; (to the right side) xiàng yòu 向右; to turn right xiàng yòu zhuǎn 向右转; (for emphasis) right now mǎshàng 马上, lìkè 立刻; she stood right in the centre of the garden tā zhàn zài huāyuán zhèng zhōngyāng 她站在花园正中央

ring 1 vb (British English) (to phone) dǎ diànhuà 打电话; to ring for a taxi dǎ diànhuà jiào chūzūchē 打电话叫出租车; (to make a sound) xiǎng xiǎng 响; the telephone rang diànhuà líng xiǎng le 电话铃响了; (to activate a door or bicycle bell) àn líng 按铃; to ring the doorbell àn ménlíng 按门铃; (to sound a church bell) qiāo zhōng 敲钟 **2** n (a piece of jewellery) a ring yìzhī jièzhi 一只戒指; a wedding ring yìzhī jiéhūn jièzhi 一只结婚戒指; (a circle) a ring yíge yuánquān 一个圆圈, yíge huán 一个环; (in a circus) the ring yuánxíng chǎngdì 圆形场地; **ring up** (British English) dǎ diànhuà 打电话

rinse vb chōngxǐ 冲洗, qīngxǐ 清洗

ripe adj shú 熟, chéngshú 成熟

rise vb (if it's the sun or moon) shēngqǐ 升起; (if it's smoke, a balloon, a plane) shàngshēng 上升; (if it's a price, a water level) shàngzhǎng 上涨; (if it's temperature) shēnggāo 升高

risk 1 n wēixiǎn 危险 **2** vb mào...wēixiǎn 冒...危险; to risk losing one's job mào shīqù gōngzuò de wēixiǎn 冒失去工作的危险

river n a river yìtiáo hé 一条河

riverbank n a riverbank yìtiáo hé'àn 一条河岸

road n a road yìtiáo (dào)lù 一条(道)路; the road to London qù Lúndūn de lù 去伦敦的路

road sign n a road sign yíge lùbiāo 一个路标

roadworks n xiū lù gōngchéng 修路工程

roar vb (if it's a lion) hóu jiào 吼叫, hóujiào 吼叫; (if it's a person) hūhǎn 呼喊, dàhǎndàjiào 大喊大叫; (if it's an engine) hōngmíng 轰鸣 上鸣; (if it's the wind) hūxiào 呼啸

roast 1 vb kǎo 烤 **2** adj kǎo 烤; to eat Peking duck chī Běijīng kǎo yā 吃北京烤鸭 **3** n a roast yíkuài kǎoròu 一块烤肉

rob *vb* qiǎng 抢, qiǎngjié 抢劫; to rob someone of his money qiǎng mǒurén de qián 抢某人的钱; to rob a bank qiǎngjié yínháng 抢劫银行

robbery *n* yícì qiǎngjié (àn) 一次抢劫(案)

robin *n* yìzhī zhīgēngniǎo 一只更鸟

robot *n* yíge jīqìrén 一个机器人

rock *n* (a large stone) a rock yíkuài shítou 一块石头, yíkuài yánshí 一块岩石; (as a material for construction) yánshí 岩石, shítou 石头; (a type of music) yáogǔn yīnyuè 摇滚音乐

rock climbing *n* pānshí yùndòng 攀石运动

rocket *n* a rocket yìkē huǒjiàn 一颗火箭

role *n* (an actor's part) jiǎosè 角色; a role yíge jiǎosè 一个角色; (a function) zuòyòng 作用; he played an important role in organizing this conference tā zài zǔzhī zhècì huìyì zhōng qǐle zhòngyào de zuòyòng 他在组织这次会议中起了重要的作用

roll 1 *vb* (to move by turning over and over) gǔn(dòng) 滚(动); the ball rolled under a car qiú gǔndàole yíliàng qìchē xiàmian 球滚到了一辆汽车下面; to roll the pastry into a ball bǎ miàn gǔnchéng yíge qiú 把面滚成一个球 **2** *n* (of paper, cloth, plastic) juǎn 卷; a roll of film yìjuǎn jiāojuǎn 一卷胶卷; (bread) a roll yíge miànbāojuǎn 一个面包卷; (US English) (at school) to call the roll diǎn míng 点名; **roll about, roll around** (if it's an object) dàochù gǔn 到处滚; **roll over** fān 翻; **roll up** juǎn 卷; to roll up a newspaper juǎnqǐ bàozhǐ 卷起报纸

roller coaster *n* a roller coaster yíliè yóulè tiānchē 一列游乐天车

roller-skate *n* hànbīng xié; a pair of roller-skates yìshuāng hànbīng xié 一双旱冰鞋

roller-skating *n* huá hànbīng 滑旱冰

romantic *adj* (characterized by romance) luómàndìkè 罗曼蒂克, làngmàn 浪漫; (passionate and imaginative) fùyú huànxiǎng 富于幻想, xiǎngrùfēifēi 想入非非

roof *n* a roof yíge wūdǐng 一个屋顶, yíge fángdǐng 一个房顶

room n a room yíge fángjiān 一个房间; (space) kōngjiān 空间, dìfang 地方; to make room kòngchū dìfang 空出地方; is there room? hái yǒu kōngjiān ma? 还有空间吗?; (scope) yúdì 余地; there is still room for improvement hái yǒu gǎijìn de yúdì 还有改进的余地

root n (of a plant) yíge gēn 一个根; (source, origin, cause) yíge gēnyuán 一个根源

rope n a rope yìgēn shéngzi 一根绳子

rose n a rose (a plant) yìkē méiguì 一棵玫瑰; (a flower) yìzhī méiguihuā 一支玫瑰花

rosy adj (rose-red) méiguìsè de 玫瑰色的; rosy cheeks hóngrùn de liǎnjiá 红润的脸颊

rotten adj fǔlàn de 腐烂的, fǔxiǔ de 腐朽的

rough adj (not smooth) bù píng 不平, bù guānghuá 不光滑; (when talking about the skin, paper) cūcāo 粗糙; rough skin cūcāo de pífū 粗糙的皮肤; (when talking about roads) qíqū bù píng 崎岖不平; the road is rough zhètiáo lù qíqū bù píng 这条路崎岖不平; (not gentle) cūbào 粗暴, cūlǔ 粗鲁; (tough) to live in a rough area zhù zài yíge zhì'ān chà de dìqū 住在一个治安差的地区; (not exact, precise) cūlüè 粗略; a rough figure yíge cūlüè de shùzì 一个粗略的数字; (difficult) jiānnán 艰难; he had a rough time there tā zài nàr guòle yíduàn hěn jiānnán de rìzi 他在那儿过了一段很艰难的日子; (caused by bad weather) a rough sea bōtāo xiōngyǒng de hǎimiàn 波涛汹涌的海面

round ! Often round occurs in combinations with verbs. For more information, see the note at around. **1** prep (on every side of) wéizhe 围着; to sit round a table wéizhe zhuōzi zuò 围着桌子坐; (to complete a circuit) rào 绕, wéirào 围绕; to sail round the world wéirào dìqiú hángxíng 围绕地球航行; (all over) zài.. gè chù 在...各处, dàochù 到处; we walked round Oxford wǒmen zài Niújīn gè chù zǒulezhōu 我们在牛津各处走了走 **2** adv (on a circular or circuitous course) zhuàn quān 转圈; to run round the track on the sports ground zài cāochǎng shang zhuàn quān pǎo 在操场上转圈跑; to go round to

John's ràodào qù Yuēhàn jiā 绕道去约翰家; **to invite someone round** yāoqíng mǒurén dào jiā li lái 邀请某人到家里来 **3** *n* **a round** *(in a quiz show or showjumping)* yìchǎng 一场; *(in boxing)* yíge huíhé 一个回合; *(in an election, a negotiation, a tournament)* yìlún 一轮 **4** *adj* *(circular)* yuán 圆, yuánxíng de 圆形的; *(spherical)* qiúxíng de 球形的; *(plump)* fēngmǎn 丰满

roundabout *n (British English)* *(in a playground or at a fair)* **a roundabout** yíge mùmǎ xuánzhuàn pán 一个木马旋转盘; *(for traffic)* **a roundabout** yíge huánxíng lùkǒu 一个环形路口

route *n (on land)* lùxiàn 路线; **a route** yìtiáo lùxiàn 一条路线; **a** [bus | train] **route** yìtiáo [qìchē | huǒchē] lùxiàn 一条 [汽车 | 火车] 路线; *(for planes and ships)* hángxiàn 航线; **a route** yìtiáo hángxiàn 一条航线

routine *n* chángguī 常规, guànlì 惯例

row¹ 1 *n (a line of persons or things)* pái 排; **a row of** [people | seats | cars...] yìpái [rén | zuòwèi | qìchē...] 一排 [人 | 座位 | 汽车...]; **the pupils were sitting in rows** xuéshengmen yìpái yìpái de zuòzhe 学生们一排一排地坐着; **in a row** liánxù 连续, yìlián 一连; **to arrive late five days in a row** liánxù wǔ tiān chí dào 连续五天迟到 **2** *vb (to propel with an oar)* huá 划; **to row a boat** huá chuán 划船; *(to transport by rowing)* huá chuán sòng 划船送; **I can row you across the river** wǒ kěyǐ huá chuán sòng nǐ guò hé 我可以划船送你过河; *(as a sport)* huá chuán bǐsài 划船比赛; **Oxford University rowed against Cambridge University on the river Thames** Niújīn Dàxué gēn Jiànqiáo Dàxué zài Tàiwúshìhé shang jìnxíngle huá chuán bǐsài 牛津大学跟剑桥大学在泰晤士河上进行了划船比赛

row² *n (British English)* **a row** yícì chǎojià 一次吵架, yícì chǎozuǐ 一次吵嘴; **to have a row with someone** gēn mǒurén chǎojià 跟某人吵架

rowing *n* huá chuán 划船

rowing boat *(British English)*, **rowboat** *(US English)* *n* **a rowing boat** yìtiáo huátǐng 一条小艇

royal *adj* **the Royal Family** wángshì 王室, huángjiā 皇家; **the Royal Navy** Huángjiā Hǎijūn 皇家海军; [Your | His | Her] **Royal**

Highness Diànxià 殿下; a royal palace (for a queen) yízuò huánggōng 一座皇宫; (for a king) yízuò wánggōng 一座王宫

rub vb (to apply pressure to with a circular or backward and forward movement) róu 揉; to rub one's eyes róu yǎnjīng 揉眼睛; **rub out** (British English) cādiào 擦掉; to rub out that character cādiào nàge zì 擦掉那个字

rubber n (the material) xiàngjiāo 橡胶; (British English) (an eraser) a rubber yíkuài xiàngpí 一块橡皮

rubbish n (refuse) lājī 垃圾; (anything worthless) fèiwù 废物; (nonsense) fèihuà 废话

rubbish bin n (British English) a rubbish bin yíge lājītǒng 一个垃圾桶

rucksack n a rucksack yíge bèibāo 一个背包

rude adj (not polite) cūlǔ 粗鲁, wúlǐ 无礼; to be rude to someone duì mǒurén hěn wúlǐ 对某人很无礼; (vulgar) dījí 低级, xiàliú 下流; a rude story yíge xiàliú gùshi 一个下流故事

rug n a rug (a floor mat) yíkuài xiǎo dìtǎn 一块小地毯; (a thick covering or wrap) yìtiáo máotǎn 一条毛毯

rugby n gǎnlǎnqiú 橄榄球

ruin 1 vb (to spoil) gǎozāo 搞糟; he's ruined this meal tā bǎ zhèdùn fàn gǎozāo le 他把这顿饭搞糟了; (to damage) huǐhuài 毁坏; you'll ruin your shoes nǐ huì huǐhuài nǐde xié 你会毁坏你的鞋; (to destroy completely) huīmiè 毁灭; his hope was ruined tāde xīwàng (bèi) huīmiè le 他的希望(被)毁灭了 **2** n (destruction) huǐmiè 毁灭; (damage) huǐhuài 毁坏; (a fallen or broken state) fèixū 废墟; the whole school is now in ruins zhěnggè xuéxiào xiànzài chéngle yípiàn fèixū 整个学校现在成了一片废墟

rule 1 n a rule (of a game, a language) yìtiáo guīzé 一条规则; (in a school, an organization) yìtiáo guīdìng 一条规定; it's against the rules zhè wéifǎn guīdìng 这违反规定 **2** vb (to govern) tǒngzhì 统治; to rule a country tǒngzhì yíge guójiā 统治一个国家; (to control) kòngzhì 控制; he ruled his family with an iron hand tā jǐnjǐn de kòngzhìzhe quán jiā 他紧紧地控

制着全家; (to determine or decree) cáijué 裁决, cáidìng 裁定;
the court ruled that he was guilty fǎyuàn cáijué tā yǒu zuì 法院
裁决他有罪

ruler n a ruler (for measuring or ruling lines) yíge chǐzi 一个尺子;
(a person who governs) yíge tǒngzhìzhě 一个统治者

rumour (British English), **rumor** (US English) n a rumour
(a statement of doubtful accuracy) yíge yáoyán 一个谣言;
(hearsay) yíge chuánwén 一个传闻

run 1 vb to run pǎo 跑; to run across the street pǎoguò mǎlù 跑
过马路; (compete in a race) sàipǎo 赛跑; to run a race cānjiā
sàipǎo 参加赛跑; (from danger) táopǎo 逃跑; (to manage)
guǎnlǐ 管理; to run a school guǎnlǐ yíge xuéxiào 管理一个学
校; (to work, to operate) yùnzhuǎn 运转, yùnxíng 运行; the
machine is running well jīqì yùnzhuǎn liánghǎo 机器运转良
好; (if it's a vehicle) xíngshǐ 行驶: the car is running at 80
kilometres per hour qìchē yǐ měi xiǎoshí bāshí gōnglǐ de sùdù
xíngshǐ 汽车以每小时八十公里的速度行驶; (to
organize) bàn 办; to run a competition bàn yíge bǐsài 办一个比
赛; (to flow) liú 流; (to fill with water) fàng shuǐ 放水; to run a bath wǎng zǎopén
li fàng shuǐ 往澡盆里放水; (to come off, as stains or make-up)
diào 掉; the rain has made her make-up run yǔshuǐ bǎ tā liǎn
shang de huàzhuāng chōngdiào le 雨水把她脸上的化妆冲掉
了; (in an election) jìngxuǎn 竞选; to run for president jìngxuǎn
zǒngtǒng 竞选总统; (other uses) it is running late shíjiān bù
duō le 时间不多了; he is running a temperature tā zài fāshāo
他在发烧 **2** n to go for a run qù pǎobù 去跑步; **run about,
run around** dàochù pǎo 到处跑, sìchù pǎo 四处跑; **run away**
(to escape) táopǎo 逃跑, qiántáo 潜逃; (to gallop away
uncontrollably) shīqù kòngzhì 失去控制; **run off** (to escape)
táopǎo 逃跑

runner n a runner (one who runs) yíge pǎobù de rén 一个跑步
的人; (one who runs in a race) yìmíng sàipǎo yùndòngyuán
一名赛跑运动员

rush 1 vb (to hurry) jímáng 急忙, cōngcōng 匆匆, cōngmáng
匆忙! Note that in this sense, the force of the word rush is often
carried by such adverbs as those in the translations above.

Where necessary, another verb functions as the predicate; to rush to finish one's homework jímáng zuòwán zuòyè 急忙做完作业; he rushed into a shop tā cōngcōng de jìnle yìjiā shāngdiàn 他匆匆地进了一家商店; to rush out of the house cōngmáng chōngchū fángzi 匆忙冲出房子; to be rushed to the hospital jímáng bèi sòngjìn yīyuàn 急忙被送进医院; (*to put pressure on*) cuī 催, cuīcù 催促; please don't rush me qǐng búyào cuī wǒ 请不要催我 **2** n to be in a rush cōngmáng 匆忙, mánglù 忙碌; to do one's homework in a rush cōngmáng de zuò zuòyè 匆忙地做作业

rush hour n the rush hour jiāotōng gāofēng shíjiān 交通高峰时间

Russia n Éguó 俄国, Éluósī 俄罗斯

Russian **1** adj Éguó de 俄国的, Éluósī de 俄罗斯的 **2** n (*the people*) the Russians Éguórén 俄国人, Éluósīrén 俄罗斯人; (*the language*) Éyǔ 俄语, Éwén 俄文

rusty adj (shēng)xiù de (生)锈的

Ss

sad adj (*sorrowful*) nánguò 难过, bēishāng 悲伤; he feels sad tā gǎndào nánguò 他感到难过; (*grave, saddening*) lìng rén nánguò de 令人难过的, lìng rén bēishāng de 令人悲伤的; sad news lìng rén nánguò de xiāoxi 令人难过的消息; (*regrettable*) yíhàn 遗憾, kěxī 可惜; it's sad that you didn't get a scholarship hěn yíhàn, nǐ méiyǒu dédào jiǎngxuéjīn 很遗憾, 你没有得到奖学金

saddle n a saddle yíge ānzi 一个鞍子, yíge mǎ'ān 一个马鞍

safe **1** adj (*free from danger, without risk*) ānquán 安全; a safe place yíge ānquán de dìfang 一个安全的地方, is it safe to go there? qù nàr ānquán ma? 去那儿安全吗?; to feel safe gǎndào ānquán 感到安全; (*sure, reliable*) yǒu bǎwò 有把握, yídìng

一定: it is safe to say that she will get the scholarship tā yídìng huì dédào jiǎngxuéjīn 她 一定会得到奖学金 **2** *n* a safe yíge bǎoxiǎnxiāng 一个保险箱

safety *n* ānquán 安全

sail 1 *n* a sail yíge fān 一个帆; to set sail kāiháng 开航, chūháng 出航 **2** *vb* (chéng chuán) hángxíng (乘船) 航行; to sail around the world wéirào shìjiè hángxíng 围绕世界航行; to go sailing qù chéng chuán hángxíng 去乘船航行

sailing *n* (*in sports*) hánghǎi yùndòng 航海运动; (*travelling by boat*) chéng chuán lǚxíng 乘船旅行

sailing boat (*British English*), **sailboat** (*US English*) *n* a sailing boat yìsōu fānchuán 一艘帆船

sailor *n* a sailor yìmíng shuǐshǒu 一名水手, yìmíng hǎiyuán 一名海员

saint *n* a saint yíge shèngrén 一个圣人, yíge shèngtú 一个圣徒

salad *n* sèlā 色拉, xīcān liángbàncài 西餐凉拌菜

salary *n* a salary yìfèn gōngzī 一份工资, yìfèn xīnshuǐ 一份薪水

sale *n* to be on sale at a reduced price jiǎnjià chūshòu 减价出售; for sale chūshòu 出售, dàishòu 待售; the total sales of this year quán nián xiāoshòu é 全年销售额

sales assistant *n* (*British English*) a sales assistant yíge tuīxiāoyuán 一个推销员, yíge xiāoshòuyuán 一个销售员

salmon *n* a salmon yìtiáo sānwényú 一条三文鱼, yìtiáo guīyú 一条鲑鱼

salt *n* yán 盐

same 1 *adj* (*identical*) tóngyī 同一; they go to the same school tāmen zài tóngyīge xuéxiào shàngxué 他们在同一个学校上学; (*similar in style or type*) tóngyàng 同样, yíyàng 一样; she has the same coat as I do tāde shàngyī gēn wǒde yíyàng 她的上衣跟我的一样; I made the same mistake as he did wǒ hé tā fànle tóngyàng de cuòwù 我和他犯了同样的错误; the houses all look the same zhèxiē fángzi kànshangqu dōu yíyàng

这些房子看上去都一样 **2** *pron* **!** *Note that in this sense, the meaning conveyed by* same *in English has to be stated overtly in Chinese;* I bought my girlfriend a bottle of perfume, and he did the same wǒ gěi wǒ nǚpéngyou mǎile yì píng xiāngshuǐ, tā yě gěi tā nǚpéngyou mǎile yì píng 我给我女朋友买了一瓶香水, 他也给他女朋友买了一瓶; to do the same as the others xiàng biéren nàyàng zuò 象别人那样做; 'Happy New Year!'—'the same to you!' 'Xīnnián kuàilè!'—'yě zhù nǐ Xīnnián kuàilè!' '新年快乐!'—'也祝你新年快乐!'

sand *n* shāzi 沙子, shā 沙

sandal *n* a sandal yìzhī liángxié 一只凉鞋; a pair of sandals yìshuāng liángxié 一双凉鞋

sandwich *n* a sandwich yíkuài sānmíngzhì 一块三明治; a ham sandwich yíkuài huǒtuǐ sānmíngzhì 一块火腿三明治

Santa (Claus) *n* Santa (Claus) Shèngdàn lǎorén 圣诞老人

sardine *n* a sardine yìtiáo shādīngyú 一条沙丁鱼

satellite TV *n* wèixīng diànshì 卫星电视

satisfactory *adj* lìng rén mǎnyì de 令人满意的

satisfied *adj* mǎnyì 满意

Saturday *n* xīngqīliù 星期六, lǐbàiliù 礼拜六

sauce *n* a sauce yìzhǒng jiàngzhī 一种酱汁, yìzhǒng tiáowèizhī 一种调味汁

saucepan *n* a saucepan yíge (chángbǐng) píngdǐguō 一个 (长柄)平底锅

saucer *n* a saucer yíge chábēidié 一个茶杯碟

sausage *n* a sausage yìgēn xiāngcháng 一根香肠

save *vb* (to rescue) jiù 救; they saved his life tāmen jiùle tāde mìng 他们救了他的命; (to avoid spending) chǔxù 储蓄, zǎn 攒; to save (up) chǔxù 储蓄; to save money zǎnqián 攒钱; (to avoid wasting) jiéshěng 节省, jiéyuē 节约; to save [time | energy | money...] jiéshěng [shíjiān | jīnglì | qián...] 节省[时间 | 精力 | 钱...]; (to keep) liú 留; to save a piece of cake for someone gěi mǒurén liú yíkuài dàngāo 给某人留一块蛋糕; (to preserve in the *computer*) cún 存, chǔcún 储存; (*to save a file*) cún yíge wénjiàn 存一个文件; (*to spare*) to save someone a lot of work jiéshěng mǒurén hěn duō gōngzuò 节省某人很多工作; it will save us from having to write to him again zhè kěyǐ shǐ wǒmen miǎnde zài gěi tā xiě xìn 这可以使我们免得再给他写信

savings n chǔxù 储蓄, cúnkuǎn 存款

saw n a saw yìbǎ jù 一把锯

saxophone n a saxophone yìgēn sàkèsīguǎn 一根萨克斯管

say vb (*to utter in words*) shuō 说; to say goodbye shuō zàijiàn 说再见; she says (*that*) she can't go out tonight tā shuō jīnwǎn tā bù néng chūqù 她说今晚她不能出去; he said to wait here tā shuō zài zhèr děng 他说在这儿等; (*to express*) shuōmíng 说明, biǎomíng 表明; what do these figures say? zhèxiē shùzì shuōmíng shénme? 这些数字说明什么?; (*to report in the newspaper, on the radio, TV*) bàodào shuō 报导说, bàogào shuō 报告说; the radio said the Queen was going to visit China shōuyīnjī bàodǎo shuō Nǚwáng yào fǎngwèn Zhōngguó 收音机报导说女王要访问中国; (*to suppose*) jiǎshè 假设; let's say there will be twenty people at the party zánmen jiǎdìng yǒu èrshíge rén cānjiā zhège jùhuì 咱们假定有二十个人参加这个聚会

scandal n a scandal yíjiàn chǒuwén 一件丑闻, yíjiàn chǒushì 一件丑事

scare vb xià 吓, jīngxià 惊吓; you scared me! nǐ xiàle wǒ yítiào 你吓了我一跳; scare away bǎ...xiàpǎo 把...吓跑; to scare someone away bǎ mǒurén xiàpǎo 把某人吓跑

scared adj I am scared wǒ hàipà 我害怕

scarf n a scarf yìtiáo wéijīn 一条围巾

scenery n fēngjǐng 风景, jǐngsè 景色

school n a school yìsuǒ xuéxiào 一所学校; to be a student at school zài shàngxué 在上学; a school bus yíliàng xiàochē 一辆校车

schoolbag n a schoolbag yíge shūbāo 一个书包

schoolboy *n* a schoolboy yígè nán xuésheng 一个男学生

schoolgirl *n* a schoolgirl yígè nǚ xuésheng 一个女学生

schoolwork *n* gōngkè 功课, zuòyè 作业

science *n* kēxué 科学; to study science xuéxí kēxué 学习科学

scientist *n* a scientist yìmíng kēxuéjiā 一名科学家

scissors *n* jiǎnzi 剪子, jiǎndāo 剪刀; a pair of scissors yìbǎ jiǎnzi 一把剪子

score 1 *vb* to score a goal jìn yígè qiú 进一个球; to score a point dé yì fēn 得一分 **2** *n* (*points gained in a game or competition*) bǐfēn 比分; the final score of the football match zúqiú bǐsài de zuìhòu bǐfēn 足球比赛的最后比分; (*result of a test or examination*) a score yígè chéngjì 一个成绩

Scotland *n* Sūgélán 苏格兰

Scottish *adj* Sūgélán(rén) de 苏格兰(人)的

scratch *vb* (*when itchy*) náo 挠, são 搔; to scratch one's arm náo gēbo 挠胳膊; (*if it's a person or an animal*) zhuā 抓; (*if it's by a bush, a thorn*) guā 刮, huá 划; (*to mark with a knife or something hard*) kè 刻

scream *vb* jiānjiào 尖叫, dàjiào 大叫

screen *n* a screen (*of a TV set or a computer*) yígè píngmù 一个屏幕; (*of a cinema*) yígè yínmù 一个银幕

screw *n* a screw yìkē luósī(dīng) 一颗螺丝(钉)

sea *n* hǎi 海, hǎiyáng 海洋; beside the sea, by the sea zài hǎi biān 在海边

seagull *n* a seagull yìzhī hǎi'ōu 一只海鸥

seal 1 *n* a seal (*the animal*) yìzhī hǎibào 一只海豹; (*a tool used to impress*) yìméi túzhāng 一枚图章 **2** *vb* (*to close up*) fēng 封; to seal the envelope bǎ xìnfēng fēngqǐlái 把信封封起来; to seal up mìfēng 密封; (*to stamp*) gài zhāng 盖章; to seal a document zài wénjiàn shang gài zhāng 在文件上盖章

search *vb* to search xúnzhǎo 寻找; to search for someone xúnzhǎo mǒurén 寻找某人; (*to examine a place, a person*) sōuchá 搜查; they searched my luggage at the airport tāmen zài fēijīchǎng sōuchále wǒde xínglǐ 他们在飞机场搜查了我的行李

seashell n a seashell yíge bèiké 一个贝壳

seasick adj to be seasick, to get seasick yūnchuán 晕船

seaside n hǎibiān; at the seaside zài hǎibiān 在海边

season n (one of the four divisions of the year) jì 季, jìjié 季节; a season yí jì 一季, yíge jìjié 一个季节; strawberries are in season xiànzài shì cǎoméi wàngjì 现在是草莓旺季

seat n a seat (something to sit on) yíge zuòwèi 一个座位, yíge wèizi 一个位子; (a right to sit in a council or committee) yíge xíwèi 一个席位

seatbelt n a seatbelt yíge ānquándài 一个安全带

second 1 adj dì'èr 第二; it's the second time I've called her zhè shì wǒ dì'èrcì gěi tā dǎ diànhuà 这是我第二次给她打电话; (of lower quality) èrděng de 二等的; a second class cabin èrděng cāng 二等舱 **2** n (in a series) the second dì'èr 第二; (in time) a second yì miǎo 一秒, yì miǎo zhōng 一秒钟; (a very short time) yíhuìr 一会儿, piànkè 片刻; (in dates) èr rì 二日, èr hào 二号; the second of May wǔyuè èr rì 五月二日 **3** adv dì'èr 第二; to come second in the race zài sàipǎo zhōng dé dì'èr 在赛跑中得第二

secondary school n a secondary school yìsuǒ zhōngxué 一所中学

second-hand adj (biéren) yòngguo de (别人)用过的, èrshǒu 二手; a second-hand table yìzhāng yòngguo de zhuōzi 一张用过的桌子; a second-hand car yíliàng èrshǒu chē 一辆二手车; a second-hand coat yíjiàn biéren chuānguo de wàiyī 一件别人穿过的外衣

secret 1 adj mìmì 秘密 **2** n a secret yíge mìmì 一个秘密; to tell someone a secret gàosu mǒurén yíge mìmì 告诉某人一个秘密 **3** adj mìmì de 秘密地

secretary n a secretary (in an office, dealing with papers, keeping records, etc.) yíge mìshū 一个秘书; (of a political *party or party organization*) yíge shūjì 一个书记: (*a government minister*) yíge dàchén 一个大臣

see *vb* to see kànjian 看见, kàndào 看到; what can you see? nǐ néng kànjian shénme? 你能看见什么?; I didn't see them wǒ méi jiàndào tāmen 我没见到他们; she can't see the words on the blackboard tā kàn bú jiàn hēibǎn shang de zì 她看不见黑板上的字 *Note* that to negate **kànjian** 看见, *the change* **bù** 不 *comes between* **kàn** 看 *and* **jiàn** 见; (*to meet*) jiànmiàn 见面: do you see each other often? nǐmen chángcháng hùxiāng jiànmiàn ma? 你们常常互相见面吗?; see you tomorrow! míngtiān jiàn! 明天见; (*to look at*) kàn 看; please let me see your ticket qǐng ràng wǒ kàn yíxià nǐde piào 请让我看一下你的票; (*to visit*) kàn 看; I'm going to see a doctor wǒ qù kàn yīshēng 我去看医生; he came to see me yesterday tā zuótiān lái kàn wǒ le 他昨天来看我了; (*to watch*) kàn 看; to see [a film | a play | an exhibition] kàn [diànyǐng | xì | zhǎnlǎnhuì] 看 [电影 | 戏 | 展览会]; (*to understand, apprehend*) dǒng 懂, lǐjiě 理解, míngbai 明白; do you see what I mean? nǐ dǒng wǒde yìsi ma? 你懂我的意思吗?; (*to accompany*) péi 陪; I'll see you home wǒ péi nǐ huí jiā 我陪你回家

seem *vb* (*to appear*) hǎoxiàng 好像, sìhū 似乎; she seems [happy | annoyed | tired...] tā hǎoxiàng [hěn gāoxìng | hěn nǎohuǒ | hěn lèi...] 她好像 [很高兴 | 很恼火 | 很累...]; (*when talking about one's impressions*) kànlai 看来, kànyàngzi 看样子; it seems (that) there are many problems kànlai yǒu hěn duō wèntí 看来有很多问题

seldom *adv* hěn shǎo 很少, bù cháng 不常

self-confident *adj* yǒu zìxìnxīn 有自信心

selfish *adj* zìsī 自私

sell *vb* mài 卖, chūshòu 出售; to sell books to the students mài shū gěi xuésheng 卖书给学生; he sold me his car tā bǎ tāde chē màigěile wǒ 他把他的车卖给了我; water is sold in bottles shuǐ àn píng chūshòu 水按瓶出售

send *vb* (*to direct someone to go on a mission*) pài 派, pàiqiǎn 派遣; to send someone to post a letter pài mǒurén qù jì xìn

派某人去寄信 (to cause to be conveyed by post) jì 寄; to **send a package to someone** jìgěi mǒurén yíge bāoguǒ 寄给某人一个包裹; **he sent her a letter** tā jìgěi tā yìfēng xìn 他寄给她一封信; (to cause to be conveyed by electronic means) fā 发; to **send an e-mail message to someone** gěi mǒurén fā yíge diànzǐ yóujiàn 给某人发一个电子邮件; to **send a pupil home from school** bǎ yíge xuésheng cóng xuéxiào dǎfā huí jiā 把一个学生从学校打发回家; **send away;** (to dismiss) jiěgù 解雇; (to expel) qūzhú 驱逐; **send back** tuìhuán 退还, sònghuán 送还; **send for** qù jiào 去叫; to **send for the doctor** qù jiào yīshēng 去叫医生; **send off** to **send a player off** bǎ yìmíng duìyuán fáxiǎ chǎng 把一名队员罚下场; **send on** to send on baggage tíqián yùnsòng xíngli 提前运送行李; to send on post zhuǎnsòng xìnjiàn 转送信件

senior high school (US English), senior school
(British English) *n* a senior (high) school yìsuǒ gāozhōng 一所高中

sense
n (the body's capacity for perception) **the sense of** [sight | hearing | taste | smell | touch] [shì | tīng | wèi | xiù | chù] jué [视 | 听 | 味 | 嗅 | 触] 觉; (meaning, significance) yìyì 意义, yìsi 意思; it **doesn't make sense** zhè méi yǒu yìyì 这没有意义; (reasonableness) dàolǐ 道理; **it makes sense to check first** xiān jiǎnchá yíxià shì yǒu dàolǐ de 先检查一下是有道理的; to **have the sense not to go** bú qù shì yǒu dàolǐ de 不去是有道理的; **common sense** chángshí 常识, chánglǐ 常理; (mental attitude) **a sense of** [honour | justice | humour | beauty] yìzhōng [róngyù | zhèngyì | yōumò | měi] gǎn 一种 [荣誉 | 正义 | 幽默 | 美] 感; (consciousness) zhījué 知觉; **he is still in hospital but has recovered his senses** tā hái zài yīyuàn li, dàn yǐjīng huīfù zhījué 他还在医院里, 但已经恢复知觉; (feeling for what is appropriate) lǐzhì 理智, lǐxìng 理性; **he has obviously lost his senses** tā xiǎnrán shīqùle lǐzhì 他显然失去了理智

sensible
adj (when describing a person) dǒngshì 懂事, míngzhì 明智; (when describing a decision, a plan) qièhé shíjì 切合实际, hélǐ 合理; (when describing clothes) shíyòng 实用

sensitive *adj* (*easily affected*) mǐngǎn 敏感; **he is very sensitive to criticism** tā duì pīpíng fēicháng mǐngǎn 他对批评非常敏感; **a sensitive market** yíge mǐngǎn de shìchǎng 一个敏感的市场

sentence 1 *n* (*in language*) jùzi 句子; **a sentence** yíge jùzi 一个句子, yíjù huà 一句话; (*for a crime*) pànjué 判决, pànxíng 判刑; **a (prison) sentence** yíxiàng pànjué 一项判决
2 *vb* pàn 判, pànjué 判决; **to sentence someone to one year in prison** pàn mǒurén yì nián túxíng 判某人一年徒刑

separate 1 *adj* (*individual*) dāndú 单独; **the children have separate rooms** háizimen yǒu dāndú de fángjiān 孩子们有单独的房间; (*distinct*) bù tóng 不同; **there are two separate problems** yǒu liǎngge bù tóng de wèntí 有两个不同的问题
2 *vb* (*if it's a couple*) fēnjū 分居; **her parents separated two years ago** tā fùmǔ liǎng nián qián fēnjū le 她父母两年前分居了; **to separate the meat from the fish** bǎ ròu gēn yú fēnkāi 把肉跟鱼分开

separated *adj* fēnkāi de 分开的, gékāi de 隔开的

separately *adv* (*apart*) fēnkāi de 分开地; (*individually*) fēnbié de 分别地

September *n* jiǔyuè 九月

serial *n* a serial (*if it's a novel*) yíbù liánzǎi xiǎoshuō 一部连载小说, (*if it's a periodical publication*) yìfèn qīkān 一份期刊, (*if it's a TV play*) yíbù diànshì liánxùjù 一部电视连续剧

series *n* (*sequence*) xìliè 系列; **a series of problems** yíxìliè wèntí 一系列问题; (*set*) **a series of stamps** yíwǎ yóupiào 一套邮票; **a new series of Chinese language textbooks** yítào xīn de Zhōngwén jiàokēshū 一套新的中文教科书

serious *adj* (*causing worry*) yánzhòng 严重; **a serious accident** yícì yánzhòng shìgù 一次严重事故; (*when describing a personality*) rènzhēn 认真; **to be serious about** [football | going to college] duì [zúqiú | shàng dàxué] hěn zhòngshì 对 [足球 | 上大学] 很重视

serve *vb* (*in a shop*) **are you being served?** yǒu rén zài jiēdài nín ma? 有人在接待您吗?; (*at table*) **to serve the soup** shàng tāng 上汤: he served the guest a cup of Chinese tea tā gěi kèrén duānshang yìbēi Zhōngguó chá 他给客人端上一杯中国茶; (to work for) ...fúwù 为...服务; can computers serve agriculture? jìsuànjī kěyǐ wèi nóngyè fúwù ma? 计算机可以为农业服务吗?; (in tennis, badminton, etc.) fāqiú 发球

service n (the act of serving) fúwù 服务; (the act of helping or assisting) bāngzhù 帮助; (in a church) yíshì 仪式; (other uses) **military service** bīngyì 兵役; **public services** gōnggòng shìyè 公共事业; there are eight bus services to Beijing everyday měi tiān yǒu bābān gōnggòng qìchē qù Běijīng 每天有八班公共汽车去北京

service station n a service station yíge jiāyóuzhàn 一个加油站

set 1 n (a collection) tào 套; a set of [keys | stamps | plates] yítào [yàoshi | yóupiào | pánzi] 一套 [钥匙 | 邮票 | 盘子]; (in tennis) pán 盘; a set yìpán 一盘 **2** vb (to decide on) (guī)dìng (规)定; **to set** [a date | a price | a goal...] (guī)dìng [yíge rìqī | yíge jiàgé | yíge mùbiāo...] (规)定 [一个日期 | 一个价格 | 一个目标...]; (to adjust for a specific time or condition) tiáo 调; **to set** [an alarm clock | a video | a camera lens] tiáo [nàozhōng | lùxiàngjī | zhàoxiàngjī jìngtóu] 调 [闹钟 | 录像机 | 照相机镜头]; (for assignments or exams) **to set homework** bùzhì zuòyè 布置作业; **to set an exam** chū kǎojuàn 出考卷; (to create) chuàngzào 创造; **to set a new world record** chuàngzào yíxiàng xīn de shìjiè jìlù 创造一项新的世界记录; (to establish) shùlì 树立; **to set a good example for someone** wèi mǒurén shùlì yíge hǎo bǎngyàng 为某人树立一个好榜样; (when talking about a story, a film, or the physical stage for a play) yǐ...wéi bèijǐng 以...为背景; the film is set in Shanghai zhèbù diànyǐng yǐ Shànghǎi wéi bèijǐng 这部电影以上海为背景; (when talking about the sun) luò 落; (other uses) **to set the table** bǎi cānzhuō 摆餐桌; **to set fire to a house** fàng huǒ shāo yízuò fángzi 放火烧一座房子; **to set someone free** shìfàng mǒurén 释放某人; **set off** (to leave) chūfā 出发, dòngshēn 动身; (to cause to go off) **to set off fireworks** ránfàng yānhuǒ 燃放烟火; **to set off a bomb** shǐ yìkē zhàdàn bàozhà 使一颗炸弹爆炸; **to set off a burglar alarm** nòngxiǎng fángdào bàojǐngqì 弄响防盗报警器; **set up** (establish) jiànlì 建立, shèlì 设立;

to set up an organization jiànlì yíge zǔzhī 建立一个组织; (to start and manage) kāibàn 开办; to set up a company kāibàn yìjiā gōngsī 开办一家公司; (to place in position) shùqǐ 竖起, dāqǐ 搭起; to set up a tent tāqǐ yíge zhàngpeng 搭起一个帐篷

settle vb (to end) jiějué 解决, tiáotíng 调停; to settle [an argument | a dispute | a problem] jiějué [yìchǎng zhēnglùn | yíge jiūfēn | yíge wèntí] 解决 [一场争论 | 一个纠纷 | 一个问题]; (to decide on) dìng dìng 定, juédìng 决定; nothing is settled yet yíqiè dōu hái méi dìng 一切还没定; (to make one's home) dìngjū 定居; settle down (to live comfortably in one's new home) ānjū 安居; (to calm down) píngjìngxialai 平静下来, ānxia xīn lai 安下心来; she settled down to her homework tā ānxia xīn lai zuò zuòyè 她安下心来做作业; settle in āndùn 安顿

seven num qī 七

seventeen num shíqī 十七

seventeenth num (in a series) dìshíqī 第十七; (in dates) the seventeenth of May wǔyuè shíqī rì 五月十七日, wǔyuè shíqī hào 五月十七号

seventh num (in a series) dìqī 第七; (in dates) the seventh of July qīyuè qī rì 七月七日, qīyuè qī hào 七月七号

seventy num qīshí 七十

several det jǐge 几个; several tables jǐzhāng zhuōzi 几张桌子; several books jǐběn shū 几本书! Note that in jǐge 几个, ge 个 is a measure word that may be replaced by a different measure word, depending on the noun that follows.

severe adj (harsh) yánlì 严厉; (giving cause for concern) yánzhòng 严重; (strict) yángé 严格

sew vb féng 缝, féngzhì 缝制

sewing n féngrèn 缝纫

sewing machine n a sewing machine yìtái féngrènjī 一台缝纫机

sex n (state of being male or female) xìngbié 性别; (sexual intercourse) xìngjiāo 性交; to have sex with someone hé mǒurén fāshēng xìng guānxi 和某人发生性关系; hé mǒurén xìngjiāo 和某人性交

shade n (out of the sun) yīn 荫, yīnliángchù 荫凉处; **to sit in the shade of a tree** zuò zài shùyìn xia 坐在树荫下; (a colour) nóngdàn 浓淡; **a shade** yìzhǒng nóngdànsè 一种浓淡色; (for a lamp) dēngzhào 灯罩; **a shade** yíge dēngzhào 一个灯罩

shadow n a shadow yíge yǐngzi 一个影子

shake vb (to move with quick vibrations) yáo(huàng) 摇(晃), yáo(dòng) 摇(动); **to shake a bottle** yáohuàng yíge píngzi 摇晃一个瓶子; (to grasp the hand of someone in greeting) wò shǒu 握手; **to shake hands with someone** hé mǒurén wò shǒu 和某人握手; (when saying no) yáo 摇; **to shake one's head** yáo tóu 摇头; (with cold, fear, shock) fādǒu 发抖; **he was shaking with fear** tā xià de fādǒu 他吓得发抖; (during an explosion, an earthquake) zhèndòng 震动; **the earthquake shook the building** dìzhèn bǎ zhěnggè dàlóu dōu zhèndòng le 地震把整个大楼都震动了

shall vb (when talking about the future) huì 会, jiāng(yào) 将(要); **I shall see you next Tuesday** xiàge xīngqī'èr wǒ huì jiàndào nǐ 下个星期二我会见到你; **we shall arrive there on time** wǒmen jiāng ànshí dàodá nàr 我们将按时到达那儿; (when making suggestions) ...hǎo ma 好吗, yào bu yào... 要不要...; **shall I set the table?** yào bu yào wǒ bǎi cānzhuō? 要不要我摆餐桌?; **shall we go to the cinema?** wǒmen qù kàn diànyǐng hǎo ma? 我们去看电影好吗?

shame n (emotion caused by a humiliating feeling) xiūkuì 羞愧, xiūchǐ 羞耻; **she felt shame at having failed the exam** tā yīn kǎoshì bù jígé ér gǎndào xiūkuì 她因考试不及格而感到羞愧; (disgrace or dishonour) chǐrǔ 耻辱, xiūrǔ 羞辱; **to bring shame on someone** gěi mǒurén dàilai chǐrǔ 给某人带来耻辱; **shame on you!** nǐ zhēn diūrén! 你真丢人!; (when expressing regret) yíhàn 遗憾, kěxī 可惜; **that's a shame** zhēn yíhàn 真遗憾

shampoo n xǐfàjì 洗发剂, xiāngbō 香波

shape n (a form) xíng 形, xíngzhuàng 形状; **a shape** yíge xíngzhuàng 一个形状; **a square shape** yíge fāngxíng 一个方形; **in the shape of an apple** chéng píngguǒ (de) xíngzhuàng 呈

苹果(的)形状; (when talking about health) qíngkuàng 情况, zhuàngtài 状态; **she is in good shape after the operation** tā shǒushù hòu shēntǐ qíngkuàng hěn hǎo 她手术后身体情况很好; **to get in shape** chǔyú liánghǎo zhuàngtài 处于良好状态

share 1 vb (to join with others in using) héyòng 合用; **to share a house** héyòng/hézhù yídòng fángzi 合用/合住一栋房子; (when talking about dividing costs, rent, work) fēndān 分担; **to share** [the cost | the petrol | the work] **(with someone)** (hé mǒurén) fēndān [fèiyòng | qíyóufèi | zhèxiàng gōngzuò] (和某人)分担[费用/汽油费|这项工作]; (to take a share of) fēnxiǎng 分享; **he shared** [the profit | the money | her joy] **(with his sister)** tā (hé tā mèimei) fēnxiǎng [lìrùn | qián | tāde huānlè] 他(和他妹妹)分享[利润|钱|她的欢乐] **2** n (portion) fènr 份儿; **a share** yífènr 一份儿; **to pay one's fair share** fù yīng fù de nà yífènr 付应付的那一份儿; (unit of ownership in a public company) gǔpiào 股票; **a share** yìgǔ 一股; **share out** (British English) (amongst others) fēn 分

shark n a shark yìtiáo shāyú 一条鲨鱼

sharp adj (when speaking of knives, blades, etc.) kuài 快; (pointed) jiān 尖; (sudden, extreme) jí 急; **a sharp bend** yíge jí zhuǎnwān 一个急转弯; (intelligent) jīngmíng 精明; (aggressive) jiānkè 尖刻, kēkè 苛刻; (when talking about a pain) jùliè 剧烈

shave vb guā liǎn 刮脸, tì xū 剃须

she pron tā 她

sheep n a sheep yìzhī yáng 一只羊

sheet n (for a bed) chuángdān 床单; **a sheet** yìzhāng chuángdān 一张床单; (a piece) **a sheet** (of paper) yìzhāng zhǐ 一张纸; (of glass) yíkuài bōli 一块玻璃

shelf n a shelf yíge jiàzi 一个架子; **a book shelf** yíge shūjià 一个书架

shell n a shell yíge ké 一个壳

shelter 1 n (from rain, danger) **a shelter** yíge duǒbìchù 一个躲避处; (for homeless people) **a shelter** yíge qīshēn zhī dì 一个

栖身之地; **a bus shelter** yíge gōnggòng qìchē hòuchētíng 一个公共汽车候车亭 **2** vb (to take shelter) duǒbì 躲避; (to give protection to) bìhù 庇护, bǎohù 保护

shin n the shin xiǎotuǐ 小腿

shine vb (if it's the sun) zhàoyào 照耀; **the sun is shining** yángguāng zhàoyào 阳光照耀; (to give off light) fā guāng 发光; **the light in the lighthouse is shining** dēngtǎ li de dēng zài shǎnshǎn fā guāng 灯塔里的灯在闪闪发光; (to reflect light) fāliàng 发亮, fā guāng 发光; **the ring on her hand shone in the sun** tā shǒu shang de jièzhǐ zài yángguāng xià shǎnshǎn fāliàng 她手上的戒指在阳光下闪闪发亮; (to point a light at) **to shine a torch at someone** yòng shǒudiàntǒng zhào mǒurén 用手电筒照某人

ship n a ship yìsōu chuán 一艘船; **a passenger ship** yìsōu kèlún 一艘客轮

shirt n a shirt yíjiàn chènshān 一件衬衫, yíjiàn chènyī 一件衬衣

shiver vb fādǒu 发抖, duōsuo 哆嗦

shock 1 n (an upsetting experience) zhènjīng 震惊, dǎjī 打击; **a shock** yíge zhènjīng 一个震惊, yíge dǎjī 一个打击; **to get a shock** shòudào zhènjīng 受到震惊; **to give someone a shock** gěi mǒurén yíge dǎjī 给某人一个打击; (the medical state) xiūkè 休克, zhòngfēng 中风; **to be in shock** chǔyú xiūkè zhuàngtài 处于休克状态; (from electricity) **a shock** yícì diànjī 一次电击; **to get a shock** chù diàn 触电 **2** vb (to upset) shǐ...zhènjīng 使...震惊; **to shock someone** shǐ mǒurén zhènjīng 使某人震惊; **we were shocked by the news** duì zhège xiāoxi wǒmen dōu gǎndào zhènjīng 对这个消息我们都感到震惊; (to cause a scandal) shǐ...fènkǎi 使...愤慨; **to shock someone** shǐ mǒurén gǎndào fènkǎi 使某人感到愤慨

shoe n (for a person) xié 鞋; **a shoe** yìzhī xié 一只鞋; **a pair of shoes** yìshuāng xié 一双鞋; (for a horse) títiě 蹄铁; **a shoe** yíge títiě 一个蹄铁

shoot vb (to aim and fire a weapon) shèjī 射击, kāi qiāng 开枪; **to shoot at someone** xiàng mǒurén shèjī 向某人射击; (to hit with a missile from a weapon) jīzhòng 击中; shèzhòng 射中; they shot him in the leg tāmen jīzhòngle tāde tuǐ 他们击中了他的腿; to shoot someone dead kāi qiāng dǎsǐ mǒurén 开枪打死某人; (to move very fast) his car shot past me tāde chē cóng wǒ pángbiān fēisù kāiguoqu 他的车从我旁边飞速开过去; (when talking about film production) pāishè 拍摄; to shoot a film pāishè yíbù diànyǐng 拍摄一部电影

shop 1 n a shop yìjiā shāngdiàn 一家商店 **2** vb to go shopping qù mǎi dōngxi 去买东西

shop assistant n (British English) a shop assistant yìmíng shòuhuòyuán 一名售货员

shopkeeper n a shopkeeper yíge diànzhǔ 一个店主

shopping n mǎi dōngxi 买东西; to do the shopping mǎi dōngxi 买东西

shopping cart n (US English) a shopping cart yíliàng gòuwù shǒutuīchē 一辆购物手推车

shopping centre (British English), **shopping center** (US English) n a shopping centre, a shopping mall yíge gòuwù zhōngxīn 一个购物中心

shopping trolley n (British English) a shopping trolley yíliàng gòuwù shǒutuīchē 一辆购物手推车

shop window n a shop window yíge chúchuāng 一个橱窗

shore n (the edge of the sea) hǎi'àn 海岸; (dry land) hǎibīn 海滨

short 1 adj (not long) duǎn 短; the days are getting shorter tiān yuèlái yuè duǎn le 天越来越短了; a short skirt yìtiáo duǎn qún 一条短裙; he has short hair tā shì duǎn tóufa 他是短头发; (not tall) ǎi 矮; he's shorter than I tā bǐ wǒ ǎi 他比我矮; (brief) jiǎnduǎn 简短; a short speech yíge jiǎnduǎn de jiǎnghuà 一个简短的讲话; (lacking, wanting) quē(shǎo) 缺(少); to be short of [money | food | ideas...] quēshǎo [qián | shípǐn | zhǔyi...] 缺少[钱 | 食品 | 主意...] **2 in short** zǒngzhī 总之

short cut n a short cut yíge jiéjìng 一个捷径

shortly adv (soon) lìkè 立刻, mǎshàng 马上; (not long) bùjiǔ
不久; shortly before we left wǒmen líkāi qián bùjiǔ 我们离开
前不久

shorts n duǎnkù 短裤; a pair of shorts yìtiáo duǎnkù 一条短裤

shot n (from a gun) a shot (kāi) yì qiāng (开)一枪, yícì shèjī
一次射击; to fire a shot at someone xiàng mǒurén kāi yì qiāng
向某人开一枪; (in sports) a shot (in football) yícì shèmén
一次射门

should vb (when talking about what is right, what one ought to
do) yīnggāi 应该, yīngdāng 应当; she should learn to drive tā
yīnggāi xué kāi chē 她应该学开车; you shouldn't be late nǐ bù
yīnggāi chídào 你不应当迟到; (when saying something may
happen) yīnggāi huì 应该会, kěnéng huì 可能会; we should
be there by midday zhōngwǔ yǐqián wǒmen yīnggāi huì dàodá
nàr 中午以前我们应该会到达那儿; it shouldn't be too
difficult zhè kěnéng bú huì tài nán 这可能不会太难; (when
implying that something, though likely, didn't happen) běnlái
(yīnggāi) 本来(应该); the letter should have arrived yesterday
zhèfēng xìn běnlái yīnggāi zuótiān dào 这封信本来应该昨天
到; (when implying that something happened though it ought to
not have) běnlái bù (yīnggāi) 本来不(应该); you shouldn't have
said that nǐ běnlái bù yīnggāi nàme shuō 你本来不应该那么
说; (when used in a conditional clause to express a hypothetical
condition) wànyī 万一; if it should rain tomorrow, we shall have
to change our plans míngtiān wànyī xiàyǔ, wǒmen jiù děi
gǎibiàn jìhuà 明天万一下雨, 我们就得改变计划; (when
asking for permission) kě(yǐ) bù kěyǐ 可(以)不可以; should I
call him? wǒ kě bù kěyǐ gěi tā dǎ diànhuà? 我可不可以给他打
电话?; (when asking for advice) yīnggāi 应(该)不
应该 hǎo ma 好吗; should I call the doctor? wǒ yīng bù
yīnggāi jiào yīshēng? 我应不应该叫医生?; (when expressing a
past expectation of a future event) jiāng 将, huì 会; they didn't
expect that I should come and attend the meeting tāmen méi
xiǎngdào wǒ huì lái cānjiā huì 他们没想到我会来参加会;
(when expressing surprise at something unexpected) huì 会,
jìng(huì) 竟(会); it is surprising that he should be so foolish tā
jìnghuì zhème shǎ, zhēn ràng rén chījīng 他竟会这么傻, 真让

人吃惊; (when used after such verbs as propose, suggest, or such adjectives as necessary, important) **!** Note that in these cases, should is often not translated; **I suggest that he should discuss this matter with you** wǒ jiànyì tā hé nǐ tǎolùn zhège wèntí 我建议他和你讨论这个问题

shoulder n jiān 肩, jiānbǎng 肩膀; **to wear a sweater over one's shoulders** bǎ yījiàn máoyī pī zài jiān shang 把一件毛衣披在肩上; **he has strong shoulders** tāde jiānbǎng hěn jiēshi 他的肩膀很结实

shout 1 vb hǎn 喊, jiào 叫; **to shout at someone** duì mǒurén hǎn 对某人喊 **2** n hūhǎn 呼喊, hǎnjiào 喊叫; **a shout** yìshēng hūhǎn 一声呼喊; **shout out** hǎnchūlái 喊出来, dàshēng shuōchūlái 大声说出来

shovel n **a shovel** yìbǎ tiěxiān 一把铁锨, yìbǎ tiěchǎn 一把铁铲

show 1 vb (to let someone see) gěi...kàn 给...看; **to show someone a photo** gěi mǒurén kàn yìzhāng zhàopiàn 给某人看一张照片; (to guide) dài 带, (dài)lǐng (带)领; **I'll show you to your room** wǒ dài nǐ qù nǐde fángjiān 我带你去你的房间; (to point to) to show someone where to go gàosu mǒurén wǎng nǎr zǒu 告诉某人在哪儿走; **there's a sign showing the way to the swimming pool** yǒu yíge lùbiāo gàosu nǐ qù yóuyǒngchí de lù zěnme zǒu 有一个路标告诉你去游泳池的路怎么走; (to be on TV, at the cinema) fàngyìng 放映; **the film is showing at that cinema** zhèbù diànyǐng zhèngzài nàjiā diànyǐngyuàn fàngyìng 这部电影正在那家电影院放映; **to be shown on TV** zài diànshì shang fàngyìng/bōfàng 在电视上放映/播放; (to indicate) biǎomíng 表明, shuōmíng 说明; **this shows that he doesn't agree with our plan** zhè biǎomíng tā bù tóngyì wǒmende jìhuà 这表明他不同意我们的计划; (to demonstrate) gěi...shìfàn 给...示范, zuògěi...kàn 做给...看; **let me show you how to use this computer** wǒ lái gěi nǐ shìfàn zěnme yòng zhètái jìsuànjī 我来给你示范怎么用这台计算机 **2** n **a show** (on a stage) yìchǎng yǎnchū 一场演出; (on TV) yíge diànshì jiémù 一个电视节目; (on radio) yíge guǎngbō jiémù 一个广播节目; (at a cinema) yìchǎng diànyǐng 一场电影; (an exhibition) a show yíge zhǎnlǎn 一个展览; **show off** màinòng 卖弄, xuànyào 炫耀; **show round** to show someone round the town dài mǒurén cānguān chéngqū 带某人参观城区; **show up** (to be present) dàochǎng 到场; (to appear) xiǎnlù 显露, xiǎnchū 显出; (to expose) jiēlù 揭露, jiēchuān 揭穿

shower n (for washing) línyù 淋浴; a shower yíge línyù 一个淋浴; to have a shower xǐ línyù 洗淋浴; (rain) zhènyǔ 阵雨; a shower yìchǎng zhènyǔ 一场阵雨

showjumping n qí mǎ yuè zhàng yùndòng 骑马越障运动

shrimp n a shrimp yíge (xiǎo)xiā 一个小虾

shrink vb (when talking about clothing) shōusuō 收缩; the shirt shrank after washing zhèjiàn chènshān xǐ hòu shōusuō le 这件衬衫洗后收缩了; (when talking about an economy, etc.) suōxiǎo 缩小, jiǎnshǎo 减少

shut 1 adj (when referring to a book) héshang de 合上的; the book was shut shū shì héshang de 书是合上的; (when describing the eyes, the mouth) bìshang 闭上; my eyes were shut wǒ bìzhe yǎnjing 我闭着眼睛; (when describing a door, a shop) guānmén 关门; all the shops are shut suǒyǒu de shāngdiàn dōu guānmén le 所有的商店都关门了 **2** vb (if it's a window, a door) guān 关; to shut [the window | the door] guān [chuānghu | mén] 关[窗户 | 门]; the door does not shut properly zhè mén guān bú shàng 这门关不上; (if it's a book, a dictionary, a magazine to be closed) héshang 合上; to shut [the book | the dictionary] héshang [shū | cídiǎn] 合上[书 | 词典]; (if it's the eyes, the mouth to be closed) bìshang 闭上; to shut [one's eyes | one's mouth] bìshang [yǎnjīng | zuǐ] 闭上[眼睛 | 嘴]; **shut down** (to close) guānbì 关闭; the factory shut down in May last year zhèjiā gōngchǎng qùnián wǔyuè guānbì le 这家工厂去年五月关闭了; **shut out** to shut someone out bǎ mǒurén guān zài wàimiàn 把某人关在外面; **shut up** (to be quiet) zhùzuǐ 住嘴; (to lock inside) to shut someone up bǎ mǒurén guānqilai 把某人关起来; to shut something up bǎ mǒuwù shōucángqilai 把某物收藏起来

shy adj (bashful) hàixiū 害羞, miǎntiǎn 腼腆; (easily frightened) dǎnqiè 胆怯

sick adj (ill) bìng 病, shēngbìng 生病: he got sick tā bìng le 他病了; she felt sick tā juéche bù shūfu 她觉得不舒服: to be sick (British English) (to vomit) ěxin 恶心, yào òutù 要呕吐; (fed up) fán le 烦了, yànjuàn le 厌倦了: he's sick of his neighbours tā duì tāde línjū yànjuàn le 他对他的邻居厌倦了

sickness n a sickness yìzhǒng jíbìng 一种疾病

side n (a line forming part of a boundary or the part near the boundary) biān 边, biān 边: a side yì biān 一边; there are shops on either side of the road mǎlù liǎng biān dōu yǒu shāngdiàn 马路两边都有商店; by the side of the river zài hé biān 在河边; the north side of Beijing Běijīng de běi biān 北京的北边; (of a person's body) cè 侧: to be lying on one's side cèzhe shēnzi tǎngzhe 侧着身子躺着; on my right side wǒ shēntǐ de yòu cè 我身体的右侧; (a surface of something flat) miàn 面: a side yí miàn 一面; please read the other side of the page qǐng kàn zhè yíyè de lìng yí miàn 请看这一页的另一面; (aspect) fāngmiàn 方面: a side yíge fāngmiàn 一个方面; to consider all sides of the problem kǎolǜ zhège wèntí de gège fāngmiàn 考虑这个问题的各个方面; (in a conflict, a contest) pài 派, fāng 方: a side yí pài 一派, yì fāng 一方; (a team) duì 队, fāng 方: a side yí duì 一队; side with zhàn zài...de yì biān 站在...的一边, zhīchí 支持

sidewalk n (US English) a sidewalk yìtiáo rénxíngdào 一条人行道

sigh vb tànxī 叹息, tànqì 叹气

sight n (faculty of seeing) shìlì 视力, shìjué 视觉: to have good sight shìlì hǎo 视力好: to be [long | short] -sighted huàn [yuǎn | jìn] shì 患 [远 | 近] 视; (view) to catch sight of someone kànjiàn mǒurén 看见某人: to be out of sight kàn bú jiàn 看不见

sightseeing n guānguāng 观光, yóulǎn 游览

sign 1 n (a mark, symbol) a sign yíge fúhào 一个符号, yíge jìhào 一个记号; the US dollar sign měiyuán de fúhào 美元的符号; (for traffic) a sign yíge biāozhì 一个标志; (for shops, *advertising*) **a sign** yíge zhāopái 一个招牌; (*a notice*) **a sign** yíge páizi 一个牌子; (*evidence, indication*) **a sign** yíge zhèngzhào 一个征兆, yíge jìxiàng 一个迹象 **2** *vb* (*to put one's signature to*) zài...shang qiān zì/míng 在...上签字/名; **to sign** (*one's name on*) **a cheque** zài zhīpiào shang qiān zì 在支票上签字; **sign on** (*British English*) (*to record one's arrival at work*) qiān dào 签到; (*to begin a new job*) **to sign on** kāishǐ yíxiàng xīn gōngzuò 开始一项新工作

signal 1 *n* **a signal** yíge xìnhào 一个信号 **2** *vb* (*using lights, flags, a coding system*) fā xìnhào 发信号; **to signal to turn left** fāchū xiàng zuǒ guǎi de xìnhào 发出向左拐的信号; (*using one's hands*) dǎ shǒushì 打手势; **to signal someone to come** dǎ shǒushì ràng mǒurén lái 打手势让某人来

signature *n* **a signature** yíge qiānmíng 一个签名

signpost *n* **a signpost** yíge lùbiāo 一个路标

silence *n* (*absence of noise*) jìjìng 寂静, wúshēng 无声; (*refraining from speech*) chénmò 沉默, mò bú zuò shēng 默不作声

silent *adj* (*quiet*) jìjìng 寂静; (*not speaking or making any sound*) chénmò 沉默, mò bú zuò shēng 默不作声

silk *n* sī 丝, sīchóu 丝绸

silly *adj* shǎ 傻, yúchǔn 愚蠢, hútu 糊涂

silver 1 *n* (*the metal*) yín 银, yínzi 银子; (*silver coins*) yínbì 银币 **2** *adj* yín 银; **a silver ring** yìzhī yín jièzhi 一只银戒指

simple *adj* (*not complicated*) jiǎndān 简单; (*plain*) pǔsù 朴素; (*unsuspecting*) dānchún 单纯; (*ordinary*) pǔtōng 普通, píngcháng 平常

since 1 *prep* ! Note that the phrase or clause beginning with since appears at the beginning of the sentence in Chinese: cóng...yǐlái 从...以来, zìcóng 自从; **I haven't been feeling well since Monday** cóng xīngqīyī yǐlái, wǒ yìzhí gǎnjué shēntǐ bù shūfu 从星期一以来, 我一直感觉身体不舒服; **she has been living in China since 1988** zìcóng yìjiǔbābā nián, tā yìzhí zhù zài Zhōngguó 自从一九八八年她一直住在中国;

I haven't seen him **since last week** wǒ zìcóng shàng xīngqī yìzhí méi jiànguo tā 我自从上星期一直没见过他 **2** conj (from the time when) yǐcóng...yǐlái, ...yǐlái, 以来, ...以来; **I haven't heard from her since she left** tā líkāi yǐhòu, wǒ hái méi shōudàoguo tāde xìn 她离开以后，我还没收到过她的信; **I've lived here since I was ten** wǒ cóng shí suì yǐlái yìzhí zhù zài zhèr 我从十岁以来一直住在这儿; **it's ten years since she died** tā sǐle shí nián le 她死了十年了; (because) yīnwèi 因为, jìrán 既然; **since she was ill, she couldn't go** jìrán tā bìng le, suǒyǐ tā bù néng qù 既然她病了，所以她不能去 **3** adv (from that time) yǐhòu 以后; (from then on) hòulái 后来; **I have been living here ever since** cóng nà yǐhòu wǒ yìzhí zhù zài zhèlǐ 从那以后我一直住在这里

sincere adj zhēnchéng 真诚, chéngkěn 诚恳

sincerely adv zhēnchéng de 真诚地, chéngkěn de 诚恳地; **Yours sincerely** (British English), **Sincerely yours** (US English) Nínde zhōngchéng de 您的忠诚的; **I sincerely hope that...** wǒ zhōngxīn xīwàng... 我衷心希望...

sing vb chàng 唱, chànggē 唱歌

singer n **a singer** (one who sings as a profession) yìmíng gēshǒu 一名歌手; (one whose fame for singing is widely recognized) yìmíng gēchàngjiā 一名歌唱家

singing n chànggē 唱歌, gēchàng 歌唱

single adj (one) yī 一; **we visited three towns in a single day** wǒmen yì tiān fǎngwènle sānge chéngzhèn 我们一天访问了三个城镇; **I didn't see a single person** wǒ méiyǒu kànjiàn yíge rén 我没有看见一个人; (without a partner) dúshēn 独身; (for one person) dānrén 单人; **a single bed** yìzhāng dānrén chuáng 一张单人床; (denoting ticket for transport valid for outward journey only) (British English) dānchéng 单程; **a single ticket** yìzhāng dānchéng piào 一张单程票

sink **1** n **a sink** (in a kitchen) yíge shuǐchí 一个水池, yíge xǐdícáo 一个洗涤槽 **2** vb (to become submerged in water) chénmò 沉没, chén 沉; **the boat sank in five minutes** nàtiáo chuán bú dào wǔ fēnzhōng biàn chénmò le 那条船不到五分钟便沉没

ʃ; (subside) xiàxiàn 下陷; (to cause to sink) to sink a ship shǐ yìsōu chuán chénmò 使一艘船沉没

sister n a sister (elder) yíge jiějie 一个姐姐; (younger) yíge mèimei 一个妹妹

sister-in-law n a sister-in-law (elder brother's wife) yíge sǎozi 一个嫂子; (younger brother's wife) yíge dìmèi/dìxí 一个弟妹/弟媳; (husband's elder sister) yíge dàgūzi 一个大姑子; (husband's younger sister) yíge xiǎogūzi 一个小姑子; (wife's elder sister) yíge dàyízi 一个大姨子; (wife's younger sister) yíge xiǎoyízi 一个小姨子

sit vb (to take a seat) zuò 坐; to be sitting on the floor zuò zài dì shang 坐在地上; (British English) (to take) to sit an exam cānjiā kǎoshì 参加考试; **sit down** zuòxia 坐下; **sit up** (to rise to a sitting position) zuòqilai 坐起来

sitting room n a sitting room yìjiān qǐjūshì 一间起居室

situated adj wèiyú 位于, zuòluòzài 坐落在; situated near the town centre wèiyú shì zhōngxīn fùjìn 位于市中心附近

situation n (location) wèizhi 位置, dìdiǎn 地点; a situation yíge wèizhi 一个位置; (momentary state) chǔjìng 处境, jìngkuàng 境况; to be in a dangerous situation chǔjìng wēixiǎn 处境危险; (a set of circumstances) xíngshì 形势, júshì 局势; [international | domestic | economic] situation [guójì | guónèi | jīngjì] xíngshì [国际 | 国内 | 经济] 形势

six num liù 六

sixteen num shíliù 十六

sixteenth num (in a series) dìshíliù 第十六; (in dates) the sixteenth of July qīyuè shíliù rì 七月十六日, qīyuè shíliù hào 七月十六号

sixth num (in a series) dìliù 第六; (in dates) the sixth of February èryuè liù rì 二月六日, èryuè liù hào 二月六号

sixty num liùshí 六十

size n (when talking about a person) shēncái 身材; she's about your size tāde shēncái gēn nǐ chàbùduō 她的身材跟你差不多, (when talking about hats, socks, shoes) hào 号; a size yíge hào

一个号; what size shoes do you wear? nǐ chuān jǐ hào de xié? 你穿几号的鞋?; (when talking about clothes) chǐcùn 尺寸; do you have trousers of this size? nǐmen yǒu zhège chǐcùn de kùzi ma? 你们有这个尺寸的裤子吗?; (when talking about how big something is) what is the size of [your house | England | that school | the apple]? [nǐde fángzi | Yīnggélán | nàsuǒ xuéxiào | píngguǒ] yǒu duō dà? [你的房子 | 英格兰 | 那所学校 | 苹果] 有多大?; I like a garden of this size wǒ xǐhuan zhème dàxiǎo de huāyuán 我喜欢这么大小的花园; the size of the window chuānghu de dàxiǎo 窗户的大小, chuānghu de chǐcùn 窗户的尺寸

skateboard n a skateboard yíge (sìlún) huábǎn 一个(四轮)滑板

skating n ice-skating huábīng 滑冰; roller-skating liūbīng 溜冰

skating rink n a skating rink (for ice-skating) yíge huábīngchǎng 一个滑冰场; (for roller-skating) yíge liūbīngchǎng 一个溜冰场

sketch n (a drawing) cǎotú 草图, sùmiáo 素描; a sketch yìzhāng cǎotú 一张草图; (a funny scene) xiǎopǐn 小品; a sketch yíge xiǎopǐn 一个小品

ski 1 n a ski yìzhī huáxuěbǎn 一只滑雪板; a pair of skis yìfù huáxuěbǎn 一副滑雪板 **2** vb to go skiing qù huáxuě 去滑雪

skiing n huáxuě 滑雪

skilful (British English), **skillful** (US English) adj shúliàn 熟练, língqiǎo 灵巧

skill n (the quality) jìyì 技艺, jìqiǎo 技巧; (a particular ability) jìnéng 技能, jìshù 技术

skin n pífū 皮肤, pí 皮

skinny adj (thin) jí shòu 极瘦, píbāogǔ de 皮包骨的

skip vb (to give little jumps) bèng 蹦; (with a rope) tiàoshéng 跳绳; to skip classes táoxué 逃学, táokè 逃课

ski resort n a ski resort yíge huáxuě shèngdì 一个滑雪胜地

skirt n a skirt yìtiáo qúnzi 一条裙子

sky n the sky tiān 天, tiānkōng 天空: a clear sky qínglǎng de tiānkōng 晴朗的天空

skydiving n tiàosǎn yùndòng 跳伞运动

slap vb to slap someone's face dǎ mǒurén ěrguāng 打某人耳光; to slap someone on the back zài mǒurén bèi shang pāi yíxià 在某人背上拍一下

sled, sledge (British English) **1** n a sled yíge xuěqiāo 一个雪橇 **2** vb to go sledging (British English) chéng xuěqiāo qù 乘雪橇去

sleep 1 n shuìjiào 睡觉, shuìmián 睡眠; to go to sleep shuìzháo 睡着, rùshuì 入睡; I cannot go to sleep wǒ shuì bù zháo 我睡不着; to go back to sleep chóngxīn shuìzháo 重新睡着; to put someone to sleep shǐ mǒurén rùshuì 使某人入睡 **2** vb (to be asleep) shuì 睡, shuìjiào 睡觉; to sleep with someone hé mǒurén fāshēng xìng guānxi 和某人发生性关系, hé mǒurén shuìjiào 和某人睡觉; **sleep in** (to let oneself sleep longer than usual) wǎn qǐchuáng 晚起床, shuìlǎnjiào 睡懒觉

sleeping bag n a sleeping bag yíge shuìdài 一个睡袋

sleepy adj to be sleepy, to feel sleepy xiǎng shuìjiào 想睡觉, gǎnjué kùn 感觉困

sleet n yǔ jiā xuě 雨夹雪

sleeve n a sleeve yìzhī xiùzi 一只袖子; to roll up one's sleeves juǎnqǐ xiùzi 卷起袖子

slice 1 n a slice of [bread | meat | lemon | cucumber] yípiàn [miànbāo | ròu | níngméng | huángguā] 一片 [面包 | 肉 | 柠檬 | 黄瓜] **2** vb to slice bread bǎ miànbāo qiēchéng piàn 把面包切成片

slide 1 vb (to slip or slide) huá 滑, huádòng 滑动; to slide on ice huábīng 滑冰; (to slip off) huáluò 滑落; the plates slid off the table pánzi cóng zhuōzi shang huáluòxiaqu 盘子从桌子上滑落下去 **2** n (an image from a photograph) a slide yìzhāng huàndēngpiàn 一张幻灯片; (in a playground) a slide yíge huátī 一个滑梯

slim 1 adj miáotiáo 苗条, xìcháng 细长 **2** vb (British English) jiǎn féi 减肥

slip vb (to glide or slide) huá huá 滑; (to fall down by sliding) huádǎo 滑倒; **she slipped when coming down the mountain** tā xià shān de shíhou huádǎo le 她下山的时候滑倒了; (to fall off by sliding) huáluò 滑落; **the glass slipped out of my hands** bōlíbēi cóng wǒ shǒu zhōng huáluòxiaqu 玻璃杯从我手中滑落下去

slipper n a slipper yìzhī tuōxié 一只拖鞋; **a pair of slippers** yìshuāng tuōxié 一双拖鞋

slippery adj huá 滑

slot machine n a slot machine yìtái tóu bì dǔbójī 一台投币赌博机

slow adj (not fast) màn 慢, huǎnmàn 缓慢; **to make slow progress** jìnbù hěn màn 进步很慢; (not bright) chídùn 迟钝, bèn 笨; (describing a watch, a clock) màn 慢; **the clock is 20 minutes slow** zhège zhōngbiǎo màn èrshí fēn zhōng 这个钟表慢二十分钟; **slow down** fàngmàn sùdù 放慢速度, mànxialai 慢下来

slowly adv mànmàn de 慢慢地, huǎnmàn de 缓慢地

sly adj jiǎohuá 狡猾, jiǎozhà 狡诈

small adj xiǎo 小; **a small car** yíliàng xiǎo qìchē 一辆小汽车; **a small quantity** shǎo liàng 少量

small ad n (British English) a small ad yíge xiǎo guǎnggào 一个小广告

smart adj (British English) (elegant) xiāosǎ 潇洒, piàoliang 漂亮; (intelligent) cōngming 聪明, jīngmíng 精明

smash vb (to break) dǎsuì 打碎, dǎpò 打破; (to get broken) pò pò 破, suì 碎; **smash up** dǎohuǐ 捣毁, dǎpò 打破

smell 1 n (an odour) a smell yìzhǒng qìwèi 一种气味; (the sense) the sense of smell xiùjué 嗅觉 2 vb (to perceive by nose) wén 闻; **I can smell burning** wǒ néng wéndào húwèir 我能闻到糊味儿; (to give off an odour) wénqilai 闻起来; **this smells nice** zhè wénqilai hěn hǎowén 这闻起来很好闻

smile 1 vb xiào 笑, wēixiào 微笑; **to smile at someone** xiàng mǒurén (wēi)xiào 向某人(微)笑 2 n a smile xiào 笑, wēixiào 微笑

smoke 1 n yān 烟, yānqì 烟气 **2** vb (to give off smoke) mào yān 冒烟; (to inhale and expel tobacco smoke) chōu yān 抽烟, xī yān 吸烟; **do you smoke?** nǐ xī yān ma? 你吸烟吗?; (to inhale and expel smoke from) xī 吸, chōu 抽; **to smoke a pipe** chōu yāndǒu 抽烟斗

smooth adj (when describing a road, the ground) píngtǎn 平坦; **a smooth road** yìtiáo píngtǎn de dàolù 一条平坦的道路; (when describing the surface of paper, glass, a table, a floor) guānghuá 光滑; **the floor is very smooth** dìmiàn hěn guānghuá 地面很光滑; (when describing an action) píngwěn 平稳; **the flight was not very smooth** fēixíng bú tài píngwěn 飞行不太平稳; (when describing a writing style) tōngshùn 通顺, liúchàng 流畅

smother vb (to suffocate by excluding air) shǐ...zhìxī 使...窒息, shǐ...tòu bú guò qì lai 使...透不过气来; **to smother someone** shǐ mǒurén zhìxī 使某人窒息

snack n xiǎochī 小吃, kuàicān 快餐

snail n a snail yíge wōniú 一个蜗牛

snake n a snake yìtiáo shé 一条蛇

snapshot n a snapshot yìzhāng kuàizhào 一张快照

sneaker n (US English) a sneaker (a shoe) yìzhī yùndòngxié 一只运动鞋; **a pair of sneakers** yìshuāng yùndòngxié 一双运动鞋

sneeze vb dǎ pēntì 打喷嚏

snobbish adj shìlì 势利, chǎnshàng qīxià 谄上欺下

snooker n táiqiú 台球

snore vb dǎ hān 打鼾, dǎ hūlu 打呼噜

snow 1 n xuě 雪 **2** vb xiàxuě 下雪; **it's snowing** zhèngzài xiàxuě 正在下雪

snowball n a snowball yíge xuěqiú 一个雪球

snowman n a snowman yíge xuěrén 一个雪人

so 1 adv (to such an extent) zhème 这么, nàme 那么; **he's so** [happy | stupid | smart...] tā nàme [gāoxìng | bèn | cōngmíng...] 他那么 [高兴 | 笨 | 聪明...]; **they speak so fast** tāmen shuō de zhème kuài 他们说得这么快; I have so much work to do wǒ yǒu zhème duō gōngzuò yào zuò 我有这么多工作要做; (also) yě 也！Note that in this sense, the meaning conveyed by so in English has to be stated overtly in Chinese; I'm fifteen and so is he wǒ shíwǔ suì, tā yě shíwǔ suì 我十五岁, 他也十五岁; if you go, so will I rúguǒ nǐ qù, wǒ yě qù 如果你去, 我也去; (very) fēicháng 非常, hěn 很; I'm so pleased to hear the news tīngdào zhège xiāoxi, wǒ fēicháng; gāoxìng 听到这个消息, 我非常高兴; (other uses) I think so wǒ xiǎng shì zhèyàng 我想是这样; I'm afraid so kǒngpà shì zhèyàng 恐怕是这样; who says so? shéi shuō de? 谁说的?; so what? nà yòu zěnmeyàng ne? 那又怎样呢?; and so on děngděng 等等 2 conj (therefore) suǒyǐ 所以, yīncǐ 因此; she was sick, so I went to see her tā bìng le, suǒyǐ wǒ qù kàn tā 她病了, 所以我去看她; so (that) yǐbiàn 以便, wèide shì 为的是; he moved to a house near his mother, so that he could look after her better tā bāndào lí tā mā hěn jìn de yísuǒ fángzi, yǐbiàn tā néng gèng hǎo de zhàogù tā 他搬到离他妈妈近的一所房子, 以便他能更好地照顾她; (then, in that case) nàme 那么, zhèyàng kànlai 这样看来; so you are going to study Chinese nàme nǐ dǎsuàn xué Zhōngwén 那么你打算学中文 3 so as yǐbiàn 以便, wèide shì 为的是; we left early so as not to miss the train wǒmen hěn zǎo jiù líkāi le, wèide shì bú wù huǒchē 我们很早就离开了, 为的是不误火车

soap n (for washing) féizào 肥皂; (on TV) a soap yíbù diànshì liánxùjù 一部电视连续剧

soccer n zúqiú 足球

social adj (relating to society) shèhuì de 社会的; (sociable) xǐhuan jiāojì de 喜欢交际的

social studies n shèhuì yánjiū 社会研究, shèhuìxué 社会学

social worker n a social worker yíge shèhuì gōngzuòzhě 一个社会工作者

sock n a sock yìzhī duǎnwà 一只短袜; a pair of socks yìshuāng duǎnwà 一双短袜

sofa n a sofa yíge shāfā 一个沙发

soft adj (not hard or tough) ruǎn 软; the ground is soft here zhèr de dì hěn ruǎn 这儿的地很软; a soft toffee yíkuài ruǎn nǎitáng 一块软奶糖; (when describing colours; lights, voice) róuhé 柔和; soft lights róuhé de dēngguāng 柔和的灯光; (when describing a manner, an action) wēnhé 温和; a soft answer yíge wēnhé de dáfù 一个温和的答复; (yielding easily to pressure) ruǎnruò 软弱, shùncóng 顺从; you are too soft with him nǐ duì tā tài ruǎnruò 你对他太软弱; soft drinks ruǎn yǐnliào 软饮料

software n ruǎnjiàn 软件

soldier n a soldier yíge shìbīng 一个士兵, yíge zhànshì 一个战士

sole n the sole (of the foot) jiǎodǐ 脚底; (of a shoe) a sole yíge xiédǐ 一个鞋底

solicitor n (British English) a solicitor yíge lǜshī 一个律师

solution n a solution yíge jiějué bànfǎ 一个解决办法

solve vb jiě 解, jiějué 解决; to solve a problem jiějué yíge wèntí 解决一个问题

some 1 det (an amount or number of); (when used in mid-sentence) yìxiē 一些; I have to buy some bread wǒ děi mǎi yìxiē miànbāo 我得买一些面包; she ate some strawberries tā chīle yìxiē cǎoméi 她吃了一些草莓; we visited some beautiful towns wǒmen fǎngwènle yìxiē měilì de chéngzhèn 我们访问了一些美丽的城镇; (when used at the beginning of a sentence) yǒuxiē 有些; some shops don't open on Sunday yǒuxiē shāngdiàn xīngqītiān bù kāimén 有些商店星期天不开门; (certain) mǒu(yī) 某(一); she is studying at some university in Beijing tā zài Běijīng de mǒu (yī)suǒ dàxué xuéxí 她在北京的某(一)所大学学习; some people don't like travelling by plane mǒu (yī)xiē rén bù xǐhuan zuò fēijī lǚxíng 某(一)些人不喜欢坐飞机旅行 **2** pron (an amount or number of); (when used in mid-sentence) yìxiē 一些; I know where you can find some wǒ zhīdào zài nǎr nǐ néng zhǎodào yìxiē 我知道在哪儿你能找到一些; (when used at the beginning of a sentence) yǒu yìxiē 有一些

有一些; some are useful yǒu yìxiē hěn yǒuyòng 有一些很有用; (certain people) yǒu (yì)xiē rén 有(一)些人; some (of them) are Chinese (tāmen dāngzhōng yǒu yìxiē rén shì) Zhōngguórén (他们当中)有一些人是中国人; (certain things) yǒu (yì)xiē dōngxi 有(一)些东西; some are quite expensive yǒu yìxiē dōngxi xiāngdāng guì 有一些东西相当贵

someone pron (also **somebody**) mǒurén 某人, mǒu (yí)ge rén 某(一)个人; someone famous mǒu yíge yǒumíng de rén 某一个有名的人

something pron (an undefined thing) yíge dōngxi 一个东西, mǒuwù 某物; I saw something interesting wǒ kàndào yíge yǒuqù de dōngxi 我看到一个有趣的东西; (an undefined matter) yíjiàn shì 一件事, mǒushì 某事; I'd like to discuss something with you wǒ xiǎng gēn nǐ tǎolùn yíjiàn shì 我想跟你讨论一件事

sometimes adv yǒushíhou 有时候, yǒushí 有时

somewhere adv zài mǒu (yí)ge dìfang 在某(一)个地方, zài shénme dìfang 在什么地方; they live somewhere in Scotland tāmen zhù zài Sūgélán de mǒu ge dìfang 他们住在苏格兰的某个地方; let's go somewhere else zánmen qù lìngwài yíge dìfang ba 咱们去另外一个地方吧

son n a son yíge érzi 一个儿子

song n a song yìshǒu gē 一首歌, yìzhī gē 一支歌

son-in-law n a son-in-law yíge nǚxu 一个女婿

soon adv (before long, in a short time) hěn kuài 很快, bùjiǔ 不久; he'll go to China soon tā hěn kuài jiùyào qù Běijīng le 他很快快要去北京了; (in a moment) yíhuìr 一会儿; I'll come back soon wǒ yíhuìr jiù huílai 我一会儿就回来; (early) zǎo 早, the sooner the better yuè zǎo yuè hǎo 越早越好; as soon as possible jìn zǎo 尽早; (quickly) jìn kuài 尽快; come as soon as you can nǐ jìn kěnéng kuài lái 你尽可能快来

sore adj to have a sore [throat | leg | back...] [sǎngzi | tuǐ | hòubèi...] téng [嗓子 | 腿 | 后背] 疼; my arm is very sore wǒde gēbo hěn téng 我的胳膊很疼

sorry adj (when apologizing) duìbuqǐ 对不起 bàoqiàn 抱歉; sorry! duìbuqǐ 对不起! I'm sorry I'm late duìbuqǐ, wǒ lái wǎn le 对不起, 我 来晚了; (to say sorry shuō duìbuqǐ 说对不起; (when expressing regret) yíhàn 遗憾; I'm sorry you can't come hěn yíhàn nǐ bù néng lái 很遗憾你不能来; (when expressing regret for what one did in the past) hòuhuǐ 后悔, àohuǐ 懊悔; I feel very sorry for what I did wǒ duì wǒ suǒ zuò de shì gǎndào hěn hòuhuǐ 我对我所做的事感到很后悔; (when expressing pity or sympathy) nánguò 难过, wǎnxī 惋惜; to feel sorry for someone wèi mǒurén nánguò 为某人难过

sort 1 n zhǒng 种, lèi 类; it's a sort of [bird | computer | loan...] zhè shì yìzhǒng [niǎo | jìsuànjī | dàikuǎn...] 这是一种 [鸟 | 计算机 | 贷款...]; he's not that sort of person tā bú shì nàlèi rén 他不是那类人 **2** vb (to classify) bǎ...fēn lèi 把...分类; to sort files bǎ dǎng'àn fēn lèi 把档案分类; (to arrange) zhěnglǐ 整理; to sort the books into piles bǎ shū zhěnglǐchéng yíluǒ yíluǒ de 把书整理成一摞一摞的; sort out (to solve) jiějué 解决; to sort out a problem jiějué yíge wèntí 解决一个问题; (to deal with) chǔlǐ 处理; I'll sort it out wǒ huì chǔlǐ zhèjiàn shì 我会处理这件事; (to arrange and organize) zhěnglǐ 整理; to sort out these documents zhěnglǐ zhèxiē wénjiàn 整理这些文件; (to classify) bǎ...fēn lèi 把...分类; to sort out the photos bǎ zhàopiàn fēn lèi 把照片分类; to sort out the old clothes from the new bǎ yīfu àn xīn jiù fēn lèi 把衣服按新旧分类

sound 1 n shēng 声, shēngyīn 声音; a sound yíge shēngyīn 一个声音; I heard the sound of voices wǒ tīngjian shuōhuà shēng le 我听见说话声了; to turn up the sound of the television bǎ diànshìjī de shēngyīn tiáo dà 把电视机的声音 调大; the sound of a piano gāngqín shēng 钢琴声 **2** vb (to give out a sound) xiǎng 响; the alarm clock sounded at 7 o'clock nàozhōng qī diǎn xiǎng le 闹钟七点响了; (to give an impression on hearing) tīngqilai 听起来; it sounds [dangerous | odd | interesting...] zhè tīngqilai [hěn wēixiǎn | hěn qíguài | hěn yǒu yìsi...] 这听起来 [很危险 | 很奇怪 | 很有意思...]; it sounds like a piano zhè tīngqilai xiàng gāngqín 这听起来像钢琴

soup n a soup yíge tāng 一个汤

sour *adj* suān 酸; the milk has gone sour niúnǎi biàn suān le 牛奶变酸了

south 1 *n* the south nánfāng 南方, nánbù 南部; in the south of China zài Zhōngguó de nánfāng 在中国的南方 **2** *adv* to go south qù nánfāng 去南方; to live south of Beijing zhù zài Běijīng de nánbù 住在北京的南部 **3** *adj* nán 南; to work in south London zài nán Lúndūn gōngzuò 在南伦敦工作

South Africa *n* Nán Fēi 南非

South America *n* Nán Měi(zhōu) 南美(洲)

southeast *n* the southeast dōngnán 东南

southwest *n* the southwest xīnán 西南

souvenir *n* a souvenir yíge jìniànpǐn 一个纪念品

space *n* (room) kōngjiān 空间; to take up space zhàn kōngjiān 占空间; (an area of land or a place) kòng dì 空地, dìfang 地方; an open space yíkuài kòng dì 一块空地; (outer space) tàikōng 太空; (a gap) kòng 空, kòngbái 空白; a space yíge kòng 一个空; fill the spaces with verbs yòng dòngcí tián kòng 用动词填空

Spain *n* Xībānyá 西班牙

Spanish 1 *adj* Xībānyá de 西班牙的, Xībānyárén de 西班牙人的 **2** *n* Xībānyáyǔ 西班牙语, Xībānyáwén 西班牙文

spare *adj* (extra) duōyú 多余; I've got a spare ticket wǒ yǒu yìzhāng duōyú de piào 我有一张多余的票; (not in actual use) kòng 空; are there any spare seats? hái yǒu kòng zuòwèi ma? 还有空座位吗?

spare part *n* a spare part yíge bèijiàn 一个备件

spare room *n* a spare room yìjiān kòng fángjiān 一间空房间

spare time *n* spare time kòngyú shíjiān 空余时间

speak *vb* (utter words) shuōhuà 说话, jiǎnghuà 讲话; to speak to a friend gēn yíge péngyou shuōhuà 跟一个朋友说话; who's speaking, please? qǐng wèn, nín shì nǎ wèi? 请问, 您是哪位?; generally speaking yìbān shuōlái 一般说来; (to utter) shuō 说, jiǎng 讲; to speak Japanese shuō Rìyǔ 说日语; speak up (to *speak boldly)* dàdǎn de shuō 大胆地说; *(to speak so as to be heard easily)* qīngchu xiǎngliàng de shuō 清楚响亮地说

special *adj (exceptional)* tèshū 特殊, tèbié 特别; **a special purpose** yíge tèshū de mùdì 一个特殊的目的; *(designed for a particular purpose)* zhuānmén 专门; **a special school** yìsuǒ zhuānmén de xuéxiào 一所专门的学校; *(intimate)* tèbié qīnmì 特别亲密; **she's a special friend of mine** tā shì wǒ tèbié qīnmì de péngyou 她是我特别亲密的朋友

speciality *(British English)*, **specialty** *(US English)* *n* **a speciality** *(an occupation or area of study)* yìmén zhuānyè 一门专业; *(a skill)* yíge tècháng 一个特长, yíge zhuāncháng 一个专长; *(a product)* yíge tèchǎn 一个特产

specially *adv* tèyì 特意, tèdì 特地

spectator *n* **a spectator** yíge guānzhòng 一个观众

speech *n* **a speech** yíge jiǎnghuà 一个讲话, yíge fāyán 一个发言

speed 1 *n (rate of progress)* sùdù 速度 **2** *vb* **to speed away** kuàisù kāizǒu 快速开走, kuàisù shǐqù 快速驶去; *(to drive too fast)* chāosù xíngshǐ 超速行驶; **speed up** jiā sù 加速, zēng sù 增速

speed limit *n* sùdù jíxiàn 速度极限

spell *vb (to give letters of a word in order)*; *(when speaking)* pīn 拼, pīndú 拼读; *(when writing)* pīn 拼, pīnxiě 拼写; **how do you spell this word?** zhège cí (nǐ) zěnme pīn? 这个词(你)怎么拼?

spelling *n* pīnfǎ 拼法

spend *vb (to pay out)* huā 花; **how much money have you spent?** nǐ huāle duōshǎo qián? 你花了多少钱? *(to give or bestow for any purpose)* huā 花, huāfèi 花费, yòng 用; **she spent lots of her time and energy in helping me** tā huāfèile hěn duō shíjiān hé jīnglì lái bāngzhù wǒ 她花费了很多时间和精力来帮助我; **he spent an hour writing a letter to his girlfriend** tā huāle yíge xiǎoshí gěi tāde nǚpéngyou xiě xìn 他花了一个小时给他的女朋友写信; *(to pass, as time)* guò 过, dùguò 度过; **I shall spend my Christmas in China** wǒ jiāng zài Zhōngguó guò Shèngdànjié 我将在中国过圣诞节

spider n a spider yíge zhīzhū 一个蜘蛛

spill vb (to cause to pour or flow over) shǐ/bǎ...sǎ 使/把...洒: don't spill the milk bié bǎ niúnǎi sǎchūlai 别把牛奶洒出来: (to flow over or fall out) yìchū 溢出, jiànchū 溅出

spinach n bōcài 菠菜

spit vb (to eject from mouth) tǔ 吐: (to eject saliva) tǔ tán 吐痰

spite: in spite of prep jǐnguǎn 尽管; we went out in spite of the rain jǐnguǎn xiàyǔ, wǒmen háishì chūqu le 尽管下雨, 我们还是出去了! Note that the phrase introduced by jǐnguǎn 尽管 must be at the beginning of the sentence.

spiteful adj yǒu èyì de 有恶意的, yǒu yuànhèn de 有怨恨的

spoil vb (to mar) huǐle 毁了, nòngzāo 弄糟, gǎozāo 搞糟; the rain spoilt [the party | the football match | the picnic] yǔ bǎ [jùhuì | zúqiú bǐsài | yěcān] huǐle 雨把 [聚会 | 足球比赛 | 野餐] 毁了, (to ruin, to damage) sǔnhuài 损坏; (as a parent) jiāoguàn 娇惯, guànhuài 惯坏; to spoil a child jiāoguàn háizi 娇惯孩子

sponge n a sponge yíkuài hǎimián 一块海绵

spoon n a spoon yìbǎ sháozi 一把勺子, yìbǎ chízi 一把匙子

sport n a sport yìzhǒng yùndòng 一种运动, yìzhǒng tǐyù 一种体育; to be good at sports shàncháng tǐyù yùndòng 擅长体育运动

sports centre (British English), **sports center** (US English) n a sports centre yíge tǐyù (yùndòng) zhōngxīn 一个体育运动中心

sports club n a sports club yíge tǐyù jùlèbù 一个体育俱乐部

spot 1 n (on an animal) a spot yíge bāndiǎn 一个斑点; (British English) (on the face or body) a spot yíge bāndiǎn 一个斑点, yíge hēidiǎn 一个黑点, (dirt mark or stain) a spot yíge wūdiǎn 一个污点; (a place) a spot yíge dìdiǎn 一个地点; on the spot dāngchǎng 当场, xiànchǎng 现场 **2** vb (to detect) fāxiàn 发现; (to see someone you recognize) rènchū 认出

sprain vb niǔshāng 扭伤; to sprain one's wrist niǔshāng shǒuwàn 扭伤手腕

spring n chūntiān 春天, chūnjì 春季; the Spring Festival (the Chinese New Year) Chūnjié 春节

spy n a spy yíge jiàndié 一个间谍, yíge mìtàn 一个密探, yíge tèwù 一个特务

square 1 n (the shape) a square yíge zhèngfāngxíng 一个正方形; (in a town) a square yíge guǎngchǎng 一个广场 **2** adj (having the geometrical form) zhèngfāngxíng de 正方形的, fāng de 方的

squash 1 n (the sport) bìqiú 壁球 **2** vb (to crush flat) bǎ...yābiǎn 把...压扁; be careful not to squash the tomatoes xiǎoxīn bié bǎ xīhóngshì yābiǎn 小心别把西红柿压扁了; (to crowd) jǐ(rù) 挤(入), jǐ(jìn) 挤(进); they managed to squash into the lift tāmen shèfǎ jǐjìnle diàntī 他们设法挤进了电梯

squeak vb zhīzhī de jiào 吱吱地叫

squeeze vb (for the purpose of getting juice) zhà 榨; to squeeze [oranges | lemons | apples...] zhà [júzi | níngméng | píngguǒ...] zhī 榨[橘子 | 柠檬 | 苹果...]汁; (to injure) jǐshāng 挤伤; to squeeze one's fingers jǐshāng shǒuzhǐ 挤伤手指; (showing affection or friendship) to squeeze someone's hand jǐnwò mǒurén de shǒu 紧握某人的手; to squeeze something into a bag wǎng yíge bāo li sāi mǒu jiàn dōngxi 往一个包里塞某件东西; all six people were squeezed into a small car liùge rén dōu jǐ zài yíliàng xiǎo qìchē li 六个人都挤在一辆小汽车里

squirrel n a squirrel yìzhī sōngshǔ 一只松鼠

stable 1 n a stable yíge mǎjiù 一个马厩, yíge mǎpéng 一个马棚 **2** adj (constant and not ready to change) wěndìng 稳定; (firmly fixed) láogù 牢固, jiāngù 坚固

stadium n a stadium yíge tǐyùchǎng 一个体育场, yíge yùndòngchǎng 一个运动场

staff n the staff (of a company, a bank) quántǐ zhíyuán 全体职员; (of a school, a college) quántǐ jiàozhíyuán 全体教职员

stage n (a step in development) jiēduàn 阶段; a stage yíge jiēduàn 一个阶段; a stage (for a performance) yíge wǔtái 一个舞台; (for a speech) yíge jiǎngtái 一个讲台

stain 1 n a stain yíge wūdiǎn 一个污点 **2** vb (to soil or change the colour of) zhānwū 沾污; (to bring disgrace upon) diànwū 玷污

stairs n lóutī 楼梯; **to fall down the stairs** cóng lóutī shang shuāixialai 从楼梯上摔下来

stamp n (for postage) a stamp yìzhāng yóupiào 一张邮票; (an imprinted mark) a stamp yíge chuō 一个戳, yíge yìn 一个印; (a tool for marking) a stamp yìméi túzhāng 一枚图章

stamp-collecting n jíyóu 集邮

stand vb zhàn 站; he stood by the window tā zhàn zài chuānghu pángbiān 他站在窗户旁边; to stay standing, to remain standing zhànzhe bú dòng 站着不动; (to be situated) zuòluò 坐落, wèiyú 位于; the house stands by a river nàzuò fángzi zuòluò zài yìtiáo hé biān 那座房子坐落在一条河边; (to put) to stand a vase on a table bǎ yíge huāpíng fàng zài zhuōzi shang 把一个花瓶放在桌子上; (to step) to stand on a nail cǎi zài yíge dīngzi shang 踩在一个钉子上; (to bear) rěnshòu 忍受, shòu de liǎo 受得了; can you stand the hot weather there? nǐ néng shòu de liǎo nàr de rè tiānqì ma? 你能受得了那儿的热天气吗? he can't stand playing football tī zúqiú tā shòu bù liǎo 踢足球他受不了; (other uses) to stand in someone's way fáng'ài mǒurén 妨碍某人, dǎng mǒurén de dào 挡某人的道; to stand for election (British English) cānjiā jìngxuǎn 参加竞选; to stand trial shòu shěn 受审; **stand back** wǎng hòu zhàn 往后站, tuìhòu 退后; **stand for** (to represent) dàibiǎo 代表; (to mean) yìsi shì 意思是, yìwèizhe 意味着; **stand out** (to be prominent) tūchū 突出, chūsè 出色; **stand up** to stand up zhànqilai 站起来; (given as an order in the classroom or the army) stand up! qǐlì! 起立; to stand someone up (fail to keep an appointment) gēn mǒurén shī yuē 跟某人失约; **stand up for** (to support) zhīchí 支持; (to defend) hànwèi 捍卫; to stand up for one's rights hànwèi zìjǐ de quánlì 捍卫自己的权利; **stand up to** (to meet face to face) yǒnggǎn de miànduì 勇敢的面对; to stand up to the hooligans yǒnggǎn de miànduì liúmáng 勇敢的面对流氓; (to show resistance to) dǐkàng 抵抗

star n (in space) **a star** yìkē xīng 一颗星; (a famous person) **a star** yíge míngxīng 一个明星

stare vb dīngzhe kàn 盯着看, mù bù zhuǎn jīng de kàn 目不转睛地看; **to stare at someone** dīngzhe kàn mǒurén 盯着看某人

start 1 vb (to begin) kāishǐ 开始; **to start** [working | writing letters | running...] kāishǐ [gōngzuò | xiě xìn | pǎo...] 开始[工作 | 写信 | 跑...]; **you should start by phoning them** nǐ yīnggāi kāishǐ xiān gěi tāmen dǎ diànhuà 你应该开始先给他们打电话; (to begin one's working life) **to start (out) as a teacher** kāishǐ dāng lǎoshī 开始当老师; (to set out) chūfā 出发, dòngshēn 动身; **when will you start for China?** nǐ shénme shíhou chūfā qù Zhōngguó? 你什么时候出发去中国?; (to cause) fādòng 发动; **to start a war** fādòng yìchǎng zhànzhēng 发动一场战争; (to begin working) fādòng 发动, qǐdòng 起动; **the car won't start** qìchē fādòng bù qǐlái 汽车发动不起来; (to put into action) kāi(dòng) 开(动); **to start** [a car | a machine] kāidòng [qìchē | jīqì] 开动[汽车 | 机器]; (to set up and run) kāibàn 开办, chuàngbàn 创办; **they've decided to start a new school in the village** tāmen juédìng zài cūn lǐ kāibàn yísuǒ xīn xuéxiào 他们决定在村里开办一所新学校 **2** n **a start** yíge kāishǐ 一个开始, yíge kāiduān 一个开端; **at the start of** [the race | the meeting | the week] [bǐsài | huìyì | zhège xīngqí] kāishǐ de shíhou [比赛 | 会议 | 这个星期]开始的时候; **start off** (to set out) chūfā 出发, dòngshēn 动身; (to begin) kāishǐ 开始; **start over** (US English) chóngxīn kāishǐ 重新开始

starter n (British English) (of a meal) tóupán 头盘; **a starter** yíge tóupán 一个头盘

state n (a country) guójiā 国家; (a constituent member of a federation) zhōu 州; **a state** yíge zhōu 一个州; (a government) **the State** zhèngfǔ 政府; (a condition) zhuàngtài 状态, zhuàngkuàng 状况; **the state of her health is worrying** tāde jiànkāng zhuàngkuàng hěn lìng rén dānyōu 她的健康状况很令人担忧; **to be in a bad state of repair** xūyào xiūlǐ 需要修理

statement n **a statement** (an account) yíge chénshù 一个陈述; (a formal declaration or account) yíxiàng shēngmíng 一项声明

station n (for trains or coaches) zhàn 站; a [train | coach] station yíge [huǒchē | qìchē] zhàn 一个 [火车 | 汽车] 站; (on TV or radio) tái 台; a [TV | radio] station yíge [diànshì | guǎngbō diàn] tái 一个 [电视 | 广播电] 台

statue n a statue yízuò diāoxiàng 一座雕像, yízuò sùxiàng 一座塑像

stay 1 vb (to remain) dāi 呆/ 待, tíngliú 停留; we stayed there for a week wǒmen zài nàr dāile yíge xīngqī 我们在那儿呆了一个星期; (to have accommodation) zhù 住; to stay with friends yǔ péngyou zhù zài yìqǐ 与朋友住在一起 **2** n she enjoyed her stay in Shanghai tā zài Shànghǎi guò de hěn yúkuài 她在上海过得很愉快; to make a short stay here zài zhèr duǎnqī zhù yíduàn shíjiān 在这儿短期住一段时间; **stay away from** bú qù 不去; to stay away from school bú qù shàngxué 不去上学; **stay in** dāi zài jiā lǐ 呆在家里, bù chū mén 不出门; **stay out** dāi zài wàimian 呆在外面, bù huí jiā 不回家; to stay out late dāi zài wàimian hěn wǎn (bù huí jiā) 呆在外面很晚(不回家); **stay up** (to keep late hours) bú shuìjiào 不睡觉

steady adj (constant, stable) wěndìng 稳定, bú biàn 不变; to keep up a steady speed bǎochí wěndìng de sùdù 保持稳定的速度; (not likely to move) wěngù 稳固

steak n a steak (beef) yíkuài niúpái 一块牛排; (fish) yíkuài yú 一块鱼

steal vb (to practise theft) tōu dōngxi 偷东西; to steal from someone cóng mǒurén nàr tōu dōngxi 从某人那儿偷东西; (to take by theft) tōu 偷; to steal money from someone cóng mǒurén nàr tōu qián 从某人那儿偷钱

steam n zhēngqì 蒸汽, shuǐzhēngqì 水蒸气

steel n gāng 钢, gāngtiě 钢铁

steep adj (when describing a rise or decline in price, living standards) jíjù 急剧; (when describing a road or a mountain) dǒu 陡, dǒuqiào 陡峭

steering wheel n a steering wheel (of a car or lorry) yíge fāngxiàngpán 一个方向盘

step 1 n (when walking) bù 步; a step yí bù 一步; to take a step mài/zǒu yí bù 迈/走一步; (in a flight of stairs) tíjí 梯级; a step yíge tíjí 一个梯级; (in front of a doorstep) táijiē 台阶; a step yíge táijiē 一个台阶; (one of a series of actions) bùzhòu 步骤; to take steps cǎiqǔ bùzhòu 采取步骤 **2** vb (to walk) zǒu 走; to step into the house zǒu jìn fángzi 走进房子; (to advance by taking a step or steps) mài bù 迈步; to step on a nail cǎi zài dīngzi shang 踩在钉子上; **step aside** zǒu dào pángbiān qu 走到旁边去, kào biān zhàn 靠边站

stepbrother n a stepbrother (elder brother by a stepmother) yíge yìmǔ gēge 一个异母哥哥; (younger brother by a stepmother) yíge yìmǔ dìdi 一个异母弟弟; (elder brother by a stepfather) yíge yìfù gēge 一个异父哥哥; (younger brother by a stepfather) yíge yìfù dìdi 一个异父弟弟

stepfather n a stepfather yíge jìfù 一个继父, yíge yìfù 一个异父

stepmother n a stepmother yíge jìmǔ 一个继母, yíge yìmǔ 一个异母

stepsister n a stepsister (elder sister by a stepfather) yíge yìfù jiějie 一个异父姐姐; (younger sister by a stepfather) yíge yìfù mèimei 一个异父妹妹; (elder sister by a stepmother) yíge yìmǔ jiějie 一个异母姐姐; (younger sister by a stepmother) yíge yìmǔ mèimei 一个异母妹妹

stereo n a stereo yìtái lìtǐshēng shōulùjī 一台立体声收录机

stewardess n a stewardess (on a plane) yíge kōng(zhōng) xiǎo)jie 一个空(中小)姐; (on a ship) yíge nǚfúwùyuán 一个女服务员

stick 1 vb (using glue or tape) tiē 贴, zhān 粘; to stick a stamp on an envelope zài xìnfēng shang tiē yóupiào 在信封上贴邮票; (to attach by a pin or clip) bié 别; she stuck her badge onto her coat tā bǎ tāde páizi bié zài wàiyī shang 她把她的牌子别在外衣上; (when something pointed is pushed into or through something else) cì 刺, chā 插; he stuck the fork into the meat tā bǎ chāzi chā jìn ròu li 他把叉子插进肉里; (to become unmovable) kǎzhù 卡住; the door is stuck mén kǎzhù le 门卡住了

住了; (to reach an obstacle, to be stumped) nánzhù 难住; **I'm stuck by this problem** wǒ bèi zhège wèntí nánzhù le 我被这个问题难住了 **2** n (a piece of wood) yìgēn zhītiáo 一根枝条; (for walking) shǒuzhàng 手杖; **a stick** yìgēn shǒuzhàng 一根手杖; **stick at** to stick at one's work jiānchí gōngzuò 坚持工作; **stick out** shēnchū 伸出, tūchū 凸出; **there's a nail sticking out** yǒu yígè dīngzi shēnchulai 有一个钉子伸出来

sticky tape n (British English) jiāodài 胶带

stiff adj (not soft, not supple) jiāngyìng 僵硬, jiāngzhí 僵直; **I had stiff legs** wǒde tuǐ gǎndào jiāngyìng 我的腿感到僵硬; (not easy to move) bù línghuó 不灵活; (rigid and hard) yìng 硬; **this pair of shoes is too stiff** zhèshuāng xié tài yìng le 这双鞋太硬了

still¹ adv (when indicating no change) hái 还, réngrán 仍然; **does she still play the piano?** tā hái tán gāngqín ma? 她还弹钢琴吗?; **I still don't understand why you left** wǒ réngrán bù míngbai nǐ wèishénme líkāi 我仍然不明白你为什么离开; **she could still win** tā hái néng yíng 她还能赢; (used in comparisons) gèng(jiā) 更(加), háiyào 还要; **it is hot today, but it'll be still hotter tomorrow** jīntiān hěn rè, dànshì míngtiān huì gèng rè 今天很热,但是明天会更热

still² adj (quiet) jìjìng 寂静, ānjìng 安静; (motionless) jìngzhǐ 静止, bú dòng 不动; **to sit still** zuòzhe búdòng 坐着不动

sting vb to sting someone (if it's a wasp or an insect) zhē mǒurén 蜇某人; (if it's a mosquito) dīng mǒurén 叮某人, yǎo mǒurén 咬某人; (feel sharp pain) gǎndào cìtòng 感到刺痛

stir vb (to use an implement to mix something) jiǎodòng 搅动, jiǎohuo 搅和; **to stir the coffee with a spoon** yòng sháozi jiǎodòng kāfēi 用勺子搅动咖啡; (to cause a sensation in) hōngdòng 轰动; **the news stirred the whole school** zhètiáo xiāoxi hōngdòngle quán xiào 这条消息轰动了全校; **stir up hatred** shāndòng chóuhèn 煽动仇恨, tiǎoqǐ chóuhèn 挑起仇恨; **stir up patriotism** jīqǐ àiguózhǔyì 激起爱国主义

stomach n the stomach wèi 胃, dùzi 肚子; **to have a pain in one's stomach** wèi téng 胃疼, dùzi téng 肚子疼

stone n a stone (a piece of rock) yíkuài shítou 一块石头; (a gem) yíkuài bǎoshí 一块宝石, yíkuài zuànshí 一块钻石; (the hard seed of a fruit) hé 核; an apricot stone yíge xìnghé 一个杏核

stop 1 vb (to put an end to) tíngzhǐ 停止; to stop [laughing | working | learning Chinese] tíngzhǐ [xiào | gōngzuò | xué Zhōngwén] 停止 [笑 | 工作 | 学中文]; to stop smoking jiè yān 戒烟; (when giving an order) bié 别, búyào 不要! Note that when bié 别 or búyào 不要 is used to stop what is going on, le 了 is required at the end of the sentence; stop [talking | writing | playing football]! bié [shuō huà | xiě | tī zúqiú] le! 别 [说话 | 写 | 踢足球] 了!; (to prevent) zǔzhǐ 阻止; to stop someone from [leaving | playing the violin | talking] zǔzhǐ mǒurén [líkāi | lā xiǎotíqín | jiǎnghuà] 阻止某人 [离开 | 拉小提琴 | 讲话]; (to come to a halt) tíng 停; the bus didn't stop qìchē méi tíng 汽车没停; (when talking about noise, weather, music) tíng 停, tíngzhǐ 停止; suddenly the noise stopped tūrán zàoyīn tíng(zhǐ) le 突然噪音停(止)了; it's stopped raining yǔ tíng le 雨停了 **2** n a (bus) stop yíge qìchēzhàn 一个汽车站; to miss one's stop zuòguòle zhàn 坐过了站

store n a store (a shop) yíge shāngdiàn 一个商店; (a place for keeping goods) yíge cāngkù 一个仓库

storey (British English), **story** (US English) n a storey yì céng 一层

storm n a storm yìchǎng fēngbào 一场风暴; (with rain) yìchǎng bàofēngyǔ 一场暴风雨; (with snow) yìchǎng bàofēngxuě 一场暴风雪

story n (a tale) a story yíge gùshi 一个故事; (a literary genre) a (short) story yíbù (duǎnpiān) xiǎoshuō 一部(短篇)小说; (in a newspaper) a story yìtiáo bàodào 一条报道; (a rumour) a story yíge yáochuán 一个谣传; (US English) ▶ **storey**

stove n (US English) a stove yíge lúzi 一个炉子

straight 1 adj zhí 直; a straight line yìtiáo zhí xiàn 一条直线; she had straight hair tāde tóufa shì zhí de 她的头发是直的; (in the right position) zhèng 正; the picture isn't straight zhèzhāng huà bú zhèng 这张画不正; (honest) chéngshí 诚实,

zhèngzhí 正直 **2** adv zhí 直; to stand up straight zhàn zhí 站直; to go straight ahead yìzhí wǎng qián zǒu 一直往前走; (without delay) lìkè 立刻, mǎshàng 马上; to go straight home lìkè huí jiā 立刻回家

strange adj (odd) qíguài 奇怪; it's strange that she didn't come tā méi lái hěn qíguài 她没来很奇怪; (unknown) mòshēng 陌生, bù shúxī 不熟悉

stranger n a stranger yíge (mò)shēngrén 一个(陌)生人; (someone from another region) yíge yìxiāngrén 一个异乡人

straw n (for feeding animals) dàocǎo 稻草, màigǎn 麦秆; (for drinking) a straw yìgēn xīguǎn 一根吸管

strawberry n a strawberry yíge cǎoméi 一个草莓

stream n a stream yìtiáo xiǎohé 一条小河, yìtiáo xiǎoxī 一条小溪

street n a street yìtiáo jiē(dào) 一条街(道), yìtiáo mǎlù 一条马路

streetlamp (British English), **streetlight** (US English) n a streetlamp yíge jiēdēng 一个街灯

strength n (quality of being strong) lìliàng 力量, lì(qi) 力(气); (capacity for exertion or endurance) qiángdù 强度

stressful adj jǐnzhāng 紧张, yālì dà de 压力大的

stretch vb (to extend in space) shēnkāi 伸开, shēnchū 伸出; to stretch one's arms shēnkāi gēbo 伸开胳膊; (to make straight by tension) bǎ...lāzhí 把...拉直; to stretch the wire bǎ diànxiàn lāzhí 把电线拉直

strict adj (stern) yángé 严格, yánlì 严厉; (observing exact rules) yánjǐn 严谨

strike n (an attack); a strike yícì dǎjī 一次打击, yícì gōngjī 一次攻击; (a cessation of work) a strike yícì bàgōng 一次罢工; to go on strike jǔxíng bàgōng 举行罢工

string n (thin cord) a piece of string yìgēn xiànshéng 一根线绳

striped adj yǒu tiáowén de 有条纹的

stroke vb (to touch lightly in an affectionate way) fǔmó 抚摩, lǚ 捋

stroller n (US English) (a push-chair) a stroller yíge yīng'ér tuīchē 一个婴儿推车

strong adj (having physical strength) qiángzhuàng 强壮, qiángjiàn 强健; she's strong tā hěn qiángzhuàng 她很强壮; (having mental strength) jiānqiáng 坚强, jiānjué 坚决; (intense) qiángliè 强烈; strong [feeling | contrast | protests] qiángliè de [gǎnqíng | duìbǐ | kàngyì] 强烈的 [感情 | 对比 | 抗议]; (not easily damaged) jiēshi 结实, láogù 牢固; (when describing one's attitude, standpoint, determination) jiānding 坚定; (having force, power) a strong wind yìcháng dà fēng 一场大风; strong tea nóng chá 浓茶; a strong wine yìzhǒng liè jiǔ 一种烈酒; (obvious, noticeable) a strong German accent yìkǒu hěn zhòng de Déyǔ kǒuyīn 一口很重的德语口音; a strong smell of garlic yìzhǒng hěn nóng de dàsuàn wèi 一种很浓的大蒜味; (having military power) qiángdà 强大

stubborn adj wángù 顽固, gùzhí 固执

student n a student yíge xuésheng 一个学生

study 1 vb (to be engaged in learning) xuéxí 学习; she is studying for an exam tā zài xuéxí zhǔnbèi kǎoshì 她在学习准备考试; (to make study of) xuéxí 学习, xué 学; to study history xué(xí) lìshǐ 学(习)历史; (to scrutinize) zǐxì kàn 仔细看 **2** n (a room) a study yìjiān shūfáng 一间书房; (act of studying) xuéxí 学习

stuff 1 n (things) dōngxi 东西; (material) cáiliào 材料 **2** vb (to pack, to fill) zhuāng 装, sāi 塞; to stuff a suitcase with clothes wǎng xiāngzi li zhuāng yīfu 往箱子里装衣服; (to feed) to stuff the children with cakes yòng dàngāo tiánbǎo háizimen de dùzi 用蛋糕填饱孩子们的肚子

stuffing n tián(sāi)liào 填(塞)料

stupid adj bèn 笨, yúchǔn 愚蠢

style n (a way of dressing, behaviour) her way of dressing always has style tā chuān de zǒngshì hěn rùshí 她穿得总是很入时; (a manner of doing things) a style yìzhǒng zuòfēng 一种

作风, yìzhǒng fēnggé 一种风格; his working style tāde gōngzuò zuòfēng 他的工作作风; (a way of writing) a style yìzhǒng wéntǐ 一种文体; (a distinctive characteristic) a style (of architecture) yìzhǒng (jiànzhù) fēnggé 一种(建筑)风格; (a design, a type) a style yìzhǒng shìyàng 一种式样, yìzhǒng yàngshì 一种样式; the style of a car qìchē de shìyàng 汽车的式样; a hair style yìzhǒng fàxíng 一种发型; (a way of life) a life style yìzhǒng shēnghuó fāngshì 一种生活方式; to live in (grand) style shēnghuó háohuá 生活豪华; (a fashion) a style yìzhǒng shímáo 一种时髦

stylish adj shímáo 时髦, piàoliang 漂亮

subject n (of a conversation) huàtí 话题; a subject yíge huàtí 一个话题; (being studied) kēmù 科目, kèchéng 课程; a subject yíge kèchéng 一个课程; (topic) tímù 题目; a subject yíge tímù 一个题目

suburb n the suburbs jiāoqū 郊区, jiāowài 郊外

subway n (US English) (the underground) the subway dìtiě 地铁; (British English) (an underground passage) a subway yìtiáo dìxià tōngdào 一条地下通道

succeed vb (to accomplish what is attempted) chénggōng 成功; (follow, take the place of) jìchéng 继承, jiētì 接替

success n chénggōng 成功

successful adj chénggōng 成功

such 1 det zhèyàng 这样, zhèzhǒng 这种; there's no such thing méi yǒu zhèyàng de dōngxi 没有这样的东西 **2** adv nàme 那么; they have such a lot of money tāmen yǒu nàme duō qián 他们有那么多钱; she's such a strange person tā shì nàme qíguài de yíge rén 他是那么奇怪的一个人

suddenly adv tūrán 突然, hūrán 忽然

suffer vb (to be affected by) zāoshòu 遭受, zāodào 遭到; to suffer [heavy casualties | enormous economic losses] zāoshòu [yánzhòng shāngwáng | jùdà jīngjì sǔnshī] 遭受 [严重伤亡 | 巨大经济损失]; (to feel pain) shòu (tòng)kǔ 受(痛)苦; to suffer from [TB | heart failure | a cold] déle [fèijiéhé | xīnlì shuāijié | gǎnmào] 得了 [肺结核 | 心力衰竭 | 感冒]

sugar n táng 糖

suggestion n a suggestion yìtiáo jiànyì 一条建议

suicide n to commit suicide zìshā 自杀

suit 1 n a suit (a man's) yítào nánshì xīfú 一套男式西服; (a woman's) yítào nǚshì xīfú 一套女式西服 **2** vb (to be convenient, to fit) héshì 合适, shìhé 适合; to suit someone duì mǒurén héshì 对某人合适; does Friday suit you? xīngqīwǔ duì nǐ héshì ma? 星期五对你合适吗? the hat suits you zhèdǐng màozi nǐ dài hěn shìhé 这顶帽子你戴很适合

suitable adj héshì 合适, shìyí 适宜; a suitable present yíge héshì de lǐwù 一个合适的礼物; these books are suitable for children zhèxiē shū shìyí értóng kàn 这些书适宜儿童看

suitcase n a suitcase yíge shǒutíxiāng 一个手提箱

sum n a sum of money yìbǐ qián 一笔钱; (a problem in arithmetic) a sum yídào suànshùtí 一道算术题; to be good at sums suànshù hěn hǎo 算术很好; **sum up** zǒngjié 总结, gàikuò 概括

summer n xiàtiān 夏天, xiàjì 夏季

summer holiday (British English), **summer vacation** (US English) n shǔjià 暑假

sun n the sun tàiyáng 太阳; (sunshine) yángguāng 阳光; to sit in the sun zuò zài yángguāng xia 坐在阳光下

sunbathe vb jìnxíng rìguāngyù 进行日光浴, shài tàiyáng 晒太阳

sunburn n shàishāng 晒伤

sunburned adj she got sunburned tā shàishāng le 她晒伤了

Sunday n xīngqīrì 星期日, xīngqītiān 星期天, lǐbàitiān 礼拜天

sunglasses n tàiyángjìng 太阳镜, mòjìng 墨镜

sunny adj qínglǎng 晴朗, yángguāng míngmèi 阳光明媚; a sunny day yíge qíngtiān 一个晴天

sunset n rìluò 日落

sunshade n a sunshade yìbǎ yángsǎn 一把阳伞

sunshine *n* yángguāng 阳光

suntan *n* shàihēi 晒黑; **you've got a suntan** nǐ shàihēi le 你晒黑了

suntan oil *n* **a suntan oil** yìzhǒng fángshàiyóu 一种防晒油

supermarket *n* **a supermarket** yìjiā chāojí shìchǎng 一家超级市场, yìjiā chāoshì 一家超市

supper *n* **a supper** yídùn wǎnfàn 一顿晚饭, yídùn wǎncān 一顿晚餐

support *vb* (*to agree with, to help*) zhīchí 支持, zhīyuán 支援; **to support the strike** zhīchí bàgōng 支持罢工; (*to keep*) **to support a family** yǎng jiā 养家; **to support oneself** yǎnghuó zìjǐ 养活自己; (*to hold up or bear the weight of*) zhīchēng 支撑; **what are we going to use to support the roof?** wǒmen yòng shénme lái zhīchēng wūdǐng? 我们用什么来支撑屋顶?

supporter *n* **a supporter** (*of a team, a party*) yíge zhīchízhě 一个支持者; (*one who supports a view, a policy*) yíge yōnghùzhě 一个拥护者

suppose *vb* (*to posit a hypothetical situation*) jiǎdìng 假定, jiǎrú 假如; **suppose you can't come, please give us a call** jiǎdìng nǐ bù néng lái, qǐng gěi wǒmen dǎ ge diànhuà 假定你不能来，请给我们打个电话; (*to incline to believe, guess*) xiǎng 想, cāixiǎng 猜想 **!** *Note that while in English the verb* **suppose** *is negated in the main clause, the negation is shifted to the subordinate clause in Chinese*; **I don't suppose you know yet?** wǒ xiǎng nǐ hái bù zhīdào ba? 我想你还不知道吧?; (*to be meant to*) **to be supposed to** yīnggāi 应该, yīngdāng 应当; **I'm supposed to arrive there at 10** wǒ yīnggāi shí diǎn dào nàr 我应该十点到那儿

sure *adj* (*certain*) gǎn kěndìng 敢肯定, yǒu bǎwò 有把握; **I'm sure he said nine o'clock** wǒ gǎn kěndìng tā shuō de shì jiǔ diǎn 我敢肯定他说的是九点; **are you sure?** nǐ yǒu bǎwò ma? 你有把握吗?; **she is not sure if she can come** tā bù gǎn kěndìng tā néng lái 她不敢肯定她能来; (*bound*) yídìng huì 一定会, kěndìng huì 肯定会; **he is sure to win** tā yídìng huì yíng 他一定会赢; **sure of oneself** yǒu xìnxīn 有信心; **she's sure of herself** tā hěn yǒu xìnxīn 她很有信心; **to make sure that...**

yídìng yào... 一定要..., bǎozhèng... 保证...; to make sure that the door is closed yídìng yào bǎ mén guānhǎo 一定要把门关好

surf vb to go surfing qù chōnglàng 去冲浪

surface 1 n a surface yíge biǎomiàn 一个表面 **2** vb (to rise to the surface of the water) lùchū shuǐmiàn 露出水面

surfboard n a surfboard yíge chōnglàngbǎn 一个冲浪板

surgeon n a surgeon yíge wàikē yīshēng 一个外科医生

surgery n to have surgery zuò/dòng shǒushù 做/动手术, kāidāo 开刀; (British English) (the place) a surgery yíge zhěnsuǒ 一个诊所

surname n a surname yíge xìng 一个姓

surprise 1 n a surprise (an event) yíjiàn yìxiǎng bú dào de shìqing 一件意想不到的事情; (a gift) yíge yìxiǎng bú dào de lǐwù 一个意想不到的礼物; (an item of news) yìtiáo yìxiǎng bú dào de xiāoxi 一条意想不到的消息 **!** Note that when a surprise is translated into Chinese, it is often necessary to categorize the thing that is surprising by using an appropriate noun, and to modify it by yìxiǎng bú dào de 意想不到的, which means unexpected or surprising; (the state of being amazed) jīngqí 惊奇, jīngyà 惊讶; to take someone by surprise shǐ mǒurén hěn jīngqí 使某人很惊奇; to someone's surprise shǐ mǒurén jīngyà de shì 使某人惊讶的是; he looked up in surprise tā jīngqí de táiqǐ tóu lai 他惊奇地抬起头来 **2** vb to surprise someone shǐ mǒurén jīngqí 使某人惊奇, shǐ mǒurén jīngyà 使某人惊讶

surprised adj gǎndào chījīng 感到吃惊, gǎndào yìwài 感到意外; I'm not surprised wǒ bù gǎndào chījīng 我不感到吃惊; to be surprised at something duì mǒushì gǎndào chījīng 对某事感到吃惊; I'm surprised that he didn't come tā méi lái, wǒ gǎndào hěn yìwài 他没来, 我感到很意外

surrender vb (to give oneself up to the police, the authorities, etc.) zìshǒu 自首; (to give up in a fight, battle, or war) tóuxiáng 投降; (to give something up to an enemy, the police, etc.) jiāochū 交出; (to give something up as a result of pressure or necessity) fàngqì 放弃

surround vb wéi 围, bāowéi 包围; the police surrounded the house jǐngchá bāowéile nàzuò fángzi 警察包围了那座房子; the house is surrounded by trees fángzi zhōuwéi dōu shì shù 房子周围都是树

surroundings n zhōuwéi 周围, huánjìng 环境

survey n a survey yíxiàng diàochá 一项调查

survive vb xìngmiǎn yú 幸免于, huóxialai 活下来; to survive an accident xìngmiǎn yú yìchǎng shìgù 幸免于一场事故; to survive the winter huóguò dōngtiān 活过冬天

suspect 1 vb (to imagine that someone is guilty of) huáiyí 怀疑; she's suspected of stealing money rénmen huáiyí tā tōu qián 人们怀疑她偷钱; (to be inclined to believe) cāixiǎng 猜想, rènwéi 认为; I suspect that this may be true wǒ cāixiǎng zhè kěnéng shì zhēn de 我猜想这可能是真的 **2** n a suspect yíge xiányífàn 一个嫌疑犯, yíge kěyí fènzǐ 一个可疑分子

suspicious adj (inclined to suspect) huáiyí 怀疑, cāiyí 猜疑; to be suspicious of someone huáiyí mǒurén 怀疑某人; (giving ground for suspicion) kěyí 可疑

swan n a swan yìzhī tiān'é 一只天鹅

swap vb jiāohuàn 交换, jiāoliú 交流

sweat vb chūhàn 出汗

sweater n (US English) a sweater (usually woolen) yíjiàn máoyī 一件毛衣; (worn before or after physical exercise) yíjiàn yùndòngyī 一件运动衣

sweatshirt n a sweatshirt yíjiàn yùndòngshān 一件运动衫, yíjiàn xiūxiánshān 一件休闲衫

Sweden n Ruìdiǎn 瑞典

Swedish 1 adj Ruìdiǎn de 瑞典的 **2** n (the people) Ruìdiǎnrén 瑞典人; (the language) Ruìdiǎnyǔ 瑞典语

sweep vb sǎo 扫, dǎsǎo 打扫

sweet 1 adj (tasting of sugar) tián 甜, tiánwèi de 甜味的; the wine is too sweet zhè jiǔ tài tián le 这酒太甜了; to have a sweet tooth xǐhuan chī tián shí 喜欢吃甜食; (fragrant) fāngxiāng 芳香; (kind, gentle) qīnqiè 亲切, hé'ǎi 和蔼; to be sweet to someone duì mǒurén qīnqiè 对某人亲切; (cute) kě'ài 可爱 **2** n (British English) a sweet yíkuài táng 一块糖

swim 1 vb (to propel oneself in water) yóuyǒng 游泳; (to travel by propelling oneself in water) yóu 游; to swim across the lake yóuguò hú qù 游过湖去 **2** n a swim yóuyǒng 游泳; to go for a swim qù yóuyǒng 去游泳

swimming n yóuyǒng 游泳

swimming pool n a swimming pool yíge yóuyǒngchí 一个游泳池

swimsuit n a swimsuit yíjiàn yóuyǒngyī 一件游泳衣

swing 1 vb (to move back and forth) bǎidòng 摆动, yáobǎi 摇摆; to swing on a gate zài mén shang bǎidòng 在门上摆动; (to move something back and forth) bǎidòng 摆动, huàngdòng 晃动; to swing one's legs huàngdòng tuǐ 晃动腿 **2** n a swing (for children) yíge qiūqiān 一个秋千

Swiss 1 adj Ruìshì de 瑞士的 **2** n the Swiss Ruìshìrén 瑞士人

switch 1 n a switch yíge kāiguān 一个开关 **2** vb (zhuǎn)huàn (转)换, gǎibiàn 改变; to switch seats huàn zuòwèi 换座位; to switch from English to Chinese cóng Yīngyǔ huànchéng yòng Hànyǔ 从英语换成用汉语; to switch off guān 关; to switch off the light guān dēng 关灯; switch on dǎkāi 打开; to switch the radio on dǎkāi shōuyīnjī 打开收音机

Switzerland n Ruìshì 瑞士

sympathetic adj (showing pity) tóngqíng 同情; (showing understanding) zànchéng 赞成, yǒu tónggǎn 有同感

syringe n a syringe yíge zhùshèqì 一个注射器

system n (a complex whole, an organization) a system yíge tǐxì 一个体系, yíge xìtǒng 一个系统; (of a society or a political organization) a system yíge zhìdù 一个制度, yíge tǐzhì 一个体制; a democratic system yíge mínzhǔ zhìdù 一个民主制度; (a method) a system yítào fāngfǎ 一套方法

table 520 **take**

Tt

table n a table yìzhāng zhuōzi 一张桌子

tablet n (when talking about medicine) a tablet yípiàn yào 一片药

table tennis n table tennis pīngpāngqiú 乒乓球

tail n a tail (of an animal) yíge wěiba 一个尾巴; (of other things) yíge wěibù 一个尾部

Taiwan n Táiwān 台湾

take vb (to take hold of in the hand) ná 拿; let me take your raincoat wǒ gěi nǐ názhe yǔyī 我给你拿着雨衣; (to take hold of in one's arms) bào 抱; I took the baby in my arms wǒ bǎ yīng'ér bào zài huái lǐ 我把婴儿抱在怀里; (to take someone by the hand) lā 拉; she took me by the hand tā lāzhe wǒde shǒu 她拉着我的手; (to carry) dài 带; I took my umbrella wǒ dàizhe yǔsǎn 我带着雨伞; I'll take the letters to her wǒ gěi tā dàiqu zhèxiē xìn 我给她带去这些信; (to accompany, lead, guide) lǐng 领, dài(lǐng) 带(领); to take the children for a walk lǐng háizi qù sànbù 领孩子去散步; to take someone home dài mǒurén huí jiā 带某人回家; (to cause to go) názǒu 拿走; who's taken my dictionary? shéi názǒule wǒde cídiǎn? 谁拿走了我的词典; (to remove) to take a book off the shelf cóng shūjià shang náxia yìběn shū 从书架上拿下一本书; (to steal) tōu 偷; (to cope with, to bear) (in the negative) shòu bù liǎo 受不了; he can't take the pain tā shòu bù liǎo téng 他受不了疼; (when talking about what is necessary) xūyào 需要; it takes [time | courage | patience...] xūyào [shíjiān | yǒngqì | nàixīn...] 需要 [时间 | 勇气 | 耐心...]; it takes two hours to get to London dào Lúndūn xūyào liǎngge xiǎoshí 到伦敦需要两个小时; to take a long time to do one's homework zuò zuòyè xūyào hěn cháng shíjiān 做作业需要很长时间; it won't take long bú yào hěn cháng shíjiān 不要很长时间; (to accept) jiēshòu 接受; to take someone's advice jiēshòu mǒurén de zhōnggào 接受某人的

忠告; (to eat, to swallow) chī 吃; **to take medicine** chī yào 吃药; **I don't take sugar in my tea** wǒ hē chá bú fàng táng 我喝茶不放糖; (when talking about travelling) zuò 坐, chéng 乘; **to take** [a taxi | the bus | the underground] zuò [chūzūchē | gōnggòng qìchē | dìtiě] 坐 [出租车 | 公共汽车 | 地铁]; **to take exams** kǎoshì 考试; (when talking about selecting courses) xué 学, xuéxí 学习; **to take** [Chinese history | computer studies | driving lessons] xué [Zhōngguó lìshǐ | jìsuànjì | kāi chē] 学 [中国历史 | 计算机 | 开车]; (to wear) chuān 穿; **to take a size 10** chuān shí hào de chuān 10 号的; (when used with various nouns) **to take** [a bath | a rest | a walk | a photograph | a look] [xǐ ge zǎo | xiūxi yíhuìr | sànbù | zhào zhāng xiàng | kàn yí kàn] [洗个澡 | 休息一会儿 | 散步 | 照张像 | 看一看]; **take apart** chāikāi 拆开; **take away to take away the rubbish** bǎ lājī nòngzǒu 把垃圾弄走; **the meeting took him away early** yīnwèi kāihuì tā děi zǎo yìdiǎnr líkāi 因为开会他得早一点离开; **take back** náhuí 拿回; **I had to take the dress back** wǒ bùdébù bǎ yīfu náhuíqu 我不得不把衣服拿回去; **take down** (to remove) náxia 拿下, qǔxia 取下; **to take the painting down** bǎ huà náxialai 把画拿下来; (to write down) jìxia 记下; **I took down his address** wǒ jìxia tāde dìzhǐ 我记下他的地址; **take hold of** názhe 拿着, zhuāzhe 抓着; **take off** (from an airport) qǐfēi 起飞; (to remove) **to take off one's** [coat | shirt | skirt | trousers | shoes...] tuōxia [wàiyī | chènshān | qúnzi | kùzi | xié...] 脱下 [外衣 | 衬衫 | 裙子 | 裤子 | 鞋...]; **to take off one's** [hat | glasses | gloves | ring | necklace...] zhāixia [màozi | yǎnjìng | shǒutào | jièzhi | xiàngliàn...] 摘下 [帽子 | 眼镜 | 手套 | 戒指 | 项链...]; **take out** (from a box, a pocket, a bag) náchū 拿出; **he took a pen out of his pocket** tā cóng kǒudài li náchū yìzhī gāngbǐ 他从口袋里拿出一支钢笔; (from a bank account) qǔ 取, tí 提; **to take money out** qǔ qián 取钱; (to release one's anger at) **to take something out on someone** yīnwèi mǒushì xiàng mǒurén fāxiè 因为某事向某人发泄; **take part** cānjiā 参加; **to take part in a game** cānjiā yíxiàng bǐsài 参加一项比赛; **take place** (if it's an unexpected incident or accident) fāshēng 发生; (if it's an organized event) jǔxíng 举行; **take up** (as a hobby) kāishǐ (cóngshì) 开始(从事); **to take up sailing** kāishǐ fānchuán yùndòng 开始帆船运动; (to use up) zhàn 占; **to take up space** zhàn kōngjiān 占空间

talented adj yǒu cáinéng de 有才能的, yǒu cáihuá de 有才华的

talk 1 vb (to speak) jiǎnghuà 讲话, tánhuà 谈话; to talk in Chinese yòng Hànyǔ jiǎnghuà 用汉语讲话; to talk to someone hé mǒurén jiǎnghuà 和某人讲话; I talked to them about the trip wǒ gēn tāmen tánle zhècì lǚxíng de qíngkuàng 我跟他们谈了这次旅行的情况; they were talking about you tāmen zài tánlùn nǐ 他们在谈论你; to talk on the phone dǎ diànhuà 打电话; (to speak at a meeting or a conference) yǎnjiǎng 演讲, jiǎnghuà 讲话; he is going to talk to the students and teachers at Peking University tā yào zài Běijīng Dàxué xiàng shīshēngmen yǎnjiǎng 他要在北京大学向师生们演讲; (to chat) xiánliáo 闲聊 **2** n (a conversation) yícì tánhuà 一次谈话, yícì jiāotán 一次交谈; (a lecture) yícì jiǎngzuò 一次讲座; (to a club, a group, a meeting) yíge bàogào 一个报告, yícì yǎnjiǎng 一次演讲; (discussions) huìtán 会谈; the two leaders had friendly talks yesterday liǎngwèi lǐngdǎorén zuótiān jìnxíngle yǒuhǎo de huìtán 两位领导人昨天进行了友好的会谈

talkative adj jiàntán 健谈, xǐhuan jiǎnghuà 喜欢讲话

tall adj gāo 高; to be six feet tall liù yīngchǐ gāo 六英尺高

tan n a tan rìshàihòu de fūsè 日晒后的肤色; to get a tan shài de hēihēi de 晒得黑黑的

tanned adj shàihēi le 晒黑了

tap 1 n (British English) a tap yíge shuǐlóng(tóu) 一个水龙(头); to turn the tap off bǎ shuǐlóng(tóu) guānshang 把水龙(头)关上 **2** vb to tap on the door qiāo mén 敲门

tape 1 n a tape (for a tape recorder) yìpán lùyīndài 一盘录音带; (for a video) yìpán lùxiàngdài 一盘录像带; (for sticking) jiāodài 胶带 **2** vb (to record) bǎ...lùxiàlai 把...录下来; she's taped that film tā bǎ nàbù diànyǐng lùxiàlai le 她把那部电影录下来了

tape recorder n a tape recorder yìtái lùyīnjī 一台录音机

target n a target (in shooting) yíge bǎzi 一个靶子; (what is aimed at) yíge mùbiāo 一个目标; (an object of criticism) yíge duìxiàng 一个对象

tart n (British English) a tart yíge xiànrbǐng 一个馅儿饼; an apple tart yíge píngguǒ xiànrbǐng 一个苹果馅儿饼

task n a task yíge rènwù 一个任务, yíxiàng gōngzuò 一项工作

taste 1 n (when eating, drinking) a taste yìzhǒng wèidào 一种味道, yìzhǒng zīwèi 一种滋味; (power of discerning and judging) taste jiànshǎng (néng)lì 鉴赏(能)力; she has good taste tā jùyǒu liánghǎo de jiànshǎng nénglì 她具有良好的鉴赏能力 **2** vb (when describing a flavour) chángqilai 尝起来, chīqilai 吃起来; to taste good chángqilai wèidào hěn hǎo 尝起来味道很好; to taste awful chángqilai wèidào hěn zāogāo 尝起来味道很糟糕; it tastes like cabbage chīqilai wèidào xiàng juǎnxīncài 吃起来味道像卷心菜; (when eating, drinking) cháng 尝, pǐncháng 品尝

tax n shuì 税

taxi n a taxi yíliàng chūzūchē 一辆出租车

taxi rank (British English), **taxi stand** (US English) n a taxi rank yíge chūzū qìchēzhàn 一个出租汽车站

tea n (the product) tea chá 茶; a cup of tea yì bēi chá 一杯茶; (British English) (a meal) fàn 饭, chádiǎn 茶点

teach vb (to train, educate, or impart knowledge) jiāo 教; to teach someone [to read | to drive | to ride a horse] jiāo mǒurén [niàn shū | kāi chē | qí mǎ] 教某人 [念书 | 开车 | 骑马]; to teach Chinese to adults jiāo chéngrén Zhōngwén 教成人中文; (to work as a teacher) jiàoshū 教书, jiàoxué 教学; where does she teach? tā zài nǎr jiāoshū? 她在哪儿教书?

teacher n a teacher yìmíng jiàoshī 一名教师, yíwèi lǎoshī 一位老师

team n a team yíge duì 一个队; a football team yìzhī zúqiúduì 一支足球队

teapot n a teapot yíge cháhú 一个茶壶

tear¹ vb (to pull apart, to rend) sī 撕, chě 扯; to tear a page out of a book cóng shū shang sīxia yíyè zhǐ 从书上撕下一页纸; (to become torn) sīpò 撕破, chěpò 扯破; this kind of paper tears easily zhèzhǒng zhǐ hěn róngyì sīpò 这种纸很容易撕破

tear off (to remove by tearing) chēdiào 扯掉; (to depart hurriedly) xùnsù zǒudiào 迅速走掉, pǎodiào 跑掉; **tear up to tear up a letter** bǎ yìfēng xìn sī de fěnsuì 把一封信撕得粉碎; **the wind tore up many houses** dà fēng cuīhuǐle hěn duō fángzi 大风摧毁了很多房子

tear² n a tear yìdī yǎnlèi 一滴眼泪; to burst into tears dàkūqilai 大哭起来

tease vb dòunòng 逗弄, xìnòng 戏弄

teaspoon n a teaspoon yìbǎ cháchí 一把茶匙

technical adj jìshù de 技术的, zhuānyèxìng de 专业性的

teenager n a teenager yígè shíjǐ suì de háizi 一个十几岁的孩子

telephone n a telephone yíbù diànhuà 一部电话

telephone directory n a telephone directory yìběn diànhuàbù 一本电话簿

telescope n a telescope yíjià wàngyuǎnjìng 一架望远镜

television n a television yìtái diànshìjī 一台电视机; I saw the film on television wǒ shì zài diànshì shang kàn de zhèbù diànyǐng 我是在电视上看的这部电影

tell vb (to say to) gàosu 告诉; did you tell your parents? nǐ gàosu nǐ fùmǔ le ma? 你告诉你父母了吗? to tell someone about a problem gàosu mǒurén yíge wèntí 告诉某人一个问题; don't tell anyone bié gàosu biérén 别告诉别人; (for telling a story, a joke) jiǎng 讲; to tell jokes jiǎng xiàohua 讲笑话; (for telling a lie, a joke) shuō 说; to tell a lie shuōhuǎng 说谎; (when giving orders or instructions) ràng 让, jiào 叫, mìnglìng 命令; to tell someone to leave the classroom ràng mǒurén líkāi jiàoshì 让某人离开教室; to tell someone not to smoke jiào mǒurén búyào chōu yān 叫某人不要抽烟; (to work out, to know) kànchū 看出, zhīdào 知道, duàndìng 断定; I can tell (that) she's disappointed wǒ néng kànchulai tā hěn shīwàng 我能看出来她很失望; you can tell he's lying wǒ néng zhīdào tā zài shuōhuǎng 你能知道他在说谎; (when making distinctions) fēnbiàn 分辨, biànbié 辨别; to tell him from his twin brother fēnbiàn tā hé tāde luánshēng xiōngdì 分辨他和他的孪生兄弟; I can't tell which is which wǒ biànbié bù chū nǎge shì nǎge 我辨别不出他们谁是哪个; **tell off** to tell someone off zébèi mǒurén 责备某人

temper n (temperament, disposition) píqì 脾气; she has a rather bad temper tā píqì hěn huài 她脾气很坏; to lose one's temper fā píqì 发脾气; (mood) xīnqíng 心情; to be in a good temper xīnqíng hǎo 心情好

temperature n (of the body) tǐwēn 体温; to have a temperature fāshāo 发烧; (degree of heat or cold) wēndù 温度; (about the weather) qìwēn 气温

temple n a temple yízuò (sì)miào 一座(寺)庙

temporary adj línshí 临时, zànshí 暂时

ten num shí 十

tennis n wǎngqiú 网球

tennis court n a tennis court yíge wǎngqiú chǎng 一个网球场

tense adj jǐnzhāng 紧张

tent n a tent yìdǐng zhàngpeng 一顶帐篷

tenth num (in a series) dìshí 第十; (in dates) shí rì 十日, shí hào 十号; the tenth of October shíyuè shí hào 十月十号

term n a term (in schools or universities) yíge xuéqí 一个学期; (of office or appointment) yíge rènqí 一个任期; (a limited period of time) yíge qīxiàn 一个期限; (a word or expression) shùyǔ 术语, cíyǔ 词语; a term yíge shùyǔ 一个术语; (conditions) term tiáojiàn 条件

terrible adj (expressing shock) kěpà 可怕, xiàrén 吓人; (used for emphasis) jídù 极度, lìhài 厉害; (awful, very bad) zāogāo 糟糕

terrified adj hàipà 害怕, xià de yàomìng 吓得要命

terror n terror kǒngbù 恐怖, kǒngjù 恐惧

terrorist n a terrorist yìmíng kǒngbù fènzǐ 一名恐怖分子

test 1 vb (to put to the proof) jiǎnyàn 检验; (to try out) shìyàn 试验; (in exams) cèyàn 测验 **2** n a test (means of trial) yícì shìyàn 一次试验; (in school, college) yícì cèyàn 一次测验; (written) yícì bǐshì 一次笔试; (oral) yícì kǒushì 一次口试; a driving test yícì jiàshǐ kǎoshì 一次驾驶考试; to have an eye test zuò yícì yǎnjīng jiǎnchá 做一次眼睛检查

than 1 prep (in comparisons) bǐ 比; to be [stronger | more intelligent | faster...] than someone bǐ mǒurén [qiángzhuàng | cōngming | kuài...] 比某人 [强壮 | 聪明 | 快...]; I've got more money than you wǒde qián bǐ nǐde duō 我的钱比你的多; (when talking about quantities) more than yǐshàng 以上; more than half of the pupils are absent yíbàn yǐshàng de xuéshēng méi lái 一半以上的学生没来; less than bú dào 不到; it's worth less than £100 tāde jiàzhí búdào yìbǎi yīngbàng 它的价值不到一百英镑 **2** conj bǐ 比; he's older than I am tā bǐ wǒ dà 他比我大

thank vb xièxie 谢谢, gǎnxiè 感谢

thanks 1 adv gǎnxiè 感谢, gǎnjī 感激; many thanks, thanks a lot duōxiè 多谢 **2** thanks to xìngkuī 幸亏, yóuyú 由于

thank you adv xièxie 谢谢, xièxie nín 谢谢您; thank you for coming xièxie nín guānglín 谢谢您光临; 'more wine?'—'thank you' 'zài jiā diǎnr jiǔ ma?'—'xièxie, qǐng zài jiā diǎnr' '再加点儿酒吗?'—'谢谢, 请再加点儿'

that ! Note that as a determiner or a pronoun, that is often translated as nàge 那个, where ge 个 is a measure word and varies with the noun that follows or with the noun to which it refers. **1** det nà 那, nàge 那个; at that time nà shíhou 那时候; who is that person? nàge rén shì shéi? 那个人是谁? I don't like that novel wǒ bù xǐhuan nàběn xiǎoshuō 我不喜欢那本小说 **2** pron nà 那, nàge 那个 ! Note that sometimes that is specified as a person or as a thing; in the former case, that is translated as nàge rén 那个人, and in the latter, nàge dōngxi 那个东西; what's that? nà(ge dōngxi) shì shénme? 那(个东西)是什么? who's that? nà(ge rén) shì shéi? 那(个人)是谁? who put that on the table? shéi bǎ nàge fàng zài zhuōzi shang? 谁把那个放在桌子上? is that Tom? shì Tāngmǔ ma? 是汤姆吗? (when used as a relative pronoun) ! Note that when used as a relative pronoun, that is not translated; the girl that I met is his

sister wǒ jiàndào de nàge gūniang shì tā mèimei 我见到的那个姑娘是他妹妹; **do you know the person that I was talking to just now?** nǐ rènshi wǒ gāngcái gēn tā jiǎnghuà de nàge rén ma? 你认识我刚才跟他讲话的那个人吗? **3** conj ! Note that when used as a conjunction, that is usually not translated; **she said that she would come** tā shuō tā huì lái 她说她会来 **4** adv nàme 那么, nàyàng 那样; **the question is not that difficult** zhège wèntí méiyǒu nàme nán 这个问题没有那么难

the det (when referring to a person or thing mentioned here or previously) zhè 这, nà 那; **the student you want to meet is not here today** nǐ yào jiàn de nàge xuésheng jīntiān bú zài 你要见的那个学生今天不在; (if you like the book, I can lend it to you) yàoshi nǐ xǐhuan zhèběn shū, wǒ kěyǐ jiègěi nǐ 要是你喜欢这本书, 我可以借给你; (when referring to something understood, something unique) ! Note that in this sense, the is not translated; **please switch off** [the radio | the TV | the light...] qǐng bǎ [shōuyīnjī | diànshìjī | dēng...] guānshang 请把[收音机 | 电视机 | 灯...] 关上; **the sun has come out** tàiyáng chūlai le 太阳出来了; (when referring to a particular type, class, or group of people or objects) ! Note that in this sense, the is not translated; **the Japanese like to eat raw fish** Rìběnrén xǐhuan chī shēng yú 日本人喜欢吃生鱼; **the rich should help the poor** fùrén yīnggāi bāngzhù qióngrén 富人应该帮助穷人; **the horse is a useful animal** mǎ shì yǒuyòng de dòngwù 马是有用的动物; (when used with the comparative or superlative) ! Note that in this sense, the is not translated; **you've made it all the worse** nǐ bǎ tā gǎo de gèng zāole 你把它搞得更糟了; **she's the most hardworking student in the class** tā shì bān li zuì nǔlì de xuésheng 她是班里最努力的学生

theatre (British English), **theater** (US English) n a theatre (a place where plays are performed) yíge jùyuàn 一个剧院, yíge xìyuàn 一个戏院; (a surgical operating room) yíge shǒushùshì 一个手术室; **a lecture theatre** yíge jiētī jiàoshì 一个阶梯教室

their det (for men, or men and women together) tāmende 他们的; **I don't like their house** wǒ bù xǐhuan tāmende fángzi 我不喜欢他们的房子; (for women) tāmende 她们的; (for non-human and inanimate beings) tāmende 它们的

theirs pron (for men, or men and women together) tāmende 他们的; which car is theirs? nǎliàng chē shì tāmende? 哪辆车是他们的?; (for women) tāmende 她们的; (for non-human and inanimate beings) tāmende 它们的

them pron (for men, or men and women together) tāmen 他们; I don't know them wǒ bú rènshi tāmen 我不认识他们; (for women) tāmen 她们; (for non-human and inanimate beings) tāmen 它们! Note that in this sense, them is usually not translated if it is an object following a verb; please put them on the table qǐng fàng zài zhuōzi shang 请放在桌子上; when you finish reading these magazines, please remember to return them nǐ kànwán zhèxiē zázhì, qǐng jìzhù huánhuilai 你看完这些杂志, 请记住还回来; I bought two gifts for my parents and they like them very much wǒ gěi wǒ fùmǔ mǎile liǎngjiàn lǐwù, tāmen hěn xǐhuan 我给我父母买了两件礼物, 他们很喜欢

themselves pron (when used as a reflexive pronoun) themselves (for men, or men and women together) (tāmen)zìjǐ (他们)自己; they didn't hurt themselves tāmen méiyǒu shāngzhe zìjǐ 他们没有伤着自己; (for women) (tāmen)zìjǐ (她们)自己; (for emphasis) zìjǐ 自己, qīnzì 亲自; they said it themselves tāmen zìjǐ shuōde 他们自己说的; they didn't attend the meeting themselves tāmen méiyǒu qīnzì cānjiā huì 他们没有亲自参加会

then adv (at that point in time) nàshí 那时, dāngshí 当时; I was living in Taiwan then dāngshí wǒ zhù zài Táiwān 当时我住在台湾; from then on cóng nàshí qǐ 从那时起; (after, next) ránhòu 然后, jiēzhe 接着; I went to Beijing and then to Shanghai wǒ qùle Běijīng, ránhòu yòu qùle Shànghǎi 我去了北京, 然后又去了上海

there 1 pron (when followed by the verb to be) yǒu 有! Note that the negative from of yǒu 有 is méi yǒu 没有; there is a problem yǒu yíge wèntí 有一个问题; there aren't any shops méi yǒu rènhé shāngdiàn 没有任何商店; (when used with verbs like to exist, to appear, etc.)! Note that in this case, there is not translated; there exist many problems cúnzài hěn duō wèntí 存在很多问题; there appears some hope chūxiànle yìxiē xīwàng 出现了一些希望 **2** adv (when talking about location) nàr 那儿, nàlǐ 那里; who's there? shéi zài nàr? 谁在那儿?; the train wasn't there huǒchē bú zài nàlǐ 火车不在那里; when will we get there? wǒmen shénme shíhou dào nàr? 我们什么时候到那儿?; they don't go there very often tāmen bù chángcháng qù nàlǐ 他们不常常去那里; (when drawing attention) there's [the sea | my watch | your mother] [dàhǎi | wǒde biǎo | nǐ māma] zài nàr [大海 | 我的表 | 你妈妈] 在那儿; there you are, there you go gěi (nǐ) 给(你)

therefore adv yīncǐ 因此. suǒyǐ 所以

these 1 det zhèxiē 这些; these books aren't mine zhèxiē shū bú shì wǒde 这些书不是我的 **2** pron zhèxiē 这些; these are your things zhèxiē shì nǐde dōngxi 这些是你的东西; these are my friends zhèxiē shì wǒde péngyou 这些是我的朋友

they pron (for men, or men and women together) tāmen 他们; they'll be there too tāmen yě huì zài nàr 他们也会在那儿; (for women) tāmen 她们; they're intelligent girls tāmen shì hěn cōngming de gūniang 她们是很聪明的姑娘; (for non-human and inanimate beings) tāmen 它们

thick adj (having a large distance between surfaces) hòu 厚; (great in diameter) cū 粗; (dense) mì 密, nóngmì 浓密; (when describing a liquid) chóu 稠, nóng 浓; (when describing smoke) nóng 浓

thief n a thief yíge xiǎotōu 一个小偷

thigh n the thigh dàtuǐ 大腿

thin adj (slim, lean) shòu 瘦; (having little distance between surfaces) báo 薄; (small in diameter) xì 细; (of little density) xīshǎo 稀少; (watery) xībó 稀薄

thing n (a material object) a thing yíge dōngxi 一个东西, yíjiàn dōngxi 一件东西; what's the thing on the table? zhuōzi shang de dōngxi shì shénme 桌子上的东西是什么?; (a matter, an affair) a thing yíjiàn shì(qing) 一件事(情); I've got things to do wǒ yǒu shìqing yào zuò 我有事情要做; (belongings) things yòngpǐn 用品, suǒyǒuwù 所有物

think vb (when talking about opinions) rènwéi 认为, juéde 觉得; **what do you think of it?** nǐ rènwéi zhège zěnmeyàng? 你认为这个怎么样?; **I think it's unfair** wǒ juéde zhè bù gōngpíng 我觉得这不公平; **'will they come?'—'I don't think so'** 'tāmen huì lái ma?'—'wǒ rènwéi bú huì' '他们会来吗?'—'我认为不会'; **who do you think will win?** nǐ juéde shéi huì yíng? 你觉得谁会赢?; (to concentrate on an idea) xiǎng 想, kǎolǜ 考虑; **think hard before answering** xiǎnghǎo le zài huídá 想好了再回答; (to remember) xiǎngqǐ 想起; **I can't think of his name** wǒ xiǎng bù qǐ tāde míngzi 我想不起他的名字; **can you think of where we met him?** nǐ néng xiǎngqǐ wǒmen zài nǎr jiànguo tā ma? 你能想起我们在哪儿见过他吗?; (to have in mind) xiǎngdào 想到, xiǎngqǐ 想起; **I thought of you when I saw the address** wǒ kàndào zhège dìzhǐ jiù xiǎngdàole nǐ 我看到这个地址就想到了你; (to have vague plans to) dǎsuàn 打算, jìhuà 计划; **to be thinking of changing jobs** dǎsuàn huàn gōngzuò 打算换工作; (to solve by a process of thought) xiǎngchū 想出; **to think of a solution** xiǎngchū yíge jiějué bànfǎ 想出一个解决办法; **he couldn't think of a better idea** tā xiǎng bù chū yíge gèng hǎo de zhǔyi 他想不出一个更好的主意! Note that when bù 不 is used to negate xiǎngqǐ 想起, xiǎngdào 想到, or xiǎngchū 想出, bù 不 comes between the verb xiǎng 想 and its complement as in xiǎng bù qǐ 想不起, xiǎng bú dào 想不到 and xiǎng bù chū 想不出

third 1 adj dìsān 第三 **2** n (in a series) the third dìsān 第三; (in dates) sān hào 三号, sān rì 三日; **the third of June** liùyuè sān rì 六月三日; (when talking about quantities) **a third of the population** sānfēn zhī yī de rénkǒu 三分之一的人口 **3** adv dìsān 第三; **to come third in a race** zài bǐsài zhōng dé dìsān 在比赛中得第三

thirsty adj kě 渴, kǒukě 口渴; **I'm very thirsty** wǒ hěn kě 我很渴

thirteen num thirteen shísān 十三

thirteenth num (in a series) the thirteenth dìshísān 第十三; (in dates) shísān hào 十三号, shísān rì 十三日; **Friday the thirteenth** shísān hào xīngqīwǔ 十三号星期五

thirty num thirty sānshí 三十

this ! *Note that as a determiner or a pronoun, this is often translated as* zhège 这个, *where* ge 个 *is a measure word that varies with the noun to which it refers.* **1** *det* zhè 这, zhège 这个; **I like** [this garden | this book | this shop...] wǒ xǐhuan [zhège huāyuán | zhèběn shū | zhèjiā shāngdiàn...] 我喜欢[这个花园 | 这本书 | 这家商店...]; *(when referring to today)* jīntiān 今天; **this** [morning | afternoon | evening] jīntiān [shàngwǔ | xiàwǔ | wǎnshang] 今天[上午 | 下午 | 晚上]; **this year** jīnnián 今年 **2** *pron* zhè 这, zhège 这个; **what's this?** zhè shì shénme? 这是什么?; **who's this?** zhè shéi? 这是谁?; **this is the kitchen** zhè shì chúfáng 这是厨房 **3** *adv* zhème 这么, zhèyàng 这样; **he is about this tall** tā chàbuduō yǒu zhème gāo 他差不多有这么高

thorn *n* a thorn yìgēn cì 一根刺

those 1 *det* those nàxiē 那些; **those books are yours** nàxiē shū shì nǐde 那些书是你的 **2** *pron* those nàxiē 那些; **what are those?** nàxiē shì shénme? 那些是什么?; **those are my friends** nàxiē shì wǒde péngyou 那些是我的朋友

though *conj* suīrán 虽然, jǐnguǎn 尽管; **though he can speak good Chinese, he can't write in Chinese** suīrán tā Hànyǔ shuō de hěn hǎo, dàn(shì) tā bú huì xiě Hànzì 虽然他汉语说得很好, 但(是)他不会写汉字 **!** *Note that in Chinese the use of* suīrán 虽然 *or* jǐnguǎn 尽管 *does not exclude the use of* kěshì 可是 *(= but) or* dànshì 但是 *(= but).*

thought *n* a thought *(an idea)* yìzhǒng xiǎngfǎ 一种想法; *(a school of thought)* yìzhǒng sīxiǎng 一种思想

thousand *num* qiān 千; **one thousand, a thousand** yìqiān 一千; **four thousand pounds** sìqiān yīngbàng 四千英镑

thread *n* a thread yìgēn xiàn 一根线

threat *n* wēixié 威胁, kǒngxià 恐吓

threaten *vb* wēixié 威胁, kǒngxià 恐吓

three *num* three sān 三; **three schools** sānsuǒ xuéxiào 三所学校

throat *n* the throat sǎngzi 嗓子, hóulóng 喉咙

through ! *Often through occurs in combinations with verbs, for example: go through, let through, read through, etc. To find the correct translations for this type of verb, look up the separate dictionary entries at go, let, read, etc.; prep (from one side to the other)* chuānguò 穿过, tōngguò 通过; **to drive through the desert** kāi chē chuānguò shāmò 开车穿过沙漠; **to go through the town centre** chuānguò shì zhōngxīn 穿过市中心; **to look out through a window** tōngguò chuānghu xiàng wài kàn 通过窗户向外看; **to go through customs** tōngguò hǎiguān 通过海关; **to go through a red light** chuǎng hóng dēng 闯红灯; *(from the beginning to the end)* cóng tóu dào wěi 从头到尾; **he didn't read through all these letters** tā méiyǒu cóng tóu dào wěi kàn suǒyǒu de zhèxiē xìn 他没有从头到尾看所有的这些信; *(by way of)* tōngguò 通过; **I came to know her through a friend** wǒ tōngguò yíge péngyou rènshile tā 我通过一个朋友认识了她; **she found a new job through the newspaper** tā tōngguò bàozhǐ zhǎodàole yíge xīn gōngzuò 她通过报纸找到了一个新工作; *(when talking about time)* **right through the day** zhěngzhěng yì tiān 整整一天; **from Friday through to Sunday** cóng xīngqīwǔ dào xīngqīrì 从星期五到星期日; **open April through September** *(US English)* cóng sìyuè dào jiǔyuè kāifàng 从四月到九月开放

throw *vb (to fling, cast)* rēng 扔; **to throw stones at someone** xiàng mǒurén rēng shítou 向某人扔石头; **throw me the ball** bǎ qiú rēng gěi wǒ 把球扔给我; **to throw a book to the floor** bǎ yìběn shū rēng zài dì shang 把一本书扔在地上; *(to cause to fall)* shuāidǎo 摔倒; **to throw someone to the ground** bǎ mǒurén shuāidǎo zài dì shang 把某人摔倒在地上; **throw away, throw out** rēngdiào 扔掉

thumb *n* the thumb dàmǔzhǐ 大拇指

thunder *n* léi 雷, léishēng 雷声

thunderstorm *n* a thunderstorm yìchǎng léibàoyǔ 一场雷暴雨

Thursday *n* Thursday xīngqīsì 星期四, lǐbàisì 礼拜四

Tibet *n* Xīzàng 西藏

ticket *n* a ticket yìzhāng piào 一张票

tickle *vb (to itch)* fāyǎng 发痒; *(to cause to produce laughter)* to tickle someone dòu mǒurén xiào 逗某人笑

tide *n* the tide cháo 潮, cháoshuǐ 潮水; the tide is out tuì cháo le 退潮了; the tide is coming in zhǎng cháo le 涨潮了

tidy *adj* zhěngjié 整洁, zhěngqí 整齐; **tidy up** zhěnglǐ 整理 shōushi 收拾

tie 1 *vb (to fasten, tether)* shuān 拴; to tie a dog to a tree bǎ yìzhī gǒu shuān zài yìkē shù shang 把一只狗拴在一棵树上; *(to bind)* kǔn 捆, zā 扎; to tie the parcel (up) with string yòng shéngzi bǎ bāoguǒ kǔnqǐlai 用绳子把包裹捆起来; *(to make a knot)* jì 系; to tie one's shoelaces jì xiédài 系鞋带; to tie one's tie dǎ lǐngdài 打领带 **2** *n (worn with a shirt)* a tie yìtiáo lǐngdài 一条领带; *(in sport)* a tie yìgé píngjú 一个平局; **tie up** *(to parcel up)* kǔnzā 捆扎; *(to tether)* shuān 拴

tiger *n* a tiger yìzhī lǎohǔ 一只老虎

tight *adj (firmly fixed)* láogù 牢固, jǐn 紧; *(taut, tense)* lājǐn 拉紧, bēngjǐn 绷紧; *(closely fitting)* are the shoes too tight for you? zhèshuāng xié nǐ chuān tài jǐn le ma? 这双鞋你穿太紧了吗?; *(air-tight, water-tight)* mìfēng de 密封的

tights *n* jǐnshēnkù 紧身裤

till¹ ▸ until

till² *n* a till yígè fàng qián de chōuti 一个放钱的抽屉

timber *n* mùcái 木材, mùliào 木料

time *n* shíjiān 时间; I don't have time to go there wǒ méi yǒu shíjiān qù nàr 我没有时间去那儿; we haven't seen them for a long time wǒmen hěn cháng shíjiān méiyǒu kànjian tāmen le 我们很长时间没有看见他们了; there is no time for you to argue méi yǒu shíjiān ràng nǐmen zhēnglùn 没有时间让你们争论; a long time ago hěn jiǔ yǐqián 很久以前; *(when talking about a specific hour or period of time)* what's the time? what time is it? jǐ diǎn le 几点了?; what time does the film start? diànyǐng jǐ diǎn kāiyǎn? 电影几点开演? diànyǐng shénme shíhou kāiyǎn? 电影什么时候开演?; on time ànshí 按时.

zhǔnshí 准时; **to arrive on time** ànshí dàodá 按时到达; **in** [**five days' | a week's | six months'**] **time** guò [wǔ tiān | yíge xīngqī | liùge yuè] 过[五天 | 一个星期 | 六个月]; **this time last year** qùnián zhège shíhou 去年这个时候; **by this time next week** xiàge xīngqī zhège shíhou (zhīqián) 下个星期这个时候(之前); **it's time we left** wǒmen gāi zǒu le 我们该走了; (a moment) **at times** yǒushí 有时, bùshí 不时; **from time to time** yǒushí 有时, bùshí 不时; **at the right time** zài shìdàng de shíhou 在适当的时候; **any time now** cóng xiànzài qǐ suíshí 从现在起随时; **he may arrive at any time now** cóng xiànzài qǐ tā suíshí dōu huì dàodá 从现在起他随时都会到达; **for the time being** zànshí 暂时; (a period in the past) **we didn't know each other at the time** nà shí(hòu), wǒmen hùxiāng bú rènshi 那时(候), 我们互相不认识; (an experience) **to have a good time** guò de hěn yúkuài 过得很愉快; **to have a hard time concentrating** wú fǎ jízhōng jīnglì 无法集中精力; (an occasion) cì 次, huí 回; [**this | last | next | first | second | the last**] **time** [zhè | shàng | xià | dìyī | dì'èr | zuìhòu yí] cì [这 | 上 | 下 | 第一 | 第二 | 最后一] 次; [**five | several | many**] **times** [wǔ | jǐ | xǔduō] cì [五 | 几 | 许多] 次; **the first time we met** wǒmen dìyīcì jiànmiàn de shíhou 我们第一次见面的时候; (-fold) bèi 倍; **three times more expensive** guì sānbèi 贵三倍; **ten times quicker** kuài shíbèi 快十倍

timetable n (for trains, buses) **a timetable** yíge shíkèbiǎo 一个时刻表; (in school, at work); **a timetable** yíge shíjiānbiǎo 一个时间表

tin n (the metal) tīn 锡; (British English) (a tin can) **a tin** yìtǒng (guàntou) 一筒(罐头); **a tin of beans** yìtǒng dòuzi guàntou 一筒豆子罐头

tin opener n (British English) **a tin opener** yìbǎ guàntoudāo 一把罐头刀, yìbǎ kāiguàntoudāo 一把开罐头刀

tiny adj jí xiǎo 极小, wēixiǎo 微小

tip n (the point) **the tip of** [**a pen | the finger | the nose | the tongue**] [bǐ | shǒuzhǐ | bízi | shétou] jiān [笔 | 手指 | 鼻子 | 舌头] 尖; (an extra sum of money given to reward good service) **a tip** yìfēn xiǎofèi 一份小费; (a piece of advice) **a tip** yíge gàojiè 一个告诫; (a hint) **a tip** yíge tíshì 一个提示, yíge ànshì 一个暗示

tire n (US English) a tire yíge lúntāi 一个轮胎, yíge chētāi 一个车胎

tired adj (needing rest) lèi 累, píláo 疲劳, píjuàn 疲倦; he is tired tā lèi le 他累了; (needing a change) to be tired of yànfán 厌烦, yànjuàn 厌倦; I'm tired of being a waitress wǒ duì dāng nǚfúwùyuán yànfán le 我对当女服务员厌烦了

tiring adj lèi rén de 累人的, lìng rén píláo de 令人疲劳的

tissue n a tissue yìzhāng wèishēngzhǐ 一张卫生纸, yìzhāng miánzhǐ 一张棉纸

to prep ! There are many adjectives like mean, nice, rude, etc., and verbs like belong, write, etc., which involve the use of to. For translations, look up the adjective entries at mean, nice, rude or the verb entries at belong, write.

toast n kǎomiànbāo 烤面包; a piece of toast yípiàn kǎomiànbāo 一片烤面包

toaster n a toaster yíge kǎomiànbāoqì 一个烤面包器

today adv jīntiān 今天, jīnrì 今日

toe n jiǎozhǐ 脚趾, jiǎojiān 脚尖

toffee n nǎitáng 奶糖, tàifēitáng 太妃糖

together adv yìqǐ 一起, yíkuàir 一块儿

toilet n a toilet yíge cèsuǒ 一个厕所

toilet paper n wèishēngzhǐ 卫生纸

tomato n a tomato yíge xīhóngshì 一个西红柿, yíge fānqié 一个番茄

tomorrow adv míngtiān 明天, míngrì 明日

tongue n shétou 舌头, shé 舌

tonight adv (this evening) jīntiān wǎnshang 今天晚上, jīnwǎn 今晚; (during the night) jīntiān yè li 今天夜里, jīn yè 今夜

too adv (also) yě 也; I'm going too wǒ yě qù 我也去; (more than is necessary or desirable) tài 太; it's too [big | expensive | far] tài [dà | guì | yuǎn] le 太 [大 | 贵 | 远] 了; there were too many people

rén tài duō le 人太多了; I ate too much wǒ chī de tài duō le
我吃得太多了

tool n a tool yíge gōngjù 一个工具

tooth n a tooth yìkē yá 一颗牙; a set of false teeth yítào jiǎyá
一套假牙

toothache n he has a toothache tā yátòng 他牙痛

toothbrush n a toothbrush yìbǎ yáshuā 一把牙刷

toothpaste n yágāo 牙膏

top 1 n (the highest part) dǐng 顶, dǐngbù 顶部; at the top of [the
hill | the tree | the tower | the stairs] (zài) [shān | shù | tǎ | lóutī]
dǐng(shang) (在) [山 | 树 | 塔 | 楼梯] 顶(上); the fourth line from
the top cóng shàngmian shǔ dìsìháng 从上面数第四行;
(a cover, a lid) a top (on a bottle, pot, pan) yíge gàir 一个盖儿,
yíge gàizi 一个盖子; (on a pen) yíge bǐmào 一个笔帽; (the
highest level) to get to the top in the competition zài bǐsài zhōng
huòdé dìyī 在比赛中获得第一; to be at the top of the class
zài bān li míngliè dìyī 在班里名列第一 **2** adj the top [shelf |
drawer | button] dǐngshang de [jiàzi | chōuti | kòuzi] 顶上的 [架子 |
抽屉 | 扣子]

torch n (a flashlight) (British English) a torch yíge shǒudiàn(tǒng)
一个手电(筒); (a portable stick of inflammable material for
producing a flame) a torch yíge huǒjù 一个火炬, yíge huǒbǎ
一个火把

torn adj sīpòle de 撕破了的, chěpòle de 扯破了的

tortoise n a tortoise yìzhī (wū)guī 一只(乌)龟

total 1 n a total zǒngshù 总数; (if it's money) zǒng'é 总额 **2** adj
zǒng 总, quánbù 全部

touch 1 vb (with one's hand) mō 摸, chùmō 触摸; (come into
contact with) pèng 碰, jiēchù 接触; (affect one's feelings)
shǐ...gǎndòng 使...感动; the story touched us all zhège gùshi
shǐ wǒmen dōu hěn gǎndòng 这个故事使我们都很感动 **2** n
to get in touch with someone yǔ mǒurén liánxì 与某人联系;
to keep/stay in touch with someone yǔ mǒurén bǎochí liánxì
与某人保持联系

tough adj (strong, resilient, not brittle) jiānrèn 坚韧, jiēshi 结实; (sturdy) jiànzhuàng 健壮; (unyielding, as a policy, attitude, or view) qiángyìng 强硬; (when describing a person) wánqiáng 顽强, jiānqiáng 坚强; (difficult) kùnnan 困难, nánbàn 难办; (rough) **a tough area** yíge hěn luàn de dìqù 一个很乱的地区

tour 1 n (by a singer, a band, a theatre group) **a tour** yícì xúnhuí yǎnchū 一次巡回演出; **on tour** zhèngzài xúnhuí yǎnchū 正在巡回演出; (by a sports person, a sports team) **a tour** yícì xúnhuí bǐsài 一次巡回比赛; (by tourists, pupils, visitors); **a tour** (when travelling from place to place) yícì lǚxíng 一次旅行, yícì lǚyóu 一次旅游; (visiting a single area) yícì yóulǎn 一次游览, yícì cānguān 一次参观; **to go on a tour of the castle** qù yóulǎn chéngbǎo 去游览城堡 **2** vb **to go touring** qù lǚxíng 去旅行; **to tour the United States** zhōuyóu Měiguó 周游美国

tourism n lǚyóuyè 旅游业

tourist n **a tourist** yíwèi yóukè 一位游客, yìmíng lǚxíngzhě 一名旅行者

tourist information office n **a tourist information office** yíge lǚyóu xìnxī fúwùchù 一个旅游信息服务处

toward(s) prep (in the direction of) xiàng 向, cháo 朝; **towards the east** xiàng dōngbiān 向东边; (shortly before) jiāngjìn 将近, jiējìn 接近; **towards evening** jiāngjìn wǎnshang 将近晚上; (when talking about attitudes, feelings) duì 对, duìyú 对于; **to be friendly towards someone** duì mǒurén hěn yǒuhǎo 对某人很友好

towel n **a towel** yìtiáo máojīn 一条毛巾

tower n **a tower** yízuò tǎ 一座塔

tower block n (British English) **a tower block** yízuò gāolóu 一座高楼

town n **a town** yíge chéng(zhèn) 一个城(镇), yíge zhèn 一个镇; **to go into town** jìn chéng 进城

town hall n **a town hall** yíge shìzhèngtīng 一个市政厅

toy n **a toy** yíge wánjù 一个玩具

track n (a path) a track yìtiáo lù 一条路, yìtiáo xiǎodào 一条小道; (in sports) a track yìtiáo pǎodào 一条跑道; (rails) the track(s) tiěguǐ 铁轨, guǐdào 轨道; (left by a person, an animal, a car) tracks xíngzōng 行踪, zōngjì 踪迹

tracksuit n a tracksuit yítào yùndòngfú 一套运动服

trade n màoyì 贸易, jiāoyì 交易; a trade yìzhǒng zhíyè 一种职业, yìzhǒng hángyè 一种行业

tradition n a tradition yíge chuántǒng 一个传统

traffic n jiāotōng 交通

traffic jam n a traffic jam jiāotōng dǔsè 交通堵塞

traffic lights n jiāotōng xìnhàodēng 交通信号灯, hónglǜdēng 红绿灯

train 1 n a train yíliè huǒchē 一列火车; the train to Shanghai qù Shànghǎi de huǒchē 去上海的火车 **2** vb (to teach, to prepare) péixùn 培训, xùnliàn 训练; to train employees péixùn gùyuán 培训雇员; to train athletes xùnliàn yùndòngyuán 训练运动员; (to learn a job) to train as a doctor jiēshòu zuò yīshēng de xùnliàn 接受做医生的训练; (for a sporting event) xùnliàn 训练, duànliàn 锻炼; to train for a better result in the sports meet wèi zài yùndònghuì shang qǔdé gèng hǎo de chéngjì ér xùnliàn 为在运动会上取得更好的成绩而训练

trainer n (a shoe) (British English) yùndòngxié 运动鞋; a pair of trainers yìshuāng yùndòngxié 一双运动鞋; (a person in sports) a trainer yíwèi jiàoliànyuán 一位教练员

training course n a training course yíge xùnliànbān 一个训练班

tramp n a tramp yíge liúlàngzhě 一个流浪者

translate vb (to turn from one language into another) fānyì 翻译, yì 译; (to interpret, to explain) jiěshì 解释, shuōmíng 说明

translator n a translator yìmíng fānyì 一名翻译

transport, transportation (US English) n yùnshū 运输, jiāotōng 交通; a means of transport yìzhǒng yùnshū gōngjù 一种运输工具, yìzhǒng jiāotōng gōngjù 一种交通工具;

public transport gōnggòng jiāotōng 公共交通, gōnggòng yùnshū 公共运输

trap n a trap (a device for catching) yíge xiànjǐng 一个陷井; (a plan to deceive, betray, etc.) yíge quāntào 一个圈套; **to set a trap for someone** wèi mǒurén shè yíge quāntào 为某人设一个圈套

trash n (US English) fèiwù 废物, lājī 垃圾

trash can n (US English) **a trash can** yíge lājīxiāng 一个垃圾箱

travel vb lǚxíng 旅行; **to travel** [abroad | to China | by bike] [qù guówài | qù Zhōngguó | qí zìxíngchē] lǚxíng [去国外 | 去中国 | 骑自行车] 旅行

travel agency n **a travel agency** yìjiā lǚxíngshè 一家旅行社

traveller (British English), **traveler** (US English) n a traveller yíge lǚxíngzhě 一个旅行者, yíge yóukè 一个游客

traveller's cheque (British English), **traveler's check** (US English) **a traveller's cheque** yìzhāng lǚxíng zhīpiào 一张旅行支票

tray n **a tray** yíge pánzi 一个盘子, yíge tuōpán 一个托盘

treat vb (to behave towards) duìdài 对待; **to treat someone** [badly | nicely | politely] duìdài mǒurén [hěn bù hǎo | hěn hǎo | hěn yǒu lǐmào] 对待某人 [很不好 | 很好 | 很有礼貌]; (to deal with, to handle) chǔlǐ 处理; **we have to treat this carefully** wǒmen děi xiǎoxīn chǔlǐ zhèjiàn shì 我们得小心处理这件事; (to give medical treatment to) yīzhì 医治, zhìliáo 治疗; **to treat someone for flu** gěi mǒurén yīzhì liúgǎn 给某人医治流感; (to pay for) to treat someone to Peking duck qǐng mǒurén chī Běijīng kǎoyā 请某人吃北京烤鸭

treatment n (behaviour towards someone) dàiyù 待遇, duìdài 对待; **to receive warm and friendly treatment from someone** shòudào mǒurén rèqíng yǒuhǎo de duìdài 受到某人热情友好的对待; (by a doctor) zhìliáo 治疗; **free treatment** miǎnfèi zhìliáo 免费治疗

tree *n* a tree yīkè shù 一棵树

tremble *vb* fādǒu 发抖, duōsuo 哆嗦; they were trembling with fear tāmen xià de fādǒu 他们吓得发抖

trendy *adj* shímáo 时髦, suí cháoliú 随潮流

trial *n* (a test or an experiment) a trial yícì shìyàn 一次试验; (in court) a trial yícì shěnwèn/shěnpàn 一次审问/审判; to go on trial shòu shěn(pàn) 受审(判)

triangle *n* a triangle yíge sānjiǎo(xíng) 一个三角(形)

trick **1** *n* (a joke) a trick yíge èzuòjù 一个恶作剧; to play a trick on someone zhuōnòng mǒurén 捉弄某人; (a means of deceiving) a trick yíge guǐjì 一个诡计, yíge piànjú 一个骗局; (to entertain) a trick yíge xìfǎ 一个戏法, yíge bǎxì 一个把戏 **2** *vb* qīpiàn 欺骗, hǒngpiàn 哄骗

trip **1** *n* (a journey) a trip yícì lǚxíng 一次旅行; to be on a business trip chūchāi 出差, zuò yícì gōngwù lǚxíng 做一次公务旅行 **2** *vb* (to stumble) bàn(dǎo) 绊(倒); I tripped over the step at the gate wǒ ràng ménkǒu de táijiē bànle yíxià 我让门口的台阶绊了一下; to trip someone (up) bǎ mǒurén bàndǎo 把某人绊倒

trouble *n* (difficulties) kùnnan 困难; he has trouble using this computer tā yòng zhètái jìsuànjī yǒu kùnnan 他用这台计算机有困难; (a scrape) kùnjìng 困境; to be in trouble chǔyú kùnjìng 处于困境; to get someone into trouble shǐ mǒurén xiànrù kùnjìng 使某人陷入困境; (disturbance) máfan 麻烦; to make trouble zhìzào máfan 制造麻烦, nàoshì 闹事; I'm sorry to have given you so much trouble duìbuqǐ, wǒ gěi nǐmen tiānle zhème duō máfan 对不起, 我给你们添了这么多麻烦; (an effort) he took the trouble to check every patient tā bù cí láokǔ wèi měige bìngrén dōu zuòle jiǎnchá 他不辞劳苦为每个病人都做了检查; to go to a lot of trouble helping others to go to a lot of trouble helping others bù cí láokǔ bāngzhù biéren 不辞劳苦帮助别人

trousers *n* kùzi 裤子; a pair of trousers yìtiáo kùzi 一条裤子

trout *n* a trout yìtiáo zhēnzūn 一条真鳟, yìtiáo guīyú 一条鲑鱼

truck *n* a truck yíliàng kǎchē 一辆卡车

truck driver n a truck driver yíwèi kǎchē sījī 一位卡车司机

true adj (genuine) zhēn 真; (in accordance with facts) zhēnshí 真实, zhēn 真; is it true that he's leaving? zhēn de tā yào zǒu ma? 真的他要走吗? a true story yíge zhēnshí de gùshi 一个真实的故事; to come true shíxiàn 实现; (faithful) zhōngshí 忠实; a true friend yíge zhōngshí de péngyou 一个忠实的朋友

trumpet n a trumpet yíge (xiǎo)hào 一个(小)号

trunk n (of a tree) a trunk yíge shùgàn 一个树干; (of an elephant) a trunk yíge xiàng bízi 一个象鼻子; (US English) (of a car) the trunk xínglixiāng 行李箱

trust vb (believe in) xìnrèn 信任, xiāngxìn 相信; I don't trust them wǒ bú xìnrèn tāmen 我不信任他们; (to rely on) xìnlài 信赖; you can't trust them nǐ bù néng xìnlài tāmen 你不能信赖他们

truth n (a proposition that agrees with actuality) a truth yìtiáo zhēnlǐ 一条真理; (the actual fact, the real situation) the truth zhēnxiàng 真相, zhēnshí qíngkuàng 真实情况

try 1 vb (to endeavour) jìnlì 尽力, jìnliàng 尽量, lìtú 力图; to try to [learn Chinese well | come early | forget that matter...] lìtú [xué hǎo Hànyǔ | zǎo lái | wàngjì nàjiàn shì...] 力图 [学好汉语 | 早来 | 忘记那件事...]; (to attempt) shì 试, chángshì 尝试; try phoning him shìzhe gěi tā dǎ diànhuà 试着给他打电话; let me try ràng wǒ shì yíxià 让我试一下; (to test) shì 试, shìyòng 试用; to try (out) a new method shìyòng yìzhǒng xīn de fāngfǎ 试用一种新的方法; to try (on) a pair of jeans shì(chuān) yìtiáo niúzǎikù 试(穿)一条牛仔裤; (to taste) (pǐn)cháng (品)尝; (in court) shěnxùn 审讯, shěnpàn 审判 **2** n let me have a try ràng wǒ shì yíxià 让我试一下

T-shirt n a T-shirt yíjiàn tìxùshān 一件T恤衫

tube n a tube yìgēn guǎnzi 一根管子; (for a wheel) a tube yíge nèitāi 一个内胎; (British English) (the underground) the tube dìtiě 地铁, dìxià tiědào 地下铁道

Tuesday n xīngqī'èr 星期二, lǐbài'èr 礼拜二

tuna n jīnqiāngyú 金枪鱼

tunnel n a tunnel yìtiáo suìdào 一条隧道

turkey n a turkey yìzhī huǒjī 一只火鸡

turn 1 vb (to rotate) zhuàn 转, zhuàndòng 转动; the wheel is turning fast lúnzi zài hěn kuài de zhuàndòng 轮子在很快地转动; to turn the handle zhuàndòng bǎshǒu 转动把手; (to move one's body) zhuǎn shēn 转身; she turned and walked away tā zhuǎn shēn zǒu le 她转身走了; (to change direction) zhuǎn 转; to turn right xiàng yòu zhuǎn 向右转; she turned her face towards the sun tā bǎ liǎn zhuǎn xiàng tàiyáng 她把脸转向太阳; (when talking about a page) fān 翻; please turn to page 10 qǐng fāndào dìshíyè 请翻到第十页; (to change) bǎ...biànchéng 把...变成; to turn the bedroom into an office bǎ wòshì biànchéng yíjiàn bàngōngshì 把卧室变成一间办公室; (to become) biànchéng 变成; to turn into a butterfly biànchéng yìzhī húdié 变成一只蝴蝶; to turn red biàn(chéng) hóng (de) 变(成)红(的); (on the road, in the corridor) guǎi 拐; don't turn left bié wǎng zuǒ guǎi 别往左拐 **2** n (a bend) a turn yígè zhuǎnwān 一个转弯; (when talking about taking turns) whose turn is it? lúndào shéi le? 轮到谁了?; it's your turn now xiànzài lúndào nǐ le 现在轮到你了; **turn around, turn round** (to face the other way) (if it's a person) zhuǎnguò shēn (qu) 转过身(去); (if it's a car) diào tóu 调头; (to go round and round) zhuǎn quān 转圈; **turn away** (to turn or look in a different direction) zhuǎnguò shēn/liǎn qu 转过身/脸去; she turned away embarrassed tā bùhǎoyìsi de zhuǎnguò shēn qu 她不好意思地转过身去; (to dismiss from service) jiěgù 解雇; (to cause to leave) dǎfā zǒu 打发走, niǎnzǒu 撵走; the police turned the students away jǐngchá bǎ nàxiē xuéshēng dǎfā zǒu le 警察把那些学生打发走了; **turn back** (to return) zhéhuí 折回, wǎng huí zǒu 往回走; he found this was the wrong road and then turned back tā fāxiàn zhètiáo lù bú duì, jiù wǎng huí zǒu le 他发现这条路不对, 就往回走了; (when dealing with pages) fān huídào 翻回到; please turn back to page 5 qǐng fānhuídào dìwǔyè 请翻回到第五页; **turn down** (to lower) guānxiǎo 关小, tiáodī 调低; to turn down the radio bǎ shōuyīnjī guānxiǎo 把收音机关小; (to reject) jùjué 拒绝; to turn someone down jùjué mǒurén 拒绝某人; **turn off**

guānshang 关上; **to turn off** [the oven | the light | the tap...] bǎ [kǎoxiāng | dēng | shuǐlóngtóu...] guānshang 把 [烤箱 | 灯 | 水龙头...] 关上; **turn on** dǎkāi 打开, kāi 开; **to turn on** [the TV | the radio | the tap...] bǎ [diànshìjī | shōuyīnjī | shuǐlóngtóu...] dǎkāi 把 [电视机 | 收音机 | 水龙头...] 打开; **turn out to turn out all right (in the end)** (zuìhòu) jiéguǒ búcuò (最后) 结果不错; **to turn out to be easy** yuánlái hěn róngyì 原来很容易; **turn over** (to roll over) dǎfān 打翻; **he turned the vase over** tā bǎ huāpíng dǎfān le 他把花瓶打翻了; **turn over the page** fāndào xià yíyè 翻到下一页; **turn up** (to arrive) lái lái, dào dào 到; (to increase) **to turn up** [the heating | the music | the TV] bǎ [nuǎnqì | yīnyuè | diànshì] kāidà 把 [暖气 | 音乐 | 电视] 开大

turtle n a (sea) turtle yíge (hǎi)guī 一个(海)龟; (US English) (a tortoise) a turtle yíge wūguī 一个乌龟

TV n a TV yìtái diànshìjī 一台电视机

twelfth num (in a series) dìshí'èr 第十二; (in dates) shí'èr rì 十二日, shí'èr hào 十二号; **the twelfth of July** qīyuè shí'èr hào 七月十二号

twelve num twelve shí'èr 十二

twenty num twenty èrshí 二十

twice adv (when talking about the number of times) liǎngcì 两次; **I met him twice** wǒ jiànguo tā liǎngcì 我见过他两次; (two-fold) liǎngbèi 两倍; **twice** [as many people | as much time] liǎngbèi [duō de rén | duō de shíjiān] 两倍 [多的人 | 多的时间]

twin 1 n a twin yíge shuāngbāotāi 一个双胞胎 **2** adj shuāngbāotāi de 双胞胎的, luánshēng de 孪生的; a twin [brother | sister] (younger) yíge shuāngbāotāi de [dìdi | mèimei] 一个双胞胎的 [弟弟 | 妹妹]; (older) yíge shuāngbāotāi de [gēge | jiějie] 一个双胞胎的 [哥哥 | 姐姐]; **twin** [brothers | sisters] luánshēng [xiōngdì | jiěmèi] 孪生 [兄弟 | 姐妹]

twist vb (to form a spiral) níng/níng 拧, niǔ 扭; **to twist a rope** níng yìgēn shéngzi 拧一根绳子; (to injure) niǔshāng 扭伤; **he twisted his ankle** tā niǔshāngle jiǎobózi 他扭伤了脚脖子

two num (in counting, in numbers, digits) èr 二; (the year) 2002 èrlínglíng'èr nián 2002年; (when used with a measure word) liǎng 两; two brothers liǎngge xiōngdì 两个兄弟

type 1 n a type (a sort, a kind) yìzhǒng (lèixíng) 一种(类型); this type of [person | book | building...] zhèzhǒng [rén | shū | lóu...] 这种[人 | 书 | 楼...]; he's not my type tā bú shì wǒ xǐhuan de nàzhǒng rén 他不是我喜欢的那种人 **2** vb dǎzì 打字

typewriter n a typewriter yìtái dǎzìjī 一台打字机

typical adj diǎnxíng 典型

typist n a typist yìmíng dǎzìyuán 一名打字员

tyre n (British English) a tyre yíge lúntāi 一个轮胎, yíge chētāi 一个车胎

....

Uu

....

ugly adj (unpleasant to the sight) chǒu(lòu) 丑陋, nánkàn 难看

umbrella n an umbrella yìbǎ (yǔ)sǎn 一把雨伞

unbelievable adj nán yǐ zhìxìn 难以置信, wúfǎ xiāngxìn 无法相信

uncle n an uncle (father's elder brother) yíge bófù 一个伯父, yíge bóbo 一个伯伯; (father's younger brother) yíge shūshu 一个叔叔; (mother's younger or elder brother) yíge jiùjiu 一个舅舅; (husband of father's sister) yíge gūfu 一个姑父; (husband of mother's sister) yíge yífu 一个姨父; (not a relation) an uncle (a man younger than one's father) yíge shūshu 一个叔叔; (a man older than one's father) yíge bóbo 一个伯伯

uncomfortable adj (awkward and uneasy) bú zìzài 不自在, bù ān 不安; to make someone (feel) uncomfortable shǐ mǒurén (gǎndào) bú zìzài 使某人感到不自在; (describing a physical feeling) bù shūfu 不舒服; I felt uncomfortable sitting in that chair wǒ zuò zài nàbǎ yǐzi shang gǎnjué bù shūfu 我坐在那把椅子上感觉不舒服; (*describing the physical condition of something*) bù shūfu 不舒服, bù shūshì 不舒适; **an uncomfortable bed** yìzhāng bù shūfu de chuáng 一张不舒服的床

unconscious *adj* (*not knowing*) bù zhīdào de 不知道的; **I was unconscious of his presence** wǒ bù zhīdào tā zài chǎng 我不知道他在场; (*lose consciousness*) shīqù zhījué de 失去知觉的, bù xǐng rénshì de 不省人事的; **to knock someone unconscious** bǎ mǒurén zhuàng de shīqù zhījué 把某人撞得失去知觉; (*not aware*) wú yìshi de 无意识的; **an unconscious act** yíge wú yìshi de dòngzuò 一个无意识的动作

under *prep* **under** zài...xiàmian 在...下面, zài...dǐxia 在...底下; **to hide under the bed** cáng zài chuáng xiàmian 藏在床下面; **I found the newspaper under the table** wǒ zài zhuōzi dǐxia zhǎodàole bàozhǐ 我在桌子底下找到了报纸; (*less than*) **to earn under three pounds an hour** měi xiǎoshí zhèng bú dào sān yīngbàng 每小时挣不到三英镑; **children under five** wǔ suì yǐxià de háizi 五岁以下的孩子, bù mǎn wǔ suì de háizi 不满五岁的孩子

underground *n* (*British English*) **the underground** dìtiě 地铁

underline *vb* (*to put a line under*) zài...xiàmian huà xiàn 在...下面划线; **to underline all the names** zài suǒyǒu de míngzi xiàmian huà xiàn 在所有的名字下面划线; (*to emphasise*) qiángdiào 强调; **to underline the importance of this meeting** qiángdiào zhècì huìyì de zhòngyàoxìng 强调这次会议的重要性

underneath 1 *adv* (zài) xiàmian (在)下面, (zài) dǐxia (在)底下; **I want to see what's underneath** wǒ xiǎng kàn yíxià xiàmian yǒu shénme 我想看一下下面有什么 **2** *prep* zài...xiàmian 在...下面, zài...xiàbian 在...下边; **underneath the building** zài dàlóu xiàmian 在大楼下面

underpants *n* nèikù 内裤

understand *vb* (*to comprehend*) dǒng 懂; **I can't understand what they're saying** wǒ bù dǒng tāmen shuō de huà 我不懂他

们说的话: do you understand Japanese? nǐ dǒng Rìyǔ ma? 你懂日语吗?; **to make oneself understood** biǎodá qīngchu zìjǐ de yìsi 表达清楚自己的意思; (to be able to follow the working, logic, or meaning of) lǐjiě 理解 **I can understand why he wants to learn Chinese** wǒ kěyǐ lǐjiě tā wèishénme xiǎng xué Zhōngwén 我可以理解他为什么想学中文; (to know) liǎojiě 了解; **he doesn't understand the difficult situation I'm in** tā bù liǎojiě wǒ suǒ chǔ de kùnjìng 他不了解我所处的困境

understanding adj (sympathetic) néng liàngjiě rén de 能谅解人的; (discerning) **an understanding smile** huìxīn de wēixiào 会心的微笑; **an understanding person** yíge shànjiě rényì de rén 一个善解人意的人

underwater adv zài shuǐ xià 在水下

underwear n nèiyī 内衣

undo vb (for buttons, knots) jiěkāi 解开; **to undo a button** jiěkāi yíge kòuzi 解开一个扣子; (for parcels, boxes) dǎkāi 打开; (to cancel, to annul) qǔxiāo 取消

undress vb gěi...tuōxià yīfu 给...脱下衣服; **she undressed her daughter** tā gěi tā nǚ'ér tuōxià yīfu 她给她女儿脱下衣服; **I undressed and went to bed** wǒ tuōxià yīfu shàng chuáng shuìjiào 我脱下衣服上床睡觉

uneasy adj (anxious) (xīnshen) bù ān (心)神不安, yōulǜ 忧虑; (uncomfortable) jūshù 拘束, bú zìzài 不自在

unemployed adj (out of work) shīyè de 失业的; **he is unemployed** tā shīyè le 他失业了; **unemployed workers** shīyè de gōngrén 失业的工人

unemployment n shīyè 失业

unfair adj bù gōngpíng 不公平, bù gōngzhèng 不公正

unfortunately adv bùxìng de shì 不幸的是, yíhàn de shì 遗憾的是

unfriendly adj bù yǒuhǎo 不友好, lěngmò 冷漠

ungrateful adj wàng'ēn fùyì 忘恩负义, bù lǐng qíng 不领情

unhappy adj (not glad) bù gāoxìng 不高兴, bù yúkuài 不愉快; (not satisfied) bù mǎnyì 不满意; **are you unhappy with your**

new job? nǐ duì nǐde xīn gōngzuò bù mǎnyì ma? 你对你的新
工作不满意吗? (without happiness) bú xìngfú 不幸福; he
had an unhappy life there tā zài nàr de shēnghuó hěn bú xìngfú
他在那儿的生活很不幸福

unhealthy adj (describing a person) bú jiànkāng de 不健康
的, yǒu bìng de 有病的; (describing a way of life, food) duì
jiànkāng yǒu hài de 对健康有害的; (not morally or spiritually
wholesome) bùliáng 不良

uniform n a uniform yítào zhìfú 一套制服; a school uniform
yítào xiàofú 一套校服; a police uniform yítào jǐngfú 一套警服;
an army uniform yítào jūnzhuāng 一套军装

union n a union yíge gōnghuì 一个工会;
(a federation) yíge liánhéhuì 一个联合会

unique adj (being the only one of its kind) wéiyī 唯一, dúyī
wú'èr 独一无二; (unusual) dútè 独特

United Kingdom n Liánhé Wángguó 联合王国, Yīngguó
英国

United States (of America) n Měilìjiān Hézhòngguó
美利坚合众国, Měiguó 美国

universe n (the whole system of things) yǔzhòu 宇宙, tiāndì
wànwù 天地万物; (the world) shìjiè 世界

university n a university yìsuǒ dàxué 一所大学

unkind adj (when describing a person, an action) bù réncí 不仁
慈, bù héshàn 不和善; (when describing a remark) kēkè 苛刻,
kèbó 刻薄

unknown adj his telephone number is unknown to me tāde
diànhuà hàomǎ wǒ bù zhīdào 他的电话号码我不知道; an
unknown number yíge wèizhī shù 一个未知数; an unknown
hero yíge wúmíng yīngxióng 一个无名英雄

unless ! conj rúguǒ (...) bù 如果 (...) 不, chúfēi...fǒuzé 除非... 否
则! Note that the clause introduced by rúguǒ 如果 bù must
precede the main clause. Note also that rúguǒ 如果 and bù 不
can be separated by the subject or put together after the
subject; she won't come unless you phone her rúguǒ nǐ bù gěi

tā dǎ diànhuà, tā bú huì lái 如果你不给她打电话，她不会来; you wouldn't understand this book unless you know Chinese history nǐ rúguǒ bù liǎojiě Zhōngguó lìshǐ, nǐ jiù huì kàn bù dǒng zhèběn shū 你如果不了解中国历史，你就会看不懂这本书; I'll cancel the meeting unless he can come chúfēi tā néng lái, fǒuzé wǒ jiù qǔxiāo zhècì huìyì 除非他能来，否则我就取消这次会议

unlock vb bǎ... (de) suǒ dǎkāi 把...(的)锁打开; to unlock the door bǎ mén suǒ dǎkāi 把门锁打开

unlucky adj (unfortunate) bú xìngyùn 不幸运, dǎoméi 倒霉; you were unlucky nǐ hěn bú xìngyùn 你很不幸运; (ill-omened) bù jíxiáng 不吉祥

unpack vb to unpack a suitcase dǎkāi xiāngzi bǎ dōngxi náchulai 打开箱子把东西拿出来

unsuitable adj bù héshì 不合适, bù shìyí 不适宜

untidy adj (describing a place) bù zhěngqí 不整齐, língluàn 凌乱; (describing a person) lāta 邋遢, bù xiū biānfú 不修边幅

until 1 prep dào 到, (zhí)dào...(wéizhǐ) (直)到...(为止); I'm staying until Thursday wǒ dāi dào xīngqīsì 我呆到星期四; until now zhídào xiànzài 直到现在; I'm going to wait until after Christmas wǒ dǎsuàn děng dào Shèngdànjié yǐhòu 我打算等到圣诞节以后; (when used in a negative sentence) **!** Note that when until is used in a negative sentence, the pattern not...until is often translated as (zhí)dào...cái... (直)到...才... or (zài)...yǐqián...bù/méi... (在)...以前...不/没...; she won't get an answer until next week xiàge xīngqī yǐqián tā bú huì dédào dáfù 下个星期以前她不会得到答复; not until yesterday did I meet him wǒ zhídào zuótiān cái jiàndào tā 我直到昨天才见到他 2 conj (zhí)dào (直)到; I'll wait until he gets back home wǒ yào děng dào tā huí jiā 我要等到他回家; we'll stay here until they come back wǒmen yào zài zhèr dāi dào tāmen huílai 我们要在这儿呆到他们回来; (when used with a negative main clause) **!** Note that when until is used with a negative main clause, the pattern not...until is often translated as (zhí)dào...cái... (直)到...才... or (zài)...yǐqián...bù/méi... (在)...

以前.... 不/没....; she didn't go to see the doctor until she was very ill tā zhídào bìng de hěn lìhài cái qù kàn yīshēng 她直到病得很厉害才去看医生; she won't go to Taiwan until her friend has found her a language school there zài tāde péngyou gěi tā zhǎodào yǔyán xuéxiào yǐqián, tā bú huì qù Táiwān 在她的朋友给她找到语言学校以前, 她不会去台湾

unusual *adj* (*rare*) hǎnjiàn 罕见, shǎoyǒu 少有; such a strong wind is quite unusual in this area zhème dà de fēng zài zhège dìqū shì shǎoyǒu de 这么大的风在这个地区是少有的; (*not ordinary*) bù xúncháng 不寻常, bù píngcháng 不平常; it's an unusual day for her today duì tā láishuō, jīntiān shì ge bù xúncháng de rìzi 对她来说, 今天是个不寻常的日子

up ! *Often up occurs in combinations with verbs, for example: blow up, give up, own up, etc. To find the correct translations for this type of verb, look up the separate dictionary entries at blow, give, own, etc.* **1** *prep* the cat's up the tree māo zài shù shang 猫在树上; to go up the street yánzhe mǎlù wǎng qián zǒu 沿着马路往前走; she ran up the stairs tā pǎoshàng lóutī 她跑上楼梯; the library is up those stairs túshūguǎn zài nàge lóutī shàngmiàn 图书馆在那个楼梯上面 **2** *adv* up in the sky zài tiān shang 在天上; up on (top of) the wardrobe zài yīguì shàngmiàn 在衣柜上面; to go up shàngqu 上去; to go up to Scotland shàng Sūgélán 上苏格兰; up there zài nàr 在那儿; put the painting a bit further up bǎ huà zài wǎng shàng fàng yìdiǎnr 把画再往上放一点儿; to climb up [a hill | a ladder | a tree] pá [shān | tīzi | shù] 爬[山 | 梯子 | 树] **3** *adj* (*out of bed*) is he up yet? tā qǐchuáng le ma? 他起床了吗?; he was up all night tā yí yè méi shuì 他一夜没睡; (*higher in amount, level*) the price of fish is up by 20% yú jià shàngzhǎngle bǎifēn zhī èrshí 鱼价上涨了百分之二十 **4** up to (*well enough*) he is not up to going out yet tā hái bù néng chūqu 他还不能出去; (*capable of*) is she up to this translation work? tā néng shèngrèn zhège fānyì gōngzuò ma? 她能胜任这个翻译工作吗?; (*when talking about who is responsible*) it's up to [me | you | them] to decide yóu [wǒ | nǐ | tāmen] (lái) juédìng 由 [我 | 你 | 他们] (来) 决定; (*until*) zhídào 直到; up to [now | 1996 | yesterday] zhídào [xiànzài | yìjiǔjiǔliù nián | zuótiān] 直到 [现在 | 一九九六年 | 昨天]

upset 1 *adj* to be/get upset (*annoyed*) fánnǎo 烦恼, nǎohuǒ 恼火; he got very upset when his car broke down on the way tāde chē zài lù shang huàile de shíhou, tā fēicháng nǎohuǒ 他的车在路上坏了的时候, 他非常恼火; (*distressed*) kǔnǎo 苦恼, yōushāng 忧伤; she was very upset to hear the news of the accident tīngdào zhège shìgù de xiāoxi, tā fēicháng yōushāng 听到这个事故的消息, 她非常忧伤 **2** *vb* (*to make someone unhappy*) shǐ...yōushāng/kǔnǎo 使...忧伤/苦恼; to upset someone shǐ mǒurén yōushāng/kǔnǎo 使某人忧伤/苦恼; (*to annoy*) shǐ...fánnǎo/nǎohuǒ 使... 烦恼/恼火; to upset someone shǐ mǒurén fánnǎo/nǎohuǒ 使某人烦恼/恼火

upside down *adv* (*turned over completely*) dào 倒, diāndǎo 颠倒; you're holding the book upside down nǐ bǎ shū ná dào le 你把书拿倒了; (*in disorder or chaos*) luànqībāzāo 乱七八糟; they turned everything in the room upside down tāmen bǎ wū lǐ de dōngxi nòng dé luànqībāzāo 他们把屋里的东西弄得乱七八糟

upstairs *adv* lóushàng 楼上; to go upstairs shàng lóu 上楼; to bring the cases upstairs bǎ xiāngzi nádào lóushàng lái 把箱子拿到楼上来

urgent *adj* jǐnjí 紧急, jíqiè 急切

us *pron* wǒmen 我们; they don't know us tāmen bú rènshi wǒmen 他们不认识我们

USA *n* Měiguó 美国

use 1 *vb* (*to make use of*) yòng 用, shǐyòng 使用; I use this car to go to work wǒ yòng zhèliàng chē shàng bān 我用这辆车上班; he uses this room as an office tā bǎ zhège fángjiān yòngzuò bàngōngshì 他把这个房间用做办公室; what is it used for? zhè shì yòng lái; zuò shénme de? 这是用来做什么的?; to use [water | petrol | electricity] (shǐ) yòng [shuǐ | qìyóu | diàn] (使)用[水 | 汽油 | 电]; to use [someone | this opportunity] lìyòng [mǒurén | zhège jīhuì] 利用[某人 | 这个机会] **2** *n* to make use of a room lìyòng yíge fángjiān 利用一个房间; he has the use of a car yǒu qìchē gòng tā shǐyòng 有汽车供他使用; she's lost the use of her legs tāde liǎngtiáo tuǐ bù néng zǒulù le 她的两条腿不能走路了; (*when talking about what is* *useful*) to be of use to someone duì mǒurén yǒuyòng 对某人有用; to be (of) no use méi yòng 没用; this bike is no use any more zhèliàng zìxíngchē méi yòng le 这辆自行车没用了; what's the use of complaining? bàoyuàn yǒu shénme yòng? 抱怨有什么用?: **use up** he's used up all the money tā bǎ qián dōu huāwán le 他把钱都花完了; have you used up the milk? nǐ bǎ niúnǎi yòngwán le ma? 你把牛奶用完了吗?

used 1 *vb* (*did so frequently or regularly*) guòqù chángcháng 过去常常; I used to go there by bike wǒ guòqù chángcháng qí zìxíngchē qù nàr 我过去常常骑自行车去那儿; (*did so formerly*) guòqù 过去; I used not to smoke wǒ guòqù bù chōuyān 我过去不抽烟; there used to be a castle here zhèr guòqù yǒu ge chéngbǎo 这儿过去有个城堡 **2** *adj* to be/get used to xíguàn 习惯; he's not used to living on his own tā bù xíguàn yíge rén shēnghuó 他不习惯一个人生活; to get used to a new job xíguàn xīn de gōngzuò 习惯新的工作; (*not new*) shǐyòngguo de 使用过的; jiù 旧; used cars shǐyòngguo de qìchē 使用过的汽车; used furniture jiù jiājù 旧家具

useful *adj* (*of use*) yǒuyòng 有用; (*helpful*) yǒu bāngzhù 有帮助

useless *adj* (*having no use, point, or purpose*) méi(yǒu) yòng 没(有)用, wú yòng 无用; it's useless complaining bàoyuàn méiyǒu yòng 抱怨没有用; (*describing a person*) wúnéng 无能; I'm useless at chemistry wǒ duì gǎo huàxué hěn wúnéng 我对搞化学很无能

usually *adv* tōngcháng 通常, yìbān 一般

vacant *adj* (*unoccupied*) kòng 空, kòngxiánzhe 空闲着; is there a vacant room in the house? fángzi li yǒu kòng fángjiān ma? 房子里有空房间吗?: (*when describing a post or a position*) kòngquē de 空缺的; a vacant post yíge kòngquē de zhíwèi 一个空缺的职位

vacation n (US English) a vacation yíge jiàqī 一个假期; to take a vacation xiū jià 休假; the [summer | winter | Christmas] vacation [shǔ | hán | Shèngdàn] jià [暑 | 寒 | 圣诞] 假

vacuum vb to vacuum a room yòng xīchénqì dǎsǎo fángjiān 用吸尘器打扫房间

vacuum cleaner n a vacuum cleaner yíge xīchénqì 一个吸尘器

vague adj (indefinite, uncertain) hánhu 含糊, bù quèqiè 不确切; a vague answer yíge hánhu de huídá 一个含糊的回答; (indistinct) móhu 模糊, bù qīngxī 不清晰; (not clearly expressed) biǎodá (de) bù qīngchu 表达(得)不清楚

vain adj (pettily self-complacent) zìfù 自负; he is vain about his learning tā duì zìjǐ de xuéwèn hěn zìfù 他对自己的学问很自负; (valuing oneself inordinately on some trivial personal distinction) ài xūróng 爱虚荣; is he a vain person? tā shì yíge ài xūróng de rén ma? 他是一个爱虚荣的人吗?; (futile) túláo 徒劳, báifèi 白费; in vain túláo 徒劳, báifèi 白费; all my efforts were in vain wǒde suǒyǒu nǔlì dōu báifèi le 我的所有努力都白费了

valid adj (legally adequate) yǒuxiào 有效; is this ticket still valid? zhèzhāng piào hái yǒuxiào ma? 这张票还有效吗?; (capable of being justified) zhèngdàng 正当; a valid reason yíge zhèngdàng de lǐyóu 一个正当的理由; (well based) quèzuò 确凿, yǒu gēnjù 有根据; valid evidence quèzuò de zhèngjù 确凿的证据

valley n a valley (a low area between hills) yíge shāngǔ 一个山谷; (the basin in which a river flows) yíge liúyù 一个流域

valuable adj (very useful) bǎoguì 宝贵, yǒujiàzhí 有价值; (worth a lot of money) zhíqián 值钱, guìzhòng 贵重; this watch is rather valuable zhèkuài biǎo xiāngdāng zhíqián 这块表相当值钱

van n a van yíliàng yùnhuòchē 一辆运货车

vandalize vb pòhuài 破坏, huǐhuài 毁坏

vanilla n xiāngzǐlán 香子兰, xiāngcǎo 香草

various adj (diverse) gè zhǒng gè yàng 各种各样, bù tóng 不同; there are various ways of saying it yǒu gè zhǒng gè yàng de shuōfǎ 有各种各样的说法; (several) jǐge 几个; they visited several schools tāmen fǎngwènle jǐge xuéxiào 他们访问了几个学校

vary vb (to differ, be different) bù tóng 不同, bù yīyàng 不一样; food prices vary from town to town shípǐn de jiàgé měi gè chéngzhèn dōu bù tóng 食品的价格每个城镇都不同; (to change intentionally) gǎibiàn 改变; to vary one's working style gǎibiàn gōngzuò fāngshì 改变工作方式

vase n a vase yíge huāpíng 一个花瓶

veal n xiǎoniúròu 小牛肉

vegetable n (shū)cài (蔬)菜; a vegetable yìkē cài 一棵菜

vegetarian n a vegetarian yíge chī sù de rén 一个吃素的人

vein n a vein (for carrying blood in the body) yìgēn xuèguǎn 一根血管

velvet n tiān'éróng 天鹅绒, sīróng 丝绒

versus prep duì 对

very 1 adv very hěn 很, fēicháng 非常; I don't know him very well wǒ bù hěn liǎojiě tā 我不很了解他; we like them very much wǒmen fēicháng xǐhuan tāmen 我们非常喜欢他们; not (...) very bù hěn 不很, bú tài 不太; it is not very hot today jīntiān bú tài rè 今天不太热; (for emphasis) ! Note that in this case, very is usually not translated: 第一次; they called me the very next day tāmen dì'èr tiān jiù gěi wǒ dǎ diànhuà le 他们第二天就给我打电话了 **2** adj ! Note that when very is used as an adjective, it is often translated as jiù 就 or zhèng 正; she studied in that very school tā jiù zài nàsuǒ xuéxiào xuéxí 她就在那所学校学习; you are the very person I need nǐ zhèng shì wǒ suǒ xūyào de rén 你正是我所需要的人; at the very beginning gāng kāishǐ de shíhou 刚开始的时候; to stay to the very end dāi dào zuìhòu 待到最后

vest n (British English) (a piece of underwear) a vest yíjiàn hànshān 一件汗衫, yìjiàn bèixīn 一件背心; (US English) (a waistcoat) a vest yíjiàn bèixīn 一件背心, yíjiàn mǎjiǎ 一件马甲

vet *n* a vet yíge shòuyī 一个兽医

via *prep* (*when talking about a route*) jīngyóu 经由, jīngguò 经过, lùjīng 路经; to go to Japan via Beijing jīngyóu Běijīng qù Rìběn 经由北京去日本; (*when talking about a means*) tōngguò 通过, liyòng 利用; I returned the book to him via a student of his wǒ tōngguò tāde yíge xuésheng bǎ shū huángěile tā 我通过他的一个学生把书还给了他

vicious *adj* (*ferocious*) xiōng'è 凶恶, xiōngcán 凶残; (*nasty, meant to hurt*) èyì 恶意, èdú 恶毒; (*addicted to vice or bad habits*) duòluò 堕落

victory *n* a victory yícì shènglì 一次胜利; to win a victory yíngdé shènglì 赢得胜利

video 1 *n* (*a recorded film, programme, event*) a video yìpán lùxiàngdài 一盘录像带; ▶ **video cassette, video recorder 2** *vb* (*to record*) lù 录; (*to film*) to video a wedding gěi yíge hūnlǐ shèxiàng 给一个婚礼摄像

video camera *n* a video camera yìtái shèxiàngjī 一台摄像机

video cassette *n* a video cassette yìpán lùxiàngdài 一盘录像带

video game *n* a video game yìpán diànzǐ yóuxì 一盘电子游戏

video recorder *n* a video recorder yìtái lùxiàngjī 一台录像机

view *n* (*a scene viewed by the eyes*) kàn 看, guānkàn 观看; if you want to get a better view, you'd better come here yàoshǐ nǐ xiǎng kàn de qīngchu, zuìhǎo dào zhèr lái 要是你想看得清楚, 最好到这儿来; (*a line of vision*) shìxiàn 视线; you're blocking my view nǐ dǎngzhùle wǒde shìxiàn 你挡住了我的视线; (*an opinion*) a view yíge guāndiǎn 一个观点, yíge yìjiàn 一个意见; a point of view yíge guāndiǎn 一个观点; I'd like to know your views on this matter wǒ xiǎng zhīdào nǐ duì zhèjiàn shì de yìjiàn 我想知道你对这件事的意见

village *n* a village yíge cūnzhuāng 一个村庄

vinegar *n* cù 醋

vineyard n a vineyard yíge pútaoyuán 一个葡萄园

violent adj (of great force) měngliè 猛烈, qiángliè 强烈, jīliè 激烈; (vicious) xiōngcán 凶残, cánbào 残暴; (marked by extreme force or fierceness) bàolì de 暴力的

violin n a violin yìbǎ xiǎotíqín 一把小提琴

visit 1 vb (to pay an official call upon) fǎngwèn 访问; the British delegation is visiting China Yīngguó dàibiǎotuán zhèngzài fǎngwèn Zhōngguó 英国代表团正在访问中国; (to come or go to see formally) cānguān 参观, fǎngwèn 访问; they visited some hospitals and schools tāmen cānguānle yìxiē yīyuàn hé xuéxiào 他们参观了一些医院和学校; (for sightseeing and pleasure) cānguān 参观, yóulǎn 游览; are you going to visit the Great Wall? nǐmen yào qù yóulǎn Chángchéng ma? 你们要去游览长城吗?; to go to visit [a patient | my grandmother | my old friend...] qù kàn [yíge bìngrén | wǒde nǎinai | wǒde lǎo péngyou...] 去看 [一个病人 | 我的奶奶 | 我的老朋友...]; (to stay with) we visited my parents for a week wǒmen zài wǒ fùmǔ nàr zhùle yíge xīngqī 我们在我父母那儿住了一个星期 **2** n a visit (an official call) yícì fǎngwèn 一次访问; (when talking about visits to institutions, museums, exhibitions, etc.) yícì cānguān 一次参观; (a sightseeing excursion) yícì yóulǎn 一次游览; (a call at someone's home) yícì bàifǎng 一次拜访, yícì tànwàng 一次探望; (a stay) I paid my elder brother a visit for two days wǒ zài wǒ gēge nàr dāile liǎngtiān 我在我哥哥那儿呆了两天

visitor n (a guest) a visitor yíge kèrén 一个客人; to have visitors yǒu kèrén 有客人; (a tourist) a visitor yíge yóukè 一个游客

vocabulary n cíhuì 词汇

voice n (the sound of a person speaking, singing, etc.) a voice yíge shuōhuà shēngyīn 一个说话声音; to speak [in a low voice | in a loud voice] [xiǎo shēng de | dà shēng de] shuōhuà [小声地 | 大声地] 说话; (the quality of the sound one makes while singing or speaking) sǎngzi 嗓子, sǎngyīn 嗓音; she has a good voice tāde sǎngzi hěn hǎo 他的嗓子很好

volleyball n páiqiú 排球

vomit vb ǒutù 呕吐, tù 吐

vote vb (to express one's choice by vote) tóupiào 投票; to vote [for | against] someone tóupiào [xuǎn | bù xuǎn] mǒurén 投票 [选 | 不选] 某人; to vote [for | against] a plan tóupiào [zànchéng | fǎnduì] yíge jìhuà 投票 [赞成 | 反对] 一个计划; (to determine by vote) tóupiào juédìng 投票决定; to vote in a new policy tóupiào juédìng yíxiàng xīn zhèngcè 投票决定一项新政策

Ww

wages n gōngzī 工资

waist n the waist yāo 腰, yāobù 腰部

waistcoat n (British English) a waistcoat yíjiàn bèixīn 一件背心, yíjiàn mǎjiǎ 一件马甲

wait vb to wait děng(hòu) 等(候); to wait for someone děng mǒurén 等某人; I'm waiting to use the phone wǒ zài děngzhe yòng diànhuà 我在等着用电话; I can't wait to see them wǒ jíqiè de xiǎng jiàndào tāmen 我急切地想见到他们; (in a restaurant) to wait on tables, to wait tables (US English) fúshì kèrén chī fàn 服侍客人吃饭; wait up wait up děng(hòu)zhe bú shuìjiào 等(候)着不睡觉; to wait up for someone wèi děnghòu mǒurén ér bú shuìjiào 为等候某人而不睡觉

waiter n a waiter yíge fúwùyuán 一个服务员

waiting room n a waiting room (at a train or a bus station) yíge hòuchēshì 一个候车室; (at an airport) yíge hòujīshì 一个候机室; (at a port) yíge hòuchuánshì 一个候船室; (in a hospital) yíge hòuzhěnshì 一个候诊室

waitress n a waitress yíge nǚzhāodài 一个女招待

wake vb (to be roused from sleep) xǐng 醒, xǐnglai 醒来; has she woken (up)? tā xǐng le ma? 她醒了吗?; (to rouse from

sleep) jiàoxǐng 叫醒, nòngxǐng 弄醒; to wake someone (up)
bǎ mǒurén jiàoxǐng 把某人叫醒

Wales *n* Wēi'ěrshì 威尔士

walk 1 *vb* (*to go on foot*) zǒu 走, zǒulù 走路; **are you walking
to the station?** nǐ yào zǒulù qù chēzhàn ma? 你要走路去车站
吗?; (*for pleasure*) sànbù 散步; **to walk in the park** zài gōngyuán
sànbù 在公园散步; (*to take an animal out on a leash, etc.*) liù
遛; **to walk the dog** liù gǒu 遛狗; (*to escort by walking*)
péi(zhe)...zǒu 陪(着)...走, sòng 送; **I'll walk you to the bus stop**
wǒ péi(zhe) nǐ zǒu dào chēzhàn 我陪(着)你走到车站 **2** *n* a
walk sànbù 散步; **to go for a walk** qù sànbù 去散步; (*act of
walking*) zǒu 走, zǒulù 走路; **my school is five minutes' walk
from here** wǒde xuéxiào lí zhèr zǒulù yào wǔ fēnzhōng 我的学
校离这儿走路要五分钟; **walk around** sànbù 散步; **to walk
around town** zài chéng li sànbù 在城里散步; **to walk around
the lake** zài hú zhōuwéi sànbù 在湖周围散步; **walk away**
zǒukāi 走开; **walk back** zǒu huí 走回; **to walk back home**
zǒu huí jiā 走回家; **walk by** zǒuguò 走过; **walk in(to)** zǒujìn
走进; **walk out** zǒuchū 走出; **to walk out of the room** zǒuchū
fángjiān 走出房间; **walk up to** zǒujìn 走近, zǒuxiàng 走向

walkman® *n* a walkman yìtái biànxiéshì lùfàngjī 一台便携式
录放机

wall *n* a wall yìdǔ qiáng 一堵墙; **the Great Wall** Chángchéng
长城

wallet *n* a wallet yíge qiánbāo 一个钱包, yíge píjiázi 一个皮
夹子

wallpaper *n* qiángzhǐ 墙纸

walnut *n* a walnut yíge hétáo 一个核桃

wander *vb* (*to ramble, to roam*) xiánguàng 闲逛, mànbù 漫步;
to wander around town zài chéng li xiánguàng 在城里闲逛;
wander away, wander off mànmàn de zǒukāi 慢慢地走开

want *vb* (*to desire something or someone*) (xiǎng)yào (想)要; **do
you want another coffee?** nǐ hái (xiǎng)yào yìbēi kāfēi ma? 你还
(想)要一杯咖啡吗?; **do you want me to go with you?** nǐ
(xiǎng)yào wǒ hé nǐ yìqǐ qù ma? 你(想)要我和你一起去吗?;

(to desire to do something) xiǎng(yào) 想(要), yào 要; he wants [to go out | to go home | to play basketball ...] tā xiǎng [chūqù | huí jiā | dǎ lánqiú...] 他想 [出去 | 回家 | 打篮球...]; she didn't want to stay there tā bù xiǎng dāi zài nàr 她不想呆在那儿; (to need) xūyào 需要; the house wants repairs zhèdòng fángzi xūyào xiūlǐ le 这栋房子需要修理了

war n a war yìchǎng zhànzhēng 一场战争

wardrobe n a wardrobe yíge yīguì 一个衣柜, yíge yīchú 一个衣橱

warm 1 adj (moderately hot) nuǎnhuo 暖和, wēnnuǎn 温暖; I'm very warm wǒ hěn nuǎnhuo 我很暖和; he doesn't feel warm tā gǎnjué bù nuǎnhuo 他感觉不暖和; the weather is getting warm tiānqì nuǎnhuoqǐlai le 天气暖和起来了; (ardent, enthusiastic) rèqíng 热情, rèliè 热烈; they gave us a warm reception tāmen rèqíng de jiēdàile wǒmen 他们热情地接待了我们; a warm welcome rèliè de huānyíng 热烈地欢迎; (hearty) rèxīn 热心, rèqíng 热情; a warm person yíge rèxīn de rén 一个热心的人; **2** vb to warm the plates bǎ pánzi rè yíxià 把盘子热一下; to warm one's hands bǎ shǒu nuǎnhuo yíxià 把手暖和一下; **warm up** (to get warm) nuǎnhuoqǐlai 暖和起来; the room is warming up fángjiān nuǎnhuoqǐlai le 房间暖和起来了; (for a sport event) zuò zhǔnbèi huódòng 做准备活动; (to make warm) rè 热, jiārè 加热; to warm up the food bǎ fàn rè yíxià 把饭热一下

warn vb jǐnggào 警告, gàojiè 告诫; to warn someone about the risks jǐnggào mǒurén yǒu wēixiǎn 警告某人有危险; to warn someone to be careful gàojiè mǒurén yào xiǎoxīn 告诫某人要小心

wash vb (to clean) xǐ 洗; to wash one's clothes xǐ yīfu 洗衣服; to wash one's face xǐ liǎn 洗脸; (to get clean) xǐ 洗; this sheet doesn't wash easily zhètiáo chuángdān bù hǎo xǐ 这条床单不好洗; **wash out** (to remove by washing) xǐdiào 洗掉, xǐqù 洗去; to wash a stain out bǎ wūdiǎn xǐdiào 把污点洗掉; **wash up** (British English) (to do the dishes) xǐ wǎn 洗碗, xǐ cānjù 洗餐具; (US English) (to clean one's hands) xǐ shǒu 洗手; (to clean one's face) xǐ liǎn 洗脸

washbasin (British English) n a washbasin yíge xǐliǎnpén 一个洗脸盆, yíge xǐshǒupén 一个洗手盆

washing n the washing (to be washed) yào xǐ de yīfu 要洗的衣服; (being washed) zhèngzài xǐ de yīfu 正在洗的衣服; (washed) xǐhǎole de yīfu 洗好了的衣服; to do the washing xǐ yīfu 洗衣服

washing machine n a washing machine yìtái xǐyījī 一台洗衣机

washing-up n (British English) the washing-up (to be washed) yào xǐ de cānjù 要洗的餐具; (being washed) zhèngzài xǐ de cānjù 正在洗的餐具; (washed) xǐhǎole de cānjù 洗好了的餐具; to do the washing-up xǐ wǎn 洗碗, xǐ cānjù 洗餐具

wasp n a wasp yìzhī huángfēng 一只黄蜂, yìzhī mǎfēng 一只马蜂

waste 1 vb làngfèi 浪费; to waste [money | time | energy…] làngfèi [qián | shíjiān | jīnglì…] 浪费 [钱 | 时间 | 精力…] **2** n làngfèi 浪费; it's a waste of [money | time | energy…] zhè shì làngfèi [qián | shíjiān | jīnglì…] 这是浪费 [钱 | 时间 | 精力…]; it's a waste of time going there qù nàr shì làngfèi shíjiān 去那儿是浪费时间; (an uncultivated region) huāngdì 荒地, huāngyě 荒野; a waste yípiàn huāngdì 一片荒地; (refuse or rejected material) lājī 垃圾, fèiwù 废物

watch 1 vb (to look at) kàn 看; to watch [television | a football match | a Peking opera] kàn [diànshì | zúqiú sài | jīngjù] 看 [电视 | 足球赛 | 京剧]; she watched me making the meal tā kàn wǒ zuò fàn 她看我做饭; (to observe, to follow) jiānshì 监视; I feel I'm being watched wǒ juéde yǒu rén zài jiānshì wǒ 我觉得有人在监视我; (to pay attention to) zhùyì 注意; please watch your spelling qǐng zhùyì nǐde pīnxiě 请注意你的拼写; (to tend) zhàokàn 照看, zhàoliào 照料 **2** n a watch (a timepiece) yíkuài shǒubiǎo 一块手表; **watch out** zhùyì 注意, dāngxīn 当心

water 1 n shuǐ 水; drinking water yǐnyòng shuǐ 饮用水 **2** vb to water [the flowers | the tree | the garden] gěi [huā | shù | huāyuán] jiāo shuǐ 给 [花 | 树 | 花园] 浇水; (to irrigate with water) guàngài 灌溉; (to salivate) liú kǒushuǐ 流口水

waterfall n a waterfall yíge pùbù 一个瀑布

water-skiing n huáshuǐ 滑水

wave 1 vb (to greet or call someone) zhāoshǒu 招手; to wave to someone xiàng mǒurén zhāoshǒu 向某人招手; (to say farewell or send signals) huīshǒu 挥手; to wave goodbye huīshǒu gàobié 挥手告别; to wave red flags huīwǔ/huīdòng hóngqí 挥舞/挥动红旗 **2** n a wave (on the surface of the sea, river, etc.) yíge (bō)làng 一个(波)浪; (in physics) yíge bō 一个波

way 1 n (a means, a method) a way yìzhǒng fāngfǎ 一种方法; it's a way of earning money zhè shì yìzhǒng zhuàn qián de fāngfǎ 这是一种赚钱的方法; it's a good way to make friends zhè shì yìzhǒng jiāo péngyou de hǎo fāngfǎ 这是一种交朋友的好方法; he does it the wrong way tā zuò de fāngfǎ bú duì 他做的方法不对; (when referring to the manner of doing something) a way yìzhǒng fāngshì 一种方式; I like their way of life wǒ xǐhuan tāmende shēnghuó fāngshì 我喜欢他们的生活方式; I don't like this way of educating children wǒ bù xǐhuan zhèzhǒng jiàoyù háizi de fāngshì 我不喜欢这种教育孩子的方式; (a route, a road) lù 路, dàolù 道路; a way yìtiáo lù 一条路; I can't remember the way to the station wǒ bú jìde qù chēzhàn de lù le 我不记得去车站的路; we can buy something to eat along the way wǒmen kěyǐ mǎi yìdiǎn dōngxi zài lù shang chī 我们可以买一点东西在路上吃; on the way back (going back) zài huíqu de lù shang 在回去的路上; (coming back) zài huílái de lù shang 在回来的路上; I met them on the way back from town wǒ zài cóng chéngli huílái de lù shang yùjiànle tāmen 我在从城里回来的路上遇见了他们; on the way to Shanghai zài qù Shànghǎi de lù shang 在去上海的路上; where's the way out? cóng nǎr kěyǐ chūqu 从哪儿可以出去? can you tell me the way to the underground qǐng wèn qù dìtiě zěnme zǒu? 请问去地铁怎么走?; to lose one's way mílù 迷路; (a direction) fāngxiàng 方向; which way are you going? nǐ qù nǎge fāngxiàng 你去哪个方向?; they went that way tāmen qùle nàge fāngxiàng 他们去了那个方向; come this way zhè biān lái 这边来; (someone's path) to be in someone's way dǎng mǒurén de dào/lù 挡某人的道/路; to be in the way dǎngdào 挡道, àishì 碍事; Get out of the way!

Gǔnkāi! 滚开*: (when talking about distances) **the airport is a long way from here** fēijīchǎng lí zhèr hěn yuǎn 飞机场离这儿很远; **to come all the way from Tibet** cóng Xīzàng yuǎndào ér lái 从西藏远道而来: (what one wants) **she always wants her own way** tā zǒngshì wǒ xíng wǒ sù 她总是我行我素; **if I had my own way, I'd go alone** jiǎrú wǒ néng shuōle suàn, wǒ jiù yíge rén qù 假如我能说了算，我就一个人去 **2 by the way** (when used with a question) **what's his name, by the way?** shùnbiàn wèn yíxià 顺便问一下，tā jiào shénme míngzi? 顺便问一下，他叫什么名字?: (when used with a statement) **by the way, I've bought the train tickets** shùnbiàn shuō yíxià 顺便说一下，wǒ yǐjīng mǎile huǒchēpiào le 顺便说一下，我已经买了火车票了

we *pron* **we** wǒmen 我们; **we didn't agree** wǒmen méi tóngyì 我们没同意

weak *adj* (having very little power) ruǎnruò 软弱, wúlì 无力; **a weak government** yíge ruǎnruò (wúlì) de zhèngfǔ 一个软弱 (无力) 的政府; (not healthy) ruò 弱, xūruò 虚弱; **she has a weak heart** tāde xīnzàng hěn xūruò 她的心脏很虚弱; (not good or able) chà 差, bóruò 薄弱; **I'm weak at foreign languages** wǒde wàiyǔ hěn chà 我的外语很差; (describing tea or coffee) dàn 淡

wealthy *adj* fù(yǒu) 富(有), yǒuqián 有钱

wear *vb* (when talking about wearing coats, shirts, dresses, trousers, socks, shoes) chuān 穿; **she's wearing jeans** tā chuānzhe niúzǎikù 她穿着牛仔裤; **to wear black** chuān hēisè de yīfu 穿黑色的衣服; (when talking about wearing hats, scarves, glasses, or accessories such as rings, necklaces, etc.) dài 戴; **he's wearing a red tie today** jīntiān tā dàizhe yìtiáo hóngsè de lǐngdài 今天他戴着一条红色的领带; (to damage, as clothes) mópò 磨破, chuānpò 穿破; **the trousers are all worn** kùzi dōu chuānpò le 裤子都穿破了; **wear out** (to damage by wearing) chuānpò 穿破; **to wear one's shoes out** bǎ xié chuānpò 把鞋穿破; (to damage through use) yònghuài

---

*in informal situations

用坏; the toothbrush is worn out yáshuā yǐjīng yònghuài le 牙刷已经用坏了; (to make tired and exhausted) the work has worn everyone out zhège gōngzuò bǎ měi ge rén dōu lèi de jīngpí lìjìn 这个工作把每个人都累得精疲力尽; I feel worn out wǒ gǎndào hěn pífá 我感到很疲乏

weather n the weather tiānqì 天气; what's the weather like? tiānqì zěnmeyàng? 天气怎么样?; [fine | cloudy | wet] weather [qíng | yīn | yǔ] tiān [晴 | 阴 | 雨] 天

weather forecast n the weather forecast tiānqì yùbào 天气预报

webpage n a webpage yìzhāng wǎngyè 一张网页

website n a website yíge wǎngzhǐ 一个网址

wedding n a wedding yíge hūnlǐ 一个婚礼; to attend a wedding cānjiā yíge hūnlǐ 参加一个婚礼

Wednesday n xīngqīsān 星期三 | lǐbàisān 礼拜三

week n a week xīngqí 一个星期, yì zhōu 一周; [this | last | next] week [zhège | shàng(ge) | xià(ge)] xīngqí [这个 | 上(个) | 下(个)] 星期

weekend n a weekend yíge zhōumò 一个周末

weigh vb (to find the weight of) chēng 称; to weigh the luggage chēng xínglǐ 称行李; to weigh oneself chēng zìjǐ de tǐzhòng 称自己的体重; (to have the weight of) zhòng 重, zhòngliàng shì 重量是; how much do you weigh nǐ yǒu duō zhòng? 你有多重?; my luggage weighs 20 kilos wǒde xínglǐ zhòng èrshí gōngjīn 我的行李重二十公斤

weight n (the heaviness of a thing) zhòngliàng 重量; (the heaviness of one's body) tǐzhòng 体重; [to lose | to gain] weight [jiǎnqīng | zēngjiā] tǐzhòng [减轻 | 增加] 体重

weird adj (strange, bizarre) qíguài 奇怪, bùkěsīyì 不可思议

welcome 1 vb huānyíng 欢迎; to welcome someone huānyíng mǒurén 欢迎某人 **2** adj (when receiving people) huānyíng 欢迎; welcome to the United States huānyíng (nǐmen) dào Měiguó lái 欢迎(你们)到美国来; suggestions are welcome huānyíng dàjiā tíchū jiànyì 欢迎大家提出建议; **a welcome guest** yíwèi shòu huānyíng de kèrén 一位受欢迎的客人; (when acknowledging thanks) **'thanks'—'you're welcome'** 'xièxie'—'bú yòng kèqì' '谢谢'—'不用客气' **3** n a welcome huānyíng 欢迎

well 1 adv (in good manner or degree) **!** Note that in this sense **well** is often translated as **hǎo** 好. However, it can also be expressed as **búcuò** 不错, **shùnlì** 顺利, etc; **well hǎo** 好; **she speaks Chinese well** tā Hànyǔ shuō de hěn hǎo 她汉语说得很好; **well done gàn de hǎo** 干得好; **he's not eating well** (because of a poor appetite) tā chī fàn bú tài hǎo 他吃饭不太好, ta shíyù bú zhèn 他食欲不振; **did everything go well?** yíqiè shùnlì ma? 一切顺利吗?; **he treated us well** tā duì wǒmen búcuò 他对我们不错; **she was dressed well** tā chuān de hěn piàoliang 她穿得很漂亮; (fully, thoroughly) **I understand her feeling well** wǒ wánquán lǐjiě tāde xīnqíng 我完全理解她的心情; **please clean the room well before you leave** qǐng nǐ líkāi qián bǎ fángjiān chèdǐ dǎsǎo yíxià 请你离开前把房间彻底打扫一下; (very possibly) **hěn kěnéng** 很可能; **you may well be right** nǐ hěn kěnéng shì duì de 你很可能是对的; **he may well come to see you** tā hěn kěnéng lái kàn nǐ 他很可能来看你; (to a considerable degree) **this is well beyond her ability** zhè dàdà chāochūle tāde nénglì 这大大超出了她的能力; **it's well worth considering** zhè hěn zhíde kǎolǜ 这很值得考虑; **his exam result is well above the average** tāde kǎoshì chéngjī gāochū píngjūn fēn hěn duō 他的考试成绩高出平均分很多 **2** adj **he's not feeling well** tā juéde bù shūfu 他觉得不舒服; **everyone is well** dàjiā dōu hěn hǎo 大家都很好; **I'm very well** wǒ hěn hǎo 我很好; **you don't look very well** nǐ (kànshangqu) liǎnsè bú tài hǎo 你(看上去)脸色不太好; **I hope you'll get well soon** wǒ xīwàng nǐ zǎorì huīfù jiànkāng 我希望你早日恢复健康 **3 as well** yě 也; **he speaks Japanese as well** tā yě huì shuō Rìyǔ 他也会说日语 **4 as well as** bùjǐn...érqiě... 不仅...而且..., jì...yòu... 既...又...; **he bought a Japanese dictionary as well as a Chinese dictionary** tā bùjǐn mǎile yìběn Zhōngwén cídiǎn, érqiě hái mǎile yìběn Rìwén cídiǎn 他不仅买了一本中文词典,而且还买了一本日文词典

well-known adj (celebrated) zhùmíng 著名, chūmíng 出名; (fully and widely known) zhòng suǒ zhōu zhī 众所周知

Welsh 1 adj Wēi'ěrshì de 威尔士的 **2** n (the people) the Welsh Wēi'ěrshìrén 威尔士人; (the language) **Welsh** Wēi'ěrshìyǔ 威尔士语

west 1 n xībù 西部, xībiān 西边; in the west of China zài Zhōngguó de xībù 在中国的西部; the West Xīfāng 西方 **2** adv to go west wǎng xī(bian) qù 往西(边)去; to live west of Beijing zhù zài Běijīng xībù 住在北京西部 **3** adj xī 西; to work in west London zài xī Lúndūn gōngzuò 在西伦敦工作

wet 1 adj (saturated with water) shī 湿; your hair is wet nǐde tóufa shīle 你的头发湿了; (damp) cháo 潮, cháoshī 潮湿; (rainy) wet weather duōyǔ de tiānqì 多雨的天气; a wet day yíge yǔ tiān 一个雨天; (not yet dry) bù gān 不干; the paint is still wet yóuqī hái méi gān 油漆还没干 **2** vb (to make wet) nòng shī 弄湿

what 1 pron (used in questions) shénme 什么; what's that box? nàge hézi shì shénme? 那个盒子是什么?; what does he look like? tā zhǎng de shénme yàng? 他长得什么样?; I don't know what he's doing wǒ bù zhīdào tā zài zuò shénme 我不知道他在做什么; what's your name? nǐ jiào shénme míngzi? 你叫什么名字?; what's the time? jǐ diǎn le? 几点了?; what's the Chinese for 'boring'? Zhōngwén 'boring' zěnme shuō? 中文'boring' 怎么说?; what's her phone number? tāde diànhuà hàomǎ shì duōshǎo? 她的电话号码是多少?; (used as a relative pronoun) what he [bought | sold | asked for...] was a computer tā(suǒ) [mǎi | mài | yào...] de shì yìtái jìsuànjī 他(所) [买 | 卖 | 要...] 的是一台计算机; is this what he [said | needed | wrote...] zhè shì tā (suǒ) [shuō | xūyào | xiě...] de ma? 这是他(所) [说 | 需要 | 写...] 的吗; do what you want nǐ xiǎng zuò shénme jiù zuò shénme 你想做什么就做什么; what [books | colours | food...] do you like? nǐ xǐhuan shénme [shū | yánse | fàn...]? 你喜欢什么 [书 | 颜色 | 饭...]?; what time is it? jǐ diǎn le? 几点了?; (in exclamations) duōme 多么; what [a good idea | cold weather | a pretty girl!] duōme [hǎo de zhǔyi | lěng de tiānqì | měilì de gūniang] a! 多么 [好的主意 | 冷的天气 | 美丽的姑娘] 啊! **3** adv

what do you think of him? nǐ juéde tā zěnmeyàng? 你觉得他
怎么样?; **what does it matter to him?** zhè gēn tā yǒu shénme
guānxi? 这跟他有什么关系?; **4 what if** (*what would happen
if*) rúguǒ...zěnme bàn 如果...怎么办; **what if I can't get there
on time?** rúguǒ wǒ bù néng ànshí dàodá nàr, zěnme bàn ne?
如果我不能按时到达那儿, 怎么办呢?; (*what would it
matter if*) jíshǐ...nǐ yǒu shénme guānxi 即使...又有什么关系;
what if I don't get there on time? jíshǐ wǒ bú ànshí dàodá nàr,
yòu yǒu shénme guānxi ne? 即使我不按时到达那儿, 又有
什么关系呢?

whatever *pron* (*when anything is possible*) take whatever you
want nǐ yào shénme jiù ná shénme ba 你要什么就拿什么吧;
whatever you think is useful fánshì nǐ xiǎng de dōu hěn yǒuyòng
凡是你想的都很有用; (*when it doesn't matter*) whatever
[happens | they do | you say...], I won't change my mind bùguǎn
[fāshēng | tāmen zuò | nǐ shuō...] shénme, wǒ dōu bú huì gǎibiàn zhǔyì
不管 [发生 | 他们做 | 你说...] 什么, 我都不会改变主意

wheat *n* xiǎomài 小麦, màizi 麦子

wheel *n* a wheel yíge lúnzi 一个轮子

wheelchair *n* a wheelchair yíge lúnyǐ 一个轮椅

when 1 *adv* shénme shíhou 什么时候; **when did she leave?**
tā shì shénme shíhou líkāi de? 她是什么时候离开的?; **when
is your birthday?** nǐ shénme shíhou guò shēngrì? 你什么时候
过生日?; **I don't know when the film starts** wǒ bù zhīdào
diànyǐng shénme shíhou kāiyǎn 我不知道电影什么时候开演
2 *conj* (dāng/zài)...de shíhou (当/在)...的时候; **he didn't study
any Chinese when he was at school** tā zài zhōngxué de shíhou
méi xué Zhōngwén 他在中学的时候没学中文; **when I'm 18,
I'll have my own car** wǒ shíbā suì de shíhou, wǒ yào yǒu yíliàng
zìjǐ de qìchē 我十八岁的时候, 我要有一辆自己的汽车;
(*when talking about something unexpected happening in the
midst of another action*) **I was asleep when the phone rang**
wǒ zhèngzài shuìjiào, tūrán diànhuàlíng xiǎng le 我正在睡觉,
突然电话铃响了; **we were playing basketball when it started
to rain** wǒmen zhèngzài dǎ lánqiú, tūrán tiān xiàqǐ yǔ lai 我们
正在打篮球, 突然天下起雨来 **3** *pron* (*used as a relative*

pronoun) **!** *Note that in this case, when is usually not translated;* **in the days when there was no TV** zài méi yǒu diànshì de rìzi li 在没有电视的日子里; *(used in questions)* shénme shíhou 什么时候; **until when did you work last night?** zuótiān yè li nǐ yìzhí gōngzuò dào shénme shíhou? 昨天夜里你一直工作到什么时候?

where 1 *adv* nǎli 哪里, nǎr 哪儿; **where are you going?** nǐ shàng nǎr? 你上哪儿?; **where do they work?** tāmen zài nǎlǐ gōngzuò? 他们在哪里工作?; *do you know where* [he is | Tom is | we're...] *going?* nǐ zhīdào [tā yào | Tāngmǔ yào | wǒmen yào...] qù nǎr ma? 你知道[他要 | 汤姆要 | 我们要...] 去哪儿吗?; **I wonder where he lives** wǒ xiǎng zhīdào tā zhù zài nǎlǐ 我想知道他住在哪里 **2** *conj* ...de dìfang ... 的地方; **that's where she fell** nà jiù shì tā diēdǎo de dìfang 那就是她跌倒的地方; **I'll leave the key where you can see it** wǒ huì bǎ yàoshi fàng zài nǐ néng kànjian de dìfang 我会把钥匙放在你能看见的地方 **3** *pron* *(used as a relative pronoun in a defining relative clause)* **!** *Note that in this case, where is usually not translated;* **the village where we live** wǒmen zhù de cūnzi 我们住的村子; *(used as a relative pronoun in a non-defining relative clause)* zài nàlǐ 在那里, zài nàr 在那儿; **I went to Shanghai last year, where I visited some Chinese families** qùnián wǒ qùle Shànghǎi, zài nàlǐ wǒ fǎngwènle yìxiē Zhōngguó jiātíng 去年我去了上海, 在那里我访问了一些中国家庭; *(used in questions)* nǎlǐ 哪里, nǎr 哪儿; **where do you come from?** nǐ cóng nǎlǐ lái? 你从哪里来?

whether *conj (if)* shìfǒu 是否, shì bú shì 是不是; **I don't know whether or not to accept her invitation** wǒ bù zhīdào shìfǒu yīnggāi jiēshòu tāde yāoqǐng 我不知道是否应该接受她的邀请; **whether... or...** *(when introducing two alternatives)* ...háishi... ... 还是...; **I wonder whether I should go to Beijing or Shanghai** wǒ bù zhīdào (wǒ) yīnggāi qù Běijīng háishi qù Shànghǎi 我不知道(我)应该去北京还是去上海; *(in any case, in any event)* bùguǎn/búlùn...háishi... 不管/不论...还是...; **whether you come to me or I go to you, we must find time to discuss this problem this week** bùguǎn nǐ lái wǒ zhèr háishi wǒ qù nǐ nàr, zhège xīngqī wǒmen bìxū zhǎo shíjiān tǎolùn zhège wèntí 不管你来

我这儿还是我去你那儿 这个星期我们必须找时间讨论
这个问题

which 1 pron (used as a relative pronoun in a defining relative
clause)！ Note that in this case, which is usually not translated;
the house which I told you about wǒ gàosu nǐ de nàzuò fángzi
我告诉你的那座房子; **the book which is on the table** (zài)
zhuōzi shang de shū (在)桌子上的书; (used as a relative
pronoun in a non-defining relative clause)！ Note that in this
case, which is often translated as the noun it refers to, or as
the pronouns, zhè 这 or nà 那; **he was teaching at Peking
University, which was very far from the city centre** tā zài
Běijīng Dàxué jiāoshū, Běijīng Dàxué lí shì zhōngxīn hěn yuǎn
他在北京大学教书, 北京大学离市中心很远; **he has given
up smoking, which makes his wife very pleased** tā jiè yān le,
zhè shǐ tā tàitai fēicháng gāoxìng 他戒烟了, 这使他太太
非常高兴; (in questions) **which...?**！ Note that in questions,
which as a pronoun is usually translated as **nǎxiē 哪些** if it
refers to a plural noun, and as **nǎ (yí)ge 哪(一)个** if it refers
to a singular noun. In **nǎ (yí)ge 哪(一)个**, the measure word
ge 个 may be replaced with a different measure word
depending on the noun being referred to; (when the noun is
plural) **nǎxiē 哪些**; **which of these books are yours?** zhèxiē
shū zhōng nǎxiē shì nǐde? 这些书中哪些是你的?; (when the
noun is singular) **nǎ (yí)ge 哪(一)个**; **of these parks, which is
the largest?** zhèxiē gōngyuán nǎ yíge zuì dà? 这些公园哪一个
最大?; **of these books, which is most useful?** zhèxiē shū nǎ
yìběn zuì yǒuyòng? 这些书哪一本最有用?; **there are three
computers; which do you want to buy?** yǒu sāntái jìsuànjī, nǐ
xiǎng mǎi nǎ yìtái? 有三台计算机, 你想买哪一台?; **2** det
(when the noun that follows is plural) **nǎxiē 哪些**; **which books
did he borrow?** tā jiè le nǎxiē shū? 他借了哪些书?; (when the
noun that follows is singular) **nǎ (yí)ge 哪(一)个**！ Note that in
nǎ (yí)ge 哪(一)个, the measure word **ge 个** may be replaced
by a different measure word depending on the noun being
referred to; **which one of the nurses speaks Chinese?** nǎ yíge
hùshi huì shuō Hànyǔ? 哪一个护士会说汉语?; **which car is
yours?** nǎ yíliàng chē shì nǐde? 哪一辆车是你的?; **he asked**

me which shirt I liked tā wèn wǒ xǐhuan nǎ yíjiàn chènshān
他问我喜欢哪一件衬衫

while conj (in the time that) (dāng)...de shíhou (当)... 的时候;
I was ill while I was on holiday in Japan wǒ zài Rìběn dùjià de
shíhou bìng le 我在日本度假的时候病了; she fell asleep
while watching TV tā kàn diànshì de shíhou shuìzháo le 她看
电视的时候睡着了, tā kànzhe diànshì shuìzháo le 她看着
电视睡着了

whisper vb (to say in soft, hushed tones) xiǎoshēng de shuō
小声地说, dīshēng de shuō 低声地说

whistle 1 vb (with the mouth) chuī kǒushào 吹口哨; (with a
whistle) chuī shàozi 吹哨子; (when referring to a train) míng dí
鸣笛 **2** n a whistle (blown with the mouth) yíge shàozi 一个
哨子; (sounded by escaping steam) yíge qìdí 一个汽笛

white adj bái 白, báisè de 白色的

who pron (used in questions) shéi/shuí 谁; who told you? shéi
gàosu nǐ de? 谁告诉你的?; who did you invite? nǐ qǐngle shéi?
你请了谁?; who did he buy the book for? tā gěi shéi mǎi de
shū? 他给谁买的书?; (used as a relative pronoun in a defining
relative clause) ▌ Note that in this case, who is usually not
translated; those who can't come by bike nàxiè bù néng qí
zìxíngchē lái de rén 那些不能骑自行车来的人; the man who
you want to see nǐ xiǎng jiàn de nàge rén 你想见的那个人;
(used as a relative pronoun in a non-defining relative clause) tā
他, tā 她, tāmen 他们 ▌ Note that in this case, who is translated
as tā 他 if it refers to a man, as tā 她 if it refers to a woman, and
as tāmen 他们 if it refers to a plural noun; I went to see my
mother, who had just come back from China wǒ qù kàn wǒ
māma, tā gāng cóng Zhōngguó huílai 我去看我妈妈, 她刚从
中国回来; he is waiting for his friends, who are coming to
celebrate his birthday tā zài děng tāde péngyou, tāmen yào lái
gěi tā guò shēngrì 他在等他的朋友, 他们要来给他过生日

whole 1 n the whole of [the country | London | August...] zhěnggè
[guójiā | Lúndūn | bāyuè...] 整个 [国家 | 伦敦 | 八月...] **2** adj a whole
day yì zhěng tiān 一整天; three whole weeks zhěngzhěng
sānge xīngqí 整整三个星期; the whole world quán shìjiè

全世界; I don't want to spend my whole life here wǒ bù xiǎng zài zhèlǐ dùguò wǒde zhěnggè yìshēng 我不想在这里度过我的整个一生

whom pron (used in questions) shéi/shuí 谁; whom did you meet? nǐ yùjiànle shéi? 你遇见了谁?; (used as a relative pronoun in a defining clause) ! Note that in this case, whom is usually not translated; the person whom you met yesterday zuótiān nǐ jiàn de nàge rén 昨天你见的那个人; (used as a relative pronoun in a non-defining clause) tā 他, tā 她, tāmen 他们! Note that in this case, whom is translated as tā 他 if it refers to a man, as tā 她 if it refers to a woman, and as tāmen 他们 if it refers to a plural noun; my younger brother, whom you met in my house, is going to Taiwan to study Chinese wǒ dìdi yào qù Táiwān xuéxí Hànyǔ, nǐ zài wǒ jiā jiànguo tā 我弟弟要去台湾学习汉语, 你在我家见过他; these students, for whom I have to arrange accommodation, came from China zhèxiē xuésheng lái zì Zhōngguó, wǒ děi gěi tāmen ānpái zhùsù 这些学生来自中国, 我得给他们安排住宿

whose 1 pron (used in questions) shéi de/shuí de 谁的; whose is this nice hat? zhèdǐng piàoliang de màozi shì shéi de? 这顶漂亮的帽子是谁的?; (used as a relative pronoun) ! Note that in this case, whose is often translated as tāde 他的 if it refers to a masculine singular noun, as tāde 她的 if it refers to a feminine singular noun, as tāde 它的 if it refers to a non-human singular noun, as tāmende 他们的 if it refers to a human plural noun, and as tāmende 它们的 if it refers to a non-human plural noun. Sometimes, whose is not translated at all in a defining relative clause; the boy whose bike was stolen (tāde) zìxíngchē bèi rén tōuzǒude de nàge nánháir (他的)自行车被人偷走了的那个男孩儿; the woman whose house I'm buying wǒ yào mǎi tāde fángzi de nàge nǚde 我要买她的房子的那个女的; they are Mr. and Mrs. Brown, whose son used to be a student of mine tāmen shì Bùlǎng xiānsheng hé Bùlǎng tàitai, tāmende érzi yǐqián shì wǒde xuésheng 他们是布朗先生和布朗太太, 他们的儿子以前是我的学生; the chair whose leg is broken duànle tuǐ de nàbǎ yǐzi 断了腿的那把椅子 **2** det shéi de/shuí de 谁的; whose car is that? nà shì shéi de chē? 那是谁的车?; whose pen did you borrow? nǐ jiè shéi de bǐ? 你借谁的笔?

why 1 adv wèishénme 为什么; why did you tell him? nǐ wèishénme gàosu tā? 你为什么告诉他?; why aren't they coming? tāmen wèishénme bù lái? 他们为什么不来?; why not? wèishénme bù? 为什么不?; why don't we eat out tonight? jīntiān wǎnshang wǒmen wèishénme bù chūqu chī ne? 今天晚上我们为什么不出去吃呢? **2** conj ...de yuányīn ...的原因; that's (the reason) why I can't stand him zhè jiù shì wǒ bù néng rěnshòu tā de yuányīn 这就是我不能忍受他的原因; please tell me why you want to learn Chinese qǐng nǐ gàosu wǒ nǐ yào xué Zhōngwén de yuányīn 请你告诉我你要学中文的原因, qǐng nǐ gàosu wǒ nǐ wèishénme yào xué Zhōngwén 请你告诉我你为什么要学中文

wide adj (in size) kuān 宽; a wide garden yíge hěn kuān de huāyuán 一个很宽的花园; the room is ten metres wide zhège fángjiān shí mǐ kuān 这个房间十米宽; (in range) a wide range of choices guǎngfàn de xuǎnzé fànwéi 广泛的选择范围; a person with wide interests yíge xìngqù guǎngfàn de rén 一个兴趣广泛的人; a wide range of games zhǒnglèi fánduō de yóuxì 种类繁多的游戏

width n (the distance between) kuāndù 宽度; (being wide) kuānkuò 宽阔; a road of great width yìtiáo kuānkuò de mǎlù 一条宽阔的马路

wife n (less formal) qīzi 妻子, àirén 爱人; (more formal) fūrén 夫人, tàitai 太太; a wife yíwèi fūrén 一位夫人

wild adj (describing animals, plants) yěshēng 野生; wild plants yěshēng zhíwù 野生植物; wild animals yěshēng dòngwù 野生动物; (noisy, out of control) fāfēng 发疯, fākuáng 发狂; he's gone wild tā fāfēng le 他发疯了; (not cultivated) huāngwú 荒芜 huāngliáng 荒凉

wildlife n yěshēng dòngwù 野生动物

will vb (when talking about the future) (in positive statements and questions) huì 会, jiāng(yào) 将(要); will she agree? tā huì tóngyì ma? 她会同意吗?; it will rain tomorrow míngtiān jiāngyào xiàyǔ 明天将要下雨; we will discuss this problem wǒmen jiāng tǎolùn zhège wèntí 我们将讨论这个问题; (in *negative sentences*) **will not** (jiāng) bú huì (将)不会; **she won't agree** tā bú huì tóngyì 她不会同意; **I won't forget** wǒ bú huì wàngjì 我不会忘记; (*when talking about willingness*) yuànyì 愿意; **I will do my best to help this child** wǒ yuànyì jìn zuì dà nǔlì bāngzhù zhège háizi 我愿意尽最大努力帮助这个孩子; **she won't come** tā bú yuànyì lái 她不愿意来; (*when talking about intentions*) xiǎng 想, yào 要; **will you visit the Great Wall?** nǐ yào qù cānguān Chángchéng ma? 你要去参观长城吗?; **we won't stay too long** wǒmen bù huì dāi hěn cháng shíjiān 我们不会呆很长时间; (*in invitations and requests*) (qǐng)...hǎo ma? (请)... 好吗?; **will you have some coffee?** nín hē diǎnr kāfēi, hǎo ma? 您喝点儿咖啡, 好吗?; **will you pass me the salt, please?** qǐng nǐ bǎ yán dìgěi wǒ, hǎo ma? 请你把盐递给我, 好吗?; (*when making an assumption about the future*) huì 会; **they won't know what's happened** tāmen bú huì zhīdào fāshēngle shénme shì 他们不会知道发生了什么事

win *vb* (*be victorious*) yíng 赢, huòshèng 获胜; (*to gain in a battle, match, contest*) yíngdé 赢得, huòdé 获得; **to win a gold medal** huòdé yìméi jīnpái 获得一枚金牌

wind *n* a wind fēng 风

window *n* a window (*in a house, a car, a plane*) yīge chuānghu 一个窗户; (*in a shop*) yīge chúchuāng 一个橱窗

windsurfing *n* fānbǎn yùndòng 帆板运动

windy *adj* guā (dà) fēng 刮(大)风, fēng dà 风大; **it's very windy outside** wàimian guā dà fēng 外面刮大风

wine *n* pútaojiǔ 葡萄酒

wing *n* a wing (*of a bird*) yìzhī chìbǎng 一只翅膀; (*for a plane*) yíge jīyì 一个机翼

winter *n* dōngtiān 冬天, dōngjì 冬季

wipe *vb* cā 擦; **to wipe** [one's nose | one's tears | the table...] cā [bízi | yǎnlèi | zhuōzi...] 擦 [鼻子 | 眼泪 | 桌子...]

wise *adj* (*when describing a person*) cōngming 聪明; (*when describing a decision, a choice, or a leader*) yīngmíng 英明, míngzhì 明智

wish 1 n (a hope) a wish yíge yuànwàng 一个愿望; **best wishes** (in greetings) zuì liánghǎo de zhùyuàn 最良好的祝愿; **to give one's best wishes to someone** xiàng mǒurén zhìyì 向某人致意; (in a letter) **with best wishes** zhù hǎo 祝好 **2** vb (to want, to be inclined) xiǎng 想, yào 要; **how long do they wish to stay here for?** tāmen xiǎng zài zhèr dāi duō jiǔ? 他们想在这儿待多久?; (to long, to hope) kěwàng 渴望; **I wish to visit Hong Kong** wǒ kěwàng qù Xiānggǎng fǎngwèn 我渴望去香港访问; (expressing what one would like to happen or to have happened) yàoshì…jiù hǎo le 要是…就好了; **I wish they could come** yàoshì tāmen néng lái jiù hǎo le 要是他们能来就好了; **she wished she hadn't lied** tā xiǎng yàoshì tā méi sāhuǎng jiù hǎo le 她想要是她没撒谎就好了; (in greetings) zhù 祝, zhùyuàn 祝愿; **to wish someone a happy birthday** zhù mǒurén shēngrì kuàilè 祝某人生日快乐

with prep (in the company of) hé…(yìqǐ) 和…(一起), gēn…(yìqǐ) 跟…(一起); **he went away with his friends** tā hé tāde péngyou (yìqǐ) zǒu le 他和他的朋友(一起)走了; **I'm living with my parents** wǒ gēn wǒ fùmǔ zhù zài yìqǐ 我跟我父母住在一起; (by means of) yòng 用; **she is wiping her tears with her hands** tā zài yòng shǒu cā yǎnlèi 她在用手擦眼泪; (in the possession of) **!** Note that in this case, with is often not translated; **a girl with black hair** yíge hēi tóufa de nǚhái 一个黑头发的女孩儿; **the boy with the broken leg** nàge duànle tuǐ de nánhái 那个断了腿的男孩儿; **a man with a great sense of humour** yíge hěn yōumò de rén 一个很幽默的人; **he left with a smile** tā xiàozhe zǒu le 他笑着走了; **she's married with two children** tā jiéhūn le, yóu liǎngge háizi 她结婚了, 有两个孩子; (denoting support) zàntóng 赞同, zhīchí 支持; **most people are with this proposal** dàduōshù rén dōu zàntóng zhège tíyì 大多数人都赞同这个提议; (denoting understanding) dǒng 懂, míngbai 明白, lǐjiě 理解; **I'm with you** wǒ dǒng nǐde yìsi 我懂你的意思; (because of) **!** Note that in this case, with is often not translated; **she jumped with joy** tā gāoxìng de tiàole qǐlai 她高兴地跳了起来; **she shivered with fear** tā xià de fādǒu 她吓得发抖; (at hand) **I haven't got any money with me** wǒ (shēn shang) méi dài qián 我(身上)没带钱; **you'd better take a dictionary with**

you nǐ zuìhǎo suíshēn dài yìběn cídiǎn 你最好随身带一本词典; (at the same time as) suízhe 随着; the living standard improves with the increase in the people's income shēnghuó shuǐpíng suízhe rénmen shōurù de zēngjiā ér gǎishàn 生活水平随着人们收入的增加而改善

without prep méiyǒu 没有; we got in without paying wǒmen méiyǒu fù qián jiù jìnqu le 我们没有付钱就进去了

wolf n a wolf yìtiáo láng 一条狼

woman n a woman yíwèi fùnǚ 一位妇女; a single woman yíge dānshēn fùnǚ 一个单身妇女

wonder vb (to ask oneself) xiǎng zhīdào 想知道; I wonder [how he came | why he came | who came...] wǒ xiǎng zhīdào [tā shi zěnme lái de | tā wèishénme lái | shéi lái le...] 我想知道 [他是怎么来的 | 他为什么来 | 谁来了...]; I was wondering when you'd arrive wǒ xiǎng zhīdào nín shénme shíhou dào 我想知道您什么时候到; (in polite requests) I wonder if you could help me? bù zhī nǐ nénɡ bù nénɡ bānɡ wǒ ge mánɡ? 不知你能不能帮我个忙?

wonderful adj (when describing a performance, a match) jīngcǎi 精彩; (when describing someone's courage, memory) jīngrén 惊人; (when describing the weather, an idea, a plan, etc.) jí hǎo 极好, jí miào 极妙; the weather is wonderful tiānqì hǎo jí le 天气好极了; what a wonderful idea! zhège zhǔyì miào jí le! 这个主意妙极了!; wonderful! tài hǎo le! 太好了!

wood n (timber) mùtou 木头; the table is made of wood zhèzhāng zhuōzi shì mùtou zuò de 这张桌子是木头做的; (a small forest) a wood yípiàn shùlín 一片树林

wool n (soft hair of a sheep, goat, etc.) yángmáo 羊毛, máo 毛; (yarn spun from sheep or goat hair) máoxiàn 毛线, róngxiàn 绒线

word n (the smallest meaningful unit in a language) a word yíge (dān)cí 一个(单)词; what's the Chinese word for 'break'? 'break' de Zhōngwén dāncí shì shénme? 'break' 的中文单词是什么?; (utterance) huà 话; I didn't say a word wǒ yíjù huà yě méi shuō 我一句话也没说; in other words huàn jù huà shuō 换句话说; (a brief conversation) can I have a word with you? wǒ kěyǐ gēn nǐ tán yíxià ma? 我可以跟你谈一下吗?

work 1 *vb (to do a job)* gōngzuò 工作; **to work at home** zài jiā li gōngzuò 在家里工作; *(to have a job)* **to work as** [a doctor | a teacher | an actor...] dāng [yīshēng | lǎoshī | yǎnyuán...] 当 [医生 | 老师 | 演员...]; *(to operate properly)* gōngzuò 工作; **the TV isn't working** diànshìjī bù gōngzuò le 电视机不工作了; *(to be successful) (if it's an idea, a plan, a trick)* xíng de tōng 行得通 **!** *Note that the negative form is* xíng bù tōng 行不通; **the plan doesn't work** zhège jìhuà xíng bù tōng 这个计划行不通; *(if it's a medicine, a treatment)* qǐ zuòyòng 起作用; *(to use, to operate)* shǐyòng 使用, cāozuò 操作; **do you know how to work the computer?** nǐ zhīdào zěnme shǐyòng zhètái jìsuànjī ma? 你知道怎么使用这台计算机吗? **2** *n* **work** gōngzuò 工作, huór 活儿; **I've got a lot of work to do** wǒ yǒu hěn duō gōngzuò yào zuò 我有很多工作要做; *(employment)* **have you found work yet?** nǐ zhǎodào gōngzuò le ma? 你找到工作了吗? **she is out of work** tā shīyè le 她失业了; *(students' work)* zuòyè 作业; *(for building, for repairs)* gōngchéng 工程; **there are road works outside at the moment** wàimian zhèngzài jìnxíng xiū lù gōngchéng 外面正在进行修路工程; *(by a writer, an artist, a musician)* **a work** yíge zuòpǐn 一个作品; *(a book)* **works** zhùzuò 著作; **work out** *(to find)* zhǎochū 找出; **to work out the answer** zhǎochū dá'àn 找出答案; *(to understand)* nòng míngbai 弄明白, nòng qīngchu 弄清楚; *(with figures)* suànchū 算出; *(to take exercise)* duànliàn 锻炼; *(to devise)* shèjìchū 设计出; *(to formulate, to make)* zhìdìngchū 制订出; **to work out a plan** zhìdìngchū yíxiàng jìhuà 制订出一项计划; **work up** *(when talking about getting excited)* **to get worked up** jīdòngqǐlai 激动起来; *(to rouse)* huànqǐ 唤起, jīqǐ 激起; **to work up enthusiasm for learning Chinese** huànqǐ xuéxí Zhōngwén de rèqíng 唤起学习中文的热情

worker *n* **a worker** *(in a factory)* yíge gōngrén 一个工人; *(in an office, a bank)* yíge gōngzuò rényuán 一个工作人员

world *n* **the world** shìjiè 世界; **all over the world** quán shìjiè 全世界; **the biggest city in the world** shìjiè shang zuì dà de chéngshì 世界上最大的城市

World Cup *n* **the World Cup** Shìjiè Bēi 世界杯

World Wide Web, WWW *n* the World Wide Web Wàn Wéi Wǎng 万维网

worm *n* a worm yìtiáo chóngzi 一条虫子

worried *adj* dānxīn 担心, bú fàngxīn 不放心; to be worried about someone dānxīn mǒurén 担心某人

worry *vb* (*to be worried*) dānxīn 担心, bú fàngxīn 不放心; there's nothing to worry about méi yǒu shénme kě dānxīn de 没有什么可担心的; (*to make someone worried*) shǐ...dānxīn 使... 担心, shǐ...bù ān 使... 不安; it's worrying me zhè shǐ wǒ hěn dānxīn 这使我很担心

worse *adj* (*evil in a higher degree*) gèng huài 更坏; this idea is worse than that one zhège zhǔyi bǐ nàge gèng huài 这个主意比那个更坏; (*when describing a standard, the weather, a condition*) gèng chà 更差, gèng zāo 更糟; she's worse than me at sports zài tǐyù fāngmiàn tā bǐ wǒ gèng chà 在体育方面她比我更差; the weather is going to get worse tiānqì huì biànde gèng zāo 天气会变得更糟; (*when describing an illness*) gèng zhòng 更重; he is getting worse tāde bìng gèng zhòng le 他的病更重了

worst 1 *n* the worst (*when talking about a wicked person*) zuì huài de rén 最坏的人; (*when talking about an ability, a condition, a standard, the weather*) zuì chà 最差, zuì zāo(gāo) de 最糟(糕)的; I'm the worst at Chinese zài xuéxí Zhōngwén fāngmiàn, wǒ shì zuì chà de 在学习中文方面，我是最差的 **2** *adj* (*most wicked or evil*) zuì huài 最坏; (*when talking about an ability, a condition, a standard, the weather*) zuì chà 最差, zuì zāo(gāo) 最糟(糕); the worst hotel in town chéng lǐ zuì chà de lǚguǎn 城里最差的旅馆; the worst film I've ever seen wǒ suǒ kànguo de zuì zāo(gāo) de diànyǐng 我所看过的最糟(糕)的电影; his worst enemy tā zuì xiōng'è de dírén 他最凶恶的敌人; (*the most severe or serious*) zuì yánzhòng 最严重; the worst accident zuì yánzhòng de shìgù 最严重的事故

worth *adj* (*equal in value to*) zhí 值; to be worth £100 zhí yìbǎi yīngbàng 值一百英镑; (*deserving of*) zhíde 值得; the exhibition is not worth visiting zhège zhǎnlǎnhuì bù zhíde cānguān 这个展览会不值得参观

would vb (when talking about hypothetical rather than real situations) huì 会, jiù huì 就会: **if I had more money, I would buy a car** wǒ yàoshì yǒu gèng duō de qián, wǒ huì mǎi yíliàng qìchē 我要是有更多的钱, 我会买一辆汽车; **we would have missed the train if we'd left later** rúguǒ wǒmén zài wǎn diǎnr zǒu, wǒmen jiù huì wùle huǒchē le 如果我们再晚点儿走, 我们就会误了火车了; (when used as the past tense of will) jiāng 将, (jiāng)huì (将)会! Note that in this sense, the negative form is (jiāng) bú huì (将)不会: **I thought you'd forget to come** wǒ yǐwéi nǐ huì wàngle lái 我以为你会忘了来; **we knew she wouldn't like it** wǒmen zhīdào tā bú huì xǐhuan 我们知道她不会喜欢; (when talking about probability or likelihood) dàgài 大概, yěxǔ 也许: **she'd be 30 now** tā xiànzài dàgài sānshí suì le 她现在大概三十岁了; **he would be in the library now** xiànzài tā yěxǔ zài túshūguǎn 现在他也许在图书馆; (to be willing to) yuànyì 愿意, yào 要: **he wouldn't listen to me** tā bú yuànyì tīng wǒde huà 他不愿意听我的话; (when talking about one's wishes) xiǎng 想: **I'd like a beer** wǒ xiǎng yào yìbēi píjiǔ 我想要一杯啤酒; **we would like to stay another night** wǒmen xiǎng zài dāi yíge wǎnshang 我们想再呆一个晚上; (when making a polite request) qǐng...hǎo ma 请... 好吗, qǐng...kěyǐ ma 请... 可以吗: **would you turn the TV off, please?** qǐng bǎ diànshì guānshang, hǎo ma? 请把电视关上, 好吗?; **would you pass the book to me, please?** qǐng bǎ nàběn shū dìgěi wǒ, kěyǐ ma? 请把那本书递给我, 可以吗?; (when talking about a habitual action in the past) zǒngshì 总是, zǒnghuì 总会: **she would sit beside me** tā zǒngshì zuò zài wǒde pángbiān 她总是坐在我的旁边

wrap vb (to cover by putting something all over) bāo 包; **to wrap (up) a present** bāo yíge lǐwù 包一个礼物; (to cover by putting something round the middle) guǒ 裹, bāo 包; **to wrap the child in a blanket** yòng tǎnzi bǎ háizi guǒqilai 用毯子把孩子裹起来

wreck 1 vb (to destroy, to ruin) pòhuài 破坏, sǔnhài 损害; **be wrecked** (if it's a ship, a train, or a plane) shīshì 失事; **the ship was wrecked** nàsōu chuán shīshì le 那艘船失事了 **2** n (if it's damaged but might be fixed) **a wreck** (of a ship) yìsōu shīshì de chuán 一艘失事的船; (of a car) yíliàng shīshì de qìchē 一辆失事的汽车; (if it's completely in ruins) cánhái 残骸; **the wreck of** [a ship | a car | a plane] de cánhái 一[艘船 | 辆汽车 | 架飞机] 的残骸

wrestling n shuāijiāo yùndòng 摔跤运动

wrist n the wrist shǒuwàn 手腕, wànzi 腕子

write vb write xiě 写; to write [an essay | a cheque | a letter...] xiě [yìpiān wénzhāng | yìzhāng zhīpiào | yìfēng xìn...] 写[一篇文章 | 一张支票 | 一封信...]; (to write a letter) xiě xìn 写信; to write (to) someone (US English) gěi mǒurén xiě xìn 给某人写信; **write back** huí xìn 回信; **write down** jìxià 记下, xiěxià 写下; **write out** (to transcribe) xiěchū 写出; (to write in full) quánbù xiěchu 全部写出

writing n (the act of one who writes) xiě 写; (a literary production or composition) xiězuò 写作; (handwriting) bǐjì 笔迹, zìjì 字迹

writing pad n a writing pad yìběn biànjiānběn 一本便笺本

wrong adj (not as it should be) there's something wrong with the TV diànshìjī yǒu diǎnr bú zhèngcháng 电视机有点儿不正常; what's wrong (with you)? (nǐ) zěnme le? (你)怎么了?; what's wrong with that? nà yǒu shénme bú duì? 那有什么不对?; there isn't anything wrong with him tā méi yǒu shénme wèntí 他没有什么问题; (not proper or suitable) bù héshì 不合适; I'm sorry I've said the wrong thing duìbuqǐ, wǒ shuōle bù héshì de huà 对不起,我说了不合适的话; that's the wrong thing to do nà yàng zuò bù héshì 那样做不合适; (not correct) cuò 错, bú duì 不对; that's wrong nà shì bú duì de 那是不对的; to dial the wrong number bōcuò hàomǎ 拨错号码; it's the wrong answer zhège dá'àn shì cuò de 这个答案是错的; you are wrong nǐ cuò le 你错了; I took the wrong key wǒ nácuòle yàoshi 我拿错了钥匙; they went the wrong way tāmen zǒucuòle lù 他们走错了路; (immoral) bú dàodé 不道德, bú duì 不对; it's wrong to steal tōu dōngxi shì bú dàodé de 偷东西是不道德的; she hasn't done anything wrong tā méiyǒu zuò shénme bú duì de shì 她没有做什么不对的事

Xx

xerox 1 *n* fùyìn 复印 **2** *vb* fùyìn 复印

X-ray 1 *n* an X-ray yìzhāng àikèsī guāng piàn 一张Ｘ光片; **to have an X-ray** jìnxíng àikèsī-guāng jiǎnchá 进行Ｘ光检查 **2** *vb* yòng àikèsī guāng jiǎnchá 用Ｘ光检查

Yy

yacht *n* a yacht; (*for pleasure*) (*US English*) yìsōu yóutǐng 一艘游艇; (*for racing*) yìsōu sàitǐng 一艘赛艇; (*for sailing*) yìsōu fānchuán 一艘帆船

yard *n* (*a measurement of length*) **a yard** yì mǎ 一码; (*area around a building*) **a yard** yíge yuànzi 一个院子; (*US English*) (*a garden*) **a yard** yíge huāyuán 一个花园

yawn *vb* dǎ hāqian 打哈欠

year *n* (*when talking about time*) **a year** yì nián 一年; **[last | this | next] year** [qù | jīn | míng] nián [去 | 今 | 明] 年; **the year** [before last | after next] **year** [qián | hòu] nián [前 | 后] 年; **two years ago** liǎng nián (yǐ)qián 两年(以)前; **to work all year round** quán nián gōngzuò 全年工作; **he's lived there for years** tā zài nàlǐ zhùle hěn duō nián le 他在那里住了很多年了; (*when talking about age*) **a year** yí suì 一岁; **he is 15 years old, he is 15 years of age** tā shíwǔ suì (le) 他十五岁(了); **a four-year old** yíge sì suì de háizi 一个四岁的孩子; (*in a school system*) **first year, year one** yī niánjí 一年级; **she is in second year, she is in year two** tā zài èr niánjí 她在二年级

yell 1 *vb* (jiào)hǎn (叫)喊; **to yell at someone** chòngzhe mǒurén hǎn 冲着某人喊 **2** *n* a yell yìshēng dàhǎn 一声大喊

yellow adj huáng 黄, huángsè de 黄色的: the leaves have gone yellow yèzi biàn huáng le 叶子变黄了

yes adv shì (de) 是(的), duì 对: 'are you going with us?'—'yes, I am' 'nǐ gēn wǒmen yìqǐ qù ma?'—'shìde, wǒ gēn nǐmen yìqǐ qù' '你跟我们一起去吗?'—'是的, 我跟你们一起去'; (when providing a positive response to a negative statement or question) bù 不: 'they don't know each other'—'yes, they do' 'tāmen hùxiāng bú rènshi'—'bù, tāmen hùxiāng rènshi' '他们互相不认识'—'不, 他们互相认识'; 'didn't he tell you?'—'yes, he did' 'tā méi gàosu nǐ ma?'—'bù, tā gàosu wǒ le' '他没告诉你吗?'—'不, 他告诉我了'

yesterday adv zuótiān 昨天: the day before yesterday qiántiān 前天

yet 1 adv (in a negative sentence) hái 还: not yet hái méiyǒu 还没(有): it's not ready yet hái méi zhǔnbèihǎo 还没准备好: I haven't told him yet wǒ hái méiyǒu gàosu tā 我还没有告诉他: (in a question) yǐjīng 已经! Note that in this case, yet is often not translated: have they arrived yet? tāmen (yǐjīng) dào le ma? 他们(已经)到了吗?: has she met them yet? tā (yǐjīng) jiàndào tāmen le ma? 她(已经)见到他们了吗? **2** conj rán'ér 然而, dànshì 但是

yogurt n suānnǎi 酸奶

you pron (singular) nǐ 你: do you speak Chinese? nǐ huì shuō Hànyǔ ma? 你会说汉语吗?: he will help you tā huì bāngzhù nǐ 他会帮助你: (plural) nǐmen 你们: are you students? nǐmen shì xuésheng ma? 你们是学生吗?: (the polite form, singular) nín 您: may I ask you a question? wǒ kěyǐ wèn nín yíge wèntí ma? 我可以问您一个问题吗?: (when used impersonally) nǐ 你, rénmen 人们: you can buy anything here zài zhèlǐ shénme nǐ dōu néng mǎi de dào 在这里什么你都能买得到: you never know what will happen shéi yě bù zhīdào huì fāshēng shénme shì 谁也不知道会发生什么事: these mushrooms can make you ill zhèxiē mógu néng shǐ rén dé bìng 这些蘑菇能使人得病

young 1 adj niánqīng 年轻, niánqīng 年青: a young lady yíwèi niánqīng de nǚshì 一位年轻的女士: young people niánqīng rén 年青人, niánqīng rén 年轻人, qīngnián 青年: she is a year younger than I tā bǐ wǒ xiǎo yí suì 她比我小一岁; to look young xiǎnde niánqīng 显得年轻; a younger brother yíge dìdi 一个弟弟; a younger sister yíge mèimei 一个妹妹; (when describing children, babies, animals) yòuxiǎo 幼小; a young [baby | animal] yíge yòuxiǎo de [ying'ér | dòngwù] 一个幼小的[婴儿 | 动物]; a young child yíge yòutóng 一个幼童 2 n the young (of people) qīngnián 青年, niánqīng rén 年轻人; (of animals) yòuzǎi 幼崽; (of birds) yòuniǎo 幼鸟, chúniǎo 雏鸟

your det (singular) nǐde 你的; is this your book? zhè shì nǐde shū ma? 这是你的书吗?; (plural) nǐmende 你们的; (the polite form, singular) nínde 您的; here is your room zhè shì nínde fángjiān 这是您的房间; (when used impersonally) ! Note that in this case, your is usually not translated; smoking is bad for your health xīyān duì shēntǐ yǒu hài 吸烟对身体有害

yours pron (singular) nǐde 你的; the red car is yours nàliàng hóng chē shì nǐde 那辆红车是你的; (plural) nǐmende 你们的; our garden is bigger than yours wǒmende huāyuán bǐ nǐmende dà 我们的花园比你们的大; (polite form, singular) nínde 您的; is this suitcase yours? zhège xiāngzi shì nínde ma? 这个箱子是您的吗?

yourself pron (when used as a reflexive pronoun) yourself (nǐ) zìjǐ (你)自己; you should trust yourself nǐ yīnggāi xiāngxìn (nǐ) zìjǐ 你应该相信(你)自己; (polite form) (nín) zìjǐ (您)自己; you haven't poured any wine for yourself nǐ hái méiyǒu gěi (nín) zìjǐ dào jiǔ ne 您还没有给(您)自己倒酒呢; (when used for emphasis) qīnzì 亲自, běnrén 本人, zìjǐ 自己; you don't have to go yourself nǐ bú bì qīnzì qù 你不必亲自去

yourselves pron (when used as a reflexive pronoun) (nǐmen) zìjǐ (你们)自己; what have you bought for yourselves? nǐmen gěi (nǐmen) zìjǐ mǎile xiē shénme? 你们给(你们)自己买了些什么?; (when used for emphasis) zìjǐ 自己, qīnzì 亲自; are you going to organize it yourselves? nǐmen dǎsuàn zìjǐ zǔzhī ma? 你们打算自己组织吗?

youth n (a young man) a youth yíge nán qīngnián 一个男青年, yíge xiǎohuǒzi 一个小伙子; (young people) the youth niánqīng rén 年轻人, niánqīng rén 年青人

youth club *n* a youth club yíge qīngnián jùlèbù 一个青年俱乐部

youth hostel *n* a youth hostel yíge qīngnián lǚguǎn 一个青年旅馆

youth worker *n* a youth worker yíwèi qīngshàonián gōngzuòzhě 一位青少年工作者

Zz

zap *vb* (*to destroy*) huǐdiào 毁掉, cuīhuǐ 摧毁; (*British English*) (*to switch channels*) (zhuǎn)huàn píndào (转)换频道; to zap from channel to channel bù tíng de (zhuǎn)huàn píndào 不停地(转)换频道

zapper *n* (*British English*) a zapper (*a remote control*) yíge yáokòngqì 一个遥控器

zebra *n* a zebra yìpǐ bānmǎ 一匹斑马

zebra crossing *n* (*British English*) a zebra crossing yìtiáo rénxíng héngdào 一条人行横道

zero *num* líng 零

zip (*British English*), **zipper** (*US English*) **1** *n* a zip yìtiáo lāliàn 一条拉链, yìtiáo lāsuǒ 一条拉锁; to undo a zip lākāi lāliàn 拉开拉链 **2** *vb* lāshang...de lāliàn 拉上...的拉链; to zip up [one's trousers | one's jacket | the bag...] bǎ [kùzi | jiákè | bāo...] de lāliàn lāshang 把 [裤子 | 夹克 | 包...] 的拉链拉上

zip code *n* (*US English*) a zip code yíge yóuzhèng biānmǎ 一个邮政编码

zone *n* a zone yíge dìdài 一个地带, yíge dìqū 一个地区

zoo *n* a zoo yíge dòngwùyuán 一个动物园